Revision Checklist

Worthwhile Content

The essay's main point is clear and sharply focused.

- ☐ Does the title attract attention and provide a forecast? (49)
- ☐ Is the topic limited enough? (21)
- ☐ Do you get to your main point quickly? (50)
- ☐ Is the thesis definite, informative, and easy to find? (22)

The discussion delivers on the promise made in your thesis.

- ☐ Will your readers learn something new and useful? (83)
- ☐ Do you support every assertion with detailed evidence and examples? (26)
- ☐ Does everything belong, or can anything be cut? (34)
- ☐ Have you used only your best material? (33)

Sensible Organization

The essay has a definite introduction, body, and conclusion.

- ☐ Will your introduction make readers want to read on? (50)
- ☐ Does each body paragraph develop one supporting point? (24)
- ☐ Does the order of major points and paragraphs reveal a clear line of thought and emphasize what is most important? (6)
- ☐ Does the conclusion give a real sense of an ending? (55)
- ☐ Is everything connected? (11)
- ☐ If you varied this organization, was it for good reason? (152)

Except for paragraphs of transition or special emphasis, each body paragraph is usually a mini-essay.

- ☐ Does the paragraph have a topic (or orienting) statement? (95)
- ☐ Does the topic statement come at the beginning or end, depending on your desired emphasis? (95)
- ☐ Does everything stick to the point (unity) and stick together (coherence), with adequate transitions to mark relationships? (97, 98, 105)
- ☐ Is the paragraph developed enough to support the point? (95)

Readable Style

Sentences are clear, concise, and fluent.

- ☐ Can each sentence be understood the first time it is read? (113)
- ☐ Are points conveyed clearly in the fewest words? (118)
- ☐ Are sentences put together with enough variety? (124)

Each word does its job.

- ☐ Is a real person speaking, and is the voice likable? (132)
- ☐ Is everything in plain English? (140)
- ☐ Is your meaning precise, concrete, and specific? (133)
- ☐ Is your tone appropriate for this situation and audience? (138)

Why Do You Need This New Edition?

Here are six good reasons why you should buy this new edition of *The Writing Process*!

1. **New Digital Tip boxes.** Practical digital tips for using various technologies during the writing and research processes have been added to every chapter in Sections One, Two, and Four. Topics include using digital tools to help you plan, write, and revise; using search engines and subject directories strategically; evaluating Web-based sources; and much more.

2. **Updated technology coverage throughout.** In addition to the new Digital Tip boxes, the text now includes the latest coverage of exploring and documenting electronic sources when doing research; new and expanded discussion of using digital media in the workplace; examples of essays revised using computerized editing tools; and more.

3. **An easier to use Section Three, "Essays for Various Goals."** In addition to more readings about "real world" topics (such as social networking, immigration, leaving a job, and more), the chapters in this section are now easier to navigate, moving straightforwardly from background concepts to practical applications. All chapters in this section now include Beyond the Writing Classroom boxes, which demonstrate how rhetorical strategies have practical uses in other courses, in the community, and in the workplace.

4. **The latest coverage of the research process.** Section Four, "The Research Process," now includes the latest information on using electronic resources and provides updated MLA and APA documentation guidelines, which have changed since the tenth edition of this text. The two annotated research reports have also been thoroughly revised to serve as up-to-date examples of researched writing.

5. **An expanded chapter on workplace writing.** Chapter 26, "Writing at Work," provides practical advice to those who are already on the job or will soon be entering the workforce. The chapter has been updated to include more coverage and examples of electronic résumés, job application letters, dossiers, portfolios, Webfolios, basic workplace correspondence, and business letters.

6. **New Learning Objectives boxes.** Each chapter now begins by previewing the knowledge and skills you will learn as you read the chapter and complete the assignments therein. These objectives are followed up at chapter's end with links to chapter-specific material available on MyCompLab, a rich online resource available with the purchase of a new book. MyCompLab provides you with interactive grammar, writing, and research resources to help you improve your writing skills and get a better grade.

PEARSON

The Writing Process

ELEVENTH EDITION

The Writing Process

A CONCISE RHETORIC, READER, AND HANDBOOK

John M. Lannon
University of Massachusetts–Dartmouth

PEARSON

Boston   Columbus   Indianapolis   New York   San Francisco
Upper Saddle River   Amsterdam   Cape Town   Dubai   London   Madrid
Milan   Munich   Paris   Montréal   Toronto   Delhi   Mexico City
São Paulo   Sydney   Hong Kong   Seoul   Singapore   Taipei   Tokyo

Executive Editor: Suzanne Phelps Chambers
Development Editor: Bruce Cantley
Senior Marketing Manager: Sandra McGuire
Editorial Assistant: Laney Whitt
Senior Supplements Editor: Donna Campion
Production Manager: Ellen MacElree
Project Coordination, Text Design, and Electronic Page Makeup: Integra Software Services, Inc.
Cover Designer/Manager: Wendy Ann Fredericks
Cover Image: © Dreamstime
Senior Manufacturing Buyer: Dennis J. Para
Printer/Binder: Edwards Brothers Malloy
Cover Printer: Edwards Brothers Malloy

For permission to use copyrighted material, grateful acknowledgment is made to the copyright holders on pp. 527–529, which are hereby made part of this copyright page.

Library of Congress Cataloging-in-Publication Data
Lannon, John M.
  The writing process : a concise rhetoric, reader, and handbook / John M. Lannon.—11th ed.
    p. cm.
  Includes bibliographical references and index.
  ISBN-13: 978-0-205-21009-1
  ISBN-10: 0-205-21009-0
  1. English language—Rhetoric.   2. Report writing.   I. Title.
  PE1408.L3188 2011
  808'.042—dc23

2011022591

10 9 8 —EBM—15

www.pearsonhighered.com

ISBN-13: 978-0-205-21009-1
ISBN-10:   0-205-21009-0

BRIEF CONTENTS

DETAILED CONTENTS

SECTION THREE	**Essays for Various Goals 149**

An Index of Useful Guidelines for Writers

PREFACE

The Writing Process, Eleventh Edition, promotes rhetorical awareness by treating the writing process as a set of deliberate and recursive decisions. It promotes rhetorical effectiveness by helping develop the problem-solving skills essential to reader-centered writing. Practical guidelines, accessible models, case studies, and checklists enable students to produce writing that works.

NEW AND SPECIAL FEATURES IN THE ELEVENTH EDITION

- **Thoroughly enhanced technology coverage.** Practical suggestions for using various technologies for writing and research now begin in the book's introduction and continue throughout via new Digital Tip boxes in every chapter in Sections One, Two, and Four. In addition to the Digital Tip boxes, *The Writing Process* now includes examples of writing revised using computerized editing tools; the latest coverage of using Web-based sources and documenting electronic sources in Section Four ("The Research Process"); and new and expanded discussion of electronic résumés, Webfolios, emails, instant messages, text messages, blogs, and wikis in Chapter 26 ("Writing at Work").
- **A revised and reconfigured Section Three, on the various rhetorical strategies.** In addition to an increased focus on "real world" readings, these chapters are now easier to navigate, moving from background concepts, to a sample essay using the particular strategy as a primary strategy, to a Case Study that compares a professional essay with an annotated student essay in response, and finally to Applications exercises at chapter's end. All chapters in this section now include a variety of special features including Beyond the Writing Classroom boxes to help students see how rhetorical strategies apply in real-world situations, such as in other courses, in the community, and in the workplace.
- **Thoroughly updated coverage of the research process.** Section Four includes the latest on using electronic resources during the research process, updated APA guidelines for documenting electronic sources, and the most recent MLA documentation guidelines. The two annotated research reports (one in APA style and one in MLA style) have been thoroughly revised to serve as up-to-date models for students.
- **An updated Section Five, "Special Issues in Writing."** Chapter 26, "Writing at Work," provides the essentials of workplace communication. Coverage includes résumés (including résumés adapted for scanning, emailing, and online posting), solicited and unsolicited job application letters, dossiers, portfolios, Webfolios, memos, emails, instant messages, text messages, blogs, wikis, letter format, and common types of business letters. Annotated examples illustrate each major type of workplace document. Chapter 27, "Taking Short-Answer, Paragraph, and Essay

Exams," offers sample test questions, annotated responses, Guidelines, and Applications to help students take in-class quizzes and tests effectively.

■ **New Learning Objectives boxes.** Each chapter now begins by spelling out the knowledge and skills students can expect to acquire from that chapter (for example, how to do peer critiquing online). These objectives are followed up at chapter's end with links to chapter-specific material available on MyCompLab.

■ **A mix of professional and student essays by diverse authors.** Although professional examples enhance skills in reading and responding, students are often more comfortable emulating essays written by other students. Therefore *The Writing Process* offers a balance. New essays in this edition deal with such topics as the struggle faced by immigrants as they strive to adapt while retaining their cultural identity, the dehumanizing aspects of certain jobs, generational differences in attitudes toward social networking, and an argument for abolishing the final two years of high school.

■ **Guidelines boxes.** The Guidelines boxes help students synthesize and apply the information in each chapter by providing a quick reference to each key topic. All the Guidelines boxes have been streamlined for this edition, and new ones have been added.

■ **End-of-chapter Checklists.** To serve as an editing guide and to enhance collaborative activities, the Eleventh Edition continues to feature Checklists throughout the text, many of which have been revised.

■ **Applications exercises.** The standard, collaborative, computer, and Web-based Applications have been revised throughout, with technology references thoroughly updated and new Applications added.

■ **Annotations, Note boxes, and Questions boxes.** Marginal annotations point out crucial information or provide helpful summaries. Note boxes highlight important side points. Finally, Questions About the Reading boxes help students focus their thoughts.

THE FOUNDATIONS OF *THE WRITING PROCESS*

The Writing Process proceeds from writer-centered to reader-centered discourse. Beginning with personal topics and a basic essay structure, the focus shifts to increasingly complex rhetorical tasks, culminating in argument. Within this cumulative structure, each chapter is self-contained for flexible course planning. The following concepts are foundational to the book:

■ Writers with no rhetorical awareness overlook the decisions that are crucial for effective writing. Only by defining their rhetorical problem and asking the important questions can writers formulate an effective response to the problem.

■ Although it follows no single, predictable sequence, the writing process is not a collection of random activities; rather it is a set of deliberate decisions in problem solving. Beyond emulating this or that model essay, students need to understand that effective writing requires critical thinking.

- Students write for audiences other than teachers and for purposes other than completing an assignment. To view the act of writing as a mere display of knowledge or fluency, an exercise in which writer and reader (i.e., "the teacher") have no higher stake or interest, is to ignore the unique challenges and constraints posed by each writing situation. In every forum beyond the classroom, we write to forge a specific connection with a specific audience.

- Students at any level of ability can develop audience awareness and learn to incorporate within their writing the essential rhetorical features: worthwhile content, sensible organization, and readable style.

- In addition to being a fluent *communicator*, today's educated person needs to be a discriminating *consumer* of information, skilled in the methods of inquiry, retrieval, evaluation, and interpretation that constitute the research process.

- As an alternative to reiterating the textbook material, classroom workshops apply textbook principles by focusing on the students' writing. These workshops call for an accessible, readable, and engaging book to serve as a comprehensive resource. (Suggestions for workshop design appear in the *Instructor's Manual*.)

- Finally, writing classes typically contain students with all types of strengths and weaknesses. *The Writing Process* offers explanations that are thorough, examples and models that are broadly intelligible, and goals that are rigorous yet realistic. The textbook is flexible enough to allow for various course plans and customized assignments.

ORGANIZATION OF THE TEXT

Section One, "The Process," covers planning, drafting, and revising. Students learn to generate, select, organize, and express their material recursively. They see how initial decisions about purpose and audience influence later decisions about what will be said and how it will be said. They see that writing is essentially a "thinking" process; they also learn to work collaboratively.

Section Two, "Specific Revision Strategies," focuses on top-down revision: content, organization, and style. Students learn to support their assertions; to organize for the reader; and to achieve prose maturity, precise diction, and appropriate tone.

Section Three, "Essays for Various Goals," shows how the *strategies* (or modes) of discourse serve the particular *goals* of a discourse; that is, how description, narration, exposition, and argument are variously employed—and often combined—for expressive, referential, or persuasive ends. The opening chapter explains how reading and writing are linked and offers guidance for reading and responding to essays by others. Subsequent chapters focus on each primary rhetorical strategy, using a balance of student and professional writing samples that touch on a wide range of themes. Beyond studying the samples and case studies as models, students are asked to respond to the issues presented—that is, to write in response to a specific rhetorical situation.

Section Four, "The Research Process," approaches research as a process of deliberate inquiry and critical thinking. Students learn to formulate significant research questions; to explore a selective range of primary and secondary sources; to record, summarize, avoid plagiarism, and document their findings; and, most important, to evaluate sources and evidence and to interpret findings accurately. Fully annotated sample research reports in APA and MLA style provide clear and engaging models.

Section Five, "Special Issues in Writing," consists of two chapters. Chapter 26, "Writing at Work," introduces students to the special considerations of on-the-job writing. Chapter 27, "Taking Short-Answer, Paragraph, and Essay Exams," provides a useful guide for taking a variety of in-class tests.

Section Six, "A Brief Handbook," covers the essentials of grammar, punctuation, and mechanics.

Finally, the "Format Guidelines for Submitting Your Manuscript" appendix offers solid advice on the visual presentation of papers and reports.

INSTRUCTIONAL SUPPLEMENTS

- **Instructor's Manual.** The *Instructor's Manual* contains general suggestions and ideas for teaching composition, sample syllabi, chapter overviews, suggested responses to exercises, additional sample essays, collaborative projects, and options for writing.
- **MyCompLab.** The only online application that integrates a writing environment with proven resources for grammar, writing, and research, MyCompLab gives students help at their fingertips as they draft and revise. Instructors have access to a variety of assessment tools including commenting capabilities, diagnostics and study plans, and an e-portfolio. Created after years of extensive research and in partnership with faculty and students across the country, MyCompLab offers a seamless and flexible teaching and learning environment built specifically for writers.
- **Interactive Pearson eText.** An eBook version of *The Writing Process* is also available in MyCompLab. This dynamic, online version of the text is integrated throughout MyCompLab to create an enriched, interactive learning experience for writing students.
- **CourseSmart.** Students can subscribe to *The Writing Process* as a CourseSmart eText (at CourseSmart.com). The site includes all of the book's content in a format that enables students to search the text, bookmark passages, save their own notes, and print reading assignments that incorporate lecture notes.
- **PowerPoint Slides.** The Instructor's Resource Center features a full set of slides that highlight the essential topics in each chapter of *The Writing Process* and help facilitate in-class presentation of the material.

ACKNOWLEDGMENTS

Much of the improvement in this edition was inspired by helpful reviews from Lisa A. Baker, Waukesha County Technical College; Jacob Bosch, Brown Mackie College; Christelle L. Del Prete, University of Massachusetts–Dartmouth and Bridgewater State University; Anna Maheshwari, Schoolcraft College; and Patricia Vázquez, College of Southern Nevada. I also continue to be grateful to the reviewers of earlier editions, with apologies that the list has grown too long over eleven editions to reproduce here.

A special thanks to the students who allowed me to reproduce versions of their work: Chris Adley, Al Andrade, Joe Bolton, Mike Creeden, Wendy Gianacoples, Liz Gonsalves, Shirley Haley, Cheryl Hebert, Pam Herbert, Jeff Leonard, Maureen Malloy, John Manning, Cathie Nichols, Julia Schoonover, Adam Szymkowicz, Patricia Williams, and the many other student writers named in the text.

From Suzanne Phelps Chambers, Joe Opiela, Mary Ellen Curley, Ellen MacElree, and Laney Whitt I received outstanding editorial guidance and support. Thanks to Bruce Cantley for his superb development help and ideas and to Martha Beyerlein for expertly managing production.

For Chega, Daniel, Sarah, and Patrick—without whom not.

John M. Lannon

The Process—Decisions in Planning, Drafting, and Revising

Introduction

Most writing is a conscious, deliberate *process*—not the result of divine intervention, magic, miracles, or last-minute inspiration. Nothing ever leaps from the mind to the page in one neat and painless motion—not even for creative geniuses. Instead, we plan, draft, and revise. Sometimes we know right away what we want to say; sometimes we discover our purpose and meaning only as we write. But our finished product takes shape through our decisions at different stages in the writing process.

Note *This book shows you how to plan, draft, and revise in a suggested sequence of activities. But just as no two people use an identical sequence of activities to drive, ski, or play tennis, no two people write in the same way. How you decide to use this book depends on your writing task and on what works for you.*

HOW WRITING LOOKS

Messiness is a natural and often essential part of writing in its early stages

Writing appears in many shapes

The neat and ordered writing samples throughout this book show the *products* of writing—not the *process*. Every finished writing task begins with messy thoughts, ideas crossed out, lists, arrows, and fragments of ideas, as in the printout of my first draft of this introduction (written using my word processor's editing tool) shown in in Figure I.1. In that figure, my revised text is shown in gray boxes and my comments are shown in blue boxes.

Just as the writing process has no one recipe, the finished products have no one shape. In fact, very little writing published in books, magazines, and newspapers looks exactly like the basic college essay discussed in this book's early chapters (an introductory paragraph beginning or ending with a thesis statement; three or more support paragraphs, each beginning with a topic sentence; and a concluding paragraph). But all effective writers use identical skills: They know how to discover something worthwhile to write about, how to organize their material sensibly, and how to express their ideas clearly and convincingly.

Why college essays are important

What any reader expects

College essays offer a good model for developing these skills because they provide you with a basic structure for shaping your thinking. They also supply an immediate, helpful audience—your instructor and classmates.

Like any audience, your classroom readers will expect you to give them something worthwhile—some useful information, a new insight on some topic, an unusual perspective, or an entertaining story—in a form easy to follow and pleasing to read.

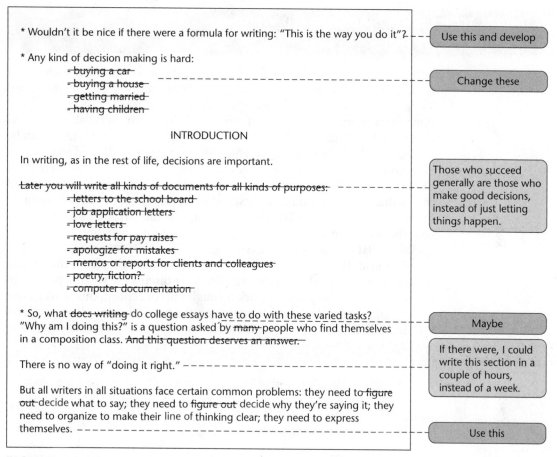

FIGURE 1.1   Part of a typical first draft

HOW WRITING MAKES A DIFFERENCE

Differences writing can make

What kind of difference can any writing make? It might move readers to act or reconsider their biases; it might increase their knowledge or win their support; it might broaden their understanding. Whether you're giving instructions for running an electric toothbrush or pouring out your feelings to a friend, effective writing brings writer and reader together.

As you read the essays in this book, you will see how student and professional writers in all kinds of situations manage to make a difference with their readers. These models, along with the advice and assignments, should help your writing make a difference of its own.

HOW DIGITAL TOOLS HAVE TRANSFORMED WRITING (AND HOW THEY HAVE NOT)

Writers today do most, if not all, of their writing onscreen, using such digital tools as word processing programs, email, blogs, and interactive Web sites. These and many other technologies enhance the speed, volume, and options for transmitting written information. Also, most materials written on paper can be scanned as PDF (Portable Document Format) files that can be posted on a Web site, sent as an email attachment, downloaded to a CD, or even converted into editable e-files, thus removing them from their print origins entirely. But no matter how efficient the writing tools and how varied the media, our communication itself still needs to be *written*. We continue to rely on the proven strategies that comprise the writing process. In the end, the *human brain* remains our ultimate tool for navigating the complex decisions that produce effective writing.

That said, the media that allow us to get our thoughts from the human brain to the page must be considered when we discuss the writing process in today's world. To help you to work through the concepts in this book as you use digital media to get your thoughts on the page, all the writing chapters now include Digital Tips, practical ideas for writing on your computer.

Decisions in the Writing Process

LEARNING OBJECTIVES FOR THIS CHAPTER

- Appreciate the importance of connecting with your reading audience
- Consider the decisions required during the planning, drafting, and revising stages of the writing process
- Understand the looping nature of the writing process
- Recognize that the writing process often involves collaboration
- Identify the benefits and limitations of using digital writing tools

During the writing process, you transform the material you discover—by inspiration, research, accident, or other means—into a message that makes a difference for readers. In short, writing is a process of making deliberate decisions.

Consider a Dear John or Jane letter, an essay exam, a job application, a letter to a newspaper, a note to a sick friend, or your written testimony as a witness to a crime. In each of these situations, you write because you have a *viewpoint*— a position on the topic—and you want to respond or speak out. By asserting your viewpoint, you let readers know exactly where you stand; you announce your position.

Here are just a few examples of viewpoints any writer might assert:

Examples of viewpoints

College is not for everyone.

I deserve a raise.

Food can be just as addictive as a drug.

I want my life to be better than that of my parents.

It's time to bring back school uniforms.

Later you will see how ideas like these serve as thesis statements for essays.

But merely expressing a viewpoint doesn't tell readers very much. To understand and appreciate your ideas, readers need clear explanations. Any useful writing—whether a book, a news article, a memo, a report, or an essay— displays a sensible line of thinking, often in a shape like this:

Much of your writing will have this basic shape

INTRODUCTION
The introduction attracts attention, announces the topic and viewpoint, and previews what will follow. All good introductions invite readers in.

BODY
The body explains and supports the viewpoint, achieving *unity* by remaining focused on the viewpoint. It achieves *coherence* by carrying a line of thinking from sentence to sentence in logical order. Body sections come in all different sizes, depending on how much readers need and expect.

CONCLUSION
The conclusion sums up the meaning of the piece or points toward other meanings to be explored. Good conclusions give readers a clear perspective on what they have just read.

Writers also make decisions about to whom they're writing (their *audience*) and how they want to sound: whether they want to sound formal, friendly, angry, or amused.

DECISION MAKING AND THE WRITING PROCESS

Composing words on paper or onscreen is only one small part of the writing process. Your real challenge lies in making those types of planning, drafting, and revising decisions diagrammed in Figure 1.1.

FIGURE 1.1
Typical decisions during
the writing process

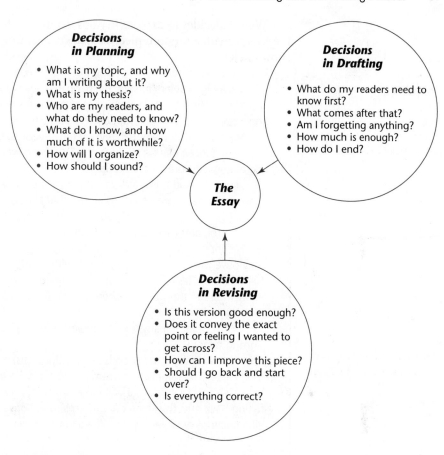

*Decisions
in Planning*

- What is my topic, and why am I writing about it?
- What is my thesis?
- Who are my readers, and what do they need to know?
- What do I know, and how much of it is worthwhile?
- How will I organize?
- How should I sound?

*Decisions
in Drafting*

- What do my readers need to know first?
- What comes after that?
- Am I forgetting anything?
- How much is enough?
- How do I end?

*The
Essay*

*Decisions
in Revising*

- Is this version good enough?
- Does it convey the exact point or feeling I wanted to get across?
- How can I improve this piece?
- Should I go back and start over?
- Is everything correct?

Note

Of course, none of these decisions necessarily occurs in the next sequence shown here. But before turning in a final draft, you will need to answer each of these questions.

CASE STUDY

ONE WRITER'S DECISION-MAKING PROCESS

To appreciate writing as a deliberate process, let's follow one student through two approaches to the same writing situation. We'll see how decisions about planning, drafting, and revising like those shown in Figure 1.1 distinguish this writer's quickest effort from her best effort.

Wendy Gianacoples has been assigned an essay on this topic: "Identify a personal trait that is so strong you cannot control it (a quick temper, shyness, fear of failure, a phobia, or the like). In a serious or humorous essay, show how this trait affects your behavior. Provide enough details for readers to gain a clear understanding of this part of your personality."

Wendy decides to explore her obsession with food. Her first response to the assignment, a random piece of freewriting, took about 20 minutes and is shown below.

Wendy's freewriting

Food is a big problem in so many people's lives these days. I guess so many of us are victims of the ad culture that promotes endless eating while offering miracle diets and contraptions for slimming down and buffing up. "Eat all you want and lose weight!" "Get in fantastic shape without exercising!" With claims like those blaring through the TV, it's no wonder that Americans are increasingly becoming fat and lazy.

For me, food is like a drug—it makes me crazy. I hate it one minute and crave it the next. The amazing thing is that I know I'm just hurting myself when I go to extremes. And I always end up feeling guilty about my lack of self-control, and then I try to undo the damage.

I suppose everyone has some little secret, something in the closet that they have to live with. But struggling with a food obsession becomes nearly a full-time task. It's almost always on my mind: how I can't stop thinking about my next secret trip to the kitchen so I can feed my insecurities with sweets and calories and everything in sight; how I then do penance by fasting and exercising; how I never tell anyone. If people could only see me, it would be a sorry sight to behold.

Not even my close friends know about this. It just seems too painful to talk about. But somehow it seems easier to write about it. I keep promising myself that I'll find the willpower to overcome this, but so far I just keep falling back into the same old patterns, and I have no idea why. I wonder if all addictions are like this one: filled with secrecy, sadness, helplessness, and self-loathing.

Discussion of Wendy's freewriting

Freewriting is a valuable invention tool—but merely a first step. Wendy's draft has potential, but she hints at lots of things in general and points at nothing in particular. Without a thesis to assert a controlling viewpoint, neither writer nor reader finds an orientation. Lacking a definite thesis, Wendy never decided which material didn't belong, which material was the most important, and which material deserved careful development.

At first, the essay seems to be about how media marketing exploits American eating habits, but the beginning of the second paragraph suggests that Wendy's topic has shifted to her own problems with food. The rest of her draft only hints at the specific problem Wendy is attempting to describe. The final sentence seems to drift off by talking about addiction in general.

The lack of an introduction and a conclusion prevents us from narrowing the possible meanings of the piece and finding a clear perspective on what we have just read. Paragraphs also either lack development or fail to focus on one specific point. And some sentences (like the second and third in paragraph four) lack logical connections to other material.

Finally, we get almost no concrete sense of a real person speaking to real people. Wendy has written only for herself—as if she were writing in a journal or diary.

A quick effort (as in a journal or diary) offers a good way to get started. But when writers go no further, they bypass the essential stages of *planning* and *revising*. In fact, putting something on the page or screen is relatively easy. But getting the piece to *succeed*, to make a difference for readers, requires tougher decisions.

Now let's follow Wendy's thinking as she returns to her freewriting and struggles through her planning decisions.

Wendy's planning decisions

What exactly is my topic, and why am I writing about it? *My intended topic was "an uncompromising look at my obsession with food," but my first draft got off track. I need to focus on the specifics!*

I'm writing this essay to discover my own feelings and to help readers understand these feelings by showing them specific parts of my lifestyle that I can finally face realistically.

What is my thesis? *After countless tries, I think I've finally settled on my rough thesis: "Food can seem like my best friend, but it actually dominates my life through endless cycles of need, indulgence, self-loathing, and guilt."*

Who are my readers, and what do they need to know? *My audience consists of my teacher and classmates. (This essay will be discussed in class.) Each reader is already somewhat familiar with the American preoccupation with eating. But I want my audience to understand specifically the consequences of my personal obsession.*

What do I know about this topic? *A better question might be, What don't I know? I've spent much of my life dealing with this issue, so I certainly don't have to do any research.*

Of all the information I have on this topic, how much of it is worthwhile (considering my purpose and audience)? *Because I could write volumes here, I'll have to resist getting carried away. I've already decided to focus on the "cycles" named in my thesis. One paragraph explaining each of these supporting points (and illustrating them with well-chosen examples) should do.*

How will I organize? *I guess I've already made this decision by settling on my thesis: moving from need to indulgence to self-loathing to guilt. Self-loathing and guilt are what I want to emphasize, so I will save them for last.*

How do I want my writing to sound? *I'm sharing something intimate with my classmates, so my tone should be intimate and personal, as when people talk to people they trust.*

In completing her essay, Wendy went on to make similar decisions for drafting and revising. Here is her final draft.

Wendy's final draft	**CONFESSIONS OF A FOOD ADDICT**
Introductory paragraph (leads into the thesis)	Like many compulsive eaters, I eat to fill a void—an emptiness within. I feed my feelings. Food can be my best friend, always dependable, always there when needed. *This friend, however, actually is a tyrant that dominates*
Thesis	*my life through endless cycles of need, indulgence, and guilt.*
Topic sentence and first support paragraph	*Thanks to my food obsession, I seem to have two personalities: the respected, self-controlled Wendy who eats properly all day, and the fat, needy Wendy who emerges after dark to gobble everything in sight.* Lying in bed, I wait for the house to be silent. Feeling excited and giddy, I sneak to the kitchen and head straight for the freezer to begin my search. My initial prize is an unopened pint of Ben & Jerry's chocolate chip ice cream. I break the container's seal, dig in with my spoon, and shovel down massive gobs. (I have a love-hate relationship with food: I want all or nothing.) Before long, the container is empty.
Topic sentence and second support paragraph (divided into three sections to parallel the phases of the "binge")	*Stashing the empty container deeply in the trash, I continue my rampage.* From the cookie drawer, I snatch a nearly full package of Fig Newtons. As I tiptoe toward the milk, I ask myself what the folks at Weight Watchers would say if they could see me standing half-awake in my ice cream–splattered Lanz nightgown, popping down Fig Newtons and swigging milk from the carton. After pushing the few remaining cookies to the front of the package to make it look fuller, I rummage around for my next "fix."
Next phase	Beneath a bag of frozen Bird's Eye vegetables lurks a frozen pizza—the ultimate midnight snack. The oven will take too long, but the microwave is too noisy—all that beeping could get me busted. Feeling daring, I turn on the kitchen faucet to drown out the beeps, place the pizza in the microwave, set the timer, grab the last handful of Fig Newtons, and wait.
Final phase	By the time the pizza gets polished off, it's 1:00 a.m. and I crave Kraft Macaroni & Cheese. Standing on a chair, I reach for a box from the overhead cabinet. Trying to be quiet, I dig out a spaghetti pot from a pile of pots and pans, holding my breath as I ease the pan from the clutter. While the water boils and the macaroni cooks, I fix a bowl of Rice Krispies. Just as I finish chowing down "Snap, Crackle, and Pop," the macaroni is ready. I eat the whole package and then bury the box in the trash.
Topic sentence and third support paragraph	*After a binge, I panic: What have I done?* I set a hand on my bulging stomach and think of the weight I'll gain this week. Climbing the stairs to my bed, I feel drained, like a person on drugs who is now "coming down." In my bedroom, I study myself in the full-length mirror, looking for visible signs of my sins. Lying in bed, I feel fat and uncomfortable. Although I usually sleep on my stomach, on binge nights I assume the fetal position, cradling my full belly, feeling ashamed and alone, as if I were the only person who overeats and uses food as a crutch. When the sugar I've consumed keeps me awake, I plead with God to help me overcome this weakness.
Topic sentence and fourth support paragraph (kept brief to emphasize the big picture—looking backward and forward)	*The next morning, I kick myself and feel guilty.* I want to block out last night's memories, but my tight clothes offer a painful reminder. My stomach is sick all day, and I have heartburn. During the following week, I'll eat next to nothing and exercise constantly, hoping to break even on the scale at Weight Watchers.

Concluding paragraph	Most people don't consider compulsive eating an addiction. Substance abusers can be easy to spot, but food addicts are less obvious. Unlike drugs, one can't live without food. People would never encourage a drug addict or an alcoholic to "have another hit" or "fall off the wagon." However, people constantly push food on overeaters: "Come on, one brownie won't hurt. I made them especially for you," says a friend. When I decline, she scowls and turns away. Little does she know, while she was in the bathroom, I had four. —*Wendy Gianacoples*

Discussion of Wendy's final draft

Here are some of Wendy's major improvements:

- The distinct shape (introduction, body, conclusion) enables us to organize our understanding and follow the writer's thinking.
- The essay no longer confuses us. We know where this writer stands because she tells us, with a definite thesis, and we know why because she shows us, with plenty of examples.
- She wastes nothing; everything seems to belong, and everything fits together.
- Now each paragraph has its own design, and each paragraph enhances the whole.
- We now see real variety in the ways in which words are put together. We hear a genuine voice.

All good writing has these qualities

Because she made careful decisions, Wendy produced a final draft that displays the qualities of all good writing: *content* that makes it worth reading, *organization* that reveals the line of thinking and emphasizes what is most important, and *style* that is economical and convincingly human.

THE LOOPING STRUCTURE OF THE WRITING PROCESS

Writing is not predictable

Writers rarely struggle with decisions about planning, drafting, and revising in a predictable sequence. Instead, writers choose sequences that work best for them. Figure 1.2 diagrams this looping ("recursive") structure of the writing process.

In some ways, the writing process is always different; in some ways, it's always the same. For example, we tackle a research paper differently from questions on an essay exam. Memos, letters, reports, emails, or other workplace documents call for their own specific approaches. In some of these cases (say, an essay exam), immediate time pressures might force you to find shortcuts. When you're writing about a topic you already know well, you might spend less time planning what to say. When you're writing a

FIGURE 1.2
The looping structure of the writing process

Decisions in the writing process are recursive; no one stage is complete until all stages are complete.

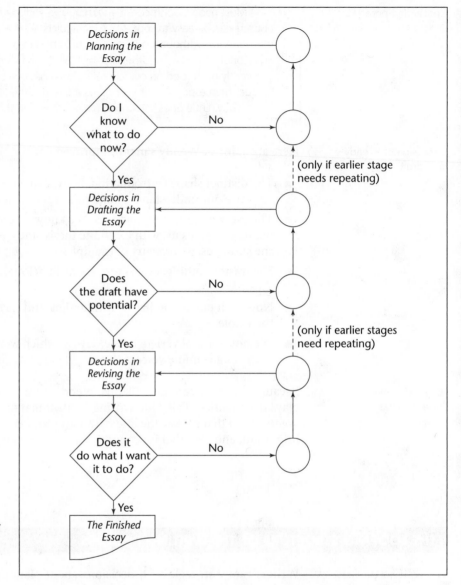

A writer might even revisit the "finished" essay for additional revision.

document that will be posted online (say, a Web page), the updating and revising might be endless. But even though any writing situation poses its own particular challenges, the basic loop of planning, drafting, and revising remains pretty much constant.

Note   *Rarely is any piece of writing ever strictly "finished." Even famous writers have returned to a successful published work years later to revise it once again.*

DECISIONS IN COLLABORATIVE WRITING

Many of the Applications exercises in this book ask you to collaborate with peers. Especially now that the Internet simplifies collaborative work, countless documents in the workplace are produced by teams; effective collaboration enables a group to synthesize the best from each member. Collaboration allows us to do the following:

Benefits of collaboration

- Share in new perspectives
- Test and sharpen ideas
- Recognize our biases and assumptions
- Get feedback from group members
- Enjoy group support instead of working alone

But like all writing, collaborative work demands decisions. Group members have to find ways of expressing their views persuasively, of accepting constructive criticism, and of getting along and reaching agreement with others who hold different views. Collaborators may face these potential problems:

Things that go wrong in collaborative work

- Differences in personality, working style, commitment, standards, or ability to take criticism
- Disagreements about exactly what or how much the group should accomplish, who should do what, or who should make the final decisions
- Feelings of intimidation or reluctance to speak out

Guidelines in the following chapters will help make collaborative projects more productive for you.

DIGITAL TIP

Know When Digital Tools Can Help and When They Cannot

Besides reducing the drudgery of writing and revising, computers can provide tremendous advantages if you understand their limitations. Here are some of those benefits and limitations:

Benefits

- As you write, you can brainstorm, develop different outlines, design countless versions of a document, and keep whatever you need on file.

- You can do much—but not all—of your research at the computer. See Chapter 21 for detailed descriptions of computerized research and reference tools.

- Using email, instant messaging, a networked classroom, a collaborative (Wiki) Web site, or a blog, people can edit, proofread, and comment on each other's writing—often without altering the text itself.

(continues)

Limitations

- The task of sorting, organizing, and interpreting information still belongs to the writer. Computers cannot do our thinking for us.

- No digital device such as a spelling or grammer checker can convert bad writing to good. Moreover, the ease of "fixing" our writing on a computer might encourage minimal revision. (Sometimes the very act of rewriting an entire page in longhand or type causes us to rethink that page or discover something new.)

- Thorough research is rarely done exclusively via the Internet. Hard copy sources that have been overseen by experts before publication and guidance from a trained librarian continue to be indispensable.

Throughout this book, further "Digital Tips" boxes will help you make thoughtful decisions about the part computers and other digital tools can serve when you write.

APPLICATIONS

1.1   We all hear and read plenty about America's social problems: poverty, inequality, racial strife, violence, and so on. How then could any "ordinary" writer be expected to contribute something new to that conversation? Could only professional writers make a difference?

Read the following essay—by a 19-year-old student—and decide for yourself whether it makes a difference for you. (Use the questions that follow the essay as a guide for your analysis.)

Essay for analysis

BREAKING THE BONDS OF HATE

Ever since I can remember, I wanted the ideal life: a big house, lots of money, cars. I wanted to find the perfect happiness that so many people have longed for. I wanted more than life in the jungle of Cambodia. America was the place, the land of tall skyscrapers, televisions, cars, and airplanes.

In the jungles of Cambodia, I lived in a refugee camp. We didn't have good sanitation or modern conveniences. For example, there were no inside bathrooms—only outside ones made from palm-tree leaves, surrounded by millions of flies. When walking down the street, I could smell the aroma of the outhouse; in the afternoon, the 5- and 6-year-olds played with the dirt in front of it. It was the only thing they had to play with, and the "fragrance" never seemed to bother them. And it never bothered me. Because I smelled it every day, I was used to it.

The only thing that bothered me was the war. I have spent half of my life in war. The killing is still implanted in my mind. I hate Cambodia. When I came to America 9 years ago at the age of 10, I thought I was being born into a new life. No more being hungry, no more fighting, no more killing. I thought I had escaped the war.

In America, there are more kinds of material things than Cambodians could ever want. And here we don't have to live in the jungle like monkeys, we don't have to hide from mortar bombing, and we don't have to smell the rotten human carrion. But for the immigrant, America presents a different type of jungle, a different type of war, and a smell as bad as the waste of Cambodia.

Most Americans believe the stereotype that immigrants work hard, get a good education, and have a very good life. Maybe it used to be like that, but not anymore. You have to be deceptive and unscrupulous in order to make it. If you are not, then you will end up like most immigrants I've known. Living in the ghetto in a cockroach-infested house. Working on the assembly line or in the chicken factory to support your family. Getting up at 3 o'clock in the morning to take the bus to work and not getting home until 5 p.m.

If you're a kid my age, you drop out of school to work because your parents don't have enough money to buy you clothes for school. You may end up selling drugs because you want cars, money, and parties, as all teenagers do. You have to depend on your peers for emotional support because your parents are too busy working in the factory trying to make money to pay the bills. You don't get along with your parents because they have a different mentality: You are an American and they are Cambodian. You hate them because they are never there for you, so you join a gang as I did.

You spend your time drinking, doing drugs, and fighting. You beat up people for pleasure. You don't care about anything except your drugs, your beers, and your revenge against adversaries. You shoot at people because they've insulted your pride. You shoot at the police because they are always bothering you. They shoot back and then you're dead like my best friend, Sinerth.

Sinerth robbed a gas station. He was shot in the head by the police. I'd known him since the sixth grade from my first school in Minneapolis. I can still remember his voice calling me from California. "Virak, come down here, man," he said. "We need you. There are lots of pretty girls down here." I promised him that I would be there to see him. The following year he was dead. I felt sorry for him. But as I thought it over, maybe it is better for him to be dead than to continue with the cycle of violence, to live with hate. I thought, "It is better to die than live like an angry young fool, thinking that everybody is out to get you."

Mad-dog mind-set: When I was like Sinerth, I didn't care about dying. I thought that I was on top of the world, being immortalized by drugs. I could see that my future would be spent working on the assembly line like most of my friends, spending all my paycheck on the weekend, and being broke again on Monday morning. I hated going to school because I couldn't see a way to get out of the endless cycle. My philosophy was "Live hard and die young."

I hated America because, to me, it was not the place of opportunities or the land of the "melting pot" as I had been told. All I had seen were broken beer bottles on the street and homeless people and drunks using the sky as their roof. I couldn't walk down the street without someone yelling out, "You f—ing gook" from his car. Once again I was caught in the web of hatred. I'd become a mad dog with the mind-set of the past: "When trapped in the corner, just bite." The war mentality of Cambodia came back: Get what you can and leave. I thought I came to America to escape war, poverty, fighting, to escape the violence, but I wasn't escaping, I was being introduced to a newer version of war—the war of hatred.

I was lucky. In Minneapolis, I dropped out of school in the ninth grade to join a gang. Then I moved to Louisiana, where I continued my life of "immortality" as a member of another gang. It came to an abrupt halt when I crashed a car. I wasn't badly injured, but I was underage, and the fine took all my money. I called a good friend of the Cambodian community in Minneapolis for advice (she'd tried to help me earlier). I didn't know where to go or whom to turn to. I saw friends landing in jail, and I didn't want that. She promised to help me get back in school. And she did.

Since then I've been given a lot of encouragement and caring by American friends and teachers who've helped me turn my life around. They opened my eyes to a kind of education that frees us all from ignorance and slavery. I could have failed so many times except for those people who believed in me and gave me another chance. Individuals who were willing to help me have taught me that I can help myself. I'm now a senior and have been at my school for three years; I plan to attend college in the fall. I am struggling to believe I can reach the other side of the mountain.

—*Virak Khiev*

Questions about the reading

Does the Content of the Essay Make It Worth Reading?

- Can you find a definite thesis that announces the writer's viewpoint? Where?
- Do you have enough information to understand the viewpoint?
- Do you learn something new and useful? Explain briefly.
- Does everything belong, or should any material be cut? Where?

Does the Organization Reveal the Writer's Line of Thinking?

- Is there an introduction to set the scene, a middle to walk through, and a conclusion to sum up the meaning?
- Does each support paragraph present a distinct unit of meaning?
- Does each paragraph stick to the point and stick together?

Is the Style Economical and Convincing?

- Can you understand each sentence the first time you read it? If not, which ones need clarification?
- Should any words be cut? If so, where?
- Are sentences varied in the way they're put together? Cite examples.
- Is the writer's meaning always clear? If not, where is it unclear?
- Can you hear a real person speaking? Describe the person you hear.
- Do you like the person you hear? Why or why not?

Write out your answers to these questions, and be prepared to discuss them in class.

1.2   **COLLABORATIVE PROJECT** In class, write a "quick effort" essay about a personal trait or about an event that left you feeling alienated. Exchange papers with a classmate, and evaluate your classmate's paper, using the questions from Application 1.1. In one or two paragraphs, give your classmate advice for revising. Don't be afraid to mark up the paper you're evaluating with your own questions, comments, and suggestions. Discuss your evaluation with your classmate. At home, review the evaluation of your paper carefully, and write your "best" version of your original essay. List the improvements you made in moving from your quick effort to your best effort. Be prepared to discuss your improvements in class.

Also, in two or three paragraphs, trace your own writing process for this essay by describing the decisions you made. Be prepared to discuss your decisions in class.

Note   *Don't expect miracles at this stage, but do expect some degree of frustration and confusion. Things will improve quickly.*

1.3   **COLLABORATIVE PROJECT** Out of class (and drawing on your personal experience with group work if possible), write down one benefit you look forward to in working with peers and one potential problem. In class, share your expectations and concerns with a small group. Do group members raise similar issues, or does everyone have different concerns? As a group, craft these issues and concerns into a list of group goals: benefits you hope to achieve and pitfalls you hope to avoid.

1.4   **WEB-BASED PROJECT** Visit the Colorado State University writing guides at <**http:///www.writing.colostate.edu/guides/**>. Under the "Writing Documents" link, explore the "Writing Academic Evaluations" and "Answering Exam Questions" sections. In 200 to 300 words, describe how the process for these types of writing projects follows the looping process shown in Figure 1.2. What are the key stages in the process? How do you know when to move forward and when to back up and repeat a stage?

Attach a copy of all relevant Web pages to your explanation.

Note   *Instead of quoting your sources directly, paraphrase (page 384). Be sure to credit each source of information (page 380).*

1.5   The following list offers ideas for essays you might write. People write best about things they know, so we begin with personal forms of writing. You might want to return to this list for topic ideas when essays are assigned throughout the early chapters of this book.

(a)   Do some music videos communicate distorted and dangerous messages? If so, what should be done? Discuss specific examples and their effect on viewers.

(b)   Our public schools have been accused of failing to educate America's students. Does your high school typify the so-called failure of American education? Why or why not? How well did your school prepare you for college—and for life?

(c) Describe the good and bad points of being a "nontraditional" student (returning to school after military service, employment, raising a family, or the like). Write for readers in a similar situation who are thinking about returning to school. What are the most important things they should know?

(d) As a part-time student who balances work and school, give advice to a friend in your situation who wants to follow your example but feels fearful or discouraged. Explain how you manage to cope.

For additional information and practice with the learning objectives in this chapter, go to www.mycomplab.com, Resources>Writing>The Writing Process.

Decisions in Planning

LEARNING OBJECTIVES FOR THIS CHAPTER

- Develop the skills for deciding about topic, purpose, thesis, and audience
- Discover useful material through freewriting, asking questions, brainstorming, mind mapping, and reading and researching

- Select and organize material effectively

- Find your own voice, connect with your audience, and avoid an overly informal tone

- Use planning skills for your own work as well as group work

Why writers need to plan

Writing is a battle with impatience, a fight against the natural urge to "be done with it." Effective writers win this battle by *planning*: analyzing their writing situation, exploring their assets, and finding a voice. Of course, planning continues throughout the writing process, but an initial plan gives you a place to start and a direction for your decisions.

DECIDING ON A TOPIC, PURPOSE, THESIS, AND AUDIENCE

Your earliest planning decisions will require that you analyze your writing situation.

Questions for Analyzing a Writing Situation

- *What, exactly, is my topic?*
- *Why am I writing about this?*

- *What is my thesis?*
- *Who are my readers?*

You won't always follow the same order in making these decisions; in Chapter 1, Wendy Gianacoples discovers her thesis before brainstorming for material. The key is to make all the decisions in whichever order works best for you.

As with any stage in the writing process, you might have to return again and again to your plan.

Decide on Your Topic

When you are asked to choose your own topic, remember one word: *focus*. Sometimes, afraid we'll have too little to say, we mistakenly choose the broadest topic. But a focused topic provides more to write about by allowing for the nitty-gritty details that show readers what we mean. A *focused topic* is something you know and can talk about from your own experience, observation, or research, something that has real meaning for you.

"What, exactly, is my topic?"

Within any subject, you need to discover a *topic*, your own angle of vision, a viewpoint. First, make the subject narrow:

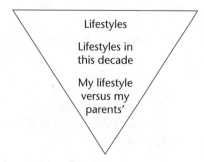

Lifestyles

Lifestyles in this decade

My lifestyle versus my parents'

Even the limited subject "my lifestyle versus my parents'" could be narrowed again—say, to one specific difference (in attitudes about money or work or education or the like).

Narrow your subject until you get to where you can take a definite position; then make it a topic by inserting your viewpoint.

SUBJECT		TOPIC
My lifestyle versus my parents'	→	How I want my life to differ from that of my parents

---

GUIDELINES for Choosing Your Essay Topic

- *Begin with something you know and can discuss in detail.*

- *Say a lot about a little rather than a little about a lot.* Sometimes, afraid we'll have too little to say, we mistakenly choose the broadest topic. But a focused topic actually provides *more* to write about by allowing for the nitty-gritty details that show readers what we mean.

- *Narrow the topic until you can express a specific point of view.*

- *Take your time.* People who begin writing too early usually hit a dead end.

> **Note** | *Use the Internet to locate topics of interest via Wikipedia, for example, or Google or Yahoo.*

You might get stuck later and have to discard the whole topic, but for now you have a clear and definite start.

Decide on Your Purpose

"Why am I writing this?"

Finding a *purpose* means asking yourself, Why am I writing this piece? Each writing situation has a specific *goal*. Perhaps you want audience members to see what you saw, to feel what you felt, or to think differently. To achieve your goal, you will need a definite *strategy*.

Goal plus strategy equals purpose. Consider one writer's inadequate answers to the familiar question "Why am I writing this paper?"

Inadequate statements of purpose

> I'm writing this essay to pass the course.
>
> My goal is to write an essay about college life.
>
> My goal is to describe to classmates the experience of being a nontraditional student.

The first two responses tell nothing about the specific goal. The third response defines the goal but offers no strategy. Here is our writer's final purpose statement (goal plus strategy):

A useful statement of purpose

> My purpose is to describe to classmates the experience of being a nontraditional student. I'll focus on the special anxieties, difficulties, and rewards.

Sometimes you might need to explore purposes until one pops up. In any case, the purpose statement should provide the raw material for your thesis.

GUIDELINES for Deciding on Your Writing Purpose

- *Specify your goal.* Perhaps you want readers to see what you saw, to feel what you felt, or to change their opinion. The goal of "writing an essay about yoga" is too general; "writing an essay to persuade my classmates to give yoga a try" is more definite.

- *Identify an effective strategy.* Here is a clear strategy for a persuasive essay about yoga: "My purpose is to write an essay persuading classmates to try yoga by explaining how it relaxes the body, clears the mind, and stimulates the imagination."

- *Take your time.* Sometimes you won't be able to define your purpose immediately. You might need to make a rough draft or outline first.

Note

The purpose statement is part of the discovery process; the thesis is part of the finished essay. (See pages 22–27.)

Decide on Your Thesis

"What is my thesis?"

Your purpose statement identifies exactly what you want to *do*. Your thesis announces exactly what you want to *say*—the "big picture" boiled down to one or two (or sometimes three) sentences. Usually appearing early in your essay, the thesis conveys two kinds of information: It names the topic, and it states your viewpoint about the topic:

	TOPIC	VIEWPOINT

Topic plus viewpoint

[Chemical pesticides and herbicides] [are not only hazardous but also ineffective].

The essay can then be built around this central idea.

What a thesis does

By telling readers exactly what to expect, your thesis makes a commitment. Besides serving as the reader's road map, the thesis is your planning tool—the thread that holds your ideas together and that clarifies your own thinking.

The thesis itself can be expressed in various ways, as in these examples:

An opinion

Starting college after the age of 30 hasn't been easy, but the good points definitely outweigh the bad.

An evaluation

I want my life to be better than that of my parents.

A suggestion

Campus security should be increased.

A question

Should college be for everyone?

A debatable claim

High school should be shortened by two years.

Each of these thesis statements creates a clear expectation. They don't keep readers guessing. They make their points quickly.

Note

Think of your thesis as "the one sentence you would keep if you could keep only one" (U.S. Air Force Academy 11).

Thesis as Framework.   Consciously or unconsciously, readers look for a thesis, usually in the essay's early paragraphs. Even a single paragraph is hard to understand if the main point is missing. For example, read this next paragraph only once, and then try answering the questions that follow it.

A paragraph with its main point omitted

This person's job is not to punish but to heal. Most students are bad writers, but the more serious the injuries, the more confusing the symptoms, the greater the need for effective diagnostic work. When an accident victim is carried into the hospital emergency ward, the doctor does not start treating the patient at the top and slowly work down without a sense of priority, spending a great deal of time on the black eye before [getting] to the punctured lung. Yet that is exactly what the English teacher too often does. The doctor looks for the most vital problem; he [or she] wants to keep the patient alive, and . . . goes to work on the critical injury.

—*Donald Murray*

Can you identify the paragraph's main idea? Probably not. Without the main point, you have no framework for understanding this information in its larger meaning.

Now insert the following sentence at the beginning and reread the paragraph.

The missing main idea

| The writing teacher must not be a judge but a physician.

This orientation makes the paragraph's exact meaning obvious.

In the basic essay framework, each body paragraph supports its own *topic statement,* which focuses on one aspect of the thesis. The thesis is the controlling idea; each topic statement treats one part of the controlling idea, as diagrammed here:

Introductory paragraph

Support paragraphs

Some writers include in the thesis an explicit preview of supporting points; some don't. For instance, an essay titled "Beef Cost and the Cattle Rancher" might have this thesis statement:

A thesis that includes a preview

| Because of rising costs, unpredictable weather, and long hours, many cattle ranchers have trouble staying in business.

An alternative is to omit such a preview:

| Cattle ranchers' biggest challenge is survival for their businesses.

Including a preview in their thesis helps some writers stay on track as they develop each support paragraph. With or without the preview, be sure that supporting points appear as topic statements in subsequent paragraphs, as in this next example:

Introductory paragraph

Thesis

| _____
_____
_____ Starting college after age 30 hasn't been easy, but the good points definitely outweigh the bad.

Although that thesis does not preview the main supporting points, each point is spelled out in respective topic statements:

First support paragraph

| My major obstacles were lack of self-confidence and fear of failure. [*topic statement*]

_____
_____

Second support paragraph	While struggling to overcome my panic, I worked at developing good study habits and sharpening my basic skills. [*topic statement*]
	_____
	_____
Third support paragraph	After realizing I could do the work, I began to relax and savor the "joy of learning." [*topic statement*]
	_____
	_____

Evaluating Your Thesis.   The first thing readers want to know is this:

What readers ask about your thesis

| What, exactly, is your point, and why is it worth reading about?

Always check to see that your thesis provides a sharp focus and a definite and significant viewpoint.

- *Is the topic sharply focused?* In a short essay, avoid broad topics:

Too broad

| Some experiences can be unforgettable.

- *Is a definite viewpoint expressed?* Convey your exact position. These thesis statements are not clear:

No clear viewpoint

| I started college at age 35. [*Merely states a fact.*]
College can be a complex experience.

- *Is the viewpoint worthwhile?* Whether your thesis is expressed as an opinion, an evaluation, a suggestion, a question, or a debatable claim, it should trigger some fresh insight or have some value or importance for readers. A thesis that contributes nothing new is worthless:

Insignificant viewpoints

| The college years can be traumatic. [*Everyone would agree, so why discuss something obvious?*]
Every nontraditional student has a unique college experience. [*No big surprise here!*]

- *Is the point supportable?* Avoid any claim that you can't back up with credible evidence (page 81):

Unsupportable claim

| Older students are more serious about schoolwork than their younger counterparts.

- *Does the thesis offer a preview?* Provide a concise but clear picture of where your essay is headed. This next sentence offers no such preview:

No preview

| My experience as a nontraditional student has been interesting, to say the least.

GUIDELINES for Developing Your Thesis

- *Allow plenty of time for getting your thinking straight.* Don't expect your thesis to pop up automatically. For any writer, deciding on a solid thesis is often half the battle.

- *Use whatever works to get yourself started.* Try writing a *working thesis,* summarizing in one or two sentences the main point you want your essay to convey. If you get stuck, try freewriting, brainstorming, or other discovery strategies from pages 30–33. Keep at it until a working thesis emerges.

- *Settle on a specific topic.* Never tackle something too broad. Instead of writing, say, about *school reform* (a huge topic), focus on *school uniforms* or *dress codes.*

- *Stick to one clear and definite main point.* Spell out your viewpoint on the topic: For example, "School uniforms offer one promising way of improving the learning environment." Take a position that leads somewhere; don't merely state a *fact,* as in "Nearly three-fourths of New York City schools now have dress codes." Facts serve as evidence to *support* a thesis, but once a fact has been verified (see page 83), there is little else to say about it. However, your viewpoint about what a fact "means" could serve as a thesis, as in "The growing popularity of dress codes is one more sign that school reform is headed back to the basics."

    Once you have settled on a position, don't be vague about it: Instead of "School dress codes have benefits and drawbacks," write "The benefits of school dress codes outweigh the drawbacks."

- *Make a worthwhile point.* Be sure that your point is worth discussing or arguing—that it offers something new or significant (see page 81). Don't merely restate the obvious, as in "School uniforms are a controversial issue."

- *Make your point supportable.* Readers always want to know "Says who?" Don't make an overstated claim, as in "Uniforms and dress codes are the best way to improve our schools." Don't make a highly opinionated claim that can't be backed up, as in "Uniforms make students look and feel more attractive." Instead, rely on the evidence: "As many schools are discovering, uniforms and dress codes can enhance the learning environment." Be sure you can support your point within the length of your essay. Also be sure that you have enough to say to justify an entire essay.

- *Get your facts straight.* Some claims will require research; some will not. For example, research would be needed to support this thesis: "Evidence increasingly suggests that dress codes promote a more disciplined learning environment."

- *Offer a preview of the whole essay.* Key words or phrases in your thesis tell readers what to expect in terms of the essay's purpose, scope, and direction. Replace abstract and general words ("good," "poor," "interesting," "significant," "complex") with concrete and specific words ("evidence suggests," "disciplined learning environment"). Avoid needless and self-evident prefaces, as in "The purpose of this essay is to…" or "In this paper, I will show…"; instead, let your key words provide the forecast.

For a more explicit preview, list your supporting points in your thesis. This might require two or more sentences, as in "School uniforms and dress codes are on the rise and for good reason: They work. School districts across the country are finding that uniforms promote discipline, safety, and learning, along with a sense of equality among differing social groups." Each of those four supporting points then will appear in its own topic sentence.

- *Use the thesis to check on your paper.* As you work on your paper, keep checking back to make sure you haven't wandered—but if you happen to discover some new and promising direction, you might rethink your thesis and adjust it as needed.

- *Always leave room for revision.* Plan on writing numerous versions and be prepared to revise the thesis while you are writing your essay, all the way to the end.

- *Decide where to place your thesis.* In a college essay, the thesis usually appears as the final sentence of the essay's introduction. But in some writing situations, it can appear elsewhere, as shown on page 301.

In this next sentence, the preview is adequate, but the preface is needless:

Needless preface

[In this essay, I will discuss how] the good points of starting college after the age of 30 definitely outweigh the bad.

How thesis form and location can vary

Variations in Your Thesis. The thesis statement can take different forms:

- The thesis need not be limited to one sentence.
- The thesis does not always explicitly preview the main supporting points.
- A thesis does not automatically call for only three supporting points. Three is a good minimum, but some topics call for more, others for only one or two.

When to Compose Your Thesis. In an ideal world, writers would be able to (1) settle on a topic, (2) compose a purpose statement, and (3) compose a thesis. But these steps rarely occur in such neat order. If you have trouble coming up with a thesis right away, go on to some other activity: List some ideas, work on an outline, do some freewriting, or take a walk. Writing, after all, is a way of discovering what you want to say. Sometimes, preliminary research is necessary.

Even if you do begin with a workable thesis, it might not be the one you end up with. As you work and discover new meanings, you might need to revise or start again.

"Who are my readers
and what do they expect?

Decide on Your Audience

Except for a diary or a journal, everything you write is for readers who will react to your information. You might write to a prospective employer who wants to know why you quit a recent job, to a committee who wants to know why you deserve a scholarship, to a classmate who wants to know you better, or to a professor who wants to know whether you understand the material. For any audience, your task is to deliver a message that makes a difference with readers and helps them see things your way.

Audiences you might
encounter

Out of school, you will write for diverse audiences (customers, employers, politicians, and so on). But in school, you can envision a definite audience besides your instructor: your classmates. Like anyone else, they expect your writing to be clear, informative, and persuasive. Whoever your readers are, they need enough material to understand your position and to react appropriately. Readers don't need repetition of material they already know. To put readers in your place, first put yourself in theirs. Anticipate their most probable questions.

What audiences expect

GUIDELINES for Analyzing Your Audience

- *Picture your readers and exactly what they need and expect.* Whether your audience is the company president or the person sitting next to you in first-year English, that audience is motivated by specific concerns and information needs. Your readers may expect to acquire information, solve a problem, make a decision, evaluate your performance, or merely be entertained.

- *When you don't know exactly who will be reading your essay, picture the "general reader."* General readers, like almost all of us, are impatient with abstract theories yet expect enough background to help them grasp your message. They are bored or confused by excessive detail, and they are frustrated by raw facts left unexplained or uninterpreted. Instead of trying to show readers how smart you are, make *them* feel smart.

- *Anticipate your readers' questions.* Based on their specific needs and concerns, readers have various questions: What is it? What does it mean? What happened? Who was involved? When, where, and why did it happen? What might happen? How do I do it? How did you do it? Why is X better than Y? Can you give examples? Says who? So what? Give readers what they need to know, not what they already know.

- *Anticipate your readers' reactions.* If your topic is controversial, will some people resist what you have to say? Will some feel threatened or offended? Should you be bold and outspoken, or tread lightly? No matter how sensible your ideas, they will be rejected out of hand by any audience you alienate. (For achieving a likable persona, see page 291.)

ANALYZING YOUR WRITING SITUATION

Assume that you are writing in response to this assignment:

> Illustrate some feature of our societal values or behavior that you find humorous, depressing, contemptible, or admirable. Possible topics: our consumer or dress habits, the cars we drive, our ideas of entertainment.

First, focus your topic:

Focusing your topic

> societal values or behavior   →
>
> the cars we drive   →
>
> our love affair with cars   →
>
> why we love our cars   →

This last topic seems focused enough for a short essay. But what in this topic do you wish to explore? What do you want readers to see and understand?

Your focused topic

> How cars appeal to our sense of individuality

Now that you have a suitable topic, you're on your way. You might get stuck later and have to start from scratch, but for now you can move forward and decide on your purpose.

Because the essay examines *how*, you organize a rough outline to lay out a sequence of examples:

Your rough outline

> 1. The car as an individual statement
> 2. The car as a political statement
> 3. The car as a personal sanctuary

Now you can compose your statement of purpose:

Your purpose statement

> My purpose is to poke fun at our obsession with cars by explaining to my classmates how cars appeal to our sense of individuality. I'll discuss uses of the car as a lifestyle statement, personal billboard, and private sanctuary.

This is your map for reaching your goal. (Keep in mind that the purpose statement is part of the discovery process, but the thesis is part of the finished essay.)

Based on the purpose statement, you might derive the following thesis:

Your thesis

> Today's self-centered consumers demand cars that satisfy their craving for individuality.

As you consider your audience (teacher and classmates), you anticipate the following general questions about your thesis:

General questions you can anticipate

- *Exactly what do you mean by "individuality"?*
- *What is the connection between cars and individuality?*
- *Can you give examples?*
- *Who cares?*

As this case study continues, after the following section, you will identify more specific audience questions you need to answer.

DISCOVERING, SELECTING, AND ORGANIZING YOUR MATERIAL

Once you have analyzed your writing situation by choosing a topic, honing your purpose, writing a thesis, and anticipating your audience, you need to ask yourself the following questions.

Questions for Exploring Your Assets

- *What do I know about the topic?*
- *How much of my material is useful in this situation?*
- *How will readers want this organized?*

Discover Useful Material

"What do I know about the topic?"

Discovering useful material is called *invention*. When you begin working with an idea or exploring a topic, you search for useful material, for content—insight, facts, statistics, opinions, examples, images—that might help answer the question "How can I find something worthwhile to say—something that will advance my meaning?"

Some people use invention as an early writing step, a way of getting started. Some save the invention stage until they've made other decisions. Regardless of the sequence, all writers use invention throughout the writing process.

The goal of invention is to get as much material as possible on paper through the use of strategies like the following.

Freewriting.   *Freewriting* is a version of the "quick effort" approach discussed in Chapter 1. Wendy Gianacoples's first attempt (see page 8) is the product of freewriting. As the term suggests, when freewriting, you simply write whatever comes to mind, hoping that the very act of recording your thinking will generate useful content.

How to freewrite

Try freewriting by exploring what makes you angry or happy or frightened or worried. Write about what surprises you or what you think is unfair or what you would like to see happen. If you keep a journal, consult it to see if you've written anything related to your topic in the past. Don't stop writing until you've filled a page or two, and don't worry about organization or correctness—just get your thoughts down. Although it will never produce a finished essay, freewriting can give you a good start by uncovering all kinds of buried ideas. It can be especially useful for curing "writer's block."

Using Journalists' Questions.   To probe the many angles and dimensions of a topic, journalists ask these questions:

Questions Journalists Ask

- *Who was involved?*
- *What happened?*
- *When did it happen?*

- *Where did it happen?*
- *How did it happen?*
- *Why did it happen?*

Unlike freewriting, the journalists' questions offer a built-in organizing strategy—an array of different "perspectives" on your topic.

Asking Yourself Questions.   If you can't seem to settle on a definite viewpoint, try answering any of these questions that apply to your topic.

Discovery Questions You Can Ask

- *What is my opinion of X?*
- *Am I for it or against it?*
- *Does it make me happy or sad?*
- *Is it good or bad?*
- *Will it work or fail?*
- *Does it make sense?*
- *What have I observed about X?*

- *What have I seen happen?*
- *What is special or unique about it?*
- *What strikes me about it?*
- *What can I suggest about X?*
- *What would I like to see happen?*
- *What should or should not be done?*

Brainstorming.   Brainstorming is a sure bet for coming up with useful material; its aim is to produce as many ideas as possible. Here is how brainstorming works:

GUIDELINES for Brainstorming

1. *Find a quiet spot, and bring an alarm clock, a pencil, and plenty of paper.* Set the alarm to ring in 30 minutes.

2. *Try to protect yourself from interruptions: phones, music, or the like.* Sit with eyes closed for 2 minutes, thinking about absolutely nothing.

(continues)

3. *Now concentrate on your writing situation.* If you've already spelled out your purpose and your audience's questions, focus on them. Otherwise, repeat this question: "What can I say about my topic, at all?"

4. *As ideas begin to flow, record every one.* Don't stop to judge relevance or worth, and don't worry about complete sentences (or even correct spelling). Simply get everything on paper. Even the wildest idea might lead to some valuable insight. Keep pushing and sweating until the alarm rings. If the ideas are still flowing, reset the alarm and go on.

5. *At the end, you should have a chaotic mixture of junk, irrelevancies, and useful material.* Take a break.

6. *Now confront your list.* Strike out what is useless, and sort the remainder into categories. Include any other ideas that crop up. Your finished list should provide plenty of raw material.

Mind-Mapping.   A more structured version of brainstorming, *mind-mapping* (see Figure 2.1a) helps visualize relationships. Begin by drawing a circle around the main issue or concept, centered on the paper or whiteboard. Then add related ideas, each in its own box, connected to the circle by a ruled line (or "branch"). Add branches as lines to some other distinct geometric shape containing supporting ideas. Unlike a traditional outline, a mind-map does not require sequential thinking: as each idea pops up, it is connected to related ideas by its own branch.

A simplified form of mind-mapping is the *tree diagram* (see Figure 2.1b), in which a major topic, minor topics, and subtopics are connected by branches that indicate their relationships.

Reading and Researching.   Some of our best ideas, insights, and questions often come from our reading (as discussed in Chapter 9). Or we might want to consider what others have said or discovered about our topic (as discussed in Chapter 20) before we reach our own conclusions. Reading and research are indispensable tools for any serious writer.

FIGURE 2.1
Two visual techniques
for thinking creatively

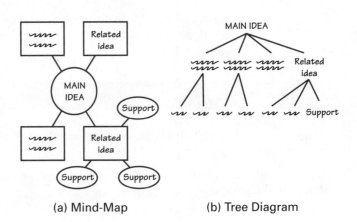

(a) Mind-Map   (b) Tree Diagram

Select Your Best Material

"How much of my material is useful in this situation?"

Invention invariably produces more material than a writer needs. Select only the material that best advances your meaning (see Chapter 5, "Revising the Content").

If you find yourself trying to include everything you've discovered, you probably need to refocus on your purpose and audience.

Organize for Readers

With an outline, you move from a random listing of items as they occurred to you to a deliberate map that will guide readers from point to point.

"How will readers want this organized?"

All readers expect a definite beginning, middle, and ending that provide orientation, discussion, and review. But specific readers want these sections tailored to their expectations. Identify your readers' expectations by (1) anticipating their probable questions about your thesis and (2) visualizing the sequence in which readers would want these questions answered.

Some writers can organize merely by working from a good thesis statement. Others prefer to begin with some type of outline. And some writers like to write a draft and then an outline to check their line of thinking. You might outline early or later. But you need to move from a random collection of ideas to an organized list that helps readers follow your material.

GUIDELINES for Selecting and Organizing Your Material

- *Never expect to use everything.* Trim your inventory—but save each version in a separate file in case you need something later.

- *Organize logically.* All readers expect a definite beginning, middle, and ending:

  —The beginning (or *introduction*) provides orientation by telling readers what they need to know first.
  —The middle (or *body*) reveals your exact meaning, with one idea logically following another.
  —The ending (or *conclusion*) emphasizes what is most important and leaves readers reflecting on what they have just read.

- *Check your outline for unity and coherence.* An outline has *unity* when everything directly supports the thesis. An outline has *coherence* when the thesis and all supporting material form one connected line of thought, like links in a chain. (See pages 97–99.)

- *Check your outline for emphasis.* An outline has suitable *emphasis* when the important things stand out. Last things are best remembered; middles are too easily forgotten.

Note | *No single form of outline should be followed slavishly. The organization of any writing is ultimately determined by its audience's needs and expectations.*

EXPLORING AND ARRANGING ASSETS

For your essay on our obsession with cars (see page 29), assume you've developed this brainstorming list:

Your brainstorming list

1. to get us from point A to point B, junkers would suffice
2. we demand variety in our lives
3. we want cars that make us look cool
4. people seem to love their bumper stickers
5. with bumper stickers we exercise our right to free speech
6. nobody likes driving an old bomber
7. no matter what the price we don't care
8. off-road vehicles are everywhere, but most of them never leave the pavement
9. "creativity is more important than knowledge"—what kind of bumper sticker logic is that?
10. Henry Ford's Model T's all looked exactly alike—they were basic transportation, not fashion statements!
11. today's cars are fiberglass and metal gods
12. today's automakers cater to our self-centered fantasies
13. we can run much of our lives without leaving the comfy car
14. the car is the ultimate personal space
15. a great way to escape the daily hassles
16. cars give us the freedom to go where we want when we want
17. we love to do our own thing—what America's all about
18. the car's popularity has led to the phenomenon of drive-up windows
19. people in other countries don't mind public transportation, but we seem to hate it
20. what about the bumper stickers that announce "I'm a tough guy" or "I'm an intellectual"?
21. we can even sing aloud in the car without seeming weird

With your raw material collected, you can now move into the selection phase—leaving open the possibility that new material may surface.

As you review your brainstorming list, you decide to cut items 11, 16, and 19.

Your selection of material to omit

- *Item 11 doesn't relate to the theme of individualism.*
- *Item 16 is a cliché and too general to have real meaning in this essay.*
- *Item 19 makes an unsupportable generalization.*

(If you end up trying to include *all* your raw material, you probably need to refocus on your purpose and audience. Chapter 5 offers advice for selecting fresh and worthwhile material.)

Next, you try to anticipate specific readers' questions about your essay, and you come up with this list of possibilities:

Specific reader questions you anticipate

- *Can you set the scene for us and give us a context for your thesis?*
- *Why do we identify so strongly with our cars?*
- *Where do bumper stickers fit in?*
- *Why do we often hang out in the car?*
- *What does all this say about us as a culture?*

Your readers' expectations give you a basis for organizing your brainstorming material into categories:

Your general outline

I. How our relationship to cars has evolved

II. How cars help us project an ideal self

III. Why we decorate our cars with stickers

IV. How cars provide a private space

V. How cars serve as the ultimate mechanism for achieving individuality

Within each category, you arrange your brainstorming items, along with any other worthwhile material that occurs to you. Your final outline might resemble this one:

Your final outline

I. Why do we love our cars so much?
   A. Originally, cars were merely basic transportation.
   B. All Model T's looked alike.
   C. Today's automakers cater to our urge to do our own thing.
   D. Consumers love this kind of attention.
   E. Thesis: Today's self-centered consumers demand cars that satisfy our craving for individuality.

II. We want cars that make a unique lifestyle statement.
   A. If basic transportation were the issue, an old junker would do.
   B. But we want to project that special image.
   C. Roughly 50 percent of consumers buy some type of off-road vehicle.
   D. Most of these Jeeps and SUVs never leave the pavement.
   E. Driving a sports car really makes us feel special.

III. Stickers serve as our own personal billboard.
   A. They allow us to exercise our right to free speech.
   B. They announce exactly where we stand.
   C. They tell the world that we're animal lovers, intellectuals, tough guys, or whatever.
   D. Volvos often display political or intellectual statements.
   E. NRA stickers, especially on trucks, intimidate wimps like me.
   F. I hurry to get out of the line of fire.

IV. Public transportation is torture for individuals like us.
   A. America's cars are personal hideaways, places to escape other humans.
   B. Drive-up windows are one popular form of escape.
   C. We can transact business, order meals, and dine without ever leaving the car.
   D. We can sing along with the radio as we gobble our fatburgers and fries.
   E. If you try singing on a bus or subway, people look at you funny.

V. Cars entice us because they provide the ultimate mechanism for achieving individuality.

   A. The cars we drive and the stickers we sport proclaim our prepackaged uniqueness.
   B. We can do what we want without seeming weird.
   C. We can avoid direct human contact.
   D. Our car is who we are.

This outline takes the form of short sentences that encapsulate key ideas for later expansion. Some writers use a less formal outline—a simple list of phrases without numerals or letters. (Use the type that works best for you.)

Later, during various drafts, you will discover more material and probably delete some original material (as in the final draft, pages 56–58).

DIGITAL TIP

Use Digital Tools to Help You Plan

Nearly every planning technique writers traditionally practiced using pen and paper has been converted into a digital tool either online, downloadable to your computer, or housed within your word-processing program. Consider the following tools to help shape your thesis statement and to help you discover and organize your ideas:

Online Thesis Creators

These simple tools (for example, those at <http://tommarch.com/electraguide/thesis.php> or <http://johnmcgarvey.com/apworld/student/thesiscreator.html>) help you convert your general topic into a focused thesis statement. (Do a Web search on "thesis creator" or "thesis builder.")

Mind-Mapping Software

A number of mind-mapping programs, such as MindMapper, MindGenius, and MindJet, are available for free trial and purchase online. These programs walk you through the mind-mapping process and allow you to revise concepts and easily add or change branches.

Computerized Outliners

Use the outlining option (sometimes called "table of contents") in your word-processing program to help organize your main topics and subtopics automatically from preselected formats. You can easily make changes to major heads and subheads without cumbersome cutting, pasting, and retyping.

If you prefer to freewrite or brainstorm on your computer rather than on paper, you can easily go back and copy and paste material from these discovery methods into your formal outline.

FINDING YOUR VOICE

Whether your writing connects with readers depends on how it "sounds." The way your writing sounds depends on its *tone,* your personal mark—the voice readers hear when reading your words. Readers who like the tone like the writer.

Consciously or unconsciously, readers ask three big questions about the writer:

Readers' questions in sizing up a writer

- *Is this person someone who is businesslike, serious, silly, sincere, phony, boring, bored, intense, stuck-up, meek, confident, friendly, hostile?*
- *Is this person treating me as a friend, acquaintance, stranger, enemy, nobody, superior, subordinate, bozo, somebody with a brain and feelings?*
- *Is this person really thinking about the topic or merely "going through the motions"?*

How readers answer these questions will depend on your voice.

Why fancy words don't always work

Some inexperienced writers mistakenly think that fancy words make them sound more intelligent and important. And sometimes, of course, only the complex word will convey your exact meaning. Instead of saying, "Sexist language **contributes to the ongoing existence of stereotypes,**" you could say more accurately and concisely, "Sexist language **perpetuates stereotypes.**" (One "fancy" word effectively replaces six "simpler" words.) But when you use fancy words only to impress, your writing sounds stuffy and pretentious.

Find a Voice That Connects with Readers

Personal essays ordinarily employ a conversational tone: You write to your readers as though you were speaking to them. Consider these opening lines:

Conversational tone

> I'm probably the only person I know who still has the same two parents she was born with. We have a traditional American family: We go to church and football games; we watch the Olympics on television and argue about politics, and we have Thanksgiving dinner at my grandmother Clancy's and Christmas dinner with my father's sister Jess, who used to let us kids put pitted olives on our fingertips when we were little.
>
> —*Shirley Haley*

Haley's tone is friendly and relaxed—the voice of a writer who seems at home with herself, her subject, and her readers. We are treated to comfortable images of family things. But the long list of "traditional" family activities also hints at the writer's restlessness and lets us share her mixed feelings of attraction and repulsion.

Suppose Haley had decided to sound more "academic":

Academic tone

> Among my friends and acquaintances, I am apparently the only individual with the good fortune to have parents who remain married. Our family activities are grounded in American tradition: We attend church services and football games; we watch televised sporting events and engage in political debates; at Thanksgiving, we dine at Grandmother's, and at Christmas, we visit an aunt who has always been quite tolerant of children's behavior.

Which tone is better? To see for yourself which version is more inviting, test each against the three big questions for readers on page 37.

Avoid an Overly Informal Tone

How tone can be too informal

Achieving a conversational tone does not mean writing in the same way we would speak to friends at the local burger joint. *Substandard usage* ("He ain't got none"; "I seen it today") is unacceptable in formal writing; so is *slang* ("hurling," "phat," "chillin"), which usually has specific meaning only for members of a particular in-group. *Profanity* ("pissed off"; "This idea sucks"; "What the hell") not only conveys contempt for the audience but often triggers contempt for the person using it. *Colloquialisms* ("OK," "a lot," "snooze") tend to crop up more in speaking than in writing.

How tone can offend

Tone is offensive when it violates the reader's expectations: when it seems disrespectful, tasteless, distant and aloof, too "chummy," casual, or otherwise inappropriate for the topic, the reader, and the situation.

When to use an academic tone

A formal or academic tone is appropriate in countless writing situations: a research paper, a job application, a report for the company president. In a history essay, for example, you would not refer to George Washington and Abraham Lincoln as "those dudes George and Abe." Whenever you begin with freewriting or brainstorming, your tone might be overly informal and is likely to require some adjustment during subsequent drafts.

THE WRITER'S PLANNING GUIDE

Decisions and strategies covered in this chapter apply to almost any writing situation. You can make sure your own planning decisions are complete by using a Planning Guide whenever you write. Items in the Planning Guide are reminders of things to be done. Your instructor might ask you to use a Planning Guide for early assignments and to submit your responses along with your completed essay. The following Planning Guide has been completed to show a typical set of decisions for "Cars R Us" (pages 56–58). Create a blank version (with just the bold categories showing) and keep a copy on your computer to "save as" and fill in for each of your writing projects.

COMPLETED PLANNING GUIDE

Broad subject: Societal values or behavior

Limited topic: How cars appeal to our sense of individuality

Purpose statement (what you want to do): My purpose is to poke fun at our obsession with cars by explaining to my classmates how cars appeal to our sense of individuality. I'll discuss uses of the car as a lifestyle statement, personal billboard, and private sanctuary.

Thesis statement (what you want to say): Today's self-centered consumers demand cars that satisfy their craving for individuality.

Audience: Classmates

Probable audience questions:

Can you set the scene for us and give us a context for your thesis?
Why do we identify so strongly with our cars?
Where do bumper stickers fit in?
Why do we often hang out in the car?
What does all this say about us as a culture?

Brainstorming list:
1. to get us from point A to point B, junkers would suffice
2. we demand variety in our lives
3. we want cars that make us look cool . . . *and so on*

Outline:
I. Why do we love our cars so much?
   A. Originally, cars were merely basic transportation.
   B. All Model T's looked alike.
   C. Today's automakers cater to our urge to do our own thing. . . . *and so on.*

Appropriate tone for audience and purpose: relaxed and humorous

> Note   *Remember that your decisions for completing the Planning Guide need not follow the strict order of the items listed, so long as you make all the necessary decisions.*

PLANNING FOR GROUP WORK

In Chapter 1, you thought ahead to the kinds of decisions groups must make if they are to benefit from all members' contributions. The following guidelines will enable your group to prepare for collaborative work.

GUIDELINES for Writing Collaboratively

- *Appoint a group manager.* The manager assigns tasks, enforces deadlines, conducts meetings, consults with the instructor, and "runs the show."

- *Prepare a project management plan.* Figure 2.2 shows a sample planning form.

- *Compose a purpose statement* (see page 21). Spell out the goal and the plan for achieving it.

- *Decide how the group will be organized.* For example, the group will research and plan together, but each person will write a different part of the document.

    Alternatively, some members will plan and research, one person will write a complete draft, and others will review, edit, revise, and produce the final version.

> Note   *The final revision should display one consistent style throughout, as though written by one person only.*

- *Divide the task.* Who will be responsible for which parts of the essay or report or which phases of the project? Who is the best at doing what (writing, editing, using a word processor, giving an oral presentation to the class)?

> Note   *Spell out—in writing—specific expectations for each team member.*

- *Establish specific completion dates for each phase.* Keep everyone focused on what is due when.

- *Decide on a meeting schedule and format.* How often will the group meet, where, and for how long? In or out of class? Who will take notes? Set a strict time limit for each discussion topic. Distribute copies of the meeting agenda and timetable beforehand, and stick to this plan. Meetings work best when each member prepares a specific contribution ahead of time.

- *Establish a procedure for responding to the work of other members.* Will reviewing and editing (see pages 71–73) be done in writing, face to face, as a group, one on one, or online? Will this process be supervised by the project manager?

(continues)

Project Planning Form

Project title:
Audience:
Project manager:
Team members:
Purpose of the project:
Type of document required:

Specific Assignments	**Due Dates**	**Person(s) Responsible**
Research:		
Planning:		
Drafting:		
Revising:		
Preparing progress report:		
Preparing oral briefing for the team:		
Final document first draft:		
Final document:		

Work Schedule

	Date	*Place*	*Time*	*Note Taker*
Team meetings:				
#1				
#2				
#3				
etc.				
Meetings with instructor				
#1				
#2				
etc.				

Miscellaneous

How will disputes and grievances be resolved?
How will performances be evaluated?
Other matters (Use of technology: email, Google Docs, Track Changes, etc.)?

FIGURE 2.2 **Project Planning Form for Managing a Collaborative Project**

To manage a team project you need to (a) spell out the project goal, (b) break the entire task down into manageable steps, (c) create a climate in which people work well together, and (d) keep each phase of the project under control.

Guidelines (continued)

- *Develop a file-naming system for various drafts.* When working with multiple drafts, it's too easy to save over a previous version and lose something important.

- *Establish procedures for dealing with group problems.* How will gripes and disagreements be aired and resolved? How will irrelevant discussion be curtailed?

- *Select a group decision-making style.* Will decisions be made alone by the group manager or by group input or majority vote?

- *Appoint a different "observer" for each meeting.* This group member will make a list of what worked and didn't work during the meeting.

- *Decide how to evaluate each member's contribution.* Figure 2.3 shows possible criteria a manager can use to evaluate members. Criteria for evaluating the manager might include open-mindedness, fairness in assigning tasks, ability to organize the team, ability to resolve conflicts, and so on. (Members might keep a journal of personal observations for overall evaluation of the project.)

Sources: Debs 38–41; Hill-Duin 45–50; Hulbert 53–54; Matson 30–31; McGuire 467–68; Morgan 540–41.

FIGURE 2.3
Sample form for evaluating team members

> **Performance Appraisal for** ___J. Fishkill___
> (Rate each element as *[superior]*, *[acceptable]*, or *[unacceptable]*, and use the "Comment" section to explain each rating briefly)
>
> - *Cooperation:* [___superior___]
>   Comment: works extremely well with others; always willing to help out
>
> - *Dependability:* [___acceptable___]
>   Comment: arrives on time for meetings; completes all assigned work
>
> - *Effort:* [___acceptable___]
>   Comment: does fair share of work; needs no prodding
>
> - *Quality of work produced:* [___superior___]
>   Comment: produces work that is carefully researched
>
> - *Ability to meet deadlines:* [___superior___]
>   Comment: delivers all assigned work on or before the deadline; helps other team members with last-minute tasks
>
> Project manager's signature ___R. P. Ketchum___

Note

Any evaluation of strengths and weaknesses should be backed up by comments that explain the ratings (as in Figure 2.3). A group needs to decide beforehand what constitutes "effort," "cooperation," and so on.

Use Your Computer to Collaborate on Group Projects

When you are working on a group writing project and not all group members are able to be at the same location at the same time, take advantage of the various online collaborative tools available to you:

Emails and Blogs

Emails and blog pages are both great ways to collaboratively edit simple pieces of writing. Team members may send or post comments and suggestions for editing to the entire group. For complex documents, use email and blog pages as the media to send or post longer documents but not to make complicated edits.

Editing Applications

These applications are built into word-processing programs and may be called "track changes" or "edit" on your word processor's menu. Editing applications allow group members to share a document, with each member inserting his or her own edits without deleting the previous version. Figure 4.2 shows an edited document. Notice how cuts are shown via strikethrough, and additions appear in a different color. (With two or more editors, each editor uses a different color, and inserted comments may be initialed to differentiate editors.) Edits may be accepted or rejected by the group member responsible for producing a final version.

Wikis and Other Intractive Web Sites

A wiki is a Web site that allows group members to post a document and to "check" the document in or out to make edits. The advantage of a wiki is that no two group members can check out and edit a document simultaneously, thus preventing duplication of work. Also, previous versions are automatically saved on the site, allowing for comparison. On an interactive Web site such as *Google Docs*, teams can create a free account and than create or upload documents to be edited by various members of the team.

When using these digital tools to collaborate, make sure that everyone in the group agrees on procedures to prevent mistakes, confusion, and needless duplication of work.

✔ A CHECKLIST for Planning

(Numbers in parentheses refer to the first page of discussion.)

Narrowing Your Topic

☐ Is the topic sufficiently **focused** for a college essay? (21)

☐ Do **I know enough** about this topic to write something worthwhile? (21)

Identifying Your Purpose

☐ Have I identified a definite **goal**? (21)

☐ Have I mapped out a clear **strategy** for achieving my goal? (22)

(continues)

Developing Your Thesis

☐ Does my thesis express a definite and worthwhile **viewpoint**? (25)

☐ Is the position expressed in my thesis one that I can **support** convincingly? (25)

Pinpointing Your Audience

☐ Have I identified my audience's **needs and expectations**? (28)

☐ Have I anticipated my audience's **major questions**? (28)

☐ Have I anticipated my audience's **reactions**? (28)

Discovering Useful Material

☐ Have I used the **invention strategies** that work best for me? (30)

☐ Have I discovered **sufficient material** to support my thesis? (30)

Selecting and Organizing Your Material

☐ Have I identified my **best material** and retained only that? (33)

☐ Have I organized so that readers can **follow my thinking**? (33)

☐ Is everything **logically connected** and **related** to my thesis? (33)

Finding Your Voice

☐ Does my **tone** fit the topic and the situation? (38)

☐ Is my tone **conversational** but **not overly informal**? (38)

APPLICATIONS

2.1   Narrow two or three of the broad topics in the list below to a topic suitable for a short essay. (Review pages 20–21.)

EXAMPLE

social rituals   →

high school proms   →

how the romantic image of prom night has become a myth   →

how today's typical prom night is based on competition and appearances and polluted by drugs, alcohol, and sex

TOPICS TO BE NARROWED

entertainment	careers	war	family
life	sports	crime	sex
social rituals	automobiles	fashion	music
marriage	alcohol	studying	drugs

2.2   Compose statements of purpose for essays on three or more of the topics in Application 2.1. (Review pages 21–22.)

EXAMPLE

Topic	The problems with prom night
Purpose Statement	My purpose is to persuade past and present high school students that high school proms have become a waste of time. I will discuss four major problems with prom night: drugs and alcohol, sexual promiscuity, competition, and danger.

2.3   Convert your statements of purpose from Application 2.2 into thesis statements. (Review pages 22–27.)

EXAMPLE

Purpose Statement	My purpose is to persuade past and present high school students that proms have become a waste of time. I will discuss four major problems with prom night: drugs and alcohol, sexual promiscuity, competition, and danger.
Thesis Statement	High school proms have lost their value as social events and have become expensive and exaggerated rituals that entrap students in situations they often despise.

2.4   For each thesis statement in Application 2.3, brainstorm and write three or four topic statements for individual supporting paragraphs. Arrange your topic statements in logical order. (Review pages 24–25.)

EXAMPLE

Thesis Statement	High school proms have lost their value as social events and have become expensive and exaggerated rituals that entrap students in situations they often despise.
First Topic Statement	Parents, teachers, coaches, and other role models seem to merely accept the fact that students are going to drink or get high on prom night.
Second Topic Statement	It is almost an unspoken law that a couple (no matter how unacquainted) should have sex on prom night.
Third Topic Statement	Competition over who has the most expensive dress, the most unusual tux, the biggest limousine, or the cutest date also detracts from the evening.

Fourth Topic Statement Not only do many students feel obliged to attend the prom in order to fit in, but they also feel obliged to participate in often dangerous after-prom events.

2.5 Revise the following thesis statements that do not already (1) focus on a limited topic, (2) establish a definite viewpoint, (3) offer a worthwhile viewpoint, (4) make a supportable claim, or (5) preview, in order, the supporting ideas.* Mark an X next to those that are adequate. (Review pages 25–27.)

EXAMPLE

Faulty Thesis Grades are a way of life in college. *[establishes no definite or worthwhile viewpoint and fails to preview the supporting ideas]*

Revised Thesis (With Supporting Idea Provided) Grades are an aid to education because they motivate students, provide an objective measure of performance, and prepare people to compete successfully in their careers.

1. Less than one semester in college has changed my outlook.
2. I have three great fears.
3. This essay concerns my attitude toward online education.
4. The Batmobile is a good car for students because it's inexpensive, fuel-efficient, and dependable.
5. My significant other is the kindest person I know.

2.6 **COLLABORATIVE PROJECT** Organize into small groups. Choose a subject from the following list. Then decide on a thesis statement and brainstorm (not necessarily in this order). Identify a specific audience, and develop an outline. When each group completes this procedure, one representative can present the outline to the class for suggestions about revision. (Review pages 31–32.)

instructions for surviving the first semester of college

suggestions for improving one's college experience

causes of teenage suicide

arguments for or against a formal grading system

an argument for an improvement you think this college needs

how you expect your country to be different in 10 years

---

*For practice, this exercise asks that each thesis statement include an explicit preview. When your own thesis statement excludes an explicit preview, you should nonetheless announce the essay's direction.

young people's needs that parents often ignore

difficulties faced by nontraditional students

 2.7   **WEB-BASED PROJECT** Go to the University of Victoria's Writer's Guide at <**http://web.uvic.ca/wguide/**>. Use the Table of Contents page to find *Audience and Tone.* Locate one item of information about audience and tone (or voice) not covered in this chapter. Take careful notes for a brief discussion of this information in class. Attach a copy of all relevant Web pages to your written notes.

ALTERNATIVE ASSIGNMENTS

a. Locate additional information on thesis statements from <**http://www.cws.Illinois.edu/workshop/writing/tips/**>. Follow the *Writing Tips* link to *Thesis Statements.*
b. For advice about organizing a paper, go to <**http://www.powa.org/organizing**>.
c. For advice about discovering useful material (invention), go to <**http://www.powa.org/discovering**>.

> **Note** | *Instead of quoting your sources directly, paraphrase (see page 384). Be sure to credit each source of information (see page 380).*

2.8   From Application 2.4, select the most promising set of materials, and write your best essay. Use selected items from your brainstorming list to develop each support paragraph. Outline as necessary. Provide an engaging introduction and a definite conclusion. Use the questions on page 16 as guidelines for revising your essay.

Works Cited

Debs, Mary Beth. "Collaborative Writing in Industry." In *Technical Writing: Theory and Practice.* Ed. Bertie E. Fearing and W. Keats Sparrow. New York: Modern Language Assn., 1989: 33–42. Print.

Hill-Duin, Ann. "Terms and Tools: A Theory and Research-Based Approach to Collaborative Writing." *Bulletin of the Association for Business Communication* 53.2 (1990): 45–50. Print.

Hulbert, Jack E. "Developing Collaborative Insights and Skills." *Bulletin of the Association for Business Communication* 57.2 (1994): 53–56. Print.

Matson, Eric. "The Seven Sins of Deadly Meetings." *Fast Company* Oct.-Nov. 1997: 27–31. Print.

McGuire, Gene. "Shared Minds: A Model of Collaboration." *Technical Communication* 39.3 (1992): 467–68. Print.

Morgan, Meg. "Patterns of Composing: Connections between Classroom and Workplace Collaborations." *Technical Communication* 38.4 (1991): 540–42. Print.

U.S. Air Force Academy. *Executive Writing Course.* Washington: GPO, 1981. Print.

For additional information and practive with the learning objectives in this chapter, go to www.mycomplab.com, Resources>Writing>The Writing Process>Planning.

CHAPTER 3

Decisions in Drafting

LEARNING OBJECTIVES FOR THIS CHAPTER

- Recognize that the drafting stage doesn't typically follow a formula
- Draft an effective essay title and introduction
- Select an effective opening strategy
- Draft the body of an essay
- Select an appropriate closing strategy

One of any writer's hardest moments is in getting the paper started. If you've completed the Planning Guide on page 39, you should have a head start—with a thesis, an outline, a list of ideas, and so on. But you still need to shape all this material into a unified and coherent essay. Here is where you decide on answers to some tough questions.

Questions for Drafting Your Essay

- *How do I begin the essay?*
- *What comes next?*
- *How will I end?*

- *How much is enough?*
- *What can I leave out?*
- *Am I forgetting anything?*

Different ways of drafting

Drafting has no simple formula. Some writers work from a brainstorming list and perhaps an outline. Others hate outlining, and they start right off writing and scribbling and rewriting. Some write a quick draft before thinking much about their writing situation. Some write a whole draft in one marathon sitting. Some write in short bursts, a few minutes at a time. Introductions are often written last.

How to beat writer's block

You might start your essay in the middle, at the end, or with whatever ideas you feel surest about. Or you might do more brainstorming (see page 31). Your best bet in any case is to read through all your planning material and then plunge right in and keep filling the pages. Take breaks if you need to, but try to stop where you'll have something left to say when you return to the paper. Sooner or later—after false starts, detours, and dead ends—the right words will begin to flow, and a useful first draft will emerge.

Note   *As you work, remember that each writing sample in this chapter and in this book is the product of multiple drafts and revisions. None of these writers expected to get it just right the first time—nor should you.*

DRAFTING THE TITLE AND INTRODUCTION

Whether you start the essay in the middle, at the end, or at the beginning, the first two parts of your completed essay will be the title and the introduction.

The Title

Why titles are important

Titles—which are sometimes chosen after the essay is complete—should forecast an essay's subject and approach. Clear, attention-getting titles, such as "Let's Shorten the Baseball Season" and "Instead of Running, Try Walking," help readers plan how to interpret what they read.

Assume that you are continuing your work from Chapter 2, where you planned your essay about America's obsession with cars. You have chosen the title "Cars R Us."

The Introductory Paragraph

Introductions differ in shape and size and may consist of more than one paragraph; however, basic introductory paragraphs often have a funnel shape:

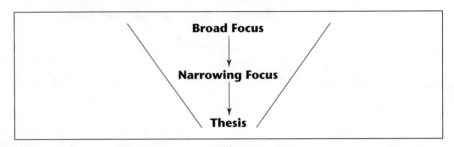

Now that you have decided on a title—"Cars R Us"—you can introduce your essay's final draft, using a funnel pattern:

CARS R US

Broad focus (1–5)

Narrowing focus (6–7)

Thesis (8)

[1]We Americans love our automobiles, no question. [2]But why is next year's new model always front-page news? [3]Cars were once merely a way to get from point A to point B faster than by foot or horse and buggy. [4]Henry Ford's Model T's all looked identical, like boxes on wheels, all painted black. [5]People bought Model T's for basic transportation, not to make a fashion statement. [6]In the twenty-first century, however, automakers cater to our desire to "do our own thing." [7]We love their attention, and they know it. [8]Today's self-centered consumers demand cars that satisfy their craving for individuality.

—*Maureen Malloy*

Why introductions are important

Introductory paragraphs do more than just lead into the essay; they invite readers in and set a tone. The first-person plural (**we, our**) invites us to look at ourselves. Amusing images (**horse and buggy, boxes on wheels**) and deliberate clichés (**front-page news, do our own thing**) signal the writer's intention to have fun with this essay. If your only aim were to lead into the main discussion, you might have given this introduction instead:

A lifeless opening

| We love our cars because they enhance our sense of individuality.

But this version lacks the inviting tone and the images that engage our attention and make us want to read on.

Placing the Thesis

In a standard essay, the thesis often appears at the end of the introductory paragraph, as a bridge to the discussion. But sometimes readers want to know where you stand immediately, especially when the topic is controversial.

A controversial thesis as opener

> *Single-sex schools offer distinct advantages over coeducational schools.* Coeducational classrooms inhibit student participation and tend to ignore gender-specific learning styles. Single-sex classrooms not only encourage participation but also allow for the kinds of gender-based teaching strategies that promote effective learning.
>
> —*Cheryl Hebert*

Sometimes even personal writing can open with the thesis, especially when the viewpoint is unexpected.

A surprising thesis as opener

> *I hate summer beaches.* Ocean swimming is impossible; upon conquering a wave, I simply lose to the next, getting pushed back onto the hard-packed, abrasive sand. Booby-traps of bottles, soda cans, toys, and rocks make walking hazardous. Heavy with the stench of suntan lotion, greasy french fries, dead fish, and sweat, the thick, searing air hangs motionless about the scorching sand. Blasting radios and growling hot rods cut the slap-swoosh of the green-gray surf to a weak hiss. People devour a summer beach, gouging the sound with umbrella spikes and gripping it with oiled limbs, leaving only trampled debris at summer's end.
>
> —*Pam Herbert*

In some essays, the thesis appears later, even toward the end (as on page 301). A delayed thesis is especially useful in a story leading to some larger meaning (*Here is what happened* and then *Here is what it means*).

Selecting an Opening Strategy

"How do I begin?"

The specifics of your introduction are determined by what you know about your readers and your purpose.

Questions for Analyzing Your Audience and Purpose

- *Are my readers likely to be interested in this topic?*
- *How can I make them want to read on?*
- *Are they likely to react defensively?*

- *Is my purpose to describe something, to tell a story, to explain something, to change somebody's mind?*

The opening strategies that follow offer various possibilities for connecting with your audience.

Open with an Anecdote.   An anecdote is a brief, personal story that makes a point.

> Last weekend, I gave a friend's younger brother a ride from the mall. As we drove, I asked him the same old questions about high school, grades, football, and girlfriends. He answered me in one-word sentences and then pulled out a cassette tape. "Wanna hear somethin' cool?" I shrugged and popped it into the tape player. What came pouring through my car speakers made me run a stop sign. The "rap" song spelled out, in elaborate detail, 101 ways to violate a woman's body. Needless to say, it was a long ride across town.
>
> I borrowed the tape and listened to every song, horrified by their recurrent theme of sexual violence and domination. But most horrifying is that a 15-year-old kid actually considers this music "cool."
>
> —*Liz Gonsalves*

Open with a Question.   An opening question can get readers thinking right away, especially when you write instructions, give advice, or argue for action.

> What do you do when you find yourself in the produce room cooler with your manager and he nonchalantly wraps his arm around your waist? Or how about when the guys you work with come out with a distasteful remark that makes you seem like a piece of meat? These are just a couple of problems you might face as the only female in a department. There are, however, ways of dealing with this kind of harassment.
>
> —*Mary Hesse*

Open with a Short Quotation.   If a quotation can summarize your point, use it—and clarify its significance immediately.

> "The XL Roadster—anything else is just a car," unless the XL happens to be mine. In that case, it's just a piece of junk.
>
> —*Jack Haskins*

Open with a Direct Address.   The second-person *you* can involve the readers and help them pay attention—especially when you are giving instructions or advice or writing persuasively.

> Does the thought of artificially preserved, chemically treated food make you lose your appetite? Do limp, tasteless, frozen vegetables leave you cold? Then you should try your hand at organic gardening.
>
> —*Sarah White*

Use direct address in ads, popular articles, and brochures but not in academic reports or most business and technical documents.

Open with a Brief, Vivid Description.   Instead of a thesis, some descriptive essays simply have an orienting sentence to set a scene or create a mood, to place readers at the center of things.

> The raft bobs gently as the four divers help each other with scuba gear. We joke and laugh casually as we struggle in the cramped space; but a

restlessness is in the air because we want to be on our way. Finally, everyone is ready, and we split into pairs. I steal a last glance over the blue ocean. I hear the waves slap the boat, the mournful cry of a seagull, and a steady murmur from the crowded beach a mile away. With three splashes my friends jump in. I follow. There is a splash and then silence. The water presses in, and all I hear is the sound of my regulator as I take my first breath. All I see is blue water, yellow light, and endless space. While the world rushes on, we feel suspended in time. Then my buddy taps me on the shoulder, and we begin a tour of a hidden world.

—George Bond

Open with Examples.   Examples enable readers to visualize the issue or problem.

Privacy in America is disappearing. New technologies enable users to unearth anyone's health, credit, email, and legal records with a few keystrokes. Beyond these computerized records, our telephones, our television sets, and even our trash can be monitored by government agencies, banks, businesses, political groups—or just plain nosy people. Current United States law does disturbingly little to protect our right to privacy.

—Chris Adey

Open with a Definition.   Clarify abstract terms for both writer and reader. This next essay, on the limits of the American dream, begins by defining that key term.

The American dream has taken on different meanings for different people, but its original meaning derived from a seemingly unlimited potential for growth in the sense of the country's great westward expansion followed by the Industrial Revolution. From this combination of geographic and economic progress emerged the correlation between the American dream and freedom. The seemingly endless supply of land and employment let people feel there was nothing stopping them from "moving up in the world." We now recognize, however, that the dream does have a limit.

—John Manning

As you draft your introduction, consider the following suggestions:

Hints for an engaging introduction

- The introduction can be the hardest part of an essay to write. Many writers complete it last. If you do write your introduction first, be sure to revise it later.
- In most college writing, avoid opening with personal qualifiers, such as "It is my opinion that…," "I believe that…," and "In this paper, I will…."
- Let your introduction create suspense that is resolved by your thesis statement, usually at the end of the opening paragraph.
- If the opening is boring, vague, long-winded, or toneless, readers may give up. Don't waste their time.

DRAFTING THE BODY

"How much is enough, and how can I shape it?"

The body of your essay delivers on the commitment made in your thesis. Readers don't want details that only get in the way or a jigsaw puzzle that they have to unscramble for themselves. To develop the body, therefore, answer the following questions:

Questions for Developing the Body of Your Essay

- *How much is enough?*
- *How much information or detail should I provide?*

- *How can I stay on track?*
- *What shape will reveal my line of thought?*

Decide about purpose and unity. Here you will discard material you thought you would keep, and maybe you will discover additional material. Look hard at everything you've discovered during freewriting, brainstorming, and questioning. Stand in the reader's place. Keep whatever belongs, and discard whatever doesn't.

Decide how many support paragraphs to include. College essays typically have three or more, but use as many as you need. Decide how to develop each support paragraph and how to arrange them. What paragraph order will make the most sense and provide the best emphasis?

Elements affecting the shape of your writing (unity, coherence, emphasis, and transition) are discussed fully in Chapter 6, "Revising the Paragraphs." Principles of developing the individual paragraph are principles as well of creating the whole essay—and of writing at any length.

DRAFTING THE CONCLUSION

Why conclusions are important

An essay's conclusion refocuses on the thesis and leaves a final and lasting impression on readers. Your conclusion might evaluate the meaning or significance of the body section, restate your position, predict an outcome, offer a solution, request an action, make a recommendation, or pave the way for more exploration. Avoid conclusions that repeat, apologize, or belabor the obvious:

Don't repeat

I have just discussed my views on the role cars play in our lives.

Don't apologize

Although some readers might disagree, this is how I see it.

Don't belabor the obvious

Now that you've read my essay, you should have a clear picture of the exaggerated importance we place on our cars.

Selecting a Closing Strategy

"How do I end?"

Forgettable endings drain the life from any writing. This list of strategies shows ways of closing with meaning and emphasis.

Close with a Summary.   A review of main points helps readers remember what is most important.

Close with a Call to Action.   Tell readers exactly what you want them to do.

> Just imagine yourself eating a salad of crisp green lettuce, juicy red tomato chunks, firm white slices of cucumber, and crunchy strips of green pepper—all picked fresh from your own garden. If this picture appeals to you, begin planning your summer garden now, and by July the picture of you eating that salad will become a reality. *Bon appétit!*
>
> —Sarah White

Close with a Quotation.   This next writer quotes from journalist Ellen Goodman's essay "Blame the Victim."

> I agree with Ellen Goodman's assertion that there is "something malignant about some of the extremists who make a public virtue of their health." The cancer is in the superior attitudes of the "healthy elite"—an attitude that actually discourages exercise and healthy habits by making average people feel too intimidated and inferior even to begin a fitness program.
>
> —Mike Creeden

Close with an Interpretation or Evaluation.   Help readers understand the meaning of things.

> A growing amount of so-called private information about American citizens is collected daily. And few laws protect our right to be left alone. In the interest of pursuing criminals, government too often sacrifices the privacy of innocent people, and new technology is making old laws obsolete. Huge collections of data are becoming available to your insurance company, to prospective employers, to companies doing mass mailings, and even to your neighbor. The invasion continues, and no one seems to know how to stop our world from fulfilling the prophecy in George Orwell's *Nineteen Eighty-Four.*
>
> —Chris Adey

Whichever strategy or combination of strategies you select, make your conclusion refocus on your main point without repeating it.

GUIDELINES for Drafting the Essay

The Title and Introduction

- *Provide a forecasting title.* Engage readers and prepare them for what follows.

- *Write your introduction last.* If you must write it first, be sure to revise it later.

- *Avoid opening with personal qualifiers.* College writing should generally be free of such qualifiers as "It is my opinion that…," "I will now discuss…," and "In this paper, I will…."

- *Place your thesis.* Your thesis usually comes at the end of the opening paragraph. However, in some essays, the thesis appears later, even near the end.

- *Grab the reader's attention and give a clear sense of what to expect.* Go for visual details.

- *Be as brief as possible.*

The Body

- *Decide* how much is enough. Give readers everything they need, and only that.

- *Support your thesis.* Present your data, discuss your evidence, lay out your case, or tell readers what to do and how to do it.

- *Develop each support paragraph.* Use one paragraph for each supporting idea.

- *Guide the reader.* Use transitional words, sentences, and paragraphs as needed (page 105).

- *Provide plenty of graphic detail.* Help readers visualize your evidence.

The Conclusion

- *Never just stop, having run out of things to say.* Help readers draw their own conclusion by summing up, interpreting, evaluating, or emphasizing your point.

- *Try to be brief, but offer some perspective.* Tell readers what they should be thinking or feeling or doing. Should they be angry, curious, supportive—or what?

CASE STUDY

DRAFTING THE ESSAY

As an illustration of how these drafting decisions produce a completed essay, consider "Cars R Us." (Chapter 4 traces the steps in revision that led to the final version presented here.)

The thesis and each topic sentence appear in italics.

CARS R US

The finished essay Introduction	We Americans love our automobiles, no question. But why is next year's new model always front-page news? Cars were once merely a way to get from point A to point B faster than by foot or horse and buggy. Henry Ford's Model T's all looked identical, like boxes on wheels, and were all painted black. People bought Model T's for basic transportation, and not to make a fashion statement. In the twenty-first century, however, automakers cater to our desire to "do our own thing." We love their attention and they know it. *Today's self-centered consumers demand cars that satisfy their craving for individuality.*

Thesis

First support paragraph

We want automobiles that make a unique lifestyle statement about who we think we are. If today's cars were only a means to cruise to the grocery store, we'd all be willing to drive junkers. But most people hate rusty old bombers. We want to be able to see our ideal (or idealized) images mirrored in our car's glossy paint job or our truck's chrome hubcaps. For example, roughly 50 percent of today's rugged individuals buy four-wheel drive, off-road vehicles that never leave the pavement. Instead we navigate our urban and suburban wilderness in Hummers, Big Wheel trucks, and SUV land barges because these vehicles symbolize toughness and an uncompromising attitude. We buy sports cars not so much to impress others as to impress ourselves: "Hey, I'm driving this red convertible Miata because I'm special."

Second support paragraph

Cars provide each individual with a personal billboard. As a way to exercise our right to free speech, bumper stickers announce exactly where we stand. They tell the world that we're intellectuals or tough guys or sensitive types. One of mine reads, "I love my humpback whale." Another promotes my favorite radio station. For some reason, Volvos often carry political statements such as "Women, unite," or "Make love, not war," or profound observations such as Einstein's "Creativity is more important than knowledge"—which might be fine for a genius like Einstein, but what about the rest of us mere mortals? Some individuals like to be more rugged than others. Pickup trucks, for instance, often sport National Rifle Association stickers, which seem to proclaim "Get out of my way!" to the rest of us wimps. I, with my stuffed Bugs Bunny doll in the back window, hurry out of their line of fire.

Third support paragraph

Owning a car means not having to rely on—yikes—public transportation, torture for individuals like us. Americans' cars are personal sanctuaries, places to escape other humans. One popular form of escape is the drive-up window. Banks, donut shops, even dry cleaners enable us to transact business without leaving the car. Snug in our mobile dining rooms, we no longer have to budge from our orthopedically correct leather seat to order a meal. A simple adjustment of the tilt-steering allows laptop dining as we savor our grease-laden food in private, far from the noisy restaurant and screaming kids. We just stay in our cars. How convenient. We can even sing along to the stereo between bites or hum along as we chew. If you sing on a bus or subway, other commuters look at you strangely and hide their valuables.

Conclusion

Cars entice us Americans because they offer the ultimate mechanism for achieving individuality. Through the kind of car we drive and how we adorn it, we can really "be somebody" and proclaim to strangers our singular selves.

We can dine "à la car" and sing aloud without seeming weird. Isolated in our climate-controlled, stereophonic capsule, we can avoid direct human contact and concentrate full time on being individuals. At the beginning of *Mother Night,* novelist Kurt Vonnegut observes, "We are what we pretend to be"—a condition made increasingly possible by the cars we choose to drive.

—*Maureen Malloy*

Discussion

This essay presents a focused picture. And the picture is unified: nothing gets in the way; everything belongs.

But thoughts also need shaping to help readers organize their own understanding. Each paragraph must help detail the prepackaged identity offered by the American automobile.

Finally, the concluding paragraph offers perspective on the whole essay, refocusing on the thesis, summing up the main points, and presenting a quotation that suggests a larger meaning. Readers remember last things best, and this conclusion leaves us with something worth remembering.

DIGITAL TIP

Use Your Computer to Draft Safely and Efficiently

Although drafting on a computer is second nature to most people, some tips may be helpful. Remember that you can easily lose work by accidentally hitting the "delete" button or experiencing a computer meltdown. Also, consider the following suggestions.

Safety Considerations

- Save and print your work often. Also make a copy of your document in a backup file (on an external hard drive or device, or saved to disc) at the end of each day in case of computer malfunction.

- Keep different files for each draft. Drafting hardly ever occurs in a neat sequence ("good," "better," "best"). Parts of an earlier draft might be better than something you've rewritten. Give each file a different name (Draft 1, Draft 2) in case you need to retrieve usable material. Use "save as" to create each new draft, and revise only the latest version.

Efficiency Considerations

- Consider the benefits of printing out a hard copy. Nothing beats making notes to yourself with pen or pencil. However, if you are more comfortable working on the computer at all times, you can insert notes on the digital page by enclosing them in brackets and perhaps by using a different font or by using Track Changes in Word.

- During the drafting stage, do not waste time on revising or proofreading. Concentrate on getting all relevant thoughts down on paper. Stay focused on the *content.*

✔ A CHECKLIST for Drafting

An Engaging Title and Introduction

☐ Does the title attract attention and forecast what follows?

☐ Does the introduction invite readers in and set a tone?

☐ Have you chosen an effective opening for your readers and purpose?

☐ Do graphic details enable readers to "see"?

☐ Does the introduction run to more than one paragraph, if needed?

☐ Is the thesis well placed?

An Informative Body Section

☐ Does the body deliver on the commitment made in your thesis?

☐ Are any details missing?

☐ Does every detail belong?

☐ Can anything be cut?

☐ Do you have as many support paragraphs as you need?

☐ Is each support paragraph well developed?

☐ Does the order of paragraphs make good sense and provide proper emphasis?

☐ Are transitional words, sentences, and paragraphs used as needed?

An Emphatic Conclusion

☐ Does the conclusion refocus the main point without repeating it?

☐ Does it tell readers what they should be thinking, feeling, or doing?

☐ Is it likely to leave a final and lasting impression on readers?

For more on these criteria, see page 56.

APPLICATIONS

3.1   Plan and draft an essay about something special to you—a place, a person, an experience, an activity, or anything else. Decide on an audience such as classmates, a friend, or someone close to you. Your purpose here is to *share* your way of seeing, and so be sure your audience comes to understand *why* the thing is special. Let readers see it and feel your responses to it. Be sure your thesis is clear.

Think about a voice that will appeal to your readers. Think about unity so that your writing sticks to the point and about order and transition so that it sticks together. Have a beginning, a middle, and an ending.

(Use the questions on page 16 for guidelines in drafting your essay.)

3.2   Now that you know more about how to begin, how to develop and shape the middle, and how to end, return to an essay you wrote earlier, and produce a better draft. List the improvements you made, and be prepared to discuss them.

3.3   **COLLABORATIVE PROJECT** Find a good introduction or conclusion to a short article in a magazine such as *Time, Newsweek,* or *Slate.* Analyze the strategies that make the writing effective. (Review pages 50–53 and 54–55.)

3.4   **COMPUTER APPLICATION** Save three copies of your essay under different file names. Redraft one copy, keeping the ideas from this chapter in mind. Take an overnight break, and then redraft a second copy of the original. Print the new versions, and compare all three. Choose your favorite version, and explain whether you think your latest changes improved the essay and, if so, in what ways.

3.5   **WEB-BASED PROJECT** Do some Web research on writer's block and how it can be overcome. You may want to start at either <**http://owl.english.purdue. edu/owl/resource/567/01/**> or <**http://grammar.ccc.commnet/edu/grammar/ composition/brainstorm_block.htm**>. Prepare a summary (see pages 384–385) of strategies classmates might use to overcome writer's block. Attach copies of the relevant Web pages.

> Note   *Instead of quoting your sources directly, paraphrase (see page 384). Be sure to credit each source of information (see page 380).*

For additional information and practice with the learning objectives in this chapter, go to www.mycomplab.com, Resources>Writing>The Writing Process>Drafting.

Decisions in Revising

LEARNING OBJECTIVES FOR THIS CHAPTER

- Understand revision and what aspects of an essay are examined during the revision process
- Appreciate the role of peer editing and identify ways to peer edit effectively
- Recognize types of errors to look for when proofreading as a final step of revision

Besides being a battle with impatience, writing is a battle with inertia: Once we've written a draft, we are often too easily satisfied with what we've done. Good writers win the battle by revising often. For the sake of clarity, earlier chapters have presented a single sequence of steps for composing an essay. To review:

One sequence for composing an essay

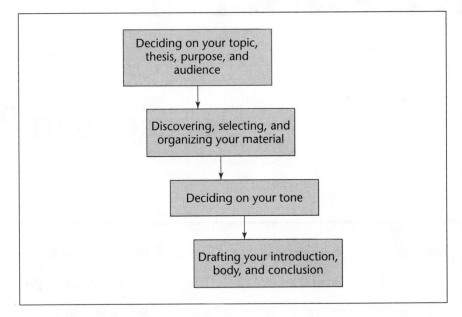

Deciding on your topic, thesis, purpose, and audience

Discovering, selecting, and organizing your material

Deciding on your tone

Drafting your introduction, body, and conclusion

You have seen that writers rarely follow this exact sequence. But no matter what the sequence, every effective writer depends on *revision*—the one constant in the writing process. When you finish a first draft, you have really only begun.

THE MEANING OF REVISION

Why rhetorical elements are important

Revision involves more than proofreading for spelling, punctuation, and other mechanical details (discussed later in this chapter). Mechanical correctness is essential, but what matters most are the essay's *rhetorical elements: worthwhile content, sensible organization,* and *readable style.* The rhetorical elements determine whether your writing connects with readers and makes a difference. Revision never means merely recopying; it always means *rethinking.*

Useful revision happens only when you can evaluate accurately what you have already written. Use the Revision Checklist below to pinpoint possible improvements in content, organization, and style. (Numbers in parentheses refer to the first page of discussion.)

✔ A CHECKLIST for Revision

Worthwhile Content

The essay's main point is clear and sharply focused.
- ☐ Does the title attract attention and provide a forecast? (49)
- ☐ Is the topic limited enough? (21)

☐ Do you get to your main point quickly? (50)

☐ Is the thesis definite, informative, and easy to find? (22)

The discussion delivers on the promise made in your thesis.

☐ Will your readers learn something new and useful? (83)

☐ Do you support every assertion with detailed evidence and examples? (26)

☐ Does everything belong, or can anything be cut? (34)

☐ Have you used only your best material? (33)

Sensible Organization

The essay has a definite introduction, body, and conclusion.

☐ Will your introduction make readers want to read on? (50)

☐ Does each body paragraph develop one supporting point? (54)

☐ Does the order of major points and paragraphs reveal a clear line of thought and emphasize what is most important? (6)

☐ Does the conclusion give a real sense of an ending? (25)

☐ Is everything connected? (11)

☐ If you varied this organization, was it for good reason? (152)

Except for paragraphs of transition or special emphasis, each body paragraph is usually a mini–essay.

☐ Does the paragraph have a topic (or orienting) statement? (95)

☐ Does the topic statement come at the beginning or end, depending on your desired emphasis? (95)

☐ Does everything stick to the point (unity) and stick together (coherence), with adequate transitions to mark relationships? (97, 98, 105)

☐ Is the paragraph developed enough to support the point? (95)

Readable Style

Sentences are clear, concise, and fluent.

☐ Can each sentence be understood the first time it is read? (113)

☐ Are points conveyed clearly in the fewest words? (118)

☐ Are sentences put together with enough variety? (124)

Each word does its job.

☐ Is a real person speaking, and is the voice likable? (132)

☐ Is everything in plain English? (140)

☐ Is your meaning precise, concrete, and specific? (133)

☐ Is your tone appropriate for this situation and audience? (138)

As you use the Revision Checklist, ask yourself questions such as the following:

Questions for Critical Evaluation and Revision

- *Have I conveyed my exact point or feeling?*
- *Do vivid details from the event come to mind now that I've finished writing?*
- *What facts or figures or ideas do I now remember?*

- *Can I reorganize for greater emphasis or clarity?*
- *Can I find a better way of saying what I want to say?*
- *Does this draft sound as I intended it to sound, or is it too corny or detached or arrogant or humble?*

Eventually you will find that you can revise almost automatically, without following the checklist item by item.

Note *Revising a draft doesn't always guarantee that you will improve it. Save each draft and then compare them to select the best material from each one.*

CASE STUDY

REVISING THE DRAFT

Assume that you've written this early draft of "Cars R Us" (the final version of which appears on pages 57–58):

A draft to be revised

CAR CRAZY

We Americans love our automobiles. No question. But why do we worship them? Nearly every country has access to cars, but not every country has the freedom to use them as they please. Cars were once merely a way to get from point A to point B faster than by foot or horse and buggy. Now cars are fiberglass and metal gods. America is founded on freedom, and our cars allow us to move.

In the early 1900s when Henry Ford began producing Model T's, they all had the same body style, sort of like rectangles on wheels. Black was a buyer's only choice of paint color. People didn't purchase Model T's because they were pretty; they were basic transportation, with no fancy options or "toys" like cars have now: tilt-steering, heated power seats, climate control, an eight-speaker stereo system with CD drive, and so on. Americans get sick of the same thing over and over. We demand variety in our lives and especially in our cars.

In the twenty-first century, automakers cater to us. We love their attention, and they know it. Americans are used to instant gratification. We want and get next year's new models *now*. Because they understand our "first person on the block to have it" mentality, the car manufacturers tantalize us with concept cars—you know, those weird, space-age-looking vehicles with gull's wings and rocket packs. To please the American sense of beauty, each year the cars get more attractive. New cars are sleeker and shinier and more pleasing to touch. With such beauty, though, comes higher sticker prices. But we don't care. We are willing to pay any price to practice the Automobile Religion.

Today, cars mean more to us than a way to cruise around town. If we saw them as only a means to get to the grocery store, we'd all be willing to drive junkers. Instead, we see our cars as reflections of our personalities. Most people don't want to drive rusty old bombers. We want to be able to see our ideal (or idealized) images mirrored in our car's glossy paint job. We want automobiles that make a statement about ourselves. People travel through the American wilderness in Jeeps and trucks because they symbolize toughness and an uncompromising attitude. We buy sports cars not so much to impress others as to impress ourselves: "Hey, I'm driving this red convertible Miata, and I feel like the master of the highway."

That's why we love our cars and decorate them as we do, to display a little of ourselves even while we drive. With bumper stickers, we exercise our constitutional rights to free speech. One of mine reads, "I love my humpback whale." Another promotes my favorite radio station. For some reason, I often see National Rifle Association stickers on pickup trucks. Again, the drivers are making a statement to the rest of us motorists: "I like to maim and kill! Get out of my way!" I, with my stuffed Bugs Bunny doll in the back window, get out of the way.

The word *automobile* means "self-moving." Cars give us the freedom to go where we want, when we want, across town or across the country. There is plenty of wide-open space for our cars. Even owners of land barge SUVs usually find a place to park. Let's consider the Japanese for a moment. They, too, love their cars (with good reason), yet their autos are stuck on a few tiny islands, and parking laws are so strict that meter-readers write in chalk on the sidewalk how long a car has been parked in a certain spot. Too long, and it's towed. In America, we can usually park our cars illegally and get away with it (for at least as long as it takes to run into the bank or the drugstore).

When we own a car, we don't have to rely on—yikes—public transportation, something people in other countries don't mind doing. Americans' cars are personal sanctuaries, places to escape other humans. The car's popularity has led to the phenomenon of drive-up windows. Banks, donut shops, even dry cleaners allow us to transact business without leaving the comfort and safety of our autos. Try getting a bus driver to stop at Dunkin' Donuts because you have a sudden urge for a cruller. We no longer have to move from the driver's seat to order a meal. We no longer have to sit in a noisy McDonald's with screaming kids to eat our grease-laden food. We just stay in our cars. How convenient. We can even sing along to the stereo if we want. Other commuters look at you strangely and hide their valuables if you sing on a subway.

Cars entice us Americans because they allow us to do the things that appeal to us: drive where we please, when we please, dine "à la car," sing aloud in public and not be thought insane. And through the kinds of cars we drive and how we adorn them, we can share with strangers our personalities. Even though we may be isolated in our automobiles, we share with other motorists the camaraderie that comes with belonging to the Car Cult.

Discussion

This draft makes a good start, but it needs substantial revision. First, there seems to be too much material. This lack of a clear focus leaves lots of reader questions unanswered:

- *What and where is the thesis?*
- *Is this essay about cars and our love of freedom, of variety, of self-esteem, of free speech, of privacy, or what?*
- *What was the meaning of this whole observation for you?*

Next, the organization of this draft hints at an introduction, body, and conclusion, but some paragraphs lack definite topic sentences and clear connections between ideas. And despite the colorful images, the conversational style (like a person talking), and the use of plain English, all this could be said in fewer words and with clearer emphasis.

Figure 4.1 shows how the Checklist for Revision (pages 62–63) can help you revise to achieve the finished essay on pages 57–58. For reference, the paragraphs from the draft are labeled A through H. Specific needed improvements are explained on the pages following the draft. Notice that the original eight-paragraph draft has been reshaped into a five-paragraph revision.

Note

This case illustrates revision for "rhetorical features" (content, organization, and style). But once the final draft is rhetorically effective, it needs to be proofread for "mechanical features" (correct grammar, punctuation, word choice, mechanics, and format)—covered in parts of Chapter 8 and in Section Six.

Revision has resulted in an essay with worthwhile content, sensible organization, and a readable style. (For detailed advice on achieving these qualities in a final draft, see Chapters 5–8.)

Rewrite introduction to invite readers in

Cars R Us

~~Car Crazy~~

We Americans love our automobiles. No question.
is next year's new model always front-page news?
But why ~~do we worship them? Nearly every country has~~

~~access to cars, but not every country has the freedom to~~

A

FIGURE 4.1   A draft edited for revision

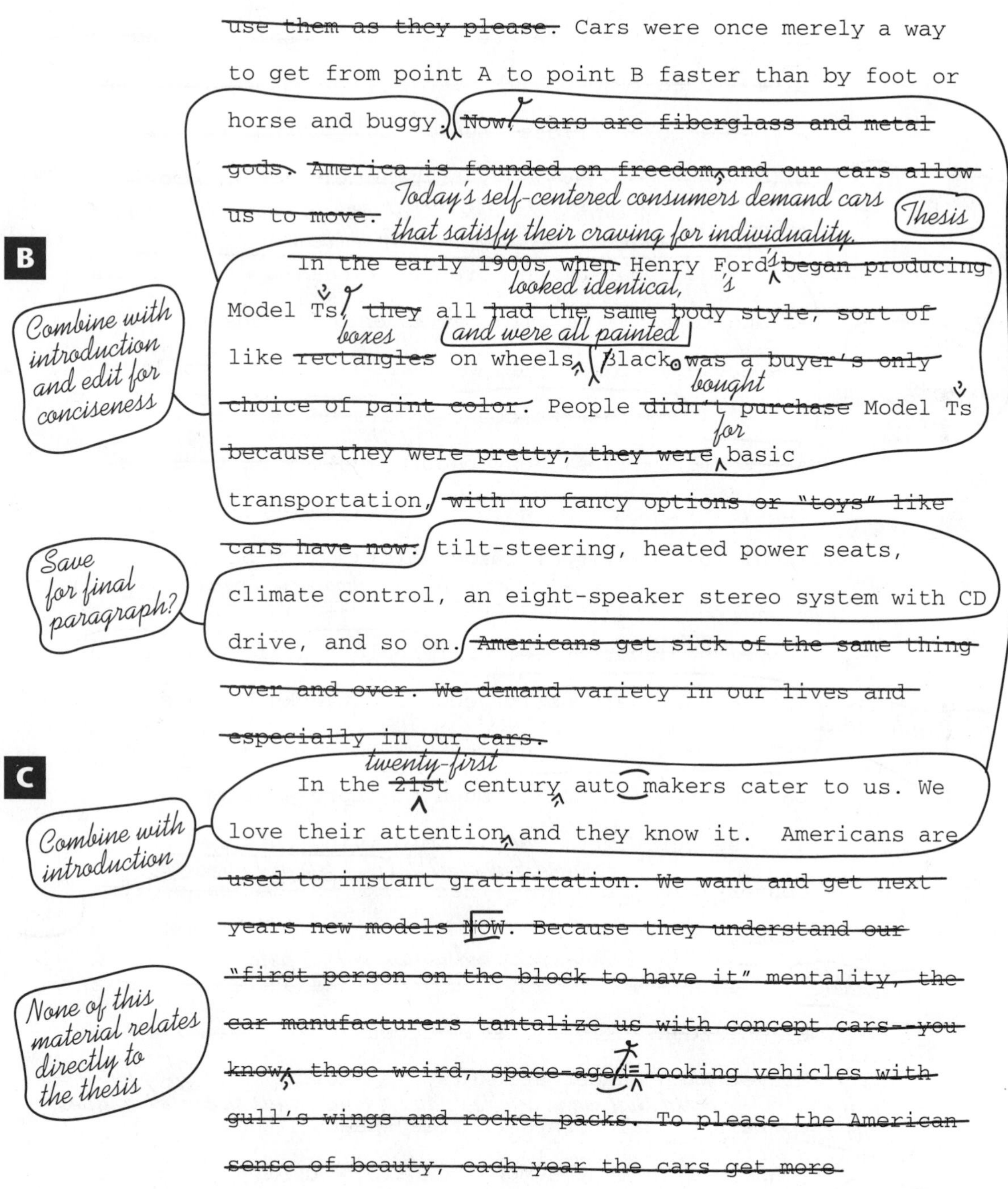

~~use them as they please.~~ Cars were once merely a way to get from point A to point B faster than by foot or horse and buggy. Now ~~cars are fiberglass and metal gods. America is founded on freedom, and our cars allow us to move.~~ *Today's self-centered consumers demand cars that satisfy their craving for individuality.* (Thesis)

B

(Combine with introduction and edit for conciseness)

In the early 1900s when Henry Ford*'s* ~~began producing~~ Model Ts, ~~they all had the same body style, sort of~~ *looked identical,* *boxes* like ~~rectangles~~ on wheels, *and were all painted* Black ~~was a buyer's only choice of paint color.~~ People ~~didn't purchase~~ *bought* Model Ts *for* ~~because they were pretty; they were~~ basic transportation, ~~with no fancy options or "toys" like cars have now:~~

(Save for final paragraph?)

tilt-steering, heated power seats, climate control, an eight-speaker stereo system with CD drive, and so on. ~~Americans get sick of the same thing over and over. We demand variety in our lives and especially in our cars.~~

C

(Combine with introduction)

In the *twenty-first* ~~21st~~ century auto makers cater to us. We love their attention, and they know it. ~~Americans are used to instant gratification. We want and get next years new models NOW. Because they understand our~~

(None of this material relates directly to the thesis)

~~"first person on the block to have it" mentality, the car manufacturers tantalize us with concept cars--you know, those weird, space-age-looking vehicles with gull's wings and rocket packs. To please the American sense of beauty, each year the cars get more~~

FIGURE 4.1 A draft edited for revision (continues)

attractive. ~~New cars are sleeker and shinier / and more pleasing to touch. With such beauty, though, comes higher sticker prices. But we don't care. We are willing to pay any price to practice the Automobile Religion.~~ *We want automobiles that make a unique lifestyle statement about who we think we are.*

(Topic sentence)

D

(Say this more concisely)

Today, cars mean more to us than a way to cruise around town. If we saw them as only a means to get to the grocery store, then we'd all be willing to drive junkers. ~~Instead, we see our cars as reflections of our personalities.~~ Most people *hate* ~~don't want to drive~~ rusty, old bombers. We want to be able to see our ideal (or idealized) images mirrored in our car's glossy paint job, *or in our truck's chrome hubcaps* ~~We want automobiles that make a statement about ourselves.~~

(Sharpen the images)

People travel through the American wilderness in jeeps and trucks because they symbolize toughness and an uncompromising attitude. We buy sports cars not so much to impress others, *as* ~~but~~ to impress ourselves: "Hey, I'm driving this red convertible Miata *because I'm special* *(relates to theme of individuality)* ~~and I feel like the master of the highway~~."

(cross-thru)

E

(Topic sentence)

Cars provide each individual with a personal billboard. ~~That's why we love our cars and decorate them as we do, to display a little of ourselves even while we drive.~~ With bumper stickers, we exercise our *They tell the world that we're intellectuals or tough guys or sensitive types.* constitutional rights to free speech. One of mine reads, "I love my humpback whale." Another promotes my favorite radio station. ~~[//////////]~~ For some

(Add more examples)

FIGURE 4.1 A draft edited for revision (continues)

reason, I often see National Rifle Association stickers on pickup trucks. Again, the drivers are making a statement to the rest of us motorists: "I like to maim ~~and kill!~~ Get out of my way!" to the rest of us *wimps* ~~motorists.~~ (Stet) I, with my stuffed Bugs Bunny doll in the back window, get out of the ~~way.~~ *line of fire.*

> *Too aggressive*

> *Avoid name-calling*

F

> *None of this material relates to the thesis*

~~The word "automobile" means self-moving. Cars give~~ ~~us the freedom to go where we want, when we want,~~ ~~across town or across the country. There is plenty of~~ ~~wide-open space for our cars. Even owners of land~~ ~~barge SUVs usually find a place to park. Let's~~ ~~consider the Japanese for a moment. They, too, love~~ ~~their cars (with good reason), yet their autos are stuck~~ *few* *s* ~~on a tiny island, and parking laws are so strict that~~ ~~meter-readers write in chalk on the sidewalk how long a~~ ~~car has been parked in a certain spot. Too long, and~~ ~~it's towed. In America, we can usually park our cars~~ ~~illegally and get away with it (for at least as long as~~ ~~it takes to ⌐run⌐ into the bank or~~ *the* ~~drugstore.)~~

G

> *Delete irrelevant comparison*

When we own a car, we don't have to rely on-- *torture for individuals like us.* yikes--public transportation, ~~something people in other~~ ~~countries don't mind doing.~~ Americans' cars are personal sanctuaries, places to escape other humans. *One popular form of escape is the* ~~The car's popularity has led to the phenomenon of~~ drive-up windows. Banks, donut shops, even dry cleaners allow us to transact business without leaving

FIGURE 4.1   A draft edited for revision (continues)

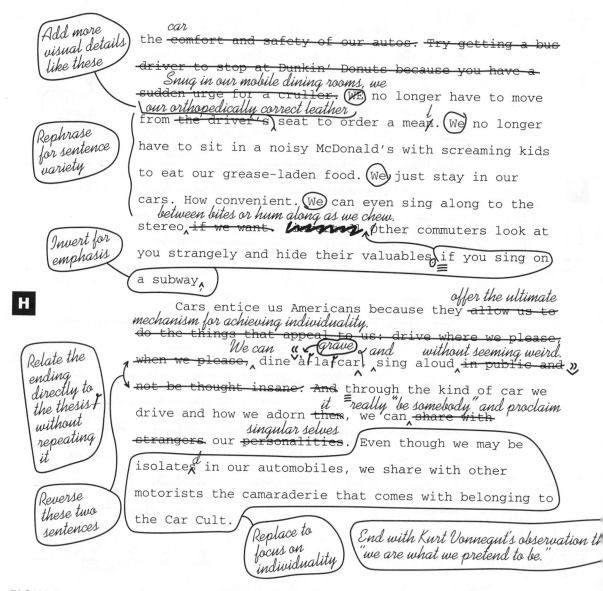

FIGURE 4.1   A draft edited for revision (continues)

Discussion of Figure 4.1

Paragraph A: The essay's title could be more specific about the theme here: namely, how we identify with our cars. The paragraph itself gives readers no clear sense of what to expect. Sentences 3 and 6 refer to car worship, while sentences 4 and 7 (the thesis?) are about freedom. If the final sentence is indeed the thesis, it seems to promise a discussion on the theme of worshiping our cars because they give us the freedom to move. But the final draft will explore other themes such as self-esteem, free speech, and privacy—all elements of our craving for individuality.

Paragraph B: Much of this material could be trimmed and combined with the introductory paragraph, to focus on consumer attitudes toward the Model T's versus today's cars. The two final sentences seem awfully general; they can be cut.

Paragraph C: The two opening sentences could be combined with the introductory paragraph to focus again on the change in consumer attitudes. The rest of the paragraph, with its wordy and irrelevant details about instant gratification, concept cars, and high sticker prices, can be cut.

Paragraph D: This paragraph provides informative details, but it lacks a topic sentence to frame readers' understanding of these details. Also, wordiness could be trimmed and images sharpened to provide a more vivid picture. Otherwise the material here is definitely worthwhile.

Paragraph E: This paragraph, too, is generally strong, but it needs a more definite topic sentence and additional examples. Also, the tone in reference to pickup trucks and NRA stickers lapses into name-calling and stereotyping.

Paragraph F: The entire paragraph strays from the essay's purpose to explore Americans' need to identify with our cars. It seems to belong to some other essay about cars and freedom or some such.

Paragraph G: This is another strong paragraph, with a basically solid topic sentence and vivid detail. The sweeping comparison with other countries and the Dunkin' Donuts reference really add nothing and can be deleted. Some sharper images would intensify the picture, and a few style changes would improve emphasis and readability.

Paragraph H: This conclusion needs a topic sentence that relates more explicitly to the thesis. The colorful images do a nice job of reflecting on the essay's main themes, but they should be followed by a closing statement that sums up the essay's larger meaning.

Figure 4.2 shows a sample page edited using a word processor's editing application.

REVISING WITH PEERS

All writing can benefit from feedback. As part of the revision process, your writing course may include workshops for peer review and editing. *Peer review* means evaluating how well your own writing and the writing of others meets its purpose and connects with its intended audience.

Questions reviewers ask

- *Is the content accurate, appropriate, and useful?*
- *Is the material organized for the reader's understanding?*
- *Is the style clear, easy to read, and engaging?*

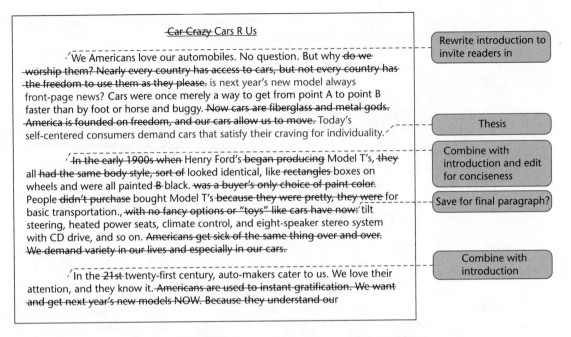

FIGURE 4.2 **A page from a draft edited using a word processor's editing application**

Through peer review, classmates point out to each other what works and what doesn't work. This commentary helps writers think about ways of revising.

Editing means actually "fixing" the piece by making it more precise and readable without altering the author's intended meaning.

Some ways in which editors "fix" writing

- Rephrasing or reorganizing sentences
- Clarifying a thesis or topic sentence
- Choosing a better word or phrase
- Correcting spelling, usage, and punctuation

GUIDELINES for Peer Review and Editing

- *Exchange drafts with a classmate.* Edit for content, organization, style, and correctness. Use the editing, revision, and proofreading symbols on the last page of this book.

- *Read the entire piece before you comment.* Get a clear sense of the assignment's purpose and audience. Try to visualize the document as a whole before you evaluate specific parts.

- *Remember that mere mechanical correctness offers no guarantee of effectiveness.* A "correct" piece of writing may still contain faulty rhetorical elements (inferior content, confusing organization, or unsuitable style).

■ *Understand the acceptable limits of editing.* In the workplace, "editing" can range from fine-tuning to an in-depth rewrite. In school, however, rewriting a piece to the extent that it ceases to belong to its author may constitute plagiarism.

■ *Be honest but diplomatic.* Begin with something positive before moving to critique. Support rather than judge.

■ *Always explain why you feel something doesn't work.* Instead of "This paragraph is confusing," say, "Because this paragraph lacks a clear topic sentence, I had trouble discovering the main idea." Help the writer identify the cause of the problem.

■ *Focus first on the big picture.* Begin with the thesis, the ideas, and the shape of the essay. (Is the thesis clear and definite? Is the supporting material relevant and convincing? Is the discussion easy to follow? Does each paragraph do its job?) Then discuss specifics of style and correctness (tone, word choice, sentence structure, and so on).

■ *Make specific recommendations.* Mark your suggested revisions clearly on the page, and write out your overall advice in enough detail for the writer to know what to do. (For reviewing, editing, and revising via computer files, see the Digital Tip box on page 74.)

■ *Be aware that not all feedback has equal value.* Even professional editors can disagree. If different readers offer conflicting opinions of your own work, give the most weight to your instructor's comments.

■ *Sign and return the edited draft.* Face-to-face or via email discuss your suggestions, as well as those you receive, with your classmate.

PROOFREADING YOUR FINAL DRAFT

No matter how engaging and informative the essay, basic errors distract the reader and make the writer look bad. Proofreading detects easily correctable errors such as these:

Errors we look for during proofreading

■ *Sentence errors,* such as fragments, comma splices, or run-ons
■ *Punctuation errors,* such as missing apostrophes or unnecessary commas
■ *Usage errors,* such as **it's** for **its, lay** for **lie,** and **their** for **there**
■ *Mechanical errors,* such as misspelled words, inaccurate dates, or incorrect abbreviations
■ *Format errors,* such as missing page numbers, inconsistent spacing, or incorrect form of documenting sources
■ *Typographical errors* (typos), such as repeated or missing words or letters, missing word endings (**-s** or **-ed** or **-ing**), or left-out quotation marks or parentheses

GUIDELINES for Proofreading

- *Save it for the final draft.* Proofreading earlier drafts might cause writer's block and distract you from the "rhetorical features" (content, organization, and style).

- *Take a break before proofreading your final draft.* You should approach your final draft alert and with fresh eyes.

- *Work from hard copy.* Research indicates that people read more perceptively (and with less fatigue) from a printed page than from a computer screen.

- *Keep it slow.* Slide a ruler under each line or move backward, sentence by sentence.

- *Be especially alert for troublesome areas in your writing.* Do you have trouble spelling? Do you get commas confused with semicolons? Do you make a lot of typos?

- *Proofread more than once.* The more often you do it, the better.

DIGITAL TIP

Use Your Computer to Revise   The Digital Tip boxes in Chapters 5 through 8 will provide specific advice for using your computer at various stages of the revision process (to revise overall content, paragraphs, sentences, and words/phrases). Below are suggestions for revising on your computer.

- Use your word processor's print preview option. The miniaturized snapshot of the essay will show where paragraphs are too long or short and whether the essay meets length requirements.

- Use the editing application in your word-processing program every time you review, edit, or revise. This feature (see Figure 4.2, which uses this application) is specifically designed for revision and/or collaboration. You can edit your paper or that of your peer so that any additions show in a different color and any deletions show as strikethroughs without deleting the original text. You can also add comments, either next to or at the bottom of the document. Once you or your peer are satisfied with the revised paper, click on the accept changes option.

- Take advantage of your computer's cut, copy, paste, and move options. Adjust your paragraphs and sentences so that they fall where they fit best. Check for effective placement of your thesis statement and topic sentences.

- Save your work regularly and back up your files at the end of each day. Save each revision as a separate document titled Revision 1, Revision 2, etc., so you can keep track of versions and go back to an earlier version if needed.

☑ A CHECKLIST for Proofreading

Sentences

☐ Are all sentences complete (no unacceptable fragments)? (494)

☐ Is the document free of comma splices and run-on sentences? (499–500)

☐ Are ideas of equal importance coordinated? (497)

☐ Are ideas of lesser importance subordinated? (497)

☐ Does each verb agree with its subject? (501)

☐ Does each pronoun refer to and agree with a specific noun? (502)

☐ Is each pronoun in the correct case (nominative, objective, possessive)? (505)

☐ Is each modifier positioned to reflect the intended meaning? (503)

☐ Is the document free of shifts in person, voice, tense, and mood? (506)

Punctuation

☐ Does each sentence conclude with appropriate end punctuation? (508)

☐ Are semicolons and colons used correctly to indicate a *break* between items? (509–510)

☐ Are commas used correctly as a grammatically warranted *pause* between items? (511)

☐ Do apostrophes signal possessives, contractions, and certain plurals? (515)

☐ Do quotation marks set off direct quotes and certain titles? (517)

☐ Is each quotation punctuated correctly? (517)

☐ Do ellipses indicate material omitted from a quotation? (518)

☐ Do italics indicate certain titles or names, emphasis, or the special use of a word? (518)

☐ Are brackets, parentheses, and dashes used correctly and as needed? (519–520)

Mechanics

☐ Are abbreviations used correctly and without confusing the reader? (520)

☐ Are hyphens used correctly and as needed? (521)

☐ Are words capitalized correctly and as needed? (522)

☐ Are numbers written out or expressed in numerals as needed? (523)

☐ Has electronic spell or grammar checking been supplemented by actual proofreading? (523)

Format, Usage, and Keyboarding

☐ Are pages numbered correctly? (525)

☐ Are sources cited in a standard form of documentation? (386)

☐ Have typographical errors been corrected? (526)

☐ Are commonly confused words used accurately? (133)

4.1 Using the Checklist for Revision on pages 62–63 as a guide, return to an essay you have written earlier, and revise it.

At this stage, you are bound to feel a little confused about the finer points of content, organization, and style. But in later chapters, you will learn to improve your skill for diagnosing problems and prescribing cures.

Along with your revised essay, submit the original essay and an explanation of the improvements you've made.

4.2 **COLLABORATIVE PROJECT** Take an essay you have written earlier, and exchange it for a classmate's. Assume that your classmate's essay has been written specifically for you as the audience. Write a detailed evaluation of your classmate's essay, making specific suggestions for revision. Using the Checklist for Revision on pages 62–63, evaluate all three rhetorical features: content, organization, and style. Use the Checklist for Proofreading (page 75) to recommend improvements in grammar, punctuation, and mechanics. Do plenty of scribbling on the essay, and sign your evaluation.

4.3 **COLLABORATIVE PROJECT** Email a copy of your essay (as a word file) to a classmate, and ask this reviewer to make specific comments using the Checklist for Revision and the editing application in your word processing program. Then forward it to a second reviewer, who will repeat the exercise. Alternatively, create a *Google Docs* account so that all team members can access your uploaded essay.

4.4 **COMPUTER PROJECT** Try out the spell checker supplied by the word-processing program you're using. First, learn how to add words you use often (your name, for example) to the computer's dictionary so that the program won't question you each time it encounters these words. Second, make a list of the words the computer lists as misspelled and the suggested corrections. Compare the computer's suggestions with the entries in a good dictionary. Do they match? Keep a log of the words you misspell.

Then proofread your paper carefully, watching for the kinds of errors computers can't catch: *homonyms,* or words that sound alike but are spelled differently and have different meanings (*their* and *there, heel* and *heal*), and *transpositions* (*form* for *from*). Also note that older spell checkers won't catch missing or extra words! How many of these corrections did you find?

4.5 **WEB-BASED PROJECT** Web pages from the Writer's Block <**www.writersblock.ca/ spring1995/feature.htm**> describe the relationship between writers and editors in the workplace. Prepare a summary of this information, in your own words, for class discussion. (Page 384 offers guidelines for summarizing information.) Attach a copy of the Web page to your summary.

PEARSON
mycomplab

For additional information and practice with the learning objectives in this chapter, go to www.mycomplab.com, Resources>Writing>The Writing Process>Revising.

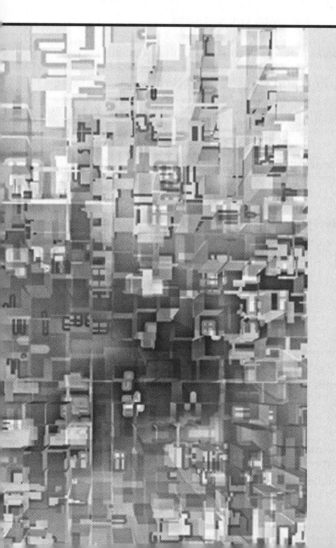

Specific Revision Strategies

Introduction

Chapter 1 reminds us that it is a rare piece of writing that is ever "finished" in the strict sense. Most writing, even at later stages, is more of a work in progress, with considerable room for improvement. Even professional writers often revisit a "finished" work for further revision.

Revising from the top down

One useful way to revise is to consider your essay from the top down. First, consider the actual content—your reason for writing in the first place; next, the shape and position of each paragraph; then, the flow of your sentences; and, finally, the quality of your phrasing and word choice. Figure II.1 shows how essay revision can move from large matters to small.

Revising the Content
- Is the thesis clear, focused, and significant?
- Is the support credible, informative, and substantial?

Revising the Organization
- Is the essay's structure visible at a glance?
- Is each support paragraph basically its own mini–essay?

Revising the Sentences
- Is each sentence immediately understandable?
- Is rich information expressed in the fewest words possible?
- Are sentences constructed with enough variety?

Revising the Words and Phrases
- Does each word clarify—rather than muddle—the meaning?
- Is the tone appropriate?

FIGURE II.1 Top-down decisions in revision

Beefing up the content

Readers expect content that rewards their effort. To make it convincing, informative, and thorough, we provide plenty of *details:* facts, ideas, examples, numbers, names, events, dates, or reasons that help readers visualize what we mean. But we trim away needless detail. Early drafts almost always need trimming.

Harnessing paragraph power

Readers look for shapes they can recognize. Instead of forcing readers to organize unstructured material for themselves, we shape it for their understanding. Our essential organizing tool is the paragraph: forming part of the essay's larger design while telling its own, self-contained story.

Honing the sentences

Readers have no patience with writing that's hard to interpret, takes too long to make the point, or reads like a Dick-and-Jane story from primary school. So we work to produce razor-sharp sentences that are clear and forceful, waste no words, and are easy to read.

Finding the perfect wording

Readers are turned off by wording that is awkward, too fancy, or stuffy and impersonal. So we fine-tune each word to convey precisely what we are seeing, thinking, and feeling.

Note

Like other decisions about writing, the revising process is not always as systematic as outlined here. For example, you might revisit the content while working on the organization, or you might think of a better word while reshaping a paragraph. Once you have learned the strategies in this section, how you decide to use them will be up to you.

CHAPTER 5

Revising the Content: Writing Something Worthwhile

LEARNING OBJECTIVES FOR THIS CHAPTER

■ Revise an essay for credibility, informative value, and completeness

■ Define plagiarism, recognize plagiarized content, and know how to avoid unintended plagiarism

Readers hate to waste time. They expect an insightful thesis backed by solid content and support.

The first requirement of worthwhile content is *unity:* every word, every detail belongs. Three other qualities are also essential to worthwhile content: *credibility, informative value,* and *completeness.**

---

*Adapted from James L. Kinneavy's assertion that discourse should be factual, unpredictable, and comprehensive. See James L. Kinneavy, *A Theory of Discourse* (Englewood Cliffs, NJ: Prentice-Hall, 1971).

MAKE IT CREDIBLE

Anyone can assert opinions; *supporting* your assertion—that is, making it credible for your readers—is the real challenge. We all have opinions about political candidates, cars, and controversial subjects such as abortion and nuclear energy. But many of our opinions are *uninformed;* instead of resting on facts, they lean mostly on a chaotic collection of beliefs repeated around us, notions we've inherited from advertising, things we've read but never checked, and assumptions we've never examined.

UNINFORMED OPINIONS

Christopher Columbus was a hero.

Christopher Columbus was an oppressor.

Grindo toothpaste is best for making teeth whiter.

In a democracy, religion deserves a voice in government.

Informed opinion, in contrast, rests on fact or good sense. Any fact ("My hair is brown"; "Americans have more televisions than bathtubs") can be verified by anyone. A fact can be verified by observation ("I saw Felix murder his friend"), by research ("Wood smoke contains the deadly chemical dioxin"), by experience ("I was hugged this morning"), or by measurement ("Roughly 60 percent of our first-year students eventually earn a degree"). Opinions based on these facts would be informed opinions.

INFORMED OPINIONS

Felix is guilty of murder.

Homes with woodstoves need good ventilation.

This has been a good day for me.

College clearly is not for everyone.

To *support an opinion,* you must often consider a variety of facts. You might be able to support with facts the claim that Grindo toothpaste makes teeth whiter, but a related fact may be that Grindo contains tiny silicone particles—abrasives that "whiten" by scraping enamel from teeth. The second fact could change your opinion about Grindo.

The Grindo example illustrates that no two facts about anything are likely to have equal relevance. Assume you've asserted this opinion:

This opinion needs supporting facts

The Diablo Canyon nuclear plant is especially dangerous.

In deciding how to support this opinion, you compare the relevance of each of these facts:

Not all supporting facts are equal

1. The road system is inadequate for rapid evacuation of local residents.
2. Nuclear plants have no suitable way to dispose of radioactive wastes.

3. The plant is only 100 miles from sizable population centers.

4. The plant is built near a major earthquake fault.

Although all these facts support the label "dangerous," the first three can apply to many nuclear plants. Only the fourth addresses the danger specific to the Diablo Canyon plant and therefore has most relevance to the thesis. Because readers can tolerate only so many details, you must decide which of your facts offer the best support.

Besides unifying your facts, you need to arrange them for emphasis. Consider this opening passage:

PASSAGE A: AN OPINION SUPPORTED BY FACT

Child abuse has become our national disgrace. In the past decade, reported incidence has increased an average of 20 percent yearly. This year alone, more than 500,000 children (fewer than 20 percent of cases) will be the reported victims of physical, sexual, or emotional violence by one or both parents. And among the reported offenders, only 3 percent are ever convicted. Even more tragic, the pattern of violence is cyclical, with many abused children later becoming abusive parents themselves.

We move from the disquieting numbers to the tragically cyclical process.

Instead of relying on facts, certain moral or emotional opinions (about prayer in public schools, the existence of God, laws against flag desecration, children's rights) often rest on common sense and insight. The following passage supports the opinion that parents should limit their role in telling their children how to live.

PASSAGE B: AN OPINION SUPPORTED BY GOOD SENSE

The idea of the child as personal property has always bothered me, for personal reasons. I lack the feeling that I own my children and have always scoffed at the idea that what they are and do is a continuation or rejection of my being. I like them, I sympathize with them, I acknowledge the obligation to support them for a term of years—but I am not so fond or foolish as to regard a biological tie as a lien on their loyalty or respect or to imagine that I am equipped with special powers of guidance as to their success and happiness. Beyond inculcating some of the obvious manners required in civilized life, who am I to pronounce on what makes for a happy or successful life? How many of us can say that we have successfully managed our own lives? Can we do better with our children?

This passage offers no statistics, research data, or observable facts. However, the support is credible because of its insight into our shared reality as parents and children.

MAKE IT INFORMATIVE

Readers expect to find *something new and useful.* Writing has informative value when it does at least one of these things:

An essay with informative value does one or more of these things

- Shares something new and significant
- Reminds us about something we know but ignore
- Offers fresh insight or perspective on something we already know

In short, informative writing gives readers exactly what they need.

Readers approach most topics with some prior knowledge (or old information). They might need reminding, but they don't need a rehash of old information; they can fill in the blanks for themselves. On the other hand, readers don't need every bit of new information you can think of, either.

As a reader of this book, for example, you expect to learn something worthwhile about writing, and my purpose is to provide that. Which of these statements would you find useful?

> Writing is hard and frustrating work.
>
> Writing is a process of deliberate decisions.

The first statement offers no news to anyone who ever has picked up a pencil. But the second statement reminds you that producing good writing can be a lot more complex than we would like. Because the second statement offers new insight into a familiar process, we can say it has informative value.

We see that passages A and B (page 82) satisfy our criteria for informative value: Passage A offers surprising evidence about child abuse; passage B gives fresh insight into the familiar issue of parent–child relations.

Sometimes we write for a mixed group of readers with varied needs. How, then, can our writing have informative value for each reader?

Imagine that you are an ex-jogger and a convert to walking for aerobic exercise. You decide to write an essay for classmates on the advantages of walking over running. You can assume that a few classmates are runners; others swim, cycle, or do other exercise; some don't do much but are thinking of starting; and some have no interest in any exercise. Your problem is to address all these readers in one essay that each reader will find worthwhile. Specifically, you want to accomplish three things:

- Persuade runners and other exercisers to consider your alternative
- Encourage the interested nonexercisers to try walking
- Spark interest among the diehard nonexercisers and perhaps even inspire them to rise up out of their easy chairs and hit the bricks

First, you will need to answer the questions that all readers share:

Audience questions you
can anticipate

- *Why is walking better than running?*
- *How are walking and running similar and different?*
- *What are the benefits of walking? Can you give examples?*
- *Why should I bother?*

Some readers will have special questions. Nonexercisers might ask, "What exactly is aerobic exercise, anyway?" And the true couch potatoes might ask, "Who cares?" Your essay will have to answer all these questions.

Assume that many hours of planning, drafting, and revising have enabled you to produce this final draft:

AN ESSAY WITH INFORMATIVE VALUE

WALK BUT DON'T RUN

Our bodies gain aerobic benefits when we exercise at a fast enough pace for muscles to demand oxygen-rich blood from the heart and lungs. During effective aerobic exercise, the heart rate increases roughly 80 percent above normal. Besides strengthening muscle groups—especially the heart—aerobic exercise makes blood vessels stronger and larger.

Running, or jogging, has become a most popular form of aerobic exercise. But millions of Americans who began running to get in shape are now limping to their doctors for treatment of running injuries. To keep yourself in one piece as you keep yourself in shape, try walking instead of running.

All the aerobic benefits of running can be yours if you merely take brisk walks. Consider this comparison. For enough aerobic training to increase cardiovascular (heart, lungs, and blood vessels) efficiency, you need to run three times weekly for roughly 30 minutes. (Like any efficient system, an efficient cardiovascular system produces maximum work with minimum effort.) You can gain cardiovascular benefits equivalent to running, however, by taking a brisk walk three times weekly for roughly 60 minutes. Granted, walking takes up more time than running, but it carries fewer risks.

Because of its more controlled and deliberate pace, walking is safer than running. A walker stands far less chance of tripping, stepping in potholes, or slipping and falling. And the slower pace causes less physical trauma. Anyone who has ever run at all knows that a runner's foot strikes the ground with sizable impact. But the shock of this impact travels beyond the foot—to the shins, knees, hips, internal organs, and spine. Walking, of course, creates an impact of its own, but the walker's foot strikes the ground with only half as much force as the runner's foot.

Beyond its apparent physical dangers, running can provoke subtle stress for the devoted exerciser. Because running is generally seen as more competitive than just walking, we can be too easily tempted to push our bodies too far, too fast. Even though we might not compete in races or marathons, we often tend to compete against ourselves—maybe just to keep up with a jock neighbor or to break a personal record. And by ignoring the signals of overexertion and physical stress, we can easily run ourselves into an injury—if not the grave. Slowing to a walk instead is a safe way of leaving the "competition" behind.

—*Jeff Leonard*

Will this essay have informative value for all readers? Probably. It seems to answer all the readers' questions we anticipated on page 84. Will all readers become converts? Probably not. But each should have something to think about. A worthwhile message makes a difference for its readers, even if it triggers only the slightest insight.

Now let's assume that you had written the walking essay by using the old high school strategy of filling up the page. Your opening paragraph might have looked like this:

AN OPENING WITHOUT INFORMATIVE VALUE

WALK BUT DON'T RUN

Medical science has made tremendous breakthroughs in the past few decades. Research has shown that exercise is a good way of staying healthy, beneficial for our bodies and our minds. More people of all ages are exercising today than ever before. Because of its benefits, one popular form of exercise for Americans is aerobic exercise.

Your readers (in the situation described on page 83) already know all this. Even new material lacks informative value when it is irrelevant:

MATERIAL IRRELEVANT TO THE SITUATION

To avoid the perils of running, the Chinese attend sessions of t'ai-chi, a dancelike series of stretching routines designed to increase concentration and agility. Although t'ai-chi is less dangerous than running, it fails to provide a true aerobic workout.

This material might serve in an essay comparing aerobic and nonaerobic exercises, but it does not belong in this comparison between walking and running.

Nor would highly technical details have informative value here, as in this example:

MATERIAL TOO TECHNICAL FOR THE SITUATION

Walking and jogging result in forward motion because you continually fall forward and catch yourself. With each stride, you lift your body, accelerate, and land. You go faster when running because you fall farther, but you also strike the ground harder and for less time. Your increase in speed and distance fallen combine with the shorter contact period to cause an impact on your body that is more than double the impact from walking.

This material would be of interest to students of biophysics, exercise physiology, or sports medicine, but it is too detailed for a mixed audience.

MAKE IT COMPLETE

All writers struggle with the question of completeness in their writing: How much is enough? (Or how long should it be?) To find the answer, you need once again to anticipate readers' questions about your thesis.

Assume, for instance, that a friend now living in another state is thinking of taking a job similar to one you held last summer. Your friend has written to ask how you liked the job; your response will influence the friend's decision. Here is a passage from a first draft that tells but doesn't show:

NOT ENOUGH DETAIL

My job last summer as a flagger for a road construction company was boring, tiresome, dirty, and painful. All I did was stand in the road and flag cars. Every day I just stood there, getting sore feet. I was always covered with dirt and breathing it in. To make matters worse, the sun, wind, and bugs ruined my skin. By the end of summer, I vowed never to do this kind of work again.

This passage has only limited informative value because it fails to make the experience vivid for the reader. The sketchy details fail to answer our obvious questions.

- *Can you show me what the job was like?*
- *What, exactly, made it boring, tiresome, dirty, and painful?*

This next passage, by contrast, includes graphic details that help readers *visualize* and feel a part of it all:

ENOUGH DETAIL

My job last summer as a flagger for a road construction company was boring, tiresome, dirty, and painful. All day I stood like a robot, waving a stupid red flag at oncoming traffic, my eardrums blasted by the racket of road machinery, each day dragging by more slowly than the last. My feet would swell, and my legs would ache from standing on the hard clay and gravel for up to fifteen hours a day. And the filth was disgusting. The fumes, oil, and grime from the road machinery and the exhaust from passing cars became like a second skin. Each breath sucked up more dust, clogging my sinuses, irritating my eyes. But worst of all was the weather. Blistering from sunburn, I was being sandblasted and rubbed raw by windstorms, pounded by hail, or chewed by mosquitoes and horseflies. By the end of summer, I was a freak with swollen feet and ankles, the skin of a water buffalo, and chronic sinusitis. I'd starve before taking that job again.

—*Regina Dumont*

Additional details (say, a day-by-day description of every event) would probably clutter the message. The reader here needed and wanted just enough information to make an informed decision.

Giving enough detail is not the same as merely adding words. Whatever does nothing but fill the page is puffery:

HOT AIR

My job last summer as a flagger for a road construction company was boring, tiresome, dirty, and painful. ~~Day in and day out,~~ I stood ~~on that road~~ for endless hours getting ~~a severe case of~~ sore feet. My face and body were ~~always completely~~ covered with the dust blown up from the ~~passing cars and various other~~ vehicles, and I was forced to breathe in all of this ~~horrible~~ junk ~~day after day. To add to the problems of boredom, fatigue, and dirt,~~ the weather murdered my skin. ~~Let me tell you that~~ by the time ~~the~~ summer ended, I ~~had~~ made ~~myself~~ a solemn promise never to ~~victimize myself by~~ taking this kind of awful job again.

Although this passage is nearly twice as long as the original first draft, it adds no meaning; hot air (the words crossed out) offers no real information.

Note

Don't worry about having too little to say. Once you have begun the writing process (searching for details, rephrasing, making connections), you will probably find it harder to stay within the limit than to reach it. Your purpose is to make your point, not to show how smart you are. Instead of including every word, fact, and idea that crosses your mind, learn to select. Sometimes one single detail is enough: To make the point about a "boring" job, the passage on page 86 describes the writer standing like a robot, waving a red flag.

The examples presented here show how you can measure the completeness of your own writing by answering questions like the following:

Details answer these questions

- *Who, what, when, where, and why?*
- *What did you see, feel, hear, taste, smell?*
- *What would a camera record?*
- *What are the dates, numbers, percentages?*
- *Can you compare it with something more familiar?*

AVOID PLAGIARISM

Whether in a brief essay or a long research paper, much of any writer's information comes from other sources, and the work of others must be properly documented. *Plagiarism* is using someone else's work—words, ideas, or illustrations, published or unpublished—without giving the creator of that work sufficient credit. A serious breach of scholarly ethics, plagiarism can have severe consequences. Students who plagiarize risk a failing grade or disciplinary action ranging from suspension to expulsion. A record of such action can adversely affect professional opportunities in the future, as well as graduate school admission.

Examples of plagiarism   Blatant cases of plagiarism occur when a writer consciously lifts passages from another work (print or online) and incorporates them into his or her own work without quoting or documenting the original source. And it isn't always intentional. Sometimes writers will fail to cite a source being quoted or paraphrased because they misplaced the original source and publication information or forgot to note it during their research (Anson and Schwegler 602–05). Whereas this more subtle and often unconscious form of misrepresentation is less blatant, it still constitutes plagiarism and can undermine a writer's credibility or worse.

Plagiarism and the Internet

The rapid development of Internet resources has spawned a wide array of misconceptions about plagiarism. Some people mistakenly assume that because material posted on a Web site is free, it can be paraphrased or copied without citation. Despite the ease of cutting and pasting from Web sites, the fact remains: Anytime you borrow someone else's words, ideas, perspectives, or images—regardless of the medium where you found them—you need to document the source—ideally, the *original* source—accurately.

The perils of obtaining plagiarized work online

It's no secret that any cheater can purchase essays, reports, and term papers on the Web. But antiplagiarism Web sites such as *<http://plagiarism.org>* now enable professors to cross-reference a suspicious paper against previously published material, flagging and identifying each plagiarized source.

To protect yourself against unintentional plagiarism, follow these steps:

How to avoid plagiarism

- Identify the sources you need to document.
- Take effective and accurate notes.
- Use quotations, paraphrases, and summaries carefully.
- Document your sources.

Each of these steps is fully explained and illustrated in Chapter 23. Consult that chapter whenever you need to credit one or more sources of information.

GUIDELINES for Revising Your Content

- *From all the material you develop during planning and drafting, select only what is worthwhile.* Keep nothing unless your reader needs to know it.

- *Assess your draft's credibility.* Credible writing is believable and convincing, with opinions based on fact or common sense. Distinguish carefully between informed versus uninformed opinion.

- *Assess your draft's informative value.* Readers always expect something new and useful. *Details* are writing's lifeblood: facts, ideas, numbers, names, events, dates, or reasons that enable readers to *visualize* your meaning. However, readers don't need every detail you can think of. Early drafts almost always need radical surgery to trim away excess material.

- *Assess your draft's completeness.* The often-stipulated 500 to 1,000 words is a realistic length for giving a well-focused topic respectable treatment. Quality, however, is far more important than quantity.

- *Whenever you paraphrase or quote someone, be sure to credit your source.*

DIGITAL TIP

Use Your Word Processor to Revise an Essay's Content

As you revise, you might have a hard time separating the process into stages: revising the content, the paragraphs, the sentences, and then the words and phrases. Try to stick to one stage at a time until you develop your own method. Here are suggestions for staying focused on content:

- Use your word processor's editing application to highlight content areas only. Turn on the highlighter feature and use the comments feature as well. Go through the essay four separate times, avoiding any edits at the paragraph, sentence, or word/phrase level.

- On your first pass, highlight portions that seem to lack credibility. Tagged to the highlighted passages, add comments to yourself about what is lacking and what corrections you plan.

- On your second pass, use a different color and highlight areas that seem to lack informative value. Add comments tagged to these areas, noting the problems and your planned solutions.

- On your third pass, use a third color and highlight areas that seem incomplete. Add tagged comments noting the problems and potential solutions.

- Finally, use a fourth color and highlight any areas that might be considered as plagiarized if you fail to document them properly. When in doubt, err on the side of caution.

- Save your multihighlighted documents as Revision 1 or use another title that indicates this file is your content revision.

☑ A CHECKLIST for Content

Credibility

☐ Does each assertion rely on **informed opinion**? (81)

☐ Is each informed opinion **supported** by verifiable facts or reasonable ideas? (82)

☐ Is the thesis **clear, focused,** and **significant**? (26)

☐ Is each supporting fact **relevant** to the thesis? (82)

☐ Are the facts and ideas arranged for best **emphasis**? (101)

☐ Does all nonfactual support appeal to our **common sense**? (82)

Informative Value

☐ Does the essay provide **fresh** and **relevant** information or insight? (83)

☐ Does it answer the **main questions** one could anticipate from readers? (84)

☐ Are readers given exactly and only **what they need**? (84)

(continues)

☐ Does the essay avoid rehashing **old information** (readers' prior knowledge)? (83)

☐ Do **graphic details** enable readers to visualize what is being discussed? (86)

Completeness

☐ Is this the **best material** readers could be given? (34)

☐ Is there **enough support** to make the point? (86)

☐ Is the piece free of **needless details**? (87)

☐ Is each **source** of quoted, paraphrased, or summarized material **properly cited**? (87)

APPLICATIONS

5.1 Each of the following sentences states either a fact or an opinion. Rewrite all statements of opinion as statements of fact. Remember that a fact can be verified. (Review pages 81–82.)

EXAMPLE

Opinion	My roommate isn't taking college work seriously.
Fact	My roommate never studies, sleeps through most classes, and has missed every exam.

1. Professor X grades unfairly.
2. My vacation was too short.
3. The salary for this position is $35,000 a year.
4. This bicycle is reasonably priced.
5. We walked 5 miles last Saturday.

5.2 Return to Maureen Malloy's essay on pages 57–58. Underline all statements of fact, and circle all statements of opinion. Are all the opinions supported by facts or by good sense? Now perform the same evaluation on an essay you have written. (Review pages 80–82.)

5.3 Assume that you live in the Northeast, and citizens in your state are voting on a solar energy referendum that would channel millions of tax dollars toward solar technology. The next paragraphs are designed to help you, as a voter, make an educated decision. Do both versions of the message have informative value? Explain your response. (Review pages 83–85.)

Solar power offers a realistic solution to the Northeast's energy problems. In recent years, the cost of fossil fuels (oil, coal, and natural gas) has risen rapidly while the supply has continued to decline. High prices and short supply will continue to cause a worsening energy crisis. Because solar energy comes directly from the sun, it is an inexhaustible resource. By using this energy to heat and air-condition our buildings, as well as to provide electricity, we could decrease substantially our consumption of fossil fuels. In turn, we would be less dependent on the unstable Middle East for our oil supplies. Clearly, solar power is a good alternative to conventional energy sources.

Solar power offers a realistic solution to the Northeast's energy problems. To begin with, solar power is efficient. Solar collectors installed on fewer than 30 percent of roofs in the Northeast would provide more than 70 percent of the area's heating and air-conditioning needs. Moreover, solar heat collectors are economical, operating for up to 20 years with little or no maintenance. These savings recoup the initial cost of installation within only 10 years. Most important, solar power is safe. It can be transformed into electricity through photovoltaic cells (a type of storage battery) noiselessly and with no air pollution—unlike coal, oil, and wood combustion. In sharp contrast to its nuclear counterpart, solar power produces no toxic wastes and poses no catastrophic danger of meltdown. Thus, massive conversion to solar power would ensure abundant energy and a safe, clean environment for future generations.

5.4   **COLLABORATIVE PROJECT** Review a classmate's essay, and eliminate all statements that lack informative value (those that offer commonly known, irrelevant, or insignificant material). Be careful not to cut material the audience needs in order to understand the essay, such as the following:

- Details that help us see
- Details that help us feel
- Numerical details
- Vivid comparisons
- Details that a camera would record
- Details that help us hear

Would some parts of your classmate's essay benefit from greater detail? Use the above list as a basis for making specific suggestions.

5.5   **COMPUTER APPLICATION** Make an electronic copy of a classmate's essay. Put the main topic in boldface, and underline all supporting material that has informative value. Save the file. Copy it and cut anything not in bold or underlined. Working with your classmate, compare the two versions.

5.6   **COMPUTER APPLICATION** Select a paragraph you have written for an earlier assignment. Using the paragraph on page 86 as a guide, create and save at least two alternative versions of this paragraph by deleting different combinations of words and phrases. Print out all three versions. Then, from among the alternatives, choose what you think is the most effective version of *each sentence.* Recombine these sentences into a fourth version of the paragraph—one that achieves completeness without clutter.

5.7   **WEB-BASED PROJECT** Prepare a brief presentation for your class in which you answer the questions "What is plagiarism?" and "How do I avoid it?" Start by exploring either <**http://www.indiana.edu/~wts/pamphlets/plagiarism.shtml**> or <**http://owl.english.purdue.edu/owl/resource/589/01/**>. Find at least one additional Web source on plagiarism.

For your class presentation, your goal is to summarize in one page or less a practical, working definition of plagiarism and a list of strategies for avoiding it. (See page 385 for guidelines for summarizing information.) Attach a copy of all relevant Web pages to your presentation. Be sure to credit each source of information (see page 87).

Work Cited

Anson, Chris M., and Robert A. Schwegler. *The Longman Handbook for Writers and Readers.* 4th ed. New York: Longman, 2005. Print.

For additional information and practice with the learning objectives in this chapter, go to www.mycomplab.com, Resources>Writing>The Writing Process>Revising.

CHAPTER 6

Revising the Paragraphs: Shaping for Readers' Access

LEARNING OBJECTIVES FOR THIS CHAPTER

- Recognize that a support paragraph has the same introduction/body/conclusion structure as a full essay

- Understand how topic statements act as paragraph introductions by providing a framework

- Define paragraph unity and know how to achieve a unified paragraph

- Define paragraph coherence and know the various methods to achieve a coherent paragraph

Essay readers expect to see an introduction (with a thesis), a body section (with topic statements), and a conclusion in an essay—as illustrated in Figure 6.1—to help them recognize the essay's overall shape and orient themselves to the reading process.

FIGURE 6.1
Support paragraphs in the basic essay

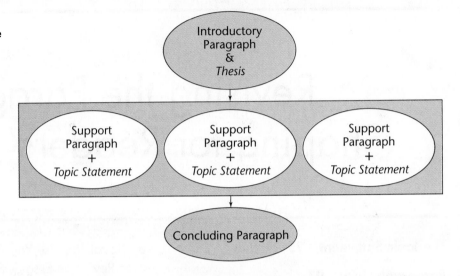

But an essay's overall shape is not enough to orient readers as they move through the essay. Readers also need to see that the paragraphs within the body of the essay—the *support paragraphs*—have their own similar shapes.

Although it is part of the essay's larger design, each support paragraph can usually stand alone in meaning and emphasis. Consider this paragraph by a noted psychiatrist.

A TYPICAL SUPPORT PARAGRAPH

Introduction
(topic statement, 1)
Body (2–9)

Conclusion (10–12)

Crime is everybody's temptation. [2]It is easy to look with proud disdain upon "those people" who get caught—the stupid ones, the unlucky ones, the blatant ones. [3]But who does not get nervous when a police car follows closely? [4]We squirm over our income-tax statements and make some "adjustments." [5]We tell the customs official that we have nothing to declare—well, practically nothing. [6]Some of us who have never been convicted of any crime picked up over two billion dollars' worth of merchandise last year from the stores we patronize. [7]Over a billion dollars was embezzled by employees last year. [8]One hotel in New York lost over seventy-five thousand finger bowls, demitasse spoons, and other objects in its first ten months of operation. [9]The Claims Bureau of the American Insurance Association estimates that 75 percent of all claims are dishonest in some respect and the amount of overpayment more than $350,000,000 a year. [10]These facts disturb us or should. [11]They give us an uneasy feeling that we are all indicted. [12]"Let him who is without sin cast the first stone."

—*Karl Menninger*

Menninger's paragraph is part of a longer work, a chapter in his book *The Crime of Punishment*. But the paragraph's shape is familiar enough: The introduction asserts a definite viewpoint, the body walks us through the writer's reasoning, and the conclusion offers perspective on what we have read.

In short, Menninger's paragraph is a mini–essay. It functions in much the same way as a complete essay. Therefore, when you revise your paragraphs, think of each one as a mini–essay. Each paragraph should have a beginning, middle, and end. Even more important, it should mirror a complete essay in that it has a topic statement to give it purpose, a sense of unity in which every part of the paragraph supports the topic statement, and a sense of coherence thanks to a connected line of thought running from the beginning of the paragraph to the end. Finally, the paragraph should be just long enough to make its point.

THE TOPIC STATEMENT

A college essay needs a thesis that asserts the main point, and each support paragraph needs a *topic statement* that asserts a supporting point. So when you revise your support paragraphs, first make sure that each contains a topic statement. Sometimes the topic statement comes at the end of the paragraph and sometimes in the middle, but usually it comes first. The paragraph's first sentence should focus and forecast.

The Topic Statement as Readers' Framework

No focus
Better

No forecast
Better

Most paragraphs in college writing begin by *telling readers what to look for.* Don't write "Some jobs are less stressful than others" when you mean "Mortuary management is an ideal major for anyone craving a stress-free job." The first topic statement doesn't give a very clear forecast; the second helps us focus. Don't write "Summers in Goonville are awful" when you mean "I hate Goonville because of the chiggers, ticks, scorpions, and rattlesnakes."

The Topic Statement as Writers' Framework

Without a topic statement, writers struggle to make their paragraphs more than a collection of random thoughts. *Always take a definite stand; assert something significant.*

Imagine that you are a member of Congress, about to vote on abortion legislation. One of your constituents has responded to your request for citizens' viewpoints with a letter that begins like this:

No focus or forecast

> *Abortion is a very complex issue.* There is a sharp division between those who are for it and those who are against it. Very few people take a neutral stand on this issue. The battle between supporters and opponents has raged for years. This is only one of the serious problems in our society. Every day, things seem to get worse.
>
> —*Carlo Melchiorre*

Because this writer never identifies his purpose or conveys his exact meaning, his paragraph merely spouts a number of unrelated thoughts that are all common knowledge. If the writer had instead refined his meaning by asserting a definite viewpoint, he might have written a worthwhile paragraph.

Better

Depending on his purpose, he might have begun with "Abortion laws in our state discriminate against the poor," or "Abortion is wrong because of the irresponsibility it allows." Before you can explain yourself, you have to figure out exactly what you mean.

How Audience and Purpose Determine a Topic Statement's Focus

Your topic statement's focus governs the level of detail in the paragraph itself. Decide carefully whom you're writing for and why. Say, for example, a friend is thinking about applying to your school and has asked about life on campus. You happen to know that this person cares especially about personal identity and hence about attending a college that appreciates each student's unique potential. In this instance, you might come up with the following topic statement and paragraph:

A broad focus

> Because you're a person who hates the idea of being lost in the crowd, I know you would enjoy Rangeley College. In a school such as this one, with limited enrollment and small classes, it's easy to make friends and get to know each professor. In no time, you'll find that all the faces look familiar and almost everyone is on a first-name basis. Also, there will be lots of people asking you to join various organizations and activities. You can count on being welcomed here, on having a real sense of belonging, on making a difference. Why not give this place a try? You won't be sorry.

Suppose now that you are instead working part time in the admissions office, helping prepare a brochure that emphasizes the various activities and organizations at the college. In this case, the focus of your topic statement would be more limited than the one in the above example, and the paragraph's details would be more specific:

A more limited focus

> Whether your interests are social, artistic, political, or athletic, you'll find plenty of ways to keep busy at Rangeley College. In addition to our eight sororities and seven fraternities, we have a social club that sponsors dances, parties, concerts, and whatever else might be needed to liven up even the dreariest weekend. If you like politics, run for the Student Senate or join the Visitor's Council, which brings social and political celebrities to campus. If you're musically inclined, join the marching band, chamber orchestra, or rock group. Also, the various clubs for painters, writers, actors, and dancers are always looking for new talent. To stay in shape, try out for varsity baseball, hockey, soccer, lacrosse, or track (all have both women's

and men's teams), or join an intramural team. All in all, if you are looking for involvement and challenge, Rangeley College is the place for you.

Depending on your purpose and the audience's needs, a topic statement about life at Rangeley College could be narrowed even further—say, with a paragraph describing the chamber orchestra, the lacrosse team, or the activities of the Visitor's Council.

PARAGRAPH UNITY

When you revise your paragraphs, keep an eye out for paragraph unity. Each paragraph in an essay requires both *external* and *internal* unity. A paragraph has external unity when (as on pages 57–58) it belongs with all of the other paragraphs in the essay. But—thinking of your individual paragraphs as mini-essays—each paragraph requires internal unity as well: Every sentence directly supports the topic statement.

Imagine that you're composing a paragraph beginning with this topic statement:

Chemical pesticides and herbicides are not only ineffective but also hazardous.

The words that signal the meaning here are **ineffective** and **hazardous;** everything in the paragraph should advance that meaning. Here is the unified paragraph:

A UNIFIED PARAGRAPH

Chemical pesticides and herbicides are not only ineffective but also hazardous. Because none of these chemicals has permanent effects, pest populations invariably recover and need to be resprayed. Repeated applications cause pests to develop immunity to the chemicals. Furthermore, most pesticides and herbicides attack species other than the intended pest, killing off its natural predators, thus actually increasing the pest population. Above all, chemical residues survive in the environment (and in living tissue) for years and are often carried hundreds of miles by wind and water. This toxic legacy includes such biological effects as birth deformities, reproductive failures, brain damage, and cancer. Although intended to control pest populations, these chemicals ironically threaten to make the human population their ultimate victims.

One way to destroy unity in this paragraph would be to veer from the focus on the ineffective and hazardous aspects to material about the cost of the chemicals, their unpleasant odor, or the number of people who oppose their use.

Every topic statement has a *signal term*, a key word or phrase that announces the viewpoint. In the following paragraph, the signal term is **intelligent,** causing readers to expect material about whale intelligence.

But the shift to food problems fails to advance the meaning of intelligence, throwing the paragraph—and the reader—off track:

A DISUNIFIED PARAGRAPH

Whales are among the most intelligent of all mammals. Scientists rank whale intelligence with that of higher primates because of whales' sophisticated group behavior. These impressive mammals have been seen teaching and disciplining their young, helping their wounded comrades, engaging in elaborate courtship rituals, and playing in definite gamelike patterns. Whales continually need to search for food in order to survive. Their search for krill and other sea organisms can cause them to migrate thousands of miles yearly.

PARAGRAPH COHERENCE

Also look for paragraph coherence when revising your support paragraphs. In a coherent paragraph, every sentence follows a *connected line of thought*, like links in a chain, from the beginning of the paragraph to the end. Not only is the paragraph tied together logically, but it is also tied together linguistically, using language devices such as parallelism; repetition and restatement; pronouns; consistent tense, point of view, and number; and transitions.

This next paragraph, written by a track team veteran who is addressing new runners, is both unified and coherent: Everything relates to the topic in a continuous line of thinking.

A COHERENT PARAGRAPH

[1]*To be among the first out of the starting blocks in any race, follow these instructions.* [2]First, when the starter says, "Into your blocks," make sure you are the last runner down. [3]Take your sweet time; make all the others wait for you. [4]You take your time for three good reasons: One, you get a little more stretching than your competitors do; two, they are down in the blocks getting cold and nervous while you're still warm and relaxed from stretching; and three, your deliberate manner tends to weaken other runners' confidence. [5]The second step is to lean forward over your shoulders, in the "set" position. [6]This way, you will come out of the blocks forward and low, meeting less wind resistance. [7]The third and final step is to pump your arms as fast as you can when you come off the blocks. [8]The faster your arms pump, the faster your legs will move. [9]By concentrating on each of these steps, you can expect your quickest possible start.

—*Sarah Michaelson*

The material in the previous paragraph seems easy enough to follow:

1. The topic statement sets a clear direction.
2. The first step is introduced.
3–4. The importance of taking your time is emphasized and explained.

5–6. The second step is introduced and its importance explained.
7–8. The third step is introduced and its importance explained.
9. The conclusion sums up.

Because the material follows a logical order (in this case, chronological), readers know exactly where they are at any place in the paragraph. Let's now examine specific ways of achieving coherence.

Ordering Ideas for Coherence

The mind works in structured ways to arrange and make sense of its many perceptions. If you decide you like a class (a general observation), you then identify your particular reasons (friendly atmosphere, interesting subject, dynamic teacher, and so on); your thinking has followed a *general-to-specific order*. Or if you tell a friend about your terrific weekend, you follow the order of events, how things happened over the weekend; your thinking has followed a *chronological order*. These are just two of several ordering patterns the mind uses to reveal a specific relationship. Here are the most common ordering patterns:

Common ways of arranging information

- general-to-specific order
- specific-to-general order
- emphatic order
- spatial order
- chronological order

These ordering patterns can help you answer the following questions:

- *What comes first?*
- *What comes next?*
- *Does the subject have any features that suggest any particular order?*

Answers will be based on your subject and purpose. In a letter describing your new car (subject) to a friend, you might decide to move from outside to inside in a spatial order, as one would when first examining the car. Or if you decided to concentrate on the car's computerized dashboard (subject), you might move from left to right (as one would view it from the driver's seat). If, instead, you were trying to persuade someone to stay in school or to quit smoking, you probably would present your reasons in an emphatic order, from least to most important, or vice versa.

As we will see, some kinds of order call for your topic statement to come last instead of first. Even then, your opening sentence should tell readers what to expect. Before considering those variations, however, let's begin with the standard ordering pattern: general to specific.

General-to-Specific Order. The most usual way of arranging a paragraph is from general to specific: *a general topic statement supported by specific details.*

Most sample paragraphs we've seen so far follow a general-to-specific order, as this next one does:

STARTING WITH THE BIG PICTURE

General assertion
(topic statement, 1)
Specific support (2–8)

Conclusion (9)

[1]Americans everywhere are obsessed with speed. [2]The airlines think it's so important that they've developed jets that can cross the ocean in a few hours. [3]Despite energy shortages, Detroit often makes the speed of a car and the power of its engine a focal point of its advertising campaign. [4]Ads for oil companies boast of 10-minute oil changes at their gas stations. [5]Even pedestrians aren't spared: Some shoemakers will put soles and heels on shoes "while you wait." [6]Fast-food restaurants prosper as increasing millions gobble increasing billions of "all-beef" hamburgers and guzzle their Cokes in seconds flat. [7]And the Day of Rest, too, has given way to the stopwatch as more and more churches offer brief evening services or customize their offerings to suit "people on the go." [8]Some churches even offer drive-in ceremonies—pay your money, spit out your prayer, and hit the road, streaking toward salvation with Ronald McDonald. [9]These days, even the road to eternity has a fast lane.

—*Lorraine Furtado*

Paragraphs of general-to-specific order are the workhorses of virtually all nonfiction writing.

Specific-to-General Order.   For some purposes, instead of narrowing and restricting your meaning, you will generalize and extend it. Thus *your support will come first and your topic statement last.* A specific-to-general order is especially useful for showing how pieces of evidence add up to a convincing conclusion, as in this next paragraph.

STARTING WITH THE SUPPORTING DETAILS

Orienting statements (1–2)
Specific details (3–7)

General conclusion
(topic statement, 8–9)

[1]I've been thinking about seeing. [2]There are lots of things to see, unwrapped gifts and free surprises. [3]The world is fairly studded and strewn with pennies cast broadside from a generous hand. [4]But—and this is the point—who gets excited by a mere penny? [5]If you follow one arrow, if you crouch motionless on a bank to watch a tremulous ripple thrill on the water and are rewarded by the sight of a muskrat paddling from its den, will you count that sight a chip of copper only, and go your rueful way? [6]It is dire poverty indeed when a man is so malnourished and fatigued that he won't stoop to pick up a penny. [7]But if you cultivate a healthy poverty and simplicity, so that finding a penny will literally make your day, then, since the world is in fact planted in pennies, you have with your poverty bought a lifetime of days. *[8]It is that simple.* *[9]What you see is what you get.*

—*Annie Dillard*

Even though the topic statement appears last, the opening statements forecast the paragraph. Whenever you decide to delay your topic sentence, be sure the paragraph's opening sentence gives readers enough orientation for them to know what's going on.

A specific-to-general order works best for supporting a position that some readers might disagree with, as in this next example:

SAVING THE BIG PICTURE FOR LAST

Specific observation in orienting statement (1)

Specific arguments (2–7)

[1]Strange that so few ever come to the woods to see how the pine lives and grows and spires, lifting its evergreen arms to the light—to see its perfect success; but most are content to behold it in the shape of many broad boards brought to market, and deem *that* its true success! [2]But the pine is no more lumber than [the person] is, and to be made into boards and houses is no more its true and highest use than the truest use of a [person] is to be cut down and made into manure. [3]There is a higher law affecting our relations to pine as well as to [people]. [4]A pine cut down, a dead pine, is no more a pine than a dead human carcass is a [person]. [5]Can [one] who has discovered only some of the values of whalebone and whale oil be said to have discovered the true use of the whale? [6]Can [one] who slays the elephant for [its] ivory be said to have "seen the elephant"? [7]These are petty and accidental uses; just as if a stronger race were to kill us in order to make buttons and flutes of our bones; for everything may serve a lower as well as a higher use. [8]*Every creature is better alive than dead, [people] and moose and pine trees, and [one] who understands it correctly will rather preserve its life than destroy it.*

General conclusion (topic statement, 8)

—*Henry David Thoreau*

Some readers (especially those in the paper and lumber industry, as well as hunters) would find Thoreau's main point harder to accept if it were placed at the beginning. By moving from the specific to the general, Thoreau presents his evidence before drawing his conclusion. Also, things that come last (last word in a sentence, last sentence in a paragraph, last paragraph in an essay) are the things readers remember best.

Emphatic Order. In earlier chapters, we've seen how emphasis can make important ideas stand out and become easier to remember. Writers *achieve emphasis within paragraphs by positioning material* in two common ways: (1) *from least to most important* or *serious* or *dramatic*, and (2) *vice versa*. The next paragraph is from an essay analyzing television advertisements for toys of violence. Joe Bolton places his strongest example last, for greatest emphasis.

HELPING READERS FOCUS

Topic statement (1–2)

Examples in increasing order of importance (3–5)

[1]*Too many toys advertised during television programs for children are of what I call the "death and destruction" variety: toys that simulate the killing of humans by humans.* [2]*Such toys make children's "war games" seem far too real.* [3]During the pre-Christmas season, children are bombarded with ads promoting all the new weapons: guns, tanks, boats, subs, helicopters, lasers, and more. [4]One new warplane is described as "the wickedest weapon yet," and a new mobile

weapon resembles an old "Nike" missile, designed to be moved around on railroad tracks to avoid an enemy strike. [5]One of the enemy dolls is even dubbed a "paranoid schizophrenic killer" and advertised as such on the side of the box.

—Joe Bolton

Spatial Order. Sometimes you create a word picture by presenting the parts of your subject in the same order that readers would follow if they were actually looking at the item. In this next paragraph, the writer describes someone who is to be picked up at a busy airport.

HELPING READERS EXPERIENCE

Topic statement

A gradually narrowing focus

Roger should be easy to recognize. When I last saw him, he was wearing dark blue jeans, a pair of dark brown hunting boots with red laces, and a light blue cableknit sweater with a turtleneck; he was carrying a red daypack with black trim filled with books. He stands about 6 feet 4 inches, has broad, slouching shoulders, and carries roughly 190 pounds on a medium frame. He walks in excessively long strides, like a cowboy. His hair is sunstreaked, sandy blond, cut just below his ears and feathered back on the sides. He has deep purple eyes framed by dark brown eyelashes and brows set into a clear, tanned complexion. The bridge of his nose carries a half-inch scar in the shape of an inverted crescent. His right front tooth has a small chip in the left corner.

—Jen James

The description follows the order of features readers would recognize in approaching Roger: first, from a distance, by his clothing, size, posture, and stride; next, from a closer view—the hair, eye color, and so on; and finally, from right up close—the scar on his nose and the chip on his tooth. The earlier details, visible from a distance, would alert readers, and the later ones would confirm their impression as they moved nearer. The writer decided to take the angle of a movie camera gradually closing in.

Chronological Order. A chronological order follows the *actual sequence of events.* Writers use chronological order to give instructions (how to be first out of the starting blocks), to explain how something works (how the heart pumps blood), or to show how something happened. This paragraph from George Orwell's essay "Shooting an Elephant" shows how something brutal happened. As with many paragraphs that tell a story, this one has no topic statement. Instead, the opening sentence places us in the middle of the action.

HELPING READERS EXPERIENCE

Orienting statement (1–2)

[1]When I pulled the trigger I did not hear the bang or feel the kick—one never does when a shot goes home—but I heard the devilish roar of glee

Sequence of events
(3–16)

that went up from the crowd. ²In that instant, in too short a time, one would have thought, even for the bullet to get there, a mysterious, terrible change had come over the elephant. ³He neither stirred nor fell, but every line on his body had altered. ⁴He looked suddenly stricken, shrunken, immensely old, as though the frightful impact of the bullet had paralyzed him without knocking him down. ⁵At last, after what seemed like a long time—it might have been five seconds, I dare say—he sagged flabbily to his knees. ⁶His mouth slobbered. ⁷An enormous senility seemed to have settled upon him. ⁸One could have imagined him thousands of years old. ⁹I fired again into the same spot. ¹⁰At the second shot he did not collapse but climbed with desperate slowness to his feet and stood weakly upright, with legs sagging and head drooping. ¹¹I fired a third time. ¹²That was the shot that did it for him. ¹³You could see the agony of it jolt his whole body and knock the last remnant of strength from his legs. ¹⁴But in falling he seemed for a moment to rise, for as his hind legs collapsed beneath him he seemed to tower upwards like a huge rock toppling, his trunk reaching skywards like a tree. ¹⁵He trumpeted, for the first and only time. ¹⁶And then down he came, his belly towards me, with a crash that seemed to shake the ground even where I lay.

—*George Orwell*

The actual chronology in Orwell's paragraph is simple:

1. With the first shot, the elephant falls to its knees.
2. With the second shot, instead of collapsing, the elephant drags itself up.
3. With the third shot, the elephant falls, rises, and then falls for good.

But note that if narrating these events in order were the writer's only purpose, the paragraph might look like this:

MERELY TRACING THE EVENT

When I pulled the trigger, a change came over the elephant. He neither stirred nor fell, but every line on his body had altered as if the impact of the bullet had paralyzed him without knocking him down. At last, he sagged to his knees. His mouth slobbered. I fired again into the same spot. At the second shot, he did not collapse but climbed slowly to his feet and stood with legs sagging and head drooping. I fired a third time. That was the shot that did it for him. But in falling he seemed for a moment to rise. And then, down he came, with his belly towards me, with a crash that shook the ground.

This paragraph presents the kinds of details a camera might record.

Compare the first and second version of Orwell's paragraph. Which has the greater impact? Why?

Note

This chapter asks you to practice specific strategies, but remember, when you write on your own, you won't begin by saying, "I've decided to write a spatial paragraph, and so now I need to find a subject that will fit that order." Instead, you will say, "I want to discuss X; therefore, I need to select the ordering pattern that best reveals my thinking." Much of your writing will call for a combination of these ordering patterns.

Using Parallelism for Coherence

Several other devices enhance coherence. The first is *parallelism*—similar grammatical structures and word order for similar items or for items of equal importance. Note how parallelism is employed in this next paragraph (parallel structures are italicized):

EXPRESSING EQUAL ITEMS EQUALLY

[1]*What is the shape of my life?* [2]*The shape of my life* today starts with a family. [3]I *have* a husband, five children, and a home just beyond the suburbs of New York. [4]I *have* also a craft, writing, and therefore work I want to pursue. [5]*The shape of my life* is, of course, determined by many other things: *my background and* childhood, *my mind and* its education, *my conscience and* its pressures, *my heart and* its desires. [6]I want to *give and take* from my children and husband, to share with friends and community, *to carry out* my obligations to [humanity] and *to the world, as a woman, as an artist, as a citizen.*

—*Anne Morrow Lindbergh*

This paragraph displays parallelism between as well as within sentences. Sentences 2 and 5 open with identical structures ("The shape of my life...") to signal that both sentences treat the same subject. Sentence 5 has four parallel phrases ("my background and..., my mind and..., my conscience and..., my heart and..."). These similar structures emphasize similarity between ideas, thereby tying the paragraph together. See page 115 for further discussion of parallelism.

Can you identify additional examples of parallelism in Lindbergh's paragraph?

Using Repetition and Restatement for Coherence

To help link ideas, you can repeat key words or phrases or rephrase them in different ways, as in this next paragraph (repeated and restated elements are italicized):

FORWARDING THE MAIN IDEA

[1]*Whales are among the most intelligent of all mammals.* [2]Scientists rank whale *intelligence* with that of higher primates because of whales' *sophisticated* group behavior. [3]These *bright* creatures have been seen teaching and disciplining their young, helping their wounded comrades, engaging in elaborate courtship rituals, and playing in definite gamelike patterns. [4]They are able to coordinate such *complex cognitive activities* through their highly effective communication

system of sonar clicks and pings. Such *remarkable social organization* apparently stems from the humanlike devotion that whales seem to display toward one another.

The signal word **intelligent** in the topic statement reappears as **intelligence** in sentence 2. Synonyms (different words with similar meaning) describing intelligent behavior (**sophisticated, bright, humanlike**) reinforce and advance the main idea throughout.

Note

Keep in mind that needless repetition makes writing tedious and annoying to read. For a clear distinction between effective and ineffective repetition, see page 119.

Using Pronouns for Coherence

Instead of repeating certain nouns, it is sometimes more natural to use pronouns that refer to an earlier key noun. Pronouns improve coherence by relating sentences, clauses, and phrases to each other. This next paragraph uses pronouns to avoid repeating *the bull fighters* (pronouns are italicized):

USING PRONOUNS AS CONNECTORS

The bull fighters march in across the sand to the president's box. *They* march with easy professional stride, swinging along, not in the least theatrical except for *their* clothes. *They* all have the easy grace and slight slouch of the professional athlete. From *their* faces *they* might be major league ball players. *They* salute the president's box then spread out along the barrera, exchanging *their* heavy brocaded capes for the fighting capes that have been laid along the red fence by the attendants.

—*Ernest Hemingway*

Be sure each pronoun refers clearly to the appropriate noun. The pronouns in Hemingway's paragraph, for example, clearly refer to the bull fighters. See page 113 for a full discussion of pronoun–antecedent agreement.

Using Consistent Tense, Point of View, and Number for Coherence

Coherence always relies on consistent tense, point of view, and number. In general, do not shift from past to present tense, from third- to first-person point of view, or from singular to plural nouns or pronouns. See Section Six for a discussion of shifts that destroy coherence.

Using Transitions for Coherence

The devices we have discussed so far for achieving coherence (order, parallelism, repetition and restatement, pronouns) *suggest* specific relations between ideas. Transitional expressions *announce* those relations. As Figure 6.2 shows,

An addition: *moreover, in addition, and, also*

> I am majoring in naval architecture; *also,* I spent three years crewing on a racing yawl.

Results: *hence, therefore, accordingly, thereupon, as a result, and so, as a consequence*

> Mary enjoyed all her courses; *therefore,* she worked especially hard last semester.

An example or illustration: *for instance, to illustrate, for example, namely, specifically*

> Competition for part-time jobs is fierce; *for example,* eighty students applied for the clerk's job at Sears.

An explanation: *in other words, simply stated, in fact*

> Louise had a terrible semester; *in fact,* she flunked three courses.

A summary or conclusion: *in closing, to conclude, to summarize, in brief, in short, in summary, to* sum up, all in all, on the whole, in retrospect, in conclusion

> Our credit is destroyed, our bank account is overdrawn, and our debts are piling up; *in short,* we are bankrupt.

Time: *first, next, second, then, meanwhile, at length, later, now, the next day, in the meantime, in turn, subsequently*

> Mow the ball field this morning; *afterward,* clean the dugouts.

A comparison: *likewise, in the same way, in comparison, similarly*

> Our reservoir is drying up because of the drought; *similarly,* water supplies in neighboring towns are dangerously low.

A contrast or alternative: *however, nevertheless, yet, still, in contrast, otherwise, but, on the other hand, to the contrary, notwithstanding, conversely*

> Felix worked hard; *however,* his grades remained poor.

FIGURE 6.2 Common transitions and the relations they indicate

words or phrases such as **for example, meanwhile, however,** and **moreover** work like bridges between thoughts. Each has a definite meaning, even without a specific context:

TRANSITION	RELATION
X; meanwhile, Y	X and Y are occurring at the same time.
X; however, Y	Y is in contrast or exception to X.
X; moreover, Y	Y is in addition to X.
X; consequently, Y	Y is a result of X.

Here is a paragraph in which transitions are used to clarify the writer's line of thinking (transitions are italicized):

USING TRANSITIONS TO BRIDGE IDEAS

Psychological and social problems of aging are too often aggravated by the final humiliation: poverty. One of every three older Americans lives near or below the poverty level. *Meanwhile*, only one of every nine younger adults lives in poverty. The American public assumes that Social Security and Medicare provide adequate support for the aged. These benefits alone, *however*, are rarely enough to raise an older person's living standards above the poverty level. *Moreover*, older people are the only group living in poverty whose population has been increasing rather than decreasing. More and more of our aging citizens *thus* confront the prospect of living with less and less.

Note

Transitional expressions should be a limited option for achieving coherence. Use them sparingly and only when a relationship is not already made clear by the devices discussed earlier.

Whole sentences can serve as transitions between paragraphs, and a whole paragraph can serve as a transition between sections of writing. Assume, for instance, that you work as a marketing intern for a stereo manufacturer. You have just completed a section of a memo on the advantages of the new AKS amplifier and are now moving to a section on selling the idea to consumers. This next paragraph might link the two sections:

A TRANSITIONAL PARAGRAPH

Because the AKS amplifier increases bass range by 15 percent, it should be installed as a standard item in all our stereo speakers. Tooling and installation adjustments, however, will add roughly $50 to the list price of each model. We must therefore explain the cartridge's long-range advantages to consumers. Let's consider ways of explaining these advantages.

Notice that this transitional paragraph *contains* transitional expressions, as well.

GUIDELINES for Shaping Your Support Paragraphs

- *Think of each support paragraph as a mini–essay (introduction, body, conclusion).* Develop each supporting point in enough detail to convey your exact meaning.

- *Build each paragraph around a clear topic statement that supports your thesis and tells readers what to expect.* Sometimes your topic statement belongs at the paragraph's end and sometimes in the middle, but usually it belongs first. When your topic sentence does come later, be sure the paragraph opens with an *orienting statement* (pages 100, 101).

- *Focus the paragraph on one limited aspect of the thesis.* Depending on your purpose and your readers' needs, you can make any topic statement increasingly specific. An essay

(continues)

assessing whale intelligence, for example, might contain this topic statement: "Whales can exhibit intelligence that is **almost human**." For a different purpose, you might narrow the paragraph's focus to one single behavior: "One indicator of whales' intelligence is the way they **play in gamelike patterns**." Note the signal terms (in boldface), the key words that announce the viewpoint.

- *Revise your topic statement as needed.* You might come up first with a topic statement, and then your support—or vice versa. The sequence is unimportant, as long as the finished paragraph offers a definite framework and solid support.

- *Make the paragraph unified.* The paragraph has external unity when it fits with all other paragraphs in the essay; it has internal unity when all its material directly relates to the signal term.

- *Make the paragraph coherent.* Make everything stick together by a combination of methods: (1) arranging ideas in logical order; (2) using parallel phrasing for similar items; (3) repeating or restating signal terms and other key words and phrases; (4) using pronouns to refer to earlier nouns; (5) using consistent tense, point of view, and number; and (6) using transitions to signal relationships.

DIGITAL TIP

Use Your Word Processor to Revise an Essay's Supporting Paragraphs

For a second round of edits (see the Digital Tip box in Chapter 5 for advice on the first round: revising the content), stick to the organization of the essay's supporting paragraphs. Here are suggestions for revising at the paragraph level:

- Open a copy of your content revision as a separate document, but retain those edits as you create a new document with paragraph-level edits overlaying the content edits. For this revision, use bold rather than highlighting so you don't confuse content-level edits with paragraph-level edits. Go through the document and examine each supporting paragraph three times.

- On the first pass, use bold to mark each paragraph's topic statement. Does every paragraph have a clear topic statement? Use the comments feature to note any topic statements that lack focus or forecast and to explain how you plan to revise.

- On your second pass, examine each paragraph for unity. Note why any paragraph may lack unity and how you intend to solve the problem.

- On the third pass, note why any paragraph seems to lack coherence and how you plan to repair any related problems.

- Save your document as Revision 2 or use another file name that indicates the document contains both content and paragraph revisions.

☑ A CHECKLIST for Support Paragraphs

Overall Shape

☐ Is each paragraph an effective **mini-essay** (introduction, body, conclusion)? (95)

☐ Is each paragraph just long enough to **make its point**? (95)

Topic Statement

☐ Does the topic statement **express a definite viewpoint** and **provide a forecast**? (95)

☐ Is the topic statement sharply and appropriately **focused**? (96)

☐ Does the topic statement contain a clear **signal term**? (97)

Unity

☐ Does the paragraph have **external unity**? (97)

☐ Does the paragraph have **internal unity**? (97)

Coherence

☐ Is the paragraph's **order of ideas** logical and recognizable? (99)

☐ Are similar items expressed in **parallel grammatical form**? (104)

☐ Does **repetition** or **restatement** help link ideas, as needed? (104)

☐ Do **pronouns** link sentences, clauses, and phrases, as needed? (105)

☐ Are **tense, point of view, and number** consistent throughout? (105)

☐ Do **transitional expressions** bridge ideas, as needed? (105)

APPLICATIONS

6.1   Identify the subject and the signal term in each of these sentences. (Review pages 97–98.)

EXAMPLE

The pressures of the sexual revolution are everywhere.

—*Joyce Maynard*

Subject	pressures of the sexual revolution
Signal term	everywhere

1. High voltage from utility transmission lines can cause bizarre human and animal behavior.

2. Nuclear power plants need stricter supervision.

3. Producers of television commercials have created a loathsome gallery of men and women patterned, presumably, on Mr. and Mrs. America.

—*Marya Mannes*

4. From the very beginning of school, we make books and reading a constant source of possible failure and possible humiliation.

—*John Holt*

5. High interest rates cripple the auto and housing industries.

6.2 **COLLABORATIVE PROJECT AND COMPUTER APPLICATION.** The following paragraph is unified but not coherent because the sentences are not in logical order. On computer disks, each member of your group should individually rearrange the sentences so that the line of thinking is clear and then print a hard copy. As a group, compare your different versions, with each member explaining the order he or she chose. Then agree on a final version, which one group member will create by rearranging the sentences on his or her disk. Print this final version for the entire class, justifying your group's decisions.

> [1]Conditions in the state mental hospital are shameful. [2]Sedatives, soothing baths, occupational therapy, and individual counseling are rarely used because the hospital cannot afford them. [3]Hundreds of patients are left in filthy conditions, never receiving the care they desperately need. [4]When my sociology class toured the hospital, we spent the entire morning walking through the wards and talking to the attendants. [5]Because the windows are kept closed, the air is damp and musty. [6]On the whole, anyone who tours the mental hospital can't help feeling ashamed of this state. [7]Patients lie for hours staring vacantly at the dirty ceiling. [8]Some of them listen to the radio or watch television hour after hour. [9]The big brick building is 2 miles from the main highway, and many people do not even know there is such a place. [10]The food is cold and unappetizing. [11]The hospital has only three physicians for more than five hundred patients. [12]Straitjackets, ropes, and leather straps are used to tie down violent patients.

6.3 Select one of these assignments and write a paragraph organized from the general to the specific.

- Picture the ideal summer job. Explain to an employer why you would like the job.
- Assume that it's time for end-of-semester student course evaluations. Write a one-paragraph evaluation of your favorite course to be read by your professor's department chair.
- Explain your views on video games. Write for your classmates.
- Describe the job outlook in your chosen field. Write for a high school senior interested in your major.

6.4 Identify a problem in a group to which you belong (such as family, club, or sorority). Or select a topic from the following list or make up one of your own. After reviewing page 101, write two emphatic paragraphs, one featuring the emphatic material at the beginning and the other positioning it at the end. Be prepared to explain which version works better and why.

- Advice about surviving in college—to an entering freshman
- Your life goal—to your academic adviser, who is recommending you for a scholarship
- Your reasons for wanting to live off campus—to the dean of students

6.5   Select the best paragraph or essay you have written thus far (or one that your instructor suggests). Using the strategies in this chapter, revise the paragraph or essay for improved coherence. After revising, list the specific strategies you employed (logical order, parallelism, repetition of key terms, restatement, pronouns, transitions).

6.6   **WEB-BASED PROJECT** Even after reading this chapter, a classmate of yours admits to not having a good understanding of how and when to start a new paragraph, let alone how to use paragraphs effectively to structure and develop an argument. "I just indent and start a new paragraph when it looks right," she says. Your project is to do some research on the Web in order to develop a one-page handout for your classmate (and others who may have similar difficulties grasping the subtleties of paragraphs) that presents some practical strategies for using paragraphs more effectively. Good places to start your search include <**http://owl.english.purdue.edu/owl/resource/606/01/**> and <**http://grammar.ccc.commnet.edu/grammar/paragraphs.htm**>.

Attach a copy of the relevant Web page(s) to your presentation. Be sure to credit each source of information (page 87).

For additional information and practice with the learning objectives in this chapter, go to www.mycomplab.com, Resources>Writing>The Writing Process>Revising.

Revising the Sentences: Writing with Style

LEARNING OBJECTIVES FOR THIS CHAPTER

■ Improve the clarity of sentences

■ Make your sentences more concise

■ Recognize ways to improve sentence flow

A definition of style

Every bit as important as *what* you have to say is *how* you decide to say it. Your particular *writing style* is a blend of these elements:

What determines your style

■ The way in which you construct each sentence
■ The length of your sentences
■ The way in which you connect sentences
■ The words and phrases you choose
■ The tone you convey

No matter how vital your content and how sensible your organization, readers' needs will not be served unless your style is *readable:* sentences easy to understand and words precisely chosen.

One requirement for readable sentences is, of course, correct grammar, punctuation, and spelling. But beyond being merely "correct," readable sentences emphasize relationships among ideas, make every word count, and flow smoothly.

AIM FOR CLARITY

These guidelines will help you write clear sentences that convey your meaning on the first reading.

ref

Keep Your Pronoun References Clear

Pronouns (**she, it, his, their,** and so on) must clearly refer to the nouns they replace.

Ambiguous referent	Our patients enjoy the warm days while **they** last. [*Are the patients or the warm days on the way out?*]

Depending on whether the referent (or antecedent) for *they* is *patients* or *warm days,* the sentence can be clarified.

Clear referent	While these warm days last, our patients enjoy them.
	or
	Our terminal patients enjoy these warm days.
Ambiguous	Sally told Sarah that **she** was obsessed with **her** job.
Revised	Sally told Sarah, "I'm obsessed with my job."
	Sally told Sarah, "I'm obsessed with your job."

What other interpretations are possible for this ambiguous sentence?

Avoid using **this, that,** or **it**—especially to begin a sentence—unless the pronoun refers to a specific antecedent (referent).

Vague	The problem with our defective machinery is only compounded by the new operator's incompetence. **This** annoys me!
Revised	I am annoyed by the problem with our defective machinery, as well as by the new operator's incompetence.

See Section Six for more on pronoun reference and page 143 for avoiding sexist bias in pronoun usage.

Avoid Ambiguous Modifiers

A modifier is a word (usually an adjective or adverb) or a group of words (usually a phrase or a clause) that provides information about other words or groups of words. If a modifier is too far from the words it modifies, the message can be ambiguous. Position modifiers to reflect your meaning.

Misplaced modifier	**Only** press the red button in an emergency. [*Does "only" modify "press" or "emergency"?*]
Revised	Press **only** the red button in an emergency.
	or
	Press the red button in an emergency **only.**

Another problem with ambiguity occurs when a modifying phrase has no word to modify, as in this next example:

Dangling modifier	**Being so well respected in the scientific field,** I would appreciate your recommendation.

The writer meant to say that the *reader* is well known, but with no word to connect to, the modifying phrase dangles. Eliminate the confusion by adding a subject:

Revised	Because **you** are so well respected in the scientific field, I would appreciate your recommendation.

See Section Six for more on modifiers.

Avoid Overstuffed Sentences

Give no more information in one sentence than readers can retain and process.

Overstuffed	A smoke-filled room not only causes teary eyes and runny noses but can also alter people's hearing and vision, as well as create dangerous levels of carbon monoxide, especially for people with heart and lung ailments, whose health is particularly threatened by secondhand smoke.

Clear things up by sorting out the relationships:

Revised	Besides causing teary eyes and runny noses, a smoke-filled room can alter people's hearing and vision. One of the biggest dangers of secondhand smoke, however, is high levels of carbon monoxide, a particular health threat for people with heart and lung ailments.

Keep Equal Items Parallel

To reflect relationships among items of equal importance, express them in identical grammatical form (see also page 104). For example, if you begin the series with a noun, use nouns throughout the series; likewise for adjectives, adverbs, and specific types of clauses and phrases.

Faulty	The new tutor is **enthusiastic, skilled,** and **you can depend on her.**
Revised	The new tutor is **enthusiastic, skilled,** and **dependable.** [*all subject complements*]

Faulty	In his new job, Ramon felt **lonely** and **without a friend.**
Revised	In his new job, Ramon felt **lonely** and **friendless.** [*both adjectives*]

Faulty	Lulu plans **to study** all this month and **on scoring** well in her licensing examination.
Revised	Lulu plans **to study** all this month and **to score** well in her licensing examination. [*both infinitive phrases*]

Arrange Word Order for Coherence and Emphasis

In coherent writing, everything sticks together; each sentence builds on the preceding sentence and looks ahead to the one that follows. In similar fashion, sentences generally work best when the beginning looks back at familiar information and the end provides new or unfamiliar information.

Effective word order

FAMILIAR		UNFAMILIAR
My dog	has	fleas.
Our boss	just won	the lottery.
This company	is planning	a merger.

This pattern also emphasizes the new information. Every sentence has a key word or phrase that sums up the new information and that is usually emphasized best at the end of the sentence.

Faulty emphasis	We expect a **refund** because of your error in our shipment.
Correct	Because of your error in our shipment, we expect a **refund.**

Faulty emphasis	After your awful behavior, an **apology** is what I expect.
Correct	After your awful behavior, I expect an **apology.**

One exception to placing key words last occurs with an imperative statement (a command, an order, an instruction) with the subject (*you*) understood. For instance, each step in a list of instructions should begin with an action verb (**insert, open, close, turn, remove, press**).

Correct	**Insert** the disk before activating the system.
	Remove the protective seal.

The opening key word tells readers immediately what action to take.

Use Active Voice Whenever Possible

A verb's *voice* signals whether a sentence's subject acts or is acted on. Active voice (**I did it**) is more direct, concise, and persuasive than passive voice (**It was done by me**). In active voice sentences, a clear agent performs a clear action on a recipient:

	AGENT	**ACTION**	**RECIPIENT**
Active	Leslie	lost	your report.
	SUBJECT	**VERB**	**OBJECT**

Passive voice, in contrast, reverses this pattern, placing the recipient of the action in the subject slot:

	RECIPIENT	**ACTION**	**AGENT**
Passive	Your report	was lost	by Leslie.
	SUBJECT	**VERB**	**PREPOSITIONAL PHRASE**

Sometimes the passive eliminates the agent altogether:

Passive	Your report was lost. [*Who lost it?*]

Passive voice is unethical if it obscures the person or other agent who performed the action when that responsible person or agent should be identified.

Some writers mistakenly rely on passive voice because they think it sounds more objective and important, but in fact it often makes sentences seem wordy and evasive.

Concise and direct (active)	**I underestimated** expenses for this semester. [*6 words*]
Wordy and indirect (passive)	Expenses for this semester **were underestimated by me.** [*8 words*]
Evasive (passive)	Expenses for this semester **were underestimated.**

In reporting errors or bad news, use active voice for clarity and sincerity. Do not evade responsibility by hiding behind passive constructions:

| **Passive** | A mistake was made in your shipment. [*By whom?*] |
| **"irresponsibles"** | It was decided not to hire you. [*Who decided?*] |

Use active voice when you want action. Otherwise, your statement will have no power:

| **Weak passive** | If my claim is not settled by May 15, the Better Business Bureau will be contacted, and their advice on legal action will be taken. |
| **Strong active** | If you do not settle my claim by May 15, I will contact the Better Business Bureau for advice on legal action. |

Notice that this active version emphasizes the new and important information by placing it at the end.

Ordinarily, use active voice for giving instructions:

Faulty passive	The door to the cobra's cage should be locked.
	Care should be taken with the dynamite.
Correct active	Lock the door to the cobra's cage.
	Be careful with the dynamite.

pv

Use Passive Voice Selectively

Passive voice is appropriate in lab reports and other documents in which the agent's identity is immaterial to the message.

Use passive voice if the person behind the action needs to be protected.

| **Correct passive** | The criminal **was identified.** |
| | The victim **was asked** to testify. |

Use passive voice when the audience has no need to know the agent:

Correct passive	Mr. Jones **was brought** to the emergency room.
	The bank failure **was publicized** statewide.
	All policy claims **are kept** confidential.

Prefer passive voice when you want to be indirect or inoffensive:

Active but offensive	**You have not paid** your bill.
	You need to overhaul our filing system.
Inoffensive passive	This bill **has not been paid.**
	Our filing system **needs overhauling.**

APPLICATIONS

7.1   Edit each sentence to eliminate faulty modification, unclear pronoun reference, overstuffing, faulty parallelism, or key words buried in midsentence. For sentences suggesting two meanings, write a version for each meaning intended. (Review pages 113–116.)

1. Bill told Fred that he was mistaken.
2. In all writing, revision is required.
3. Only use this elevator in a fire.
4. Making the shelves look neater was another of my tasks at X-Mart that is very important to a store's business because if the merchandise is not always neatly arranged, customers will not have a good impression, whereas if it is neat they probably will return.
5. Student nurses are required to identify diseases and how to treat them.

7.2   Convert these passive voice sentences to concise, forceful, and direct expressions in active voice. (Review pages 116–117.)

1. The evaluation was performed by us.
2. The essay was written by me.
3. Unless you pay me within three days, my lawyer will be contacted.
4. Hard hats should be worn at all times.
5. It was decided to decline your invitation.

7.3   The following sentences lack proper emphasis because of improper use of active voice. Convert each to passive voice. (Review page 117.)

1. Joe's company fired him.
2. You are paying inadequate attention to student safety.
3. A power surge destroyed more than two thousand lines of our new computer program.
4. You did a poor job editing this report.
5. The selection committee awarded Mary a Fulbright Scholarship.

TRIM THE FAT

Concise writing conveys the most information in the fewest words. But it does not omit the details necessary for clarity. Use fewer words whenever fewer will do.

Cluttered   At this point in time I must say that I need a vacation.

Concise   I need a vacation now.

First drafts are rarely concise. Trim the fat.

Avoid Wordy Phrases

Each of the following phrases can be reduced to one word.

Revising wordy phrases

at this point in time	=	now
has the ability to	=	can
due to the fact that	=	because
the majority of	=	most
on a daily basis	=	daily

Eliminate Redundancy

A redundant expression says the same thing twice in different words, as in *fellow classmates.*

Spotting redundant phrases

[utmost] perfection	[totally] oblivious
[mental] awareness	[past] experience
[the month of] August	[future] prospects
[mutual] cooperation	[free] gift

Avoid Needless Repetition

Unnecessary repetition clutters writing and dilutes meaning.

Repetitious In trauma victims, breathing is restored by **artificial respiration.** Techniques of **artificial respiration** include mouth-to-mouth **respiration** and mouth-to-nose **respiration.**

Repetition in this next passage disappears when sentences are combined.

Concise In trauma victims, breathing is restored by artificial respiration, either mouth-to-mouth or mouth-to-nose.

Note *Don't hesitate to repeat, or at least rephrase, if you feel that readers need reminders. Effective repetition helps avoid cross-references like these: "See page 3" or "Review page 1."*

Avoid *There* and *It* Sentence Openers

Many **There is, There are,** and It sentence openers can be eliminated.

Faulty **There were** several good reasons why Boris dropped out of school.

Concise Boris dropped out of school for several good reasons.

In some contexts, proper emphasis does call for a There opener.

> **Correct**   People have often wondered about the rationale behind Boris's sudden decision. **There were** several good reasons for his dropping out of school.

Most often, however, **There** openers are best dropped.

> **Faulty**   **There is** a fire danger created by your smoking in bed.
> **Concise**   Your smoking in bed creates a fire danger.

Avoid beginning a sentence with **It** unless **It** clearly points to a specific referent in the preceding sentence: "This document is excellent. **It** deserves special recognition."

> **Wordy**   **It** gives me great pleasure to introduce our speaker.
> **Concise**   I am pleased to introduce our speaker.

Delete Needless Phrases

To be, as well as **that** and **which** phrases, can often be cut.

> **Wordy**   She seems [to be] upset.
> **Wordy**   I consider some of my classmates [to be] brilliant.
> **Wordy**   The Hydromobile is a car [that is] worth buying.
> **Wordy**   This [is a] math problem [that] is impossible to solve.
> **Wordy**   The book [,which is] about Hemingway [,] is fascinating.

Avoid Weak Verbs

Prefer verbs that express a definite action: **open, close, move, continue, begin.** Avoid verbs that express no specific action: **is, was, are, has, give, make, come, take.** All forms of the verb **be** are weak.

> **Note**   *In some cases, such verbs are essential to your meaning: "Dr. Johnson is operating at 7 a.m." or "Take me to your leader."*

Substitute a strong verb for conciseness:

> **Weak and wordy**   Please **take into consideration** my application.
> **Concise**   Please **consider** my application.

Here are examples of weak verbs converted to strong verbs:

Revising weak verbs

give a summary of	=	summarize
make an assumption	=	assume
come to the conclusion	=	conclude
take action	=	act
make a decision	=	decide

Strong verbs, or action verbs, suggest an assertive and confident writer.

Avoid Excessive Prepositions

Wordy   Some **of** the members **of** the committee made these recommendations.

Concise   Some committee members made these recommendations.

Wordy   I gave the money **to** Sarah.

Concise   I gave Sarah the money.

Avoid Nominalizations

Nouns manufactured from verbs (nominalizations) are harder to understand than the verbs themselves.

Weak and wordy   We ask for the **cooperation** of all students.

Strong and concise   We ask that all students **cooperate.**

Weak and wordy   Give **consideration** to the possibility of a career change.

Strong and concise   **Consider** a career change.

Besides causing wordiness, nominalizations can be vague—by hiding the agent of an action. Verbs are generally easier to read because they signal action.

Wordy and vague   A need for immediate action exists. [*Who should take the action? We can't tell.*]

Precise   We must act immediately.

Nominalizations drain the life from your style. For example, in cheering for your favorite team, you wouldn't say "Blocking of that kick is a necessity!" instead of "Block that kick!"

Note   *Avoid excessive economy. For instance, "All students must cooperate" would not be an acceptable alternative to the first example in this section. But for the final example, "Block that kick!" would be.*

Here are nominalizations restored to their action verb forms:

Trading nouns for verbs

conduct an investigation of	=	investigate
provide a description of	=	describe
conduct a test of	=	test

Make Negatives Positive

A positive expression is easier to understand than a negative one.

Indirect and wordy   Please do not be late in submitting your report.

Direct and concise   Please submit your report on time.

Sentences with multiple negative expressions are even harder to translate:

Confusing and wordy   Do **not** distribute this memo to employees who have **not** received security clearance.

Clear and concise   Distribute this memo only to employees who have received security clearance.

Besides the directly negative words (**no, not, never**), some indirectly negative words (**except, forget, mistake, lose, uncooperative**) also force readers to translate.

Confusing and wordy   **Do not neglect** to activate the alarm system.
My diagnosis was **not inaccurate.**

Clear and concise   **Be sure** to activate the alarm system.
My diagnosis was **accurate.**

Some negative expressions are perfectly correct of course, as when expressing disagreement.

Correct negatives   This is **not** the best plan.
Your offer is **unacceptable.**
This project will **never** succeed.

Prefer positives to negatives, though, whenever your meaning allows:

Trading negatives for positives

did not succeed	=	failed
does not have	=	lacks
did not prevent	=	allowed
not unless	=	only if

Clear Out Clutter Words

Clutter words stretch a message without adding meaning. Here are some of the most common: **very, definitely, quite, extremely, rather, somewhat, really, actually, situation, aspect, factor.**

Cluttered	**Actually,** one **aspect** of a relationship **situation** that could **definitely** make me **very** happy would be to have a **somewhat** adventurous partner who **really** shared my **extreme** love of traveling.
Concise	I'd like to meet an adventurous person who loves traveling.

Delete Needless Prefaces

Instead of delaying the new information in your sentence, get to the point.

Wordy	[I am writing this letter because] I wish to apply for the position of dorm counselor.
Wordy	[The conclusion we can draw is that] writing is hard work.

Delete Needless Qualifiers

Qualifiers such as **I feel, it would seem, I believe, in my opinion,** and **I think** express uncertainty or soften the tone and force of a statement.

Appropriate qualifiers	Despite Frank's poor academic performance last semester, he will, **I think,** do well in college.
	Your product **seems to be** what I need.

But when you are certain, eliminate the qualifier so as not to seem tentative or evasive.

Needless qualifiers	[It seems that] I've wrecked the family car.
	[It would appear that] I've lost your credit card.
	[In my opinion,] you've done a good job.

Note   *When communicating across cultures, keep in mind that a direct, forceful style might be considered offensive (page 144).*

APPLICATIONS

7.4   Make these sentences more concise by eliminating redundancies and needless repetition. (Review page 119.)

1. She is a woman who works hard.
2. I am aware of the fact that Sam is a trustworthy person.
3. Clarence completed his assignment in a short period of time.

4. Bruno has a stocky build.

5. Sally is a close friend of mine.

6. I've been able to rely on my parents in the past.

7.5 Make these sentences more concise by eliminating **There is** and **There are** sentence openers, and the needless use of **it, to be, is, of, that,** and **which.** (Review pages 119–120.)

1. Our summer house, which is located on Cape Cod, is for sale.

2. Another reason the job is attractive is because the salary is excellent.

3. Smoking of cigarettes is considered by many people to be the worst habit of all habits of human beings.

4. There are many students who are immature.

5. It is necessary for me to leave immediately.

7.6 Make these sentences more concise by replacing weak verbs with strong ones and nouns with verbs, by changing negatives to positives, and by clearing out clutter words, needless prefatory expressions, and needless qualifiers. (Review pages 120–123.)

1. I have a preference for Ferraris.

2. I am not unappreciative of your help.

3. Actually, I am very definitely in love with you.

4. It seems that I've made a mistake in your order.

5. In my opinion, winter is an awful season.

6. A need for your caution exists.

7. Never fail to attend classes.

HELP SENTENCES FLOW

Fluent sentences are easy to read because they provide clear connections, variety, and emphasis. Varied sentence length and word choices eliminate choppiness and monotony. Fluent sentences enhance *clarity,* emphasizing the most important idea. They convey information more concisely by replacing short, repetitious sentences with longer, more economical sentences. The following strategies will help you write fluently.

 Combine Related Ideas

Disconnected   Jogging can be healthful. You need the right equipment. Most necessary are well-fitting shoes. Without this equipment, you take the chance of injuring your legs. Your knees are especially prone to injury. [*5 sentences*]

Clear, concise, and fluent Jogging can be healthful if you have the right equipment. Shoes that fit well are most necessary because they prevent injury to your legs, especially your knees. [*2 sentences*]

Most information can be rearranged to place the focus on what you want to emphasize. Imagine that this set of facts describes an applicant for a ski instructor's position:

- Sarah James has been skiing since age 3.
- She has no experience teaching skiing.
- She has won several slalom competitions.

Assume that you are Snow Mountain Ski Area's head instructor, conveying your impression of this candidate to the manager. To convey a negative impression, you might combine the information in this way:

Strongly negative emphasis Although Sarah James has been skiing since age 3 and has won several slalom competitions, **she has no experience teaching skiing.**

The *independent clause* (in boldface) receives the emphasis (also see page 497, on subordination). But if you are undecided yet leaning in a negative direction, you might write this:

Slightly negative emphasis Sarah James has been skiing since age 3 and has won several slalom competitions, **but** she has no experience teaching skiing.

In this sentence, the information both before and after **but** appears in independent clauses. Joining them with the coordinating word **but** suggests that both sides of the issue are equally important (or "coordinate"). Placing the negative idea last, however, gives it a slight emphasis. (See also page 497, on coordination.)

To emphasize strong support for the candidate, you could say this:

Positive emphasis Although Sarah James has no experience teaching skiing, **she has been skiing since age 3 and has won several slalom competitions.**

Here the initial information is subordinated by **although,** giving the final information the weight of an independent clause.

Note

Combine sentences only to simplify the reader's task. Overstuffed sentences with too much information and too many connections can be hard for readers to sort out.(See page 114.)

Vary Sentence Construction and Length

Related ideas often need to be linked in one sentence so that readers can grasp the connections.

Disconnected The nuclear core reached critical temperature. The loss-of-coolant alarm was triggered. The operator shut down the reactor.

Connected As the nuclear core reached critical temperature, triggering the loss-of-coolant alarm, the operator shut down the reactor.

But an idea that should stand alone for emphasis needs a sentence of its own:

Correct Core meltdown seemed inevitable.

However, an unbroken string of long or short sentences can bore and confuse readers, as can a series with identical openings:

Dreary There are some drawbacks about diesel engines. They are difficult to start in cold weather. They cause vibration. They also give off an unpleasant odor. They cause sulfur dioxide pollution.

Varied Diesel engines have some drawbacks. Most obvious are their noisiness, cold-weather starting difficulties, vibration, odor, and sulfur dioxide emissions.

Similarly, when you write in the first person, overusing *I* makes you appear self-centered. Do not, however, avoid personal pronouns if they make the writing more readable (say, by eliminating passive constructions).

Use Short Sentences for Special Emphasis

All this talk about combining ideas might suggest that short sentences have no place in good writing. Wrong. Short sentences (even one-word sentences) provide vivid emphasis. They stick in a reader's mind. Consider this student pilot's description of taking off:

Our airspeed increases. The plane vibrates. We reach the point where the battle begins.

Instead, the student might have written:

As our airspeed increases, the plane vibrates, and we reach the point where the battle begins.

However, she wanted to emphasize three discrete aspects of the experience: (1) the acceleration, (2) the vibration, and (3) the critical point of lifting off the ground.

DIGITAL TIP

Use Your Word Processor to Revise Sentences

Here are suggestions for revising sentences effectively on your computer:

- Do not rely solely on computerized tools. Grammar checkers may help, but they are not intuitive like the human brain and therefore cannot evaluate stylistic matters.

- Open your content and paragraph revision (Revision 2, page 108) and use "save as" to preserve the previous version; then create a new version with your sentence-level edits overlaying the previous content and paragraph edits. To avoid copying over the previous draft, give this "save as" version a new file name. Use italic rather than bold or highlighting so you don't confuse your content- and paragraph-level edits with sentence-level edits.

- On your first pass, italicize any sentences that seen unclear. Use the comments feature to note why the sentences are unclear and how you will fix them.

- On your second pass, italicize sentences that lack conciseness. Use the comments feature again to describe problems and plan solutions.

- On your third pass, italicize sentences that lack fluency. Explain the problems and how you plan to repair them.

- Save your document as Revision 3 or under its new file name.

✔ A CHECKLIST for Sentence Style

Clarity

- ☐ Does each pronoun clearly refer to the noun it replaces? (113)
- ☐ Is each modifier close enough to the word or words it defines or explains? (114)
- ☐ Does each sentence provide only as much information as readers are able to process easily? (114)
- ☐ Are items of equal importance expressed in parallel grammatical form (all nouns, all adverbs, all adjectives, and so on)? (115)
- ☐ Do most sentences begin with **familiar** information and end with **new** information? (115)
- ☐ Are sentences mostly in **active voice** rather than passive voice? (116)
- ☐ Is passive voice used only when the agent of an action is immaterial? (117)

Conciseness

- ☐ Can **wordy** and **redundant** expressions be replaced by single words? (119)
- ☐ Is the piece free of **needless repetition** of words or ideas? (119)
- ☐ Is it free of **needless sentence openers** ("There is," "There are," "It")? (119)
- ☐ Is it free of **needless phrases** ("which," "that," "to be")? (120)
- ☐ Have **needless weak verbs** ("is," "was," "has") been converted to verbs that express a definite action? (120)

(continues)

☐ Have **excessive prepositions** been removed? (121)

☐ Have **nominalizations** been restored to their action verb forms? (121)

☐ Have **negative constructions** been converted to positive ones, as needed? (122)

☐ Is the piece free of **clutter words, needless prefaces, and needless qualifiers**? (123)

Fluency

☐ Are related ideas **combined** within a single sentence, as needed? (124)

☐ Does **subordination or coordination** provide the appropriate emphasis in the combined sentence? (125)

☐ Does an idea that should **stand alone** for emphasis get a sentence of its own? (126)

☐ Are sentences **varied** in construction and length? (126)

☐ Are **short sentences** used for special emphasis? (126)

APPLICATIONS

7.7   These sentence sets lack fluency because they are disconnected, lack variety, or have no clear emphasis. Combine each set into one or two fluent sentences.

Choppy   The world's forests are now disappearing. The rate of disappearance is 18 to 20 million hectares a year (an area half the size of California). Most of this loss occurs in humid tropical forests. These forests are in Asia, Africa, and South America.

Revised   The world's forests are now disappearing at the rate of 18 to 20 million hectares a year (an area half the size of California). Most of this loss is occurring in the humid tropical forests of Africa, Asia, and South America.*

1. The world's population is growing.

   It has grown from 4 billion in 1975.

   It will exceed 6.5 billion by 2012.

   This is an increase of more than 50 percent.

2. In sheer numbers, population is growing.

   It is growing faster than in 1975.

   It adds 100 million people each year.

   This figure compares with 75 million in 1975.

---

*Sample sentences are adapted from *Global Year 2000 Report to the President: Entering the 21st Century* (Washington: GPO, 1980).

3. Energy prices are expected to rise.

   Many less-developed countries will have increasing difficulty.

   Their difficulty will be in meeting energy needs.

4. One-quarter of humanity depends primarily on wood.

   These people depend on wood for fuel.

   For them, the outlook is bleak.

5. The world has finite fuel resources.

   These include coal, oil, gas, oil shale, and uranium.

   These resources, theoretically, are sufficient for centuries.

   These resources are not evenly distributed.

7.8 Combine each set of sentences into one or two fluent sentences that provide the requested emphasis.

Sentence set	John is a loyal employee.
	John is a motivated employee.
	John is short-tempered with his colleagues.
Combined for positive emphasis	Even though John is short-tempered with his colleagues, he is a loyal and motivated employee.
Sentence set	This word processor has many excellent features.
	It includes a spelling checker.
	It includes a thesaurus.
	It includes a grammar checker.
Combined to emphasize the thesaurus	Among its many excellent features, such as spelling and grammar checkers, this word processor includes a thesaurus.

1. The job offers an attractive salary.

   It demands long work hours.

   Promotions are rapid.

   (*Combine for negative emphasis.*)

2. The job offers an attractive salary.

   It demands long work hours.

   Promotions are rapid.

   (*Combine for positive emphasis.*)

3. Company X gave us the lowest bid.

   Company Y has an excellent reputation.

   (*Combine to emphasize Company Y.*)

4. Superinsulated homes are energy-efficient.

   Superinsulated homes can promote indoor air pollution.

   The toxins include radon gas and urea formaldehyde.

   (*Combine for negative emphasis.*)

5. Computers cannot think for the writer.

   Computers eliminate many mechanical writing tasks.

   They speed the flow of information.

   (*Combine to emphasize the first assertion.*)

7.9   **COLLABORATIVE PROJECT AND COMPUTER APPLICATIONS** Have each group member revise this passage to improve fluency by combining related ideas; by varying sentence structure, openings, and length; and by using short sentences for special emphasis. (*Note:* When rephrasing to achieve conciseness, be sure to preserve the meaning of the original.) Then compare your versions and collaborate on an effective revision to present to the class.

Each summer, semitropical fish appear in New England salt ponds. They are carried northward by the Gulf Stream. The Gulf Stream is a warm ocean current. It flows like a river through the cold Atlantic. It originates in the Caribbean. It winds through the Florida straits. It meanders northward along the eastern coast of the United States. Off the shore of Cape Hatteras, North Carolina, the Gulf Stream's northerly course veers. It veers slightly eastward. This veering moves the stream and its warming influence farther from the coast. Semitropical fish are swept into the Gulf Stream from their breeding ground. The breeding ground is south of Cape Hatteras. The fish are carried northward. The strong current carries them. The current is often 20 degrees warmer than adjacent waters. Some of these fish are trapped in eddies. Eddies are pools of warm water that split from the Gulf Stream. These pools drift shoreward. By midsummer, the ocean water off the New England coast is warm. It is warm enough to attract some fish out of the eddies and nearer to shore. In turn, even warmer water flows from the salt ponds. It flows to the ocean. It attracts these warm-water fish. They are attracted into the ponds. Here they spend the rest of the summer. They die off in the fall. The ponds cool in the fall.

For additional information and practice with the learning objectives in this chapter, go to www.mycomplab.com, Resources>Writing>The Writing Process>Revising.

Revising the Words and Phrases: Fine-Tuning

LEARNING OBJECTIVES FOR THIS CHAPTER

- Know how to say something genuine
- Choose precise words
- Sharpen the visual details
- Add personality to your writing
- Write in ways that invite readers in
- Recognize the legal and ethical implications of word choice

The quality of our contact with an audience ultimately depends on the wording we choose and the tone we convey. When revising words and phrases, aim for genuineness, precision, sharp visual details, personality, and inclusion.

SAY SOMETHING GENUINE

Readers look between the lines for a real person; don't disappoint them.

Avoid Triteness

Worn-out phrases (clichés) make writers seem too lazy or too careless to find exact, unique ways of saying what they mean:

Worn-out phrases

first and foremost	tough as nails
in the final analysis	holding the bag
needless to say	up the creek
work like a dog	over the hill
last but not least	bite the bullet

Avoid Overstatement

Exaggeration sounds phony. Be cautious when using superlatives such as **best, biggest, brightest, most,** and **worst.** Recognize the differences among **always, usually, often, sometimes,** and **rarely;** among **all, most, many, some,** and **few.**

Overstated You never listen to my ideas.

Everything you say is obnoxious.

This is the worst essay I've ever read.

Avoid Misleading Euphemisms

A form of understatement, a euphemism is an expression aimed at politeness or at making unpleasant subjects seem less offensive. Thus, we **powder our noses** or **use the boy's room** instead of **going to the bathroom;** we **pass away** or **meet our Maker** instead of **dying.**

When euphemisms avoid offending or embarrassing people, they are perfectly legitimate. For example, instead of telling a job applicant he or she is unqualified, we might say, "Your background doesn't meet our needs." But euphemisms are unethical if they understate the truth when only the truth will serve. For example, don't say an employee has been "surplused" or "deselected" when truthfully that person was "laid off" or "fired."

APPLICATION

8.1 Revise these sentences to eliminate triteness, overstatement, and euphemism.

1. This course gives me a pain in the neck.
2. There is never a dull moment in my dorm.

3. Television is rotting everyone's brain.

4. I was less than candid.

5. This student is poorly motivated.

AIM FOR PRECISION

Words listed as synonyms usually carry different shades of meaning. Do you mean to say, "I'm slender, you're slim, he's lean, and she's scrawny"? The wrong choice could be disastrous.

Be especially aware of similar words with dissimilar meanings, as in Table 8.1.

Be on the lookout for imprecisely phrased (and therefore illogical) comparisons:

Faulty	Your bank's interest rate is higher than BusyBank. [*Can a rate be higher than a bank?*]
Revised	Your bank's interest rate is higher than BusyBank's.

Imprecision can create ambiguity. For instance, is **send us more personal information** a request for more information that is personal or for information that is more personal? Does your professor expect **fewer** or **less** technical details in your essay?

Precision ultimately enhances conciseness when one exact word replaces multiple inexact words.

Wordy and less exact	I have **put together** all the financial information. **Keep doing** this exercise for 10 seconds.
Concise and more exact	I have **assembled** all the financial information. **Continue** this exercise for 10 seconds.

Table 8.1 COMMONLY CONFUSED WORDS

SIMILAR WORDS	USED CORRECTLY IN A SENTENCE
Affect means "to have an influence on."	Meditation positively *affects* one's concentration.
Affect can also mean "to pretend."	Boris likes to *affect* a French accent.
Effect used as a noun means "a result."	Meditation has a positive *effect* on one's concentration.
Effect used as a verb means "to make happen" or "to bring about."	Meditation can *effect* an improvement in one's concentration.

(continues)

Table 8.1 COMMONLY CONFUSED WORDS

SIMILAR WORDS	USED CORRECTLY IN A SENTENCE
Already means "before this time."	Our new laptops are *already* sold out.
All ready means "prepared."	We are *all ready* for the summer tourist season.
Among refers to three or more.	The prize was divided *among* the four winners.
Between refers to two.	The prize was divided *between* the two winners.
Continual means "repeated at intervals."	Our lower field floods *continually* during rainy season.
Continuous means "without interruption."	His headache has been *continuous* for three days.
Criteria is the plural form of *criterion*.	Our school's *criteria* for applicants are demanding.
Criterion is the singular form.	The most important *criterion* is grade-point average.
Differ from refers to unlike things.	This plan *differs* greatly *from* our earlier one.
Differ with means "to disagree."	Mary *differs with* John about the feasibility of this project.
Disinterested means "unbiased" or "impartial."	Good science calls for *disinterested* analysis of research findings.
Uninterested means "not caring."	Middle school students are often *uninterested* in science.
Eminent means "famous" or "distinguished."	Dr. Ostroff, the *eminent* physicist, is lecturing today.
Imminent means "about to happen."	A nuclear meltdown seemed *imminent*.
Farther refers to physical distance (a measurable quantity).	The school is 20 miles *farther west*.
Further refers to extent (not measurable).	*Further* discussion of this issue is vital.
Fewer refers to things that can be counted.	*Fewer* than fifty students responded to our survey.
Less refers to things that can't be counted.	This survey had *less* of a response than our earlier one.

Table 8.1   COMMONLY CONFUSED WORDS

SIMILAR WORDS	USED CORRECTLY IN A SENTENCE
Good is always an adjective.	The food here is *good.* The young chef does a *good* job.
Well is usually an adverb.	The young chef cooks *well.*
In referring to health, *well* is an adjective.	When I feel *well,* I feel good.
Imply means "to hint at" or "to insinuate."	This report *implies* that a crime occurred.
Infer means "to reason from evidence."	From this report, we can *infer* that a crime occurred.
Its means "belonging to it."	The cost of the project has exceeded *its* budget.
It's is a contraction for "it is." (See page 516 for use of *they're, who's,* and other contractions.)	*It's* a good time for a club meeting.
Lay means "to place or set something down." It always takes a direct object.	Please *lay* the blueprints on the desk.
Lie means "to recline." It takes no direct object.	This patient needs to *lie* on his right side all night.
(Note that the past tense of *lie* is *lay.*)	The patient *lay* on his right side all last night.
Precede means "to come before."	Audience analysis should *precede* a written report.
Proceed means "to go forward."	If you must wake the cobra, *proceed* carefully.
Principle is always a noun that means "basic rule or standard."	Ethical *principles* should govern all our communications.
Principal, used as noun, means "the major person."	All *principals* in this purchase must sign the contract.
Principal, used as adjective, means "leading."	Martha was the *principal* negotiator for this contract.
Who refers to a grammatical subject.	*Who* let the tarantulas out of their cage?
Whom refers to a grammatical object. (See page 505 for *she/her, we/us,* and other forms of pronoun case.)	To *whom* was tarantula security assigned?

APPLICATION

8.2   Revise these sentences to make them precise.

1. Our outlet does more business than San Francisco.
2. Low-fat foods are healthy.
3. Marie's license is for driving an automatic car only.
4. This is the worse course I've taken.
5. Unlike many other children, her home life was good.
6. State law requires that restaurant personnel serve food with a sanitation certificate.

SHARPEN THE VISUAL DETAILS

General terms traded for specific terms

General words name broad classes of things, such as job, car, and person. Such terms usually need to be clarified by more *specific* ones:

> job = senior accountant for Rockford Press
>
> person = male Caucasian, with red hair and blue eyes

The more specific your words, the sharper your meaning:

How the level of generality affects writing's visual quality

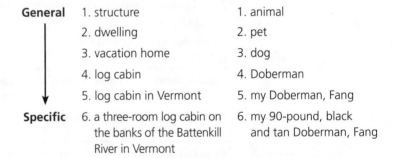

General	1. structure	1. animal
	2. dwelling	2. pet
	3. vacation home	3. dog
	4. log cabin	4. Doberman
	5. log cabin in Vermont	5. my Doberman, Fang
Specific	6. a three-room log cabin on the banks of the Battenkill River in Vermont	6. my 90-pound, black and tan Doberman, Fang

The picture becomes more vivid as we move to lower levels of generality.

Abstract words name qualities, concepts, or feelings (beauty, luxury, depression) whose exact meaning has to be nailed down by *concrete* words—words that name things we can visualize:

Abstract terms traded for concrete terms

> a beautiful view = snowcapped mountains, a wilderness lake, pink granite ledge, 90-foot blue spruce trees
>
> a depressed person = suicidal urge, feelings of worthlessness, no hope for improvement, insomnia

Your discussion must be concrete and specific enough to provide clear and convincing support. Let's say that your topic statement is this one:

> Pedestrians crossing the street in front of my house place their lives in danger.

In supporting your main point, you need to show with concrete and specific examples.

General	A person was injured there by a vehicle recently.
Specific	My Uncle Albert was hit by a speeding garbage truck last Tuesday and had his leg broken.

Similarly, don't write **thing** when you mean **problem, pencil,** or **gift.** Instead of evaluating a coworker as **nice, great,** or **terrific,** use terms that are more concrete and verifiable, such as **reliable, skillful,** and **competent** or **dishonest, irritable,** and **awkward**—further clarified by examples (**never late for work**).

Note

In some instances, you will want to generalize. Instead of writing **Bill, Mary, and Sam have been tying up the office phones with personal calls,** *you might prefer* **Some employees have been tying up....** *The second version gets your message across without pointing the finger.*

Most good writing offers both general and specific information. The more general material usually appears in the topic statement and sometimes in the conclusion because these parts, respectively, set the paragraph's direction and summarize its content. Informative writing invariably has a balance of *telling* and *showing.* Abstract and general expressions tell, and concrete and specific expressions show.

Meaningless abstraction	Professor Able's office is a sight to behold. [*What does "a sight to behold" mean?*]
Informative abstraction	Professor Able's office looks like a dump.

Now the telling needs clarification through concrete and specific showing:

Concrete showing	The floor is strewn with books, the desk is buried beneath a mountain of uncorrected papers, and the ashtrays overflow with cigar butts.

APPLICATION

8.3   In each set of terms, identify the most abstract or general and the most concrete or specific. Give reasons for your choices.

1. a presidential candidate, a U.S. senator, Barack Obama, a politician
2. a favorite spot, a beautiful place, an island in the Bahamas, a hideaway
3. woman, surgeon, person, professional individual
4. an awful person, a cruel and dishonest person, a nasty person
5. a competitor, a downhill racer, an athlete, a skier, a talented amateur
6. violence, assassination, terrorism, political action

ADD PERSONALITY

Your tone is your personal stamp—the personality that takes shape between the lines. The tone you create depends on (1) the distance you impose between yourself and the reader and (2) the attitude you show toward the subject.

How tone is created

Assume, for example, that a friend is going to take over a job you've held. You're writing your friend instructions for parts of the job. Here is your first sentence:

Informal

> Now that you've arrived in the glamorous world of office work, put on your track shoes; this is no ordinary clerical job.

This sentence imposes little distance between you and the reader (it uses the direct address, **you,** and the humorous suggestion to **put on your track shoes**). The ironic use of **glamorous** suggests just the opposite, that the job holds little glamor.

For a different reader (say, the recipient of a company training manual), you would choose some other opening:

Semiformal

> As an office assistant with Acme Explosives Corporation, you will spend little of your day seated at your desk.

The tone now is serious, no longer intimate, and you express no distinct attitude toward the job. For yet another audience (say, clients or investors who will read an annual report), you might alter the tone again:

Formal

> Office assistants at Acme Explosives are responsible for duties that extend far beyond desk work.

Here the businesslike shift from second- to third-person address makes the tone too impersonal for writing addressed to the assistants themselves.

Similarly, letters to your professor, your grandmother, and a friend, each about a disputed grade, would have a different tone:

Formal

> Dear Professor Snapjaws:
>
> I am convinced that my failing grade in calculus does not reflect a fair evaluation of my work over the semester.

Semiformal

> Dear Granny,
>
> Thanks for your letter. I'm doing well in school, except for my unfair grade in calculus.

Informal

Dear Carol,

Have I been shafted or what? That turkey, Snapjaws, gave me an F in calculus.

Establish an Appropriate Distance

We already know how tone works in speaking. When you meet someone new, for example, you respond in a tone that defines your relationship.

Tone announces
interpersonal distance

Honored to make your acquaintance. [*formal tone—greatest distance*]

How do you do? [*formal*]

Nice to meet you. [*semiformal—medium distance*]

Hi. [*informal*]

Wuzzup? [*informal—least distance*]

Each of these responses is appropriate in some situations and inappropriate in others.

GUIDELINES for Deciding About Tone

- *Use a formal or semiformal tone in writing for superiors, professionals, or academics (depending on what you think the reader expects).*

- *Use a semiformal or informal tone in essays and letters (depending on how close you feel to your reader).*

- *Use an informal tone when you want your writing to be conversational (to sound like a person talking).*

- *Above all, find out what tone your particular readers prefer.* When in doubt, do not be too casual!

Whichever tone you decide on, be consistent throughout your message:

Inconsistent tone	My dorm room isn't fit for a pig; it is ungraciously unattractive.
Revised	My dilapidated dorm room is unfit to live in.

In general, lean toward an informal tone without falling into slang. Make your writing conversational by following these suggestions:

GUIDELINES for Achieving a Conversational Tone

- *Prefer simple and familiar words.*
- *Use an occasional contraction.*
- *Address readers directly when appropriate.*
- *Use **I** and **We** when appropriate.*
- *Prefer active voice to passive voice.*

Prefer Simple and Familiar Wording. Say it in plain English. Try not to use a three-syllable word when one syllable will do.

Inflated	Upgrade your present employment situation. [*5 words, 12 syllables*]
Revised	Get a better job. [*4 words, 5 syllables*]

Whenever possible, choose words you use and hear in everyday speaking.

to utilize	=	to use
to be cognizant	=	to know
to endeavor	=	to try
to secure employment	=	to find a job
to concur	=	to agree
to purchase	=	to buy

Every now and then, a more complex or more elaborate word best expresses your meaning or replaces a handful of simpler words.

Weak	Six loops around **the outside edges** of the dome tent **are needed for** the pegs **to fit into.**
Informative and precise	Six loops around the dome tent's **perimeter accommodate** the pegs.
Weak	We need a **one-to-one exchange of ideas and opinions.**
Informative and precise	We need a **dialogue.**

Use an Occasional Contraction. Unless you have reason to be formal, use (but *do not* overuse) contractions. Balance an **I am** with an **I'm**, a **you are** with a **you're**, an **it is** with an **it's**. Generally, use contractions only with pronouns, not with nouns or proper nouns (names).

Awkward contractions	Barbara'll be here soon.
	Health's important.
Ambiguous contractions	The dog's barking.
	The baby's crying.

The ambiguous contractions could be mistaken for possessive constructions.

> **Note** *The contracted version often sounds less emphatic than the two-word version: for example, "**Don't** handle this material without protective clothing" versus "**Do not** handle this material without protective clothing." If your message requires emphasis, do not use a contraction.*

Address Readers Directly. Use the personal pronouns **you** and **your** to connect with readers.

Impersonal tone	Students at our college will find the faculty always willing to help.
Personal tone	As a student at our college, **you** will find the faculty always willing to help.

Readers relate better to something addressed to them directly.

> **Note** *Use **you** and **your** only to speak directly to the reader, as in a letter, instructions, or some form of advice, encouragement, or persuasion. By using **you** and **your** in a situation that calls for first or third person, you might write something like this:*

Wordy and awkward	When **you** are in northern Ontario, **you** can see wilderness lakes everywhere around **you.**
Appropriate	In northern Ontario, wilderness lakes are everywhere.

Use "I" and "We" When Appropriate. Instead of disappearing behind your writing, use **I** or **we** when referring to yourself or your group.

Distant	This writer would like a refund.
Revised	**I** would like a refund.
Distant	The fear was awful until the police arrived.
Revised	**We** were terrified until the police arrived.

Prefer Active Voice. Because active voice is more direct and economical than passive voice, it generally creates a less formal tone. Review pages 116–117 for use of active and passive voice.

Express a Clear and Appropriate Attitude

In addition to setting the distance between writer and reader, your tone implies your *attitude* toward the subject and the reader:

Tone announces attitude

We dine at seven.

Dinner is at seven.

> We eat at seven.
>
> We chow down at seven.
>
> We strap on the feedbag at seven.
>
> We pig out at seven.

The words you choose tell readers a great deal about where you stand. Try to convey an attitude that reflects your relationship with the reader. For instance, in an upcoming conference about a paper, does the professor expect to **discuss the situation, talk it over, have a chat,** or **chew the fat?** Decide how casual or serious your attitude should be.

Don't be afraid to inject personal commentary when it's called for. Consider how the following message, part of an argument for lower speed limits, increases in force and effectiveness with the boldfaced commentary:

> In 1972, some 56,000 people died on America's highways; 200,000 were injured, and 15,000 children were orphaned. In that year, if you were a member of a family of five, chances were that someone related to you, by blood or law, was killed or injured by **one of the most violent forms of self-elimination ever devised by humanity**—an auto accident.

If, however, your job is to report objectively, try to suppress any bias you might have; do not reveal your attitude.

Avoid Personal Bias

If people expect an impartial report, keep your own biases out of it. Imagine that you are a campus newspaper reporter investigating a confrontation between part-time faculty and the administration. Your initial report, written for tomorrow's edition, is intended simply to describe what happened. Here is how an unbiased description might begin:

A factual account

> At 10:00 a.m. on Wednesday, October 24, eighty adjunct faculty members set up picket lines around the college's administration building, bringing business to a halt. The protesters issued a formal complaint, claiming that their salary scale is unfair, their fringe benefits (health insurance and so on) are inadequate, and their job security is nonexistent.

Notice the absence of implied judgments. A less impartial version of the event, from a protester's point of view, might read like this:

A biased version

> Last Wednesday, adjunct faculty struck another blow against exploitation when eighty members paralyzed the college's repressive administration for more than six hours. The timely and articulate protest was aimed against unfair salary scales, inadequate fringe benefits, and lack of job security.

| Note | *Writing teacher Marshall Kremers (59) reminds us that being unbiased doesn't mean remaining "neutral" about something you know to be wrong or dangerous. If, for instance, you conclude that the college protest was clearly justified, say so.* |

INVITE EVERYONE IN

Not only do the words you choose reveal your way of seeing, but they also influence your reader's way of seeing. Insensitive language carries built-in judgments. And as the renowned linguist S. I. Hayakawa reminds us, judgment stops thought. Writing that creates human contact excludes no one.

Avoid Sexist Usage

Language that makes unwarranted assumptions will offend readers. Women, for example, who receive a letter addressed to **Dear Sir** will probably throw the letter out without reading it. Avoid sexist usage such as referring to doctors, lawyers, and other professionals as **he** or **him** while referring to nurses, secretaries, and homemakers as **she** or **her.** Words such as **foreman** or **fireman** automatically exclude women; terms such as **supervisor** or **firefighter** are far more inclusive.

GUIDELINES for Nonsexist Usage

- Use neutral expressions such as **chair** or **chairperson** rather than **chairman, mail carrier** rather than **postman.**

- Rephrase to eliminate the pronoun, but only if you can do so without altering your original meaning. For instance, change *A writer will succeed if **he** revises* to *A writer **who** revises will succeed.*

- Use plural forms: For example, **Writers** *will succeed if **they** revise* (but not **A writer** *will succeed if **they** revise*). For pronoun–referent agreement, see page 502.

- Use occasional paired pronouns (**him or her, she or he, his or hers**): **A writer** *will succeed if **she or he** revises.*

- Drop condescending diminutive endings such as **-ess** and **-ette** used to denote females (**poetess, drum majorette, actress**).

- Use **Ms.** instead of **Mrs.** or **Miss,** unless you know that person prefers a traditional title. Or omit titles: Roger Smith and Jane Kelly; Smith and Kelly.

- In quoting sources that ignore nonsexist standards, consider these options:
  - Insert [sic] ("thus" or "so") following the first instance of sexist usage.
  - Use ellipses (see page 518) to omit sexist phrasing.
  - Substitute or insert nonsexist words between brackets.
  - Paraphrase instead of quoting.

Avoid Offensive Usage of All Types

bias

Enlightened communication respects all people regardless of cultural, racial, ethnic, or national background; sexual and religious orientation; age; or physical condition. References to individuals and groups should be as neutral as possible. Avoid any expression that is condescending or judgmental or that might violate a reader's sense of appropriateness.

GUIDELINES for Inoffensive Usage

- Be as specific as possible, when referring to a particular culture, about that culture's identity. Instead of **Latin American** or **Asian** or **Hispanic,** prefer **Cuban American** or **Korean** or **Nicaraguan.** Use **United States** or **U.S.** rather than **American.**

- Avoid potentially judgmental expressions. Instead of **Third World** or **undeveloped nations** or the **Far East,** prefer **developing** or **newly industrialized nations** or **East Asia.** Instead of **nonwhites,** refer to **people of color.**

- Use person-first language when addressing people with disabilities. Avoid terms that could be considered either pitying or overly euphemistic, such as **victim, challenged,** or **differently abled.** Focus on the individual instead of the disability: **person who is blind** rather than **blind person, person who has lost an arm** rather than **amputee, person with AIDS** rather than **AIDS sufferer** or **AIDS victim.**

- Avoid expressions that demean people who have medical conditions: such terms as **retard, mental midget, insane idea, lame excuse, the blind leading the blind,** and **able-bodied workers.**

- Use age-appropriate designations for both genders: **girl** or **boy** for people age 14 or under; **young person, young adult, young man,** or **young woman** for those of high school age; and **woman** or **man** for those of college age. (**Teenager** or **juvenile** carries certain negative connotations.) Instead of **the elderly,** prefer **older persons** or **seniors.**

Consider the Cultural Context

The style guidelines in Chapters 7 and 8 apply to standard English in North America. But practices and preferences differ widely in various cultural contexts. Certain cultures prefer long sentences and elaborate language, to convey an idea's full complexity. Others value expressions of respect, politeness, praise, and gratitude more than clarity or directness (Hein 1225–26; Mackin 349–50).

Cultures differ in their style preferences

Writing in other languages tends to be more formal than in English, and some languages rely heavily on passive voice (Weymouth 144). French readers, for example, may prefer an elaborate style that reflects sophisticated and complex modes of thinking. In contrast, our "plain English" conversational style may connote simplemindedness, disrespect, or incompetence (Thrush 277).

In translation or in a different cultural context, certain words carry offensive or unfavorable connotations. For example, certain cultures use *male* and *female* in referring only to animals (Coe 17).

Idioms (**strike out, over the top**) make no literal sense outside U.S. culture. Slang (**bogus, phat**) and colloquialisms (**You bet, Gotcha**) can seem too informal and crude.

In short, offensive writing can alienate audiences—from both you *and* your culture (Sturges 32).

DIGITAL TIP

Use Your Word Processor to Revise Words and Phrases

For the fourth and final round of edits to a document (see the Digital Tips in Chapters 5, 6, and 7 for the earlier rounds), focus on fine tuning—revising the words and phrases. Here are suggestions:

- Do not rely solely on computerized tools when revising words and phrases. For example, spell checkers cannot differentiate among correctly spelled homonyms (such as *their, they're,* and *there*). Computerized thesauruses may suggest alternate words that distort your intended meaning.

- Open your content, paragraph, and sentence revision (Revision 3, page 127) and use the "save as" function to preserve the previous version and create a new version. Give this "save as" revision its own file name. In this new version, input the edits you highlighted, bolded, or italicized in the previous rounds (your previous version will act as a record should you need to refer back to it later).

- Then go ahead and fine tune.

- Save this final draft as Revision 4 or under its new file name.

✔ A CHECKLIST for Word Choice and Tone

Genuineness

☐ Have **trite, worn-out phrases** such as "up the creek" and "over the hill" been traded for fresh expressions? (132)

☐ Are **superlatives** such as "always," "never," "best," and "worst" used only when warranted and without overstatement? (132)

☐ Is the piece free of misleading **euphemisms**? (132)

Precision

☐ Does the **wording** precisely convey the intended meaning? (133)

☐ Are **commonly confused words** such as "affect/effect" and "fewer/less" used correctly? (133)

(continues)

☐ Does **one precise** word replace multiple inexact words, as needed? (133)

☐ Could any **ambiguous terms** be rephrased more clearly? (133)

Sharp Visual Details

☐ Are **general terms** ("student") clarified by more specific descriptions ("first-year finance major")? (136)

☐ Are **abstract terms** ("nice person") clarified by more concrete terms ("kind," "loving," "generous")? (136)

☐ Does the piece offer an appropriate balance of **telling** and **showing?** (137)

Personality

☐ Is the tone **appropriate** to the situation and audience? (138)

☐ If the situation requires, is the tone **formal** without being stuffy and impersonal? (139)

☐ For most situations, is the tone **conversational** but not overly informal? (140)

☐ Does the language generally reflect what is used and heard in **everyday speaking**—without lapsing into slang? (138)

☐ Is the tone **consistent** throughout the piece? (139)

☐ Does the occasional **contraction** lend informality, as needed? (140)

☐ Are readers **addressed directly** ("you," "your") whenever appropriate? (141)

☐ Is **first person** ("I," "we") used whenever you refer to yourself? (141)

☐ Is **active voice,** rather than passive voice, predominant? (141)

Inclusion

☐ Is the piece inviting and free of **implied bias, sexist language, and potentially offensive usage?** (143)

☐ Does the piece display **sensitivity to cultural differences?** (144)

LEGAL AND ETHICAL IMPLICATIONS OF WORD CHOICE

We are each accountable for the words we use—intentionally or not—in framing the audience's perception and understanding. Imprecise or inappropriate word choice in the workplace, for example, can spell big trouble, as in the following examples.

Situations in which word choice has ethical or legal consequences

- *Assessing risk.* Is the investment you are advocating "a sure thing," merely "a good bet," or even "somewhat risky"? Are you announcing a "caution," a "warning," or a "danger"? Never downplay the risks involved.
- *Offering a service or product.* Are you proposing to "study the problem," to "explore solutions to the problem," or to "eliminate the problem"? Do you "stand behind" your product, or do you "guarantee" it? Never promise more than you can deliver.

- *Giving instructions.* Before inserting the widget between the grinder blades, should you "switch off the grinder," "disconnect the grinder from its power source," "trip the circuit breaker," or do all three things? Always triple-check the clarity of your instructions.
- *Comparing your product with competing products.* Instead of referring to a competitor's product as "inferior," "second-rate," or "substandard," talk about your own "first-rate product" that "exceeds (or meets) all standards." Never run down the competition.
- *Evaluating an employee* (Clark 75–76). In a personnel evaluation, don't refer to the employee as "a troublemaker," "unprofessional," "too abrasive," "too uncooperative," "incompetent," or "too old" for the job. Focus on the specific requirements of this job, and offer factual instances in which these requirements have been violated: "Our monitoring software recorded five visits by this employee to X-rated Web sites during working hours" or "This employee arrives late for work on average twice weekly, has failed to complete assigned projects on three occasions, and has difficulty working with others." Instead of expressing personal judgments, offer the facts. Otherwise, you risk violating federal laws against discrimination and libel (damaging someone's reputation) and may face lawsuits.

APPLICATIONS

8.4   Rewrite these statements in plain, precise English, with special attention to tone.

1. This writer desires to be considered for a position with your company.
2. My attitude toward your behavior is one of disapproval.
3. Replacement of the weak battery should be effectuated.
4. Make an improvement in your studying situation.
5. We should inject some rejuvenation into our lifeless and dull relationship.

8.5   Find examples of overly euphemistic language (such as "chronologically challenged") or of insensitive language—possibly on the Internet or in a newsgroup.

8.6   **COLLABORATIVE PROJECT AND COMPUTER APPLICATION** A version of the following letter was published in a local newspaper. Working on the computer, each group member should rewrite the letter in plain English and then email his or her version to group members. Discuss the changes electronically and agree on a final version that one group member will compose. Print this final version for the whole class, justifying your group's revision.

> In the absence of definitive studies regarding the optimum length of the school day, I can only state my personal opinion based upon observations made by me and upon teacher observations that have been conveyed to me. Considering the length of the present school day, it is my opinion that the school

day is excessive lengthwise for most elementary pupils, certainly for almost all of the primary children.

To find the answer to the problem requires consideration of two ways in which the problem may be viewed. One way focuses upon the needs of the children, while the other focuses upon logistics, scheduling, transportation, and other limits imposed by the educational system. If it is necessary to prioritize these two ideas, it would seem most reasonable to give the first consideration to the primary and fundamental reason for the very existence of the system itself, i.e., to meet the educational needs of the children the system is trying to serve.

8.7   Rewrite these statements to eliminate sexist and other offensive expressions without altering the meaning.

1. The future of mankind is uncertain.
2. Being a stewardess is not as glamorous as it may seem.
3. Everyone has the right to his opinion.
4. The accident left me blind as a bat for nearly an hour.
5. What a dumb idea!

8.8   **WEB-BASED PROJECT** Look up "online style guides" using Google, Bing, or Yahoo! search engines. Find an online style guide that expands on the advice about tone offered in this chapter. Then prepare a one-page presentation about the guide you consulted. Attach copies of all relevant Web pages to your presentation. Be sure to credit each source of information (page 380).

Works Cited

Clark, Thomas. "Teaching Students How to Write to Avoid Legal Liability." *Business Communication Quarterly* 60.3 (1997): 71–77. Print.

Coe, Marlana. "Writing for Other Cultures." *Intercom* Jan. 1997: 17–19. Print.

Hein, Robert G. "Culture and Communication." *Technical Communication* 38.1 (1991): 125–26. Print.

Kremers, Marshall. "*IEEE Transactions on Professional Communication.*" 32.2 (1989): 58–61. Print.

Mackin, John. "Surmounting the Barrier between Japanese and English Technical Documents." *Technical Communication* 36.4 (1989): 346–51. Print.

Sturges, David L. "Internationalizing the Business Communication Curriculum." *Bulletin of the Association for Business Communication* 55.1 (1992): 30–39. Print.

Thrush, Emily A. "Bridging the Gap: Technical Communication in an Intercultural and Multicultural Society." *Technical Communication Quarterly* 2.3 (1993): 271–83. Print.

Weymouth, L. C. "Establishing Quality Standards and Trade Regulations for Technical Writing in World Trade." *Technical Communication* 37.2 (1990): 143–47. Print.

Essays for Various Goals

Introduction

Sections One and Two of this book have stressed the importance of planning, drafting, and revising to produce an essay that has been carefully considered, written, and refined. This section shows you how to focus on specific strategies to achieve a variety of writing goals.

THREE MAJOR GOALS OF WRITING

Most writing can be categorized according to three major goals: expressive, referential, and persuasive.

Expressive writing is mostly about you, the writer (your feelings, experiences, impressions, personality). This personal form of writing helps readers understand something about you or your way of seeing.

Expressive writing situations

- You write to cheer up a sick friend with a tale about your latest blind date.
- You write a Dear John (or Jane) letter.
- You write to your parents, explaining why you've been feeling down in the dumps.

Examples of expressive writing appear in the sample essays in Section One on pages 10 and 14. Many of us find expressive writing easiest because it is a kind of storytelling.

Instead of focusing on the writer, *referential* (or explanatory) *writing* refers to some outside subject. Your goal might be to inform readers about something they need to know or to explain something they need to understand. Referential writing focuses not on your feelings and experiences but on the subject at hand.

Referential writing situations

- You write to describe the exterior of your new dorm so that your parents can find it next weekend.
- You define *condominium* for your business law class.
- You report on the effects of budget cuts at your college for the campus newspaper.

An example of referential writing appears on page 64.

Persuasive writing is mostly about your audience. Beyond merely imparting information or making something understandable, your goal is to win readers' support, to influence their thinking, or to motivate them in some way. Persuasive writing appeals to both the audience's reason and to their emotions.

Persuasive writing
situations

- You write an editorial for the campus newspaper, calling for a stricter alcohol policy in the dorms.
- You write to ask a professor on sabbatical to reconsider the low grade you received in history.
- You write to persuade citizens in your county to vote against a proposal for a toxic-waste dump.

When goals overlap

These three goals—expressive, referential (or explanatory), and persuasive—often overlap. For example, persuading the dean to beef up campus security might involve discussing your personal fears (expressive goal), explaining how some students have been attacked (referential goal), and requesting specific action (persuasive goal). But most writing situations have one primary goal. Keeping that goal in focus can help you choose the best strategies for getting the job done.

Traditionally, the strategies for writing are considered to be *description, narration, exposition* (informing or explaining), and *argument*. But description, narration, and exposition can be used for expressive, referential, or persuasive goals. While Chapter 1 focuses on expressive writing, Section Three is mostly about communication between readers and writers on subjects of interest to both. Therefore, it focuses primarily on referential and persuasive uses of these strategies—that is, writing to inform, explain, or make a point. Persuasive writing raises special concerns that we will cover in Chapters 18 and 19.

Note

Keep in mind that none of these development strategies is an end in itself. In other words, we don't write merely for the sake of contrasting or of discussing cause and effect. Instead, we use a particular strategy because it provides the best framework for organizing our information and clarifying our thinking on a particular topic. Each strategy is merely one way of looking at something—another option for gaining control of the countless writing situations we face throughout our lives and careers.

MAJOR DEVELOPMENT STRATEGIES

A *development strategy* is a plan for coming up with the details, events, examples, explanations, and reasons that convey your exact meaning—a way of answering readers' questions. *Description* paints a word picture, while *narration* tells a story or depicts a series of related events, usually in chronological order. Narration relies on descriptive details to make the events vivid. *Exposition,* meanwhile, relies on description and narration, but it does more than paint a picture or tell a story: This strategy explains the writer's viewpoint. Strategies of exposition include *illustration, classification, process analysis, cause-and-effect analysis, comparison and contrast,* and *definition,* all of which are explored in the following chapters. Essays almost always employ some combination of these strategies but usually have one primary strategy.

Finally, *argument* strives to win readers to our point of view. Whereas the main point in exposition can usually be shown to be true or valid, the main point in an argument is debatable—capable of being argued by reasonable people on either side. The stronger argument, then, would be the one that makes the more convincing case.

> **Note**   *Although argument follows its own specified patterns of reasoning, it also relies on the strategies of description, narration, and exposition.*

USING THIS SECTION

This section begins with a chapter on methods for reading and responding to essays written by others. The chapters that follow then introduce a particular strategy and show how the strategy can support referential and persuasive writing.

The chapters also provide guidelines for using the strategy yourself, along with sample essays and case studies for your analysis and response. When you read these sample essays, refer to the Chapter 9 questions, as well as to the more specific questions provided in each chapter. Then examine the case study that shows one student's response to the sample essay.

A WORD ABOUT STRUCTURAL VARIATIONS

Most sample essays in earlier chapters have a basic introduction-body-conclusion structure: a one-paragraph introduction that leads into the thesis; several support paragraphs, each developed around a topic statement that treats one part of the thesis; and a one-paragraph conclusion that relates to the main point. But published writing can vary considerably from this formula. Some topics call for several introductory paragraphs; some supporting points require that one topic statement serve two or more body paragraphs; some paragraphs may be interrupted by digressions, such as personal remarks or flashbacks that are linked to the main point; some conclusions take up more than one paragraph. Single-sentence paragraphs will open, support, or close an essay.

Instead of being the final sentence in the introduction, the thesis might be the first sentence of the essay, or it may be saved for the conclusion or not stated at all, although a definite thesis is almost always unmistakably implied.

Still other essays have neither introductory nor concluding paragraphs. Instead, the opening or closing is incorporated into the main discussion. Such *structural variations are a part of a writer's deliberate decisions*—decisions that determine the ultimate quality of an essay. Many of the essays in the following chapters embody one or more of these variations. Use them as inspiration for your own writing, but remember that *effective writing always reveals a distinct beginning, middle, and ending*—and a clear line of thought.

Reading and Responding to Writing

LEARNING OBJECTIVES FOR THIS CHAPTER

- Recognize that different levels of reading an essay include reading to be entertained, get information, make a critical judgment, and discover personal meaning

- Appreciate that different readers discover different meanings in a given essay

- Respond to an essay by rereading, taking notes, and using other active reading skills

This book asks you to read other people's writing (the writing of students and professionals) in order to consider their ideas and trace their decision making. Reading also provides raw material that helps you craft your own writing. But not all reading requires the same level of interaction.

DIFFERENT LEVELS OF READING

Reading to be entertained

Different reasons for reading call for different levels of interacting with a piece of writing. In reading a Stephen King novel, for instance, we tend to skim the surface, flipping pages to find the juicy scenes and basically enjoying the ride.

Reading to get information

In reading a textbook in psychology or some other discipline, we work to grasp important facts and main ideas. Later, we often write to demonstrate our knowledge or understanding.

Reading to make a critical judgment

For this course, we go beyond merely retrieving and absorbing information. In *critical reading,* we dig beneath the surface and examine the writing itself—its content, organization, and style. Instead of accepting ideas at face value, we weigh the evidence, the assumptions, and the reasoning behind those ideas.

Questions for Critical Reading

ABOUT PURPOSE

- *What is the author asking us to think or do?*
- *In what ways does this piece succeed or fail in its purpose?*

ABOUT CONTENT

- *Is the title effective? Why?*
- *What is the thesis? Is it stated or implicit? Where does it appear?*
- *Does this placement contribute to the main point?*
- *Does the piece offer something new and useful?*
- *Does the reasoning make sense?*
- *Is the essay convincing? What kinds of support does the writer offer for the main points?*
- *Are other conclusions or interpretations possible?*

ABOUT ORGANIZATION

- *Is the discussion easy to follow?*
- *How is the introduction structured? Are the writer's decisions effective? Why?*
- *Does the essay vary the standard introduction-body-conclusion format (page 6)? If so, how? Do the writer's decisions help promote the purpose?*
- *How is the conclusion structured? Is it effective? Why?*

ABOUT STYLE

- *What is the outstanding style feature of this essay? Give examples.*
- *How effective is the tone? Give examples of word choice and sentence structure that contribute to the tone.*

This critical evaluation provides essential groundwork for writing about reading. But much of the energy for *any* writing comes from our *personal* response to something we read.

Reading to discover
personal meaning

In reading for personal meaning, we join a "conversation": Reacting to something that was said, we offer something of our own. We read to explore and inspire our own thinking, to make up our minds, or to discover buried feelings or ideas. Then we reinvent that material with a force and passion that will make a difference to our own readers.

Questions for Personal Responses to Reading

- *What special meaning does this piece have for me?*
- *What grabs my attention?*
- *Does this piece make me angry, defensive, supportive, or what?*
- *Why do I feel this way?*

- *With which statements do I agree or disagree?*
- *Has the piece reminded me of something, taught me something, changed my mind, or what?*
- *How do I want to reply?*

DIFFERENT READERS, DIFFERENT MEANINGS

The connection that writing creates is both public and private. On the one hand, a piece of writing connects publicly with its entire audience; on the other hand, the writing connects privately with each of its readers. Consider, for example, "Confessions of a Food Addict" (pages 10–11): Most readers of this essay feel the writer's anxiety and sense of failure. Beyond our common reaction, however, each of us has a unique and personal reaction as well— special feelings or memories or thoughts.

You as the reader interpret and complete the "private" meaning of anything you read. And like you, other readers come away from the same piece with personal meanings of their own. It is personal meaning that ultimately inspires your own writing.

READING STRATEGIES FOR WRITERS

A worthwhile critical and personal response to writing calls for a good strategy. Instead of just a single reading, you need to get into the piece. And you do this by rereading and by writing *while* you read: First you take notes, underline, scribble questions and comments in the margins, and summarize the main ideas. Then you examine the author's technique, evaluate the ideas, and discover what the piece means to you personally. Once you have a genuine grasp of the piece, you can decide exactly how you want to respond.

The following case study shows how student writer Jacqueline LeBlanc employs each of these strategies in preparing her response to a reading.

CASE STUDY

ONE WRITER'S RESPONSE TO READING

Judy Brady's "Why I Want a Wife" was published in the very first issue of *Ms.* magazine in spring 1972. Even though Brady seems to write for married readers in particular, her essay speaks to anyone familiar with married people in general.

As you read, consider this question: Based on your experience, how much have male and female roles really changed since this essay was written?

Essay for analysis and response

Why I Want a Wife

I belong to that classification of people known as wives. I am A Wife. And, not altogether incidentally, I am a mother.

Not too long ago a male friend of mine appeared on the scene fresh from a recent divorce. He had one child, who is, of course, with his ex-wife. He is looking for another wife. As I thought about him while I was ironing one evening, it suddenly occurred to me that I, too, would like to have a wife. Why do I want a wife?

I would like to go back to school so that I can become economically independent, support myself, and, if need be, support those dependent upon me. I want a wife who will work and send me to school. And while I am going to school I want a wife to take care of my children. I want a wife to keep track of the children's doctor and dentist appointments. And to keep track of mine, too. I want a wife to make sure my children eat properly and are kept clean. I want a wife who will wash the children's clothes and keep them mended. I want a wife who is a good nurturant attendant to my children, who arranges for their schooling, makes sure that they have an adequate social life with their peers, takes them to the park, the zoo, etc. I want a wife who takes care of the children when they are sick, a wife who arranges to be around when the children need special care, because, of course, I cannot miss classes at school. My wife must arrange to lose time at work and not lose the job. It may mean a small cut in my wife's income from time to time, but I guess I can tolerate that. Needless to say, my wife will arrange and pay for the care of the children while my wife is working.

I want a wife who will take care of my physical needs. I want a wife who will keep my house clean. A wife who will pick up after my children, a wife who will pick up after me. I want a wife who will keep my clothes clean, ironed, mended, replaced when need be, and who will see to it that my personal things are kept in their proper place so that I can find what I need the minute I need it. I want a wife who cooks the meals, a wife who is a good cook. I want a wife who will plan the menus, do the necessary grocery shopping, prepare the meals, serve them pleasantly, and then do the cleaning up while I do my studying. I want a wife who will care for me when I am sick and sympathize with my pain and loss of time from school. I want a wife to go along when our family takes a vacation so that someone can continue to care for me and my children when I need a rest and change of scene.

I want a wife who will not bother me with rambling complaints about a wife's duties. But I want a wife who will listen to me when I feel the need to explain a rather difficult point I have come across in my course of studies. And I want a wife who will edit my papers for me when I have written them.

I want a wife who will take care of the details of my social life. When my wife and I are invited out by my friends, I want a wife who will take care of the babysitting arrangements. When I meet people at school that I like and want to entertain, I want a wife who will have the house clean, will prepare a special meal, serve it to me and my friends, and not interrupt when I talk about things that interest me and my friends. I want a wife who will have arranged that the children are fed and ready for bed before my guests arrive so that the children do not bother us. I want a wife who takes care of the needs of my guests so that they feel comfortable, who makes sure that they have an ashtray, that they are passed the hors d'oeuvres, that they are offered a second helping of the food, that their wine glasses are replenished when necessary, that their coffee is served to them as they like it. And I want a wife who knows that sometimes I need a night out by myself.

I want a wife who is sensitive to my sexual needs, a wife who makes love passionately and eagerly when I feel like it, a wife who makes sure that I am satisfied. And, of course, I want a wife who will not demand sexual attention when I am not in the mood for it. I want a wife who assumes the complete responsibility for birth control, because I do not want more children. I want a wife who will remain sexually faithful to me so that I do not have to clutter up my intellectual life with jealousies. And I want a wife who understands that my sexual needs may entail more than strict adherence to monogamy. I must, after all, be able to relate to people as fully as possible.

If, by chance, I find another person more suitable as a wife than the wife I already have, I want the liberty to replace my present wife with another one. Naturally, I will expect a fresh, new life; my wife will take the children and be solely responsible for them so that I am left free. When I am through with school and have a job, I want my wife to quit working and remain at home so that my wife can more fully and completely take care of a wife's duties.

My God, who *wouldn't* want a wife?

—*Judy Brady*

Discussion

Now let's examine our critical and personal opinions of "Why I Want a Wife." Is this view of the "housewife's" destiny basically accurate, in your opinion? What particular meaning does this essay have for you?

Maybe Brady's essay leaves you feeling irate toward (1) men, (2) the writer, (3) yourself, or (4) someone else. Or maybe you feel threatened or offended. Or maybe you feel amused or confused about your own attitudes toward gender roles. The questions on pages 154 and 155 will help you explore your reactions.

Before you decide on a response to Brady's essay, see how another student responded. Here are some of the notes Jacqueline LeBlanc wrote in her journal after first reading the essay:

One of LeBlanc's journal entries

This essay is annoying because it reminds me too much of some women in my own generation who seem to want nothing more than a wifely role for themselves. For all we hear about "equal rights," women still feel the pressure to conform to old-fashioned notions. I can really take this essay personally.

After rereading the essay and reviewing her journal entries, LeBlanc identified and annotated key passages. Here is what she jotted on one paragraph of the Brady essay:

LeBlanc's annotations of one paragraph

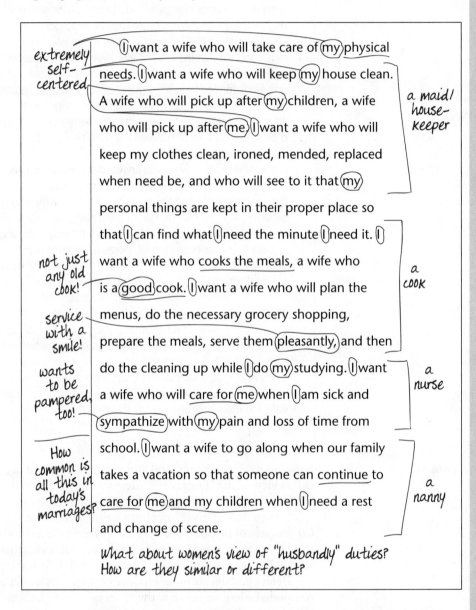

extremely self-centered

I want a wife who will take care of (my) physical needs. I want a wife who will keep (my) house clean. A wife who will pick up after (my) children, a wife who will pick up after (me.) I want a wife who will keep my clothes clean, ironed, mended, replaced when need be, and who will see to it that (my) personal things are kept in their proper place so that (I) can find what (I) need the minute (I) need it. (I)

a maid/house-keeper

not just any old cook!

want a wife who cooks the meals, a wife who is a (good) cook. (I) want a wife who will plan the

a cook

service with a smile!

menus, do the necessary grocery shopping, prepare the meals, serve them (pleasantly,) and then

wants to be pampered, too!

do the cleaning up while (I) do (my) studying. (I) want a wife who will care for (me) when (I) am sick and (sympathize) with (my) pain and loss of time from

a nurse

How common is all this in today's marriages?

school. (I) want a wife to go along when our family takes a vacation so that someone can continue to care for (me) and my children when (I) need a rest and change of scene.

a nanny

What about women's view of "husbandly" duties? How are they similar or different?

To ensure her grasp of Brady's position, LeBlanc follows the guidelines on page 163 to summarize the essay in her own words:

LeBlanc's summary of the essay

In "Why I Want a Wife," Judy Brady offers a graphic view of the lowly status of women in marriage. The typical wife is expected to serve as financial provider, nanny, nurse, maid, cook, secretary, and sex slave. And no matter how well she performs these and other oppressive duties, this wife is ultimately disposable in the event that the husband finds someone "more suitable" for the role.

Sometimes a direct quotation is necessary to preserve a special meaning or emphasis (page 383). Notice that LeBlanc is careful to place Brady's exact wording in quotation marks.

Next, LeBlanc uses the critical reading questions on page 154 to evaluate Brady's case. She measures the piece's strengths and weaknesses in terms of its purpose, thesis, support, line of reasoning, accuracy, and style. Here is part of her analysis:

LeBlanc's partial analysis

Brady sets out here to shock women (as well as men) out of traditional attitudes by defining her concept of "wife." Even though she offers no explicit thesis, her main point might be stated like this: *Women in the traditional "wifely" role are exploited and unappreciated.*

Her many vivid examples are extremely depressing and somewhat exaggerated, but most of them should be familiar to anyone who has experienced the "traditional" family—and they really don't seem all that outdated, either.

Brady's tone certainly is sarcastic, but given the situation, her sarcasm seems justified, and it adds to the essay's shock value.

She continues her critical evaluation using the Revision Checklist that faces the inside front cover.

Now that she has a solid handle on the essay, LeBlanc uses the personal response questions on page 155 to explore the special meaning she finds here. Finally, she decides on the viewpoint that will guide her own response:

LeBlanc's own viewpoint as a basis for responding

The stereotypical role condemned by Brady more than three decades ago continues to be disturbingly evident.

LeBlanc expresses her viewpoint in a definite thesis statement:

LeBlanc's thesis

Although today's "equality-minded" generation presumably sees marriage as more than just an occupation, the wifely stereotype persists.

Here, after several revisions, is the essay that explains LeBlanc's viewpoint:

LeBlanc's final response to Brady's essay

A LONG WAY TO GO

Judy Brady's portrait of a servile wife might appear somewhat dated—until we examine some of today's views about marriage. Brady defines a wife by the work she does for her husband: She is a secretary, housemaid, babysitter, and sex object. She is, in a word, her husband's employee. Although today's "equality-minded" generation presumably sees marriage as more than an occupation, the wifely stereotype persists.

Among a few of my women friends, I continue to encounter surprisingly traditional attitudes. Last week, for instance, I was discussing my career possibilities with my roommate, who added to the list of my choices by saying, "You can always get married." In her view, becoming a wife seems no different from becoming a teacher or journalist. She implied that marriage is merely another way of making a living. But where do I apply for the position of wife? The notion struck me as absurd. I thought to myself, "Surely, this person is an isolated case. We are, after all, in the twenty-first century. Women no longer get married as a substitute for a job—do they?"

Of course, many women do have both job and marriage, but as I look closely at others' attitudes, I find that my roommate's view is not so rare. Before the recent wedding of a female friend, my conversations with the future bride revolved around her meal plans and laundry schedule. To her vows "to love, honor, and cherish" she could have added "to cook, serve, and clean up." She had been anticipating the first meal she would prepare for her husband. Granted, nothing is wrong with wanting to serve and provide for the one you love—but she spoke of this meal as if it were a pass-or-fail exam given by her employer on her first day on the job. Following the big day of judgment, she was elated to have passed with flying colors.

I couldn't help wondering what would have happened if her meal had been a flop. Would she have lost her marriage as an employee loses a job? As long as my friend retains such a narrow and materialistic view of wifely duties, her marriage is not likely to be anything more than a job.

Not all my friends are obsessed with wifely duties, but some do have a definite sense of husbandly duties. A potential husband must measure up to the qualifications of the position, foremost of which is wealth. One of the first questions about any male is, "What does he do?" Engineering majors or premed students usually get highest ranking, and humanities or music majors end up at the bottom. College women are by no means opposed to marriage based on true love, but as we grow older, the fantasy of a Prince Charming gives way to the reality of an affluent provider. Some women look for high-paying marriages just as they look for high-paying jobs.

Some of my peers may see marriage as one of many career choices, but my parents see it as the only choice. To my parents, my not finding a husband is a much more terrifying fate than my not finding a job. In their view, being a wife is no mere occupation but a natural vocation for all women. But not just any man will do as a husband. My parents have a built-in screening procedure for each man I date. Appearance, money, and general background are the highest qualifications. They ignore domestic traits because they assume that his parents will be screening me for such qualifications.

I have always tried to avoid considering male friends simply as prospective husbands; likewise, I never think of myself as filling the stereotypical position of wife. But sometimes I fall into my parents' way of thinking. When I invite a friend to dinner at my house, I suddenly find myself fretting about his hair, his religion, or his job. Will he pass the screening test? Is he the right man for the role of husband? In some ways, my attitudes seem no more liberated than those of my peers or parents.

Today's women have made a good deal of progress, but apparently not enough. Allowing the practical implications of marriage to overshadow its emotional implications, a surprising number of us seem to feel that we still have to fit much of the stereotype that Brady condemns.

—Jacqueline LeBlanc

In writing about reading, each of us expresses a unique and personal response. Maybe, like Jacqueline LeBlanc, you will respond in a way that sticks closely to what you've read. Or maybe you will decide to use the reading as a launch toward new exploration.

CASE STUDY

A SECOND WRITER'S RESPONSE TO READING

Our second writer, David Galuski, discovered in the Brady essay the possibility for humor, summed up in this thesis:

Instead of a wife, I need an assistant.

He uses his response to poke fun at his own inability to cope with an impossibly busy schedule and to discover that, like all of us at times, he is just looking for a little sympathy.

Galuski's response to the Brady essay

I NEED AN ASSISTANT

I am much too busy. Being eighteen takes a lot out of a person—especially anyone who attends college full time, works two part-time jobs, plays sports, and tries to have a social life. I need someone to help me get through the day. Instead of a wife, I need an assistant.

For one thing, my assistant would help with school chores. Although I usually find time to do my homework, it is never without a good deal of pain. My assistant could ease the pain by doing some of my reading, which he could then summarize and explain to me. Maybe he could do some of my research and edit the papers I write as well. Fluent in all subjects, my assistant would be able to transfer his knowledge to me.

Studying is easy—when I have enough time. But keeping up grades while holding down two part-time jobs is another story. I spend twenty hours a week at Max's, a gourmet restaurant, where I am expected to continuously cater to my customers. But when I'm exhausted from studying, I'm likely to be forgetful and irritable. I want an assistant who will stand by me at all times at work. He could help with the work and also cover for any lapses in my patience or attention.

My work as timekeeper for hockey games at the skating rink consumes five hours weekly out of my busy schedule. I need an assistant to cover the games I cannot time because of homework or conflicting hours at the restaurant. My assistant would also stand by my side and take over when I fall asleep because of the late hours at which the games are scheduled. Although I must work at these jobs to pay college expenses, my life isn't all work and studying.

Sports are a big part of my life. I set aside at least one hour every day to run, cycle, or swim. No matter what my other commitments are, without daily exercise I feel I've accomplished nothing. I need an assistant to encourage me to run that extra step or to swim one more pool length. He would push me out the door to exercise in the cold and in the rain. My assistant would compete alongside me in the six triathlons I do each year. He would also be a good hockey player, who would attend practice sessions in my place, leaving the team happy and giving me time to finish homework or earn money.

Besides school, work, and sports, I have other commitments to consider. I try—without much success—to maintain an active social life. I need an assistant to keep me up to date on my friends and girlfriend. I never have time to call them. When I do manage to see them, it is briefly. Even though they understand my obligations, they can't help being annoyed occasionally. My assistant would make my phone calls and arrange dates for me at times when I can squeeze them in.

Dates are something I really can't make with my family. But I see my parents as much as possible. I try to help out at home, but that would be a job for my assistant. He would do my household chores, wash the cars, and mow the lawn. My assistant would make my bed and wash my clothes while I hurry off to some pressing engagement.

Finally, I need an assistant who will give me emotional support. I want an assistant to whisper in my ear, telling me that everything will turn out all right—one who will sing me to sleep and hold me when I cry. Maybe all I'm looking for after all is a little pity.

—David Galuski

We have seen how two student writers reached deep into their reading and into themselves to discover a real connection. Their writing, in turn, makes us part of that connection.

SUGGESTIONS FOR READING AND RESPONDING

Some of the readings in later chapters are professionally written; others are student written. Besides triggering your own writing, each reading provides a model of worthwhile content, sensible organization, and readable style.

Here are suggestions for reading to respond to the selections assigned throughout the semester.

GUIDELINES for Reading to Respond

- *Read the piece at least three times.* First, get a sense of the geography; next, explore your reactions; finally, see what you find most striking or important or outrageous.

- *Record initial impressions, ideas, or other reactions to the piece.*

- *Highlight and annotate passages.* Underline the statements that strike you or set you off, and jot questions and comments in the margins.

- *Summarize the entire piece.* This will ensure that you understand the author's purpose, meaning, and main ideas. (See the guidelines on page 385.)

- *Use the critical reading questions on page 154.* Evaluate the content, organization, and style to see exactly how well the author connects with readers.

- *Answer the personal response questions on page 155.*

- *Once you see what makes the piece tick, settle on the main point you want to convey in reply.*

- *Express your viewpoint in a thesis statement.* (See pages 22–28.)

APPLICATIONS

9.1   ESSAY PRACTICE: WRITING TO RESPOND

Respond to Brady's essay with an essay of your own. Share with us a new way of seeing. Imagine you are conversing with the writer: How would you reply if someone had just spoken what you have read? The guidelines will help you reach deep into your reading experience. Record your responses in a hard-copy or electronic reading journal. Base the essay on your responses.

9.2   **COLLABORATIVE PROJECT** Share or email your essay from Application 9.1 with others in your group who have completed the same assignment. Can you pinpoint places where your responses were very similar or where they were radically different? As a group, discuss the possible reasons for the differences. Have one group member record the reasons for discussion with the entire class.

9.3   **ONLINE PROJECT** Using your group's network, conduct Application 9.2 online. Transmit and exchange documents electronically.

9.4   **WEB-BASED PROJECT** Does Brady's essay describe an essentially timeless situation? Have gender roles changed at all since this essay was written (1972)? Do some roles never change? Are there valid male points of view on these issues as well?

For contrasting perspectives, visit the National Organization for Women (<*http://www.now.org*>) or Men's Issues Virtual Library (<*http://www.menweb .org/*>) Web sites, but do not limit yourself to them.

Identify one issue in the ongoing gender debate (say, workplace equity, scholastic performance, or health care differences), and compare the prevailing female and male viewpoints on the issue. In your own words, summarize each contrasting viewpoint in a one-page presentation for your classmates. Attach a copy of the relevant Web pages to your presentation. Be sure to credit each source of information.

For additional information and practice with the learning objectives in this chapter, go to www.mycomplab.com, Resources>Writing>Writing Purpose.

Description: Writing to Help Others See

LEARNING OBJECTIVES FOR THIS CHAPTER

- Understand the role of *description* as a basic writing strategy
- Differentiate description used to inform from description used to make a point
- Write an effective description using the chapter guidelines

Description creates a word picture, a clear mental image of how something looks. Because it helps readers *visualize*, description is a common denominator in all writing.

What readers expect to
learn from a description

- *What is it?*
- *What does it look like?*

165

- *How could I recognize it?*
- *What is it made of?*
- *What does it do?*
- *How does it work?*
- *What is your impression of it?*
- *How does it make you feel?*

Because any topic or event can be viewed in countless ways, your decisions about descriptive details depend on your purpose and the reader's needs. Description can either serve *objective (referential) goals*—that is, it can merely report—or it can be used differently by different writers. In such cases, description fills *subjective (and often persuasive) goals*—it makes a point.

THE LANGUAGE OF DESCRIPTION

A good description conveys an unmistakable picture, but objective description and subjective description provide different views. Objective description focuses on details any observer could recognize, details that are measurable, details that a camera would record. Subjective description looks beyond and beneath those observable details to convey the writer's unique perspective on what is observed.

Objective description relies on precise and informative language: words that specify location and position, exact measurements, weights, and dimensions. For example, instead of **large, long,** and **near,** objective description would specify **above, oblique, tangential, adjacent, interlocking, overlapping, horizontal, vertical, in cross section,** and so on.

Moving beyond precise language, subjective description employs sensory and judgmental words that convey a personal impression about what the writer is seeing. For example, a crowded rock concert audience might be described objectively as **tightly packed and enthusiastic** but subjectively as **a suffocating and chaotic mob** or **an undulating wave of youthful energy,** depending on the author's opinion. In short, objective description shows us *what it is,* while subjective description also tells us *what to think about it.*

Whether primarily objective or subjective, the effectiveness of any description is measured by the *visual quality* of its language.

USING OBJECTIVE DESCRIPTION TO INFORM

Objective description filters out—as much as is appropriate—personal impressions and focuses on observable details. It provides factual information about something for someone who will use it, buy it, or assemble it or who needs to know more about it for some good reason. Objective description records exactly what is seen from the writer's vantage point. If your CD player has been stolen, the police will want a description that includes the brand name, serial number, model, color, size, shape, and identifying marks or scratches. For this audience, a subjective description (that the item was a handsome addition to your car, that its sound quality was superb, that it made driving a pleasure) would be useless.

AN OBJECTIVE DESCRIPTION

[1]The 2-acre building lot for my proposed log cabin sits on the northern shore of Moosehead Lake, roughly 1,000 feet east of the Seboomook Point camping area. [2]The site is marked by a granite ledge, 30 feet long and 15 feet high. [3]The ledge faces due south and slopes gradually east. [4]A rock shoal along the westerly frontage extends about 30 feet from the shoreline. [5]On the easterly end of the frontage is a landing area on a small gravel beach immediately to the right of the ledge. [6]Lot boundaries are marked by yellow stakes a few feet from the shoreline. [7]Lot numbers are carved on yellow-marked trees adjacent to the yellow stakes.

This paragraph, written to help a soil engineer locate the property by boat, follows a spatial order, moving from a whole to its parts—the same order in which we would actually view the property. Instead of a standard topic statement, the paragraph begins with a simple description that gives us a definite sense of what to expect.

Because the goal is referential, only factual information appears: a brief but specific catalog of the lot's major features. Other situations might call for more specifics. For instance, the soil engineer's evaluation of the Moosehead site, written for officials who approve building permits, might look like this:

Hand-dug test holes revealed a well-draining granular material with a depth of at least 48 inches to bedrock.

The quantity of detail in a description is keyed to the writer's purpose and the audience's needs.

Note   *Pure objectivity is humanly impossible. Each writer has a unique perspective on the facts and their meaning, and each writer chooses what to put in and what to leave out.*

USING SUBJECTIVE DESCRIPTION TO MAKE A POINT

No useful description can be strictly subjective; to get the picture, readers need observable details. Subjective description colors objective details with personal impressions and metaphors. It usually strives to draw readers into the writer's view of the world, often by creating a mood or sharing a feeling, as shown in the italicized expressions in the following paragraph.

A SUBJECTIVE DESCRIPTION

GRANDMA

Orienting sentences (1–2) set the scene

The portrait, from toes to halo (3–13)

[1]Disturbing the *bleak* stillness of the room, she heaves her *ample body* from the sunken settee. [2]She releases a heavy grunt. [3]Misshapen toes protrude from the holes of sagging gray socks that once hugged her drooping calves. [4]Her form casts an *eerie shadow* as she *shuffles* across the dirty mismatched-tile floor, her *generous buttocks* rising and falling in a *wavelike motion*. [5]Pouches on either side of a belly that hangs below her waist *dance with each billow*. [6]Her bosom appears ready to rupture the stitches of her faded lavender frock. [7]*Mercifully,* the wide v-shaped neckline allows her *fleshy* neck to recline freely upon hunched shoulders—shoulders that are the *flabby bases of even meatier limbs*. [8]"Hello?" she answers the *screaming telephone* resting on the teetering old table. [9]Multiple chins form as her thick chapped lips erupt into an almost toothless grin. [10]Her nostrils flare as she *snorts* into the receiver. [11]Brown cheeks *darkened by age* form bubbles as she talks. [12]*Sagging bags under rheumy eyes lighten as mellow laughter booms* from deep within. [13]Thick earlobes peer from behind *kinky silver-gray tresses that form a halo around her worn, weary demeanor.*

Topic statement

[14]And she is beautiful.

—*Patricia Williams*

Williams blends objective and subjective description (in italics) to help us visualize the person a camera might record as well as the person beneath the mere physical details. The writer's impressions give us a genuine feel for her grandmother as well as a different way of appreciating old age.

Beyond creating a mood or sharing a feeling, description can serve practical purposes. The following selection conveys personal impressions to make a persuasive point.

SUBJECTIVE DESCRIPTION IN PERSUASIVE WRITING

Close your eyes for a moment, and picture a professional baseball game. You probably see something like this: a hot summer afternoon complete with sizzling bats, fans clad in the reds and yellows and pastels of summer, and short-sleeved vendors yelling "ICE CREAM HEEERE!" If you recall some recent World Series, though, you might envision a scene more like this: a c-c-cold starlit night highlighted by players in Thinsulate gloves and turtlenecks, fans in ski hats instead of baseball caps, and vendors hurriedly hawking coffee. This "football-like" image suggests that baseball season is just plain too long!

—*Mike Cabral*

Similarly, a colorful description of your messy dorm (as on pages 327–328) or apartment might encourage roommates to clean up their act. Or a nauseating catalog of greasy food served in the college dining hall might prompt school officials to improve the menu. Subjective writing can move readers to see things your way.

USING DESCRIPTION

- **In other courses:** Whether you are describing a lab experiment, a field trip, or a fire hazard in the dorm, you would focus on the observable details, not on your feelings. What specific types of objective description have you written in other courses?

- **In the workplace:** Your descriptions might inform customers about a new product or service. Banks require applicants for loans to describe the property or venture. Architects and engineers would describe their proposed building on paper before construction begins. Medical professionals write detailed records of a patient's condition and treatment. Whenever readers need to visualize the item itself, objective description is essential. What specific types of objective description do you expect to write in your career?

- **In the community:** You might describe the problems with discipline or drugs or violence or overcrowding at the local junior high in an attempt to increase community awareness.

Can you think of other situations in which objective description could make a difference?

GUIDELINES for Description

- *Take a long, hard look at your subject, purpose, and audience.* Precise description begins with careful observation. Your subject, your intention, and what you know of your readers' needs determine the angle you might take and the type and amount of detail to include.

- *Always begin with some type of orienting statement.* Objective descriptions rarely call for a standard topic or thesis statement. Any description, however, should begin by telling readers what to look for.

- *Choose descriptive details to suit your purpose and the readers' needs.* Use objective details to provide a picture of something exactly as a camera would record it. Use subjective details to convey your impressions—to give us a new way of seeing or appreciating something, as in "A Special Place" (page 174).

- *For subjective description, focus on a dominant impression.* What specific feeling or sensation about your subject do you want readers to experience? Do you want your picture to be scary, ugly, humorous, relaxed? The particular impression you decide on will help you select what to include in your description and what to leave out.

- *For objective description, focus on the physical characteristics.* Study your subject. Get your hands on it if you can; weigh it, measure it, take it apart.

(continues)

■ *Select details that are concrete and specific enough to convey an unmistakable picture.* Most often description works best at the lowest levels of abstraction and generality.

VAGUE	EXACT
at high speed	80 miles an hour
a tiny office	an 8-by-12-foot office
some workers	the accounting staff

■ *Use plenty of sensory details.* In describing your favorite beach, for example, allow readers to *see* "gulls cracking crabs on the rocks," *hear* "the slap-swoosh of the surf," *smell* "the stench of suntan lotion and greasy french fries," *feel* "the hard-packed, abrasive sand." Let readers touch and taste. Rely on *action verbs* to convey the energy of movement, to show how the erosion fences "whistle and ripple and clack."

■ *Arrange details in a clear sequence.* Descriptions generally follow a spatial or general-to-specific order—whichever parallels the angle of vision readers would have if they were viewing the item.

DESCRIPTION AS A PRIMARY ESSAY STRATEGY

In this next essay, a returning student who continues to work full time to support his family blends subjective and objective description to paint a sobering portrait of a factory worker's existence. As you read, think about some similar situation you might have experienced or witnessed.

SWING SHIFT

Have you ever worked in a factory? Have you ever worked swing shift? Can you stand to function like a machine in 95-degree heat or more? Let alone stand it—can you work in it for eight hours of endless repetition and mindless labor? I did, for more than eight years.

The Acme Tire and Rubber Company, about 5 miles east of our campus, resembles a prison. (Look for a massive and forbidding three-story building occupying two city blocks on Orchard Street.) The plant was built 50 years ago, and its windows, coated by the soot and grit of a half-century, admit no light, no hope of seeing in or out. Add to this dismal picture the drab red bricks and the stench of burned rubber. This is what I faced five nights a week at 10:00 p.m. when I reported for work.

A worker's life inside the plant is arranged so as not to tax the mind. At exactly 10:00 p.m. a loud bell rings. Get to work. The bell has to be loud in order to be heard over the roar of machinery and hissing steam escaping from the high-pressure lines. In time you don't even notice the noise. It took me about two weeks. At midnight the bell rings again: a 10-minute break. At 2:00 a.m. it rings again: lunch, 20 minutes. Two hours later, it rings for the last break of the night. At 6:00 a.m. the final bell announces that the long night is over; it's time to go home.

My dreary job was stocking tires. (I say "was" because I quit the job last year.) I had to load push trucks, the kind you see in railroad depots. I picked the tires up from the curing presses. A curing press is an 8-foot-high by 6-foot-wide by 6-foot-deep pressure cooker. There are eighteen curing presses all in a row, and the temperature around them is over 100 degrees. Clouds of steam hang just below the 20-foot ceiling. By the time I had worked for 10 minutes, my clothes were drenched with sweat and reeked with the acrid stench of steamed rubber. Once the truck was full, I'd push it to the shipping department on the other side of the plant. It's quiet there; they ship only during the day. And it's cooler. I'd feel chilled even though the temperature was around 75 degrees. Here I would leave the full truck, look for an empty one, push it back, and start again.

It was the same routine every night: endless truckloads of tires, five nights a week, week after week. Nothing ever changed except the workers; they got older and worn out.

I wasn't surprised to hear that a worker had hanged himself there a few weeks ago. He was a friend of mine. Another friend told me that the work went on anyway. The police said to leave the body hanging until the medical examiner could clear it—like meat hanging on a hook. Someone put a blanket around the hanging body. They had to move around it. The work went on.

—*Glenn Silverberg*

Glenn Silverberg enables readers to *visualize* by structuring his description as follows: an introduction that confronts readers directly with a series of questions, an overall description of the plant, a description of a typical night shift, the specific job, a brief but forceful overview of the drudgery, and a horrifying conclusion that reinforces the themes of dehumanization and hopelessness.

Can you identify five striking subjective details in the essay? Five objective ones?

CASE STUDY

READING AND RESPONDING

In this case study, student writer Ellen Cayer relies primarily on description in her response to the following professional essay.

ESSAY FOR ANALYSIS AND RESPONSE

The widely published author of this next selection, born to Chinese immigrants, describes challenges faced by immigrants in their efforts to adapt to the realities of life in their new country: the United States. As you read, think about problems you may have encountered in trying to adapt to a new situation.

COMING INTO THE COUNTRY

In the Old World, there was one way of life, or 2, maybe 10. Here there are dozens, hundreds, all jammed in together, cheek by jowl, especially in the dizzying cities. Everywhere has a somewhere else just around the corner. We newish Americans leap-frog from world to world, reinventing ourselves en route. We perform our college selves, our waitress selves, our dot-com selves, our parent selves, our downtown selves, our Muslim, Greek, Hindi, South African selves. Even into the second or third generation, we speak different languages—more languages, often, than we know we know. We sport different names. I am Gish, Geesh, Jen, Lillian, Lil, Bilien, Ms. Jen, Miss Ren, Mrs. O'Connor. Or maybe we insist on one name. The filmmaker Mira Nair, for example, will be called *NICH-ear*, please; she is not a depilatory product.

Of course, there are places where she does not have to insist, and places that don't get the joke, that need—that get—other jokes. It's a kind of high, switching spiels, eating Ethiopian, French, Thai, getting around. And the inventing! The moments of grand inspiration: *I think I will call myself Houdini.* Who could give up even the quotidian luxury of choosing, that small swell of power: to walk or to drive? The soup or the salad? The green or the blue? We bubble with pleasure. *It's me. I'm taking the plane. I'll take the sofa, the chair, the whole shebang—why not?*

Why not, indeed? A most American question, a question that comes *to* dominate our most private self-talk. In therapy-speak, we Americans like to *give ourselves permission.* To do what? To take care of ourselves, to express ourselves, to listen to ourselves. We tune out the loudspeaker of duty, tune in to the whisper of desire. This is faint at first, but soon proves easily audible; indeed, irresistible. *Why not go to town? Why not move away? Why not marry out? Why not? Why not? Why not?*

To come to America is to be greatly disoriented for many a day. The smell of the air is wrong, the taste of the water, the strength of the sun, the rate the trees grow. The rituals are strange—the spring setting out of mulch, the summer setting out of barbecues. How willingly the men heat themselves with burgers! Nobody eats the wildlife, certainly not the bugs or leaves. And beware, beware the rules about smoking. Your skin feels tight, your body fat or thin, your children stranger than they were already. Your sensations are exhausting.

Yet one day a moment comes—often, strangely, abroad—when we find ourselves missing things. Our choice of restaurants, perhaps, or our cheap gas and good roads; or, more tellingly, our rights. To be without freedom of movement, to be without freedom of speech—these things pain everyone. But to be without *our* freedom of movement, without *our* freedom of speech is an American affliction; and in this, as in many facets of American life, possession matters. The moment we feel certain rights to be inalienable, when we feel them to be ours as our lungs are ours, so that their loss is an excision and a death, we have become American.

It's not always a happy feeling. For the more at home we become with our freedom, the more we become aware of its limits. There's much true opportunity in the land of opportunity, but between freedom in theory and freedom in practice gapes a grand canyon. As often as not, what we feel is the burn of injustice. A rise of anger, perhaps followed by a quick check on our impulse to act rashly; perhaps followed by a decision to act courageously. *We gather here today to make known our grievance. For is this not America?*

We wonder who we are—what does it mean to be Irish-American, Cuban-American, Armenian-American?—and are amazed to discover that others wonder, too. Indeed, nothing seems more typically American than to obsess about identity. Can so many people truly be so greatly confused? We feel very much a part of the contemporary gestalt.

Yet two or three generations later, we still may not be insiders Recently, I heard about a basketball game starring a boy from the Cochiti pueblo in Santa Fe. The kids on his team, a friend reported, had one water bottle, which they passed around, whereas the kids on the other team each had his own. This was a heartening story, signaling the survival of a communal culture against the pressures of individualism. But did the Cochiti boy notice the other team? I couldn't help wondering. Did he feel the glass pane between himself and the mainstream, so familiar, so tangible, so bittersweet? *Nobody has been here longer than we; how come our ways need protecting?* Later a member of the pueblo told me that the Cochiti have started a language-immerison program for the younger generation, and that it has been a success. They are saving their language from extinction.

Hooray! The rest of us cheer. How awed we feel in the presence of tradition, of authenticity. How avidly we will surf to such sites, some of us, and what we will pay to do so! We will pay for bits of the Southwest the way we will pay handsomely, in this generation or the next, for a home. Whatever that looks like; we find ourselves longing for some combination of Martha Stewart and what we can imagine, say, of our family seat in Brazil. At any rate, we can say this much: the home of our dreams is a safe place, a still place. A communal place, to which we contribute; to which we have real ties; a place that feels more stable, perhaps, than ourselves. How American this is—to long, at day's end, for a place where we belong more, invent less; for a heartland with more heart.

—*Gish Jen*

Questions About the Reading

Refer to the general questions on page 154 as well as these specific questions.

CONTENT

- *Instead of stating a thesis directly, this author describes people, places, and circumstances through a series of sketches that create a dominant impression. What is the implied thesis in this description? State it in your own words.*

- *What is the dominant impression created by this description?*

(continues)

■ *List five objective and five subjective details in the essay.*

■ *What does the author want her audience to be thinking or feeling after reading this piece?*

ORGANIZATION

■ *How does the writer order her details in the first paragraph?*

■ *Trace the movement of the description.*

■ *Is this selection of sketches unified? Explain.*

■ *What major devices lend coherence to this selection? Give examples of each.*

■ *Does the conclusion create a sense of completeness? Does it relate to the introduction? Explain how it reinforces the implied thesis.*

STYLE

■ *What notable style features can you identify? Explain and give examples.*

■ *What is the writer's attitude toward what she witnessed? How do we know? What are the signals?*

■ *Describe the tone that emerges from this essay. What kind of person does the author seem to be? How do you know?*

RESPONDING TO READING

Afer reading the selection by Gish Jen, Ellen Cayer decided to share her own impressions about a special—and welcoming—place fondly remembered from her childhood. To analyze Gish Jen's technique, and respond to that essay, Cayer combined the guidelines on page 169 with the previous questions about that reading.

Working toward the final draft shown here, Cayer consulted the description checklist (page 176) and the revision checklist (pages 62–63).

A SPECIAL PLACE

The opening sets the scene

Each of our minds has a special section where the well-preserved files of childhood lie gathering dust. It is to these special memories that we can sometimes escape the drudgery and pressures of our grown-up lives. We sneak back into the carefree days, when our biggest problems were learning how to ride a bike, sharing a bedroom with a brother or sister, and fearing braces. When life starts closing in, I love to drift from reality and responsibility, finding myself in pigtails and freckles, sitting alone in a battered treehouse, watching lazy summer days skip by.

Orienting statement creates a dominant impression

² Although dilapidated, our treehouse was the perfect haven. Built out of discarded lumber from a chicken house, it sat more than eight feet above the swampy everglades of an abandoned cow pasture. The steps leading up the smooth trunk were made of various-sized fence posts nailed haphazardly to the bark. Hanging next to the steps was a long, thick rope, its hairy back bleached by the sun, used for lifting supplies and buckets of ammunition. The two small rooms in the treehouse had slanted floors, making it impossible to

Paragraphs 2 and 3 provide objective details

play a decent game of jacks or marbles. The main room was large enough to hold three of us, one bucket of ammunition, and a bag of peanut-butter sandwiches. About one foot above the center room was a smaller one. Extending over a shallow ditch and resting on a sagging branch, this space was used for storage, unless we had guests. Above this room was a crow's nest, or lookout, where we could climb and watch out across the corn field or up toward the barn, keeping tabs on any would-be invaders or advancing enemies.

3 The "fort" (as we called it) was a great place to stage wars. The walnut tree that held it supplied ample ammunition for overpowering opponents—providing that the battles were fought during the right season. Most major outbreaks were between my little brother, who would dodge in and out among the ditch banks and wild roses, hurling handsful of dried cow chips and mud clods up at the tree, and the combined forces of one or two of my younger sisters and me, who fought back, flinging thousands of moldy walnuts. Nobody ever won—but then again, nobody ever cared.

Paragraph 4 signals a shift in focus to subjective details

4 I loved the tree blazing in battle, but it was after the others had left for dinner, chores, or new adventures that I would sit alone on the splintering planks and the treehouse would become mine.

Paragraphs 5 and 6 provide mostly subjective details that reinforce the dominant impression

5 When I was alone in the treehouse, my daydreams would run free. As I stared out over the countryside, fields of corn, alfalfa, and potatoes, and pastures dotted with livestock were all magically transformed into whatever setting I desired. I could see myself on the Starship Enterprise aiding Captain Kirk on a mission in another galaxy, or standing on the Golden Gate Bridge in a thick mist, watching the last mast disappear into the fog. Sometimes I'd be a lone scout for an Oregon-bound wagon train; trapped in an Indian uprising, I'd have to shoot my way back to the train. There was no limit to who I could be or where I could go, without ever leaving the tree.

A shift from daydreaming to "thinking"

6 As I grew older, the treehouse became a great place for thinking. Closer to reality in my teen years, I often had days when I didn't feel like pretending, serious days when I'd climb the crooked steps, or shinny up the rope to the highest point in the lookout, where I would rest in the shade and think about my future. I'd worry over days to come and how I would turn out. I'd discuss with the birds how things were going to run "when I grew up." Almost always, I'd just sit for hours and watch the sun drop behind the ridge, until the quail started calling and the evening gray covered the valley. During these times, my spot became even more special.

Sensory details throughout enable readers to visualize

Ends with an emphasis on pleasant memories

7 Our treehouse is still there, clinging to the walnut tree by rusty nails and rotting twine. The rope still hangs, three feet shorter and unraveled almost to the top. The only inhabitants of the lookout are Banty chickens and occasional cats on the prowl for unsuspecting sparrows. Those of us who played in the branches and swung on the rope have outgrown such pleasures. Still, sometimes when I'm sad or nostalgic, I tramp over the crusty pasture, jump the muddy ditch, climb the walnut tree, and think about what I'll be "when I grow up."

—Ellen Cayer

> ☑ **A CHECKLIST for Description**
>
> ☐ In the absence of a thesis, does the piece provide an **orienting statement**?
> ☐ Are any **supporting details** missing or confusing for the intended audience and purpose?
> ☐ Are any details **excessive** or **needless**?
> ☐ Are details sufficiently **concrete** and **specific**?
> ☐ Does the **descriptive sequence** parallel the reader's probable angle of vision?
> ☐ Do sensory details and judgmental words allow readers to **visualize,** as needed?
> ☐ Does **objective description** focus on details any observer would recognize?
> ☐ Does **subjective description** offer a dominant impression about the observable details?
>
> (See page 169 for more on these criteria.)

APPLICATIONS

10.1   **PARAGRAPH WARM-UP: DESCRIPTION THAT INFORMS** Assume that a close friend has been missing for two days. The police have been called in. Because you know this person well, the police have asked you for a written description. Write an objective description that would help the police identify this person. To create a clear picture, stick to details any observer could recognize. If possible, include one or more unique identifying features (scar, mannerisms, and so on). Leave out personal comments, and give only objective details. Refer to the Guidelines for Description, page 169. Use the paragraph on page 167 as a model.

10.2   **PARAGRAPH WARM-UP: DESCRIPTION THAT MAKES A POINT** Assume that your college newspaper runs a weekly column titled "Memorable Characters." You have been asked to submit a brief sketch of a person you find striking in some way. Create a word portrait of this person in one paragraph. Your description should focus on a dominant impression, blending objective details and subjective commentary. Be sure to focus on personal characteristics that support your dominant impression. Develop your description according to the Guidelines for Description on page 169.

10.3   **ESSAY PRACTICE**

   a. Explore your reactions to "Swing Shift" (page 170) using the personal response question on page 155. Then respond with an essay of your own. As you reread the essay, try to recall an intolerable situation that you or someone close to you has had to confront and endure. In your essay, work to convey a clear dominant impression for your audience.

b. Explore your reactions to "Coming into the Country" using the questions on pages 173–174. Then respond with an essay of your own.

   Perhaps you or someone you know has had to abandon something comfortably familiar (a place, a lifestyle, a relationship, a culture) for something unfamiliar or alien. Or perhaps you can describe a decision that involved great promise, risk, and personal cost. As you reread the Jen essay, think of all the things you would like to say in reply, and then settle on the main thing you want to say.

c. Explore your reactions to "A Special Place" (page 174) by using the personal response questions on page 155. Then respond with an essay of your own. If you describe a special place, give a clear picture as well as your dominant impression of the place.

d. In an essay for your classmates, describe a memorable scene—something that left a deep impression. Blend objective and subjective details to convey a dominant impression. For precision and vividness, make your details specific and concrete.

e. Do you have a hero or know a villain? Describe this person in an essay for your classmates. Provide enough descriptive details for your audience to understand why you admire or despise this person. Supply at least three characteristics to support your dominant impression.

10.4   **WEB-BASED PROJECT** Describe a special place you've lived in or visited or would like to visit. Prepare two descriptions, one objective and one subjective, in which you convey a dominant impression of the place. For ideas, visit either Fodor's Online (<*http://www.fodors.com*>) or the Tourism Office Worldwide Directory (<*http://www.towd.com*>), but do not limit yourself to these sites.

   Be sure to credit each source of information and to attach copies of relevant Web pages to your descriptions.

   Be prepared to explain to the class the differences in your two versions.

For additional information and practice with the learning objectives in this chapter, go to www.mycomplab.com, Resources>Writing>Writing Purposes.

CHAPTER 11

Narration: Writing to Help Others Share an Experience

LEARNING OBJECTIVES FOR THIS CHAPTER

- Understand the role of *narration* as a writing strategy
- Differentiate narration used to explain from narration used to make a point
- Write an effective narrative essay using the chapter guidelines

Like description (Chapter 10), narration creates a word picture, telling how events occur in time. Narration relies on the showing power of descriptive details to make the story vivid, but its main goal is to help readers follow events.

What readers expect to learn from a narrative

- *What happened?*
- *Who was involved?*
- *When did it happen?*

- *Where did it happen?*
- *Why did it happen?*

Narration sometimes answers these questions as well:

- *What were your impressions of the event?*
- *How did the event make you feel?*

Narration can serve a number of roles: In a novel or other fiction, the narrative stimulates our imagination; a newspaper feature story attempts to explain or report events as objectively as possible; in essays, the narrative often makes a definite point. Our interest here is not in fiction narratives but rather in those designed to report objectively or to make a point.

USING OBJECTIVE NARRATION TO EXPLAIN

To see how narration can serve both referential and persuasive purposes, let's look first at narration that informs, reports, or explains. These narratives simply give a picture of what happened, without stating—or even implying—any particular viewpoint. Newspaper stories and courtroom testimony often provide only the bare facts. This next paragraph simply describes events without overtly inserting personal impressions—except, perhaps, at the very end.

A NARRATIVE THAT MERELY REPORTS

The climactic scene (1)

A related detail (2)

Background (3–9)

Conclusion (10–11)

[1]Two [suspects] hobbled into Federal Court in Brooklyn on crutches yesterday, each with a leg missing and each charged with smuggling cocaine and marijuana stored in the hollowed-out parts of their confiscated artificial limbs. [2]A third suspect, a... woman, was also accused of taking part in the smuggling of $1 million worth of cocaine from Bogota to Kennedy International Airport. [3]Acting on confidential information, customs agents took the three into custody Monday night. [4]The agents took one of the suspects... to St. Vincent's Hospital in Manhattan, where physicians removed his plastic leg. [5]Inside, they said, they found one kilo (2.2 pounds) of cocaine wrapped in plastic bags. [6]The suspect told them he had lost his leg during a guerrilla uprising in Colombia two years ago. [7]Agents said they found six ounces of marijuana in the artificial right limb worn by... another suspect. [8]The woman... was allegedly found to be wearing three girdles, each concealing quantities of plastic-wrapped cocaine totaling one kilo. [9]Agents reported that each suspect had more than $400 and return tickets to Bogota. [10]United States Magistrate Vincent A. Catoggio held each in $100,000 bail. [11]Expressing concern over the missing artificial limbs, which had been described as damaged, he directed that customs agents return them in good condition.

—*New York Times*

This paragraph implies no main point. The writer simply reports the details of the bizarre smuggling strategy.

Note, however, that the writer juggles the sequence of events to attract our interest. The first two sentences place us at the story's climax. Then the background details follow strict chronological order so that we can keep track of events leading to the courtroom scene. Consistent use of past tense and third-person point of view helps us follow the story. Finally, the tongue-in-cheek observation in sentence 11 lends a slightly comical tone to the events.

USING SUBJECTIVE NARRATION TO MAKE A POINT

Narration can be an excellent strategy for advancing a definite viewpoint or thesis because a well-told story is easy to remember. When you recount last night's date, your purpose is usually to suggest a particular viewpoint: that some people can be fickle, say, or that first dates can be disastrous. The following brief story shares a special moment in the author's favorite activity—flying a small plane.

A NARRATIVE THAT MAKES A POINT

Orienting sentence

Rolling down Runway Alpha, I feel so intensely alone that I become part human, part machine—everything working together. My mind's eye is locked on the runway's center line while my eyes flash from windshield to instruments, reading, calculating, missing nothing. Meanwhile, feet and hands make delicate adjustments on the pedals and control yoke, gently... gently. Relaxed, yet poised, I concentrate so intensely that I and the plane are one. Our airspeed increases. The plane vibrates. We reach the point where the battle begins. Time stops as *83 Bigdog* and I wage silent war with gravity. It pulls at us, insisting that we are bound to the earth, slaves of its laws, this vibrating second seeming like an eternity. But in the end we win. The wheels leave the ground and we climb, that empty-stomach feeling one gets in an elevator intensified threefold. As the ground recedes, we glide above the stress of life down below. *This burst of sensations, these physical and emotional responses to each takeoff, draw me back to the cockpit again and again.*

Main point

—Phoebe Brown

Notice how the entire event is filtered through the author's impressions. The subjective details make the author's sensations real and vivid to readers and support her point about the thrill of taking off. Her sensory descriptions create a tone of excitement, placing the reader at the center of the action. In this way, telling a story can be an effective way of *showing*.

Using present tense and first-person point of view, the author tells of her experience. An alternative point of view for narration is third person (telling of someone else's experience).

Narratives can move readers to change attitudes or take action. For instance, you might tell about a boating accident to elicit voter support for tougher boating laws. You might recount the details of a conflict among employees to persuade your boss to institute a stress management program. By telling the story, you can help readers see things your way.

SUBJECTIVE NARRATION IN PERSUASIVE WRITING

> I entered community college at 17 and began taking classes with some 25- and 30-year-old students. Such an age difference made me feel much luckier than these older people. What were they doing in a freshman class, anyway? Compared to them, I had unlimited time to succeed—or so I thought. Soon after my eighteenth birthday, the horrid piece of lung tissue I coughed into the sink gave a whole new meaning to my notion of "youth." Five years of inhaling hot smoke, carbon monoxide, nicotine, and tobacco pesticides finally had produced enough coughing and sickness to terrify me. "Oh, my God, I'm going to die young; I'm going to die before all those 30-year-olds." For years, I had heard my mother tell me that I was committing suicide on the installment plan. Now I seemed to be running out of installments.
>
> —Chris Adey

By letting the story make the point, Adey's narrative seems more persuasive than the usual "Smoking is bad for you" sermon.

The main point in a narrative might be expressed as a topic or thesis statement at the beginning or end of the story. Or as in the first and third previous narratives, the main point might not be stated at all but merely implied by the story. But even when its point is saved for last or implied, the story often opens with some statement that orients readers to the events.

GUIDELINES for Narration

- *Decide on your tone.* Narrative tells a story, and tone provides the emotional component of that story. Narrative reports usually have a neutral, detached tone, whereas narratives designed to make a point or persuade usually convey a definite attitude or impression: playful, sarcastic, respectful, angry, and so on. For more on tone, see pages 37 and 138.

- *Set the scene immediately.* Place readers right at the center of the action. If you open with some sort of background explanation (as in "Back at the Ranch," page 185), keep it short. Be clear about when and where the event occurred and about who was involved.

- *Convey your main point, whether stated or implied, through the narrative details.* A narrative that simply reports has no main point. But if your narrative does make a point, consider delaying that point until the end; use an earlier orienting statement to let us know what's going on.

- *Choose details to serve specifically your purpose and the readers' needs.* Focus on the important details, but don't leave out lesser details that hold the story together. Decide when to describe events objectively and when to filter events through your own impressions.

(continues)

- *Choose details that are concrete and specific enough to show clearly what happened.* Use plenty of visual details—the details of real life. Try to show people "doing," and let us hear them talking.

- *Order details in a clear sequence.* Chronological ordering often works best in a narrative because it describes events as they occurred. But for special emphasis, you might use a *flashback* or a *flashforward* to present certain events out of sequence.

- *Control your tenses.* To keep readers on track, indicate a clear time frame for each event: present, past, past perfect ("had been"), or even future tense (as in paragraph 5, page 189. If you move from one time frame to another, be sure to keep the tense consistent within each frame (as in "The Old Guy," page 188. To create a sense of immediacy, use the present tense.

- *Use transitions to mark time and sequence.* (Review pages 105–107.)

- *Keep the point of view straight.* Decide whether you are describing an event from the perspective of a participant (first-person point of view) or an observer (third person). Narratives designed to make a point (as in "Back at the Ranch," page 185) often blend both perspectives. If you shift from one perspective to another, be sure to maintain a consistent point of view for each perspective.

- *Explore the larger meaning of the events.* Help readers process the story; tell us what it all means and what we should remember about it.

USING NARRATIVE REPORTS

BEYOND THE WRITING CLASSROOM

- **In other courses**: You might report on experiments or investigations in chemistry, biology, or psychology. Or you might retrace the events leading up to the Russian Revolution or the 1929 stock market crash. What specific types of narrative reports have you written in other courses?

- **On the job**: You might report on the events that led up to an accident on the assembly line or provide daily accounts of your crew's progress on a construction project. Whenever readers need to understand what happened, narrative reporting is essential. What specific types of narrative reports might you write in your career?

- **In the community**: As a witness to an accident, a crime, or some other incident, you might report what took place.

In what other situations might a narrative report make a difference?

NARRATION AS A PRIMARY ESSAY STRATEGY

The most powerful narratives are often those that combine objective and subjective details to reveal their point. In the following essay, a noted African American writer explores how a black man can induce paranoia among people who react to a racial stereotype. As you read, think about the hasty assumptions you may have made on the basis of a person's appearance.

BLACK MEN AND PUBLIC SPACE

My first victim was a woman—white, well dressed, probably in her early twenties. I came upon her late one evening on a deserted street in Hyde Park, a relatively affluent neighborhood in an otherwise mean, impoverished section of Chicago. As I swung onto the avenue behind her, there seemed to be a discreet, uninflammatory distance between us. Not so. She cast back a worried glance. To her, the youngish black man—a broad six feet two inches with a beard and billowing hair, both hands shoved into the pockets of a bulky military jacket—seemed menacingly close. After a few more quick glimpses, she picked up her pace and was soon running in earnest. Within seconds she disappeared into a cross street.

That was more than a decade ago. I was twenty-two years old, a graduate student newly arrived at the University of Chicago. It was in the echo of that terrified woman's footfalls that I first began to know the unwieldy inheritance I'd come into—the ability to alter public space in ugly ways. It was clear that she thought herself the quarry of a mugger, a rapist, or worse. Suffering from a bout of insomnia, however, I was stalking sleep, not defenseless wayfarers. As a softy who is scarcely able to take a knife to a raw chicken—let alone hold one to a person's throat—I was surprised, embarrassed, and dismayed all at once. Her flight made me feel like an accomplice in tyranny. It also made it clear that I was indistinguishable from the muggers who occasionally seeped into the area from the surrounding ghetto. That first encounter, and those that followed, signified that a vast, unnerving gulf lay between nighttime pedestrians—particularly women—and me. And I soon gathered that being perceived as dangerous is a hazard in itself. I only needed to turn a corner into a dicey situation, or crowd some frightened, armed person in a foyer somewhere, or make an errant move after being pulled over by a policeman. Where fear and weapons meet—and they often do in urban America—there is always the possibility of death.

In that first year, my first away from my hometown, I was to become thoroughly familiar with the language of fear. At dark, shadowy intersections, I could cross in front of a car stopped at a traffic light and elicit the thunk, thunk, thunk, thunk of the driver—black, white, male, or female—hammering down the door locks. On less traveled streets after dark, I grew accustomed to but never comfortable with people crossing to the other side of the street rather than pass me. Then there were the standard unpleasantries with policemen, doormen, bouncers, cabdrivers, and others whose business it is to screen out troublesome individuals before there is any nastiness.

I moved to New York nearly two years ago and I have remained an avid night walker. In central Manhattan, the near-constant crowd cover minimizes tense one-on-one street encounters. Elsewhere—in SoHo, for example, where sidewalks are narrow and tightly spaced buildings shut out the sky—things can get very taut indeed.

After dark, on the warrenlike streets of Brooklyn where I live, I often see women who fear the worst from me. They seem to have set their faces on neutral, and with their purse straps strung across their chests bandolier-style, they forge ahead as though bracing themselves against being tackled. I under-stand, of course, that the danger they perceive is not a hallucination. Women are particularly vulnerable to street violence, and young black males are dras-tically overrepresented among the perpetrators of that violence. Yet these truths are no solace against the kind of alienation that comes of being ever the suspect, a fearsome entity with whom pedestrians avoid making eye contact.

It is not altogether clear to me how I reached the ripe old age of twenty-two without being conscious of the lethality nighttime pedestrians attributed to me. Perhaps it was because in Chester, Pennsylvania, the small, angry industrial town where I came of age in the 1960s, I was scarcely noticeable against a backdrop of gang warfare, street knifings, and murders. I grew up one of the good boys, had perhaps a half-dozen fistfights. In retrospect, my shyness of combat has clear sources.

As a boy, I saw countless tough guys locked away; I have since buried several, too. They were babies, really—a teenage cousin, a brother of twenty-two, a childhood friend in his mid-twenties—all gone down in episodes of bravado played out in the streets. I came to doubt the virtues of intimidation early on. I chose, perhaps unconsciously, to remain a shadow—timid, but a survivor.

The fearsomeness mistakenly attributed to me in public places often has a perilous flavor. The most frightening of these confusions occurred in the late 1970s and early 1980s, when I worked as a journalist in Chicago. One day, rushing into the office of a magazine I was writing for with a deadline story in hand, I was mistaken for a burglar. The office manager called security and, with an ad hoc posse, pursued me through the labyrinthine halls, nearly to my editor's door. I had no way of proving who I was. I could only move briskly toward the company of someone who knew me.

Another time I was on assignment for a local paper and killing time before an interview. I entered a jewelry store on the city's affluent Near North Side. The proprietor excused herself and returned with an enormous red Doberman pinscher straining at the end of a leash. She stood, the dog extended toward me, silent to my questions, her eyes bulging nearly out of her head. I took a cursory look around, nodded, and bade her good night.

Relatively speaking, however, I never fared as badly as another black male journalist. He went to nearby Waukegan, Illinois, a couple of summers ago to work on a story about a murderer who was born there. Mistaking the reporter for the killer, police officers hauled him from his car at gunpoint and but for his press credentials would probably have tried to book him. Such episodes are not uncommon. Black men trade tales like this all the time.

Over the years, I learned to smother the rage I felt at so often being taken for a criminal. Not to do so would surely have led to madness. I now take pre-cautions to make myself less threatening. I move about with care, particularly late in the evening. I give a wide berth to nervous people on subway platforms during the wee hours, particularly when I have exchanged business clothes for jeans. If I happen to be entering a building behind some people who appear skittish, I may walk by, letting them clear the lobby before I return, so as not to seem to be following them. I have been calm and extremely congenial on those rare occasions when I've been pulled over by the police.

And on late-evening constitutionals I employ what has proved to be an excellent tension-reducing measure: I whistle melodies from Beethoven and Vivaldi and the more popular classical composers. Even steely New Yorkers bunching toward nighttime destinations seem to relax, and occasionally they even join in the tune. Virtually everybody seems to sense that a mugger wouldn't be warbling bright, sunny selections from Vivaldi's Four Seasons. It is my equivalent of the cowbell that hikers wear when they know they are in bear country.

—*Brent Staples*

Staples analyzes the links between events to argue that a racial stereotype has a double effect: in narrowing the perceptions of those who impose the stereotype and in narrowing the choices of those who endure the stereotype. To convey an unemotional and almost clinical tone, Staples carefully allows his choice of language and details to understate his feelings of humiliation and rage.

Can you identify five memorable objective details in Staples's narrative? Five subjective ones?

CASE STUDY

READING AND RESPONDING

In this case study, student writer Al Andrade relies primarily on narration in his response to the following professional essay.

ESSAY FOR ANALYSIS AND RESPONSE

In his narrative, "Back at the Ranch," journalist Jay Allison recalls how a dreadful moment during adolescence changed his perception of "manhood." As you read, try to think about an event in your own life that changed your attitude.

BACK AT THE RANCH

A young boy molts. Tender skin falls off, or gets scraped off, and is replaced by a tougher, more permanent crust. The transition happens in moments, in events. All of a sudden, something is gone and something else is in its place. I made a change like that standing in the back of a pickup truck when I was 15.

It was 1967 and I had a summer job at a camp in Wyoming. It was beautiful there, high-pasture country with a postcard view of the Tetons. As an apprentice counselor I straddled the worlds of boys and men, breathing the high air, watching over kids, hanging out with cowboys. The cowboys wrangled the horses for the camp and were mostly an itinerant group, living in summer cabins below the barn, and they tolerated my loitering down there.

I hitched up my jeans just like them, braided my lasso like them, smoked and cursed and slouched like them.

On the day it happened, I was standing with a group of cowboys by the ranch office. We heard the sound of a big engine coming in the long driveway, and after a while a red Corvette Sting Ray convertible, of all things, motored up in front of us. Conversation stopped. In the driver's seat was a hippie. His hair fell straight down his back and a bandanna was tied around his head. His style may have been standard for somewhere, but not for Jackson, Wyo.

The guy was decked out with beads and earrings, and dressed in fantastic colors, and next to him his girlfriend, just as exotic, with perfect blond hair, looked up at us over little square glasses with a distracted, angelic expression. All in a red Corvette.

I was fascinated, mesmerized. I looked around me with a big grin and realized that I was alone in this feeling. The cowboys all had hard stares, cold eyes. I adjusted, a traitor to myself, and blanked out my expression in kind.

The hippie opened up a big smile, and said: "I went to camp here when I was a kid... came by to say hi. Is Weenie around?"

In that moment, Weenie, the owner of the place, having heard the throb of the engine, appeared in the ranch office door and walked toward us with a bowlegged stride, his big belt buckle coming first. He walked right up to the driver and looked down on him.

"Get out." Weenie didn't say hi. "Get out of here now."

"What? Wait a minute. I came to say hi. I went to camp here. I just came to say hi."

"Get the hell off this ranch. Now." And staring at the hippie, Weenie kicked some dust up on the side of the Corvette.

"What's wrong with you, man?"

"You're what's wrong with me, son."

I noticed the cowboys were nodding. I nodded. Weenie's right. The guy should leave. He doesn't belong here.

"But you sent me a Christmas card!" By this time, the hippie had choked up a little. "I don't believe it. You sent me a goddamn Christmas card!"

The group of us closed in a little around the car. We-don't-like-that-kind-of-talk-from-a-hippie was the feeling I was getting. Thumbs came out of belt-loops. Jaws began to work.

"Looks like the little girlie's cryin'," said one of the cowboys, a tough one named Hondu. He spoke with his lips turned down on one side as if he was mouthing a cigarette. "Maybe so," said another, with mock consideration.

The notion rested in the air peacefully for a moment, then, in a sudden whipping motion, Hondu's jackknife was out, open and raised. With his other hand, he reached down and grabbed a fat bunch of the hippie's hair and pulled it toward him. Smiling grimly, he hacked it off and held it up for us to see.

During this, I looked down at the hippie's face, which was lifted up and sideways in such a way that he was looking right at me. Involuntarily, my head titled just like his and we froze like that for a second.

"There now, that's better, ain't it?" asked Hondu.

The hippie, stunned, turned to his girlfriend, whose eyes and mouth had been wide open as long as he had been sitting there. Then he turned back to us, his face contorted, helpless. And then he went wild. He threw open his door and tried to jump up from the seat, but forgot that his seat belt was fastened and it held him in place. He struggled against it, screaming, swinging his arms like a bar fighter trying to shrug off his buddies restraining him. It was funny. Like a cartoon.

I looked around. We were all laughing. Our group closed up a little more, and came toward the car. The air bristled. He was the one who started the trouble. Well, he would get what he was looking for, all right.

The hippie stopped struggling, threw the Vette into gear, and fishtailed in the dust. We all jumped out of the way, but the open door of the car bumped into Weenie's favorite dog, a Rhodesian Ridgeback, an inside-out-looking animal that gave a wild yelp and ran straight into a willow thicket. We could hear his yips over the sound of the big engine as the hippie gunned it and took off.

That settled it. The hippie hit the dog.

Without hesitation, we jumped into one of the trucks. Rifles were drawn from the rack in the cab. Other weapons were thrown up into the bed of the pickup. I was standing there and caught one.

We took off, and because the rough road slowed down the Corvette, we were gaining. I was filled with a terrible, frightening righteousness. I was holding a rifle, chasing a man and a woman with a rifle in my hand. I looked around at my partners in the truck, and the air came out of me. We meant harm. We didn't care. I wondered who I was exactly. I needed to know. And in that moment, it happened: I switched sides and never said a word about it.

We hit the asphalt road and floored it, but we couldn't catch the Corvette. No way. The smoke from its exhaust settled around us like fog in the valley.

Still, 23 years later, I can see the two of us clearly, chosen by the same moment. Memory cuts back and forth between our faces. The wind pulls tears from the hippie's eyes; his long hair waves behind him in his fiery convertible rocketing down Route 191 under the Tetons. I with my short hair stand in the back of a pickup truck watching after him, chasing after him, following, facing the same wind.

—*Jay Allison*

Questions About the Reading

Refer to the general questions on page 154, as well as these specific questions:

PURPOSE

- *In your view, what does Allison want the audience to be thinking or feeling after reading this piece?*
- *Does the essay succeed in making a difference with readers? If so, how?*

CONTENT

- *Does this essay merely inform or does it make a point, and if so, what is the point?*
- *Can you identify any new insights or unusual perspectives?*

(continues)

ORGANIZATION

■ *What major devices lend coherence to this narrative? Give examples of each.*

STYLE

■ *Are the short sentences and paragraphs effective? Explain.*

■ *How would you characterize the tone of this piece? Explain and give examples.*

■ *What is the writer's attitude toward his subject? Toward his audience? How do we know? What are the signals?*

■ *Which images here most help us visualize?*

RESPONDING TO READING

After reading Jay Allison's "Back at the Ranch," Al Andrade decided to write about a turning point in his own awareness of his coming of age. To analyze Allison's technique and respond to that essay, Al combined the reading response guidelines on page 163 with the questions about the reading, pages 155 and 187. As he worked through various drafts, Al relied on the narration guidelines on pages 181–182, the narration checklist on pages 189–190, and the revision checklist on pages 62–63 to produce the final draft that follows.

THE OLD GUY

Alternates first- and third-person points of view throughout

Paragraph 1 sets the scene

Begins in the past tense

Uses the present tense to give background

Early paragraphs convey a largely neutral tone, merely describing events

Paragraph 2 leads into orienting statement

Returns to the past tense for main events

Events throughout follow chronological order

Paragraphs 1–4 offer a participant's perspective

Shows someone talking

Orienting statement previews the main point

Transitions throughout mark time and sequence

[1]The workout was progressing as it usually does. My father and I took turns grunting the weights up and down off our chests. Our pectorals, shoulders, and arms were shaking. Throughout the one-hour session, we encouraged and coached one another. Fortunately, weight lifting demands short breaks after each set. Without these breaks our workouts might last only two minutes. The time spent preparing for the next set (or recovering from the last one) is important, not because I'm lazy but because it gives me a chance to catch up on things with Dad. Since we don't get to see each other very often, the latest news, gossip, and philosophies get aired in the weight room.

[2]While I was changing the weight on the barbell for our next set, Dad was hanging around the exercise room. We'd been talking about the possibility of building an apartment on the lot next door. This discussion led to real estate, which led to the stock market, which led to his retirement. Lately Dad has been complaining a lot about his company's lousy retirement plan. I figured he was just a practical guy planning for more comfortable retirement. Then he looked up from behind the squat rack and said, "You know, Al, if I'm lucky, I have only twenty or twenty-five years left, and I don't want to be eating dog food when I retire." I snickered at the dog food remark. He's always overstating things for emphasis. The other part of his remark—the part about having only twenty or twenty-five years left—seemed a bit melodramatic. At first, Dad's comment rolled off me like a bead of sweat, until I began doing some personal arithmetic of my own.

[3]Our workout moved from the bench press to the chinning bar. I went first. Then I watched while Dad strained to pull himself up for the tenth repetition. "Not bad for an old guy," he said after he jumped down off the bar. I looked at

Shows someone "doing"

Paragraphs 4–5 focus on the author's impressions

These later paragraphs convey a more reflective tone

Paragraphs 5–6 offer an observer's perspective

Uses the future tense for flashforward

Uses the present tense to explore the larger meaning of these events

Paragraph 7 returns to the participant's perspective and the past tense

Ends with implied thesis (main point)

him and thought he really wasn't bad. Aside from a minor middle-aged belly, he is more powerful now than ever. He routinely dead lifts 450 pounds. And even with a bad shoulder, Dad can still bench press over 250 pounds. Not bad for an old guy is right—or a young guy, for that matter. This time, however, the reference to his age wasn't as easy for me to shrug off.

[4]No longer concentrating on the weights, I thought about aging. The thought of Dad aging didn't overly distress me. I mean, the man was healthy, strong, and sweating just a few feet away. But then I pictured myself getting old, considered what I'd be doing and saying in twenty-five years. Would I be grousing about retirement plans? Would I be working out twice as hard with the notion that I might live a little longer?

[5]Most likely I'll be doing the same things Dad is doing now. A 50-year-old family man counting the years he has left. I'll be a man too busy making a living to ever make enough money. Instead of counting up the years, I'll be counting them down: five years until my retirement, ten years until I can withdraw money from my IRA without penalty, and two years before my son's twenty-fifth birthday. The cycle will be complete. I will replace my father and a son will replace me.

[6]I understand how "life goes on" and how "we're not getting any younger." But I now worried about the inevitability of middle age. I couldn't help putting myself in the Old Guy's place—of retirement worries and declining chin-ups. Twenty-three-year-old people aren't supposed to worry about retirement, or even middle age. Brilliant careers and healthy, productive lives lie ahead for us, right? We've got everything to look forward to. We think about raising families, achieving goals, and becoming successful—not about our own mortality. But we all eventually reach a time when thoughts of our own old age and death become an everyday reality.

[7]Dad wrapped his hands around the chinning bar for his last set. This time he struggled to get six repetitions. I jabbed him and jokingly scolded, "What's the matter with you?" He turned and grinned and shook his finger at me and said, "We'll see what you can do at fifty years old." *I told him I could wait.*

—Al Andrade

✔ A CHECKLIST for Narration

☐ Does the narrative set the scene immediately with an **orienting statement**?

☐ If opening background is required, is it as **concise** as possible?

☐ In a narrative that makes a point, is that point **explicitly stated** or at least **clearly implied**?

☐ Does the **tone** convey the appropriate emotional impression?

☐ Are there **enough details** to hold the story together and to show clearly what happened?

☐ Is the piece free of **excessive details**?

(continues)

☐ Does the **sequence** of details enable readers to follow events as they occurred?

☐ For events out of sequence, are **flashbacks** or **flashforwards** provided?

☐ Do **tenses** and **transitions** indicate a clear time frame for each event?

☐ Is the **point of view** (first, second, or third person) consistent and appropriate for the narrative's intended perspective?

☐ Are the events framed in their **larger meaning**?

APPLICATIONS

✗**11.1**   **PARAGRAPH WARM-UP: NARRATION THAT INFORMS** Assume that you have recently witnessed an event or accident in which someone has been accused of an offense. Because you are an objective witness, the authorities have asked you to write a short report telling them exactly what you saw. Your report will be used as evidence. Tell what happened without injecting personal impressions or interpretations. Refer to the Guidelines for Narration on pages 181–182.

11.2   **PARAGRAPH WARM-UP: NARRATION THAT MAKES A POINT** Tell about a recent experience or incident you witnessed that made a strong impression on you. Write for your classmates, and be sure to include the facts of the incident as well as your emotional reaction to it. In other words, give your readers enough details so that they will understand and, ideally, share your reaction. Use Chris Adey's paragraph (page 181) as a model, letting the details of the story imply your main point. Refer to the Guidelines for Narration.

11.3   **ESSAY PRACTICE**

    a. Explore your reactions to "Black Men and Public Space" by using the questions on page 155 and writing a narrative essay in response. Try to recall a situation in which you or someone close to you was the object of someone's hostility or rejection—say, because of resentment, fear, anger, or scorn. Describe the events and your reactions in enough detail for readers to visualize what happened and what resulted. Without preaching or moralizing, try to explain your view of this experience's larger meaning.

    b. "Back at the Ranch" proves that an essay about "what I did last summer" can be much more than a list of tired images and travel clichés—that telling your own story can make a difference. Explore your personal reactions to this essay using the personal response questions on page 155. Then respond with your own narrative about an event that has made a difference in your life. Work to recapture for us the force of the event and its impact on you. Tell us what happened, but be sure to let us know what meaning the event ultimately had for you.

c. Assume that you are applying for your first professional job after college. Respond to the following request from the job application:

> Each of us has been confronted by an "impossible situation"—a job that appeared too big to complete, a situation that seemed too awkward to handle, or a problem that felt too complex to deal with. Describe such a situation and how you dealt with it. Your narrative should make a point about the situation, problem solving, or yourself.

d. Write about the event that has caused you the greatest guilt, anger, joy, or other strong emotion and your reaction to it.

11.4   **WEB-BASED PROJECT** To get ideas for a compelling narrative, visit either the University of Oregon resources on literary nonfiction (<**http://www.lnf.uoregon. edu**>) or Storyteller.net (<**http://www.storyteller.net**>) Web sites, but do not limit yourself to them.

In a one-page presentation for your class, describe the kinds of helpful advice about nonfiction narratives that visitors can find online. Trace the links they should follow to reach advice that relates to college essays. Attach a copy of all Web pages relevant to your presentation.

For additional information and practice with the learning objectives in this chapter, go to www.mycomplab.com, Resources>Writing>Writing Purposes.

CHAPTER 12

Illustration: Writing to Provide Examples

LEARNING OBJECTIVES FOR THIS CHAPTER

- Understand the role of *illustration* as a writing strategy
- Differentiate illustration designed to explain from illustration used to make a point
- Write an effective illustrative essay using the chapter guidelines

The backbone of illustration, examples help people visualize and remember the point.

What readers expect to learn from examples

- *Who, what, where, when, how, why?*
- *What makes you think so?*
- *Can you show me?*

Examples provide the evidence that enables readers to understand your meaning and accept your viewpoint. The best way to illustrate what you mean by "an inspiring teacher" is to use one of your professors as an example. You might illustrate this professor's qualities by describing several of her teaching strategies. Or you might give an extended example (say, how she helped you develop confidence). Either way, you have made the abstract notion "inspiring teacher" concrete and thus understandable. (Notice how this paragraph's main point is clarified by the professor example.)

USING EXAMPLES TO EXPLAIN

In referential writing, examples help readers grasp an abstract term or a complex principle. You could explain what grunge music is by pointing out examples of well-known bands that have incorporated its influence. Or suppose you wanted to explain how the liberal arts have practical value in one's career; for this purpose, the following paragraph would not be very helpful.

A PASSAGE NEEDING EXAMPLES

The irony of the emphasis being placed on careers is that nothing is more valuable for anyone who has had a professional or vocational education than to be able to deal with abstractions or complexities, or to feel comfortable with subtleties of thought or language, or to think sequentially. People who have such skills will have a major advantage in just about any career. In all these respects, the liberal arts have much to offer. Just in terms of career preparation, therefore, a student is shortchanging himself or herself by shortcutting the humanities.

Because this paragraph tells but doesn't show, it fails to make a convincing case for a liberal arts education. Any reader will have unanswered questions:

- *What do you mean by "abstractions or complexities," "subtleties of thought or language," and "to think sequentially"?*
- *How exactly do students "shortchange" themselves by "shortcutting" the humanities?*
- *Can you show me how a liberal arts education is useful in one's career?*

Now consider the revised version of the previous paragraph:

A REVISION THAT INCLUDES EXAMPLES

Main point (1)

[1] The irony of the emphasis being placed on careers is that nothing is more valuable for anyone who has had a professional or vocational education than to be able to deal with abstractions or complexities, or to feel comfortable with subtleties of thought or language, or to think

Examples (italicized) (2–5)

Summary (6)

Conclusion explains how the examples fit the main point (7)

sequentially. [2]*The doctor* who knows only disease is at a disadvantage alongside the doctor who knows at least as much about people as he [or she] does about pathological organisms. [3]*The lawyer* who argues in court from a narrow legal base is no match for the lawyer who can connect legal precedents to historical experience and who employs wide-ranging intellectual resources. [4]*The business executive* whose competence in general management is bolstered by an artistic ability to deal with people is of prime value to his [or her] company. [5]For *the technologist,* the engineering of consent can be just as important as the engineering of moving parts. [6]In all these respects, the liberal arts have much to offer. [7]Just in terms of career preparation, therefore, [students are shortchanging themselves] by shortcutting the humanities.

—*Norman Cousins*

The examples help convince us that the author has a valid point.

USING EXAMPLES TO MAKE A POINT

Because examples so often provide the evidence to back up assertions, they have great persuasive power. For one thing, they make writing more convincing simply by making it more interesting. This next writing sample employs vivid examples as a basis for the author's judgment about a controversial trend in American society.

EXAMPLES THAT MAKE A POINT

Main point (1)

Examples (3–9)

Conclusion explains how the examples fit the main point (10–12)

[1]*In a society based on self-reliance and free will, the institutionalization of life scares me.* [2]Today, America has government-funded programs to treat all society's ills. [3]We have day-care centers for the young, nursing homes for the old, psychologists in schools who use mental health as an instrument of discipline, and mental hospitals for those whose behavior does not conform to the norm. [4]We have drug-abuse programs, methadone-maintenance programs, alcohol programs, vocational programs, rehabilitation programs, learning-how-to-cope-with-death-for-the-terminally-ill programs, make-friends-with-your-neighborhood-policeman programs, helping-emotionally-disturbed-children programs, and how-to-accept-divorce programs. [5]Unemployment benefits and welfare are programs designed to institutionalize a growing body of citizens whose purpose in life is the avoidance of work. [6]They are dependent on the state for their livelihood. [7]We can't even let people die in peace. [8]We put them in hospitals for the dying, so that they can be programmed into dying correctly. [9]They don't need to be hospitalized; they would be better off with their families, dying with dignity instead of in these macabre halfway houses. [10]All this is a displacement of confidence from the individual to the program. [11]We can't rely on people to take care of themselves anymore so we have to funnel them into programs.

[12]This is a self-perpetuating thing, for the more programs we make available, the more people will become accustomed to seeking help from the government.

—*Ted Morgan*

In what order (chronological, general-to-specific, and so on) are the examples in the previous paragraph presented? To what extent is this order effective?

In contrast to Ted Morgan's paragraph with its series of brief examples, this next persuasive paragraph presents a single extended example.

Acid rain indirectly threatens human health. Besides containing damaging chemicals, acid rain percolates through the soil, leaching out naturally present heavy metals, such as arsenic and mercury. Surface runoff then carries these pollutants into streams, lakes, and ponds, where they accumulate permanently in the fatty tissue of fish. In turn, any organisms eating the fish—or drinking the water—build up these poisons in their own body tissue. Moreover, acidified water can release strong concentrations of lead, copper, and aluminum from metal plumbing, making ordinary tap water hazardous. Even in the tiniest amounts, the gradual ingestion of these heavy metals has been shown to cause cancer, birth defects, and a host of other ailments.

—*Bill Kelly*

To support his point about the dangers of acid rain, Bill Kelly offers a vivid example of how the process occurs.

GUIDELINES for Illustrating with Examples

- *Fit the examples to your purpose and the readers' needs.* An effective example fits the point it is designed to illustrate. Also, the example is familiar and forceful enough for readers to recognize and remember.

- *Use brief or extended examples.* Some examples need more explanation than others. For example, Bill Kelly (above) spells out the details of a single process, whereas Ted Morgan catalogs the many threats to self-reliance that he observes.

- *Make the example more specific and concrete than the point it illustrates.* Vivid examples enable readers to *visualize.*

- *Arrange examples in a series in accessible order.* If your illustration is a narrative (as in "Fallen Arches," page 200) or a historical catalog, arrange examples chronologically. Otherwise, try a "least to most" (dramatic or important or useful) order. Placing the most striking example last ensures greatest effect.

- *Know how much is enough.* Overexplaining insults a reader's intelligence.

- *Explain how the example fits the point.* Close by refocusing on your example's larger meaning.

USING ILLUSTRATION

BEYOND THE WRITING CLASSROOM

- **In other courses:** For a psychology course, you might give examples of paranoid behavior among world leaders; for an ecology course, an example of tree species threatened by acid rain.

- **On the job:** You might give examples of how the software developed by your company can be used in medical diagnosis or examples of how certain investments have performed in the past decade.

- **In the community:** You might give examples of how your town can provide a favorable economic climate for new industry or examples of how other towns have coped with cutbacks in school funding.

What other specific uses of examples can you envision in any of these three areas?

ILLUSTRATION AS A PRIMARY ESSAY STRATEGY

The following essay by Patricia Raybon, journalist essayist, lecturer, and author, appeared in *Newsweek* magazine. As you read, think about examples in which media stereotypes may have influenced your own opinions about people.

A CASE OF "SEVERE BIAS"

This is who I am not. I am not a crack addict. I am not a welfare mother. I am not illiterate. I am not a prostitute. I have never been in jail. My children are not in gangs. My husband doesn't beat me. My home is not a tenement. None of these things defines who I am, nor do they describe the other black people I've known and worked with and loved and befriended over these 40 years of my life.

Nor does it describe most of black America, period.

Yet in the eyes of the American news media, this is what black America is: poor, criminal, addicted and dysfunctional. Indeed, media coverage of black America is so one-sided, so imbalanced that the most victimized and hurting segment of the black community—a small segment, at best—is presented not as the exception but as the norm. It is an insidious practice, all the uglier for its blatancy.

In recent months, oftentimes in this very magazine, I have observed a steady offering of media reports on crack babies, gang warfare, violent youth, poverty and homelessness—and in most cases, the people featured in the photos and stories were black. At the same time, articles that discuss other aspects of American life—from home buying to medicine to technology to nutrition—rarely, if ever, show blacks playing a positive role, or for that matter, any role at all.

Day after day, week after week, this message—that black America is dysfunctional and unwhole—gets transmitted across the American landscape. Sadly, as a result, America never learns the truth about what is actually a wonderful, vibrant, creative community of people.

Most black Americans are not poor. Most black teenagers are not crack addicts. Most black mothers are not on welfare. Indeed, in sheer numbers, more white Americans are poor and on welfare than are black. Yet one never would deduce that by watching television or reading American newspapers and magazines.

Why does the American media insist on playing this myopic, inaccurate picture game? In this game, white America is always whole and lovely and healthy while black America is usually sick and pathetic and deficient. Rarely, indeed, is black America ever depicted in the media as functional and self-sufficient. The free press, indeed, as the main interpreter of American culture and American experience, holds the mirror on American reality—so much so that what the media says is, even if it's not that way at all. The media is guilty of a severe bias and the problem screams out for correction. It is worse than simply lazy journalism, which is bad enough; it is inaccurate journalism.

For black Americans like myself, this isn't just an issue of vanity—of wanting to be seen in a good light. Nor is it a matter of closing one's eyes to the very real problems of the urban underclass—which undeniably is disproportionately black. To be sure, problems besetting the black underclass deserve the utmost attention of the media, as well as the understanding and concern of the rest of American society.

But if their problems consistently are presented as the only reality for blacks, any other experience known to the black community ceases to have validity, or to be real. In this scenario, millions of blacks are relegated to a sort of twilight zone, where who we are and what we are isn't based on fact but on image and perception. That's what it feels like to be a black American whose lifestyle is outside of the aberrant behavior that the media presents as the norm.

For many of us, life is a curious series of encounters with white people who want to know why we are "different" from other blacks—when, in fact, most of us are only "different" from the now common negative images of black life. So pervasive are these images that they aren't just perceived as the norm; they're accepted as the norm.

I am reminded, for example, of the controversial Spike Lee film *Do the Right Thing* and the criticism by some movie reviewers that the film's ghetto neighborhood isn't populated by addicts and drug pushers—and thus is not a true depiction.

In fact, millions of black Americans live in neighborhoods where the most common sights are children playing and couples walking their dogs. In my own inner-city neighborhood in Denver—an area that the local press consistently describes as "gang territory"—I have yet to see a recognizable "gang" member or any "gang" activity (drug dealing or drive-by shootings), nor have I been the victim of "gang violence."

Yet to students of American culture—in the case of Spike Lee's film, the movie reviewers—a black, inner-city neighborhood can only be one thing to be real: drug-infested and dysfunctioning. Is this my ego talking? In part, yes. For the millions of black people like myself—ordinary, hard-working, law-abiding, tax-paying Americans—the media's blindness to the fact that we even exist, let alone to our contributions to American society, is a bitter cup to drink. And as self-reliant as most black Americans are—because we've had to be self-reliant—even the strongest among us still crave affirmation.

I want that. I want it for my children. I want it for all the beautiful, healthy, funny, smart black Americans I have known and loved over the years.

And I want it for the rest of America, too.

I want America to know us—all of us—for who we really are. To see us in all our complexity, our subtleness, our artfulness, our enterprise, our specialness, our loveliness, our American-ness. That is the real portrait of black America—that we're strong people, surviving people, capable people. That may be the best-kept secret in America. If so, it's time to let the truth be known.

—Patricia Raybon

Raybon presents a vivid portrait by offering specific and concrete examples that virtually any observer of American media will find all too familiar.

CASE STUDY

READING AND RESPONDING

In this case study, student writer Sophia Rothberg relies primarily on illustration through examples in her response to the following professional essay.

ESSAY FOR ANALYSIS AND RESPONSE

In the next selection, "All You Can Eat," journalist and lucid social observer Michelle Stacey combines brief and extended examples as vivid evidence of our national addiction to excessive eating and to our collective denial of its consequences. Notice that she supports her personal observations by citing an authoritative source, nutritionist Lisa Young.

ALL YOU CAN EAT

The capacity of the human mind for self-deception is, it appears, bottomless. I plow into the vast, raisin-dotted pillowiness of my New York–style, bakery-made morning bagel and think, bagel and coffee for breakfast, no butter, no cream cheese—pretty virtuous, *n'est-ce pas?* But this is not a bagel as nature or the U.S. government intended, which would be a moderate 2 to 3 ounces and 150 to 250 calories; instead, this is a behemoth, puffed up to 5 or 6 ounces and probably 400 calories, accounting for almost half of the six to eleven daily bread servings recommended by the USDA's Food Guide Pyramid. If I continue my see-no-evil approach, I can easily rack up innumerable quantities of fat and calories in a day of restaurant meals: steaming heaps of pasta, usually 8 ounces instead of the USDA's suggested 2; gargantuan chicken breasts that look as if they were cut from a 3-foot-tall hen; baked potatoes that take up half the plate. Americans are on a portion pig-out, a swing to the far side of last decade's dainty nouvelle cuisine. "I don't care," proclaims a fast-food customer in a recent TV commercial; "just SuperSize me."

The problem goes beyond a simple ratcheting-up that leaves the door open for studied ignorance ("But I ate only *one!*"). American food has strayed so far from its original standards that our eyes and instincts can hardly be trusted anymore. Even nutrition experts can no longer guess what's in a portion. Further complicating things are the standards put out by the government—"airline portions," according to one expert. "Portion size is reaching a crisis," says Lisa Young, a nutritionist and adjunct faculty member at New York University who is writing her doctoral dissertation on the subject. "The problem is that there's a huge discrepancy between oversize restaurant portions and tiny government portions. So while 3 cups of pasta, the usual restaurant size, is too much, the ½ cup on the USDA chart isn't a realistic serving either."

Young, who notes that "portion sizes have gotten a lot larger in the last decade, and so have people," conducted a test of two hundred dietitians and nutritionists at a 1996 convention of the American Dietetic Association. She asked them to guess the fat and calorie content of various popular dishes, including Caesar salad with grilled chicken and a tuna salad sandwich. All participants underestimated by about 20 percent. The average estimate for a hamburger and onion rings was 863 calories and 44 grams of fat; the reality was 1,550 calories and 101 grams of fat. Similarly, a study several years ago found that a group of severely overweight people trying to lose weight— people "fairly well educated in terms of nutrition," according to the study's head researcher—were actually eating twice as many calories per day as they thought they were. Such wishful thinking may account for the fact that official dietary intake surveys in the past few years, based on daily food diaries, showed people eating barely enough calories to maintain body weight, while actual weights have been increasing dramatically.

The inability to estimate a total calorie count may have been beside the point in the days before the car-and-computer culture, but in this stationary age, calorie creep has put a lot of people over the edge. It's terribly tempting to let restaurant chefs or even grocery stores be one's authority on how much to eat, but mostly they're authorities on pleasing people. Listen to them for a while, and your eye gets retrained; pretty soon you'll think a 10-ounce steak is average (a USDA "serving" of meat is 2 to 3 ounces, about the size of a deck of cards).

There's a route to be charted between restaurant-gargantuan and USDA-ascetic, says Young. First, fight the food-as-bargain impulse: It is not a mortal sin to leave food on your plate, even though you paid for it. Next, plan in advance: If you're going out to dinner, try to imagine what you'll want, and adjust the rest of your day accordingly. "It's absurd to go to an Italian restaurant and order the broiled filet of sole, dry," Young says. "You want pasta. So eat less bread earlier in the day and more protein. Then, for dinner, consider getting an appetizer portion of pasta—that's usually a cup and a half. By USDA standards, that's three portions of bread, but I think that's a reasonable amount of food, along with a salad."

So if you want to splurge, go ahead—just don't kid yourself that a stack of pancakes that stretches across a 12-inch plate is magically the same as the 4-inch pancakes described in the average calorie chart. The clean-plate club closed its doors a long time ago.

—Michelle Stacey

Questions About the Reading

Refer to the general questions on page 154, as well as these specific questions.

CONTENT

- *What are Stacey's assumptions about her audience's knowledge and attitudes? Are these assumptions accurate? Why or why not?*
- *Identify one paragraph developed through an extended example and one through a series of brief examples.*
- *Should the examples be more specific? Why or why not?*

ORGANIZATION

- *Is the order of the examples effective? Explain.*
- *Are the two single-sentence paragraphs appropriate? Explain.*

STYLE

- *What is the writer's attitude toward her subject? Toward her audience? How do we know? Where are the signals?*
- *Is the tone appropriate for this writer's audience and purpose? Explain.*

RESPONDING TO READING

After reading the "All You Can Eat," by Michelle Stacey, Sophia Rothberg decided to share a personal experience, illustrating chronological details that prompted a spontaneous decision on her part: namely, to quit her job. To analyze Michelle Stacey's technique, and respond to that essay, Rothberg combined the guidelines on page 195 with the previous questions about that reading.

Working toward the final draft shown here, Rothberg consulted the illustration checklist (page 202) and the revision checklist (pages 62–63).

FALLEN ARCHES

Paragraphs 1 and 2 invite us in and set the scene

[1]As my battered blue van pulled up alongside the golden arches, I did not pause to wonder why I was one of the many teenagers employed here. I sensed that there would be plenty of chances in the course of my eight-hour day to ponder why, after a year and a half, I was still working as a McDonald's crew person.

The two final sentences in paragraph 2 preview the main point

[2]On a normal eleven-to-seven shift, I would have anticipated both a lunch rush (an overflow of customers and not enough crew people) and a dinner rush. But realizing that this was a beautiful September Saturday, I knew there would only be one big rush, starting at eleven and finally ending at seven. "I should feel privileged," I thought, "after all, they only schedule the best workers to come in for the busiest part of the day." But somehow I didn't feel any better.

One extended example

[3]Approaching the store by shuffling through endless Big Mac boxes and shake cups strewn about the parking lot, I caught a glimpse of my next image, reflected in McDonald's newly washed glass door. My creased black pants, baggy brown shirt, and freshly polished black working shoes complemented my hair, which was neatly bundled up in my neat little black cap. My name tag, neatly secured in the upper right corner of my blouse, carried the slogan, "We do it all for you." I knew that all this mirror image of mine lacked was a neat plastic smile.

Gives vivid and visual examples throughout

[4]Opening the door, I entered a room filled with identically dressed crew people waiting on customers, sweeping floors, cleaning tables, emptying trash cans, doling out fresh hot french fries, toasting bakery fresh buns, and cooking 100 percent pure beef hamburgers almost as quickly as the customers could swill them down. All this to the tune of various buzzers signaling the happy workers to follow various procedures. The twelve hamburger patties lying on the grill had a buzzer sound exactly twenty seconds after being carefully laid on the hottest part of the grill. This buzzer prompted Mike, our "meatman," to sear in the juices (fat) of each individual meat patty. Forty seconds later, Mike turned the meat patties at the prodding of a second buzzer, and forty seconds and another buzzer after that Mike removed the meat from the grill that was set at exactly 350 degrees F. Mike always moved quickly and efficiently. He was a human robot, capable of cooking $1,700 worth of food for McDonald's in one hour. And of that $1,700, Mike would receive approximately seven dollars and twenty-five cents.

Strongest example of the writer's intolerable situation

[5]My appraisal of this scene was soon interrupted, however, when I heard a customer bellowing to the whole store that his hamburger had catsup and mustard on it, and that he had specifically told the counter server that he did not like mustard. I didn't need to listen any further. The number one rule at McDonald's is that the customer is always right. The crew person is always mistaken, and it is the job of the manager to soothe the temper of the dissatisfied customer. Soon the bellowing customer would receive a new hamburger with catsup only, and a "Be Our Guest" card entitling him "to one free hamburger and french fries." The customer would then walk away feeling satisfied, and the server at the counter, temporarily embarrassed, would then begin to scurry again.

Concludes with the example that triggers her spontaneous decision

[6]Realizing that it was near eleven, I started my walk toward the time clock, when I was confronted by an assistant manager, Ken. "How much money are you going to pull in this hour Sophia? The record for the highest window server is $572, but I'm sure that if you really try you can break

Closing sentence presents the implied main point | it today." Remaining silent, I looked up into his serious, neat brown eyes, listened to the click of the time clock, signaling 11 A.M., and punched my time card, ready, I thought, to begin work. But then I hesitated. As if by instinct alone, I turned around, reached again for my card, and punched it out for the last time.

—*Sophia Rothberg*

✔ A CHECKLIST for Using Illustration

☐ Does each example **fit the point** it is designed to illustrate?

☐ Is each example **familiar enough** for readers to recognize?

☐ Is each example **specific and concrete enough** for readers to visualize?

☐ Is each example **forceful enough** for readers to remember?

☐ Is the example **appropriately brief or extended**, depending on how much explanation it needs?

☐ Are the examples arranged in an **order** that provides access and impact?

☐ Are there **enough examples** to make the point—but **not too many**?

☐ Does the piece close by focusing on the **larger meaning** of the examples?

(See page 195 for more on each of these criteria.)

APPLICATIONS

12.1 **PARAGRAPH WARM-UP: USING EXAMPLES TO EXPLAIN** Pierre Rouleau, a French student who plans to attend an American university, has asked what the typical American college student is like. He has inquired about interests, activities, attitudes, and tastes. Selecting one or more characteristics you think typify American college students, write a response to Rouleau.

12.2 **PARAGRAPH WARM-UP: USING EXAMPLES TO MAKE A POINT** Assume that your campus newspaper is inviting contributions for a new section called "Insights," a weekly collection of one-paragraph essays by students. Student contributors should focus on examples gained by close observation of campus life and American values or habits to offer some fresh insight on a problem facing our culture. Using Ted Morgan's paragraph (pages 194–195) as a model, write such a paragraph for the newspaper. Choose examples to convince your audience that the problem you discuss is real.

12.3 **ESSAY PRACTICE**

a. Explore your personal reactions to "A Case of Severe Bias" using the questions on page 155. Then respond with an essay of your own, using powerful examples to make your point.

Perhaps someone has misjudged or stereotyped you or a group to which you belong. If so, set the record straight in a forceful essay to a specified audience. Or perhaps you can think of other types of media messages that seem to present a distorted or inaccurate view (say, certain commercials, sports reporting, or war movies). For instance, do certain movies or TV programs send the wrong message? Give your readers examples they can recognize and remember.

Or you might challenge readers' assumptions by asserting a surprising or unorthodox viewpoint: that some natural foods can be hazardous, that exercise can be bad for health, or that so-called advances in electronics or medical science leave us worse off.

Or maybe you want to talk about examples of things we take for granted or what makes a good friend. Whatever the topic, be sure your examples illustrate and explain a definite viewpoint.

b. Write a human interest essay for your campus newspaper in which you illustrate some feature of our society that you find humorous, depressing, contemptible, or admirable. Possible subjects: our eating, consumer, or dress habits; our idea of a vacation or a good time; the cars we drive. Provide at least three well-developed examples to make your point. Michelle Stacey's essay (page 198) provides a useful model.

c. At some point we all make what seem to outsiders (and maybe even to ourselves!) split-second decisions—actually based on some earlier events. Write an essay to a stipulated audience (classmates, close friend, parent, employer), illustrating the events that led up to a decision you've made. Topics might include these decisions: to quit school, to buy something extravagant, to do something dangerous, to run away from something, or to take a stand on an issue. Your goal could be to entertain a friendly reader or to placate an angry one, or some such. Identify your goal beforehand.

Your story should have a point. Illustrate the events in enough detail for readers to understand how you arrived at your decision. Include both your physical and psychological sensations. To increase interest, begin with the action, saving the main point for last. Or, without stating the main point directly, simply imply it in the narrative, as the writer of "Fallen Arches" illustrates an intolerable situation as the motivation to quit her job.

d. What pleases, disappoints, or surprises you most about college life? Illustrate this topic for your family (or some other specific audience) with at least three examples.

12.4   **COLLABORATIVE PROJECT AND COMPUTER APPLICATION** Use email or your electronic mailing list to brainstorm collectively for examples to support one or more claims your group has generated in response to one of the readings or essay options in this chapter.

12.5   **WEB-BASED PROJECT** Look up the home page for a business, and pretending you're the public relations manager for that company, write an essay to convince a new client to use the business's services or products. Use the Web to find specific examples to support your claim.

For additional information and practice with the learning objectives in this chapter, go to www.mycomplab.com, Resources>Writing>Writing Purposes.

CHAPTER 13

Division and Classification: Writing to Explain Parts and Categories

LEARNING OBJECTIVES FOR THIS CHAPTER

- Understand the role of *division and classification* as writing strategies
- Recognize how division and classification may both be used either to explain or to make a point
- Write an effective essay employing division, classification, or a combination

Division and classification are both strategies for sorting things out, but each serves a distinct purpose. *Division* deals with *one thing only.* It separates that thing into parts, pieces, sections, or categories for closer examination (say, an essay divided into introduction, body, and conclusion).

What readers expect to learn from a division

■ *What are its parts?*
■ *What is it made of?*

Classification deals with *an assortment of things* that share certain similarities. It groups these things systematically (say, a CD collection into categories—jazz, rock, country, classical, and pop).

What readers expect to learn from a classification

■ *What relates to what?*
■ *In what categories do X, Y, and Z belong?*

We use division and classification in many aspects of our lives. Say you are shopping for a refrigerator. If you are mechanically inclined, you could begin by thinking about the major parts that make up a refrigerator: shelving, storage compartments, cooling element, motor, insulation, and exterior casing. You can ask questions about these individual parts to determine the efficiency or quality of each part in different kinds of refrigerators. You have *divided* the refrigerator into its components.

After shopping, you come home with a list of twenty refrigerators that seem to be built from high-quality parts. You make sense of your list by grouping items according to selected characteristics. First, you divide your list into three *classes* according to size in cubic feet of capacity: small, midsize, and large refrigerators. But you want economy, too, so you group the refrigerators according to cost. Or you might *classify* them according to color, weight, or energy efficiency. Here is how division and classification are related:

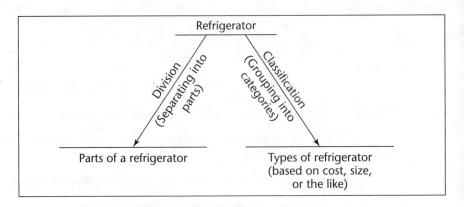

Whether you choose to apply division or classification depends on your purpose. An architect designing a library will think almost entirely of *division.* Once she has defined the large enclosed area that is needed, she must identify the parts into which that space must be divided: the reference area, reading areas, storage areas, checkout facilities, and office space. She might consider providing space for special groups of users (such as reading areas for children). In very large libraries, she might need to divide further into specialized kinds of space (such as highly secure areas for rare manuscripts or special collections or areas with special acoustic provisions for listening to recorded materials). However simple or complex her problem, this architect is thinking now only about the appropriate division of space. She is not worrying about how the library will classify its books and other material.

Classification is one of the library staff's main problems. The purpose of a library is not only to store books and other forms of information but above all to make the information retrievable. In order for us to find a book or item, the thousands or millions of books stored in the library must be arranged in logical categories. That arrangement becomes possible only if the books are carefully classified.

USING DIVISION TO EXPLAIN

We encounter referential uses of division every day. Division is used in manuals to help us understand, for example, how a computer or a car engine works. Division allows readers to tackle a complex task one aspect at a time, as in the following instructions for campers.

A DIVISION THAT EXPLAINS

Before pitching your tent, take the time to prepare the area that will be under the tent. Not only does this step prevent damage to the tent floor, but it also helps you get a good night's sleep. Begin by removing all stones, branches, and other debris. Use your camping shovel for anything too large or deep to remove by hand. Next, fill in any holes with dirt or leaves. Finally, make a few light sweeps with the shovel or a leafy branch to smooth the area.

To increase readability, the steps or substeps in a complex task often appear in list form.

USING DIVISION TO MAKE A POINT

In the following paragraph, Alan Watts uses division to explain his view of the ideal education. If we accept his divisions, we are more likely to agree that his opinion makes sense.

DIVISION THAT MAKES A POINT

Lead-in to main point
(1–3)

[1]It is perhaps idle to wonder what, from my present point of view, would have been an ideal education. [2]If I could provide such a curriculum for my children they, in their turn, might find it all a bore. [3]But the fantasy of what I would

Main point (4)

Parts of the "ideal education" (5)

Most important part (6)

have liked to learn as a child may be revealing, since I feel unequipped by education for problems that lie outside the cloistered, literary domain in which I am competent and at home. [4]Looking back, then, I would have arranged for myself to be taught survival techniques for both natural and urban wildernesses. [5]I would want to have been instructed in self-hypnosis, in aikido (the esoteric and purely self-defensive style of judo), in elementary medicine, in sexual hygiene, in vegetable gardening, in astronomy, navigation, and sailing; in cookery and clothesmaking, in metalwork and carpentry, in drawing and painting, in printing and typography, in botany and biology, in optics and acoustics, in semantics and psychology, in mysticism and yoga, in electronics and mathematical fantasy, in drama and dancing, in singing and in playing an instrument by ear; in wandering, in advanced daydreaming, in prestidigitation, in techniques of escape from bondage, in disguise, in conversation with birds and beasts, in ventriloquism, in French and German conversation, in planetary history, in morphology, [the structure of organisms], and in Classical Chinese. [6]Actually, the main thing left out of my education was a proper love for my own body, because one feared to cherish anything so obviously mortal and prone to sickness.

—*Alan Watts*

The topic statement tells; the rest *shows* by dividing the ideal education into specific kinds of instruction. This writer knew the following guidelines.

GUIDELINES for Division

- *Apply the division to a singular item.* Only one item at a time can be divided (*ideal education*; not *ideal education* and *ideal career*).

- *Make the basis of your division consistent with your purpose.* Most things can be divided in different ways for different purposes. For example, Watts could have divided education according to all sorts of different bases: primary, secondary, and higher education; or social sciences, sciences, mathematics, and humanities—and so on. But his purpose was to explain a view that goes beyond traditional categories. And so we are given "parts" of an education that few of us may have considered.

- *Make your division complete.* Only 100 percent of something can be divided, and the parts, in turn, should add up to 100 percent. If a part is omitted, the writer should say so ("some of the parts of an ideal education").

- *Subdivide the subject as needed to make the point.* Watts's first division is into survival techniques for natural and urban wildernesses. He then subdivides each of these into the specific parts listed in sentences 5 and 6. If he had stopped after the first division, he would not have made his point.

- *Keep parts from overlapping.* The logic of division requires that each item exclude all others. Consider this faulty partition of a college's governance structure: trustees, president, provost, deans, administration. These parts overlap because the second, third, and fourth positions can be listed under the heading "administration."

- *Follow a logical sequence.* In Watts's sentence 5, the parts of an ideal education range from practical to recreational to intellectual skills. In sentence 6, the most important part appears last, for emphasis.

USING CLASSIFICATION TO EXPLAIN

Like division, classifying as a referential or informative strategy is a part of our lives. Your biology textbook shows you how scientists have classified lifeforms into plants, animals, bacteria, and other categories; scientists examining fossils write up their discoveries by assigning them to one of these classes. A city planner might write a report classifying plans for conserving water on the basis of cost, efficiency, or some other basis. The following classification explains major career specialties in computer science on the basis of their central tasks.

CLASSIFICATION THAT EXPLAINS

Specialties in computer science can be grouped into three major categories. First, systems programmers write programs that run the computer equipment itself. Next, applications programmers develop programs that put the computer to work on specific jobs (such as keeping track of bank accounts). Finally, systems analysts troubleshoot, debug, and update both systems and applications programs, and they develop specifications for new computer systems. All three specialties involve analyzing a problem and then reducing it to a sequence of small, deliberate steps that a computer can carry out.

—*Pat Peterson*

USING CLASSIFICATION TO MAKE A POINT

Like division, classification can serve persuasive goals. The author of the following paragraph uses classification in considering the motives behind attending the high school prom.

CLASSIFICATION THAT MAKES A POINT

Why must everyone who counts be at the prom? The answer is simple: peer pressure. Promgoers often feel compelled to attend, as the prom represents in many ways their last chance, their last hurrah. For the popular, it is their final opportunity to saunter into a room filled with people who admire them not so much for who they are or what they've achieved but instead for the shallow ideal they represent—the football star, the homecoming queen, the rich kid. For the borderline types, the prom is their final chance to mimic the popular, to rub elbows with those who really matter. For the losers—the nerds, geeks, dweebs, wallflowers, and other loners—prom night is their last, desperate chance to try fitting in, to matter at all.

—*Julia Schoonover*

In developing her message, Schoonover observed the following guidelines.

GUIDELINES for Classification

- *Apply the classification to a plural subject.* In Schoonover's paragraph, the subject is types who attend the prom.

- *Limit the scope of your classification.* The sharper its focus, the more useful the classification. A résumé classification headed "Work Experience" is more informative than one merely labeled "Experience." A classification titled "Vegetables" would require a listing of every vegetable ever grown.

- *Make the basis of the classification consistent with your purpose.* To make her point about needs, Schoonover classifies the three groups on the basis of their respective popularity. For a different purpose, she might have classified students on prom night on some other basis, say, according to their behavior or style of dress.

- *Make the classification complete.* All three broad stereotypes of high school culture are represented.

- *Arrange the categories in a logical sequence.* For example, the categories Schoonover uses move from "winners" to "losers."

- *Don't let categories overlap.* If she had added the category "truly needy" to the three stereotypes she identifies, Schoonover's classification would overlap because all three categories represent some type of need. Or suppose a supermarket classified its meats as "pork," "beef," "ham," and "lamb." This classification would overlap because ham is a pork product rather than a separate type of meat.

USING DIVISION AND CLASSIFICATION

- **In other courses:** All academic fields divide and classify information to make sense of it and make it easier to learn. For example, in biology, organisms are divided into parts to clarify how those parts work together as a whole. In literature, types of literature are classified into genres (fiction, poetry, drama, essay), styles within genres (surrealist poetry, Elizabethan drama, gothic fiction), and so on.

- **On the job:** Businesses are organized into and within departments using division and classification. For example, a typical publishing house will classify its departments into editorial, production, sales, marketing, administrative, legal, and so on; within those departments they will divide employee roles into a hierarchy of parts (Editor in Chief, Acquisitions Editor, Development Editor, Associate Editor, Editorial Assistant). At the same time, businesses also divide and classify their products and services for planning and sales tracking reasons.

- **In the community:** Community, state, and national governments are organized using division and classification. For example, a city might be subdivided (Queens, Brooklyn, Manhattan, Staten Island, and the Bronx in New York City). Each subdivision might respond to community needs by classifying its population into categories (the elderly, working families, the Asian-American community, and so on), studying the needs of each group when social or budget decisions are made.

In what other situations might division and classification make a difference?

DIVISION AND CLASSIFICATION AS PRIMARY ESSAY STRATEGIES

In this next essay, a journalist, biographer, and historian dissects rock music as a genre that he considers simplistic, uninspired, and uninspiring As you read, think about some aspect of popular culture that you consider disappointing.

ALL JUNK, ALL THE TIME

Like a turtle egg buried on the beach, the thought warmed, out of sight, all summer. The Olympics and the political conventions helped it grow, but the key stimulus was a passing sentence in a *New York Times Magazine* article on megachurches, which are evangelical churches that number their congregations in the thousands. The article was discussing the music used in the services, and said something to the effect that the megachurches favored rock. Just like the conventions. Just like the Olympics. Just like everyone everywhere.

Megachurches keep their eye on eternity. In the here and now, rock is triumphant and universal. Its empire will only expand, ferreting out the few nooks it does not yet command, and filling them. Francis Fukuyama alerted us (wrongly) to the End of History. But rock has ended the history of music. There are no ideological, religious, or ethnic redoubts. I once read a profile of the commander of a Salvadoran death squad. He was a Deadhead. Iranian mullahs, Chinese Communists, skinheads, rabbis expecting the return of

Menachem Schneerson, Papuan savages dressed only in penis wrappers, all listen, openly or in secret, or their children will.

What is rock? A certain set of musicians—drums, guitars, a voice or two. A beat that, well, rocks. Lyrics. Pare down the music until it almost vanishes, as in rap; soften the beat until it becomes easy listening; give the songwriter the equipment and the ambitions of Brian Wilson: but the form never quite disappears. It hasn't changed for forty years, and it never will, because it is so easy to do well enough.

Consider the elements.

Music. The guitar is the ultimate E-Z-2-Play instrument. Why else was it the lyre of the American peasantry? If rock depended on some instrument—trumpet, clarinet, fiddle, piano—that required some tone of the lips or lightness of the fingers to play even barely competently, its pool of potential performers would have shrunk by 90 percent. There is only one instrument easier to fake: drums. The low standards also apply to rock vocalists. Remember Mick Jagger when he was in his prime? Heard him now, when he sounds like a voice on the subway PA system? Mr. Jagger could actually move his notes around, but they were always harsh and homely notes. That's OK—they were good enough for rock.

Words. The rock critic Elizabeth Wurtzel, reviewing an album of covers of Cole Porter songs by rock musicians, hoped the experience might inspire rock songwriters to be a little more careful of their rhyme schemes. Wrong! The whole point is not to have to worry about rhyme schemes. If you start worrying, not everyone will be able to do it. So rock will keep on rhyming "pain" and "shame," and "stop" and "stuck."

Dancing. I was in fifth and sixth grade just after kids stopped taking solemn little lessons, in gym class or after school, in the box step and the cha-cha. Those who still dance these, and all the other dances of mankind, do it, like fox hunters or Greek scholars, as a passion or a hobby. To fulfill the necessities of social intercourse, it will never be necessary to take a dance lesson again. Slow dancing to rock is what you hope to be doing horizontally with your clothes off afterward. Fast dancing is—well, look at it, at any wedding or bar mitzvah, where even the grown-ups shake their aged hams. The abolition of dance steps was a great relief to the awkward, especially the men, who once had to lead—no more visualizing the points of the compass, no more shame when you crunched the foot you were supposed to be guiding.

Entrepreneurs. There is a final way in which rock is easy, which impels the other three. It is easy to make a buck selling it. Because the product is so generic, primitive, and witless, the distributors and marketers can know nothing, ingest huge quantities of drugs, and still not be too addled to make millions. The fields I know best are journalism, publishing, and politics, and so I do know something about laziness and empty pretensions. But if there were ever a land of opportunity for the feckless, the modern music industry is it.

Rock is a form of popular culture that aims downward in terms of class and age, instead of aiming up. Rather than aspiring, it *despires*. Astronomers speak of the red shift, the change in the spectrum of the light of receding galaxies. Rock is redneck shift. The preceding phase of popular music, encompassing jazz, dance bands, and show tunes, was urban and adult. Rock is kids channeling the rhythms of bumpkins.

But the worst thing about rock is not that it fails the culture, but that it fails on its own terms. Popular music is a marker and a memory aid. Most of the important events in life—romance, courtship, celebration—are accompanied by it. We remember them because of their importance to us, no matter what was on the radio. But if the music is crude and blank, does not some of its crudity and blankness infect the experience, and the memory?

And while popular music mostly amplifies pre-existing emotions, at its best it can tug us, tease us, make us grow. Not rock. For all its supposedly revolutionary ethos, rock is a binary switch of angst and hormones—Kafka without humor, or centerfolds in notes. The emotions that unsettle, like stones under a sleeping bag—hope, regret—are beyond its ken. And they are beyond our ken, to the extent rock stuffs our ears.

It's Bottom 40, all junk, all the time. And it's here to stay.

—*Richard Brookhiser*

Notice how Brookhiser organizes his essay, identifying the key components and then grouping them into categories on the basis of their shared characteristics: first, the music, with its elementary instruments and mediocre performers; next, the simplistic words and weak rhyme schemes; and then the mindless and sloppy dance steps.

CASE STUDY

READING AND RESPONDING

In this case study, student writer Patrice LaChane relies primarily on classification in her response to the following professional essay.

ESSAY FOR ANALYSIS AND RESPONSE

In his essay, "Doubts about Doublespeak," Professor William Lutz, distinguished author and editor, categorizes four major types of language that are intended to deceive or to camouflage. As you read, think about language you may have encountered that was deceptive or downright impossible to understand.

DOUBTS ABOUT DOUBLESPEAK

During the past year, we learned that we can shop at a "unique retail biosphere" instead of a farmers' market, where we can buy items made of "synthetic glass" instead of plastic, or purchase a "high-velocity, multipurpose air circulator," or electric fan. A "waste-water conveyance facility" may "exceed the odor threshold" from time to time due to the presence of "regulated human nutrients," but that is not to be confused with a sewage plant that stinks up the neighborhood with sewage sludge. Nor should we confuse a "resource development park" with a dump. Thus does doublespeak continue to spread.

Doublespeak is language which pretends to communicate but doesn't. It is language which makes the bad seem good, the negative seem positive, the unpleasant seem attractive, or at least tolerable. It is language which avoids, shifts or denies responsibility; language which is at variance with its real or purported meaning. It is language which conceals or prevents thought.

Doublespeak is all around us. We are asked to check our packages at the desk "for our convenience" when it's not for our convenience at all but for someone else's convenience. We see advertisements for "preowned," "experienced" or "previously distinguished" cars, not used cars, and for "genuine imitation leather," "virgin vinyl" or "real counterfeit diamonds." Television offers not reruns but "encore telecasts." There are no slums or ghettos, just the "inner city" or "substandard housing" where the "disadvantaged" or "economically nonaffluent" live and where there might be a problem with "substance abuse." Nonprofit organizations don't make a profit, they have "negative deficits" or experience "revenue excesses." With doublespeak it's not dying but "terminal living" or "negative patient care outcome."

There are four kinds of doublespeak. The first kind is the euphemism, a word or phrase designed to avoid a harsh or distasteful reality. Used to mislead or deceive, the euphemism becomes doublespeak. In 1984 the U.S. State Department's annual reports on the status of human rights around the world ceased using the word "killing." Instead the State Department used the phrase "unlawful or arbitrary deprivation of life," thus avoiding the embarrassing situation of government-sanctioned killing in countries supported by the United States.

A second kind of doublespeak is jargon, the specialized language of a trade, profession or similar group, such as doctors, lawyers, plumbers or car mechanics. Legitimately used, jargon allows members of a group to communicate with each other clearly, efficiently and quickly. Lawyers and tax accountants speak to each other of an "involuntary conversion" of property, a legal term that means the loss or destruction of property through theft, accident or condemnation. But when lawyers or tax accountants use unfamiliar terms to speak to others, then the jargon becomes doublespeak.

In 1978 a commercial 727 crashed on takeoff, killing three passengers, injuring 21 others and destroying the airplane. The insured value of the airplane was greater than its book value, so the airline made a profit of $1.7 million, creating two problems: the airline didn't want to talk about one of its airplanes crashing, yet it had to account for that $1.7 million profit in its annual report to its stockholders. The airline solved both problems by inserting a footnote in its annual report which explained that the $1.7 million was due to "the involuntary conversion of a 727."

A third kind of doublespeak is gobbledygook or bureaucratese. Such doublespeak is simply a matter of overwhelming the audience with words—the more the better. Alan Greenspan, a polished practitioner of bureaucratese, once testified before a Senate committee that "it is a tricky problem to find the particular calibration in timing that would be appropriate to stem the acceleration in risk premiums created by falling incomes without prematurely aborting the decline in the inflation-generated risk premiums."

The fourth kind of doublespeak is inflated language, which is designed to make the ordinary seem extraordinary, to make everyday things seem impressive, to give an air of importance to people or situations, to make the simple seem complex. Thus do car mechanics become "automotive internists," elevator operators become "members of the vertical transportation corps," grocery store checkout clerks become "career associate scanning professionals," and smelling something becomes "organoleptic analysis."

Doublespeak is not the product of careless language or sloppy thinking. Quite the opposite. Doublespeak is language carefully designed and constructed to appear to communicate when in fact it doesn't. It is a language designed not to lead but to mislead. Thus, it's not a tax increase but "revenue enhancement" or "tax-base broadening." So how can you complain about higher taxes? Those aren't useless, billion-dollar pork barrel projects; they're really "congressional projects of national significance," so don't complain about wasteful government spending. That isn't the Mafia in Atlantic City; those are just "members of a career-offender cartel," so don't worry about the influence of organized crime in the city.

—William Lutz

Questions About the Reading

Refer to the general questions on page 154, as well as these specific questions.

CONTENT

- *What basis can you identify in Lutz's classification? Is this basis consistent with the writer's purpose? Explain.*
- *Is the classification offered there complete? Explain.*

ORGANIZATION

- *Does the arrangement of supporting paragraphs help make the classification convincing? Explain.*
- *What major devices lend coherence to this essay? Give samples of each.*

STYLE

- *What is the writer's attitude toward his subject? Toward his audience? How do we know? Where are the signals?*
- *Is the tone appropriate for this writer's audience and purpose? Explain.*

RESPONDING TO READING

After reading and analyzing William Lutz's essay and answering the questions about the reading, Patrice LaChane decided to diverge from the focus on language and to examine her neighborhood on the basis of the characteristics that make it such a likable place to live. To sort out the elements of this complex subject, LaChane settles on three main categories: the neighborhood's convenience, housing, and people.

In drafting and revising, LaChane relied on the division and classification guidelines (pages 208–209 and 210) and the revision checklists (pages 62–63 and 217).

Note

Even though classification is the dominant strategy in LaChane's essay, note that she also relies on the strategies of description, narration, and illustration to get his point across.

WE LIKE IT HERE

Title gives a clear forecast
Opening uses descriptive and narrative details to set the scene and give background

Our family lives on Elgin Avenue, a busy one-way street near Rideau Park in Bitmore, Michigan, an industrial city of fifty thousand. Sixteen years ago when we first bought the house we planned to live there only a few years before we could afford to realize the all-American dream of buying property in the suburbs. But as the years have passed, we've come to love our blue-collar neighborhood and to feel that it truly is "home." *What makes this place special for us is the convenient location, the modest character of the houses, and—most of all—the special people we call neighbors.*

Thesis divides the neighborhood into three categories, in logical order: location, architecture, people

Within easy walking distance are all kinds of stores: barbershop, pharmacy, bakery, jeweler, hardware store, convenience store, and even a clothing store. All the shopkeepers know most of the local people by name, take an interest in them, and often go out of their way to provide great service. Because fast food has yet to invade the neighborhood, we still savor "slow" food—mashed potatoes, pork chops, and ham sandwiches on fresh-baked bread—right around the corner at Ellie's diner. Schools, churches, and all the facilities at Rideau Park are easily accessible, and the bus stops right at the corner every half hour.

First category: types of convenient facilities
Uses visual examples throughout

Second category: types of houses

Since our neighborhood was built nearly sixty years ago to house factory workers, the homes are not exactly fancy; they aren't even modern. No gambrels, split-levels, or ranchers here. Instead we have a mixture of nondescript bungalows, brick row houses, two-family, three-family, and even six-family tenements, most of them no more than twenty feet apart. Many of the houses have been remodeled inside and most are well kept, both inside and out. Because of the number of multiple-family dwellings, however, parking spaces are at a premium in the evenings, when everyone is home from work. Neighborly cooperation helps alleviate the parking problem, though.

Third category: types of people

Because of the various kinds of affordable housing available in our neighborhood, we have a complex mix of generations and ethnic groups. Originally a French Canadian area, Elgin Avenue has gradually welcomed people from various ethnic backgrounds. All of them have shared their native foods, their gardening tricks, and their child-rearing theories. But the glue that holds the neighborhood together is its children. Almost forty children under age fifteen keep our homes, yards, porches, and sidewalks very lively. They rollerskate, play street hockey and kickball, douse each other with water balloons, invite one another to share a meal, sleep out in tents, and fight and make up. They watch the little babies and run errands for the elderly. They grow up and move away, only to be replaced by a new crop of kids. The older generations get along because the children do.

Conclusion reemphasizes the main point

We have seen and shared many sides of life during our sixteen years on this street. Having so many stores and other facilities nearby has been very convenient for our family. Seeing the homes being kept up has increased our pride in the neighborhood. Learning to love and respect our neighbors—and enjoying lifelong friendships—has been our greatest privilege.

—*Patrice LaChane*

☑ A CHECKLIST for Division and Classification

Division

☐ Is the division applied to a **singular** item?

☐ Is the **basis** of the division consistent with your purpose?

☐ Is the division **complete** in that it includes 100 percent of the parts?

☐ Is the item **divided** and **subdivided** as far as necessary?

☐ Have you avoided **overlapping** the parts in your division?

☐ Does the division follow a **logical sequence** (spatial, chronological, and so on)?

Classification

☐ Is the classification applied to a **plural** subject?

☐ Is the classification appropriately **limited** in scope?

☐ Is the **basis** of the classification consistent with your purpose?

☐ Is the classification **complete**?

☐ Are the categories arranged in a **logical sequence**?

☐ Have you avoided **overlapping** the categories in your classification?

(See pages 208–209 and 210 for more on each of these criteria.)

APPLICATIONS

13.1   **PARAGRAPH WARM-UP: DIVIDING TO EXPLAIN** Addressing a prospective new member, use division to explain either the organization or the function of committees in a social or service group you belong to.

13.2   **PARAGRAPH WARM-UP: DIVIDING TO MAKE A POINT** Using the paragraph on pages 207–208 as a model, write a paragraph for the college curriculum committee, explaining your idea of an ideal education.

13.3   **PARAGRAPH WARM-UP: CLASSIFYING TO EXPLAIN** You are helping prepare the orientation for next year's incoming students. Your supervisor asks you to write a paragraph outlining the jobs available to graduates in your major by organizing the jobs into major categories. Your piece will be published in a career pamphlet for new students. (You may need to do some research, say, in *The Occupational Outlook Handbook*.)

13.4   **PARAGRAPH WARM-UP: CLASSIFYING TO MAKE A POINT** Identify a group you find in some way interesting. Sort the members of that group into at least three categories. Your basis for sorting (say, driving habits, attitudes toward marriage, hairstyles) will depend on the particular point you want to make about the group.

13.5   **ESSAY PRACTICE**

   a. Explore your reactions to "All Junk, All the Time" by using the questions on page 155. Then respond with an essay of your own that relies primarily on division and classification.

   b. Explore your reactions to the Lutz essay (page 213) using the questions on page 155. Then respond with an essay of your own that supports a particular point about uses of language. You might describe an experience in which you have been misled by doublespeak. Or you might discuss situations in which doublespeak can be beneficial. Whether your approach is humorous or serious, be sure your essay makes a definite point.

   Or instead of writing about language, you might write about different types of people in your life, different places you've lived or schools you've attended, different types of students you've known or friends you've had, and so on.

   c. Assume that you've been assigned a faculty adviser who likes to know as much as possible about each advisee. The adviser asks each student to write an essay on this topic:

   Is your hometown (city, neighborhood) a good or a bad place for a child to grow up?

   Patrice Lachane's essay offers a model for response.

   d. Television seems to invade every part of our lives. It can influence our buying habits, political views, and attitudes about sex, marriage, family, and violence.

Identify a group of commercials, sitcoms, talk shows, sports shows, or the like that have a bad (or good) influence on viewers. Sort the group on a clear basis, using at least three categories, and be sure your essay supports a definite thesis.

13.6   **WEB-BASED PROJECT*** Harvard researcher Howard Gardner and others have classified nine different categories of "intelligence," or styles of thinking and learning. To learn more about multiple intelligences, search the Web for sites that will help you answer this question: Which one or more of the basic intelligence categories seem to fit your thinking and learning styles?

Prepare an essay that explains the categories you have identified. Work from a clear and definite thesis. Be sure to provide convincing personal examples and to document all sources of information.

For additional information and practice with the learning objectives in this chapter, go to www.mycomplab.com, Resources>Writing>Writing Purposes.

*I thank Georgia State University's George Pullman for inspiring this exercise.

CHAPTER 14

Process Analysis: Writing to Explain Steps and Stages

LEARNING OBJECTIVES FOR THIS CHAPTER

■ Understand the role of *process analysis* as a writing strategy

■ Recognize how process analysis can be used to give instructions or to explain how something happens

■ Write an effective process analysis using the chapter guidelines

A *process* is a sequence of actions or changes leading to a product or to a result (say, in producing maple syrup). A *procedure* is a way of carrying out a process (say, in swinging a golf club). A *process analysis* explains these various steps and stages in order to instruct or inform readers.

USING PROCESS ANALYSIS TO EXPLAIN

The most common referential uses of process analysis are to give instructions and to explain how something happens.

Explaining How to Do Something

As the examples suggest, anyone might need to write instructions. And everyone reads some sort of instructions. The new employee needs instructions for operating the office machines; the employee going on vacation writes instructions for the person filling in. A car owner reads the manual for service and operating instructions.

What readers want to know about a procedure

- *How do I do it?*
- *Why do I do it?*
- *What materials or equipment will I need?*
- *Where do I begin?*
- *What do I do next?*
- *Are there precautions I need to take?*

Instructions emphasize the reader's role, explaining each step in enough detail for the reader to complete the task safely and efficiently. This next passage is aimed at inexperienced joggers:

EXPLAINING HOW TO DO SOMETHING

Main point (1)
First step (2)
Supporting detail (3)
Second step (4)
Supporting detail (5)

Transitional sentence (6)
Third step (7–8)

Precaution (9–10)
Supporting details
(11–15)

[1]Instead of breaking into a jog too quickly and risking injury, take a relaxed and deliberate approach. [2]Before taking a step, spend at least ten minutes stretching and warming up, using any exercises you find comfortable. [3](After your first week, consult a jogging book for specialized exercises.) [4]When you've completed your warm-up, set a brisk pace walking. [5]Exaggerate the distance between steps, taking long strides and swinging your arms briskly and loosely. [6]After roughly 100 yards at this brisk pace, you should feel ready to jog. [7]Immediately break into a very slow trot: Lean your torso forward, and let one foot fall in front of the other (one foot barely leaving the ground while the other is on the pavement). [8]Maintain the slowest pace possible, just above a walk. [9]Do not bolt like a sprinter! [10]The biggest mistake is to start fast and injure yourself. [11]While jogging, relax your body. [12]Keep your shoulders straight and your head up, and enjoy the scenery—after all, it is one of the joys of jogging. [13]Keep your arms low and slightly bent at your sides. [14]Move your legs freely from the hips in an action that is easy, not forced. [15]Make your feet perform a heel-to-toe action: land on the heel; rock forward; take off from the toe.

Note that these instructions do not explain terms such as *long stride, torso,* and *sprinter* because these should be clear to the general reader. But *slow trot* is explained in detail; different readers might have different interpretations of this term.

GUIDELINES for Giving Instructions

- *Know the procedure.* Unless you have performed the task, do not try to write instructions for it.

- *Explain the purpose of the procedure.* Give readers enough background to understand why they need your instructions.

- *Make instructions complete but not excessive.* Don't assume that people know more than they really do, especially when you can perform the task almost automatically. (Think about when someone taught you to drive a car—or perhaps you have tried to teach someone else.) As in the jogging instructions, include enough detail for readers to understand what to do, but omit general and obvious steps such as "Put on your jogging shoes." Excessive details merely get in the way.

- *Show what to do.* Give them enough examples to visualize the procedure clearly.

- *Divide the procedure into simple steps and substeps.* Allow readers to focus on one task at a time.

- *Organize for the readers' understanding.* Instructions are almost always arranged in chronological order, with notes and precautions inserted for specific steps.

- *Make instructions immediately readable.* Instructions must be understood upon first reading because readers usually take immediate action. Because they emphasize the readers' role, write instructions in the second person, as direct address.

  Begin all steps and substeps with action verbs by using *active voice* ("move your legs" rather than "your legs should be moved") and the *imperative mood* ("rock forward" instead of "you should rock forward"), giving an immediate signal about the specific action to be taken.

  Use shorter sentences than usual: Use one sentence for one step, so readers can perform one action at a time.

  Finally, use transitional expressions (**while, after, next**) to show how the steps are connected.

- *Maintain a user-friendly and supportive tone.* Be encouraging instead of bossy.

- *Include troubleshooting advice.* Explain what to do when things go wrong ("If X doesn't work, first check Y and then do Z"). Place this advice near the end of your instructions.

Explaining How Something Happens

Besides showing how to do something, you often have to explain how things occur: how sunlight helps plants make chlorophyll; how a GPS system works;

how your town decided on its zoning laws. *Process explanation* emphasizes the process itself rather than the reader's or writer's role.

What readers want to know about a process

- *How does it happen? Or how is it made?*
- *When and where does it happen?*
- *What happens first, next, and so on?*
- *What is the result?*

The following example, written by a marine biologist, explains the process by which sea levels worldwide are rising. (This paragraph is part of the complete essay that appears on page 231.)

EXPLAINING HOW SOMETHING HAPPENS

Main point (1)
Order of events in the process (2–5)

Results of the process (6)

[1]The rise in sea level has been constant and gradual, but its effect on the shoreline has been dramatic. [2]Fifteen thousand years ago, much of the earth's water was locked up in glaciers and polar ice caps. [3]At that time, the shoreline was about 120 miles farther out. [4]Since then, the ice has been melting slowly and releasing its water into the oceans. [5]Sea level is now rising by nearly 1½ feet every hundred years—a rise caused both by polar ice cap and glacial melting, and by the actual settling of the land mass. [6]Because much of our coastal land is quite flat, for every rise of one foot in sea level, the shoreline retreats about 30 to 50 feet.

—Jane Lowe

Notice that the concrete, plain English style in the previous paragraph enables a broad and general audience to visualize the process. (For more on sharpening your visual details, see page 136.)

USING PROCESS ANALYSIS TO MAKE A POINT

Process explanations sometimes have a more persuasive purpose. In these cases, providing complete explanations and clear connections between steps helps convince readers that the process you're describing does happen as you say. These kinds of causal chains often support larger arguments. In the next example, Julia Schoonover uses a process analysis to support her claim that credit cards and college students are a dangerous combination.

PROCESS ANALYSIS THAT MAKES A POINT

Orienting statement (1)

Details of the process and its results (2–8)

[1]Granted, the temptation is hard to refuse. [2]Credit card companies marketing on campus offer free cards and sign-up gifts "with no obligation." [3]The "gifts" might include candy, coffee mugs, T-shirts, sports squeeze bottles, hip bags, and other paraphernalia. [4]The process seems harmless enough: Just fill in your Social Security number and other personal information, take your pick from the array of gifts, and cancel the card when it arrives. [5]But

these companies know exactly what they're doing. [6]They know that misusing the card is often easier than canceling it. [7]They know that many of us work part time and are paid little. [8]They know that most of us will be unable to pay more than the minimum balance each month—meaning big-time interest for years. [9]Don't be seduced by instant credit.

Main point (9)

—*Julia Schoonover*

GUIDELINES for Explaining How Something Happens

■ *Introduce the process by explaining what it is and why, when, and where it happens.*

■ *Divide the process into clear and distinct steps.*

■ *Present each phase of the process in logical order.*

■ *Use language that enables readers to visualize the process.*

■ *Use transitional expressions (pages 105–107) to keep readers oriented and to guide them through the phases.*

■ *Provide all the details your audience will need in order to understand the process.*

BEYOND THE WRITING CLASSROOM

USING PROCESS ANALYSIS

■ **In other courses:** You might instruct a classmate in dissecting a frog or in using the school's email network. You might answer an essay question about how economic inflation occurs or how hikers and campers can succumb to hypothermia.

■ **On the job:** You might instruct a colleague or customer in accessing a database or shipping radioactive waste. You might explain to coworkers how the budget for various departments is determined or how the voice-mail system works.

■ **In the community:** You might instruct a friend in casting for largemouth bass or preparing for a job interview. You might explain to parents the selection process for new teachers followed by your local parent–teacher group.

What additional audiences and uses for process analysis can you think of?

PROCESS ANALYSIS AS A PRIMARY ESSAY STRATEGY

Processes occur in our personal experiences as well—for example, our stages of maturation, of emotional growth and development, of intellectual awareness. The following essay traces a personal process some readers might consider horrifying: the stages of learning to live by scavenging through garbage. As you read, think about how the factual and "objective" style paints a gruesome portrait of survival at the margin of American affluence.

DUMPSTER DIVING

I began Dumpster diving about a year before I became homeless.

I prefer the term *scavenging*. I have heard people, evidently meaning to be polite, use the word *foraging*, but I prefer to reserve that word for gathering nuts and berries and such, which I also do, according to the season and opportunity.

I like the frankness of the word *scavenging*. I live from the refuse of others. I am a scavenger. I think it a sound and honorable niche, although if I could I would naturally prefer to live the comfortable consumer life, perhaps —and only perhaps—as a slightly less wasteful consumer owing to what I have learned as a scavenger.

Except for jeans, all my clothes come from Dumpsters. Boom boxes, candles, bedding, toilet paper, medicine, books, a typewriter, a virgin male love doll, coins sometimes amounting to many dollars: all came from Dumpsters. And, yes, I eat from Dumpsters, too.

There is a predictable series of stages that a person goes through in learning to scavenge. At first the new scavenger is filled with disgust and self-loathing. He is ashamed of being seen.

This stage passes with experience. The scavenger finds a pair of running shoes that fit and look and smell brand-new. He finds a pocket calculator in perfect working order. He finds pristine ice cream, still frozen, more than he can eat or keep. He begins to understand: people do throw away perfectly good stuff, a lot of perfectly good stuff.

At this stage he may become lost and never recover. All the Dumpster divers I have known come to the point of trying to acquire everything they touch. Why not take it, they reason; it is all free. This is, of course, hopeless, and most divers come to realize that they must restrict themselves to items of relatively immediate utility.

The finding of objects is becoming something of an urban art. Even respectable, employed people will sometimes find something tempting sticking out of a Dumpster or standing beside one. Quite a number of people, not all of them of the bohemian type, are willing to brag that they found this or that piece in the trash.

But eating from Dumpsters is the thing that separates the dilettanti from the professionals. Eating safely involves three principles: using the senses and common sense to evaluate the condition of the found materials; knowing the Dumpsters of a given area and checking them regularly; and seeking always to answer the question "Why was this discarded?"

Yet perfectly good food can be found in Dumpsters. Canned goods, for example, turn up fairly often in the Dumpsters I frequent. I also have few qualms about dry foods such as crackers, cookies, cereal, chips, and pasta if they are free of visible contaminants and still dry and crisp. Raw fruits and vegetables with intact skins seem perfectly safe to me, excluding, of course, the obviously rotten. Many are discarded for minor imperfections that can be pared away.

A typical discard is a half jar of peanut butter—though nonorganic peanut butter does not require refrigeration and is unlikely to spoil in any reasonable time. One of my favorite finds is yogurt—often discarded, still sealed, when the expiration has passed—because it will keep for several days, even in warm weather.

No matter how careful I am I still get dysentery at least once a month, oftener in warm weather. I do not want to paint too romantic a picture. Dumpster diving has serious drawbacks as a way of life.

I find from the experience of scavenging two rather deep lessons. The first is to take what I can use and let the rest go. I have come to think that there is no value in the abstract. A thing I cannot use or make useful, perhaps by trading, has no value, however fine or rare it may be. The second lesson is the transience of material being. I do not suppose that ideas are immortal, but certainly they are longer-lived than material objects.

The things I find in Dumpsters, the love letters and rag dolls of so many lives, remind me of this lesson. Now I hardly pick up a thing without envisioning the time I will cast it away. This, I think, is a healthy state of mind. Almost everything I have now has already been cast out at least once, proving that what I own is valueless to someone.

I find that my desire to grab for the gaudy bauble has been largely sated. I think this is an attitude I share with the very wealthy—we both know there is plenty more wherever we have come from. Between us are the rat-race millions who have confounded their selves with the objects they grasp and who nightly scavenge the cable channels for they know not what.

I am sorry for them.

—*Lars Eighner*

Identify some of the referential details Eighner has selected to make his point: Do his details have sufficient visual quality? Notice also the tone: What does the tone tell us about this writer's attitude toward his subject and audience? How do we know? What are the signals?

CASE STUDY

READING AND RESPONDING TO INSTRUCTIONS

In this case study, student writer Cathy Nichols develops her own set of instructions in her response to the following professional essay.

ESSAY FOR ANALYSIS AND RESPONSE

Frank White, author of these instructions, is a counselor at the North American Survival School, which offers courses ranging from mountaineering to desert survival. Besides being a certified emergency medical technician, White has had extensive experience hiking and camping in snake-infested terrain. The school is preparing a survival manual for distribution to all its students. This writer's contribution is a set of instructions on dealing with snakebites. Many of the readers will have no experience with snakes (or first aid), so White decided to be brief and simple, for quick, easy reading as needed. As you read, think about some procedure that you would know how to explain.

HOW TO DEAL WITH SNAKEBITES

Every year, thousands of Americans are injured—sometimes fatally—by poisonous snakebites. Fewer than 1 percent of poisonous snakebites are fatal. But many of the injuries and most fatalities can be avoided as long as you are alert and cautious and follow a few instructions.

Although most snakes bite, in the United States only rattlesnakes, copperheads, coral snakes, and water moccasins are poisonous. All these are most dangerous in early spring, when venom sacs are full from winter hibernation. Rattlers are found in most of the United States, while copperheads are only in the East. Coral snakes range throughout the South, while water moccasins live in Southern lowlands and swampy areas. Some simple precautions can help you avoid snakebites. Since most bites occur around the ankles, wear long, thick pants and high boots of heavy rubber or leather. Also, watch where you walk, swim, or sleep. As you walk, watch where you put your feet, especially in climbing over fallen trees or stone walls. In moccasin country, swim only where the water is moving and the shoreline is free of heavy vegetation. If you cannot sleep in a closed tent with a snakeproof floor, place your sleeping bag on a high, dry, open spot, and keep it zipped. When you do encounter a snake, freeze! Then move backward *very* slowly, making no moves that will frighten the snake. In case these precautions fail, always carry a snakebite kit.

Most poisonous snakebites are easy enough to recognize. Within minutes the wound will swell and change color, often bright red. You will feel a throbbing pain that radiates from the bite. The swelling, redness, and pain will spread gradually and steadily. (Bites from nonvenomous snakes, in contrast, resemble mere pinpricks.) You may experience nausea or hot flashes. In any case, if you are uncertain whether the bite is poisonous, treat it as poisonous.

If you have been bitten, *do nothing to hasten the spread of the poison.* Above all, don't panic. Resist the temptation to walk, run, or move quickly. And stay away from stimulants such as coffee, tea, cola, alcohol, or aspirin. In fact, don't ingest anything. Do not raise the area of the bite above the level of your heart. Do not apply a tourniquet. Do not try to cut into the wound and to suck out the poison by mouth. Instead, take a minute to think calmly about what you *should* do.

Take the following steps immediately. Remain calm and move as little as possible. Remove any rings, belts, or other constricting items. Keep the wound lower than the rest of your body so the poison remains localized. Have companions get you to a hospital as quickly as possible, without causing you needless exertion. If the hospital is more than an hour away, and you have a snakebite kit, use it. If the snake can be killed—safely—bring the dead snake with you—securely encased—to the emergency room, for precise identification. If possible, notify the emergency room by phone of your impending arrival.

By taking precautions and remaining alert, you should not have to fear snakebites. But if you are bitten, your best bet is to remain calm and seek medical help.

—*Frank White*

Questions About the Reading

CONTENT

- *What opening strategy is used to create interest?*
- *Is the information adequate and appropriate for the stated audience and purpose? Explain.*
- *What specific readers' questions are answered here?*

ORGANIZATION

- *What is the order of the body paragraphs? Is this the most effective order? Explain.*
- *Is the conclusion adequate and appropriate? Explain.*

STYLE

- *Are these instructions immediately readable? Explain.*
- *Is the tone of these instructions too bossy? Explain.*

RESPONDING TO READING

After reading and analyzing Frank White's essay and answering the questions on pages 154 and 155, Catherine Nichols recalled her own experience as a new commuter student and decided to write a basic "survival guide" for commuters during their first week of school. To keep her instructions brief and straightforward, Nichols divided the procedure into four basic steps: getting essential items, checking out the library, meeting one's adviser, and establishing a support network.

In drafting and revising her essay, Nichols followed the instruction guidelines on page 222 and the revision checklists on pages 62–63 and 230.

> Note

Even though process analysis is the dominant rhetorical strategy in Nichols's essay, she also relies on other strategies, such as description, illustration, division, and classification.

Title gives a forecast
Uses encouraging tone

Establishes writer's
knowledge on this topic

A FIRST-WEEK SURVIVAL GUIDE FOR COMMUTERS

Welcome, first-year students! You've probably read most of the "official" literature provided by this university. But as a recent first-year commuter who spent most of her first week lost, I'd like to offer some "unofficial" advice! If, like many commuters, you've managed to avoid freshman orientation, I hope you'll consider this a crash course for avoiding needless stress and dodging some common headaches.

Begin by getting the essential items: campus map, ID card, books, and a parking sticker. First, pick up a campus map at the Registrar's office or print one from the office Web site. Next, find the Campus Center, and go to the Student Services office to pick up your student ID. Adjacent to Student Services is your next stop, the bookstore. Bring your class schedule so that you buy the right books for your class "section." If your schedule says "ENL 101-09," that means the subject is English, the class name is Reading and Writing I, and at least nine separate classes of that course exist. (Different teachers assign different texts.) Finally, head for the Campus Police office to pick up your parking sticker. Bring your student ID and car registration. *Note:* Try to do these things *before* classes begin.

As a commuter, your best bet for studying on campus is the school library, so get to know it right away. Jot down the library hours, usually posted by the entrance. (The library closes for federal holidays and has some quirky weekend hours but its online resources are always available.) Library seating is ample, but noisy groups tend to collect at the larger tables. Look for a quiet corner on one of the upper floors. English 101 classes usually take a group library tour during the semester. If your class doesn't, or if you miss it, make an appointment with one of the librarians. No one graduates without producing research papers, so acquainting yourself with the print as well as electronic resources ahead of time will save valuable study hours.

As soon as classes begin, get to know your adviser—the person you see for choosing or adding and dropping courses and for any kind of advice. Offices are usually on the third floor of academic buildings, organized by departments. Each department has a main office and a secretary. If you don't know who your adviser is, the secretary can tell you. The department office (or Web site) can also provide you with a course "checklist." This will tell you which courses you need to complete your degree. Unlike high school teachers, college professors are not required to be on campus all day. Jot down your adviser's office hours (posted outside individual offices or in the department), office phone number, and email address.

Commuters don't have the luxury of always being on campus, so establish a support network during your first week of classes. As corny as it sounds, find a buddy in each class. Or better yet, find someone who shares more than one class with you. Exchange phone numbers (and email addresses if possible). This way, if you do have to miss a class, you will be able to keep up with the assignments. Also, check out the Tutoring Center (Blake Hall, second floor) in case you ever need help. Paid for by your basic tuition, tutors are available for most subjects. They are fellow students who are familiar not only with the university but with the specific courses and professors as well. Tutoring is available on a walk-in basis or by regular appointment.

You're being asked to adjust to many different expectations, all at the same time. A little confusion and anxiety are understandable. But the entire university community is committed to helping its new students.

Margin annotations:

Explains the procedure's purpose, in a friendly tone

First major step (classifies "essential items")

Transitions throughout mark time and sequence

Gives example

Uses chronological order for steps and substeps

Uses note to emphasize vital information

Second major step (divides each major step into simple substeps)

Addresses the readers directly throughout

Third major step (gives just enough detail for this audience)

Fourth major step (uses a short sentence for each substep)

Includes detail as needed

Maintains an encouraging tone throughout

Includes troubleshooting advice	*Note:* If you have any questions about these steps—or about anything else—*ask someone!* Chances are other people have asked the same question or experienced the same problem. Best of luck.
	—*Catherine Nichols*

✔ A CHECKLIST for Giving Instructions

- ☐ Have you **performed** this procedure, and do you **know enough** about it?
- ☐ Is the **purpose** of the procedure explained?
- ☐ Is the amount of **detail** appropriate for the intended audience?
- ☐ Is all **needless** and **obvious** information omitted?
- ☐ Do **explanations** enable readers to understand what to do?
- ☐ Do **examples** enable readers to visualize how to do it correctly?
- ☐ Do **steps and substeps** allow readers to **focus on one task** at a time?
- ☐ Do the instructions follow the **exact sequence** of steps?
- ☐ Do **notes, cautions, or warnings** appear when needed **before** the step?
- ☐ Is each step phrased in **second-person, direct address**?
- ☐ Does each step begin with an **action verb**?
- ☐ Are all steps in **active voice** and the **imperative mood**?
- ☐ Do steps generally have **short sentences**?
- ☐ Are **transitions** adequate for marking time and sequence?
- ☐ Is the **tone** encouraging and supportive, not bossy?
- ☐ Is **troubleshooting advice** included as needed?

(See page 222 for more on each of these criteria.)

CASE STUDY

READING AND RESPONDING TO A PROCESS EXPLANATION

In this case study, student writer Bill Kelly develops his own process essay in his response to the following professional essay.

ESSAY FOR ANALYSIS AND RESPONSE

Jane Lowe, marine biologist, wrote this process explanation as part of a pamphlet for a general audience on oceanside parks in her state. As you read, try to think of a process that you could explain to general readers.

How Barrier Beaches Survive and Renew Themselves

Barrier beaches are sand ridges that rim more than 50 percent of the southern shore of our state. These ridges rise above the high-tide line, running parallel with the mainland, but separated from it by a string of salt ponds. Barrier beaches are not fixed, stable structures. Like a flexible living organism they are continually moving and adjusting in response to rising sea levels and storms.

The rise in sea level has been constant and gradual, but its effect on the shoreline has been dramatic. Fifteen thousand years ago, much of the earth's water was locked up in glaciers and polar ice caps. At that time, the shoreline was about 120 miles farther out. Since then, the ice has been melting slowly and releasing its water into the oceans. Sea level is now rising by nearly 1½ feet every hundred years—a rise caused both by polar ice cap and glacial melting, and by the actual settling of the land mass. Because much of our coastal land is quite flat, for every rise of one foot in sea level, the shoreline retreats about 30 to 50 feet.

The barrier beach responds to the rising sea level, as well as to the violent storms that drive water against the shore. Sands of the barrier beach are constantly shifted by these forces and redistributed in such a way that the barrier remains intact. In order to survive, the barrier must possess an adequate sand supply in its beaches, dunes, and areas behind the dunes. Storm waves strike the barrier, picking up sand from the beach and foredunes. This sand is carried farther into the barrier and deposited as the waves lose their energy and slow down. Thus, a coastal barrier serves as an "energy sponge," absorbing the full impact of natural forces rather than being destroyed by them.

The sand's movement is the key to the barrier's flexible response to natural forces. Although the coastal mainland is slowly being drowned by rising seas, barrier beaches and their vegetation move landward and survive. Three processes make this survival possible: overwash, inlet formation, and dune migration (which depends on beachgrass for support).

Overwash occurs when storms force ocean water between or over the dunes onto the back of the barrier beach. The water carries sand from the beach and foredunes to the back of the dunes, depositing it in the form of layered shelves, or "overwash fans." The surf in a violent storm can deposit more than one hundred tons of sand as a single overwash fan. If this sand were not carried to the back of the barrier, it could be washed out to sea. So through continual movement the barrier is able to retreat before a rising sea and storms, thereby preserving its system of beach and dunes.

Inlets are formed during storms as rushing water carves channels through a barrier beach, providing an entry for sand to move behind the barrier. After the water passes through the inlets and slows down, it deposits its load of sand, creating shallow areas on the salt-pond side of the inlet. These shoals, or "inlet deltas," will provide a base for the retreating barrier beach.

Instead of being washed away, the dunes gradually migrate landward. On many of our state's barrier beaches, overwash becomes a basic mechanism for this movement. Overwash builds up the back side of the barrier; the new layers of sand provide the foundation for the dunes to build on as they are forced back. Through a process called "roll-over," what is now the back of the barrier will one day be the beach. In as little as 25 years, the landward migration has been extensive—about 30 feet for many barrier beaches.

In addition to withstanding destructive forces, the barrier beach can renew itself as it moves landward, both abilities derived mainly from its system of plants. American beachgrass, a natural stabilizer of barrier beaches, thrives in this environment of blowing sand and salt spray. Its network of roots and underground stems holds the existing dunes and limits erosion caused by waves. Also, blades of beachgrass trap windblown sand. As main stems are buried, new stems grow up from the roots.

When overwash occurs, beachgrass stems are torn loose from the foredunes and deposited, with the overwash sand, in the fans behind the dunes. New grasses grow from these fragments and the overwash fans become vegetated, preventing overwash sand from blowing away. As the plants grow, the grass blades trap even more sand, helping the overwash fan become a base for new dune formation as the barrier beach retreats landward.

—*Jane Lowe*

Questions About the Reading

CONTENT

- *Is the title too long? Explain.*
- *Is there a thesis? If so, where?*
- *Is the four-paragraph introduction necessary? Explain the role of each of the four paragraphs.*
- *Is the information appropriate for the intended audience? Explain.*
- *What specific reader questions are answered in the body?*

ORGANIZATION

- *Are the body paragraphs arranged in the best order for readers to follow the process? Explain.*

- *Why does this essay have no specific conclusion?*

STYLE

- *What is the outstanding feature of this essay? Give an example.*
- *Give one example of each of the following sentence constructions and explain briefly how each reinforces the writer's meaning: passive construction, subordination, short sentence.*

RESPONDING TO READING

After reading and analyzing the selection by Jane Lowe, part-time student Bill Kelly decided on a process he could explain clearly. Kelly belongs to an environmental group studying the problem of acid rain in its Massachusetts community. (Massachusetts is among the northeastern states most affected by acid rain.) To gain community support, the environmentalists must educate citizens about the problem. In his essay Bill explains the acid rain process by dividing it into three major phases.

Working toward the final draft shown here, Kelly relied on the page 224 guidelines and the previous questions about Lowe's essay. He also consulted the checklist for process analysis (page 234) and the revision checklist (pages 62–63).

HOW ACID RAIN DEVELOPS, SPREADS, AND DESTROYS

Paragraph 1 introduces the overall process and closes with an orienting sentence

[1]Acid rain is environmentally damaging rainfall that occurs after fossil fuels burn, releasing nitrogen and sulfur oxides into the atmosphere. Acid rain, simply stated, increases the acidity level of waterways because these nitrogen and sulfur oxides combine with the air's normal moisture. The resulting rainfall is far more acidic than normal rainfall. Acid rain is a silent threat because its effects, although slow, are cumulative. This analysis explains the cause, the distribution cycle, and the effects of acid rain.

Paragraph 2 provides detail about the first phase of the process (how acid rain is created)

[2]Most research shows that power plants burning oil or coal are the primary cause of acid rain. Fossil fuels contain a number of elements that are released during combustion. Two of these, sulfur oxide and nitrogen oxide, combine with normal moisture to produce sulfuric acid and nitric acid. The released gases undergo a chemical change as they combine with atmospheric ozone and water vapor. The resulting rain or snowfall is more acid than normal precipitation.

Paragraph 3 and 4 define "acid level"

[3]Acid level is measured by pH readings. The pH scale runs from 0 through 14; a pH of 7 is considered neutral. (Distilled water has a pH of 7.) Numbers above 7 indicate increasing degrees of alkalinity. (Household ammonia has a pH of 11.) Numbers below 7 indicate increasing acidity. Movement in either direction on the pH scale, however, means multiplying by 10. Lemon juice, which has a pH value of 2, is 10 times more acidic than apples, which have a pH of 3, and 1,000 times more acidic than carrots, which have a pH of 5.

Technical details throughout are explained clearly, enabling readers to visualize the process

[4]Because of carbon dioxide (an acid substance) normally present in air, unaffected rainfall has a pH of 5.6. At this time, the pH of precipitation in the northeastern United States and Canada is between 4.5 and 4. In Massachusetts, rain and snowfall have an average pH reading of 4.1. A pH reading below 5 is considered to be abnormally acidic and therefore a threat to aquatic populations.

Paragraphs 5, 6, and 7 explain the second phase (how acid rain travels)

[5]Although it might seem that areas containing power plants would be most severely affected, acid rain can in fact travel thousands of miles from its source. Stack gases escape and drift with the wind currents. The sulfur and nitrogen oxides are thus able to travel great distances before they return to earth as acid rain.

[6]For an average of two to five days after emission, the gases follow the prevailing winds far from the point of origin. Estimates show that about 50 percent of the acid rain that affects Canada originates in the United States; at the same time, 15 to 25 percent of the U.S. acid rain problem originates in Canada.

Paragraphs 8, 9, and 10 explain to the third phase (how acid rain destroys)

[7]The tendency of stack gases to drift makes acid rain a widespread menace. More than two hundred lakes in the Adirondacks, hundreds of miles from any industrial center, are unable to support life because their water has become so acidic.

[8]Acid rain causes damage wherever it falls. It erodes various types of building rock, such as limestone, marble, and mortar, which are gradually eaten away by the constant bathing in acid. Damage to buildings, houses, monuments, statues, and cars is widespread. Some priceless monuments and carvings have already been destroyed, and even trees of some varieties are dying in large numbers.

[9]More important, however, is acid rain damage to waterways in the affected areas. Because of its high acidity, acid rain dramatically lowers the pH in lakes and streams. Although its effect is not immediate, acid rain eventually can make a waterway so acidic it dies. In areas with natural acid-buffering elements such as limestone, the diluted acid has less effect. The northeastern United States and Canada, however, lack this natural protection and so are continually vulnerable.

[10]The pH level in an affected waterway drops so low that some species cease to reproduce. In fact, a pH level of 5.1 to 5.4 means that fisheries are threatened; once a waterway reaches a pH level of 4.5, no fish reproduction occurs. Because each creature is part of the overall food chain, loss of one element in the chain disrupts the whole cycle.

Conclusion re-emphasizes the destructive effects of this process

[11]In the northeastern United States and Canada, the acidity problem is compounded by the runoff from acid snow. During the cold winter months, acid snow sits with little melting so that by spring thaw, the acid released is greatly concentrated. Aluminum and other heavy metals normally present in soil also are released by acid rain and runoff. These toxic substances leach into waterways in heavy concentrations, affecting fish in all stages of development.

—*Bill Kelly*

✔ A CHECKLIST for Process Explanation

☐ Have you **introduced** the process by explaining what it is and why, when, and where it happens?

☐ Have you **divided** the process into clear and distinct steps or phases?

☐ Is each phase presented in **logical order?**

☐ Are technical details explained in **clear language** that enables readers to visualize what is happening?

☐ Are there enough **transitions** to guide readers through the process?

☐ Is the amount of **detail** appropriate for the intended audience?

APPLICATIONS

14.1 **PARAGRAPH WARM-UP: GIVING INSTRUCTIONS** Choose an activity you perform well. Think of a situation requiring that you write instructions for that activity. Single out a major step in the process (such as pitching a baseball or adjusting ski bindings for safe release). Provide enough details so that the reader can perform that step safely and efficiently.

14.2 **PARAGRAPH WARM-UP: EXPLAINING HOW SOMETHING HAPPENS** Select some process in your university—admissions, registration, changing majors, finding a parking place. Write a process analysis that could anchor an argument for changes in the procedure.

14.3 **ESSAY PRACTICE: USING PROCESS ANALYSIS TO MAKE A POINT** Explore your reactions to "Dumpster Diving" using the questions on pages 154–155. What is Eighner's point about values? What are the main issues? How has this essay affected your thinking about these issues? As you reread the essay, try to recall some process that has played a role for you personally or for someone close to you. Perhaps you want to focus on the process of achievement (say, preparing for academic or athletic or career competition). Perhaps you have experienced or witnessed the process of giving in to human frailty (say, addiction to drugs, tobacco, alcohol, or food). Perhaps you know something about the process of enduring and recovering from personal loss or misfortune or disappointment. Identify your audience, and decide what you want these readers to do, think, or feel after reading your essay. Should they appreciate this process, try it themselves, avoid it, or what?

Whatever you write about—college or high school or family life or city streets—make a definite point about the larger meaning beyond the details of the process, about the values involved.

14.4 **ESSAY PRACTICE: GIVING INSTRUCTIONS** Assume a specific situation and audience (like those for snakebite procedures or for coping with one's first week in college), and write instructions for a specialized procedure or for anything that you can do well (no recipes, please). Be sure you know the process down to the smallest detail. Narrow your subject (perhaps to one complex activity within a longer procedure) so you can cover it fully. Avoid day-to-day procedures that college readers would already know (brushing teeth, washing hair, and other such elementary activities).

14.5 **ESSAY PRACTICE: EXPLAINING HOW SOMETHING HAPPENS** Select a specialized process that you understand well (from your major or from an area of interest), and explain that process to uninformed readers. Choose a process that has several distinct steps, and write so that your composition classmates gain detailed understanding. Do not merely generalize; get down to specifics.

14.6   **WEB-BASED PROJECT** Assume that you and your classmates are preparing to spend a semester abroad in an international exchange program in one particular country. People from different cultures will need to communicate effectively and sensitively, so your group will need to develop a measurable degree of cultural awareness.

Your assignment is to select a country and to research that culture's behaviors, attitudes, values, and social system in terms of how these variables influence the culture's communication preferences and expectations. For example, some cultures are offended when confronted with argument, criticism, or expressions of emotion. Some cultures observe special formalities in communicating (say, friendly inquiries and displays of concern about one's family). Some cultures observe rigidly pre-scribed etiquette while dining or visiting other people's homes.

What should you and your colleagues know about this culture in order to communicate effectively and diplomatically? Prepare a set of instructions for the basic dos and don'ts. Visit either the American University's Education Lab on Cross Cultural Communication at <**http://www.maec.org/cross/**> or Executive Planet at <**http://www.executiveplanet.com**> Web sites to get started, but don't limit yourself to these.

Be sure to credit each source of information and to attach copies of relevant Web pages to your instructions.

CHAPTER 15

Causal Analysis: Writing to Explain Why Something Happened or What Will Happen

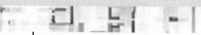

LEARNING OBJECTIVES FOR THIS CHAPTER

- Understand the role of *causal analysis* as a writing strategy
- Recognize that causal analysis can explain definite causes, as well as possible or probable causes

- Differentiate between effect-to-cause analysis and cause to-effect analysis
- Write an effective causal analysis (effect to cause or cause to effect) essay using the chapter guidelines

Analysis of reasons (causes) or consequences (effects) explains why something happened or what happens as a result of some event or incident.

What readers of causal analysis want to know

- *Why did it happen?*
- *What caused it?*
- *What are its effects?*
- *What will happen if it is done?*

If you awoke this morning with a sore shoulder (effect), you might recall exerting yourself yesterday at the college Frisbee Olympics (cause). You take aspirin, hoping for relief (effect). If the aspirin works, it will have *caused* you to feel better. But some causes and effects are harder to identify, such as the following example:

> CAUSE   EFFECT
>
> I tripped over a chair and broke my nose.

Other causes or effects could be identified for this statement:

> EFFECT   CAUSE
> I tripped over the chair because my apartment lights were out.
>
> EFFECT   CAUSE
> The lights were out because the power had been shut off.
>
> EFFECT   CAUSE
> The power was off because my roommate forgot to pay the electric bill.

In the above example, the *immediate* cause—the one most closely related to the effect—is that the writer tripped over the chair because the lights were out. However, if the true cause is more distant, be sure to make the chain of causality clear in your writing:

> CAUSE   EFFECT
> Because my roommate forgot to pay the electric bill, I tripped over a chair in the dark and broke my nose.

USING CAUSAL ANALYSIS TO EXPLAIN: DEFINITE CAUSES

As in process analysis (Chapter 14), writing that connects definite causes to their effects clarifies the relations among events in a causal chain. A *definite cause is apparent and verifiable* ("The engine's overheating is caused by a faulty radiator cap"). You write about definite causes when you explain why the combustion in a car engine causes the wheels to move or why the moon's orbit makes the tides rise and fall.

EXPLAINING A DEFINITE CAUSE

Topic sentence (1)
Causal chain (2–3)

Effects (4)
Conclusion (5)

[1]Some of the most serious accidents involving gas water heaters occur when a flammable liquid is used in the vicinity. [2]The heavier-than-air vapors of a flammable liquid such as gasoline can flow along the floor—even the length of a basement—and be explosively ignited by the flame of the water heater's pilot light or burner. [3]Because the victim's clothing often ignites, the resulting burn injuries are commonly serious and extremely painful. [4]They may require long hospitalization and can result in disfigurement or death. [5]Never, under any circumstances, use a flammable liquid near a gas heater or burner.

—*Consumer Product Safety Commission*

USING CAUSAL ANALYSIS TO MAKE A POINT: POSSIBLE OR PROBABLE CAUSES

Causal writing often explores *possible or probable causes—causes that are not apparent.* In these cases, thorough research, careful thought, and much effort are usually needed to argue for a specific cause.

Suppose you ask, "Why are there no children's day care facilities on our college campus?" Brainstorming leads to a number of possible causes, such as lack of need among students, faculty, and staff; high cost of liability insurance; lack of trained personnel; and lack of funding. You may find through your research that none of the above reasons are really the explanation, but that there is a lack of space on campus for a day care facility. If you were to make a case to the campus finance department to add a new day care facility on campus, your argument would need to focus on the most likely cause—lack of available space—and provide a solution, such as asking that funding for this facility become a priority given the genuine need for it and lack of anything else standing in the way. You would need to back up your argument by being clear, providing ample evidence, and using sound reasoning.

REASONING FROM EFFECT TO CAUSE

In reasoning from effect to cause, we examine a particular result, consequence, or outcome and try to determine the circumstances that might have produced such a result.

AN EFFECT-TO-CAUSE ANALYSIS

Effect (main point) (1)
Distant cause and examples (2)

[1]In the right situation, a perfectly sane person can hallucinate. [2]It is most likely to happen...in a place that provides little stimulation to [the] senses, such as a barren, unbroken landscape or a quiet, dimly lit room.

Examples (3–4)

Evidence (5)

Immediate cause (6–7)

[3]Hallucinations are an occupational hazard of truck drivers, radar scanners, and pilots. [4]These occupations have in common long periods of monotony: lengthy stretches of straight highway, the regular rhythms of radar patterns, the droning hum of engines. [5]A. L. Mosely of the Harvard School of Public Health found that every one of 33 long-distance truck drivers he surveyed could recall having at least one hallucination. [6]Monotony means that the brain gets fewer sensory messages from the outside. [7]As external stimulation drops off, the brain responds more to messages from inside itself.

—*Daniel Goleman*

Note

Keep in mind that faulty causal reasoning is extremely common, especially when we ignore other possible causes or we confuse mere coincidence with causation. (See page 369 for examples and discussion.)

GUIDELINES for Effect-to-Cause Analysis

- *Be sure the cause fits the effect.* Identify the immediate cause as well as any distant causes. For example, the immediate cause of a particular airplane crash might be a fuel tank explosion, in turn caused by a short circuit in frayed wiring, by faulty design, or by poor quality control by the manufacturer. Discussing only the immediate cause often merely scratches the surface of the problem.

- *Make the links between effect and cause clear.* To clarify his point, Daniel Goleman shows examples of "right" situations and "sane" persons. Research from Harvard provides convincing support. Goleman's reasoning follows:

    DISTANT CAUSE   IMMEDIATE CAUSE   EFFECT

    nonstimulating places ⟶ monotony ⟶ hallucination

    The distant cause is discussed first so that the immediate cause will make sense.

- *Distinguish clearly among possible, probable, and definite causes.* Unless the cause is obvious, limit your assertions by using *perhaps, probably, maybe, most likely, could, seems to, appears to,* or similar qualifiers that prevent you from making an unsupportable claim.

REASONING FROM CAUSE TO EFFECT

In reasoning from cause to effect, we examine a given set of circumstances and try to ascertain the outcome of those circumstances.

A CAUSE-TO-EFFECT ANALYSIS

What has the telephone done to us, or for us, in the hundred years of its existence? A few effects suggest themselves at once. It has saved lives by getting rapid word of illness, injury, or famine from remote places. By joining with the elevator to make possible the multistory residence or office building, it has made possible—for better or worse—the modern city. By bringing about a quantum leap in the speed and ease with which information moves from place to place, it has greatly accelerated the rate of scientific and technological change and growth in industry. Beyond doubt it has crippled if not killed the ancient art of letter writing. It has made living alone possible for persons with normal social impulses; by so doing, it has played a role in one of the greatest social changes of this century, the breakup of the multigenerational household. It has made the waging of war chillingly more efficient than formerly. Perhaps (though not probably) it has prevented wars that might have arisen out of international misunderstanding caused by written communications. Or perhaps—again not probably—by magnifying and extending irrational personal conflicts based on voice contact, it has caused wars. Certainly it has extended the scope of human conflicts, since it impartially disseminates the useful knowledge of scientists and the babble of bores, the affection of the affectionate and the malice of the malicious.

—*John Brooks*

GUIDELINES for Cause-to-Effect Analysis

- *Show that the effects fit the cause.* To clarify and support his point, John Brooks (above) shows the telephone's effects on familiar aspects of modern life. Because his purpose is to discuss effects in general (not only positive effects), the author balances his development with both positive and negative effects.

- *Make links between cause and effects clear.* The reasoning goes like this:

     CAUSE   IMMEDIATE EFFECT   ULTIMATE EFFECTS

telephone ⟶ created rapid communication ⟶ saved lives, led to the modern city, and so on

     CAUSE   IMMEDIATE EFFECT   ULTIMATE EFFECT

telephone ⟶ enabled people to live alone ⟶ led to breakup of multigenerational household

Without the link provided by the immediate effects, the ultimate effects would make no sense:

The telephone has saved lives. [*Why?*]

It has made possible the modern city. [*Why?*]

It has perhaps caused wars. [*Why?*]

- *Consider confounding factors (alternative explanations for a particular effect).* For instance, studies indicating that regular exercise improves health might be overlooking the fact that healthy people tend to exercise more often than those who are unhealthy.

USING CAUSAL ANALYSIS

BEYOND THE WRITING CLASSROOM

- **In other courses:** A research paper might explore the causes of the Israeli-Palestinian conflict or the effects of stress on college students. A report for the dean of students might explain students' disinterest in campus activities or the effect of a ban on smoking in public buildings.

- **On the job:** In workplace problem solving, you might analyze high absenteeism among company employees or the malfunction of equipment.

- **In the community:** Perhaps local citizens need to know how air quality will be affected if your power plant changes from coal to oil or how increasing enrollment has affected the quality of education at your local high school.

In what other situations might causal analysis make a difference?

CAUSAL ANALYSIS AS A PRIMARY ESSAY STRATEGY

In this selection, a psychologist points out the dangers of inflated self-esteem. As you read, think about how certain school experiences affected your self-esteem. In what ways has your own sense of self-esteem differed in high school versus college? What were the causes of that change?

SHOULD SCHOOLS TRY TO BOOST SELF-ESTEEM?

Beware the Dark Side

"We must raise children's self-esteem!" How often has this sentiment been expressed in recent years in schools, homes, and meeting rooms around the United States? The sentiment reflects the widespread, well-intentioned, earnest, and yet rather pathetic hope that if we can only persuade our kids to love themselves more, they will stop dropping out, getting pregnant, carrying weapons, taking drugs, and getting into trouble, and instead will start achieving great things in school and out.

Unfortunately, the large mass of knowledge that research psychologists have built up around self-esteem does not justify that hope. At best, high self-esteem is a mixed blessing whose total effects are likely to be small and minor. At worst, the pursuit of high self-esteem is a foolish, wasteful, and self-destructive enterprise that may end up doing more harm than good.

Writers on controversial topics should acknowledge their biases, and so let me confess mine: I have a strong bias in favor of self-esteem. I have been excited about self-esteem ever since my student days at Princeton, when I first heard that it was a topic of study. Over the past two decades I have probably published more studies on self-esteem than anybody else in the United States (or elsewhere). It would be great for my career if self-esteem could do everything its boosters hope: I'd be dining frequently at the White House and advising policy-makers on how to fix the country's problems.

It is therefore with considerable personal disappointment that I must report that the enthusiastic claims of the self-esteem movement mostly range from fantasy to hogwash. The effects of self-esteem are small, limited, and not all good. Yes, a few people here and there end up worse off because their self-esteem was too low. Then again, other people end up worse off because their self-esteem was too high. And most of the time self-esteem makes surprisingly little difference.

Self-esteem is, literally, how favorably a person regards himself or herself. It is perception (and evaluation), not reality. For example, I think the world would be a better place if we could all manage to be a little nicer to each other. But that's hard: We'd all have to discipline ourselves to change. The self-esteem approach, in contrast, is to skip over the hard work of changing our actions and instead just let us all *think* we're nicer. That won't make the world any better. People with high self-esteem are not in fact any nicer than people with low self-esteem—in fact, the opposite is closer to the truth.

High self-esteem means thinking well of oneself, regardless of whether that perception is based on substantive achievement or mere wishful thinking and self-deception. High self-esteem can mean *confident* and *secure*—but it can also mean *conceited, arrogant, narcissistic,* and *egotistical.*

A recent, widely publicized study dramatized the fact that self-esteem consists of perception and is not necessarily based on reality. In an international scholastic competition, American students achieved the lowest average scores among all participating nationalities. But the American kids rated themselves and their performance the highest. This is precisely what comes of focusing on self-esteem: poor performance accompanied by plenty of empty self-congratulation. Put another way, we get high self-esteem as inflated perceptions covering over a rather dismal reality.

Looking ahead, it is alarming to think what will happen when this generation of schoolchildren grows up into adults who may continue thinking they are smarter than the rest of the world—while actually being dumber. America will be a land of conceited fools.

All of this might fairly be discounted if America were really suffering from an epidemic of low self-esteem, such as if most American schoolchildren generally had such negative views of themselves that they were unable to tackle their homework. But that's not the case. On the contrary, as I'll explain shortly, self-esteem is already inflated throughout the United States. The average American already regards himself or herself as above average. At this point, any further boosting of self-esteem is likely to approach the level of grandiose, egotistical delusions.

Boosting Self-Esteem: The Problem of Inflation

Most (though not all) of the problems linked to high self-esteem involve inflated self-esteem, in the sense of overestimating oneself. Based on the research findings produced in laboratories all over North America, I have no objection to people forming a sober, accurate recognition of their actual talents and accomplishments. The violence, the self-defeating behaviors, and the other problems tend to be most acute under conditions of threatened egotism, and inflated self-esteem increases that risk. After all, if you really are smart, your experiences will tend to confirm that fact, and so there's not much danger in high self-esteem that is based on accurate recognition of your intelligence. On the other hand, if you overestimate your abilities, reality will be constantly showing you up and bursting your bubble, and so your (inflated) self-opinion will be bumping up against threats—and those encounters lead to destructive responses.

Unfortunately, a school system that seeks to boost self-esteem in general is likely to produce the more dangerous (inflated) form of self-esteem. It would be fine, for example, to give a hard test and then announce the top few scores for general applause. Such a system recognizes the successful ones, and it shows the rest what the important criteria are (and how much they may need to improve). What is dangerous and worrisome is any procedure that would allow the other students to think that they are just as accomplished as the top scorers even though they did not perform as well. Unfortunately, the self-esteem movement often works in precisely this wrong-headed fashion.

Some students will inevitably be smarter, work harder, learn more, and perform better than others. There is no harm (and in fact probably some positive value) in helping these individuals recognize their superior accomplishments and talents. Such self-esteem is linked to reality and hence less prone to causing dangers and problems.

On the other hand, there is considerable danger and harm in falsely boosting the self-esteem of the other students. It is fine to encourage them to work harder and try to gain an accurate appraisal of their strengths and weaknesses, and it is also fine to recognize their talents and accomplishments in other (including nonacademic) spheres, but don't give them positive feedback that they have not earned. (Also, don't downplay the importance of academic achievement as the central goal of school, such as by suggesting that success at sports or crafts is just as good.) To encourage the lower-performing students to regard their performance just as favorably as the top learners—a strategy all too popular with the self-esteem movement—is a tragic mistake. If successful, it results only in inflated self-esteem, which is the recipe for a host of problems and destructive patterns.

The logical implications of this argument show exactly when self-esteem should be boosted. When people seriously underestimate their abilities and accomplishments, they need boosting. For example, a student who falsely believes she can't succeed at math may end up short-changing herself and failing to fulfill her potential unless she can be helped to realize that yes, she does have the ability to master math.

In contrast, self-esteem should not be boosted when it is already in the accurate range (or higher). A student who correctly believes that math is not his strong point should not be given exaggerated notions of what he can accomplish. Otherwise, the eventual result will be failure and heartbreak. Along the way he's likely to be angry, troublesome, and prone to blame everybody else when something goes wrong.

In my years as an educator I have seen both patterns. But which is more common? Whether boosting self-esteem in general will be helpful or harmful depends on the answer. And the answer is overwhelmingly clear. Far, far more Americans of all ages have accurate or inflated views of themselves than underestimate themselves. They don't need boosting.

Dozens of studies have documented how inflated self-esteem is. Research interest was sparked some years ago by a survey in which 90 percent of adults rated themselves as "above average" in driving ability. After all, only half can really be above average. Similar patterns are found with almost all good qualities. A survey about leadership ability found that only 2 percent of high school students rated themselves as below average. Meanwhile, a whopping 25 percent claimed to be in the top 1 percent! Similarly, when asked about ability to get along with others, no students at all said they were below average.

Responses to scales designed to measure self-esteem show the same pattern. There are always plenty of scores at the high end and plenty in the middle, but only a few struggle down toward the low end. This seems to be true no matter which of the many self-esteem scales is used. Moreover, the few individuals who do show the truly low self-esteem scores probably suffer from multiple problems that need professional therapy. Self-esteem boosting from schools would not cure them.

Obviously there's precious little evidence of low self-esteem in such numbers. By definition, plenty of people are in reality below average, but most of them refuse to acknowledge it. Meanwhile large numbers of people clearly overestimate themselves. The top 1 percent can really only contain 1 percent, not the 25 percent who claim to belong there. Meanwhile, the problem that would justify programs aimed at boosting self-esteem—people who significantly underestimate themselves—is extremely rare.

—*Roy F. Baumeister*

By analyzing the causes and the effect of the self-esteem movement Baumeister presents his convincing critique of a widely popular notion.

CASE STUDY

READING AND RESPONDING

In this case study, student writer John Saurette relies primarily on causal analysis in his response to the following professional essay.

ESSAY FOR ANALYSIS AND RESPONSE

This next selection, "Don't Like What You're Wearing," appeared in *Newsweek*. In his essay, a father ponders why he disapproves of his 9-year-old son's clothing choices and asks himself "What's my problem?"

As you read, think about disagreements you've had with adults (or children) over clothing styles. What were the causes of such disagreements? What were the effects?

CLOTHES WOES

My son turned 9 recently, and I am surprised to find myself party to a subtle, low-grade tussle with him over his clothes. In the last few months he has taken up a style of dressing that, for reasons not entirely clear to me, I do not particularly like: large, baggy pants; big sneakers that bear the name of famous young basketball players; any shirt or sweat shirt with writing on it. Hats, too, he loves, and wears constantly—baseball hats, usually, though recently he has become enamored of a blue, camouflage number, pulled tightly onto his head, visor curled ominously around his eyes. No matter which corner of the cluttered closet I throw it into with my private hopes, it always reappears on his head.

Attempts to get him to wear shirts without writing on them—nice, simple, collared shirts from the Gap, for example—are all for naught. They remain neatly folded in his top drawer. Nice, khaki pants remain untouched for weeks, then months, until, one morning after the usual struggle, he pulls them out and triumphantly announces, "Dad, they don't fit anymore. They're too tight!" (Time is on his side.)

The struggle, I realize, is an ancient one, and I am surprised to find myself cast in the role of a doughty Ward Cleaver to the rebellious young Beaver. It's odd, as I've never been held up as a paragon of fashion myself. As a child I tended toward the conservative, and I remember a couple of titanic struggles with my parents over a pair of pants that seemed to me a half inch too short. And I was heartbroken to discover that the blue camping shorts and plaid shirt that I begged my mother to order out of a catalog did not turn me into the cherubic blond boy in the photograph. In college I grew my hair long and took on a look that now I recognize as a precursor to grunge—baggy polyester work pants and ill-fitting coats that I bought at the old-men's store.

My wife does not fully share my anxieties about our son's clothes. It was she who caved in and bought him the Iverson sneakers ($69.99) and, in a moment of weakness and flagging judgment, succumbed to the camouflage hat. She is less bothered by the sight of him playing basketball with his hat on sideways, one pants leg halfway up his shin, Iversons barely attached to his feet. But she was on the front lines of a struggle the other day at the mall, where the only coats for sale featured, in large, bold letters, the name of their manufacturer: ADIDAS, NIKE, or HILFIGER.

Am I actually a cultural conservative dressed in liberal tweed, out of step with the times, nervous that my son is affecting the style of a hip-hop culture that makes me nervous? Is there a racial aspect to my ambivalence? Am I overly sensitive to the remarks of the playground moms who, as we watch our children play basketball, observe, "He's really changed!" followed by meaningful silence? Am I fearful of his going the way of the shy, smiling boys I knew when they were children, and have watched slowly turn into cigarette-smoking teenagers who glower at me? When I say hello, sometimes, they look up, surprised, and the shy smile of their childhood briefly returns.

But what I once took as a largely urban phenomenon clearly is not: we went out to the small town where I grew up, the other day, an hour from the city, and as we played in the yard three or four boys strolled by, their enormous pants billowing like sails in the warm spring wind. I don't want to be an old stick-in-the-mud, but I draw the line at pants trying to slide down the backside. "Dad," he protests, "I have no belt!" Nor do I want my good-looking son turned into an unpaid walking billboard for Nike or Adidas or Hilfiger. Beyond that, I've probably got some work to do myself, updating my own antiquated and overly mythologized sense of fashion and cultural iconography.

The baseball hat, after all, is as American as apple pie, emblematic of virility and a peculiar brand of American male self-satisfaction. The fact that he likes to wear his sideways shouldn't send shivers of dread and alarm down my spine, should it? I was driven from the sport myself in the late 1960s by an overzealous coach who thought he was going to save America from communists by making me get my hair cut. When I did, finally, he said "shorter," and I quit instead.

Baseball catchers wear their hats backward, and football players in postgame interviews, and half the male college students in America, drifting around in their smug little packs, looking for a woman or a beer. But sideways? What does it mean? Why does it bother me?

"Dad!" my son asks during one of our morning skirmishes, rejected garments strewn around the floor, his hands raised and shoulders shrugged in an eternal gesture of astonishment and dismay. "What's your problem?"

—David Updike

Questions About the Reading

Refer to the general questions on page 154 as well as these specific questions.

PURPOSE

- *In your view, what does Updike want the audience to be thinking or feeling after reading this piece?*
- *Does the essay succeed in making a difference with readers? If so, how?*

CONTENT

- *Are the causes presented here definite, probable, or possible? Explain.*

- *Has the author explored distant or alternative causes adequately? Explain.*
- *What assumptions does the author make about his audience's attitudes and awareness? Are these assumptions accurate? Explain.*
- *What are the main issues here? How has this essay affected your thinking about these issues?*

ORGANIZATION

- *What combination of opening strategies is used in the introduction?*

- *Are the body paragraphs arranged in an order that emphasizes the thesis? If so, what is that order?*

STYLE

- *What is the author's attitude toward his subject? Toward his*

audience? How do we know? What are the signals?

- *Is the tone appropriate for the intended audience and purpose? Explain.*

RESPONDING TO READING

After reading David Updike's essay (page 246), John Saurette, an education major and a parent of school-age children, decided to explore this question facing his family directly: How effective are school uniforms? Perhaps the question should be recast—What are the pros and cons of school uniforms? or How does requiring school uniforms affect children's education? Saurette knows that this complex topic will require research on his part.

In drafting and revising his essay, Saurette relied on the Guidelines for Cause-to-Effect Analysis (page 241) and the revision checklists (pages 62–63 and 251.)

Note

Even though causal analysis is the dominant rhetorical strategy in Saurette's essay, he also relies on other strategies, such as vivid narration and description, colorful illustration, and process analysis.

Title announces the topic
Opens with strategies being proposed
Describes the overall desired effects

Focuses on one beneficial strategy
Thesis statement is set off in its own paragraph, for emphasis
Thesis includes a forecast of supporting points

Cites research findings here and throughout

Gives one example of beneficial effects

SCHOOL UNIFORMS: A RECIPE FOR SCHOOL REFORM

Standardized testing, teacher certification, school vouchers, metal detectors—needless to say, education reform is a top priority, from the White House to teachers' lounges to our own kitchen tables. Political candidates, parents, and school officials across the country are looking at ways to improve our schools. Various groups argue for what they believe are the correct ways to improve education, be it testing or police in the schools. However, one controversial measure is gaining popularity from New York to Long Beach. This measure is also one of the simplest: school uniforms.

School uniforms and dress codes are on the rise and for good reason: They work. School districts across the country are finding that uniforms promote order, discipline, safety, and learning, along with a sense of equality among differing social groups.

Distractions in schools over clothing seem to be an ongoing problem. For example, in a 1992 survey, 77 percent of parents in the Chicago public school system reported that their children experienced peer pressure at school over clothing (Spring 101). In hopes of improving the learning environment, New York City, the nation's largest school district, implemented standardized dress codes in nearly three-quarters of its elementary and middle schools in 1997. After two years, 95 percent of these schools reported improved discipline and a more orderly learning environment (Coles 6).

How researchers view the effects

Gives another example

Shows people talking

How educators view the effects

How parents view the effects

How opponents and courts view the effects

How negative effects of uniforms can be avoided

How students view the effects

Experts suggest that dress codes keep the school environment more orderly by reducing incidents of theft and violence over designer clothes and sneakers and provide some protection against gang activity by prohibiting the wearing of gang colors and badges. Uniforms also enable school officials to identify intruders among the student body (Spring 103–05). In 1994, students in Long Beach, California, began wearing uniforms. The effects seem impressive: Within three years, the system reported a 36 percent reduction in overall crime, 51 percent reduction in fights, 34 percent reduction in assault and battery, and 18 percent reduction in vandalism. School officials admit that uniforms were implemented as part of a larger overall reform plan, but in the words of one principal, "Though we can't attribute the improvement exclusively to uniforms...we think that it is more than coincidental" (United States, Dept. of Education 1).

Evidence suggests that dress codes also help promote discipline and reduce distractions in the classroom. In the more businesslike environment created by uniforms, teachers find it easier to keep students on task. At the same time, uniforms seem to "promote a sense of pride and a sense of calmness" (United States, Dept. of Education 1). Says one Seattle middle school principal, "[Before we had uniforms] there were many more distractions [and] my kids were really into what others were wearing" (Coles 6).

From a parent's point of view, uniforms also make sense, especially in terms of convenience and economics. Uniforms free parents from the chore of deciding what their children will wear each day. This can be especially trying as students reach middle school and high school age. Economically, just a few uniforms, and a child is set for the year. As children outgrow them, uniforms can be passed on to younger children or donated to the school for someone else's use. Even though the children will still want to buy new clothes to wear after school, the savings are real, compared to buying the latest styles in order to be part of the "in" crowd.

Dress code opponents argue that uniforms violate a student's freedom of expression. However, federal courts so far have ruled that the benefits outweigh the drawbacks. Says one federal judge, "When we weigh all the evidence involved, [uniforms] seem to have had a real positive effect" (United States, Dept. of Education 1).

Still, the latest court rulings do lean toward having an "opt out" clause for parents who strongly oppose the dress code.

In response to legal questions surrounding uniform requirements, federal officials have created a handbook for school districts that are considering dress codes. The U.S. Department of Education's *Manual on School Uniforms* provides guidelines for parent involvement, financial aid, protection of student rights, and use of uniforms as part of an overall safety plan.

Perhaps the greatest motivation for uniforms comes from students themselves. Researcher Richard Murray found that students in a middle school that required uniforms viewed their school much more positively than those in a school without such a requirement (cited in Isaacson 2). My own brief interviews of sixteen eighth graders (eight males and eight females) seem to support this observation.

Author describes own research findings

All the participants in my survey presently wore uniforms. Ten had been wearing uniforms since kindergarten, and six were transfers from schools without dress codes. Two of the six had transferred within the past year. Complaints about the dress code were mainly aesthetic, ranging from "uncomfortable" to "ugly." This seems to indicate a greater need for flexibility in style selection. But overwhelmingly, the students expressed satisfaction. When asked about suppression of individuality, the students cited ample opportunity for self-expression, including "dress-down days, hairstyles, backpacks, and school accessories."

Surprisingly, those who had transferred most recently were also the most vocal in favor of uniforms. One female student accurately summed up the overall attitude of the participants:

Offers a representative quotation

In my old school, it wasn't cool to talk to kids who wore the wrong clothes. There was always one or two kids whose parents were older and didn't dress their kids in style. They weren't bad kids, but they always got made fun of because of their clothes. It's much easier to come to school here, where having the latest or most expensive clothes is not needed to be cool. We get to know other kids for who they are, not what they wear.

Admits the limitations of this solution

Conclusion reemphasizes the main point

Granted, dress codes alone are no panacea for all of education's ills. However, at a time in which calls for school reform are loud and clear, we must take advantage of all good opportunities. Uniforms offer one of these opportunities. The evidence indicates that dress codes cut down on classroom distractions and school violence, improve discipline, promote positive attitudes, and help in student socialization—all of which are needed if our schools are to recover. Simply stated, uniforms just may be an important first step on America's road to educational excellence.

—*John Saurette*

Works Cited

Cites each source used in the essay

Albright Middle School Students. Personal interviews. 1 Oct. 2010.

Coles, Adrienne D. "NYC Joins Growing List of Districts Dressing the Same." *Education Week* 24 Nov. 1994: 6. Web. 3 Oct. 2010 <www.edweek.org>.

Isaacson, Lynne. "Student Dress Policies." *ERIC Digests* 117 (Jan. 1998): 1–4. Web. 3 Oct. 2010 <www.ed.gov/databases/ERICDigests/ed415570.html>.

Murray, Richard, J. "The Impact of School Uniforms on School Climate." *NASSP Bulletin* 81 (Dec. 1997): 106–112. Print.

Spring, Joel H. *American Education: An Introduction to Social and Political Aspects.* 12th ed. New York: Longman, 2006. Print.

United States Dept. of Education. *Manual on School Uniforms.* Washington: GPO, 1996. Web. 4 Oct. 2010 <www.ERIC.gov.80PDFS/ED387947.pdf>.

✔ A CHECKLIST for Causal Analysis

Reasoning from Effect to Cause

☐ Does the **cause** fit the **effect**?

☐ Are **immediate** as well as **distant** causes identified?

☐ Are the **links** between effects and causes clear?

☐ Are **possible, probable**, and **definite** causes clearly differentiated?

☐ Are causal claims limited by **qualifying terms** such as *perhaps, most likely,* or *seems to,* as needed?

☐ Is the relationship clearly **causal** and not merely **coincidental**?

Reasoning from Cause to Effect

☐ Do the **effects** fit the **cause**?

☐ Are **immediate** as well as distant effects identified?

☐ Are the **links** between causes and effects clear?

☐ Have **confounding factors** been ruled out?

(*See pages 240 and 241 for more on each of these criteria.*)

APPLICATIONS

15.1 **PARAGRAPH WARM-UP: USING CAUSAL ANALYSIS TO EXPLAIN** Ordinary life today depends on technology, and technology often frustrates us by letting us down when we most need it. Think of the last time you found yourself screaming at a machine. Using research if necessary, explain the immediate and distant causes of the problem you experienced, limiting your discussion to definite causes as much as possible. Think of your paragraph as the heart of a letter to a friend explaining how to avoid the problem in the future.

15.2 **PARAGRAPH WARM-UP: USING CAUSAL ANALYSIS TO MAKE A POINT** Identify a problem that affects you, your community, your family, your school or dorm, or some other group ("The library is an awful place to study because…"). In a paragraph, analyze the causes of this problem as a prelude to an argument for change. Choose a subject you know about or one you can research to get the facts. Identify the situation, the audience, and your purpose.

15.3 **ESSAY PRACTICE**

a. Explore your reactions to "Should Schools Try to Boost Self-Esteem?" using the questions on page 155. Then respond with an essay about your own views on a related issue.

b. Explore your reactions to David Updike's essay using the questions on page 155. Think about how this essay has made a difference for you, and then respond with an essay of your own that examines the causes of one of your personal likes or dislikes.

Specifically, you might analyze the appeal of some activity or behavior (harmful or beneficial, pleasurable or painful) that takes up much of your (and other people's) time. Feel free to inject humor, as in Maureen Malloy's essay on page 57. Here are activities or behaviors whose causes you could analyze:

- Why do I (or we Americans) spend so much time watching football games (or some other sport)?
- Why am I so obsessed with exercise, fashion, or diet?
- Why are we college students such party animals?

Be sure your analysis supports some definite thesis.

c. Explore your reactions to John Saurette's essay (page 248) by using the personal response questions on page 155. Then respond with an essay of your own that analyzes causes and effects of some proposed or recent innovation or change in your school or community. If, like Saurette, you use research material to support your viewpoint, be sure to document each source (see pages 386–388).

15.4 **WEB-BASED PROJECT** Assume that classmates will be serving six months as volunteers in agriculture, education, or a similar capacity in a developing country. Research and prepare an essay that alerts readers to the area's major health hazards and their causes: for example, contagious diseases or food-, water-, and insect-borne illnesses. *Hint:* Begin your research for this project by checking out the Centers for Disease Control and Prevention's Travelers' Health Web site at **<http://www.ncdc.gov>**.

For additional information and practice with the learning objectives in this chapter, go to www.mycomplab.com, Resource>Writing>Writing Purposes.

CHAPTER 16

Comparison and Contrast: Writing to Explain Similarities and Differences

LEARNING OBJECTIVES FOR THIS CHAPTER

- Understand *comparison and contrast* as writing strategies
- Recognize how to develop a comparison, a contrast, or a combined comparison/contrast

- Understand that comparison and contrast can be used to explain or to make a point

- Differentiate analogy from standard comparison

- Write a comparison-and-contrast essay using the chapter guidelines

*C*omparison examines similarities; *contrast* examines differences. Comparison and contrast (sometimes called just *comparison*) help us evaluate things or shed light on their relationship; they help us visualize the big picture.

What readers of comparison and contrast want to know

- *In what significant ways are X and Y similar or alike?*
- *In what significant ways are X and Y different?*
- *Can something about X help us understand Y?*
- *In what significant ways is one preferable to the other?*

DEVELOPING A COMPARISON

Comparison offers perspective on one thing by pointing out its similarities to something else. The two items compared are of the same class: two cars, two countries, two professors. The following paragraph compares drug habits among people of all times and places to those among people of modern times.

A COMPARISON

Main point (1)

Historical similarity to modern habits (2–3)

Religious similarity to modern habits (4–5)

Modern continuation of habit (6–7)

[1]All the natural narcotics, stimulants, relaxants, and hallucinants known to the modern botanist and pharmacologist were discovered by primitive [people] and have been in use from time immemorial. [2]One of the first things that *Homo sapiens* did with his newly developed rationality and self-consciousness was to set them to work finding out ways to bypass analytical thinking and to transcend or, in extreme cases, temporarily obliterate the isolating awareness of the self. [3]Trying all things that grew in the field or forest, they held fast to that which, in this context, seemed good—everything, that is to say, that would change the quality of consciousness, would make it different, no matter how, from everyday feeling, perceiving, and thinking. [4]Among the Hindus, rhythmic breathing and mental concentration have, to some extent, taken the place of mind-transforming drugs used elsewhere. [5]But even in the land of yoga, even among the religious and even for specifically religious purposes, *Cannabis indica* (marijuana) has been freely used to supplement the effects of spiritual exercises. [6]The habit of taking vacations from the more-or-less purgatorial world, which we have created for ourselves, is universal. [7]Moralists may denounce it; but, in the teeth of disapproving talk and repressive legislation,

Concluding point (8)

the habit persists, and mind-transforming drugs are everywhere available. [8]The Marxian formula, "Religion is the opium of the people," is reversible, and one can say, with even more truth, that "Opium is the religion of the people."

—Aldous Huxley

DEVELOPING A CONTRAST

A contrast is designed to point out differences between one thing and another. This next paragraph contrasts the beliefs of Satanism with those of Christianity.

A CONTRAST

Main point (1)
First difference (2–3)

Second difference (4)

Third difference (5–8)

[1]The Satanic belief system, not surprisingly, is the antithesis of Christianity. [2]Their theory of the universe, their cosmology, is based upon the notion that the desired end state is a return to a pagan awareness of their humanity. [3]This is in sharp contrast to the transcendental goals of traditional Christianity. [4]The power associated with the pantheon of gods is also reversed: Satan's power is waxing (increasing); God's, if he still lives, waning. [5]The myths of the Satanic church purport to tell the true story of the rise of Christianity and the fall of paganism, and there is a reversal here too. [6]Christ is depicted as an early "con man" who tricked an anxious and powerless group of individuals into believing a lie. [7]He is typified as "pallid incompetence hanging on a tree." [8]Satanic novices are taught that early church fathers deliberately picked on those aspects of human desire that were most natural and made them sins, in order to use the inevitable transgressions as a means of controlling the populace, promising them salvation in return for obedience. [9]And finally, their substantive belief, the very delimitation of what is sacred and what is profane, is the antithesis of Christian belief. [10]The Satanist is taught to "be natural; to revel in pleasure and in self-gratification; to emphasize indulgence and power in this life."

Final—and major— difference (9–10)

—Edward J. Moody

DEVELOPING A COMBINED COMPARISON AND CONTRAST

A combined comparison and contrast examines similarities and differences displayed by two or more things. This next paragraph first contrasts education with training and, second, compares how each serves important needs of society:

A COMBINED COMPARISON AND CONTRAST

Main point (1)

Difference of purpose (2)

[1]To understand the nature of the liberal arts college and its function in our society, it is important to understand the difference between education and training. [2]Training is intended primarily for the service of society; education is primarily for the individual. [3]Society needs doctors, lawyers, engineers,

How "trained" people serve society (3–5)

Similarity of effects (6)

How "educated" people serve society (7–11)

Conclusion (12)

and teachers to perform specific tasks necessary to its operation, just as it needs carpenters and plumbers and stenographers. [4]Training supplies the immediate and specific needs of society so that the work of the world may continue. [5]And these needs, our training centers—the professional and trade schools—fill. [6]But although education is for the improvement of the individual, it also serves society by providing a leavening of men and women of understanding, of perception and wisdom. [7]They are our intellectual leaders, the critics of our culture, the defenders of our free traditions, the instigators of our progress. [8]They serve society by examining its function, appraising its needs, and criticizing its direction. [9]They may be earning their livings by practicing one of the professions, or in pursuing a trade, or by engaging in business enterprise. [10]They may be rich or poor. [11]They may occupy positions of power and prestige, or they may be engaged in some humble employment. [12]Without them, however, society either disintegrates or else becomes an anthill.

—Harry Kemelman

USING COMPARISON AND CONTRAST TO EXPLAIN

Referential comparison usually helps readers understand one thing in terms of another. For example, we could explain the effects of high-fat diets on heart disease and cancer by comparing disease rates in Japan (with its low-fat diet) with those in North America. To explain how new knowledge of earthquakes has affected the way engineers design buildings, we can contrast modern buildings with buildings constructed years ago.

Referential comparison also often permits us to explain a complex or abstract idea in terms of another. For example, it's easier to understand how earlier civilizations understood a term such as *honor* if we contrast their concept with our own today.

USING COMPARISON AND CONTRAST TO MAKE A POINT

Like other development strategies, comparison and contrast can support persuasion. For example, it is often used in evaluation, in which we judge the merits of something by measuring it in relationship to something else.

We might compare two (or more) cars, computers, political candidates, college courses, or careers to argue that one is superior.

Comparisons can support other kinds of arguments as well. Huxley's comparison of past and present drug habits (page 254) supports the thesis that any habit so long entrenched will be hard to eliminate. Kemelman's analysis of the differences and similarities between training and education (page 255) supports his claim that the liberal arts college has an important function in our society.

Do you think that Moody's contrast of Christians and Satanists (page 255) also supports an implied argument, or is it mainly referential? Explain.

As always, the evidence with which you support your content, your organizational skills, and your command of style are what make your argumentative comparisons persuasive.

A SPECIAL KIND OF COMPARISON: ANALOGY

Ordinary comparison shows similarities between two things of the same class (two teachers, two styles of dress, two political philosophies). *Analogy,* on the other hand, shows similarities between two things of *different classes* (writing and skiing, freshman registration and a merry-go-round, a dorm room and a junkyard). Analogy answers the reader's question "Can you explain *X* by comparing it to something I already know?"

Analogies are useful in explaining something abstract, complex, or unfamiliar, as long as the easier subject is familiar to readers. This next analogy helps clarify an unfamiliar technical concept (dangerous levels of a toxic chemical) by comparing it to something more familiar (a human hair).

ANALOGY

A dioxin concentration of 500 parts per trillion is lethal to guinea pigs. One part per trillion is roughly equal to the thickness of a human hair compared to the distance across the United States.

—*Congressional Research Report*

By comparing new information to information your audience already understands, analogy helps build a bridge between their current knowledge and the new ideas.

USING COMPARISON AND CONTRAST

BEYOND THE WRITING CLASSROOM

- **In other courses:** In sociology, you might assess the economic progress made by minority groups by comparing income figures from earlier decades with today's figures.

- **On the job:** You might compare the qualifications of various job applicants or the performance of various stock and bond portfolios.

- **In the community:** You might compare the voting records of two politicians or the SAT scores of local students to the national average.

In what other situations might comparison and contrast make a difference?

GUIDELINES for Comparison and Contrast

- *Compare or contrast items in the same class.* Compare dogs and cats, but not dogs and trees; men and women, but not men and bicycles. Otherwise you have no logical basis for comparison. If an item is unfamiliar, define it immediately, as Moody does with Satanism.

- *Base the comparison on clear and definite criteria: costs, uses, benefits, drawbacks, appearance, results.* Huxley compares people of all times for their drug habits; Moody compares Satanism and Christianity for their primary beliefs; Kemelman compares education and training by their function in our society. Rank your criteria in order of importance. For example, Kemelman asserts that training supplies society's "immediate needs" but education supplies "the instigators of our progress" and the leadership required for cultural survival.

- *Establish your credibility for evaluating items.* Instead of merely pointing out similarities and differences (as in Moody), comparisons often evaluate competing items or viewpoints. (See page 263.) Answer readers' implied question "How do you know X is better than Y?" by briefly describing your experience with (or research on) this issue.

- *Give each item balanced treatment.* Discuss points of comparison for each item in identical order. Both Moody and Kemelman give roughly equal space to each item. In Huxley's paragraph, the other item in the comparison, modern drug use habits, is only briefly mentioned, but readers can infer its place in the discussion from their own general knowledge.

- *Support and clarify the comparison or contrast through credible examples.* Use research, if necessary, to find examples that readers can visualize.

- *Follow either a block pattern or a point-by-point pattern.* In the block pattern, one item is discussed fully and then the next, as in Kemelman: "trained" people in the first block; "educated" people in the second. Choose a block pattern when the overall picture is more important than the individual points.

- In the point-by-point pattern, one point about both items is discussed, then the next point, and so on, as in Moody: The first difference between Satanism and Christianity is in their respective cosmologies, the second is in their view of God's power, the third is in their myths about the rise of Christianity, and so on. Choose a point-by-point pattern when specific points might be hard to remember unless placed side by side.

BLOCK PATTERN	POINT-BY-POINT PATTERN
Item A	first point of A
first point	first point of B, etc.
second point, etc.	
Item B	second point of A
first point	second point of B, etc.
second point, etc.	

■ *Arrange your supporting points for greatest emphasis.* Try ordering your points from least to most important, dramatic, useful, or reasonable. Placing the most striking point last emphasizes it best.

■ *In an evaluative comparison ("X is better than Y"), offer your final judgment.* Base your judgment squarely on the criteria presented.

COMPARISON AND CONTRAST AS A PRIMARY ESSAY STRATEGY

In this next essay, an educator, columnist, and book author scrutinizes popular assumptions about the achievements of Latino immigrants relative to those of European immigrants. As you read, think about the role of cultural stereotypes in our world today and how such ignorance can be dispelled through knowledge.

Debunking Myths about Latinos

The myth endures that immigrants from Mexico and Central America don't perform as well in the United States as the European immigrants of days gone by.

For this, it is said, the Latino immigrants have only themselves to blame. It is supposed that they make no effort to assimilate. They refuse to learn English. And they lack the ambition to excel beyond low-wage jobs where they are exploited and discriminated against.

Now a study by RAND, the nonprofit think tank based in Southern California, debunks the myth. The research suggests that there is not all that much difference between the immigrants who crossed the Rio Grande to get here and those who had to cross the Atlantic. And there is even less difference between their children and grandchildren a generation or two down the line.

"There's a widespread view among both scholars and the general public that the Latino experience has been very different than the European experience," economist James Smith, author of the study, told the Associated Press. "That view is just wrong."

By examining census data and other material going back over a century, Smith was able to measure the educational and economic progress of Latino men and their children and compare it with that of other nationalities. What he found was that many popular assumptions don't hold true.

"Across generations, Latinos have done just as well as the Europeans who came in the early part of this [twentieth] century, and in fact slightly better," Smith said.

The RAND study found that although Latino immigrants who were born in the early 1900s averaged just a fifth-grade education, their sons made it as far as the ninth grade and their grandsons graduated from high school.

According to Smith, those advances were greater than those of European immigrants born in the same era. The bad news: By the third generation, the educational gains taper off.

When it comes to earnings, the news is more encouraging. Over their lifetimes, Latino immigrants born in the early 1900s earned about three-fourths as much as U.S.-born descendants of European immigrants. Their sons earned about 79 percent as much, and their grandsons nearly 83 percent as much. With every generation, the earning gap closed bit by bit, as one might expect. And while this study focused on men, Smith claims that his research on Hispanic women shows much the same thing.

Sure, this is just one study. There may be others that offer assessments that are less optimistic. There are some scholars, for instance, who argue that America is headed for a rough patch because many of the immigrants it now takes in are less educated and less skilled than those of a century ago. Others sound the alarm over language, insisting that Latino immigrants who refuse to learn English immediately are destined to flounder in the United States.

Rubbish. Regardless of ethnicity or nationality or economic resources, immigrants are the same the world over. That's because a big part of what shapes their character is not the country they come from but the fact that they leave it in the first place, risking whatever they have—including their lives—in search of a better life. Once here, they work hard in any job they can find. They instill in their children an appreciation for education and teach them the value of a dollar. And one day those children, in turn, pass on these things to theirs.

That's how it was in my family, whose American journey took it from grape fields to graduate school in three generations. Not that one should expect any of this to resonate with those Americans who remain intent on differentiating between immigrants and putting some above others.

You can't really blame them. They're in a tough spot. After all, how does a nation of immigrants reconcile the fact that so many of its people espouse views that suggest they resent immigrants? There is one way:

Convince yourself that your ancestors were of a better stock than immigrants of today, and don't let the facts get in the way. Of course, the facts at hand deal only with the progress of the immigrants of the past. The matter is settled—Latino immigrants in the 20th century matched and in some cases bettered their European counterparts. But what about the immigrants of today? My bet is that the same will be true for them.

Stay tuned.

—*Ruben Navarrette Jr.*

Navarrette systematically examines the key criteria of educational level, earnings, job skills, work ethic, and upward mobility to illustrate his point about Latino achievements. He supports his comparison by referring to a recent study by RAND, a highly regarded research group.

READING AND RESPONDING

In this case study, student writer John Manning relies primarily on comparison and contrast in his response to the following professional essay.

ESSAY FOR ANALYSIS AND RESPONSE

The next selection, by syndicated columnist Reid Goldsborough, examines the generation gap regarding attitudes about social networking and its benefits. As you read, think about your own views on this topic and about how they might differ from those in a different generation.

SOCIAL NETWORKING: CROSSING DIGITAL DIVIDE CAN PAY DIVIDENDS

There's always been a generation gap, more or less, with the younger generation trying to improve on the latter. Seeing things differently and trying for new solutions to old problems can be seen as agents of progress.

Today's generation gap manifests itself perhaps most with digital social networking. Unlike in the 1960s, when those younger than 30 couldn't trust those older about politics, lifestyles and other issues, today's young people are more likely to heavily use digital social networks whereas those older are less likely.

Whether the digital device used for social networking is a cell phone, MP3 player or personal computer connected to such Web-based social networking services as MySpace (www.myspace.com) and Facebook (www.facebook.com), the imperative is to stay connected. Social scientists call it "ambient awareness."

It can get taken to an absurd extreme. For instance, when you're waiting in line as an 18-year-old clerk texts his buddy about the moron he just waited on—the customer standing in front of you—it can elicit the same annoyance in you, for the very same reason, as that previous customer experienced.

Are other people really interested in the mundane minute-by-minute minutiae of your existence?

Apparently the answer is "yes," judging by the popularity of such newer offerings as Twitter (www.twitter.com), which promotes itself as a "microblogging" service where you can stay "hyper-connected" to your friends.

People use Twitter, a free advertising-supported service, by sending and receiving short text messages, 140 words or less, using a PC or cell phone, about what they're doing. It even includes the question, "What are you doing?" after its name in the title line of its web site. As of this writing, more than two million people have signed up to use Twitter to broadcast, you guessed it, what they're doing.

The absurdity, or fun, of spending your time this way gets hotly debated online, as does just about everything else. The sometimes nonverbal context of the debate relates to age, with many older folks regarding digital social networking as narcissistic and many younger folks contending their elders just don't get it.

The fact is that new techniques have always been adopted more readily by young people.

Computer-phobia has been around since the inception of computers, and it afflicts those who came of age using typewriters and slide rules much more than those weaned on PCs.

The adage about old dogs and new tricks is partially true here. Older folks tend to get complacent, finding what works and sticking to it, which can sometimes land them in a rut. Young people, with minds more malleable, have an easier time learning new ways. Trying out the new, however, takes not only intellectual curiosity but also time, which younger people typically have more of than those with jobs, families to support and other responsibilities.

Still, even with people pressed for time, digital social networks can be useful. Many people, both young and mature, have reported using these services to find jobs, an online extension and improvement of traditional networking using the phone, the mail and the visit. Those who travel a lot through their jobs or are self-employed use digital social networks as a weapon against solitude.

Just as with other forms of online communication, digital social networking can be a good way to get consumer advice when making a purchase and point you in the right direction or provide support when confronting a health problem.

No matter what your age, social networking works best socially when it brings people together in real life. It can be a great way, for instance, to quickly organize a social event among your friends, from a dinner party to a meeting at a local club.

Despite its reliance on cutting-edge technology, digital social networking can take you back in time, adding a small-town flavor to your life, where your circle knows everything about everybody, for better or worse. Frequently updating others on what you're up to can also increase your self-awareness, helping you take stock and make better choices in the future.

As with many things, balance here is key. Digital social networks used judiciously can improve the quality of life. But they should't replace face time—contact of the genuine kind. One of the negative consequences of the computer revolution is the digital shut-in.

In Isaac Asimov's 1957 novel *The Naked Sun*, people avoid personal contact in the flesh and relate to one another through holographic projection. That's one computer-aided future best relegated to science fiction.

—*Reid Goldsborough*

Questions About the Reading

Refer also to the general questions on page 154.

CONTENT

- *In addition to comparison and-contrast, what other development strategies support the purpose of this essay?*
- *In your own words, restate the point of the comparison in a complete sentence.*

pattern, or a combination? Comment on the effectiveness of the pattern.
- *Do both sides of the issue receive balanced treatment? Explain.*
- *Does the essay, offer a final judgment? If so, is it based convincingly on the evidence presented?*

ORGANIZATION

- *Does this comparison follow a block pattern, a point-by-point*

STYLE

- *Is the tone appropriate for the audience and purpose? Explain.*

RESPONDING TO READING

After reading and analyzing Reid Goldsborough's essay, John Manning decided to evaluate both sides of an issue very familiar to him: the pros and cons of online education.

Manning presents an implied comparison here, focusing on the benefits and drawbacks of an online "classroom," which is the less familiar item in this comparison. He can reasonably expect readers to visualize for themselves the familiar, traditional classroom.

| Note |

Even though comparison and contrast is the dominant rhetorical strategy in Manning's essay, other strategies, such as narration, illustration, and causal analysis, play supporting roles.

IS ONLINE EDUCATION TAKING US ANYWHERE?

Title gives an immediate forecast

Defines the unfamiliar item in the comparison

As a growing alternative to the traditional classroom, we hear more and more about Internet-based learning, variously known as "cybereducation," "on-line education," and "virtual education." In this model, each student's computer is "wired" to an instructor's Web site at which course material and assignments are transmitted, posted, and discussed electronically. "Virtual universities" even offer entire degrees online. After taking two of these courses, I asked myself this question: Compared with a physical classroom setting, what is gained and lost in a "virtual" classroom? *While the actual benefits are undeniable, the drawbacks or potential consequences are also worth considering.*

Writer establishes credibility

Thesis announces the basis for comparison: benefits and drawbacks

Point-by-point comparison

In terms of access and convenience, online education definitely holds the winning edge. This is especially true in Canada and Australia or parts of the

First benefit (or criterion): access and convenience

American West in which relatively small populations are scattered thinly over a vast landmass. Students working online from any location now benefit from an endless variety of courses that require no travel whatsoever. Even though I live in a suburb, I personally enjoyed the luxury of commuting by computer.

Next benefit: economy and efficiency

Online education is also more economical and efficient than traditional schooling. The "school" itself has no need to maintain a physical structure with classrooms, faculty offices, and other expensive facilities. In the face of rising tuitions and room and board costs, the potential savings passed along to students are tremendous. Also students can participate and do most of their work at their convenience—without the time constraints of regularly scheduled classes. With work and family commitments in addition to my student responsibilities, I found this aspect especially appealing.

Major benefit: student interest

Uses causal analysis

Gives vivid examples throughout

In terms of student interest, online courses stimulate concentration and interactivity on the student's part. Motivated students can focus their energies on the computer screen, in the relative peace and quiet of their own room, without the usual distractions in an actual classroom. Shy students might feel more comfortable about interacting in a social networking atmosphere. Also, the Web's graphics capabilities are more dynamic than the static pages of a textbook—in a medium that today's college-age students have grown up with (video games, email, net surfing, and so on). I found the graphics especially useful in my online Introduction to Statistics course.

First drawback: lack of interpersonal relations

Gives equal attention to "benefits" and "drawbacks"—with criteria for each ranked in order of increasing importance

Despite all these benefits, does the online learning experience itself carry interpersonal drawbacks? I personally missed the human element of getting to know my teachers and having an adviser to turn to whenever some problem arose. I also missed face-to-face discussions. It seems easier to absorb what others are saying from hearing their actual voices and seeing their faces rather than reading their words from a computer screen. (Think of a poetry reading, for example.) For me, an inspiring lecture or a heated class discussion can only happen "in person."

Writer uses narrative examples throughout to reinforce his credibility

Next drawback: practical problems

I also worry about some practical drawbacks. For instance, online courses demand a strong desire to learn and the self-discipline and skills—and confidence—to manage one's education on one's own. I wonder how many students are ready to do this. (It was extremely hard for me.) Also, some people could abuse the system. For example, how can anyone know for sure whether other people are doing a student's work or whether unqualified students are walking away with degrees based on work others have done for them? And what about studying a language online—how does one learn pronunciation without live conversation?

Major drawback: social costs

My biggest concern is with the potential social costs of online education. While online dollar costs for access are low, those for training and equipment are high—in terms of fairly high-level computer skills and expensive hardware. For example, it takes nearly a top-of-the-line computer to run increasingly complex software—a computer that soon becomes obsolete. This investment in skills and equipment automatically rules out those people who can't afford it. Once again, it seems that the affluent will get another leg up based on this technology while the have-nots stay down in the dark.

Conclusion refocuses on the main question Sums up the comparison	All in all, do the benefits of online courses outweigh the drawbacks? On the plus side, the convenience, price, and dynamics of online education can't be beat. On the minus side, for people who come to school looking for human contact, transacting exclusively online seems awfully impersonal. Also, it's hard keeping up the motivation and self-discipline needed to do all one's work online. Finally, we have to consider the potential for creating an educated elite and even greater social division between the haves and have-nots. And so
Closes with a judgment based on the evidence	while online education seems a powerful *supplement* to live classrooms, it's scary to think of it as a complete *substitute*.

—*John Manning*

☑ A CHECKLIST for Comparison and Contrast

☐ Do all items have enough in common to provide a **logical basis** for comparison and contrast?

☐ Is the comparison and contrast based on clear and definite **criteria**?

☐ Do you describe briefly your **qualifications** for evaluating related items?

☐ Is each item given **balanced** treatment?

☐ Are the similarities or differences illustrated through concrete **examples**?

☐ When the overall picture is more important than the individual points, does the comparison and contrast follow a **block pattern**?

☐ When individual points need to be remembered, are items compared and contrasted **point-by-point**?

☐ Are supporting points arranged for greatest **emphasis**?

☐ In any type of evaluative comparison, is the **final judgment** based squarely on the criteria presented?

(For more on each of these criteria, see page 258.)

APPLICATIONS

16.1 **PARAGRAPH WARM-UP: COMPARISON AND CONTRAST** Using comparison or contrast (or both), write a paragraph discussing the likenesses or differences between two people, animals, attitudes, activities, places, or things. Clearly identify the situation, the audience, and your purpose. Then classify your paragraph: Does it primarily inform, or does it make a point? Some possible topics are two places you know well, two similar consumer items, two pets you've had, and the benefits of two kinds of exercise.

16.2 **PARAGRAPH WARM-UP: ANALOGY** Develop a paragraph explaining something abstract, complex, or unfamiliar by comparing it to something concrete, simple, or familiar. ("Writing is like…"; "Love is like…"; "Osmosis works like…"). Identify a specific purpose or audience. Do you have an informative or a persuasive goal?

16.3   ESSAY PRACTICE

a. Explore your reactions to "Debunking Myths About Latinos" (page 259) using the personal response questions on page 155. Then respond with an essay of your own. As you reread the essay, think about unfair or inaccurate comparisons made by or against you or a group you know or to which you belong. Identify a specific audience, and base your comparison on clearly stipulated criteria.

b. If you had your high school years to relive, what would you do differently?

c. Explore your reactions to Reid Goldsborough's essay or to John Manning's essay by using the personal response questions on page 155. Then respond with an essay of your own that evaluates the pros and cons of social networking, ebooks, or some other electronic resource such as laptops in the classroom (which some schools now ban because of the distractions they create for some students). If you use research findings to support your viewpoint, be sure to document each source (see pages 386–388.)

16.4   WEB-BASED PROJECTS

a. Many schools now have writing centers online. These centers often have exercises or tip sheets you can browse or download. Some even have opportunities for collaboration and consultation via email or chat rooms. Do a Web search, and compare and contrast two online writing centers, assessing the quality of the services and the information provided.

b. Compare two popular Internet search engines (*Google, Alta Vista, Lycos,* etc.) on the basis of specific criteria, such as the following:

- search page (interface) is easy to use
- searches are fast
- categories are well organized and easy to browse
- offers customizable features for finding information
- offers good navigational aids
- offers good Help, FAQ, and Search Tips pages
- lists a large index of sites
- ratings system identifies quality sites
- site listings are up to date
- searches are easy to limit by topic or user
- images are easy to download and waste no screen space
- supports advanced searches using keywords

Be sure to specify the criteria you have chosen.

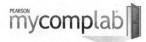

For additional information and practice with the learning objectives in this chapter, go to www.mycomplab.com, Resource>Writing>Writing Purposes.

CHAPTER 17

Definition: Writing to Explain the Exact Meaning

LEARNING OBJECTIVES FOR THIS CHAPTER

- Understand *definition* as a writing strategy
- Differentiate between denotative and connotative definition
- Choose the right level of detail in a definition
- Write an effective definition essay using the chapter guidelines

All successful writing shares one feature: clarity. Clear writing begins with clear thinking; clear thinking begins with an understanding of what all the terms mean. Therefore, clear writing depends on definitions upon which both reader and writer agree.

Definitions answer the question "What exactly are we talking about?" by spelling out the precise meaning of a term that can be interpreted in different ways; for example, a person buying a new computer needs to understand exactly what *manufacturer's guarantee* or *expandable memory* means in the context of that purchase.

Definitions can also answer the question "What exactly is it?" by explaining what makes an item, concept, or process unique; for example, an engineering student needs to understand the distinction between *elasticity* and *ductility*. Inside or outside any field, people have to grasp precisely what "makes a thing what it is and distinguishes that thing from all other things" (Corbett 38).

What readers of
definition want to know

- *What exactly are we talking about?*
- *What exactly is it?*
- *What is its accepted meaning?*
- *What personal meanings does it suggest?*

Words can signify two kinds of meaning: *denotative* and *connotative*. Denotations—the meanings in a dictionary—usually appear in referential writing. A word's denotation means the same thing to everyone. *Apple* denotes the firm, rounded, edible fruit of the apple tree.

But words have connotations as well, overtones or suggestions beyond their dictionary meanings. A word can have different connotations for different people. For example, *apple* might connote Adam and Eve, apple pie, Johnny Appleseed, apple polisher, a popular computer maker, or good health. Connotations play an important part in persuasive writing as writers rely on the possible meanings audiences find in words to elicit their emotions or to underscore a viewpoint.

USING DENOTATIVE DEFINITIONS TO EXPLAIN

Denotative definitions either explain a term that is specialized or unfamiliar to your readers or convey your exact definition of a word that has more than one meaning.

Most fields have specialized terms. Engineers talk about *prestressed concrete, tolerances,* and *trusses;* psychologists refer to *sociopathic behavior* and *paranoia;* attorneys discuss *liens, easements,* and *escrow accounts.* For readers outside the field, these terms must be defined.

Sometimes a term will be unfamiliar to some readers because it is new or no longer in use (*future shock, meltdown, doublespeak*) or slang (*props, diss, phat*).

Some readers, though, are unaware that more familiar terms, such as *guarantee, disability, lease,* and *consent,* take on very specialized meanings in some contexts. What *consent* means in one situation is not necessarily what it means in another. Denotative definition then becomes crucial if all parties are to understand.

The following paragraph explains the meaning of a once-popular slang term no longer in use.

A DENOTATIVE DEFINITION

Main point (1)

Contrast and division (2)

Division (3)

Cause-effect (sentence definition) (4)

Cause-effect as analogy (5)

[1]During my teen years I never left the house on my Saturday night dates without my mother slipping me a few extra dollars—Mad Money, it was called. [2]I'll explain what it was for the benefit of the new generation in which people just sleep with each other: the fellow was supposed to bring me home, lead me safely through the asphalt jungle, protect me from slithering snakes, rapists, and the like. [3]But my mother and I knew that young men were apt to drink too much, to slosh down so many rye-and-gingers that some hero might well lead me in front of an oncoming bus, smash his daddy's car into Tiffany's window, or, less gallantly, throw up on my dress. [4]Mad Money was for getting home on your own, no matter what form of insanity your date happened to evidence. [5]Mad Money was also a wallflower's rope ladder; if a guy you came with suddenly fancied someone else, you didn't have to stay there and suffer; you could go home.

—Anne Roiphe

USING CONNOTATIVE DEFINITIONS TO MAKE A POINT

A denotative definition cannot communicate the personal or special meaning a writer may intend. But connotative definitions explain terms that hold personal meanings for the writer.

In the next paragraph, the denotative definition of "house" (a structure serving as a dwelling) is replaced by a more personal, artistic, and spiritual definition.

A CONNOTATIVE DEFINITION

Main point (1)

Analogies (2–4)

[1] What is a house? [2]A house is a human circumstance in Nature, like a tree or the rocks of the hills; a good house is a technical performance where form and function are made one; a house is integral to its site, a grace, not a disgrace, to its environment, suited to elevate the life of its individual inhabitants; a house is therefore integral with the nature of the methods and materials used to build it. [3]A house to be a good home has throughout what is most needed in American life today—integrity. [4]Integrity, once there, enables those who live in that house to take spiritual root and grow.

—Frank Lloyd Wright

Connotative definition is especially useful when we want people to accept a particular definition of a term that carries multiple, conflicting meanings (*freedom, love, patriotism*) and especially when the meaning we advocate is unconventional or controversial.

Unless you are sure that readers know the exact or special meaning you intend, always define a term the first time you use it.

CHOOSING THE LEVEL OF DETAIL IN A DEFINITION

How much detail will readers need to understand a term or a concept? Can you use a synonym (a term with a similar meaning)? Will you provide a sentence, a paragraph—or an essay?

Parenthetical Definition

Often you can clarify the meaning of an unfamiliar word by using a more familiar synonym or a clarifying phrase:

Parenthetical definitions

> To **waffle** means to be evasive and misleading.
>
> The **leaching field** (sievelike drainage area) requires 15 inches of crushed stone.

Note *Be sure that the synonym clarifies your meaning instead of obscuring it. Don't say, "A tumor is a neoplasm." Say, "A tumor is a growth of cells that occurs independently of surrounding tissue and serves no useful function."*

Sentence Definition

More complex terms may require a sentence definition (which may be stated in more than one sentence). These definitions follow a fixed pattern: (1) the name of the item to be defined, (2) the class to which the item belongs, and (3) the features that differentiate the item from all others in its class.

Elements of sentence definitions

Term	Class	Distinguishing Features
carburetor	a mixing device	in gasoline engines that blends air and fuel into a vapor for combustion in the cylinders
diabetes	a metabolic disease	caused by a disorder of the pituitary gland or pancreas and characterized by excessive urination, persistent thirst, and inability to metabolize sugar
stress	an applied force	that strains or deforms a body

These elements are combined into one or more complete sentences:

A complete sentence definition

> Diabetes is a metabolic disease caused by a disorder of the pituitary gland or the pancreas and characterized by excessive urination, persistent thirst, and an inability to metabolize sugar.

Sentence definition is especially useful if you need to stipulate your precise definition for a term that has several possible meanings. For example, *qualified buyer* can have different meanings for different readers in construction, banking, and real estate.

Expanded Definition

A sentence definition of *carburetor* (see previous table) is adequate for a general reader who simply needs to know what a carburetor is. An instruction manual for mechanics, however, would define *carburetor* in much greater detail; these readers need to know how a carburetor works, how it is made, what conditions cause it to operate correctly, and so on.

Your choice of parenthetical, sentence, or expanded definition depends on the amount of information your readers need. Consider the two examples that follow.

A SENTENCE DEFINITION

> It [paranoia] refers to a psychosis based on a delusionary premise of self-referred persecution or grandeur (e.g., "The Knights of Columbus control the world and are out to get me"), and supported by a complex, rigorously logical system that interprets all or nearly all sense impressions as evidence for that premise.

This definition is taken from an article published in *Harper's*, a magazine with a general readership. That audience will require a more detailed definition of such a specialized term. The expanded version uses several explanatory strategies.

EXPANDED DEFINITION OF A SPECIALIZED TERM

Main point (1)
Sentence definition (2)

Effect-cause analysis (3)

Process analysis (4)

Cause-effect analysis
(5–7)

Contrast (8)

> [1]Paranoia is a word on everyone's lips, but only among mental-health professionals has it acquired a tolerably specific meaning. [2]It refers to a psychosis based on a delusionary premise of self-referred persecution or grandeur (e.g., "The Knights of Columbus control the world and are out to get me"), and supported by a complex, rigorously logical system that interprets all or nearly all sense impressions as evidence for that premise. [3]The traditional psychiatric view is that paranoia is an extreme measure for the defense of the integrity of the personality against annihilating guilt. [4]The paranoid (so goes the theory) thrusts his guilt outside himself by denying his hostile or erotic impulses and projecting them onto other people or onto the whole universe. [5]Disintegration is avoided, but at high cost; the paranoid view of reality can make everyday life terrifying and social intercourse problematical. [6]And paranoia is tiring. [7]It requires exhausting mental effort to construct trains of thought demonstrating that random events or details "prove" a wholly unconnected premise. [8]Some paranoids hallucinate, but hallucination is by no means obligatory; paranoia is an interpretive, not a perceptual, dysfunction.
>
> —*Hendrik Hertzberg and David C. K. McClelland*

General readers are much more likely to understand this expanded definition than the sentence definition alone.

As you have seen in earlier chapters, synonyms and sentence definitions are part of most writing. But notice in turn how various development strategies from earlier chapters are employed in an expanded definition.

The following expanded definition, from an auto insurance policy, defines damages for bodily injury to others, a phrase that could have many possible meanings.

EXPANDED DEFINITION OF A FAMILIAR TERM WITH A SPECIAL MEANING

Main point (1)
Sentence definition (2)
Cause-effect (3-6)

Negation (7)

[1]Under this coverage, we will pay damages to people injured or killed by your auto in Massachusetts accidents. [2]Damages are the amount an injured person is legally entitled to collect through a court judgment or settlement. [3]We will pay only if you or someone else using your auto with your consent is legally responsible for the accident. [4]The most we will pay for injuries to any one person as a result of any one accident is $5,000. [5]The most we will pay for injuries to two or more people as a result of any one accident is a total of $10,000. [6]This is the most we will pay as the result of a single accident no matter how many autos or premiums are shown on the Coverage Selections page. [7]We will not pay for injuries to guest occupants of your auto; for accidents outside of Massachusetts or in places in Massachusetts where the public has no right of access; or for injuries to any employees of the legally responsible person if they are entitled to Massachusetts workers' compensation benefits.

This definition is designed to answer two basic questions:

- *Under what conditions will the insurer pay damages?*
- *Under what conditions will the insurer not pay?*

Thus the development strategy of cause and effect, aided by *negation* (showing what something isn't), most logically serves the purpose of this definition.

Note   *Because they are designed to draw readers into the writer's complex, private associations, connotative definitions almost always call for expanded treatment.*

Note   *An increasingly familiar (and user-friendly) format for expanded definition, especially for Web users, is a listing of frequently asked questions (FAQs), which organizes chunks of information as responses to questions users are likely to ask.*

GUIDELINES for Definition

- *Decide on the level of detail.* Definitions vary greatly in length and detail, from a few words in parentheses to a complete essay. How much does this audience need in order to follow your explanation or grasp your point in this particular situation?

- *Use plain English.* Use language your audience will understand. For example, in defining a **tumor** for a general audience, don't call it "a neoplasm" but rather "an uncontrolled growth of cells occurring independently of surrounding tissue and serving no useful function." This second version enables a reader to *visualize* the meaning.

- *Classify the term precisely.* The narrower your class, the clearer your meaning. **Diabetes** is precisely classified as a **metabolic disease,** not as a **medical term.**

- *Differentiate the term accurately.* If the distinguishing features are too broad, they will apply to more than this one item. A definition of **brief** as a "legal document used in court" fails to differentiate **brief** from all other legal documents (**wills, affidavits**, and the like).

- *Avoid circular definitions.* Do not repeat, as part of the distinguishing feature, the word you are defining. "**Stress** is an applied force that places stress on a body" is a circular definition.

- *Expand your definition selectively.* Begin with a sentence definition, and select from the best combination of development strategies for your audience and purpose: description or narration, illustration, division or classification, process analysis, cause-and-effect analysis, and comparison and contrast.

- *Know how much is enough.* Don't insult people's intelligence by giving needless details or spelling out the obvious.

- *Use negation to show what a term does not mean.* For example, raw data do not constitute "information"; data become information only after they have been evaluated, interpreted, and applied.

- *Explain the term's etymology (its origin).* For example: Biological control of insects is derived from the Greek **bio,** meaning "life or living organism," and the Latin **contra,** meaning "against or opposite." Biological control, then, is the use of living organisms against insects. Check your college dictionary or, preferably, *The Oxford English Dictionary* (or its Web site).

- *Consider the legal implications of your definition.* What does an "unsatisfactory job performance" mean in an evaluation of a company employee: that the employee could be fired, required to attend a training program, given one or more chances to improve, or what (*The Employee* 3–4)? Failure to spell out your meaning invites a lawsuit.

- *Consider the ethical implications of your definition.* Be sure your definition of a fuzzy or ambiguous term, such as **safe levels of exposure, conservative investment,** or **acceptable risk,** is based on fair and accurate interpretation of the facts.

USING DEFINITION

BEYOND THE WRITING CLASSROOM

- **In other courses:** Whatever your major, much of your education focuses on definition of a virtually endless array of terms: *capitalism, sonnet, osmosis, existentialism,* and thousands more.

- **On the job:** Contracts are detailed (and legally binding) definitions of the specific terms of a business agreement. If you lease a car for company travel, for example, the printed contract will define the specific responsibilities of both the *lessee* and the *lessor.* An employment contract will spell out responsibilities for both employer and employee. Many other documents, such as employee

(*continues*)

handbooks, are considered implied contracts (*The Employee* 5). In preparing an employee handbook for your company, you would need to define such terms as *acceptable job performance* on the basis of clear objectives that each employee can understand, such as "submitting weekly progress reports," "arriving on time for meetings," and so on (5–6). Because you are legally responsible for any document you prepare, clear and precise definitions are essential.

■ **In the community:** Clear and accurate definitions help the general public understand and evaluate complex technical and social issues. For example, we hear and read plenty about the debates over genetic engineering.

DEFINITION AS A PRIMARY ESSAY STRATEGY

In this following essay, Mexican American news columnist Rose del Castillo Guilbault explores the contrast between the original, Hispanic meaning of *macho* (as a term of respect) and its acquired meaning in American English (as a term of contempt). The way we use language reflects the way we think about ourselves as a culture. As you read, think about how this essay compels us to reconsider certain attitudes, values, and popular notions of desirable behavior.

THE MEANING OF *MACHO*

What is *macho*? That depends which side of the border you come from.

Although it's not unusual for words and expressions to lose their subtlety in translation, the negative connotations of *macho* in this country are troublesome to Hispanics.

Take the newspaper descriptions of alleged mass murderer Ramon Salcido. That an insensitive, insanely jealous, hard-drinking, violent Latin male is referred to as *macho* makes Hispanics cringe.

"*Es muy macho*," the women in my family nod approvingly, describing a man they respect. But in the United States, when women say, "He's so *macho*," it's with disdain.

The Hispanic *macho* is manly, responsible, hardworking, a man in charge, a patriarch. A man who expresses strength through silence. What the Yiddish language would call a *mensch*.

The American *macho* is a chauvinist, a brute, uncouth, selfish, loud, abrasive, capable of inflicting pain, and sexually promiscuous.

Quintessential *macho* models in this country are Sylvester Stallone, Arnold Schwarzenegger, and Charles Bronson. In their movies, they exude toughness, independence, masculinity. But a closer look reveals their machismo is really violence masquerading as courage, sullenness disguised as silence and irresponsibility camouflaged as independence.

If the Hispanic ideal of *macho* were translated to American screen roles, they might be Jimmy Stewart, Sean Connery and Laurence Olivier.

In Spanish, *macho* ennobles Latin males. In English, it devalues them. This pattern seems consistent with the conflicts ethnic minority males experience in this country. Typically the cultural traits other societies value don't translate as desirable characteristics in America.

I watched my own father struggle with these cultural ambiguities. He worked on a farm for twenty years. He laid down miles of irrigation pipe, carefully plowed long, neat rows in fields, hacked away at recalcitrant weeds and drove tractors through whirlpools of dust. He stoically worked twenty-hour days during harvest season, accepting the long hours as part of agricultural work. When the boss complained or upbraided him for minor mistakes, he kept quiet, even when it was obvious the boss had erred.

He handled the most menial tasks with pride. At home he was a good provider, helped out my mother's family in Mexico without complaint, and was indulgent with me. Arguments between my mother and him generally had to do with money, or with his stubborn reluctance to share his troubles. He tried to work them out in his own silence. He didn't want to trouble my mother—a course that backfired, because the imagined is always worse than the reality.

Americans regarded my father as decidedly un-*macho*. His character was interpreted as nonassertive, his loyalty non-ambition, and his quietness, ignorance. I once overheard the boss's son blame him for plowing crooked rows in a field. My father merely smiled at the lie, knowing the boy had done it, but didn't refute it, confident his good work was well known. But the boss instead ridiculed him for being "stupid" and letting a kid get away with a lie. Seeing my embarrassment, my father dismissed the incident, saying "They're the dumb ones. Imagine, me fighting with a kid."

I tried not to look at him with American eyes because sometimes the reflection hurt.

Listening to my aunts' clucks of approval, my vision focused on the qualities America overlooked. "He's such a hard worker. So serious, so responsible." My aunts would secretly compliment my mother. The unspoken comparison was that he was not like some of their husbands, who drank and womanized. My uncles represented the darker side of *macho*.

In a patriarchal society, few challenge their roles. If men drink, it's because it's the manly thing to do. If they gamble, it's because it's how men relax. And if they fool around, well, it's because a man simply can't hold back so much man! My aunts didn't exactly meekly sit back, but they put up with these transgressions because Mexican society dictated this was their lot in life.

In the United States, I believe it was the feminist movement of the early '70s that changed *macho*'s meaning. Perhaps my generation of Latin women was in part responsible. I recall Chicanas complaining about the chauvinistic nature of Latin men and the notion they wanted their women barefoot, pregnant and in the kitchen. The generalization that Latin men embodied chauvinistic traits led to this interesting twist of semantics. Suddenly a word that represented something positive in one culture became a negative prototype in another.

The problem with the use of *macho* today is that it's become an accepted stereotype of the Latin male. And like all stereotypes, it distorts truth.

The impact of language in our society is undeniable. And the misuse of *macho* hints at a deeper cultural misunderstanding that extends beyond mere word definitions.

—*Rose del Castillo Guilbault*

By *showing* instead of merely *telling*, del Castillo Guilbault enables readers to visualize the important distinctions that support her larger point about cultural differences.

What are the major expansion strategies in this definition? Illustrate and explain.

READING AND RESPONDING

In this case study, student writer Haley relies on definition in her response to the following professional essay.

ESSAY FOR ANALYSIS AND RESPONSE

In "For My Indian Daughter," Native American author Lewis P. Johnson traces the struggle to define his cultural identity in an often unwelcoming world. He also explores his relationship with his young daughter and his hopes and expectations for quality in her life as she seeks her own identity. As you read, try to think about how you may have to define some aspect of your own identity.

FOR MY INDIAN DAUGHTER

My little girl is singing herself to sleep upstairs, her voice mingling with the sounds of the birds outside in the old maple trees. She is two and I am nearly 50, and I am very taken with her. She came along late in my life, unexpected and unbidden, a startling gift.

Today at the beach my chubby-legged, brown-skinned daughter ran laughing into the water as fast as she could. My wife and I laughed watching her, until we heard behind us a low guttural curse and then an unpleasant voice raised in an imitation war whoop.

I turned to see a fat man in a bathing suit, white and soft as a grub, as he covered his mouth and prepared to make the Indian war cry again. He was middle-aged, younger than I, and had three little children lined up next to him, grinning foolishly. My wife suggested we leave the beach, and I agreed.

I knew the man was not unusual in his feelings against Indians. His beach behavior might have been socially unacceptable to more civilized whites, but his basic view of Indians is expressed daily in our small town, frequently on the editorial pages of the country newspaper, as white people speak out against Indian fishing rights and land rights, saying in essence, "Those Indians are taking our fish, our land." It doesn't matter to them that we were here first, that the U.S. Supreme Court has ruled in our favor. It matters to them that we have something they want, and they hate us for it. Backlash is the common explanation of the attacks on Indians, the bumper stickers that say, "Spear an Indian, Save a Fish," but I know better. The hatred of Indians goes back to the beginning when white people came to this country. For me it goes back to my childhood in Harbor Springs, Michigan.

THEFT

Harbor Springs is now a summer resort for the very affluent, but a hundred years ago it was the Indian village of my Ottawa ancestors. My grandmother, Anna Showanessy, and other Indians like her, had their land there taken by treaty, by fraud, by violence, by theft. They remembered how whites had burned down the village at Burt Lake in 1900 and pushed the Indians out. These were the stories in my family.

When I was a boy my mother told me to walk down the alleys in Harbor Springs and not to wear my orange football sweater out of the house. This way I would not stand out, not be noticed, and not be a target.

I wore my orange sweater anyway and deliberately avoided the alleys. I was the biggest person I knew and wasn't really afraid. But I met my comeuppance when I enlisted in the U.S. Army. One night all the men in my barracks gathered together and, gang-fashion, pulled me into the shower and scrubbed me down with rough brushes used for floors, saying, "We won't have any dirty Indians in our outfit." It is a point of irony that I was cleaner than any of them. Later in Korea I learned how to kill, how to bully, how to hate Koreans. I came out of the war tougher than ever and, strangely, white.

I went to college, got married, lived in La Porte, Indiana, worked as a surveyor and raised three boys. I headed Boy Scout groups, never thinking it odd when the Scouts did imitation Indian dances, imitation Indian lore.

One day when I was 35 or thereabouts I heard about an Indian powwow. My father used to attend them and so with great curiosity and a strange joy at discovering a part of my heritage, I decided the thing to do to get ready for this big event was to have my friend make me a spear in his forge. The steel was fine and blue and iridescent. The feathers on the shaft were bright and proud.

In a dusty state fairground in southern Indiana, I found white people dressed as Indians. I learned they were "hobbyists," that is, it was their hobby and leisure pastime to masquerade as Indians on weekends. I felt ridiculous with my spear, and I left.

It was years before I could tell anyone of the embarrassment of this weekend and see any humor in it. But in a way it was that weekend, for all its silliness, that was my awakening. I realized I didn't know who I was. I didn't have an Indian name. I didn't speak the Indian language. I didn't know the Indian customs. Dimly I remembered the Ottawa word for dog, but it was a baby word, *kahgee,* not the full word, *muhkahgee,* which I was later to learn. Even more hazily I remembered a naming ceremony (my own). I remembered legs dancing around me, dust. Where had that been? Who had I been? "Suwaukquat," my mother told me when I asked, "where the tree begins to grow."

That was 1968, and I was not the only Indian in the country who was feeling the need to remember who he or she was. There were others. They had powwows, real ones, and eventually I found them. Together we researched our past, a search that for me culminated in the Longest Walk, a march on Washington in 1978. Maybe because I now know what it means to be Indian, it surprises me that others don't. Of course there aren't very many of us left. The chances of an average person knowing an average Indian in an average lifetime are pretty slim.

CIRCLE

Still, I was amused one day when my small, four-year-old neighbor looked at me as I was hoeing in my garden and said, "You aren't a real Indian, are you?" Scotty is little, talkative, likable. Finally I said, "I'm a real Indian." He looked at me for a moment and then said, squinting into the sun, "Then where's your horse and feathers?" The child was simply a smaller, whiter version of my own ignorant self years before. We'd both seen too much TV, that's all. He was not to be blamed. And so, in a way the moronic man on the beach today is blameless. We come full circle to realize other people are like ourselves, as discomfiting as that may be sometimes.

As I sit in my old chair on my porch, in a light that is fading so the leaves are barely distinguishable against the sky, I can picture my girl asleep upstairs. I would like to prepare her for what's to come, take her each step of the way saying, there's a place to avoid, here's what I know about this, but much of what's before her she must go through alone. She must pass through pain and joy and solitude and community to discover her own inner self that is unlike any other and come through that passage to the place where she sees all people are one, and in so seeing may live her life in a brighter future.

—*Lewis P. Johnson*

Questions About the Reading

Refer to the general questions on page 154 and the specific ones here.

CONTENT

- *What is the major expansion (or development) strategy in this definition? Which additional strategies can you identify?*
- *For whom, besides his daughter, does Johnson appear to be writing?*
- *What are Johnson's assumptions about his audience's knowledge and attitudes? Are these assumptions accurate? Why or why not?*
- *What and where is the thesis? Why does it appear at that point in the essay? Is this placement effective? Explain.*

ORGANIZATION

- *Trace the line of thought in this essay. Is this the most effective order? Explain.*
- *Does the organization make the expansion strategies easier to follow? Explain.*

STYLE

- *What is the writer's attitude toward his subject? Toward his audience? How do we know? What are the signals?*
- *Is the tone appropriate for this writer's audience and purpose? Explain.*

RESPONDING TO READING

After reading "For My Indian Daughter," Shirley Haley decided to explore her feelings about her relationship with her parents and to define her own expectations of a "Life in Full Color."

During her planning, drafting, and revising, Haley relied on the Guidelines for Definition on page 272 and the revision checklists on pages 62–63 and 280 in producing the following final draft

Note

Haley's expanded definition relies on a combination of development strategies, such as comparison and contrast, description, narration, illustration, and cause and effect.

Title attracts attention and previews the topic

Opening narrative leads into the thesis

Thesis (as sentence definition)

Paragraphs 2, 3 and 4 rely on comparison/ contrast and examples

Paragraphs 3 and 4 include causal analysis

LIFE IN FULL COLOR

1 I'm probably the only person I know who still has the same two parents she was born with. We have a traditional American family: we go to church and football games; we watch the Olympics on television and argue about politics; and we have Thanksgiving dinner at my grandmother Clancy's and Christmas dinner with my father's sister Jess, who used to let us kids put pitted olives on our fingertips when we were little. Most of my friends are struggling with the problems of broken homes; I'll always be grateful to my parents for giving me a loving and stable background. *But sometimes I look at my parents' life and hope my life will be less ordinary, less duty-bound, and less predictable.*

2 *I want my life to be imaginative, not ordinary.* Instead of honeymooning at Niagara Falls, I want to go to Paris. In my parents' neighborhood, all the houses were built alike about twenty years ago. Different owners have added on or shingled or painted, but the houses basically all look the same. The first thing we did when we moved into our house was plant trees; everyone did. Now the neighborhood is full of family homes on tree-lined streets, which is nice; but I'd prefer a condo in a renovated brick building in Boston. I'd have dozens of plants, and I'd buy great furniture one piece at a time at auctions and dusty shops and not by the roomful from the local furniture store. Instead of spending my time trying to be similar to everyone else, I'd like to explore ways of being different.

3 *My parents have so many obligations, they barely have time for themselves; I don't want to live like that.* I'm never quite sure whether they own the house or the house owns them. They worry constantly about taxes, or the old furnace, or the new deck, or mowing the lawn, or weeding the garden. After spending every weekend slaving over their beautiful yard, they have no time left to enjoy it. And when they're not buried in household chores, other people are making endless demands on their time. My mother will stay up past midnight because she promised some telephone voice 3 cakes for the church bazaar, or 5 dozen cookies for the Girl Scout meeting, or 76 little sandwiches for the women's club Christmas party. My father coaches Little League, wears a clown suit for the Lion's flea markets, and both he and my mother are volunteer firefighters. In fact, both my parents get talked into

Negative definition in closing sentence helps clarify meaning

volunteering for everything. I hate to sound selfish, but my first duty is to my-self. I'd rather live in a tent than be owned by my house. And I don't want my life to end up being measured out in endless chores.

Descriptive and narrative details throughout enable readers to *visualize*

4 *Although it's nice to take things such as regular meals and paychecks for granted, many other events in my parents' life are too predictable for me.* Every Sunday at two o'clock we dine on overdone roast beef, mashed potatoes and gravy, a faded green vegetable, and sometimes that mushy orange squash that comes frozen in bricks. It's not that either of my parents is a bad cook, but Sunday dinner isn't food anymore; it's a habit. Mom and Dad have become so predictable that they can order each other's food in restaurants. Just once I'd like to see them pack up and go away for a weekend, without telling anybody; they couldn't do it. They can't even go crazy and try a new place for their sum-mer vacation. They've been spending the first two weeks in August on Cape Cod since I was two years old. I want variety in my life. I want to travel, see this country and see Europe, do things spontaneously. No one will ever be able to predict my order in a restaurant.

Conclusion reinforces the writer's definition of "life in full color"

5 Before long, Christmas will be here, and we'll be going to Aunt Jess's. Mom will bake a walnut pie, and Grandpa Frank will say, "Michelle, you sure know how to spoil an old man." It's nice to know that some things never change. In fact, some of the ordinary, obligatory, predictable things in life are the most comfortable. But too much of any routine can make life seem dull and gray. I hope my choices lead to a life in full color.

—*Shirley Haley*

☑ A CHECKLIST for Definition

☐ Does the **level of detail** meet the audience's needs?

☐ Is the definition in **plain English?**

☐ Has the term been **classified** precisely?

☐ Has the term been **differentiated** accurately?

☐ Have you avoided **circular definition?**

☐ Is the definition **expanded** adequately?

☐ Have **needless details** been eliminated?

☐ Has definition through **negation** been used?

☐ Has the term's **etymology** been provided, as needed?

☐ Have you considered the **legal implications** of your definition?

☐ Have you considered the **ethical implications** of your definition?

(For more on each of these criteria, see pages 272–273.)

APPLICATIONS

17.1 **PARAGRAPH WARM-UP: DENOTATIVE DEFINITION THAT EXPLAINS** Using denotative definition, write a paragraph explaining the meaning of a term that is specialized, new, or otherwise unfamiliar to your reader. List in the margin the strategies for expansion you've used. Begin with a formal sentence definition (term, class, differentiation). Select a term from your major (such as *capitalism*, defined for a nonmajor) or from your daily conversation with peers (such as *phat*, defined for a senior citizen). Clearly identify the situation, the audience, and your purpose.

17.2 **PARAGRAPH WARM-UP: CONNOTATIVE DEFINITION THAT MAKES A POINT** Using connotative definition, write a paragraph explaining the special meaning or associations that a term holds for you. Select a term that can be defined in multiple—and often conflicting—ways, such as *patriotism, education, freedom,* or *morality*. List in the margin the expansion strategies you've used. Clearly identify the situation, the audience, and your purpose.

17.3 **ESSAY PRACTICE**

a. Explore your reactions to "The Meaning of *Macho*" (page 274) using the personal response questions on page 155. Then respond with an essay that supports or challenges the assertion that meaning is determined by the social or cultural context in which a word is used. Perhaps you belong to an in-group (family, friends, club, ethnic group) that uses certain words in ironic or special ways to signify meanings that could be appreciated only by members of that particular group. Perhaps you could discuss a slang term or a term of alienation used in a personal context as a term of affection or respect. Your essay should make a clear and definite point about the larger meaning behind the examples you provide.

b. Explore your reactions to "For My Indian Daughter" using the questions on page 155. Then respond with your own essay that examines the connotations of a familiar term that evokes positive or negative feelings. For instance, you might define a term of recent vintage, like *rap, grunge,* or *skater,* or you might examine the connotations of *fraternity, sorority, jock,* or some other campus-related term.

   Perhaps you have wrestled with issues of personal identity in relation to your background. Perhaps certain experiences caused you to discover a sense of alienation or a sense of belonging. Perhaps something made you appreciate your background or made you realize you were "different." Perhaps you struggled to meet certain cultural expectations or to overcome a sense of inferiority.

   Your essay should make a clear and definite point about the larger meaning behind the examples you provide.

c. Along with changing times come changes in our way of seeing. Some terms that held meanings for us two or three years ago may have acquired radically different meanings by now. If we once defined *success* narrowly as social status and income bracket, we might now define it in broader words: leading a life that puts us in touch with ourselves and the world around us. Similarly, the meanings of other terms (*education, friendship, freedom, maturity, self-fulfillment, pain, love, home, family, career, patriotism*) may have changed. Although some terms take on more positive meanings, others acquire more negative ones. Your connotations of *marriage* may depend on whether you have witnessed or experienced marriages that have been happy and constructive or bitter and destructive. And quite often an entire society's definition of something changes over time, *marriage* being a good example.

Identify something that has changed in meaning, either for you individually (as with Shirley Haley's expectations about her adult life) or for our society as a whole—such as the *American dream*. Discuss both the traditional and the new meanings (choose a serious, ironic, or humorous point of view) in such a way that your definition makes a specific point or commentary, either stated or implied, about society's values or your own.

17.4   WEB-BASED PROJECTS

a. Consult an online computer manual, a computer publication, or a newsgroup for computer enthusiasts. Find at least five technical terms that you—and probably most of your classmates—aren't familiar with or don't fully understand. Research these terms; then, for your classmates, write both sentence and expanded definitions for two of them. Some possibilities: *FTP, IRC, HTML, memory bus, firewall, RISC, LAN, CGI, JavaScript, cloud.*

b. Compare two Internet dictionaries on the basis of specific criteria, such as the following:

■ search page (interface) is easy to use
■ searches are fast
■ offers links to other dictionaries and language resources
■ provides good navigational aids
■ offers good Help, FAQ, and Search Tips pages
■ entries are easy to browse

Be sure to specify the criteria you have chosen.

Works Cited

Corbett, Edward P. J. *Classical Rhetoric for the Modern Student*. 3rd ed. New York: Oxford, UP, 1990. Print.

The Employee Problem Solver. Ramsey: Alexander Hamilton Inst., 2000. Print.

Office of Technology Assessment. *Harmful Non-Indigenous Species in the United States*. Washington: GPO, 1993. Print.

For additional information and practice with the learning objectives in this chapter, go to www.mycomplab.com, Resource>Writing>Writing Purposes.

Argument: Writing to Persuade Your Readers

LEARNING OBJECTIVES FOR THIS CHAPTER

- Understand the role of *persuasion* as a writing strategy composed of various earlier strategies
- Recognize the various ways writers can support their claims
- Understand the importance of connecting with readers in a persuasive essay
- Appreciate the different goals persuasive essays may take
- Write a persuasive essay using the chapter guidelines

As you have seen, the strategies in Chapters 10–17 can be used to draw readers into the writer's special way of seeing. This purpose can be called "persuasive" because it asks readers to agree with particular viewpoints such as these:

- The "wifely" stereotype persists in today's generation (page 159)
- Media reports on African Americans are often biased (page 196)
- Most people have too much self-esteem rather than too little (page 242)
- Prejudice against American Indians persists to this day (page 276)

Writing for the *primary* goal of persuasion, however, often takes a stand on even more controversial topics—issues on which people always disagree. For example, do the risks of nuclear power outweigh its advantages? Should marijuana be legalized? Are liberal arts degrees worth the money? We write about these issues in hopes of winning readers over to our side—or at least inducing them to appreciate our position. Although these arguments employ various development strategies (description, comparison and contrast, and so on), their underlying goal is to persuade readers to see things the writer's way.

In a free society, you can expect some readers to disagree with your stand on a controversy no matter how long and how brilliantly you argue. But even though you won't change *everyone's* mind, a strong persuasive argument can make a difference to *some people.*

Note   *Argument, in this context, means a process of careful reasoning in support of a claim, not a quarrel or dispute. People who argue skillfully connect with others in a rational, sensible way, without animosity. People who are **argumentative**, by contrast, simply make others defensive.*

ANTICIPATING AUDIENCE RESISTANCE

Argument focuses on its audience; it addresses issues in which people are directly involved. But people rarely change their minds about such issues without good reason. Expect resistance from your readers and defensive questions such as these:

What readers of argument want to know

- *Why should I even read this?*
- *Why should I change my mind?*
- *Can you prove it?*
- *How do you know?*
- *Says who?*
- *So what?*

Getting readers to admit that *you* might be right means getting them to admit that *they* might be wrong. The more strongly they identify with their position, the more resistance you can expect. To overcome this resistance, you have to put yourself in your readers' position and see things their way before you argue for your way. The persuasiveness of any argument ultimately depends on how convincing it is to its *audience*.

Making a good argument requires that you bring together all the strategies you've learned so far, along with features specific to any type of argumentative writing:

Features of an effective argument

1. a main point or claim that the audience finds debatable
2. convincing support for the claim
3. a clear and unmistakable line of thought
4. a good relationship with the audience
5. attention to the ethics of argument

HAVING A DEBATABLE CLAIM

The claim in an argument must be debatable (something open to dispute, something that can be viewed from more than one angle). Statements of fact are not debatable:

A fact is something whose certainty is established

> Several near-disastrous accidents have occurred recently in nuclear power plants.
>
> On average, women outlive men.
>
> Government economic policies have led to decreases in student loan programs.
>
> More than 50 percent of traffic deaths are alcohol-related.

Because these statements can be verified (shown to be true or accurate, at least with enough certainty that reasonable people would agree), they cannot be debated. Similarly, questions of taste or personal opinion can never be debated because they rest on no objective reasons:

Personal taste and opinion are based on preference, belief, or feeling instead of fact

> I love oatmeal.
>
> Catholics are holier than Baptists.
>
> Professor Dreary's lectures put me to sleep.
>
> I hate the taste of garlic.

Even many assertions that call for expository support are not debatable for most audiences:

Once reasonable people know the facts, they would have to agree with these claims

> Competition for good jobs is now fiercer than ever.
>
> Police roadblocks help deter drunk driving.
>
> Lowering the drinking age increases alcohol-related traffic fatalities.
>
> High gas prices have caused people to rethink their financial priorities.

Writing that demonstrates the truth of these assertions is primarily referential. Once the facts are established, the audience will almost certainly agree, "Yes, it's true."

What, then, is a *debatable claim?* It is *one that cannot be proved true but is more or less probable.* For example, few readers would debate the notion that electronic games have altered the play habits of millions of American children. But some would disagree that electronic games are dominating children's lives.

No amount of evidence can prove or disprove these claims

> The political activities of the Religious Right violate the constitutional separation of church and state.
>
> Schools should place more emphasis on competition.
>
> Police roadblocks are a justifiable deterrent against drunk driving.
>
> All states should maintain the drinking age at 21.

Even though the rightness or wrongness of these controversial issues can never be proved, writers may argue more or less persuasively for one side or the other. And unlike an assertion of personal opinion or taste, an arguable assertion can be judged by the quality of support the writer presents. How does the assertion hold up against *opposing* assertions?

Always state your arguable point directly and clearly as a thesis. Whereas other development strategies (especially description and narration) may allow the thesis to be merely implied, argumentative writing almost never does. Let readers know exactly where you stand.

SUPPORTING YOUR CLAIM

Chapter 5 shows that any credible assertion rests on opinions derived from facts. But facts out of context can be interpreted in various ways. Legitimate argument offers convincing reasons, reliable sources, careful interpretation, and valid conclusions.

Offer Convincing Reasons

An argument is only as convincing as the reasons that support it. Before people will change their minds, they need to know why. They expect you to complete a version of this statement, in which your reasons follow "because":

| My position is _____ because _____.

Arguing effectively means using *only* those reasons likely to move your specific audience. Assume, for instance, that all students living on your campus have a meal plan with a fifteen-meal requirement (for weekdays), costing $3,500 yearly. You belong to a group trying to reduce the required meals to ten weekly. Before seeking students' support and lobbying the administration, your group constructs a list of reasons for its position. A brainstorming session produces this list:

Subjective support offers reasons that matter to the writer—but not always to the reader.

The number of required meals should be reduced to ten per week for these reasons:

1. Many students dislike the food.
2. Some students with only afternoon classes like to sleep late and should not have to rush to beat the 9:00 a.m. breakfast deadline.
3. The cafeteria atmosphere is too noisy, impersonal, and dreary.
4. The food selection is too limited.
5. The price of a yearly meal ticket has risen unfairly and is now more than 5 percent higher than last year's price.

You quickly spot a flaw in this list: All these reasons rest almost entirely on *subjective* grounds, on personal taste or opinion. For every reader who dislikes the food or sleeps late, another may like the food or rise early—and so on. Your intended audience (students, administrators) probably won't think these reasons are very convincing. Your reasons should be based on *objective* evidence and on goals and values you and your readers share.

Provide Objective Evidence

Evidence (factual support from an outside source) is objective when it can be verified (shown to be accurate) by everyone involved. Common types of objective evidence include factual statements, statistics, examples, and expert testimony.

A *fact* is something that can be demonstrated by observation, experience, research, or measurement—and that your audience is willing to recognize:

Offer the facts

| Each dorm suite has its own kitchen.

Be selective. Decide which facts best support your case (page 81).

Numbers can be highly convincing. Most people focus on the bottom line (percentages, costs, savings, profits):

Cite the numbers

> Roughly 30 percent of the five hundred students we surveyed in the cafeteria eat only two meals per day.

But numbers can mislead. Your statistics must be accurate, trustworthy, and easy to understand and verify (see pages 369–374). Always cite your source.

Examples help people visualize and remember the point. For instance, the best way to explain what you mean by "wasteful" is to show "waste" occurring:

Show what you mean

> From 20 to 25 percent of the food prepared is never eaten.

Use examples your audience can identify with. Explain how each example fits the point it is designed to illustrate.

Expert testimony—if it is unbiased and if people acknowledge and accept the expert—lends authority and credibility to any claim:

Cite the experts

> Food service directors from three local colleges point out that their schools' flexible meal plans have been highly successful.

See pages 340–341 for the limits of expert testimony.

Appeal to Shared Goals and Values

Evidence alone isn't always enough to change a person's mind. Identify at least one *goal* you and your audience have in common. In the meal plan issue, for example, we can assume that everyone wants to eliminate wasteful practices. A persuasive argument will therefore take this goal into account:

Appeal to shared goals

> These changes in the meal plan would eliminate waste of food, labor, and money.

People's goals are shaped by their *values* (qualities they believe in, ideals they stand for): friendship, loyalty, honesty, equality, fairness, and so on (Rokeach 57–58). Look for a common, central value. In the meal plan case, *fairness* might be an important value:

Appeal to shared values

> No one should have to pay for meals one doesn't eat.

Here is how your group's final list of reasons might read:

Persuasive claims are backed up by reasons that matter to the reader

> The number of required weekday meals should be reduced to ten per week for these reasons:
>
> 1. No one should have to pay for meals one doesn't eat.
> 2. Roughly 30 percent of the five hundred students we surveyed in the cafeteria eat only two meals per day.

3. From 20 to 25 percent of the food prepared is never eaten—a waste of food, labor, and money.

4. Each dorm suite has its own kitchen, but these kitchens are seldom used.

5. Relying on kitchen suites and local restaurants, students on the Monday-through-Friday plan do survive on weekends. Why couldn't they survive just as well during the week?

6. Food service directors from three local colleges point out that their schools' flexible meal plans have been highly successful.

Reasonable audiences should now find this argument compelling because each reason is based on a verifiable fact or (as in item 1) good sense. Even audience members not moved to support your cause will understand why you've taken your stand.

Give people reasons that have meaning for *them* personally. For example, in a study of teenage attitudes about smoking, respondents listed these reasons for not smoking: bad breath, difficulty concentrating, loss of friends, and trouble with adults. No respondents listed dying of cancer—presumably because this last reason carries little meaning for young people personally (Bauman et al. 511).

Note *Finding objective evidence to support a claim often requires that we go beyond our own experience by doing some type of research (see Section Four).*

SHAPING A CLEAR LINE OF THOUGHT

Like other types of writing, a persuasive essay has an introduction, body, and conclusion. But within this familiar shape, your argument should do special things as well. Readers need to follow your reasoning; they expect to see how, exactly, you support your claim. The model in Figure 18.1 lays out a standard shape that can be adapted for most arguments. Select those elements appropriate to your situation, and arrange them in a sequence that reveals a clear line of thought.

CONNECTING WITH YOUR AUDIENCE

In any attempt at persuasion, the *audience* is the main focus. Whenever you set out to influence someone's thinking, remember this:

No matter how brilliant, any argument rejected by its audience is a failed argument.

If readers dislike what you have to say or decide that what you say has no meaning for them personally, they reject your argument. Instead of insisting

FIGURE 18.1
Shaping a clear line of thought
Give the audience a clear and logical path, but remember that no argument rigidly follows the order of elements shown here.

Standard Shape for an Argument

Introduction: *Attract and Invite Your Audience and Provide a Forecast*
- Identify the issue clearly and immediately. Show that your argument deserves attention.
- Be clear about the points over which you and opponents disagree.
- Acknowledge the opposing viewpoint accurately, and concede its merit.
- Offer at least one point of your own that your audience will agree with.
- Give enough background for people to understand your position accurately.
- State a clear, concrete, and definite claim (or thesis). Never delay your claim without good reason; however, if the issue is highly controversial, you might want to delay it until you've offered some convincing evidence.
- Keep the introduction short—no more than a few brief paragraphs.

Body: *Offer Support and Refutation*
- Focus on reasons that your audience will consider important.
- Organize your supporting points for best emphasis. If you think the audience has little interest, begin with the strongest material. Sometimes you can sandwich weaker points between stronger ones. But if all points are more or less equal, begin with the most familiar and acceptable to your audience, to elicit early agreement. In general, try to save the strongest points for last.
- Reinforce each supporting point with concrete, specific details (facts, examples, narratives, quotations, or other verifiable evidence).
- String your supporting points and evidence together along a definite line of reasoning.
- In at least one separate paragraph, refute any flawed assumptions and faulty logic in opposing arguments (including any anticipated but invalid objections to your points).

Conclusion: *Sum Up Your Case and Make a Direct Appeal*
- Summarize—without merely repeating—your main points and your counterarguments, emphasizing your strongest material. Offer a view of the big picture.
- Appeal directly to the audience for definite action (where appropriate).
- Let people know what they should do, think, or feel.

that people see things your way, try to see things from their perspective. The Guidelines for Persuasion (page 291) should help.

Note

Keep in mind that no cookbook formula exists and that in many situations, even the best persuasive attempts may be rejected.

GUIDELINES for Persuasion

Develop a Clear and Credible Plan

- *Define your precise goal.* Develop the clearest possible view of what you want to see happen. Then write it out: "My goal is to persuade my dorm mates to support a mandatory 3-hour 'quiet' policy Sunday through Thursday evenings."

- *Do your homework.* Carefully weigh the costs (or risks) versus the benefits. Be sure your facts are straight, your figures are accurate, and your evidence supports your claim.

- *Think your idea through.* Are there holes in this argument? Will it stand up under scrutiny?

- *Anticipate audience reaction.* Will people be defensive, shocked, annoyed, angry? Try to neutralize major objections beforehand. Express your judgments on the issue ("We could do better") without blaming people ("It's all your fault"). Consider some possible middle ground that your audience might accept.

- *Never make a claim or ask for something that people will reject outright.* Consider how much is achievable in this situation by asking what people are thinking. Invite them to share in decision making. Offer real choices.

Prepare Your Argument

- *Be clear about what you want.* Diplomacy is always important, but don't leave people guessing about your purpose.

- *Project a likable and reasonable persona.* Persona is the image or impression you project in your tone and diction. Audiences are wondering, "What do I think about the person making the argument?" "Do I like and trust this person?" "Does this person seem to know what he or she is talking about?" "Is this person trying to make me look stupid?"

  Audiences tune out aggressive people, no matter how sensible the argument. Resist the urge to preach, to sound off, or to be sarcastic. Admit the imperfections or uncertainty in your case. Invite people to respond. A little humility never hurts.

- *Find points of agreement with your audience.* "What do we *all* want?" Focus early on a shared value, goal, or experience. Emphasize your similarities. Pat deserving people on the back.

- *Never distort the opponent's position.* A sure way to alienate people is to cast the opponent in a more negative light than the facts warrant.

- *Try to concede something to the opponent.* Reasonable people respect an argument that is fair and balanced. Admit the merits of the opposing case before arguing for your own. Show empathy and willingness to compromise. Encourage people to air their own views.

- *Do not merely criticize.* If you're arguing that something is wrong, be sure you can offer realistic suggestions for making it right.

- *Stick to claims you can support.* Show people what's in it for them—but never distort the facts just to please the audience. Be honest about the risks.

(continues)

- *Stick to your best material.* Not all points are equal. Decide what material—in your audience's view—best advances your case.

- *Use your skills responsibly.* The obvious power of persuasive skills creates tremendous potential for abuse. People who feel they have been bullied or deceived will likely become your enemies.

USING ARGUMENT

BEYOND THE WRITING CLASSROOM

- **In other courses:** Much academic writing (and oral presentation) is designed to persuade others to accept a particular point of view. In a public speaking course, classmates might debate a controversial issue such as gun control; in sociology, a student might write a paper arguing that health care ought to be socialized; or a nursing student might argue that herbal remedies are largely ignored by the Food and Drug Administraction.

- **On the job:** Much business writing is persuasive. For example, a businessperson wiriting a sales letter will try to persuade customers that her company's products or sevices are superior to those of the competition. Or an executive might write a business proposal designed to persuade the Board of Directors to support a particular course of action. Or an employee might write a simple email to a coworker, briefly arguing why meeting Tuesday's deadline is vital.

- **In the community**: Argument, or debate, is a cornerstone of all democratic societies. Arguments for or against social reforms may be made by lobby groups, individuals speaking up at town mettings, politicians in a debate, citizens writing to their congresspeople, and so on.

In what other situations might argument make a difference?

Note

Remember that people rarely change their minds quickly or without good reason. A truly resistant audience will dismiss even the best arguments and may end up feeling threatened and resentful. Even with a receptive audience, attempts at persuasion can fail. Often the best you can do is avoid disaster and give people the chance to appreciate the merits of the case.

VARIOUS ARGUMENTS FOR VARIOUS GOALS

"What do I want people to be doing or thinking?"

Arguments differ considerably in the level of involvement they ask from people. Is your goal to influence people's opinions, seek their support, or induce direct action?

Arguing to Change People's Thinking

Asking only for a change in thinking

Some arguments ask for minimal audience involvement. Maybe you want people to agree that the benefits of bioengineered foods outweigh the risks or that your company's monitoring of employee emails is hurting morale. The goal here is merely to move readers to change their thinking, to say, "I agree."

Arguing to Enlist People's Support

Asking for active support

Some arguments ask people to take a definite stand. Maybe you want readers to vote for a specific candidate, lobby for additional computer equipment at your school, or enforce dorm or library "quiet" rules. The goal here is to get people actively involved, to get them to ask, "How can I help?"

Presenting a Proposal

Asking for direct action

The world is full of problems to solve. And proposals are designed precisely to solve problems. The type of proposal we examine here typically asks readers to take—or to approve—some form of direct action (to bolster campus security, to fund a new campus organization, to improve working conditions). But before you can induce people to act, you must complete these preliminary persuasive tasks:

A proposal involves persuasive tasks

1. Spell out the problem (and its causes) in enough detail to convince readers of its importance.
2. Point out the benefits of solving the problem.
3. Offer a realistic, cost-effective solution.
4. Address anticipated objections to your plan.
5. Give reasons why your readers should be the ones to act.

Your proposal goal is achieved when people say, "OK, let's do this project."

These categories can—and often do—overlap, depending on the situation. Never launch an argument without a clear view of exactly what you want to see happen.

Each of the three case studies that follow shows essays addressed to readers who have an increasing stake or involvement in the issue. Comparing these essays will demonstrate how writers in various situations can convey their way of seeing.

CASE STUDY

READING AND RESPONDING TO AN ARGUMENT FOR A CHANGE IN THINKING.

In this case study, student writter Julia Schoonover persents an argument that attempts to change readers' opinions as she responds to the following professional essay.

ESSAY FOR ANALYSIS AND RESPONSE

In this next essay *Miami Herald* columnist Bob Swift argues that "trash" fiction (about Tarzan, Nancy Drew, Conan the Barbarian, and so on) offers children a good preparation for reading great literature. As you read, think about the kinds of books, magazines, and print or online news sources you most enjoy reading. Could some of them be considered "trash"? If so, what arguments could you make for the benefits of this type of reading?

ON READING TRASH

If you want kids to become omnivorous readers, let them read trash. That's my philosophy, and I speak from experience.

I don't disagree with the National Endowment for the Humanities, which says every high school graduate should have read 30 great works of literature, including the Bible, Plato, Shakespeare, Hawthorne, the Declaration of Independence, *Catcher in the Rye, Crime and Punishment* and *Moby Dick.*

It's a fine list. Kids should read them all, and more. But they'll be better readers if they start off on trash. Trash? What I mean is what some might call "popular" fiction. My theory is, if you get kids interested in reading books— no matter what sort—they will eventually go on to the grander literature all by themselves.

In the third grade I read my first novel, a mystic adventure set in India. I still recall the sheer excitement at discovering how much fun reading could be.

When we moved within walking distance of the public library a whole new world opened. In the library I found that wonder of wonders, the series. What a thrill, to find a favorite author had written a dozen or more other titles.

I read a series about frontiersmen, learning about Indian tribes, beef jerky and tepees. A Civil War series alternated young heroes from the Blue and the Gray, and I learned about Grant and Lee and the Rock of Chickamauga.

One summer, in Grandpa Barrow's attic, I discovered the Mother Lode, scores of dusty books detailing the adventures of Tom Swift, the Rover Boys, the Submarine Boys, the Motorcycle Boys and Bomba the Jungle Boy. It didn't matter that some were written in 1919; any book you haven't read is brand new.

Another summer I discovered Edgar Rice Burroughs. I swung through jungles with Tarzan, fought green Martians with John Carter, explored Pellucidar at the Earth's core, flew through the steamy air of Venus with Carson Napier. Then I came across Sax Rohmer and, for book after book, prowled opium dens with Nayland Smith, in pursuit of the insidious Fu Manchu.

In the seventh grade I ran across Booth Tarkington's hilarious Penrod books and read them over and over.

My cousin went off to war in 1942 and gave me his pulp magazines. I became hooked on Doc Savage, the Shadow, G8 and His Battle Aces, the Spider, *Amazing Stories*. My folks wisely did not object to them as trash. I began to look in second-hand book shops for past issues and found a *Blue Book Magazine*, with an adventure story by Talbot Mundy. It led me back to the library, for more of Mundy's Far East thrillers. From Mundy, my path led to A.

Conan Doyle's *The Lost World*, Rudyard Kipling's *Kim*, Jules Verne, H. G. Wells and Jack London.

Before long I was whaling with Herman Melville, affixing scarlet letters with Hawthorne and descending into the maelstrom with Poe. In due course came Hemingway, Dos Passos, *Hamlet, The Odyssey, The Iliad, Crime and Punishment.* I had discovered "real" literature by following the trail of popular fiction.

When our kids were small, we read aloud to them from Doctor Dolittle and Winnie the Pooh. Soon they learned to read, and favored the *Frog and Toad* and *Freddie the Pig* series.

When the old Doc Savage and Conan the Barbarian pulps were reissued as paperbacks, I brought them home. The kids devoured them, sometimes hiding them behind textbooks at school, just as I had. They read my old Tarzan and Penrod books along with Nancy Drew and *The Black Stallion.*

Now they're big kids. Each kid's room is lined with bookshelves, on which are stacked, in an eclectic mix, Doc Savage, Plato, Louis L'Amour westerns, Thomas Mann, Gothic romances, Agatha Christie, Sartre, Edgar Allan Poe, science-fiction, Saul Bellow, Shakespeare, Pogo, Greek tragedies, Hemingway, Kipling, Tarzan, *Zen and the Art of Motorcycle Maintenance*, F. Scott Fitzgerald, *Bomba the Jungle Boy*, Nietzsche, *The Iliad, Dr. Dolittle*, Joseph Conrad, Fu Manchu, Hawthorne, Penrod, Dostoevsky, Ray Bradbury, Herman Melville, Conan the Barbarian...more. Some great literature, some trash, but all good reading.

—*Bob Swift*

Questions About the Reading

Refer also to the general questions on page 154.

PURPOSE

- *Who is Swift's intended audience here? How do we know?*
- *Does Swift succeed in connecting with his audience? If so, how?*

CONTENT

- *What is the primary development strategy used here? Which other strategies can you identify?*
- *Does the writer acknowledge the opposing viewpoint? If so, where?*

- *Does the thesis grow out of sufficient background details? Explain.*

ORGANIZATION

- *Is the material arranged in the best order? Explain.*
- *Are most paragraphs too short? Explain.*

STYLE

- *How would you characterize the tone? Is it appropriate for the audience and purpose?*
- *Does the writer appear likable? Is he ever too extreme? Explain.*

RESPONDING TO READING

After reading and analyzing Swift's argument that reading trash can be more useful than it seems, Julia Schoonover decided to persuade fellow students that credit cards can be far more dangerous than they appear.

While planning, drafting, and revising, Schoonover refers to the Guidelines for Persuasion, the Model Outline for Argument, and the revision checklists on pages 62–63, 290, 291, and 306, respectively.

Note	*Like most arguments, Schoonover's piece relies on multiple development strategies, especially causal analysis, process analysis, and illustration.*

Title announces the essay's purpose

Opens directly with the thesis

Acknowledges opposing view

Vivid examples help establish agreement and neutralize objections

Transition to upcoming refutation

Cause-and-effect analysis
Process analysis

Uses examples as objective evidence
Process analysis
Gives striking statistics

Gives additional examples readers can identify with

CREDIT CARDS: LEAVE HOME WITHOUT THEM

Credit cards are college students' best friends and potentially their worst enemy. Credit cards provide a convenient means of purchasing much-needed textbooks, food, and dorm room essentials. Credit cards enable students to purchase plane tickets to fly home or to Bermuda for spring break. Credit cards even make money available for those little extras that Mom and Dad would never buy—like a state-of-the-art stereo system or a new wardrobe. Long-distance calls and Christmas shopping are also made a lot easier by credit cards.

Although credit cards can be very helpful to the struggling student, they can also spell big trouble. The most obvious danger comes from their misuse: that is, the temptation to go on a spending spree. It is very easy for students to run up huge debt because credit card companies don't require cardholders— indeed, they don't *want* cardholders—to pay off their debts when the bill comes in at the end of each month. Although these cards are promoted with a teaser "low interest rate," that rate soon triples. As a result, many students end up owing more than they originally borrowed, even with regular minimum monthly payments.

Three coworkers of mine who are also students know what it's like to be in debt to credit card companies. Ron, a Fallow State College junior, owes more than $5,200 to credit card companies. Ron claims that when he first got a card, he "went crazy" with it. He bought exercise equipment, a couch, a CD player, and clothes for himself and his girlfriend. Ron now makes about $120 weekly at his part-time job, goes to school full time, and knows that because the interest rate for each of his three cards is around 17 percent and he pays only the $98 monthly minimum, it will take him about 10 years to repay his debt. By then Ron will have paid the credit card companies more than double the amount he charged.

Another coworker, Jane, a sophomore at Walloon College, says she owes $1,300 on one card and $1,100 on another. Jane says most of the money she owes is from last Christmas. She tries to pay the minimum combined charge of $40 monthly, but even $40 takes a big chunk out of her $64 weekly salary after she pays for meals, movies, gas, and a steep phone bill (her boyfriend goes to the University of Florida). Dave, a senior at the University of

Gives striking quotation
Gives striking statistic

Projects a reasonable,
empathetic persona
throughout
Cites an expert
Cause-and-effect analysis
Process analysis

Acknowledges opposing
view
Relies on visual details
throughout
Conclusion refutes
opposing view and
reemphasizes the main
point

Appeals directly to
readers

Massachusetts, worries how he will ever pay his $3,500 credit card debt on his $70 weekly paycheck. Dave can't even remember what he spent this money on. "You spend it here and there and it adds up fast." Meanwhile, Dave's debt is increasing at the rate of 18.9 percent yearly.

Because of the immediate money problems that credit cards seem to solve, it's easy to ignore the long-term effects of a bad credit history. According to accountant John Farnes, former mortgage officer at Town Savings Bank, when people apply for any type of loan, the bank immediately obtains a credit report, which lists the applicant's number of credit cards, total debt, and the amount that person is eligible to borrow. The report also shows whether the applicant has ever "maxed out" all credit cards or missed any minimum monthly payments. Applicants who have missed payments—or have been late with a payment—are usually rejected. Even people who make all minimum payments but still have outstanding or excessive credit card debt are turned down for loans. Farnes cautions that students who "run up credit card bills" can dig a big hole for themselves—a hole from which they might never climb out.

Granted, the temptation is hard to refuse. Credit card companies marketing on campus offer free cards and sign-up gifts "with no obligation." The "gifts" might include candy, coffee mugs, T-shirts, sports squeeze bottles, hip bags, and other paraphernalia. The process seems so easy and harmless: Just fill in your Social Security number and other personal information, take your pick from the array of gifts, and cancel the card when it arrives. But these companies know exactly what they're doing. They know that misusing the card is often easier than canceling it. They know that many of us work part time and are paid little. They know that most of us will be unable to pay more than the minimum balance each month—meaning big-time interest for years. Don't be seduced by instant credit.

—Julia Schoonover

Beyong merely influcing people's thinking about an issue as in the previous case, certain types of arguments ask their audience to become directly involved, as in the following case.

CASE STUDY

READING AND RESPONDING TO AN ARGUMENT SEEKING ACTIVE SUPPORT

In response to the following professional essay, student writer Suzanne Gilbertson presents an argument that attempts to enlist readers' support.

ESSAY FOR ANALYSIS AND RESPONSE

In this next essay, *Washington Post* columnist William Raspberry argues that school athletes should be required to meet minimum grade requirements. As you read, think about the academic standards at your old high school. Did your school have minimum grade standards for particpation in sports and other extracurricular activities. Were these standards fair, in your view? Should they be more strict or more lenient? If so, why?

Standards you Meet and Don't Duck

I'm telling you about my son Mark, not because I want to embarrass him, but because I find it useful in discussing public-policy questions to ask what I would advocate if the people affected by my policy proposals were members of my own family.

Mark, who is not quite twelve, is a good kid: friendly, bright, a good athlete, and (potentially) a very good student. But he has a tendency to be lazy about his studies.

So at the beginning of the year, I issued an edict: He would perform acceptably well in school or he wouldn't be allowed to play organized sports outside school.

He talked me into a modification: Rather than penalize him for last year's grades, earned before the new rule was announced, let him sign up for the Boys Club league now, and take him off the team if his mid-terms weren't up to par.

Well, the mid-terms came out, and the basketball team is struggling along without the assistance of my son the shooting guard.

All of which is a roundabout and perhaps too personal a way of saying my sentiments are with the Prince George's County (Maryland) school officials. My suburban Washington neighbors, confronted with angry parents, disappointed students, and decimated athletic teams, are under pressure to modify their new at-least-C-average-or-no-extracurriculars policy.

I hope they will resist it. The new policy may not be perfect, but it reflects a proper sense of priorities, which is one of the things our children ought to be learning. It may turn out to be a very good thing for all concerned—including the 39 percent of the county's students who are temporarily ineligible for such outside activities as athletics, cheerleading, dramatics, and band.

I've heard the arguments on the other side, and while I don't dismiss them out of hand, they fall short of persuading me that the new standards are too tough or their application too rigid. I know that for some students, the extracurriculars are the only thing that keeps school from being a complete downer. I know that some youngsters will be tempted to pass up Algebra II, chemistry, and other tough courses in order to keep their extracurricular eligibility (weighted grade points could solve that problem). And I know that for students whose strengths are other than academic, success in music or drama or sports can be an important source of self-esteem.

Still I support the C-average rule—partly because of my assumption that it isn't all that tough a standard. We're not talking here about bell-shaped curves that automatically place some students above the median and some below it. I suspect that we're talking less about acceptable academic achievement than about acceptable levels of exertion. I find it hard to believe that Prince George's teachers will flunk kids who really do try: who pay attention in class, turn in all their work, seek special assistance when they need it, and also bring athletic glory to their schools. (If it turns out that some youngsters are being penalized for inadequate gifts rather than insufficient effort, I'd support some modification of the rule.)

The principal value of the new standard is that it helps the students, including those in the lower grades, to get their own priorities right: to understand that while outside activities can be an ego-boosting adjunct to classroom work, they cannot be a substitute for it. Even the truly gifted, whose non-academic talents might earn them college scholarships or even professional careers, need as solid an academic footing as they can get.

Pity, which is what we often feel for other people's children, says give the poor kids a break. Love, which is what we feel for our own, says let's help them get ready for real life—not by lowering the standards but by providing the resources to help them meet the standards. One principal who saw 38 percent of his students fall below the eligibility cutoff agrees. Said Thomas Kirby: "I don't see any point in having a kid who can bounce a basketball graduate from high school and not be able to read."

—*William Raspberry*

Questions About the Reading

Refer also to the general questions on page 154.

PURPOSE
- *Does Raspberry succeed in making his point? If so, how?*

CONTENT
- *Does the writer acknowledge the opposing viewpoint, and does he address opponents' biggest objections to his position?*
- *Where is the thesis? Is it easily found?*
- *Does the writer offer sound reasons for his case? Explain.*
- *Does the writer offer impersonal (as well as personal) support? Explain.*

ORGANIZATION
- *Is the introduction effective? Which of the tasks listed on page 290 does it perform? Explain.*
- *Is the strongest material near the beginning or the end of the essay? Is this placement effective?*
- *How does the writer achieve coherence and smooth transitions between paragraphs?*

STYLE
- *Does the writer avoid an extreme persona here (say, sounding like a righteous parent)? Explain.*

RESPONDING TO READING

After reading and analyzing William Raspberry's essay, Suzanne Gilbertson thought about a controversy at her own university: In an age when jobs require increasing specialization, the importance of the liberal arts is being questioned. Some people argue that students in career-oriented majors, such as computer science and engineering, are hurt by the university's humanities, social science, and language requirements because these students are prevented from taking enough courses in their specialties. Beyond advocating that such requirements be dropped, some people argue that certain majors (such as fine arts and philosophy) and upper-level courses should be eliminated, thereby freeing more resources for career programs.

Gilbertson decided to refute the assertion that the liberal arts have become an unaffordable luxury at her school. Her essay was published in the campus newspaper as an open letter to faculty, administrators, trustees, and students.

| Note |

In shaping her argument, Gilbertson combines an array of development strategies.

Title announces the argument's purpose

Opens with a familiar question

Gives visual examples readers can identify with

Projects a reasonable persona throughout

Acknowledges opposing view without distorting it

Refutes opposing view

Offers clear definitions

SAVE LIBERAL ARTS

You may be one of them. As a child, you could never give a confident answer to the question "What do you want to be when you grow up?" In high school, while your friends fingered through various issues of *National Geographic* during study hall in the library, you hovered near the fiction section or lost yourself in *The Last Days of Pompeii*. Once in college, you couldn't bring yourself to declare a major, instead picking and choosing courses from an array of disciplines, like someone filling a plate at a breakfast buffet. Recognize the type? If you find yourself enjoying freshman English, if you register for beginning Spanish one semester and elementary Russian the next, or if you combine obscure philosophy courses with biology and write a poem on the similarities of the two, you might just be a closet liberal arts major.

Many folks tend to believe that education should provide the student with concrete skills that can later be applied to specific tasks. Historically, young children were apprenticed to a craftsperson to learn a skill by constant observation and imitation. Today, most people still prefer to specialize in a single field. They feel comfortable on a career track. In our high-tech age, the liberal arts major seems to have lost its appeal. Some people even label a liberal arts degree self-indulgent and impractical and encourage students to take courses that will "guarantee" them employment after graduation.

But some students find it harder to narrow their interests and sharpen their talents to fit a practical field. Are liberal arts majors simply choosing an easy or irrelevant way to a college diploma?

Maybe we need first to examine the meaning of "education" as opposed to "schooling." The "Renaissance person" is so named after the philosophers, poets, and artists who illuminated three centuries of Western civilization

Defines by negation	through a rebirth of classical learning. Such a person is characterized by an intense love of learning, a search for excellence. Far from being self-indulgent or withdrawn from worldly and practical affairs, the Renaissance person is committed to serving the needs of society by studying humanity and the life of citizens in society.
Thesis	Beyond merely imparting information or training, education in the Renaissance prepared students to be concerned citizens *in the world.* Career training alone was considered far inferior to a liberal education. *Likewise today, a liberal education teaches us to observe the human condition, synthesize what we know of that condition from our study of history and philosophy, and verbalize and communicate our perception of the needs of others besides ourselves.*
Offers a contrast Gives objective evidence to support the contrast	The twentieth century produced complex problems beyond the comprehension of Renaissance thinkers such as da Vinci, Galileo, or More. Our world seems smaller and more crowded. We are threatened by poisons in our air and water. Many nations are hungry and oppressed. We live under the constant fear of the ultimate weapons of destruction we have created to protect our freedoms. We continue to need skilled doctors to cure our ills,
Offers points of agreement	dedicated farmers to feed us, and politicians and managers to lead us. And the advanced technology at the disposal of our specialists may well be the key to our survival.
Expands on earlier points Cause-and-effect analysis Offers vivid examples throughout	Yet in order to understand and cope with the challenges of the twenty-first century, we must be able to see where we have come from. Even our present technological breakthroughs are made possible because of the questions first asked by the scholars of the Renaissance: Are there limits to what humanity can accomplish? What are the possibilities for human achievement? How can we best take advantage of our human and natural resources?
Appeals to shared goals and values	In the Renaissance tradition, the liberal arts graduate is well equipped to meet the broadest challenges of our technological society. Now more than ever, we need people who can step back and monitor our "progress." We need minds that can synthesize our many achievements and our aspirations, to guide us toward a safe and improved existence. In the end, what will bind us together will be our ability to formulate and question our goals
Reemphasizes the main idea	and to communicate our global needs. Questioning, synthesizing, and communicating—these are the broad skills liberal arts graduates bring to the enrichment of their world.

—Suzanne Gilbertson

The previous two cases have shown arguments that either seek to influence people's opinions or to encourage audience involvement in the issue at hand. *Proposals* on the other hand offer solutions to problems and make specific recommendations for how to implement those solutions, as in the following case study.

READING AND RESPONDING TO A PROPOSAL

In this case study, student writer Kerry Donahue presents an argument in the form of a proposal as she responds to the following professional essay from the *New York Times*.

ESSAY FOR ANALYSIS AND RESPONSE

In this next essay, Bard College President Leon Botstein proposes that high school should be shortened by two years and that students should enter college that much earlier. As you read, think about whether your own high-school years were, essentially, well spent.

LET TEENAGERS TRY ADULTHOOD

The national outpouring after the Littleton* shootings has forced us to confront something we have suspected for a long time: the American high school is obsolete and should be abolished. In the last month, high school students present and past have come forward with stories about cliques and the artificial intensity of a world defined by insiders and outsiders, in which the insiders hold sway because of superficial definitions of good looks and attractiveness, popularity, and sports prowess.

The team sports of high school dominate more than student culture. A community's loyalty to the high school system is often based on the extent to which varsity teams succeed. High school administrators and faculty members are often former coaches, and the coaches themselves are placed in a separate, untouchable category. The result is that the culture of the inside elite is not contested by the adults in the school. Individuality and dissent are discouraged.

But the rules of high school turn out not to be the rules of life. Often the high school outsider becomes the more successful and admired adult. The definitions of masculinity and femininity go through sufficient transformation to make the game of popularity in high school an embarrassment. No other group of adults young or old is confined to an age-segregated environment, much like a gang in which individuals of the same age group define each other's world. In no workplace, not even in colleges or universities, is there such a narrow segmentation by chronology.

Given the poor quality of recruitment and training for high school teachers, it is no wonder that the curriculum and the enterprise of learning hold so little sway over young people. When puberty meets education and learning in modern America, the victory of puberty masquerading as

---

*On April 20, 1999, two heavily armed students entered Columbine High School in Littleton, Colorado, shortly after 11 a.m. and began a shooting rampage that lasted nearly an hour. After killing 12 students and one teacher and wounding more that 20 other students, the shooters committed suicide.

popular culture and the tyranny of peer groups based on ludicrous values meet little resistance.

By the time those who graduate from high school go on to college and realize what really is at stake in becoming an adult, too many opportunities have been lost and too much time has been wasted. Most thoughtful young people suffer the high school environment in silence and in their junior and senior years mark time waiting for college to begin. The Littleton killers, above and beyond the psychological demons that drove them to violence, felt trapped in the artificiality of the high school world and believed it to be real. They engineered their moment of undivided attention and importance in the absence of any confidence that life after high school could have a different meaning.

Adults should face the fact that they don't like adolescents and that they have used high school to isolate the pubescent and hormonally active adolescent away from both the picture-book idealized innocence of childhood and the more accountable world of adulthood. But the primary reason high school doesn't work anymore, if it ever did, is that young people mature substantially earlier in the late 20th century then they did when the high school was invented. For example, the age of first menstruation has dropped at least two years since the beginning of this century, and not surprisingly, the onset of sexual activity has dropped in proportion. An institution intended for children in transition now holds young adults back well beyond the developmental point for which high school was originally designed.

Furthermore, whatever constraints to the presumption of adulthood among young people may have existed decades ago have now fallen away. Information and images, as well as the real and virtual freedom of movement we associate with adulthood, are now accessible to every fifteen- and sixteen-year-old.

Secondary education must be rethought. Elementary school should beign at age four or five and end with the sixth grade. We should entirely abandon the concept of the middle school and junior high school. Beginning with the seventh grade, there should be four years of secondary education that we may call high school. Young people should graduate at sixteen rather than eighteen.

They could then enter the real world, the world of work or national service, in which they would take a place of responsibility alongside older adults in mixed company. They could stay at home and attend junior college, or they could go away to college. For all the faults of college, at least the adults who dominate the world of colleges, the faculty, were selected precisely because they were exceptional and different, not because they were popular. Despite the often cavalier attitude toward teaching in college, at least physcists know their physics, mathematicians know and love their mathematics, and music is taught by musicians, not by graduates of education schools, where the disciplines are subordinated to the study of classroom management.

For those sixteen-year-olds who do not want to do any of the above, we might construct new kinds of institutions, each dedicated to one activity, from science to dance, to which adolescents could devote their energies while working together with professionals in those fields.

At sixteen, young Americans are prepared to be taken seriosuly and to develop the motivations and interests that will serve them well in adult life. They need to enter a world where they are not in a lunchroom with only their peers, estranged from other age groups and cut off from the game of life as it is really played. There is nothing utopian about this idea; it is immensely practical and efficient, and its implementation is long overdue. We need to face biological and cultural facts and not prolong the life of a flawed institution that is out of date.

—Leon Botstein

Questions About the Reading

Refer also to the general questions on page 154.

CONTENT

- *Does the proposal fulfill the tasks outlined on page 293? Explain.*
- *Is this argument primarily inductive or deductive? (See page 310.)*
- *Does the writer establish agreement with the reader? If so, where?*

ORGANIZATION

- *Which expository strategy is mainly used in this essay?*

- *Is the narrative introduction effective? Explain.*
- *Does the conclusion perform all the tasks listed on page 290?*

STYLE

- *Should the tone of this essay be more or less formal for this audience and purpose? Or is it appropriate? Explain.*
- *Is the writer's voice likable? Explain.*

RESPONDING TO READING

After reading "Let Teenagers Try Adulthood," Kerry Donahue settled on a unifying goal for her own proposal: As a campus newspaper columnist, she decided to prepare the following editorial in hopes of promoting campuswide support for a community service requirement for all students. Donahue knew that, to succeed, she would have to present community service in a new light.

During her planning, drafting, and revising, Donahue relied on the Guidelines for Persuasion on page 291 and the revision checklists on pages 62–63 and 306 in producing the final draft.

| Note |

As Donahue's essay illustrates, persuasion relies on a rich combination of development strategies, such as comparison and contrast and cause and effect.

	COMMUNITY SERVICE SERVES EVERYONE
Title announces topic Opens with vivid examples of need	On Horseneck Beach in Westport, a seagull lies tangled in a web of old fishing nets that washed ashore after the last high tide. It will probably die in those nets because no one is on the beach to clean up the nets or to notice the bird trapped inside. Across town in a nursing home, an elderly man struggles to read his favorite book. He has trouble making out the words. No one is around to read to him, and so he merely sits silently on the edge of his bed, anxiously awaiting a visitor—any visitor. Scenarios like these are all too
Lead-in to the thesis	common, which is why I propose that all students at our university do roughly ten hours of community sevice each semester as a graduation requirement.
Thesis	*Community service should be required for two excellent reasons: First, countless people and animals in need of help every day could use our assistance; second, we students would enjoy future benefits in more ways than one.*
Compares different connotations of community service Gives examples of voluntary service opportunities Discusses benefical effects for the community	For some people, community service connotes a form of punishment for breaking the law. Although certain lawbreakers are routinely assigned community sevice, plenty of law-abiding citizens volunteer their time as well. Examples include working in soup kitchens, organizing food drives for the homeless, helping with after-school youth programs, visiting the elderly, cleaning up the environment, and walking or campaigning for afflictions such as AIDS, cancer, and drug addiction. These and countless other activities could benefit from the help of energetic, idealistic college students. Despite our busy schedules of going to class, working, studying, sleeping, and partying, it's hard to imagine that most of us couldn't spend an extra hour here and there to make a difference in the community.
Anticipates objections to this proposal Refutes objections by pointing out harmful effects of doing nothing Acknowledges further objections Offers a reasonable limitation	Some people may object to the idea of forced service in order to graduate. They may think it unfair to ask students to devote time and energy to something that has nothing to do with their lives. But that is where they are wrong. The events in our surrounding communities do affect our lives in some way or other. If nets and dead sea animals pollute the beaches, we will not be able to use them when school gets out for the summer. Homelessness, hunger, and drug addiction drive people to crime. Misguided and mistreated children often disrupt learning in lower grades. Ultimately, no one is immune from what goes on in our community. It is true that many students have after-school jobs. Some of us take five or six classes per semester and have tons of homework. Athletes have to juggle class, practice, and games as it is. But early in the semester, when the workload is light and sports are just getting started, asking students to spend an hour or so here and there to help those in need seems hardly a lot. (Of course, those students with genuine hardships of their own would be exempted.) I realize that winning games and getting good grades fill students with pride and statisfaction. However, helping the less fortunate can be just as rewarding.
Discusses beneficial effects for students	Academically, community service can help students prepare for life beyond the walls of our campus. Working with others and interacting on a personal level can help us all broaden our horizons and open our eyes to what the real world is like. For students of all majors, this is a chance to develop career credentials in public leadership and public relations—as well as to prepare ourselves for helping improve the communities in which we eventually settle.

Illustrates how a model program works

For a model community service program, we need only look down the road: At Polk University's Stanton Center, students can work as service coordinators or can get advice on how to get involved in the community. The Stanton Center has various programs, including Music in Hospitals, Project HIV/AIDS, after-school programs for helping children with literacy and self-confidence, and help with domestic abuse for both students and non-students. The center itself it funded by federal and state grants. Our school could explore similar sources of funding.

Conclusion reemphasizes main idea

Some students may gripe at the notion of community service as a graduation requirement. But I firmly believe that the benefits far outweigh the costs. A little time each semester helping others could prepare each of us for the future while making life more pleasant for those in need. Teaching a child to read, saving animals, feeding those who are hungry, and walking to raise money for people with diseases—these are the biggest reasons why each of us at this university should do community service. We will be benefiting not only ourselves but the broader world as well.

Urges readers to act

Focuses on the larger meaning

—*Kerry Donahue*

✔ A CHECKLIST for Persuasion

Planning the Argument

☐ Have you defined your **goal** sufficiently to be able to write it out?

☐ Have you done all the necessary **homework** on this issue?

☐ Is the argument free of any obvious **weakness**?

☐ Have you addressed likely **objections** and other reactions from your audience?

☐ Are you seeking an outcome that is **achievable** in this situation?

Preparing the Argument

☐ Do you state your **purpose** clearly?

☐ Is your **persona** likable and reasonable?

☐ Do you focus on **points of agreement** with the audience?

☐ Do you portray the opposing position **fairly and accurately**?

☐ Do you **acknowledge the merits** of the opposing case?

☐ Do you go beyond merely criticizing by offering **realistic alternatives**?

☐ Do you make only claims that you can **support** with evidence?

☐ Do you present only your **best** material?

☐ Do you use your persuasive skills **responsibly**?

(*For more on each of these criteria, see page 291.*)

APPLICATIONS

18.1   **ESSAY PRACTICE: ARGUING TO INFLUENCE READERS' OPINIONS**

a. Explore your reactions to "On Reading Trash" using the questions on page 295. You might wish to challenge the author's view by arguing your own ideas about what constitutes worthwhile reading. You might support his view by citing evidence from your own experience. Or you might set out to influence reader opinion on some other topic of interest. Decide carefully on your audience and on what you want these readers to do, think, or feel. Be sure your essay supports a clear and definite point.

b. Explore your reactions to Julia Schoonover's essay using the questions on page 155. Then respond with your own essay that supports your position on some controversial topic. For example, are grades an aid or a detriment to education? Should your school adopt a voluntary pass/fail system? Be sure your essay has a clear and definite thesis and addresses a specific audience affected by the issue in some way.

18.2   **ESSAY PRACTICE: ARGUING TO ENLIST READERS' SUPPORT**

a. Explore your reactions to "Standards You Meet and Don't Duck" using the questions on page 155. Then respond with your own essay supporting or opposing the author's view. Your goal is to get readers involved. Perhaps you will want to argue from the viewpoint of athletes who are affected by grade standards.

   Or you might argue for some other school requirement, as in urging your old high school (or your college) to require an exit essay of its graduating seniors to ensure an acceptable level of literacy.

   Or maybe you believe that some school requirements are unfair. Whatever your position, be sure that your essay has a clear thesis and that you address a specific audience whose support you seek. In order to be persuasive, base your support not only on personal grounds (how you feel about it) but also on impersonal grounds (verifiable evidence) as well.

b. After reading Suzanne Gilbertson's essay, respond to the assertion that the liberal arts have become an unaffordable luxury. Be sure to consider the arguments for and against specialized vocational education versus a broadly humanistic—but less "practical"—education.

   Your college is thinking of abolishing core requirements. Write a letter to the dean in which you argue for or against this change.

   Should first-year composition be required at your school? Argue your position to the faculty senate.

18.3   **ESSAY PRACTICE: MAKING A PROPOSAL** After reading the proposals by Leon Botstein and Kerry Donahue, respond with a proposal of your own that offers an alternative to the Botstein proposal. Or propose a plan that will improve a situation in your school, job, or community. Be sure to stipulate a definite audience for your proposal. Possible topics may include improving living conditions in your dorm, improving workplace conditions, saving money at your job, and so on. Be sure to spell out the problem, explain the benefits of change, offer a realistic plan, and urge your readers to definite action.

18.4   **COLLABORATIVE PROJECT AND COMPUTER APPLICATION** Select one of the types of essays presented in this chapter. Using your electronic mailing list or email, collaborate with a group of classmates on a joint paper addressed to an appropriate audience. Use the Guidelines for Writing Collaboratively on page 40 to brainstorm electronically for a topic, thesis, and support. Then distribute writing tasks, exchange and peer-review your work, and construct a draft using transitions to knit the sections together. Submit edited versions to your group members, and confer electronically about final decisions. As you work, take notes for a future paper about how the electronic process makes working together easier, more complex, or both.

Works Cited

Bauman, K. E., et al. "Three Mass Media Campaigns to Prevent Adolescent Cigarette Smoking." *Preventive Medicine* 17 (1988): 510–30. Print.
Rokeach, Milton. *The Nature of Human Values.* New York: Free, 1973. Print.

For additional information and practice with the learning objectives in this chapter, go to www.mycomplab.com, Resource>Writing>Writing Purposes.

Special Issues in Persuasion

LEARNING OBJECTIVES FOR THIS CHAPTER

- Explain how induction and deduction appeal to reason
- Recognize the types of fallacies that result in invalid or deceptive reasoning
- Appreciate the ethical dimension of persuasive writing
- Understand the role of emotional appeals in persuasion

A persuasive argument connects with readers by appealing to their reason and often to their emotions as well.

APPEALING TO REASON

Although argument relies on some combination of description, narration, and exposition, many persuasive arguments are built around one or both of these specific reasoning patterns: *induction* (reasoning from specific evidence to a general conclusion) and *deduction* (applying a proven generalization to a specific case).

Just about any daily decision (including the ones you're asked to make in this book) is the product of inductive or deductive reasoning or both. Consider this example: You suffer from a bad case of math anxiety. On registration day, you're trying to decide on a course to fulfill your math requirement. After speaking with friends and reviewing the available evidence, you decide to register for Math 101 with Professor Digit. Let's trace the reasoning that led to your decision.

First, you reasoned inductively from this specific evidence to a generalization:

Inductive evidence

- Fact: Your older brother, a poor mathematician but a hard worker, took Professor Digit's course 2 years ago, mastered his own anxiety, and earned a B-minus.
- Fact: Although his course is demanding, Professor Digit is known for being friendly, encouraging, and always willing to help his students.
- Fact: The students you've talked to all praise Professor Digit's ability to make math "fun and understandable."
- Fact: Many of Professor Digit's students go on to take his upper-level math courses as electives.

Based on this evidence, you reached this generalization about Professor Digit's teaching skills:

A generalization based on inductive evidence

Professor Digit seems to be an excellent math teacher.

The evidence led you to an informed opinion (a probability, not a fact). You reached this opinion through inductive reasoning. You then used deductive reasoning to move from this generalization to a conclusion:

Generalization

Specific instance

Conclusion

Students willing to work hard succeed in Professor Digit's Math 101 course.

I am a hard worker.

I am likely to succeed in Professor Digit's course.

This conclusion led you to register for his section.

We use induction and deduction repeatedly, often unconsciously. Specific facts, statistics, observations, and experiences lead us inductively to generalizations such as these:

Other inductively based generalizations

Premed majors must compete for the highest grades.

Politicians can't always be trusted.

> Big cities can be dangerous.
>
> A college degree alone does not ensure career success.

On the other hand, deductive reasoning leads us from generalizations to specific instances to conclusions.

Generalization	Big cities can be dangerous.
Specific instance	New York is a big city.
Conclusion	New York can be dangerous.
Generalization	Premed majors must compete for the highest grades.
Specific instance	Brigitte will be a premed major next year.
Conclusion	Brigitte will have to compete for the highest grades.

When we write to persuade others, we need to use these processes deliberately and consciously.

Using Induction

We use induction in two situations: (1) to move from specific evidence to a related generalization or (2) to establish the cause or causes of something. Assume that you've been dating your significant other for a while, but recently you've made these observations:

Reviewing the evidence	My significant other (SO) hasn't returned my phone calls in a week.
	My SO always wants to go home early.
	My SO yawns a lot when we're together.
	My SO talks to everyone but me at parties.

This evidence leads to an inductive generalization:

Generalizing from the evidence	My SO is losing interest in me.

The same kind of reasoning establishes the possible or probable causes of your SO's aloofness. As you reflect on the relationship, you recall a number of inconsiderate things you've done recently:

Establishing the cause	I've been awfully short-tempered lately.
	I forgot all about my SO's birthday last week.
	I'm usually late for our dates.
	A few times, I've made wisecracks about my SO's creepy friends.

And so you conclude that your own inconsiderate behavior probably damaged the relationship.

Although generalizations aren't proof of anything, the better your evidence, the more likely it is that your generalizations are accurate. Avoid generalizing from too little evidence. That your significant other yawns a lot would not be a sufficient basis to conclude that she is losing interest. (Maybe she's ill or tired.) Or if your SO had yawned during only one evening, that fact alone would not support the hasty generalization that your relationship is on the rocks. Provide enough facts, examples, statistics, and informed opinions to make your assertions believable.

Consider the inductive reasoning in this passage from a 1963 letter by Martin Luther King Jr. to white clergy after he had been jailed for organizing a civil rights demonstration in Birmingham, Alabama.

AN INDUCTIVE ARGUMENT

A key statistic (1)
Informed opinion (2)

Acknowledgment of opposing views (3)
Examples (4)

A generalization from specifics (5)

Main point as a direct appeal (6)

[1]We have waited for more than 340 years for our constitutional and God-given rights. [2]The nations of Asia and Africa are moving with jetlike speed toward gaining political independence, but we still creep at horse-and-buggy pace toward gaining a cup of coffee at a lunch counter. [3]Perhaps it is easy for those who have never felt the stinging darts of segregation to say, "Wait." [4]But when you have seen vicious mobs lynch your mothers and fathers at will and drown your sisters and brothers at whim; when you have seen hate-filled policemen curse, kick, and even kill your black brothers and sisters; when you have seen the vast majority of your twenty million Negro brothers smothering in an airtight cage of poverty in the midst of an affluent society; when you suddenly find your tongue twisted and your speech stammering as you seek to explain to your six-year-old daughter why she can't go to the public amusement park that has just been advertised on television, and see tears welling up in her eyes when she is told that Funtown is closed to colored children, and see ominous clouds of inferiority beginning to form in her little mental sky, and see her beginning to distort her personality by developing an unconscious bitterness toward white people; when you have to concoct an answer for a five-year-old son who is asking, "Daddy, why do white people treat colored people so mean?"; when you take a cross-country drive and find it necessary to sleep night after night in the uncomfortable corners of your automobile because no motel will accept you; when you are humiliated day in and day out by nagging signs reading "white" and "colored"; when your first name becomes "nigger," your middle name becomes "boy" (however old you are) and your last name becomes "john," and your wife and mother are never given the respected title "Mrs."; when you are harried by day and haunted by night by the fact that you are a Negro, living constantly at tiptoe stance, never quite knowing what to expect next, and are plagued with inner fears and outer resentments; when you are forever fighting a degenerating sense of "nobodiness"—then you will understand why we find it difficult to wait. [5]There comes a time when the cup of endurance runs over, and [people] are no longer willing to be plunged into the abyss of despair. [6]I hope, sirs, you can understand our legitimate and unavoidable impatience.

—*Martin Luther King Jr.*

Notice how the inductive argument is organized: Sentence 4 carries the burden of support for King's stand. And the support itself is organized for greatest effect, with examples that progress from the injustice he has witnessed to the injustice he and his family have suffered to the humiliation he feels. Not only does he provide ample evidence to support his closing generalization (African Americans have reason to be impatient), but his evidence also adds up logically—and leads dramatically—to his conclusion.

Using Deduction

You reason deductively when you use generalizations to arrive at specific conclusions. Once the generalization "African Americans have legitimate cause for impatience" is established *inductively* (and accepted), one can argue deductively by applying the generalization to a specific instance:

Generalization	African Americans have legitimate cause for impatience.
	↓
Specific instance	Ms. Gomes is African American.
	↓
Conclusion	Ms. Gomes has legitimate cause for impatience.

The conclusion is valid because (1) the generalization is accepted and (2) the specific instance is a fact. Both these conditions must exist in order for the conclusion to be sound.

Here is how you might use deductive reasoning daily:

Examples of deductive reasoning

- If you know that Professor Jones gives no makeup exams, and you sleep through her final, then you can expect to flunk her course.
- If you know that Heapmobiles need frequent repairs, and you buy a Heapmobile, then you can expect many repairs.

The soundness of deductive reasoning can be measured by sketching an argument in the form of a *syllogism*, the basic pattern of deductive arguments. Any syllogism has three parts: a major premise, a minor premise, and a conclusion:

A valid syllogism

All humans are mortal. [*Major premise*]

↓

Feliciana is human. [*Minor premise*]

↓

Feliciana is mortal. [*Conclusion*]

If readers accept both premises, they must also accept your conclusion. For the conclusion to be valid, the major premise must state an accepted generalization, and the minor premise must state a factual instance of that generalization. Moreover, the conclusion must express the same degree of certainty as the premises (that is, if *usually* appears in a premise, it must appear in the conclusion as well). Finally, the syllogism must be stated correctly, the minor premise linking its subject with the subject of the major premise; otherwise, the syllogism is faulty:

A faulty syllogism

All humans are mortal.

↓

John is mortal. [*Minor premise is stated incorrectly; all creatures are mortal, but not all are human.*]

↓

John is human.

Each premise in a syllogism is derived from inductive reasoning. Because every human being we've known so far has been mortal, we can reasonably conclude that all human beings are mortal. And once we have examined John thoroughly and classified him as human, we can connect the two premises to arrive at the conclusion that John is mortal.

Illogical deductive arguments may result from a faulty major premise (or generalization). We can usually verify a minor premise (in the last example, merely by observing John to determine whether he is human). But the major premise is a generalization; unless we have enough inductive evidence, the generalization can be faulty. How much evidence is enough? Let your good judgment tell you. Base your premise on *reasonable* evidence so that your generalization reflects reality as discerning people would recognize it. Avoid unreasonable premises such as these:

Faulty generalizations

All men are male chauvinists.

School is boring.

Long-haired men are drug addicts.

People can't be trusted.

Frailty, thy name is woman.

Notice the problem when one such generalization appears as the major premise in an argument:

What happens when the major premise is faulty

People can't be trusted. [*Major premise*]

↓

My grandparents are people. [*Minor premise*]

↓

My grandparents can't be trusted. [*Conclusion*]

In ordinary conversation, deductive arguments are often expressed as *enthymemes*, implicit syllogisms in which the generalizations are not stated explicitly; instead they are implied or understood:

Enthymemes are implicit syllogisms

Joe is ruining his health with cigarettes. [*Implied generalization: Cigarette smoking ruins health.*]

Sally's low verbal scores on her college entrance exam suggest that she will need remedial help in composition. [*Implied generalization: Students with low verbal scores need extra help in composition.*]

Here's what happens to the conclusion when the unstated generalization is faulty:

Faulty enthymemes

Martha is a feminist, and so she obviously hates men. [*All feminists hate men.*]

He's a member of the clergy, and so what he says must be true. [*Clergy members are never mistaken or dishonest.*]

Another danger in deductive arguments is the overstated generalization, that is, making a limited generalization apply to all cases. Be sure to modify your assertions with qualifying words such as *usually, often, sometimes,* and *some* instead of absolute words such as *always, all, never,* and *nobody:*

Overstated generalizations

All Dobermans are vicious. [*Revised: "Some Dobermans can be..."*]

Politicians never keep their promises. [*Revised: "Some politicians fail to keep..."*]

In such cases, remember that the conclusion that follows must also be qualified.

A DEDUCTIVE ARGUMENT

By focusing more on bits of knowledge rather than on critical thinking skills, standardized tests tend to hinder, rather than encourage, student achievement. Critics claim that standardized tests place excessive emphasis on recall and rote learning at the expense of analysis, judgment, inspiration, and reflection. Such tests encourage students to be passive learners who need only recognize—not construct—answers and solutions. They also promote the misleading impression that every problem or question has a single right answer. Finally, they trivialize knowledge and skill development by reducing whatever is taught to a fill-in-the-best-choice format. Aware of these objections, progressive learning communities nationwide are working to develop testing tools that stimulate the student's analytical and imaginative powers.

—*Cheryl Hebert*

The deductive argument in this paragraph runs like this:

Implied generalization	Tests that focus on bits of knowledge rather than on critical thinking seem to do more harm than good.
Specific instance	Standardized tests often focus on bits of knowledge.
Conclusion	Therefore, standardized tests do more harm than good.

The argument is valid because it meets these criteria:

- The major premise is acceptable.
- The minor premise is verifiable.
- The argument is not overstated. Notice the limiting words: **tend to** [not **do**] critics claim [not **critics have proved**].
- The author limits her argument to *one* problem: how such tests may be defeating the aims of education (not how they might provide inaccurate assessment, favor certain groups, or the like).

RECOGNIZING INVALID OR DECEPTIVE REASONING

Errors in inductive or deductive reasoning are called *fallacies*. Fallacies weaken an argument by either breaking the chain of logic or evading the issue.

Fallacies That Break the Chain of Logic

In any valid reasoning pattern, one element logically follows from another (say, when a generalization is derived from credible evidence). But that logical chain can be broken by reasoning errors such as the following.

Faulty Generalizations.   We engage in faulty generalization when we jump from a limited observation to a sweeping conclusion. Even "proven" facts can invite mistaken conclusions.

Factual observations	"For the period 1992–2005, two-thirds of the fastest-growing occupations [have called] for no more than a high school degree" (Harrison 62).
	"Adult female brains are significantly smaller than male brains—about 8% smaller, on average" (Seligman 74).

How much can we generalize from these findings?

Invalid generalizations	Higher education—who needs it?
	Women are less intelligent than men.

When we accept findings uncritically and jump to conclusions about their meaning (as in the first example), we commit the error of *hasty generalization*.

When we overestimate the extent to which the findings reveal some larger truth (as in the second example), we commit the error of *overstated generalization.*

The following generalizations are often repeated—but how true are they?

Faulty generalizations

Teachers are mostly to blame for low test scores and poor discipline in public schools.

Television is worthless.

Humanities majors rarely get good jobs.

A common version of faulty generalization is *stereotyping,* the simplistic assignment of characteristics to all members of a group.

Stereotypes

All politicians are crooks.

Southern cops are brutal.

The Irish are big drinkers.

Note

*We often need to generalize, and we should. For example, countless studies support the generalization that fruits and vegetables help lower cancer risk. But we ordinarily limit general claims by inserting qualifiers such as **usually, often, sometimes, probably, possibly,** and **some.***

Faulty Causal Reasoning. Causal reasoning tries to explain *why* something happened or *what* will happen, often in very complex situations. Anything but the simplest effect is likely to have multiple causes. Faulty causal reasoning oversimplifies or distorts the cause-effect relationship through errors like these:

Ignoring other causes

Investment builds wealth. [*Ignores the role of knowledge, wisdom, timing, and luck in successful investing.*]

Ignoring other effects

Running improves health. [*Ignores the fact that many runners get injured and that some even drop dead while running.*]

Inventing a causal sequence

Right after buying a rabbit's foot, Felix won the state lottery. [*Posits an unwarranted causal relationship merely because one event follows another—the* post hoc *fallacy.*]

Confusing correlation with causation

Poverty causes disease. [*Ignores the fact that disease, while highly associated with poverty, has many causes unrelated to poverty.*]

Rationalizing

My grades were poor because my exams were unfair. [*Denies the real causes of one's failures.*]

Media researcher Robert Griffin identifies three criteria for demonstrating a causal relationship:

Along with showing correlation [say, a measurable association between smoking and cancer], evidence of causality requires that the alleged causal agent occurs prior to the condition it causes (e.g., that smoking precedes the development of cancers) and—the most difficult task—that other explanations are discounted or accounted for. (240)

For example, studies found this correlation: People who eat lots of broccoli, cauliflower, and other cruciferous vegetables have lower rates of some cancers. But other explanations (say, that big veggie eaters might have many other healthful habits as well) could not be ruled out until lab studies showed how a special protein in these vegetables actually protects human cells. (Wang 182)

Slippery Slope. We ski the slippery slope when we make an overstated prediction that one action will initiate other actions or events that produce dire consequences.

Slippery-slope assertions

> Distributing condoms to high school students will lead to rampant promiscuity.
>
> Negotiating with governments that support terrorism will only lead to more terrorism.

Faulty Analogy. An analogy is faulty when it overstates the similarities between the two items being compared.

Faulty analogies

> All my friends' parents are allowing them to hitchhike across the country. Why can't I?
>
> In many instances, cancer cells can be eliminated by the appropriate treatment. Since violent criminals are a societal cancer, they should be eliminated through capital punishment.

Question Begging. You beg the question when you base your argument on a claim that has not been proved. In other words, you commit the fault of circular reasoning by asking readers to accept an unproven premise:

Assertions that beg the question

> Useless subjects like composition should not be required.
>
> Voters should reject candidate X's unfair accusation.
>
> Books like *X* and *Y*, which destroy the morals of our children, should be banned from school libraries.

If a subject is useless, obviously it should not be required. But a subject's uselessness is precisely what has to be established. Likewise, candidate X's accusation has to be proved unfair, and books such as *X* and *Y* have to be proved corrupting.

Either-Or Thinking. You commit the either-or fallacy when you reduce an array of choices to a dilemma: only two extreme positions or sides—black or white—even though other choices exist.

False dilemmas

> Students deserve the opportunity to do their best work. But deadlines force students to hand in something not carefully done, just to make sure it's on time. [*Ignores the possibility of doing it on time* and *doing it well.*]
>
> We have the choice between polluting our atmosphere or living without energy. [*Leaves out the possibility of generating clean energy.*]
>
> Marry me or I'll join the monastery.

Arguing from Ignorance. We argue from ignorance when we contend that an assertion is true because it has not been proved false or that the assertion is false because it has not been proved true.

Arguments from ignorance

> Drunk driving laws are absurd: I know loads of people who drink and drive and who have never had an accident.
>
> Since the defendant can't offer evidence to prove her innocence, she must be guilty.

Fallacies That Evade the Issue

A deceptive argument clouds the main issue with fallacies such as the following.

Red Herring. Named after the practice of dragging a dead herring across a game trail to distract hunting dogs from their prey, this strategy aims at deflecting attention from the main issue. The distraction commonly involves an attempt to rationalize one's bad action by making it seem insignificant or by pointing to similar actions by others.

Trivializing one's bad action

Asserting that two wrongs make a right

> Except for my drunk driving arrest, I've always been a law-abiding citizen.
>
> Sure, I bought my term paper from the CollegeSucks Web site, but so do lots of other students.

Bandwagon Appeal. The bandwagon approach urges readers to "climb aboard" by claiming that everyone else is doing so.

Bandwagon appeals

> This book is a best-seller. How could you ignore it?
>
> More Cadillac owners are switching to our insurance company than ever before. [*Of course, if this were indeed statistically true, the assertion would be legitimate.*]

Irrational Appeals to Emotion. Some appeals to emotions (pity, fear, and the like) are perfectly legitimate. But you avoid the question when you distract readers from the real issue with material that is irrelevant or that obscures the issue by making an irrational appeal to emotions.

An appeal to pity	He should not be punished for his assault conviction because as a child he was beaten severely by his parents. [*Has no legal bearing on the real issue, his crime.*]
An appeal to fear	If we outlaw guns, only outlaws will have guns. [*Ignores the deaths and injuries caused by "legally owned" guns.*]
An appeal to normalcy	She is the best person for the teaching job because she is happily married and has two lovely children. [*Has nothing to do with the real issue, her qualifications as a teacher.*]
An appeal to flattery	A person with your sophistication will surely agree that marriage is outmoded. [*Has nothing to do with the conclusion, which remains to be verified.*]
An appeal to authority or patriotism	Uncle Sam stands behind savings bonds. [*Ignores the question of whether savings bonds are a good investment: Although they are safe, they pay lower interest than many other investments.*]

The snob appeal to emotion persuades readers to accept your assertion because they want to be identified with respected or notable people.

Snob appeal	"I want to be like Mike." [*Has nothing to do with the quality of the sneakers or hamburgers or other items being marketed.*]
	No all-American sports hero could be guilty of such a horrible crime. [*Ignores the evidence.*]

Attacking Your Opponent.   Another way to ignore the real question is by attacking your opponent through name-calling or derogatory statements about this person on the basis of age, sex, political or sexual orientation, or the like (ad hominem argument):

Ad hominem attacks	The effete intellectual snobs in academia have no right to criticize our increase in military spending. [*Calling people names does not discredit their argument.*]
	How could any man be expected to understand a woman's emotional needs?
	College students are too immature to know what they want, so why should they have a say in the college curriculum?

Instead of attacking the person, focus on refuting the argument.

Attacking a Straw Person.   You commit a straw person fallacy when you distort your opponent's position on the issue and use that distortion as a basis for attack.

Straw person fallacy

> Feminists won't be satisfied until men are powerless.
>
> People oppose affirmative action because they refuse to give up their own long-standing privileges.

When you set out to refute an argument, be sure to represent the opposing position accurately.

CONSIDERING THE ETHICAL DIMENSION

Arguments can "win" without being ethical if they "win" at any cost. For instance, advertisers effectively win customers with an implied argument that "our product is just what you need!" Some of their more specific claims can be "Our artificial sweetener is made of proteins that occur naturally in the human body [amino acids]" or "Our potato chips contain no cholesterol." Such claims are technically accurate but misleading: Amino acids in artificial sweeteners can alter body chemistry to cause headaches, seizures, and possibly brain tumors; potato chips often contain saturated fat, from which the liver produces cholesterol.

We are often tempted to emphasize anything that advances our case and to ignore anything that impedes it. But a message is unethical if it exploits fallacies or otherwise prevents readers from making their best decision. To help ensure that your writing is ethical, keep it accurate, honest, and fair.

✔ A CHECKLIST for Ethics in Persuasive Writing

Accuracy

☐ Have I explored **all sides of the issue** and **all possible alternatives**?

☐ Do I provide enough information and interpretation for readers to understand **the facts as I know them**?

☐ Do I avoid exaggeration, understatement, sugarcoating, or any **distortion or omission that leaves readers at a disadvantage**?

☐ Do I **state the case clearly** instead of hiding behind fallacies and generalities?

Honesty

☐ Do I make a **clear distinction** between *certainty* and *probability?*

☐ Are my information sources **valid, reliable**, and relatively **unbiased**?

☐ Do I actually **believe what I'm saying**, instead of advancing a hidden agenda?

☐ Would I still advocate this position if I were held **publicly accountable** for it?

(continues)

☐ Do I inform people of all the **consequences or risks** (as I am able to predict) of what I am advocating?

☐ Do I give candid **feedback** or **criticism**, if it is warranted?

Fairness

☐ Am I reasonably sure this document will **harm no innocent persons** or damage their reputations?

☐ Am I respecting all legitimate rights to **privacy** and **confidentiality**?

☐ Am I **distributing copies** of this document to every person who has the right to know about it?

☐ Do I **credit all contributors and sources** of ideas and information?

Adapted from Brownell and Fitzgerald 18; Bryan 87; Johannesen 21–22; Larson 39; Unger 39–46; Yoos 50–55.

APPEALING TO EMOTION

Emotion is no substitute for reason, but some audiences are not persuaded by reason alone. In fact, an audience's *attitude toward the writer* is often the biggest factor in persuasion, no matter how solid the argument. Audiences are more receptive to people they like, trust, and respect.

Appeals to honesty, fairness, humor, and common sense are ethical and legitimate ways of enhancing a supportable argument. On the other hand, appeals to closed-mindedness, prejudice, paranoia, and ignorance (as in the logical fallacies covered earlier) merely hide the fact that an argument offers no authentic support.

Emotional transactions between writer and reader are complex, but the following strategies offer guidance.

GUIDELINES for Making Emotional Appeals

- *Try to identify—empathize—with the reader's feelings.*
- *Show respect for the reader's views.*
- *Try to appear reasonable.*
- *Know when and how to be forceful or satirical.*
- *Know when to be humorous.*

Showing Empathy

To show empathy is to identify with the reader's feelings and to express genuine concern for the reader's welfare. Consider the lack of empathy in the following paragraph:

A MESSAGE THAT LACKS EMPATHY

Dear Buck,

After a good deal of thought, I've decided to write to you about your weight problem. Let's face it: You're much too fat. Last week's shopping trip convinced me of that. Remember the bathing suit you liked, the one that came only in smaller sizes? If you lost weight, you might be able to fit into those kinds of suits. In addition to helping you look attractive, the loss of 30 or 40 pounds of ugly fat would improve your health. All you have to do is exercise more and eat less. I know it will work. Give me a call if you need any more help or suggestions.

This writer's superior tone can only alienate the reader. In this next version, he makes a distinct effort to empathize.

A MORE EMPATHETIC VERSION

Dear Buck,

Remember that great bathing suit we saw in Stuart's the other day, the one you thought would be perfect for the beach party but that didn't come in your size? Because the party is still three weeks away, why not begin dieting and exercising so you can buy the suit? I know that losing weight is awfully hard because I've had to struggle with that problem myself. Buck, you're one of my best friends, and you can count on me for support. A little effort on your part could make a big difference in your life.

Empathy is especially important in arguments that try to get the reader to *do* something.

Acknowledging Opposing Views

Before making your case, acknowledge the opposing case. This next writer takes a controversial position on a turning point in the high school experience. But by showing respect for the traditional view, she decreases readers' resistance to her own position.

AN ACKNOWLEDGMENT OF OPPOSING VIEWS

Orienting statement (1)

Acknowledgment of opposing view (2–3)

Writer's argument (4)

[1]From our first steps into high school we learn to anticipate an essential rite of passage: the senior prom—one of those memories that last a lifetime. [2]Traditionally, prom night suggests a magical time when it's fun to get dressed up, have pictures taken with your date, enjoy a fancy dinner, and party with your friends; then, after a perfect evening, you kiss your date goodnight and go home. [3]This fairy-tale chain of events is how our parents recount their long-ago experiences, and it persists as part of the prom image. [4]But this benign image too often masks the reality of a night polluted by drugs and sex, a night based on competition and looks, a night hyped to unbelievable proportions, only to become a total letdown.

—*Julia Schoonover*

Maintaining a Moderate Tone

What determines whether your argument creates contact with readers is *how* you say what you have to say. Different purposes and audiences invariably call for different tones.

Ultimately, people are more inclined to accept the viewpoint of someone they like and who seems *reasonable*. Never overstate your case to make your point. Stay away from emotionally loaded words that boil up in the heat of argument. This next writer is unlikely to win converts:

VOICE OF THE HOTHEAD

Scientists are the culprits responsible for the rape of our environment. Although we never see these beady-eyed, amoral eggheads actually destroying our world, they are busy in their laboratories scheming new ways for industrialists and developers to ravage the landscape, pollute the air, and turn all our rivers, lakes, and oceans into stinking sewers. How anybody with a conscience or a sense of decency would become a scientist is beyond me.

Granted, this piece is forceful and sincere and does suggest the legitimate point that scientists share responsibility—but the writer doesn't seem very likable. The paragraph is more an attack than an argument. Besides generalizing recklessly and providing no evidence for the assertions, the writer uses emotionally loaded words (**eggheads, stinking sewers**) that overstate the position and will surely make readers skeptical.

Here is another version of the paragraph. Understating the controversial point makes the argument more convincing:

A MORE REASONABLE TONE

[1]It might seem unfair to lay the blame for impending environmental disaster at the doorstep of the scientists. [2]Granted, the rape of the environment has been carried out, not by scientists, but by profiteering industrialists and myopic developers, with the eager support of a burgeoning population greedy to consume more than nature can provide and to waste more than nature can clear away. [3]But to absolve the scientific community from complicity in the matter is quite simply to ignore that science has been the only natural philosophy the western world has known since the age of Newton. [4]It is to ignore the key question: who provided us with the image of nature that invited the rape, and with the sensibility that licensed it? [5]It is not, after all, the normal thing for people to ruin their environment. [6]It is extraordinary and requires extraordinary incitement.

—Theodore Roszak

Notice how this argument begins by acknowledging the opposing view (sentences 1–2). The tone is firm yet reasonable. When the writer points the blame at scientists, in sentences 3–4, he offers evidence.

Roszak softens his tone while making his point by using a rhetorical question in sentence 4. *Rhetorical questions* are really statements in the form of questions; because the answer is obvious, readers are invited (or challenged) to provide it for themselves. A rhetorical question can be a good way of impelling readers to confront the issue (as does the question in the second sentence of the more empathetic letter to Buck on page 323) without offending them.

But use rhetorical questions with caution. They can easily alienate readers, especially when the issue is personal.

RHETORICAL QUESTIONS USED OFFENSIVELY

Your constant tardiness is an inconvenience to everyone. It's impossible to rely on a person who is never on time. Do you know how many times I've waited in crummy weather for you to pick me up? What about all the appointments I've been late for? Or how about all the other social functions we haven't "quite" made it to on time? It's annoying to everyone when you're always late.

The tone seems far too aggressive for the situation.

Some strong issues may deserve the emotional emphasis created by rhetorical questions. This is another kind of decision you need to make continually about your audience and purpose.

Maintaining a moderate tone, however, does not mean being voiceless. People expect to sense a real person behind the words on the page. In the following essay, addressed to students and parents, Laurie Simoneau is quite forceful in soliciting their support for lobbying the school administration for individual thermostats in each dorm room. As you read this essay, think about how the objective evidence, the appeals, and the tone connect with the audience to make a persuasive argument.

THE SWEATBOX AND THE ICEBOX: DORM STUDENTS NEED THERMOSTATS

A forceful bul effective tone

It's 9:00 a.m. I peel my sweat-soaked body off the soggy sheet and turn off my alarm. I wipe my moist forehead and chin with a tissue and lick my parched lips. Even though my window is wide open, the heat repels the cold November air. After showering, I study my cracked lips and dry, blotchy skin. Infuriated, I dress and head for class.

Upstairs, my friend Lisa crawls out of bed at the sound of her own alarm. She shivers—despite the flannel pajamas, sweatshirt, and wool socks she put on last night in a vain attempt to retain body heat. Her window is shut tight, and so is her heating vent. Lisa complains often to the Housing Office, but her room still freezes.

Within days, the Student Health Office is overrun by sniffling, hacking, sneezing, retching students who must each day either leave the dorms in a sweat, only to face harsh November winds, or who freeze all night long, take hot morning showers, and then freeze again until they reach the warmth of the classroom. And these aren't isolated cases: I've surveyed all students in my dorm, and 80 percent complained about room temperatures.

The extreme temperatures of many dorm rooms are hurting students' health and performance. Students are getting sick. They are unable to study in the discomfort of their own rooms. They sleep poorly, and they are furious.

The problem has an obvious cause: Among the eight rooms in each suite are only two thermostats. And so the occupants of these two rooms adjust the heat to a temperature they find comfortable. As a result, rooms at other points on the heating pipe receive too little or too much heat. The logical solution: Install thermostats in the remaining six rooms of every suite.

The cost of dorm housing more than doubles the cost of tuition (for state residents). Students choose dorms over off-campus housing because of the "positive living-learning environment" promised in the college brochures. But many of us, I think, would now scoff at the mention of such a promise. What these sweating shivering, sniffling, hacking, sneezing, retching students request is a comfortable room temperature *throughout* the dorms. What they need are thermostats.

I ask all students and parents involved to please phone or write the Housing Office (555-1515) to voice your complaint and your request. With your support, we can create the "positive living-learning environment" all residential students desire and deserve.

—Laurie Simoneau

Is Laurie Simoneau's forceful tone appropriate to her situation? Explain and illustrate.

Using Satire in Appropriate Circumstances

Satire can be one vehicle for expressing forceful anger, frustration, or outrage without alienating readers. No one enjoys being told off or ridiculed, but sometimes a jolt of lucid observation—telling it like it is—might help readers overcome denial in order to face an issue realistically.

Satire usually relies on irony and sarcasm. *Irony* is a form of expression that states one thing while clearly meaning another, as in proclaiming a day in which everything has gone wrong as "simply wonderful!" *Sarcasm* employs a more blatant form of irony to mock or to ridicule. For instance, in the essay that follows, an undergraduate takes a hard look at the policy of eliminating "offensive" books from high school curricula.

As you read, think about how the satirical perspective forces a reexamination of attitudes.

SATIRE AS A PERSUASIVE STRATEGY

BONFIRE

I've uncovered the root of all evil today. It lurks in our schools and in our communities. It hides in children's rooms and sits on our coffee tables. Books cause all of society's problems, from drugs to homosexuality to irreverence.

Books like *Of Mice and Men* and *The Adventures of Huckleberry Finn* teach children violence, hatred, and blasphemy. After children read words like *damn, hell,* and *nigger,* they will begin to use them. If they witness violence in literature, they will hit one another. After reading about George shooting Lenny in *Of Mice and Men,* they will regard killing their friends and carrying guns as acceptable. If they view a story like *Children of the Rainbow,* which contains homosexual characters, they will look at homosexuality in a positive light. Kids wouldn't think to become gay if they didn't read about it. *Brave New World* and books of that type teach our children to have sex. Teen pregnancy and overpopulation originate from romance novels about fornication. *Go Ask Alice* introduces readers to drugs and therefore contributes to our society's drug problems. Kids won't participate in such evils if they don't know they exist.

If we shield our children from the world's harsh realities, they will grow up respectable citizens. We do this by burning books. Nothing makes me smile more than the flaming corpse of a smutty novel. While other families make hamburgers and hot dogs on their grills, I barbecue Twain. The smoke of *War and Peace* refreshes my nostrils after a long day. I bought twenty-seven copies of *Catcher in the Rye* for a bonfire last August, and this Christmas my living room will glow with the flames of that ancient pornography, the Bible.

No writing conveys a positive message, for even Dr. Seuss distorts reality for children. We should shut down all libraries, all bookstores, and all schools and end the use of the written word. After burning all books, we should eliminate magazines, newspapers, and credits at the ends of movies.

Libraries house Satan worshipers. Their message reaches our children through the schools. If you see your children with a library card, a membership card to Lucifer's kingdom, I urge you to destroy it and punish them. The future depends on eliminating texts that show the horrors of society. Keep the fires of hell away from your doorstep by setting aflame the contents of our libraries and the volumes in your bathrooms.

—Adam Szymkowicz

Some readers might feel offended or defensive about Adam Szymkowicz's harsh assessment; however, satire deliberately seeks confrontation. So be sure that you understand its potential effect on your audience before you decide on a satirical perspective in your own writing.

Adding Humor Where Appropriate

Sometimes a bit of humor can rescue an argument that might cause hard feelings. In this next paragraph, the writer wanted to call attention to the delicate issue of his roommate's sloppiness.

HUMOR AS A PERSUASIVE STRATEGY

Jack,

If you never see me alive again, my body will be at the bottom of your dirty clothes pile that rises like a great mountain in the center of our room.

How did I end up there? Well, while doing my math, I ran out of paper and set out for my desk to get a few pieces—despite the risk I knew I was taking. I was met by a 6-foot wall of dirty laundry. You know how small our room is; I could not circumnavigate the pile. I thought I'd better write this note before going to the janitor's room for a shovel to dig my way through to my desk. The going will be tough, and I doubt I'll survive. If the hard work doesn't kill me, the toxic fumes will. Three years from now, when you finally decide to do your wash, just hang my body up as a reminder to stash your dirty clothes in your closet where they will be out of sight and out of smelling range.

—*Your late roommate*

Again, anticipate how your audience will react; otherwise, humor can backfire.

Whichever strategies you employ, don't allow your tone to be voiceless. Readers need to sense a real person behind the words.

✔ A CHECKLIST for Persuasive Appeals

Appealing to Reason

☐ Is the argument's **inductive reasoning** sound? (311)

☐ Is the argument's **deductive reasoning** sound? (313)

☐ Are all **syllogisms** and **enthymemes** valid? (313, 314)

☐ Is the argument free of **fallacies that break the chain of logic**? (316)

☐ Is the argument free of **fallacies that evade the issue**? (319)

Appealing to Emotion

☐ Are emotional appeals **appropriate** and **sincere**? (322)

☐ Does the argument convey **empathy** for the reader's feelings? (322)

☐ Does the argument respect **opposing views**? (323)

☐ Is the **tone** moderate and reasonable? (324)

☐ Is **satire** used only as appropriate? (326)

☐ Is **humor** used when appropriate? (327)

APPLICATIONS

19.1   The following statements are followed by false or improbable conclusions. What specific supporting evidence would be needed to justify each conclusion so that it is not a specious generalization? (First, you need to infer the missing generalization or premise; then you have to decide what evidence would be needed for the premise to be acceptable.) (Review pages 310–311.)

EXAMPLE

> Only 60 percent of incoming first-year students eventually graduate from this college. Therefore, the college is not doing its job.

To consider this conclusion valid, we would have to be shown

- that all first-year students want to attend college in the first place
- that they are all capable of college-level work
- that they did all assigned work promptly and responsibly

1. Abner always speeds but never has an accident. Therefore, he must be an excellent driver.
2. Fifty percent of last year's college graduates did not find the jobs they wanted. Therefore, college is a waste of time and money.
3. Olga never sees a doctor. Therefore, she must be healthy.
4. This house is expensive. Therefore, it must be well built.
5. Felix is flunking first-year composition. Therefore, he must be stupid.

19.2 **PARAGRAPH WARM-UP: INDUCTIVE REASONING** Using Martin Luther King's paragraph (page 312) as a model, write a paragraph in which you use inductive reasoning to support a general conclusion about highway safety, credit cards, the legal drinking age, the changing role of women, or a subject of your own choosing. Identify your audience and purpose. Provide enough evidence so that readers can follow your line of reasoning to its conclusion.

19.3 **PARAGRAPH WARM-UP: DEDUCTIVE REASONING** Select an accepted generalization from this list, or choose one of your own, and use it as the topic statement in a paragraph using deductive reasoning. (Review pages 313–316.)

- "Beauty is in the eye of the beholder."
- "That person is richest whose pleasures are the cheapest."
- Some teachers can have a great influence on a student's attitude toward a subject.
- A college degree doesn't guarantee career success.

19.4 Identify the fallacy in each of these sentences, and revise the assertion to eliminate the error. (Review pages 316–321.)

EXAMPLE

Faulty	Television is worthless. [*sweeping generalization*]
Revised	Commercial television offers too few programs of educational value.

1. Big Goof received this chain letter, sent out twenty copies, and 3 days later won the lottery. Little Goof received this chain letter, threw it away, and fell off a cliff the next day.

2. Because our product is the best, it is worth the high price.

3. America—love it or leave it.

4. Three of my friends praise their Jettas, proving that Volkswagen makes the best cars.

5. My grades last semester were poor because my exams were unfair.

6. Anyone who was expelled from Harvard for cheating could not be trusted as a president.

7. Until college students contribute to our society, they have no right to criticize our government.

8. Because Angela is a devout Christian, she will make a good doctor.

9. Anyone with common sense will vote for this candidate.

10. You should take up tennis; everyone else around here plays.

11. Hubert, a typical male, seems threatened by feminists.

12. Convex running shoes caused Karl Crane to win the Boston Marathon.

13. "My doctor said Mylanta."

14. How could voters expect any tax-and-spend liberal to know or understand the concerns of working people like us?

15. Sky diving is perfectly safe. After thirty dives, it hasn't killed me yet!

16. If nonsmokers think their lungs are being violated by smokers, it's a fact of life. Fumes from vehicles, woodstoves, and incinerators all damage everyone's lungs. Should we ban these things too?

17. Vote for me, or our nation is doomed.

18. How could we trust any promise made by that radical, right-wing nut?

19. Killing a bald eagle (a sacred American symbol) is a crime; therefore, burning the flag (another sacred American symbol) should also be a crime.

20. If the present rate of immigration continues, U.S. workers will soon have no jobs left.

21. Gay rights activists won't be satisfied until schools promote gay lifestyles for all students.

22. If everyone else filed honest tax returns, I would too.

23. "Among 20-year-olds in 1979, those who said that they smoked marijuana 11 to 50 times in the past year had an average IQ 15 percentile points higher than those who said they'd only smoked once" (Sklaroff and Ash 85). Weed, therefore, increases brain power.

19.5 Revise this paragraph so that its tone is more moderate and reasonable, more like an intelligent argument than an attack. Feel free to add personal insights that might help the argument.

People who argue that marijuana should remain outlawed are crazy. Beyond that, many of them are mere hypocrites—the boozers of our world who squander their salary in bars and come home to beat the wife and kids. Any intelligent person knows that alcohol burns out the brain, ruins the body, and destroys the personality. Marijuana is definitely safer: It leaves no hangover; it causes no physical damage or violent mood changes, as alcohol does; and it is not psychologically or physically addictive. Maybe if those redneck jerks who oppose marijuana would put down the beer cans and light a joint, the world would be a more peaceful place.

19.6   WEB-BASED PROJECT

a. Follow a blog for a couple of days, and collect examples of faulty logic used by people who post. *Hint:* visit Stephen's Guide to the Logical Fallacies at <**http://onegoodmove.org/fallacy/**> for additional advice on logical fallacies.

b. Look at advertisements on the Web, and discuss the types of arguments and fallacies used.

Works Cited

Brownell, Judi, and Michael Fitzgerald. "Teaching Ethics in Business Communication: The Effective/Ethical Balancing Scale." *Bulletin of the Association for Business Communication* 55.3 (1992): 15–18. Print.

Bryan, John. "Down the Slippery Slope: Ethics and the Technical Writer as Marketer." *Technical Communications Quarterly* 1.1 (1992): 73–88. Print.

Griffin, Robert J. "Using Systematic Thinking to Choose and Evaluate Evidence." *Communicating Uncertainty: Media Coverage of New and Controversial Science.* Ed. Sharon Friedman, Sharon Dunwoody, and Carol Rogers. Mahwah: Erlbaum, 1999: 225–48. Print.

Harrison, Bennett. "Don't Blame Technology This Time." *Technology Review* July 1997: 62. Print.

Johannesen, Richard L. *Ethics in Human Communications.* 2nd ed. Prospect Heights: Waveland, 1983. Print.

Larson, Charles U. *Persuasion: Perception and Responsibility.* 7th ed. Belmont: Wadsworth, 1995. Print.

Seligman, Dan. "Gender Mender." *Forbes* 6 Apr. 1998: 72+. Print.

Sklaroff, Sara, and Michael Ash. "American Pie Charts." *Civilization* Apr.-May 1997: 84–85. Print.

Unger, Stephen H. *Controlling Technology: Ethics and the Responsible Engineer.* New York: Holt, 1982. Print.

Wang, Linda. "Veggies Prevent Cancer through Key Protein." *Science News* 159.12 (2001): 182. Print.

Yoos, George. "A Revision of the Concept of Ethical Appeal." *Philosophy and Rhetoric* 12.4 (1979): 41–58. Print.

For additional information and practice with the learning objectives in this chapter, go to www.mycomplab.com, Resource>Writing>Writing Purposes.

The Research Process

Introduction

We do research to obtain facts or expert opinions or to understand issues. Suppose you learn that your well water is contaminated with benzene. Should you merely ask your neighbor's opinion about the dangers, or should you track down the answers for yourself?

In the workplace, professionals need to locate all kinds of information daily (*How do we market this product? How do we avoid accidents like this one? Are we headed for another recession?*). We all have to know where and how to look for answers and how to communicate them *in writing*. Research is the way to find your own answers; a *research report* records and discusses your findings.

A research report involves a lot more than cooking up any old thesis, settling for the first material you happen to find, and then blending in a few juicy quotations and paraphrases to "prove" you've done the assigned work. Research is a deliberate form of inquiry, a process of *problem solving*. And we cannot begin to solve the problem until we have clearly defined it.

Parts of the research process follow a recognizable sequence. The steps shown in Figure IV.1 are treated in Chapters 20–25.

FIGURE IV.1
Procedural stages in the research process

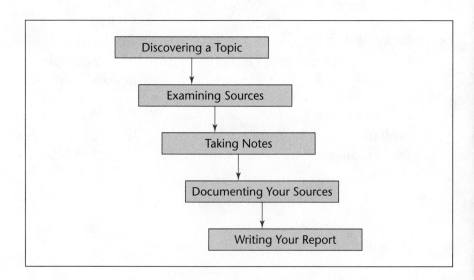

But research writing is never merely a "by the numbers" procedure ("First, do this; then do that"). The procedural stages depend on the many careful decisions that accompany any legitimate inquiry, depicted in Figure IV.2.

FIGURE IV.2
Inquiry stages in the
research process

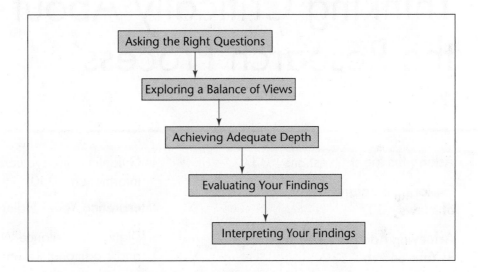

These inquiry stages of the research process (discussed in Chapter 20) lead to the kind of conclusions that make a real difference.

CHAPTER 20

Thinking Critically About the Research Process*

LEARNING OBJECTIVES FOR THIS CHAPTER

- Know how to define your research goal and examine a range of perspectives
- Know how to explore a research topic with adequate breadth and depth
- Understand that good research involves critical evaluation and interpretation of findings

Not all information is equally valuable. Not all interpretations are equally valid. In *critical thinking*, we assess the quality of our information and the accuracy of our interpretations. We use critical thinking to examine our evidence and our reasoning, to discover new connections and new possibilities, and to test the effectiveness and limits of our conclusions. The following strategies help us uncover those answers that stand the best chance of being the right answers.

---

*I thank University of Massachusetts Dartmouth librarian Shaleen Barnes for inspiring this chapter.

336

ASKING THE RIGHT QUESTIONS

The answers you uncover will only be as good as the questions you ask. Suppose, for instance, you've decided to research the topic of violent crime on college campuses.

DEFINING AND REFINING A RESEARCH QUESTION

The problem of violent crime on college campuses has received a good deal of recent publicity. So far, your own school has been spared, but as a precautionary measure, campus decision makers are considering doubling the police force and allowing police to carry guns. Some groups are protesting, claiming that guns pose a needless hazard to students or that funding for additional police should be devoted to educational programs instead. In the student senate, you and your colleagues have discussed the controversy, and you have been appointed to prepare a report that examines the trends regarding violent crime on campuses nationwide. Your report will form part of a document to be presented to the student and faculty senates in 6 weeks.

First, you need to identify your exact question or questions. Before settling on a definitive question, you need to navigate a long list of possible questions, like those in the Figure 20.1 tree chart. Any one of those questions could serve as the topic of a worthwhile research report on such a complex topic. (Perhaps you can think of other questions we might add to our chart.)

EXPLORING A BALANCE OF VIEWS

Instead of settling for the most comforting or most convenient answer, pursue the *best* answer. Even "expert" testimony may not be enough because experts can disagree or be mistaken. To answer fairly and accurately, consider a balance of perspectives from up-to-date and reputable sources.

Try to consider all the angles

- *What do informed sources have to say about this topic?*
- *On which points do sources agree?*
- *On which points do sources disagree?*

Note

Recognize the difference between "balance" (sampling a full range of opinions) and "accuracy" (getting at the facts). The media, for example, might present a more negative view than the facts warrant. Not every source is equal, nor should we report points of view as though they were equal (Trafford 137).

Let's say you've chosen this question: *Violent crime on college campuses: How common is it?* Now you can consider sources to consult (journals, reports, news articles, Internet sites, database searches, and so on). Figure 20.2 lists likely sources of information on college crime.

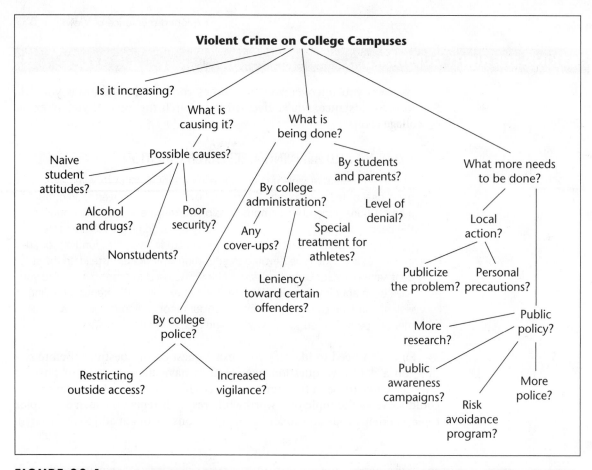

FIGURE 20.1

How the right questions help define a research problem. You cannot begin to solve a problem until you have defined it clearly.

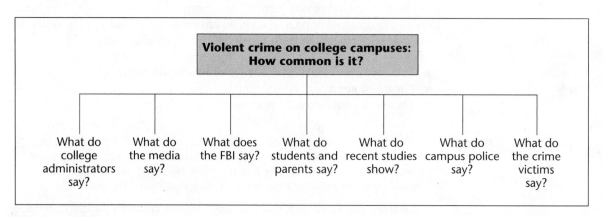

FIGURE 20.2

A range of essential viewpoints. No single source is likely to offer the final word. Ethical researchers rely on evidence that represents a fair balance of views.

ACHIEVING ADEQUATE DEPTH IN YOUR SEARCH*

Balanced research examines a *broad range* of evidence; thorough research, however, examines that evidence in sufficient *depth*. Different sources of information represent different levels of detail and dependability (see Figure 20.3).

The depth of a source determines its quality

1. The surface layer offers items from the popular press (newspapers, radio, TV, magazines, certain Internet discussion groups, blogs, and Web sites). Designed for general consumption, this layer of information often merely skims the surface of an issue.

2. At the next level are trade, business, and technical publications or Web sites (*Law Enforcement Digest, Chronicle of Higher Education,* and so on). Often available in print and Web-based formats, these publications are designed for readers who range from moderately informed to highly specialized. This layer of information focuses more on practice than on theory, on issues affecting the field, and on public relations. While the information is usually accurate, viewpoints tend to reflect a field's particular biases.

3. At a deeper level is the specialized literature (journals from professional associations: academic, medical, legal, engineering, and so on). Designed for practicing professionals, this layer of information focuses

FIGURE 20.3
Effective research achieves adequate depth

The depth of a source often determines its quality

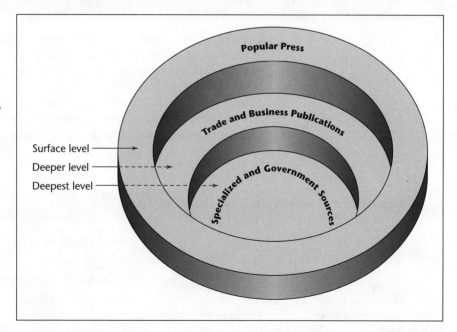

Surface level
Deeper level
Deepest level

*I thank University of Massachusetts Dartmouth librarian Ross LaBaugh for inspiring this section.

on theory as well as on practice: on descriptions of the latest studies (written by the researchers themselves and scrutinized by peers for accuracy and objectivity), on debates among scholars and researchers, and on reviews and critiques of prior studies and publications.

Also at this deepest level are government sources (reports by NASA, EPA, Congress) and corporate documents available through the Freedom of Information Act (see page 352). Designed for anyone willing to investigate its complex resources, this information layer offers hard facts and highly detailed and (in many instances) *relatively* impartial views.

Most of these sources are accessible via the Internet through specialized search engines such as LexisNexis. Ask your librarian.

> **Note**
>
> *Web pages, of course, offer links to increasingly specific levels of detail, but the actual depth and quality of a Web site's information depend on the sponsorship and reliability of that site (see page 363).*

How deep is deep enough? This depends on your purpose, your audience, and your topic. But the real story more likely resides at deeper levels. Research on college crime, for instance, would need to look beneath the media headlines, focusing instead on studies by a wide range of experts.

EVALUATING YOUR FINDINGS

Not all findings have equal value. Information might be distorted, incomplete, or misleading. Information might be tainted by *source bias,* in which a source understates or overstates certain facts, depending on whose interests that source represents—say, college administrators, students, or a reporter seeking headlines. To evaluate a particular finding, ask the questions listed on page 341. To use information from experts effectively, follow the Guidelines for Evaluating Expert Information.

GUIDELINES for Evaluating Expert Information

- *Look for common ground.* When opinions conflict, consult as many experts as possible and try to identify those areas in which they agree (Detjen 170).

- *Consider all reasonable opinions.* The science writer Richard Harris notes that "Often [extreme views] are either ignored entirely or given equal weight in a story. Neither solution is satisfying.... Putting [the opinions] in balance means... telling... where an expert lies on the spectrum of opinion.... The minority opinion isn't necessarily wrong—just ask Galileo" (170).

- *Be sure the expert's knowledge is relevant in this context.* Don't seek advice about a brain tumor from a podiatrist.

- *Don't expect certainty.* In complex issues, experts cannot *eliminate* uncertainty; they can merely help us cope with it.

- *Don't expect objectivity in all cases.* For example, the expert might have a financial or political stake in the issue or might hold a radical point of view.

- *Expect special interests to produce their own experts to support their position.*

- *Learn all you can about the issue before accepting anyone's final judgment.*

Questions for Evaluating a Particular Finding

- *Is this information accurate, reliable, and relatively unbiased?*
- *Do the facts verify the claim?*

- *How much of the information is useful?*
- *Is this the whole or the real story?*
- *Do I need more information?*

Instead of merely emphasizing findings that support their own biases or assumptions, ethical researchers seek out and report the most *accurate* answer. Only near the end of your inquiry can you settle on a *definite* thesis, based on what the facts suggest.

INTERPRETING YOUR FINDINGS

Once you have decided which of your findings seem legitimate, you must decide what they mean by asking these questions:

Questions for Interpreting Your Findings

- *What are my conclusions, and do they address my original research question?*
- *Do any findings conflict?*

- *Are other interpretations possible?*
- *Should I reconsider the evidence?*
- *What actions, if any, do these findings suggest?*

Even the best research can produce contradictory or indefinite conclusions. For example (Lederman 5): What does a reported increase in violent crime on U.S. college campuses mean—especially in light of national statistics that show overall violent crime decreasing?

Some possible
interpretations

- That college students are becoming more violent?
- That some drugs and guns from high schools end up on campuses?
- That off-campus criminals see students as easy targets?

Or could these findings mean something else entirely?

Other possible
interpretations

- That increased law enforcement has led to more campus arrests—and hence greater recognition of the problem?
- That crimes have not increased but that fewer now go unreported?

Depending on our interpretation, we might conclude that the problem is worsening—or improving!

| Note | *Not all interpretations are equally valid. Never assume that any interpretation that is possible is also allowable, especially in terms of its ethical consequences. Certain interpretations in the college crime example, for instance, might justify an overly casual or overly vigilant response, either of which could have disastrous consequences.* |

Figure 20.4 shows the critical-thinking decisions crucial to worthwhile research: asking the right questions about your topic, your sources, your findings, and your conclusions. Like the writing process (see Figure 1.2), the research process is *recursive*: Stages are revisited and repeated as often as necessary.

| Note | *Never force a simplistic conclusion on a complex issue. Sometimes the best you can offer is an indefinite conclusion. For example, "Although controversy continues over the causes of increased campus crime, we can all take simple precautions to reduce our exposure." A wrong conclusion is far worse than no definite conclusion at all.* |

DIGITAL TIP

Balance Web-based and Traditional Research

With such easy access to the Internet and its seemingly endless information, doing all of one's research online can be tempting. Many of us may ask, "Why bother to use the traditional printed sources like those at the library at all?"

Chapter 21 explores the traditional and Web-based resources researchers consult most often. Many traditional print-only sources are now available online via online databases, PDF files, and e-versions of reference works such as encyclopedias and dictionaries. However, consider the following cautions about relying solely on the Internet for your research:

- *Not everything is available online.* Many print sources continue to exist only in hard copy.

- *Online resources are often limited in length.* No one likes to toggle endlessly down a Web page. Many longer works are only available in hard copy.

- *Traditional sources are reviewed and edited more often than online sources.* Before a book, article, or other published work goes to press, it is carefully edited by professionals and may also be peer-reviewed by subject-matter experts. A document originating on the Internet is far less likely to have undergone the same scrutiny.

FIGURE 20.4
Critical thinking in the research process

No single stage is complete until all stages are complete. Stages are revisited as often as necessary.

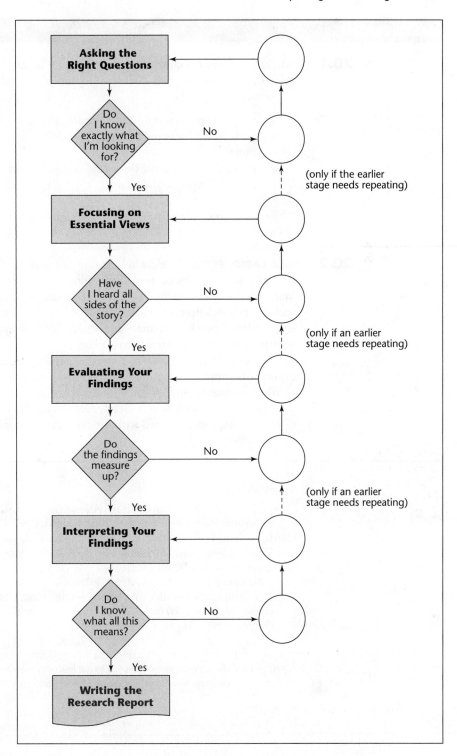

APPLICATIONS

20.1   Students in your major want to know of at least two discipline-specific information sources with different depths of specialization in the following categories:

- the popular press (newspaper, radio, TV, magazines, Web sites)
- trade or business publications (newsletters and trade magazines, or Web sites)
- professional literature (journals) and government sources (corporate data, technical reports, and so on)

Write a memo introducing these sources, giving a one-paragraph description of each.

20.2   **WEB-BASED PROJECT** Select a topic of interest from science or technology (benefits versus risks of genetically modified foods, feasibility of colonizing Mars, or the like). Survey expert opinions on this issue by consulting sources such as Ask (**<http://www.ask.com>**), *Scientific American's* "Ask the Experts" link (**<http://www.sciam.com>** and search for "ask expert"), or Expert Central (**<http://www.expertcentral.com>**).

Identify: 1) a point on which most experts agree; 2) a point on which many experts disagree; 3) an opinion at the radical end of the spectrum (with source clearly identified); and 4) an opinion that seems influenced by financial or political motives (with source clearly identified). Then, prepare a written report of your findings to be shared with the class. Attach copies of relevant Web pages to your report.

Works Cited

Detjen, Jim. "Environmental Writing." *A Field Guide for Science Writers.* Ed. Deborah Blum and Mary Knudson. New York: Oxford, 1997. 173–79. Print.

Harris, Richard F. "Toxics and Risk Reporting." *A Field Guide for Science Writers.* Ed. Deborah Blum and Mary Knudson. New York: Oxford, 1997. 166–72. Print.

Lederman, Douglas. "Colleges Report Rise in Violent Crime." *Chronicle of Higher Education* 3 Feb. 1995, sec. A: 5+. Print.

Trafford, Abigail. "Critical Coverage of Public Health and Government." *A Field Guide for Science Writers.* Ed. Deborah Blum and Mary Knudson. New York: Oxford, 1997. 131–41. Print.

For additional information and practice with the learning objectives in this chapter, go to www.mycomplab.com, Resources>Research>Understanding a Research Assignment.

Asking Questions and Finding Answers

LEARNING OBJECTIVES FOR THIS CHAPTER

■ Know how to choose a fresh and feasible research topic

■ Differentiate between primary and secondary sources

■ Recognize and use the various Web-based and traditional secondary sources

■ Understand how to conduct primary research, including interviews and surveys

DECIDING ON A RESEARCH TOPIC

A crucial step in developing a research report is deciding on a worthwhile topic. Begin with a subject with real meaning for you; then decide on the specific question you want to ask about it. Pages 337–338 show how the subject of campus crime might be narrowed. Now let's try another subject.

Say you're concerned about all the chemicals used to preserve or enhance flavor and color in foods—**food additives and preservatives**. On what specific part of this subject would you like to focus? This will be your *topic,* and it should be phrased as a question. To identify the possible questions you might ask, develop a tree chart (as on page 338). Your interests might lead you to this question: *What effects, if any, do food additives and preservatives have on children's behavior?*

> **Note**   *Far more important than the topic you choose is the question you decide to ask about it. Plan to spend many hours in search of the right question.*

GUIDELINES for Choosing a Research Topic

- *Avoid topics that are too broad for a six- to twelve-page research report.* The topic "Do food additives and preservatives affect children?" would have to include children's growth and development, their intelligence, their susceptibility to diseases, and so on.

- *Avoid topics that limit you to a fixed viewpoint before you've done your research,* such as "Which behavior disorders in children are caused by food additives and preservatives?" Presumably, you haven't yet established that such chemicals have any harmful effects. Your initial research is meant to find the facts, not to prove some point. Allow your thesis to grow from your collected facts instead of manipulating the facts to fit your thesis.

- *Avoid topics that have been exhausted,* such as abortion, capital punishment, or gun control— unless you can approach them in a fresh way: "Could recent technological developments to help a fetus survive outside the womb cause the Supreme Court to reverse its 1973 ruling on abortion?"

- *Avoid topics that can be summed up in an encyclopedia entry or in any one source:* "the life of Thoreau," "how to cross-country ski," or "the history of microwave technology." From a different angle, of course, any of these areas might allow you to draw your own, more interesting conclusions: "Was Thoreau ever in love?" "How do injury rates compare between cross-country and downhill skiing?" "How safe are microwave ovens?"

- *Avoid religious, moral, or emotional topics that offer no objective basis for informed conclusions,* such as "Is euthanasia moral?" "Will Jesus save the world?" or "Should prayer be allowed in public schools?" Questions debated throughout the ages by philosophers, judges, and social thinkers are unlikely to be definitively answered in your research paper.

PRIMARY VERSUS SECONDARY SOURCES

How primary and secondary research differ

Primary research means getting information directly from the source by conducting interviews and surveys and by observing people, events, or processes in action. *Secondary research* is information obtained secondhand by reading what other researchers have compiled in books and articles in print or online. Most information found on the Internet would be considered a secondary source.

Why you should combine primary and secondary research

Whenever possible, combine primary and secondary research. Typically, you would start by using secondary sources because they are readily available and can help you get a full background understanding of your topic. However, don't neglect to add your own findings to existing ones by doing primary research.

EXPLORING SECONDARY SOURCES

Secondary sources include some Web sites; online news outlets and magazines; blogs and wikis; books in the library; journal, magazine, and newspaper articles; government publications; and other public records. Research assignments begin more effectively when you first uncover and sort through what is already known about your topic before adding to that knowledge yourself.

Web-based Secondary Sources

To find various sites on the Web, use two basic tools: *subject directories* and *search engines*.

Subject directories are maintained by editors

- **Subject Directories.** Subject directories are indexes compiled by editors who sift through Web sites and sort the most useful links. Popular general subject directories include *Yahoo! Directory* <dir.yahoo.com>, *Google Directory* <www.google.com/dirhp>, and *About.com* <www.about.com>. Specialized directories focus on a single topic such as software, health, or employment. See *Beaucoup!*, a "directory of directories," at <www.beaucoup.com> for listings of specialized directories organized by category.

Most search engines are maintained by computers, not people

- **Search Engines.** Search engines, such as Yahoo <www.yahoo.com> and Google <www.google.com>, scan for Web sites containing key words. Even though search engines yield a lot more information than subject directories, much of it can be irrelevant. Some search engines, however, are more selective than others, and some focus on specialized topics.

Use Search Engines and Subject Directories Strategically

Most people begin their research of secondary sources by using a search engine or a subject directory. But you need to use these tools strategically to avoid being overwhelmed with excessive "hits" (search engines) or sifting through information that is much too general (subject directories). For instance, using a search engine for the topic "violent crime on college campuses" (sample report on page 420) yields more than 400,000 results. A search on "stress-induced illness" (sample report on page 434) will pull up over 25,000 results. Meanwhile the first options offered by a subject directory for these topics will be as broad as "society" and "health." Here are suggestions for using search engines and subject directories:

- *Focus your search beforehand.* Identify the precise information you seek.

- *When using a search engine, select keywords or search phrases that are varied and technical rather than general.* Some search terms generate more useful hits than others. In addition to "electromagnetic radiation," for example, try "electromagnetic fields," "power lines and health," or "electrical fields." Specialized terms (say "vertigo" versus "dizziness") offer the best access to reliable sites. However, if you are not able to locate much by using a specialized term, widen your search somewhat.

- *When using a subject directory, drill down to an appropriate level of specificity.* Don't rely on finding what you need at the top, or most general, topic level (e.g., "business" or "education"). The best subject directories are organized into multiple levels of specificity. Keep digging until you find what you want or discover that the subject directory doesn't list topics relevant to your research.

- *Use a variety of search engines and subject directories.* No single search engine can index more than a fraction of material available online, and no subject directory will list all of the same Web sites as another.

- *Think critically about the sites you do locate.* For more information on evaluating your sources, see the Digital Tip box on page 363 (Chapter 22).

- *Use bookmarks and hotlists for quick access to favorite Web sites located.*

General Commercial, Organizational, and Academic Web Sites. Search engines pull up a wide variety of hits, most of which will be commercial (.com), organizational (.org), and academic (.edu) Web sites. If a commercial site looks relevant to your search, by all means use it, as long as you think critically about the information presented. Does the company's effort to sell you something affect the content? Be careful also of organizational Web sites, which are likely to be well-researched, but may have a particular social or political agenda. Academic Web sites tend to be credible. However, some academics may also have biases, so never stop thinking critically about what you find on the Web.

Government Web Sites.   Search engines will also pull up government Web sites, but your best access route is through the United States government's Web portal at <www.usa.gov>. Most government organizations (local, state, and federal) offer online access to research and reports. Examples include the Food and Drug Administration's site at <www.fda.gov>, for information on food recalls, clinical drug trials, and countless related items; and the Federal Bureau of Investigation's site at <www.fbi.gov>, for information about fugitives, crime statistics, and much more. State and local sites provide information on auto licenses, state tax laws, and local property issues. From some of these sites you can link to specific government-sponsored research projects.

| Note | *Be sure to check the dates of reports or data you locate on a government Web site, and find out how often the site is updated.*

Online News Outlets and Magazines.   Most major news organizations offer online versions of their broadcasts and print publications. Examples include the *New York Times,* the *Wall Street Journal,* CNN, and National Public Radio. Magazines such as *Time, Newsweek,* and *Forbes* also offer Web versions. Some news is available online only, as in the online magazines *Slate* and *Salon.*

| Note | *Make sure you understand how the publication obtains and reviews information. Is it a major news site, such as CNN, or is it a smaller site run by a special-interest group? Each can be useful, but you must evaluate the source. Also keep in mind that many online magazines have a political bias.*

Blogs.   *Blogs* (short for *Web logs*) are Web sites on which the blogs' authors posts ideas, and other readers reply. The postings and attached discussions are displayed in reverse chronological order. Links that the owner has selected also supply ways to connect to other blogs on similar topics. Blogs can provide current information about specific topics from individuals, companies, and nonprofit organizations.

Wikis.   *Wikis* are community encyclopedias that allow anyone to add to or edit the content of a listing. The most popular wiki is Wikipedia <www.wikipedia.org>. The theory of a wiki is that if the information in one posting is wrong, someone will correct it, and over time the site will achieve accuracy and reliability.

Internet Forums.   For almost any topic imaginable, you will find a Web forum, or discussion group (see, for example, <discussions.apple.com/index.jspa>, for people who use Apple products). Locate relevant forums by searching one of the major Internet forum providers. For instance, in researching an issue such as stress among college students, you might visit *Google Groups* <groups.google.com> or *Yahoo! Groups* <groups.yahoo.com> and join a related group. You can subscribe to and visit the forum via the Web or receive messages directly into your email inbox.

Use Information from Blogs, Wikis, and Internet Forums Cautiously

Blogs, wikis, and internet forums are valid sources to consult during the research process, but observe the following cautions when using them. Be especially cautious when using Wikipedia.

- *Blogs.* Information on a blog usually represents the particular views of the blog author (whether an individual, company, organization, or academic institution) and of those who reply to the postings. Decide which blogs are most relevant and reliable, and evaluate the information carefully. Check any information on a blog against a professionally edited or peer-reviewed source.

- *Wikis.* Many wikis have no oversight. Aside from a few people who determine whether to delete articles based on requests from readers, the content on a wiki is not checked by editors for accuracy. Use a wiki entry to get an overview of a topic and to help you locate other sources (usually listed at the bottom of the entry on Wikipedia). Always check the information against peer-reviewed or traditional sources.

- *Internet forums.* Material from Internet forums may be insightful but biased. Visit a variety of forums for a broad perspective on the issue. Information posted on forums often is not moderated (approved by a reviewer prior to being posted). Unmoderated material can be unreliable.

E-libraries.   Entirely searchable via the Internet, e-libraries are excellent research tools. Aside from the online sites sponsored by public libraries, the most notable and reliable e-library is the Internet Public Library at <www.ipl.org>. E-libraries include links to online books, magazines, newspapers, periodical databases, and other resources including "live" librarians.

Although e-libraries can be efficient stand-ins for traditional, physical libraries, they can never replace such libraries. Resources available in electronic form will not include current books under copyright or a wide range of magazine and news articles and other publications. Supplement what you discover at an e-library with hard-copy materials from a traditional library.

Periodical Databases.   Virtually all libraries have their own Web site where a library cardholder or student can access periodical databases. These are electronic collections of articles from newspapers, magazines, journals, and other publications. You can search by title, author, keyword, and so on.

Some of the most popular general periodical databases include *InfoTrac*, *NewsBank*, *ProQuest*, and *EBSCOHost*. Your library may also subscribe to specialized databases in a variety of subject areas.

Before initiating a periodical database search, meet with your reference librarian for a tour of the various databases and instructions for searching effectively. Also be aware that some databases may not be accessible from school or home—you may need to visit your library in person.

Traditional Secondary Sources

As noted earlier, traditional secondary research tools are still of great value. Most hard-copy secondary sources are carefully reviewed and edited before they are published. Although the digitizing of hard-copy materials continues, many of these printed sources are not yet available on the Web, particularly the full texts of books.

Locate hard-copy sources by using your library's online public access catalog (OPAC). This catalog can be accessed through the Internet or at terminals in the library. You can search a library's holdings by subject, author, title, or keyword. Visit the library's Web site, or ask a librarian for help. To search catalogs from libraries worldwide, go to the *Library of Congress Gateway* at <www.loc.gov/z3950> or *LibrarySpot* at <www.libraryspot.com>.

Locate hard-copy secondary sources using your library's OPAC

Following are the principal categories of hard-copy sources found at libraries, as well as one type of source material (gray literature) that you will need to track down on your own.

Books and Periodicals. The larger or more specialized the library you visit, the more likely you are to find books by specialist publishers and periodicals that delve into more specific subject areas. When consulting books and periodicals, always check the copyright date and supplement the source with additional information from more recent sources, if necessary.

Reference Works. Reference works are general information sources that provide background and can lead to more specific information.

- **Bibliographies.** Bibliographies are lists of books and/or articles categorized by subject. To locate bibliographies in your field, begin by consulting the *Bibliographic Index Plus*, a list (by subject) of major bibliographies, which indexes over 500,000 bibliographies worldwide. You can also consult such general bibliographies as *Books in Print* or the *Readers' Guide to Periodical Literature*. Or examine subject area bibliographies, such as *Bibliography of World War II History*, or highly focused bibliographies, such as *Health Hazards of Video Display Terminals: An Annotated Bibliography.*

- **Indexes.** Book and article bibliographies may also be referred to as "indexes." Yet there are other types of indexes that collect information not likely to be found in standard bibliographies. Examples include *Associated Press News Index, Reader's Guide to Periodical Literature, Index of Patents Issued from the United States Patent and Trademark Office, Index to Scientific and Technical Proceedings*, and many more. While limited versions of some indexes may be available for free online, most are only available via a library subscription.

- **Encyclopedias.** Encyclopedias are alphabetically arranged collections of articles. You may want to start by consulting a general encyclopedia, such as *Encyclopedia Britannica* or the *Columbia Encyclopedia*, but then examine more subject-focused encyclopedias, such as *Encyclopedia* *of Nutritional Supplements, Encyclopedia of Business and Finance,* or *Illustrated Encyclopedia of Aircraft.*

- **Dictionaries.** Dictionaries are alphabetically arranged lists of words, including definitions, pronunciations, and word origins. If you can't locate a particular word in a general dictionary (e.g., a highly specialized term or jargon specific to a certain field), consult a specialized dictionary, such as *Dictionary of Engineering and Technology, Dictionary of Psychology,* or *Dictionary of Media and Communication Studies.*

- **Handbooks.** Handbooks offer condensed facts (formulas, tables, advice, examples) about particular fields. Examples include the *Civil Engineering Handbook* and *The McGraw-Hill Computer Handbook.*

- **Almanacs.** Almanacs are collections of factual and statistical data, usually arranged by subject area and published annually. Examples include general almanacs, such as the *World Almanac and Book of Facts,* or subject-specific almanacs, such as the *Almanac for Computers* or *Baer's Agricultural Almanac.*

- **Directories.** Directories provide updated information about organizations, companies, people, products, services, or careers, often listing addresses and phone numbers. Examples include *The Career Guide: Dun's Employment Opportunities Directory* and the *Directory of American Firms Operating in Foreign Countries.* For electronic versions, ask your librarian about *Hoover's Company Capsules* (for basic information on thousands of companies) and *Hoover's Company Profiles* (for detailed information).

- **Abstracts.** Abstracts are collected summaries of books and/or articles. Reading abstracts can help you decide whether to read or skip an article and can save you from having to track down a journal you may not need. Abstracts usually are titled by discipline: *Biological Abstracts, Computer Abstracts,* and so on. For some current research, you might consult abstracts of doctoral dissertations in *Dissertation Abstracts International.*

Although the reference works mentioned here are available mainly as print documents, some are available on the Internet. Go to the Internet Public Library at <www.ipl.org> for links to many online reference works. When using a reference work, check the copyright date to make sure you are accessing the most current information available.

Government Publications.   The federal government publishes maps, periodicals, books, pamphlets, manuals, research reports, and other information. Examples include the *Journal of Research of the National Bureau of Standards,* the *Monthly Catalog of the United States Government,* the *Government Reports Announcements and Index,* and the *Statistical Abstract of the United States.*

In addition, many unpublished documents are available under the Freedom of Information Act (FOIA). FOIA grants public access to all federal agency records except for classified documents, trade secrets, certain law enforcement files, records protected by personal privacy law, and the like. Contact the agency that would hold the records you seek: say, for workplace accident reports, the Department of Labor; for industrial pollution records, the Environmental Protection Agency; and so on.

Gray Literature.   Some useful printed information may be unavailable at any library. This is known as "gray literature," or materials that are unpublished or not typically catalogued. Examples include pamphlets published by organizations or companies (such as medical pamphlets or company marketing materials), unpublished government documents (available under the Freedom of Information Act), dissertations by graduate students, papers presented at professional conferences, or self-published works.

The only way to track down gray literature is to contact those who produce such literature and request anything available in your subject area. For instance, you could contact a professional organization and request any papers on your topic that were delivered at their recent annual conference, or contact a government agency for statistics relevant to your topic. Before doing so, be knowledgeable about your topic and know specifically whom to contact. Don't make vague, general requests.

Keep in mind that gray literature, like much material found on the Web, is often not carefully scrutinized for content by editors. Therefore, it may be unreliable and should be backed up by information from other sources.

EXPLORING PRIMARY SOURCES

Types of primary sources

Once you have explored your research topic in depth by finding out what others have uncovered, supplement that knowledge with information you discover yourself by doing primary research. Primary sources include unsolicited inquiries, informational interviews, surveys, and observations or experiments.

Unsolicited Inquiries

Unsolicited inquiries uncover basic but important information

The most basic form of primary research is a simple, unsolicited inquiry. Letters, phone calls, or email inquiries to experts listed in Web pages or to people you identify in other ways can clarify or supplement information you already have. Try to contact the right individual instead of a company or department. Also, ask specific questions that cannot be answered elsewhere. Be sure what you ask about is not confidential or otherwise sensitive information.

Unsolicited inquiries, especially by phone or email, can be intrusive or even offensive. Therefore, limit yourself to a few questions that don't require extensive research or thought on the part of the person you contact.

Informational Interviews

Informational interviews can lead to original, unpublished material

An excellent primary source of information is the informational interview. Much of what an expert knows may never be published. Therefore, you can uncover highly original information by spending time with your respondent and asking pertinent questions. In addition, an interviewee might refer you to other experts or sources of information.

Expert opinion is not always reliable

Of course, an expert's opinion can be just as mistaken or biased as anyone else's. Like patients who seek second opinions about medical conditions, researchers must seek a balanced range of expert opinions about complex problems or controversial issues. In researching the safety measures at a nearby nuclear power plant, for example, you would seek opinions not only from company engineers and environmentalists, but also from presumably more objective third parties such as a professor or journalist who has studied the issue.

GUIDELINES for Informational Interviews

Planning the Interview

- *Know exactly what you're looking for.* Write out your purpose.

  Purpose statement   I will interview Carol Bono, campus police chief, to ask her about specific campus safety measures being proposed and implemented.

- *Do your homework.* Learn all you can. Be sure the information this person might provide is unavailable in print.

- *Request the interview at your respondent's convenience.* Ask whether this person objects to being quoted or taped. If possible, submit your questions beforehand.

Preparing the Questions

- *Make each question clear and specific.* Avoid questions that can be answered yes or no:

  An unproductive question   In your opinion, can campus safety be improved?

Instead, phrase your question to elicit a detailed response:

  A productive question   Of the various measures being proposed or considered, which do you consider most effective?

- *Avoid loaded questions.* A loaded question invites or promotes a particular bias:

  A loaded question   Wouldn't you agree that campus safety problems have been overstated?

Ask an impartial question instead:

  An impartial question   In your opinion, have campus safety problems been accurately stated, overstated, or understated?

- *Save the most difficult, complex, or sensitive questions for last.*

- *Write out each question on a separate notecard.* Use the notecard (or your laptop) to summarize responses during the interview.

Conducting the Interview

- *Make a courteous start.* Arrive on time; express your gratitude; explain why you believe the respondent can be helpful; explain clearly how you will use the information.

- *Let the respondent do most of the talking.*

- *Be a good listener.* Don't fidget, doodle, or let your eyes wander.

- *Stick to your interview plan.* If the conversation wanders, politely nudge it back on track (unless the peripheral information is useful).

- *Ask for clarification if needed.* Keep asking until you understand.

  Clarifying questions   Could you go over that again?
  Is there a simpler explanation?

- *Repeat major points in your own words, and ask if your interpretation is correct.* But do not put words into the respondent's mouth.

- *Be ready with follow-up questions.* Some answers may reveal new directions for the interview.

  Follow-up questions   Why is it like that?
  Could you say something more about that?
  What more needs to be done?
  What happened next?

- *Keep note-taking to a minimum.* Record statistics, dates, names, and other precise data, but don't record every word. Jot key terms or phrases that can refresh your memory later.

Concluding the Interview

- *Ask for closing comments.* Perhaps these can point to additional information.

  Concluding questions   Would you care to add anything?
  Is there anyone else I should talk to?
  Can you suggest other sources that might help me understand this issue?

- *Request permission to contact your respondent again if new questions arise.*

- *Invite the respondent to review your version for accuracy.* If the interview is to be published, ask for approval of your final draft. Offer to provide copies of any document in which this information appears.

- *Say your thank-yous and leave promptly.*

- *As soon as possible, write a complete summary or record one verbally.*

Surveys

Surveys provide multiple, fresh viewpoints on a topic

Surveys help you form impressions of the concerns, preferences, attitudes, beliefs, or perceptions of a large, identifiable group (a *target population*) by studying representatives of that group (a *sample*). While interviews allow for greater clarity and depth, surveys offer an inexpensive way to get the viewpoints of a large group. Respondents can answer privately and anonymously—and often more candidly than in an interview.

Surveys help answer questions like these

Do consumers prefer brand A or brand B?

How many students on this campus are "nontraditional"?

Is public confidence in technology increasing or decreasing?

The tool for conducting surveys is the questionnaire.

GUIDELINES for Developing a Survey Questionnaire

- *Define the survey's purpose and target population.* Ask yourself, "Why is this survey being performed?" "What, exactly, is it measuring?" "How much background research do I need?" "How will the survey findings be used?" and "Who is the exact population being studied?"

- *Identify the sample group.* Determine how many respondents you need. Generally, the larger the sample surveyed, the more dependable the results (assuming a well-chosen and representative sample). Also determine how the sample will be chosen. Will they be randomly chosen? In the statistical sense, *random* does not mean "haphazard": A random sample means that each member of the target population stands an equal chance of being in the sample group.

- *Define the survey method.* How will the survey be administered—by phone, by mail, or online? Each method has benefits and drawbacks: Phone surveys yield fast results and high response rates; however, they take longer than written surveys. Also, many people find them annoying and tend to be less candid when responding in person. Mail surveys promote candid responses, but many people won't bother returning the survey, and results can arrive slowly. Surveys via the Web or email yield quick results, but computer connections can fail, and (with Web surveys) you have less control over how often the same person responds.

- *Decide on the types of questions.* Questions can be *open-* or *closed-ended.* Open-ended questions allow respondents to answer in any way they choose. Measuring the data gathered from such questions is more time-consuming, but they do provide a rich source of information. An open-ended question would be worded like this:

Open-ended question   What do you think should be done about crime at our school?

- Closed-ended questions give people a limited number of choices, and the data gathered are easier to measure. Here are some types of closed-ended questions:

Closed-ended questions   Are you interested in joining a group of concerned students?

YES _____ NO _____

Rate your degree of concern about crime problems at our school.

HIGH _____ MODERATE _____

LOW _____ NO CONCERN _____

Circle the number that indicates your view about the administration's proposal to allow campus police to carry handguns.

1 . . . . 2 . . . . 3 . . . . 4 . . . . 5 . . . . 6 7

STRONGLY   NO   STRONGLY
DISAPPROVE   OPINION   APPROVE

How often do you ...?

ALWAYS _____ OFTEN _____

SOMETIMES _____ RARELY _____

NEVER _____

To measure exactly where people stand on an issue, choose closed-ended questions.

- *Develop an engaging introduction and opening questions.* Persuade respondents that the questionnaire relates to their concerns, that their answers matter, and that their anonymity is ensured.

A survey introduction   Your answers will enable our senate representative to convey your views about handguns for the campus police. Results of this survey will appear in our campus newspaper. Thank you.

Researchers often include a cover letter with the questionnaire.

Begin with the easiest questions, usually the closed-ended ones. Respondents who commit to these are likely to answer later, more difficult questions.

- *Make each question unambiguous.* All respondents should be able to interpret identical questions identically. An ambiguous question allows for misinterpretation:

An ambiguous question   Do you favor weapons for campus police?

YES _____ NO _____

(*continues*)

"Weapons" might mean tear gas, clubs, handguns, Tasers, or some combination of these. The limited yes-or-no format reduces an array of possible opinions to an either-or choice. Here is an unambiguous version:

A clear question   Do you prefer that campus police (check all that apply):

_____ carry mace and a club?

_____ carry nonlethal "stun guns"?

_____ store handguns in their cruisers?

_____ carry small-caliber handguns?

_____ carry large-caliber handguns?

_____ carry no weapons?

_____ Don't know

To account for all possible responses, include options such as "Other," "Don't know," "Not applicable," or an "Additional comments" section.

■ *Avoid loaded questions that invite or advocate a particular viewpoint or bias:*

A loaded question   Should our campus tolerate the needless endangerment of innocent students by lethal weapons?

YES _____   NO _____

Emotionally loaded and judgmental words (**endangerment, innocent, tolerate, lethal**) in a survey are unethical because they manipulate people's responses (Hayakawa 40).

■ *Make your questionnaire brief, simple, and inviting.* Long questionnaires usually get few replies. And people who do reply tend to give less thought to their answers. Limit the number and types of questions. If conducting the survey by mail, include a stamped, return-addressed envelope, and stipulate a return date.

■ *Have an expert review your questionnaire before use whenever possible.*

Personal Observation

Observation should be your final step because you now know what to look for. Have a plan. Know how, where, and when to look, and jot down observations immediately. You might even take photos or draw sketches.

| Note | *Even direct observation is not foolproof: You might be biased about what you see (focusing on wrong events or ignoring something important); or people conscious of being observed might alter their normal behavior (Adams and Schvaneveldt 244).* |

APPLICATIONS

21.1   Prepare a research report by completing these steps. (Your instructor may establish a timetable for your project.)

PHASE ONE: PRELIMINARY STEPS

1. Choose a topic that affects you, your workplace, or your community directly. Develop a tree chart (see page 338) to help you ask the right questions.
2. Identify a specific audience and its intended use of your information.
3. Narrow your topic, checking with your instructor for approval and advice.
4. Identify the various viewpoints that will lead to your own balanced viewpoint.
5. Make a working bibliography to ensure sufficient primary and secondary sources. Don't delay this step!
6. List what you already know about your topic.
7. Submit a clear statement of purpose to your instructor.
8. Make a working outline.

PHASE TWO: COLLECTING, EVALUATING, AND INTERPRETING DATA

Read Chapter 22 in preparation for this phase.

1. In your research, begin with general reference works for an overview, and then consult more specific sources.
2. Skim the sources, looking for high points.
3. Evaluate each finding for accuracy, reliability, fairness, and completeness.
4. Take notes *selectively.* Use notecards or electronic file software.
5. Plan and administer questionnaires, interviews, and inquiries.
6. Try to conclude your research with direct observation.
7. Decide what your findings mean.
8. Settle on your thesis.
9. Use the checklist on page 375 to reassess your methods, interpretation, and reasoning.

PHASE THREE: ORGANIZING YOUR DATA AND WRITING THE REPORT

1. Revise your working outline as needed.
2. Follow the introduction-body-conclusion format.
3. Document each source of information (page 386).
4. Write your final draft according to the checklist on page 375.
5. Proofread carefully.

DUE DATES: TO BE ASSIGNED BY YOUR INSTRUCTOR

- List of possible topics due: _____
- Final topic due: _____
- Working bibliography and working outline due: _____

- Notecards (or note files) due: _____
- Revised outline due: _____
- First draft of report due: _____
- Final draft of report with supplements and full documentation due: _____

21.2 **COLLABORATIVE PROJECT** (For this assignment, read Chapter 22, pages 362–363.) Divide into small groups, and prepare a comparative evaluation of literature search media. Each group member will select one of the resources listed here and create an individual bibliography (of at least twelve recent and relevant works on a specific topic of interest selected by the group).

- conventional print media
- electronic catalogs
- CD-ROM services
- a commercial database service such as Dialog
- the Internet and Web
- an electronic consortium of local libraries, if applicable

After carefully recording the findings and keeping track of the time spent in each search, compare the ease of searching and quality of results obtained from each type of search on your group's selected topic. Which medium yielded the most current sources (page 362)? Which provided abstracts and full texts as well as bibliographic data? Which consumed the most time? Which provided the most dependable sources (page 362)? The most diverse or varied sources (pages 339–340)? Which cost the most to use? Finally, which yielded the greatest depth of resources (pages 337–339)? Prepare a brief report, and present your findings to the class.

Works Cited

Adams, Gerald R., and Jay D. Schvaneveldt. *Understanding Research Methods.* New York: Longman, 1985. Print.

Hayakawa, S. I. *Language in Thought and Action.* 3rd ed. New York: Harcourt, 1972. Print.

U.S. General Services Administration. *Your Rights to Federal Records.* Washington: GPO, 1995. Print.

For additional information and practice with the learning objectives in this chapter, go to www.mycomplab.com, Resources>Research>Finding Sources.

Evaluating and Interpreting Your Findings

LEARNING OBJECTIVES FOR THIS CHAPTER

- Understand how to evaluate print and Web-based sources for reliability
- Know how to evaluate evidence
- Appreciate the importance of interpreting your own findings
- Identify and correct errors in reasoning

Not all information is equal. Not all interpretations are equal either. For instance, if you really want to know how well the latest innovation in robotic surgery works, you need to check with other sources besides, say, the device's designer (from whom you could expect an overly optimistic or insufficiently critical assessment).

Whether you work with your own findings or the findings of other researchers, you need to decide if the information is valid and reliable. Then you need to decide what your information means. Figure 22.1 outlines your critical thinking decisions and the potential for error at any stage during the process.

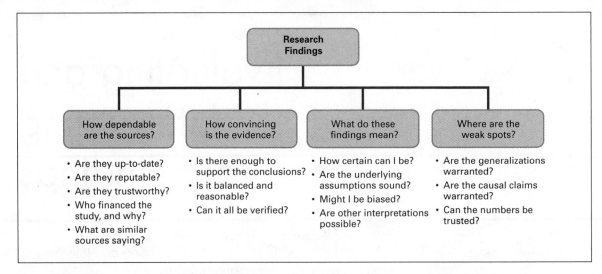

FIGURE 22.1 Decisions in evaluating and interpreting information
Collecting information is often the easiest part of the research process. Your larger challenge is in getting the exact information you need, making sure it's accurate, figuring out what it means, and then double-checking for possible errors along the way.

EVALUATE THE SOURCES

Sources are not equally dependable. A source might offer information that is out of date, inaccurate, incomplete, mistaken, or biased.

Determine the Currency of the Source

"Is the source up-to-date?"

Information, especially technical information, can go out of date very quickly. Even newly published books or journal articles may contain information that can be more than a year old, due to long processes of peer review and production.

Assess the Reputation of the Source

"Is the source dependable?"

Determine if the work is published by a university, professional society, museum, or respected news organization; if the members of the editorial board have distinguished titles and degrees; if the publication is *refereed* (all submissions reviewed by experts before acceptance); and if the bibliography demonstrates a thorough depth of research. All of the above demonstrate a high degree of dependability.

Consider the Motives of the Study's Financers

"Who financed the study, and why?"

Much of today's research is paid for by private companies or special-interest groups who have their own agendas (Crossen 14, 19). For example, medical research may be sponsored by drug or tobacco companies; nutritional research by food manufacturers; environmental research by oil or chemical companies. Typically, this type of "strategic" research is designed to support one special interest or another. Try to determine exactly what those who have funded a particular study stand to gain or lose from the results.

Cross-Check the Source against Other, Similar Sources

"What are similar sources saying?" Most studies have some type of flaw or limitation. Therefore, instead of relying on a single source or study, you should seek a consensus among various respected sources.

Evaluate Web-based Sources Effectively The Internet offers information that may never appear elsewhere—for example, from blogs and Web sites. But much of this material may reflect the bias of the special-interest groups that provide it. Moreover, anyone can publish almost anything on the Internet—including misinformation—without having it verified, edited, or reviewed for accuracy. Therefore, spend extra time evaluating information you locate online. Here are suggestions:

- *Consider the domain type.* Standard domain types in the United States include *.com* (commercial organization), *.edu* (educational institution), *.gov* or *.mil* (government or military organization), *.net* (general usage), and *.org* (nonprofit organization). The domain type might alert you to bias or a hidden agenda. For example, a .com site might provide accurate information but also some type of sales pitch. A .org site might reflect a political or ideological bias.

- *Identify the site's sponsor.* Is the sponsor a special interest group with a particular agenda or point of view? If so, balance this site's information with information from a variety of sources, including peer-reviewed publications, government Web sites, and special interest sites that offer differing perspectives. Consider, for example, how Figure 22.2, a Web page from a group that opposes genetically modified foods, might be balanced against other sources.

- *Look beyond the style of the site.* Sometimes the most reliable material resides in less attractive, text-only sites. The fact that a site looks professional doesn't mean its content is reliable.

- *Assess the currency of the site's materials.* When was the material created, posted, and updated? Many sites have not been updated in months or even years.

- *Assess the author's credentials and assertions.* Check the author's reputation, expertise, and institutional affiliation (university, company, environmental group). Do not confuse the *author* (the person who wrote the material) with the *Webmaster* (the person who created and maintains the site). Follow links to other sites that mention the author. Where, on the spectrum of expert opinion and accepted theory, does this author fall? Is each of the author's assertions supported by solid evidence? Verify any extreme claim through other sources, such as a professor or expert in the field. Consider whether you own biases might predispose you to accept certain ideas.

- *Compare the site with other sources.* Comparing similar sites helps you create a *benchmark* (a standard for evaluating any site based on criteria in these guidelines). Ask a librarian for help.

- *Look for other indicators of quality.* Does the Web site have worthwhile content? Is it sensibly organized? Is it written in a readable and credible expert style? Does it demonstrate objective coverage? Is there an indication that the site's content has been peer-reviewed? Are the links to other sites up to date? Is there a way to contact the author or organization to follow up?

THE CAMPAIGN FOR HEALTHIER EATING IN AMERICA
No Genetically Modified Organisms

ARE YOU ONE OF THE 9 OUT OF 10 AMERICANS OPPOSED TO UNLABELED GM FOODS?

PEW RESEARCH

This guide will help you determine which products are made from genetically modified organisms (GMOs) so you can make healthier non-GMO brand buying choices. GMOs are made by transferring genes from one species, such as bacteria, viruses, or animals, into the DNA of other species, such as corn.

Though most industrialized countries require labeling of GMOs, the U.S. does not. 9 out of 10 Americans want genetically modified (GM) foods to be labeled. Most people say they would avoid brands if labeled as GM.

This guide is produced by The Institute For Responsible Technology, your consumer safety partner and a world leader in exposing the health risks of GMOs. Look for our Non-GMO Shopping Guide coming in mid-2008. For more details or to make a donation, please go to www.responsibletechnology.org.

FIGURE 22.2 A special interest web page
Source: <www.responsibleTechnology.org/docs/141.pdf>.

EVALUATE THE EVIDENCE

Evidence is any finding used to support or refute a particular claim. Although evidence can serve the truth, it can also distort, misinform, and deceive. For example:

Questions that invite distorted evidence

> How much money, material, or energy does recycling really save?
>
> How well are public schools educating children?
>
> Which investments or automobiles are safest?
>
> How safe and effective are herbal medications?

Competing answers to such questions often rest on evidence that has been chosen to support a particular view or agenda.

Determine the Sufficiency of the Evidence

"Is there enough evidence?"

Evidence is sufficient when nothing more is needed to reach an accurate judgment or conclusion. Say you are researching the stress-reducing benefits of low-impact aerobics among employees at a fireworks factory. You would need to interview or survey a broad sample: people who have practiced aerobics for a long time; people of both genders, different ages, different occupations, different lifestyles before they began aerobics; and so on. But responses even from hundreds of practitioners might be insufficient unless those responses were supported by laboratory measurements of metabolic and heart rates, blood pressure, and so on.

Note   *Although anecdotal evidence ("This worked great for me!") might offer a good starting point for investigation, your personal experience rarely provides enough evidence from which to generalize. No matter how long you have practiced aerobics, for instance, you need to determine whether your experience is representative.*

Differentiate Hard from Soft Evidence

"Can the evidence be verified?"

Hard evidence consists of facts, expert opinion, or statistics that can be verified. *Soft evidence* consists of uninformed opinion or speculation, data that were obtained or analyzed unscientifically, and findings that have not been replicated or reviewed by experts.

Decide Whether the Presentation of Evidence Is Balanced and Reasonable

"Is this claim too good to be true?"

"Is there a downside?"

Evidence may be overstated, such as when overzealous researchers exaggerate their achievements without revealing the limitations of their study. Or vital facts may be omitted, as when acetaminophen pain relievers are promoted as "safe," even though acetaminophen is the leading cause of U.S. drug fatalities (Easton and Herrara).

Consider How the Facts Are Being Framed

Is the glass "half full" or "half empty"?

A *frame of reference* is a set of ideas, beliefs, or views that influences our interpretation or acceptance of other ideas. In medical terms, for example, is a "90 percent survival rate" more acceptable than a "10 percent mortality rate"? Framing sways our perception (Lang and Secic 239–40). For instance, what we now call a "financial recession" used to be a "financial depression," which was originally coined as a euphemism for "financial panic" (Bernstein 183). For more on euphemisms, see page 132.

Whether the language is provocative ("rape of the environment," "soft on terrorism"), euphemistic ("teachable moment" versus "mistake"), or demeaning to opponents ("bureaucrats," "tree huggers"), deceptive framing—all too common in political "spin" strategies—obscures the real issues.

INTERPRET YOUR FINDINGS

Interpreting means trying to reach the truth of the matter: an overall judgment about what the findings mean and what conclusion or action they suggest.

Unfortunately, research does not always yield answers that are clear or conclusive. Instead of settling for the most *convenient* answer, we pursue the most *reasonable* answer by critically examining a full range of possible meanings.

Identify Your Level of Certainty

Research can yield three distinct and very different levels of certainty.

1. The ultimate truth—the *conclusive answer:*

A practical definition of "truth"

> Truth is *what is so* about something, as distinguished from what people wish, believe, or assert to be so. In the words of Harvard philosopher Israel Scheffler, truth is the view "which is fated to be ultimately agreed to by all who investigate."[1] The word *ultimately* is important. Investigation may produce a wrong answer for years, even for centuries. For example, in the second century A.D., Ptolemy's view of the universe placed the earth at its center—and though untrue, this judgment was based on the best information available at that time. And Ptolemy's view survived for 13 centuries, even after new information had discredited this belief. When Galileo proposed a more truthful view in the fifteenth century, he was labeled a heretic.
>
> One way to spare yourself further confusion about truth is to reserve the word *truth* for the final answer to an issue. Get in the habit of using the words *belief, theory,* and *present understanding* more often. (Ruggiero 21–22)

---

[1]From *Reason and Teaching.* New York: Bobbs-Merrill, 1973.

Conclusive answers are the research outcome we seek, but often we have to settle for answers that are less than certain.

2. The *probable answer:* the answer that stands the best chance of being true or accurate, given the most we can know at this particular time. Probable answers are subject to revision in light of new information. This is especially the case with *emergent science,* such as gene therapy or food irradiation.

3. *inconclusive answer:* the realization that the truth of the matter is more elusive, ambiguous, or complex than we expected.

"Exactly how certain are we?"

We need to decide what level of certainty our findings warrant. For example, we are *highly certain* about the perils of smoking and sunburn, *reasonably certain* about the health benefits of fruits and vegetables, but *less certain* about the perils of genetically modified foods or the benefits of vitamin supplements.

Can you think of additional examples of information about which we are *highly, reasonably,* or *less* certain?

Examine the Underlying Assumptions

Assumptions are notions we take for granted, ideas we often accept without proof. The research process rests on assumptions such as these: that a sample group accurately represents a larger target group, that survey respondents remember certain facts accurately, that mice and humans share enough biological similarities for meaningful research. For a study to be valid, the underlying assumptions have to be accurate.

How underlying assumptions affect research validity

Consider this example: You are an education consultant evaluating the accuracy of IQ testing as a predictor of academic performance. Reviewing the evidence, you perceive an association between low IQ scores and low achievers. You then verify your statistics by examining a cross section of reliable sources. Should you feel justified in concluding that IQ tests do predict performance accurately? This conclusion might be invalid unless you can verify the following assumptions:

1. That neither parents nor teachers nor children had seen individual test scores, which could produce biased expectations

2. That regardless of score, each child had completed an identical curriculum, instead of being "tracked" on the basis of his or her score

Note

Assumptions can be easier to identify in someone else's thinking than in our own. During team discussions, ask members to help you identify your own assumptions.

Be Alert for Personal Bias

Personal bias is a fact of life

To support a particular version of the truth, our own bias might cause us to overestimate (or deny) the certainty of our findings.

> Unless you are perfectly neutral about the issue, an unlikely circumstance, at the very outset... you will believe one side of the issue to be right, and that belief will incline you to... present more and better arguments for the side of the issue you prefer. (Ruggiero 134)

Because personal bias is hard to transcend, *rationalizing* often becomes a substitute for *reasoning*:

Reasoning versus rationalizing

> You are reasoning if your belief follows the evidence—that is, if you examine the evidence first and then make up your mind. You are rationalizing if the evidence follows your belief—if you first decide what you'll believe and then select and interpret evidence to justify it. (Ruggiero 44)

Personal bias is often unconscious until we examine our attitudes long held but never analyzed, assumptions we've inherited from our backgrounds, and so on. Recognizing our own biases is a crucial first step in managing them.

Consider Other Possible Interpretations

"What else could this mean?"

Perhaps other researchers would disagree about the meaning of certain findings. Settling on a final meaning can be difficult—and sometimes impossible. For example, issues such as the need for defense spending or the causes of inflation are always controversial and will never be resolved. Although we can get verifiable data and can reason persuasively on many subjects, no close reasoning by any expert and no supporting statistical analysis will "prove" anything about a controversial subject. Some problems are simply more resistant to solution than others, no matter how dependable the sources.

Note

Not all interpretations are equally valid. Never assume that any interpretation that is possible is also allowable, especially in terms of its ethical consequences.

AVOID ERRORS IN REASONING

Finding the truth, especially in a complex issue or problem, often is a process of elimination, of ruling out or avoiding errors in reasoning. As we interpret, we make *inferences*: We derive conclusions about what we don't know by reasoning from what we do know (Hayakawa 37). For example, we might infer that a drug that boosts immunity in laboratory mice will boost immunity in humans or that a rise in campus crime statistics is caused by the fact that young people have become more violent. Whether a particular inference is on target or dead wrong depends largely on our answers to one or more of these questions:

Questions for testing inferences

- *To what extent can these findings be generalized?*
- *Is Y really caused by X?*
- *To what extent can the numbers be trusted, and what do they mean?*

Three major reasoning errors that can distort our interpretations are faulty generalization, faulty causal reasoning, and faulty statistical reasoning.

Faulty Generalization

The temptation to generalize on the basis of limited evidence can be hard to resist. Consider, for example, the highly controversial war in Iraq. Our political leaders initially justified this war by citing limited and often inaccurate evidence to support the general conclusion that Iraq possessed weapons of mass destruction and had collaborated with al-Qaeda in planning the 9/11 attacks on New York City and Washington, D.C. For more on faulty generalization, see page 316.

Faulty Causal Reasoning

Designed to attack a problem at its source, causal analysis addresses questions such as these:

Typical questions addressed by causal analysis

- *Why do so many students drop out of our college?*
- *Why have medical costs risen so rapidly in recent years?*

A different version of causal analysis involves reasoning from effect to cause, to address questions such as these:

- *What are possible negative effects of genetic testing on young adults?*
- *Has the so-called war on terrorism made the United States any safer?*

Faulty causal reasoning is extremely common, especially when we ignore other possible causes or when we confuse *correlation* with *causation* (see page 372). For more on causal reasoning, see page 317.

Faulty Statistical Reasoning

How numbers can mislead

The purpose of statistical analysis is to determine the meaning of a collected set of numbers. In primary research, our surveys and questionnaires often lead to some kind of numerical interpretation ("What percentage of respondents prefer *X*?" "How often does *Y* happen?"). In secondary research, we rely on numbers collected by survey researchers.

Numbers seem more precise, more objective, more scientific, and less ambiguous than words. They are easier to summarize, measure, compare, and analyze. But numbers can be totally misleading. For example, radio or television phone-in surveys often produce distorted data: Although "90 percent of callers" might express support for a particular viewpoint, people who bother to respond tend to have the greatest anger or extreme feelings, representing only a fraction of overall attitudes (Fineman 24). Mail-in or Internet surveys can produce similar distortion. Before relying on any set of numbers, we need to know exactly where they come from, how they were collected, and how they were analyzed.

Faulty statistical reasoning produces conclusions that are unwarranted, inaccurate, or deceptive. Following are typical fallacies.

Common statistical fallacies

"Exactly how well are we doing?"

The Sanitized Statistic.   Numbers can be manipulated (or "cleaned up") to obscure the facts. For instance, the College Board's 1996 "recentering" of SAT scores has raised the "average" math score from 478 to 500 and the average verbal score from 424 to 500 (boosts of almost 5 and 18 percent, respectively), although actual student performance remains unchanged (Samuelson).

"How many rats was that?"

The Meaningless Statistic.   Exact numbers can be used to quantify something so inexact or vaguely defined that it should only be approximated (Huff 247; Lavin 278): "Boston has 3,247,561 rats." "Zappo detergent makes your laundry 10 percent brighter." An exact number looks impressive, but it can hide the fact that certain subjects (child abuse, cheating in college, drug and alcohol abuse, eating habits) cannot be quantified exactly because respondents don't always tell the truth (on account of denial or embarrassment or guessing). Or they respond in ways they think the researcher expects.

"Why is everybody griping?"

Three ways of reporting an "average"

The Undefined Average.   The mean, median, and mode can be confused in determining an average (Huff 244; Lavin 279). (1) The *mean* is the result of adding up the value of each item in a set of numbers and then dividing that total by the number of items in the set. (2) The *median* is the result of ranking all the values from high to low and then identifying the middle value (or the 50th percentile, as in calculating SAT scores). (3) The *mode* is the value that occurs most often in a set of numbers.

Each of these measurements represents some kind of average. But unless we know which "average" (mean, median, or mode) is being presented, we cannot possibly interpret the figures accurately.

Assume that we want to determine the average salary among female managers at XYZ Corporation (ranked from high to low):

MANAGER	SALARY
"A"	$90,000
"B"	$90,000
"C"	$80,000
"D"	$65,000
"E"	$60,000
"F"	$55,000
"G"	$50,000

In the above example, the *mean* salary (total salaries divided by number of salaries) is $70,000, the *median* salary (middle value) is $65,000, and the *mode* (most frequent value) is $90,000. Each is, legitimately, an "average," and each could be used to support or refute a particular assertion (for example, "Women managers are paid too little" or "Women managers are paid too much").

Research expert Michael Lavin sums up the potential for bias in the reporting of averages:

> Depending on the circumstances, any one of these measurements may describe a group of numbers better than the other two.... [But] people typically choose the value which best presents their case, whether or not it is the most appropriate to use. (279)

Although the mean is the most commonly computed average, this measurement is misleading when one or more values on either end of the scale (*outliers*) are extremely high or low. Suppose, for instance, that manager "A" (above) was paid a $200,000 salary. Because this figure deviates so far from the normal range of salary figures for managers "B" through "G," it distorts the average for the whole group, increasing the mean salary by more than 20 percent (Plumb and Spyridakis 636).

"Is 51 percent really a majority?"

The Distorted Percentage Figure.   Percentages are often reported without explanation of the original numbers used in the calculation (Adams and Schvaneveldt 359; Lavin 280): "Seventy-five percent of respondents prefer our brand over the competing brand"—without mention that, say, only four people were surveyed.

| Note |

> *In small samples, percentages can mislead because the percentage size can dwarf the number it represents: "In this experiment, 33% of the rats lived, 33% died, and the third rat got away" (Lang and Secic 41). When your sample is small, report the actual numbers: "Five out of ten respondents agreed...."*

Another fallacy in reporting percentages occurs when the *margin of error* is ignored. This is the range within which the true figure lies, based on estimated sampling errors in a survey. For example, a claim that "most people surveyed prefer brand X" might be based on the fact that 51 percent of respondents expressed this preference; but if the survey carried a 2 percent margin of error, the real figure could be as low as 49 percent or as high as 53 percent. In a survey with a high margin of error, the true figure may be so uncertain that no definite conclusion can be drawn.

"Which car should we buy?"

The Bogus Ranking.   This distortion occurs when items are compared on the basis of ill-defined criteria (Adams and Schvaneveldt 212; Lavin 284): For example, the statement "Last year, the Tankmobile was the number-one selling car in America" does not mention that some competing carmakers actually sold *more* cars to private individuals and that the Tankmobile figures were inflated by hefty sales—at huge discounts—to rental-car companies and corporate fleets. Unless we know how the ranked items were chosen and how they were compared (the *criteria*), a ranking can produce a seemingly scientific number based on a completely unscientific method.

"Does X actually
cause Y?"

Confusion of Correlation with Causation. *Correlation* is a numerical measure of the strength of the relationship between two variables (say smoking and increased lung cancer risk, or education and income). *Causation* is the demonstrable production of a specific effect (smoking causes lung cancer). Correlations between smoking and lung cancer or between education and income signal a causal relationship that has been demonstrated by many studies. But not every correlation implies causation. For instance, a recently discovered correlation between moderate alcohol consumption and decreased heart disease risk offers no sufficient proof that moderate drinking *causes* less heart disease.

"Could something else
have caused Y?"

In any type of causal analysis, be on the lookout for *confounding factors,* other possible reasons or explanations for a particular outcome. For instance, studies indicating that regular exercise improves health might be overlooking the confounding factor that healthy people tend to exercise more than those who are unhealthy.

Many highly publicized correlations are the product of *data mining:* In this process, computers randomly compare one set of variables (say, eating habits) with another set (say, range of diseases). From these countless comparisons, certain relationships or associations are revealed (say, between coffee drinking and pancreatic cancer risk). As dramatic as such isolated correlations may be, they constitute no proof of causation and often lead to hasty conclusions (Ross 135).

Note

Tom Maeglin points out, however, that despite its limitations, data mining is valuable for "uncovering correlations that require computers to perceive but that thinking humans can evaluate and research further."

"Who selected which
studies to include?"

The Biased Meta-Analysis. In a *meta-analysis,* researchers examine a whole range of studies that have been done on one topic (say, high-fat diets and cancer risk). The purpose of this "study of studies" is to decide the overall meaning of the collected findings. Because results ultimately depend on which studies have been included and which omitted, a meta-analysis can reflect the biases of the researchers who select the material. Also, because small studies have less chance of being published than large ones, they may get overlooked (Lang and Secic 174–76).

GUIDELINES for Evaluating and Interpreting Information

Evaluate the Sources

- *Check the posting or publication date.* The latest information is not always the best, but keeping up with recent developments is vital.

- *Assess the reputation of each source.* Check the copyright page for background on the publisher, the bibliography for the quality of research, and (if available) the author's brief biography.

■ *Identify the study's sponsor.* If a study proclaiming the crashworthiness of the Tankmobile has been financial by the Tankmobile Auto Company, be skeptical about the findings.

■ *Look for corroborating sources.* A single study rarely produces definitive findings. Learn what other sources say, why they agree or disagree, and where most experts stand.

Evaluate the Evidence

■ *Decide whether the evidence is sufficient.* Evidence should surpass personal experience, anecdotes, or media reports. Reasonable and informed observers should be able to agree on its credibility.

■ *Look for a fair and balanced presentation.* Suspect any claims about "breakthroughs" or "miracle cures" or the like.

■ *Try to verify the evidence.* Examine the facts that support the claims. Look for replication of findings.

Interpret Your Findings

■ *Don't expect certainty.* Complex questions are mostly open-ended, and a mere accumulation of facts doesn't prove anything. Even so, the weight of evidence usually suggests some reasonable conclusion.

■ *Examine the underlying assumptions.* As opinions taken for granted, assumptions are easily mistaken for facts.

■ *Identify your personal biases.* Examine your own assumptions. Don't ignore evidence simply because it contradicts your original assumptions.

■ *Consider alternative interpretations.* What else might this evidence mean?

Check for Weak Spots

■ *Scrutinize all generalizations.* Decide whether the evidence supports the generalization. Suspect any general claim not limited by a qualifier such as "often," "sometimes," or "rarely."

■ *Treat causal claims skeptically.* Differentiate correlation from causation, as well as possible from probable or definite causes. Consider *confounding factors* (other explanations for the reported outcome).

■ *Look for statistical fallacies.* Determine where the numbers come from and how they were collected and analyzed—information that legitimate researchers routinely provide. Note the margin of error.

■ *Consider the limits of computer analysis.* Data mining often produces intriguing but random correlations; a meta-analysis might be biased; a computer model is only as accurate as the assumptions and data that were programmed in.

(continues)

- *Look for misleading terminology.* Examine terms that beg for precise definition in their specific context: **survival rate, success rate, customer satisfaction, risk factor,** and so on.

- *Interpret the reality behind the numbers.* Consider the possibility of alternative, more accurate interpretations of the data.

"How have assumptions influenced this computer model?"

The Fallible Computer Model.   Computer models process complex *assumptions* (see page 367) to predict or estimate costs, benefits, risks, and probable outcomes. But answers produced by any computer model depend on the assumptions (and data) programmed in. Assumptions might be influenced by researcher bias or the sponsors' agenda. For example, a prediction of human fatalities from a nuclear reactor meltdown might rest on assumptions about the availability of safe shelter, evacuation routes, time of day, season, wind direction, and the structural integrity of the containment unit. But these assumptions could be manipulated to overstate or understate the risk (Barbour 228). For computer-modeled estimates of accident risk (oil spill, plane crash) or of the costs and benefits of a proposed project or policy (international space station, welfare reform), consumers rarely know the assumptions behind the numbers.

"Do we all agree on what these terms mean?"

Misleading Terminology.   The terms used to interpret statistics sometimes hide their real meaning. For instance, the widely publicized figure that people treated for cancer have a "50 percent survival rate" is misleading in two ways: (1) *Survival* to laypersons means "staying alive," but to medical experts, staying alive for only 5 years after diagnosis qualifies as survival; (2) the "50 percent" survival figure covers *all* cancers, including certain skin or thyroid cancers that have extremely high *cure rates,* as well as other cancers (such as lung or ovarian) that are rarely curable and have extremely low *survival rates* ("Are We" 6).

"Is this news good, bad, or insignificant?"

Even the most valid and reliable statistics require that we interpret the reality behind the numbers. For instance, the overall cancer rate today is "higher" than it was in 1910. What this may mean is that people are living longer and thus are more likely to die of cancer and that cancer today rarely is misdiagnosed or mislabeled because of stigma ("Are We" 4). The finding that rates for certain cancers "double" after prolonged exposure to electromagnetic waves may really mean that cancer risk actually increases from 1 in 10,000 to 2 in 10,000.

The numbers may be "technically accurate" and may seem highly persuasive in the interpretations they suggest. But the actual truth behind these numbers is far more elusive. Any interpretation of statistical data carries the possibility that other, more accurate interpretations have been overlooked or deliberately excluded (Barnett 45).

ASSESS YOUR INQUIRY

The inquiry phases of the research process present a minefield of potential errors in where we search, how we interpret, and how we reason. Therefore, before you prepare the actual report, critically examine your methods, interpretations, and reasoning using the Checklist for the Research Process.

☑ A CHECKLIST for the Research Process

(Numbers in parentheses refer to the first page of discussion.)

Methods

☐ Did I ask the right questions? (337)

☐ Are the sources appropriately up-to-date? (362)

☐ Is each source reputable, trustworthy, relatively unbiased, and borne out by other sources? (362)

☐ Does the evidence clearly support the conclusions? (365)

☐ Can all the evidence be verified? (365)

☐ Is a fair balance of viewpoints presented? (337)

☐ Has my research achieved adequate depth? (339)

Reasoning

☐ Am I reasonably certain about the meaning of these findings? (366)

☐ Can I discern assumption from fact? (81, 367)

☐ Am I reasoning instead of rationalizing? (368)

☐ Can I rule out other possible interpretations or conclusions? (368)

☐ Am I confident that my causal reasoning is correct? (369)

☐ Are my generalizations warranted? (369)

☐ Can all the numbers, statistics, and interpretations be trusted? (369)

☐ Have I resolved (or at least acknowledged) any conflicts among my findings? (341)

☐ Have I decided whether my final answer is conclusive, probable, or inconclusive? (366)

☐ Is this the most reasonable conclusion or merely the most convenient? (342)

☐ Have I accounted for all sources of bias, including my own? (367)

☐ Am I getting the whole story and getting it straight? (341)

☐ Should the evidence be reconsidered? (365)

APPLICATIONS

22.1 From print or broadcast media, personal experience, or the Internet, identify an example of each of the following sources of distortion or of interpretive error: 1) a study with questionable sponsorship or motives; 2) reliance on insufficient evidence; 3) unbalanced presentation; 4) deceptive framing of facts; 5) overestimating the level of certainty; 6) biased interpretation; 7) rationalizing; 8) unexamined assumptions; 9) faulty causal reasoning; 10) hasty generalization; 11) overstated generalization; 12) sanitized statistics; 13) meaningless statistic; 14) undefined average; 15) distorted percentage figure; 16) bogus ranking; 17) fallible computer model; and 18) misinterpreted statistic.

Submit your examples to your instructor, and be prepared to discuss your materials in class.

22.2 Referring to the list in Application 22.1, identify the specific distortion or interpretive error in these examples:

(a) *The federal government excludes from unemployment figures an estimated 5 million people who remain unemployed after one year* (Morgenson 54).

(b) *Only 38.268 percent of college graduates end up working in their specialty.*

(c) *Sixty-six percent of employees we hired this year are women and minorities, compared to the national average of 40 percent.* No mention is made of the fact that only three people have been hired this year, by a company that employs three hundred (mostly white males).

(d) *Are you pro-life or pro-choice?*

22.3 Identify confounding factors (page 372) that may have been overlooked in the following interpretations and conclusions:

(a) *One out of every five patients admitted to Central Hospital dies* (Sowell). Does this mean that the hospital is bad?

(b) *In a recent survey, rates of emotional depression differed widely among different countries—far lower in Asian than in Western countries* (Horgan). Are these differences due to culturally specific genetic factors, as many scientists might conclude? Or is this conclusion confounded by other variables?

(c) *"Among 20-year-olds in 1979, those who said that they smoked marijuana 11 to 50 times in the past year had an average IQ 15 percentile points higher than those who said they'd only smoked once"* (Sklaroff and Ash 85). Does this indicate that pot increases brain power, or could it mean something else?

(d) *Teachers are mostly to blame for low test scores and poor discipline in public schools.* How is our assessment of this claim affected by the following information? *From age 2 to 17, children in the U.S. average 12,000 hours in school and 15,000 to 18,000 hours watching TV* ("Wellness Facts").

22.4   **WEB-BASED PROJECT** Uninformed opinions are usually based on assumptions we've never really examined. Examples of popular assumptions that are largely unexamined:

- Bottled water is safer and better for you than tap water.
- Forest fires should always be prevented or suppressed immediately.
- The fewer germs in their environment, the healthier the children.
- The more soy we eat, the better.

Your assignment is to identify and examine one popular assumption for accuracy. For example, you might tackle the bottled water assumption by visiting the FDA Web site at <**http://www.FDA.gov**> and the Sierra Club site at <**http://www.sierraclub.org**> for starters. (Unless you get stuck, try to work with an assumption not listed here.) Trace the sites and links you followed to get your information, and write up your findings in a report to be shared with the class.

Works Cited

Adams, Gerald R., and Jay D. Schvaneveldt. *Understanding Research Methods.* New York: Longman, 1985. Print.

"Are We in the Middle of a Cancer Epidemic?" *University of California, Berkeley, Wellness Letter* 10.9 (1994): 4–6. Print.

Barbour, Ian. *Ethics in an Age of Technology.* New York: Harper, 1993. Print.

Barnes, Shaleen. "Evaluating Sources Checklist." Information Literacy Project. 10 June 1997. Web. 23 June 1998 <http://www.lib.umassd.edu/infolit/infolit.html>.

Barnett, Arnold. "How Numbers Can Trick You." *Technology Review* Oct. 1994: 38–45. Print.

Bernstein, Peter L. *Against the Gods: The Remarkable Story of Risk.* New York: Wiley, 1998. Print.

Crossen, Cynthia. *Tainted Truth: The Manipulation of Fact in America.* New York: Simon, 1994. Print.

Easton, Thomas, and Stephen Herrara. "J&J's Dirty Little Secret." *Forbes* 12 Jan. 1998: 42–44. Print.

Facklemann, Kathleen. "Science Safari in Cyberspace." *Science News* 152.50 (1997): 397–98. Print.

Fineman, Howard. "The Power of Talk." *Newsweek* 8 Feb. 1993: 24–28.

Hall, Judith. "Medicine on Web: Finding the Wheat, Leaving the Chaff." *Technology Review* Mar.–Apr. 1998: 60–61. Print.

Hayakawa, S. I. *Language in Thought and Action.* 3rd ed. New York: Harcourt, 1972. Print.

Horgan, John. "Multicultural Studies." *Scientific American* Nov. 1996: 24+. Print.

Huff, Darrell. *How to Lie with Statistics.* New York: Norton, 1954. Print.

Lang, Thomas A., and Michelle Secic. *How to Report Statistics in Medicine.* Philadelphia: Amer. Coll. of Physicians, 1997. Print.

Lavin, Michael R. *Business Information: How to Find It, How to Use It.* 2nd ed. Phoenix: Oryx, 1992. Print.

Maeglin, Thomas. Unpublished review of *The Writing Process.* Print.

Morgenson, Gretchen. "Would Uncle Sam Lie to You?" *Worth* Nov. 1994: 53+. Print.

Plumb, Carolyn, and Jan H. Spyridakis. "Survey Research in Technical Communication: Designing and Administering Questionnaires." *Technical Communication* 39.4 (1992): 625–38. Print.

Raloff, Janet. "Chocolate Hearts: Yummy and Good Medicine." *Science News* 157.12 (2000): 188–89. Print.

Ross, Philip E. "Lies, Damned Lies, and Medical Statistics." *Forbes* 14 Aug. 1995: 130–35. Print.

Ruggiero, Vincent R. *The Art of Thinking.* 3rd ed. New York: Harper, 1991. Print.

Samuelson, Robert. "Merchants of Mediocrity." *Newsweek* 1 Aug. 1994: 44. Print.

Sklaroff, Sara, and Michael Ash. "American Pie Charts." *Civilization* Apr.–May 1997: 84–85. Print.

Sowell, Thomas. "Magic Numbers." *Forbes* 20 Oct. 1997: 120. Print.

"Wellness Facts." *University of California, Berkeley, Wellness Letter* 14.10 (1998): 1. Print.

For additional information and practice with the learning objectives in this chapter, go to www.mycomplab.com, Resources>Research>Evaluating Sources.

CHAPTER 23

Avoiding Plagiarism, Documenting Your Sources, and Respecting Copyright*

LEARNING OBJECTIVES FOR THIS CHAPTER

- Define plagiarism and identify its consequences
- Take accurate and effective notes and quote, paraphrase, and summarize correctly

(*continues*)

---

*Portions of this chapter were written by Linda Stern, Publishing School of Continuing and Professional Studies, New York University, and adapted by the author.

- Understand why, what, and how you should document
- Document a wide variety of source types in MLA and APA styles
- Know how to avoid copyright violations

WHAT IS PLAGIARISM?

Definition and consequences of plagiarism

As introduced in Chapter 5 and repeated here, *plagiarism* is using someone else's work—words, ideas, or illustrations, published or unpublished—without giving the creator of that work sufficient credit. A serious breach of scholarly ethics, plagiarism can have severe consequences. Students risk a failing grade or disciplinary action ranging from suspension to expulsion. A record of such action can adversely affect professional opportunities in the future. Scholars and teachers can face public disgrace and even be forced out of a position. In the business world, plagiarism leads to distrust and can damage careers.

Three reasons why avoiding plagiarism is important

The importance of avoiding plagiarism revolves around three significant points: preserving intellectual honesty, giving credit to the work of others, and promoting intellectual growth. First, the academic community relies on the reciprocal exchange of ideas and information to further knowledge and research. Using material without acknowledging its source violates this expectation and consequently makes it hard for researchers to verify and build on others' results. Second, plagiarism cheats writers and researchers of the credit they deserve for their work and creativity. Even with the writer's permission, presenting another's work as one's own is equivalent to lying: It's a form of dishonesty. Finally, and perhaps most important for students, plagiarizing negates the very reason for attending college. A student who hands in a plagiarized paper has missed an opportunity for growth and learning.

Plagiarism is obvious

Ethical considerations aside, it's hard to get away with plagiarism. Experienced professors can easily tell when a paper is not written in a student's own style or is more professionally prepared than they would expect. In addition, online services can now identify plagiarized papers, and academic institutions are subscribing to such services. Students at these schools will have a hard time getting away with submitting unoriginal papers.

Most plagiarism is unintentional, but unintentional plagiarism is still plagiarism. To avoid unintentional plagiarism, you need to do all of the following:

Ways to avoid unintentional plagiarism

- Identify sources and information to be documented in your paper.
- Take effective and accurate notes.
- Understand how to quote, paraphrase, and summarize properly.
- Know how to document sources both in the text itself and at the end of your report.

IDENTIFYING SOURCES AND INFORMATION THAT MUST BE CREDITED

The importance of crediting sources

The legal doctrine of *fair use* allows writers to use a limited amount of another's work in their own papers and books, as long as its origin is explicitly acknowledged. How to credit your sources, known as *documentation*, is a detailed process that will be discussed later in this chapter.

What needs to be documented and what does not

But even when you are just beginning your research, how will you know which sources will and won't need to be documented? The answer to this question is relatively simple. Whenever you use information from an *outside source* (any source that isn't your own brain), credit the source. The one major exception to this rule is that you do not have to document *common knowledge*—widely known information about current events, famous people, geographical facts, or familiar history. When in doubt if something is common knowledge, the safest strategy is to credit the source.

TAKING EFFECTIVE AND ACCURATE NOTES

Why note-taking is important

Another way to avoid unintentional plagiarism is to follow a systematic method of note-taking. Take detailed notes that identify those sources; otherwise you may forget about a source you have used, thereby unintentionally plagiarizing.

How to take notes

If you want, you may use old-fashioned notecards to record your sources and material you use from those sources. However, researchers today increasingly take notes on electronic file programs or database management software that allows notes to be filed, shuffled, and retrieved by author, title, topic, date, or keywords. You can also take notes in a single word processing file and then use the "Find" command to locate notes quickly. Whether you use a computer or notecards, your notes should be easy to organize and reorganize.

GUIDELINES for Taking Notes

- *Keep copies of your documentation information.* For all sources that you use, keep photocopies or digital records of the title and copyright pages and the pages with quotations you need. Highlight the relevant citation information in color. Keep these materials until you've completed your paper.

- *Create the Works Cited or References list first.* Before you start writing your paper, your list can start out as a working bibliography, a list of possible sources to which you add entries as you discover them. When you finalize your list, you can delete entries you've decided not to use.

(continues)

■ *Write down bibliographical information for each source you consult.* Record complete information for that source using the citation format that will appear in your document (see Figure 23.1). Record the information accurately so you won't need to track down a source at the last minute. When searching online, you can often print out or save the full bibliographic record for each source or copy and paste the URL into your document, thereby ensuring an accurate citation.

■ *Determine whether to quote, paraphrase, or summarize.* When quoting others directly, be sure to record words and punctuation accurately. When restating material in your own words (paraphrasing and summarizing), preserve the original meaning and emphasis. Double-check if any portions of paraphrases or summaries are actually quotations, and insert the necessary quotation marks.

Record each bibliographic citation exactly as it will appear in your final report

Pinsky, Mark A. *The EMF Book: What You Should Know About Electromagnetic Fields, Electromagnetic Radiation, and Your Health.* New York: Warner, 1995.

FIGURE 23.1 Record for a bibliographic citation in MLA style

QUOTING, PARAPHRASING, AND SUMMARIZING

Three ways to use outside sources

To avoid plagiarism, you must use material from outside sources properly. You can integrate outside material into your paper in three ways—by quoting, paraphrasing, or summarizing. Each quotation, paraphrase, or summary must be used in a way that accurately conveys the meaning expressed in the original source.

Quoting the Work of Others

Definition of a quotation

A *quotation* reproduces a portion of a source, word for word, for a purpose of your own: to support a statement or idea, to provide an example, to advance an argument, or to add interest or color to a discussion. The length of a quotation can range from a word or phrase to several paragraphs. In general, quote the least amount possible that gets your point across to the reader.

In your notes, you must place quotation marks around all exact wording you borrow, whether the words were written or spoken (as in an interview or presentation) or appeared in electronic form. Even a single borrowed sentence or phrase or a single word used in a special way needs quotation marks, with the exact source properly cited. These sources include people with whom you collaborate.

GUIDELINES for Quoting the Work of Others

- *Use a direct quotation only when absolutely necessary.* Sometimes a direct quotation is the only way to do justice to the author's own words. Use direct quotations when you want to preserve the original line of reasoning, special phrasing or emphasis, precise meaning, or an especially striking or colorful example. You may also quote directly when you want to convey the authority and complexity of expert opinion or the original's voice, sincerity, or emotional intensity.

- *Copy the material from your source to your paper exactly as it appears in the original.* Do not alter the spelling, capitalization, or punctuation of the original. If a quotation contains an obvious error, insert [*sic*], which is Latin for "so" or "thus," to show that the error appeared in the original. Record the exact page numbers, and double-check that you haven't altered the original expression in any way (see Figure 23.2).

- *Keep quotations as brief as possible.* For conciseness and emphasis, use ellipses. Ellipses are three spaced periods (…) to indicate that words have been omitted within a single sentence. Add a fourth period to indicate the end of a sentence or the omission of more than a sentence. The elliptical passage must be grammatical and must not distort the original meaning. For more on ellipses, see page 518.)

- *Use square brackets to insert your own clarifying comments or to add transitions between various parts of the original.* For example, "This occupation [campus police officer] requires excellent judgment."

- *Embed quoted material into your sentences clearly and grammatically.* Introduce embedded quotations with phrases such as "Jones agrees that…" or "Gomez concludes that…."

- *Quote passages four lines or longer in block form.* Avoid long quotations except in these instances: to provide an extended example, definition, or analogy or to analyze or discuss a complex idea or concept. Start on a separate line. Double-space a block quotation, and indent the entire block one inch. Do not indent the first line of the passage, but do indent first lines of subsequent paragraphs three spaces. Do not use quotation marks.

- *Cite the source of each quoted passage.* Immediately follow each quotation with a parenthetical reference indicating the source of the quotation. For instruction on how to format parenthetical references, see pages 388, 401.

In your notes, place quotation marks around all directly quoted material

Pinsky, Mark A. pp. 29–30

"Neither electromagnetic fields nor electromagnetic radiation causes cancer per se, most researchers agree. What they may do is promote cancer. Cancer is a multistage process that requires an 'initiator' that makes a cell or group of cells abnormal. Everyone has cancerous cells in his or her body. Cancer—the disease as we think of it—occurs when these cancerous cells grow uncontrollably."

FIGURE 23.2   Record for a quotation

Paraphrasing the Work of Others

Definition of a
paraphrase

Research writing is a process of independent thinking in which you work with the ideas of others in order to reach your own conclusions; unless the author's exact wording is essential, try to paraphrase instead of quoting borrowed material. A *paraphrase* is a restatement, in your own words and using your own sentence structure, of specific ideas or information from a source. The chief purpose of a paraphrase is to *maintain your own writing style* throughout your paper. A paraphrase can be about as long as the original passage.

Paraphrasing means more than changing or shuffling a few words; it means restating the original idea in your own words—sometimes in a clearer, more direct and emphatic way—and giving full credit to the source. To offer as a paraphrase an original passage only slightly altered is plagiarism. Equally unethical is offering a paraphrase, although documented, that distorts the original meaning. Figure 23.3 shows an entry paraphrased from the passage in Figure 23.2. Paraphrased material is not enclosed within quotation marks, but it is documented to acknowledge the source.

GUIDELINES for Paraphrasing the Work of Others

- *Refer to the author early in the paraphrase.* This will signal the beginning of the paraphrased passage.

- *Retain key words from the original to preserve its meaning.* Use quotation marks within your paraphrase to indicate quoted material.

- *Use your own words and sentence structure.* Do not duplicate the source's words (unless quoting), and write the sentences in your own style.

- *Make sure your readers know when the paraphrase begins and ends.* Identify the source at the start of the paraphrase or as early into it as possible.

- *Be sure to preserve the author's original intent.* Check that your paraphrase is an accurate and objective restatement of the source's specific ideas.

- *Cite the exact source of each paraphrased passage.* Immediately follow each paraphrase with a parenthetical reference indicating the exact location of the material in the source. For instruction on formatting parenthetical references, see pages 388, 401.

Signal the beginning
of the paraphrase by
identifying the source
and the end by citing the
location

> According to Pinsky, most researchers doubt that cancer is caused by either electromagnetic fields or electromagnetic radiation. These electrical currents, however, may "promote" cancer by initiating the "multistage process" that leads to proliferation of cancer cells that are otherwise present in small amounts in the healthy human body (29–30).

FIGURE 23.3 Record for a paraphrase

Summarizing the Work of Others

Definition of a summary

Like a paraphrase, a *summary* is a restatement in your own words of the source ideas. A summary, however, restates a large portion of the original text briefly, rather than restating a small portion of the original in about the same number of words. Summary is used to convey the general meaning of the ideas in a source without specific details or examples that may appear in the original. Give the essential information clearly and concisely in your own words.

GUIDELINES for Summarizing Information

- *Use your own words and sentence structure.* If you must quote a crucial word or phrase directly, use quotation marks around the quoted words.

- *Make sure your readers know where the summary begins and ends.* As with a paraphrase, identify the source early in the summary.

- *Make sure your summary is an accurate restatement of the source's main ideas.*

- *Indicate the exact source of the summarized material.* Immediately follow each summary with a parenthetical reference indicating the exact location of the material in the source. For instruction on how to format parenthetical references, see pages 388, 401.

Figure 23.4 shows an entry summarized from the passage in Figure 23.2. It captures the original's main ideas in compressed form. Summarized material is not enclosed within quotation marks, but it is documented to acknowledge your debt to the source.

Signal the beginning of the summary by identifying the source and the end by citing the location

> Pinsky explains that electromagnetic waves probably do not directly cause cancer. However, they might contribute to the uncontrollable growth of cancer cells that are normally present—but controlled—in the human body (29–30).

FIGURE 23.4   Record for a summary

Preparing an Abstract

Researchers and readers who must act on information need to identify quickly what is most important in a long document. An abstract is a type of summary that does three things: (1) shows what the document is all about; (2) helps readers decide whether to read all of it, parts of it, or none of it; and (3) gives readers a framework for understanding what follows. (See the sample abstract on page 422.)

Readers expect an abstract to accurately sketch the content, emphasis, and line of reasoning from the original. Although the abstract is written last, it is read first; to do a good job writing an abstract, follow the suggestions below.

GUIDELINES for Preparing an Abstract

- *Pare down the original material.* Omit technical details, examples, explanations, and any background readers won't need. Focus on the major ideas: thesis, topic sentences, findings, conclusions, and recommendations. Even if this draft is too long, include everything essential for this version to stand alone; you can trim later.

- *Edit for conciseness and fluency.* When you have everything readers need, trim the word count. (Review pages 118–123.)
  a. Cross out all needless words, but keep sentences clear and grammatical.
  b. Combine related ideas (see page 124) to emphasize connections.
  c. Add transitional expressions (see page 105) to emphasize connections.
  d. Respect any stipulated word limit.

- *Check your version against the original.* Verify accuracy and completeness.

DOCUMENTATION: THE KEY TO AVOIDING PLAGIARISM

Documentation is the the key to avoiding plagiarism. Proper documentation satisfies professional requirements for ethics, efficiency, and authority.

Why You Should Document

Documentation is a matter of *ethics,* for the originator of borrowed material deserves full credit and recognition. Moreover, all published material is protected by copyright law. Failure to credit a source could make you liable to legal action, even if your omission was unintentional.

Documentation is also a matter of *efficiency.* It provides a network for organizing and locating the world's recorded knowledge. If you cite a particular source correctly, your reference will enable interested readers to locate that source themselves.

Finally, documentation is a matter of *authority.* In making any claim (say, "A Mercedes is more reliable than a Ford") you invite challenge: "Says who?" Data on road tests, frequency of repairs, resale value, workmanship, and owner comments can help validate your claim by showing its basis in *fact.* A claim's credibility increases in relation to the expert references supporting it. For a controversial topic, you may need to cite several authorities who hold various views. Readers of your research report expect the *complete picture.*

What You Should Document

Document any insight, assertion, fact, finding, interpretation, judgment, or other "appropriated material that readers might otherwise mistake for your own" (Gibaldi and Achtert 155)—whether the material appears in published form or not. Specifically, you must document these sources:

Sources that require documentation

- any source from which you use exact wording
- any source from which you adapt material in your own words
- any visual illustration: charts, graphs, drawings, or the like

How to document a confidential source

In some instances, you might have reason to preserve the anonymity of unpublished sources—say, to allow people to respond candidly without fear of reprisal (as with employee criticism of the company) or to protect their privacy (as with certain material from email inquiries or electronic newsgroups). You must still document the fact that you are not the originator of this material. Do this by providing a general acknowledgment in the text ("A number of faculty expressed frustration with…"), along with a general citation in your list of References or Works Cited ("Interviews with campus faculty, May 2008").

Common knowledge need not be documented

As stated earlier, you don't need to document anything considered *common knowledge:* material that appears repeatedly in general sources. For instance, it has become common knowledge that foods containing animal fat (meat, butter, cheese, whole milk) raise blood cholesterol levels. Therefore, in a report on fatty diets and heart disease, you probably would not need to document that well-known fact. But you would document information about how the fat–cholesterol connection was discovered, what subsequent studies have found (say, on the role of saturated versus unsaturated fats), and any information for which some other person could claim specific credit. If the borrowed material can be found in only one specific source, not in multiple sources, document it. When in doubt, document the source.

How You Should Document

Cite borrowed material twice: at the exact place you use that material and at the end of your paper. Documentation practices vary widely, but all systems work almost identically: A brief reference in the text names the source and refers readers to the complete citation, which allows readers to retrieve the source if they wish.

This chapter illustrates citations and entries for two styles that are widely used for documenting sources in college writing:

- Modern Language Association (MLA) style, for the humanities
- American Psychological Association (APA) style, for social sciences

Unless your audience or your instructor has a preference, either style can be adapted to most research writing. Use one style consistently throughout your paper.

MLA DOCUMENTATION STYLE

Cite a source briefly in your text and fully at the end

Most writers in English and other humanities fields follow the *MLA Handbook for Writers of Research Papers, 7th ed.* New York: Modern Language Association, 2009. In MLA style, in-text parenthetical references briefly identify each source. Full documentation then appears in a Works Cited section at the end of the document. The parenthetical reference usually includes the author's surname and the exact page number where the borrowed material can be found:

Parenthetical reference in the text

```
One notable study indicates an elevated risk of leukemia for
children exposed to certain types of electromagnetic fields
(Bowman et al. 59).
```

Readers seeking the complete citation for Bowman can refer easily to the Works Cited section, listed alphabetically by author:

Full citation at document's end

```
Bowman, J. D., et al. "Hypothesis: The Risk of Childhood Leukemia Is
        Related to Combinations of Power-Frequency and Static Magnetic
        Fields." Bioelectromagnetics 16.1 (1995): 48-59. Print.
```

This complete citation includes page numbers for the entire article.

MLA Parenthetical References

For clear and informative parenthetical references, observe these rules:

How to cite briefly in text

- If your discussion names the author, do not repeat the name in your parenthetical reference; simply give the page number(s):

Citing page numbers only

```
Bowman et al. explain how their study indicates an elevated risk of
leukemia for children exposed to certain types of electromagnetic
fields (59).
```

■ If you cite two or more works in a single parenthetical reference, separate the citations with semicolons:

Three works in a single
reference

(Jones 32; Leduc 41; Gomez 293-94)

■ If you cite two or more authors with the same surnames, include the first initial in your parenthetical reference to each author:

Two authors with identical
surnames

(R. Jones 32)

(S. Jones 14-15)

■ If you cite two or more works by the same author, include the first significant word from each work's title, or a shortened version:

Two works by one author

(Lamont, *Biomedicine* 100–01)

(Lamont, *Diagnostic Tests* 81)

■ If the work is by an institutional or corporate author or if it is unsigned (author is unknown), use only the first few words of the institutional name or the work's title in your parenthetical reference:

Institutional, corporate,
or anonymous author

(American Medical Assn. 2)

("Distribution Systems" 18)

Keep parenthetical references brief; when possible, name the source in your discussion and place only the page number(s) in parentheses.

Where to place a
parenthetical reference

For a paraphrase, place the parenthetical reference *before* the closing punctuation mark. For a quotation that runs into the text, place the reference *between* the final quotation mark and the closing punctuation mark. For a quotation set off (indented) from the text, place the reference in the second character space *after* the closing punctuation mark.

MLA Works Cited Entries

How to format the Works
Cited list

The Works Cited list includes each source that you have paraphrased or quoted. Place your Works Cited list on a separate page at the end of the document. Arrange entries alphabetically by authors' surnames. When an author is unknown, list the title alphabetically according to its first word (excluding introductory articles such as *A, An, The*). For a title that begins with a numeral, alphabetize the entry as if the number were spelled out. In preparing the list, type the first line of each entry flush with the left margin. Indent the second and subsequent lines 1/2 inch (five spaces). Double-space within and between entries. Use one character space after all concluding punctuation marks (period, question mark).

How to cite fully at the document's end

Following are examples of complete citations as they would appear in the Works Cited section of your document. Shown below each citation is its corresponding parenthetical reference as it would appear in the text.

INDEX TO SAMPLE MLA WORKS CITED ENTRIES

What to include in an MLA citation for a book

MLA Works Cited Entries for Books.   Any citation for a book should contain the following information: author, title, editor or translator, edition, volume number, and facts about publication (city, publisher, date, type of medium—"Print").

1. Book, Single Author—MLA

Kerzin-Fontana, Jane B. *Technology Management: A Handbook.* 3rd

   ed. Delmar, NY: American Management Assn., 2010. Print.

Parenthetical reference: (Kerzin-Fontana 3-4)

Identify the state of publication by U.S. Postal Service abbreviations. For well-known U.S. cities, omit the state. If several cities are listed on the title page, give only the first. For unfamiliar cities in Canada, include the two-letter abbreviation for the province. For unfamiliar cities in other countries, include an abbreviation of the country name.

2. Book, Two or Three Authors—MLA

Aronson, Linda, Roger Katz, and Candide Moustafa. *Toxic Waste*

Disposal Methods. New Haven: Yale UP, 2009. Print.

Parenthetical reference: (Aronson, Katz, and Moustafa 121-23)

Shorten publisher's names, as in "Simon" for Simon & Schuster, "GPO" for Government Printing Office, or "Yale UP" for Yale University Press. For page numbers with more than two digits, give only the final two digits for the second number when the preceding digits in the first number are identical.

3. Book, Four or More Authors—MLA

Santos, Ruth J., et al. *Environmental Crises in Developing*

Countries. New York: Harper, 2006. Print.

Parenthetical reference: (Santos et al. 9)

The abbreviation "et al." is a shortened version of the Latin "et alia," meaning "and others."

4. Book, Anonymous Author—MLA

Structured Programming. Boston: Meredith, 2010. Print.

Parenthetical reference: (Structured 67)

5. Multiple Books, Same Author—MLA

Chang, John W. *Biophysics.* Boston: Little, 2010. Print.

---. *Diagnostic Techniques.* New York: Radon, 1997. Print.

Parenthetical references: (Chang, Biophysics 123-26), (Chang,

Diagnostic 87)

When citing more than one work by the same author, do not repeat the author's name; simply type three hyphens followed by a period. List the works alphabetically.

6. Book, One or More Editors—MLA

Morris, A. J., and Louise B. Pardin-Walker, eds. *Handbook of New*

Information Technology. New York: Harper, 2010. Print.

Parenthetical reference: (Morris and Pardin-Walker 34)

For more than three editors, name only the first, followed by "et al."

7. Book, Indirect Source—MLA

Kline, Thomas. *Automated Systems*. Boston: Rhodes, 2007. Print.

Stubbs, John. *White-Collar Productivity*. Miami: Harris, 2010.

   Print.

Parenthetical reference: (qtd. in Stubbs 116)

When your source (as in Stubbs, above) has quoted or cited another source, list each source in its alphabetical place on your Works Cited page. Use the name of the original source (here, Kline) in your text and precede your parenthetical reference with "qtd. in," or "cited in" for a paraphrase.

8. Anthology Selection or Book Chapter—MLA

Bowman, Joel P. "Electronic Conferencing." *Communication and*

   Technology: Today and Tomorrow. Ed. Al Williams. Denton,

   TX: Assn. for Business Communication, 1994, 123-42. Print.

Parenthetical reference: (Bowman 129)

The page numbers are for the selection cited from the anthology.

What to include in an MLA
citation for a periodical

MLA Works Cited Entries for Periodicals.   Give all available information in this order: author, article title, periodical title, volume or number (or both), date (day, month, year), and page numbers for the entire article—not just pages cited—along with medium: "Print."

9. Article, Magazine—MLA

DesMarteau, Kathleen. "Study Links Sewing Machine Use to

   Alzheimer's Disease." *Bobbin* Oct. 1994: 36-38. Print.

Parenthetical reference: (DesMarteau 36)

No punctuation separates the magazine title and date.
   If no author is given, list all other information:

"Distribution Systems for the New Decade." *Power Technology*

   Magazine 16 Oct. 2007: 18+. Print.

Parenthetical reference: ("Distribution Systems" 18)

This article begins on page 18 and continues on page 21. When an article does not appear on consecutive pages, give only the number of the first page, followed immediately by a plus sign. Use a three-letter abbreviation for any month spelled with five or more letters.

10. Article, Journal with New Pagination for Each Issue—MLA

Thackman-White, Joan R. "Computer-Assisted Research." *American*

Librarian 51.1 (2010): 3-9. Print.

Parenthetical reference: (Thackman-White 4-5)

Because each issue for a given year will have page numbers beginning with "1," readers need the number of this issue. The "51" denotes the volume number; "1" denotes the issue number. Omit "The," "A," or "An" if it is the first word in a journal or magazine title.

11. Article, Journal with Continuous Pagination—MLA

Barnstead, Marion H. "The Writing Crisis." *Journal of Writing*

Theory 12.1 (2008): 415-33. Print.

Parenthetical reference: (Barnstead 415-16)

The "12" denotes the volume number; "1" denotes the issue number.

How to cite an abstract   If, instead of the complete work, you are citing merely an abstract found in a bound collection of abstracts and not the full article, include the information on the abstracting service right after the information on the original article.

Barnstead, Marion H. "The Writing Crisis." *Journal of Writing*

Theory 12 (2008): 415-33. *Rhetoric Abstracts* 67 (2009):

item 1354. Print.

If citing an abstract that appears with the printed article, add "Abstract," followed by a period, immediately after the original work's page number(s).

12. Article, Newspaper—MLA

Baranski, Vida H. "Errors in Technology Assessment." *Boston*

Times 15 Jan. 2010, evening ed., sec. 2: 3. Print.

Parenthetical reference: (Baranski 3)

When a daily newspaper has more than one edition, cite the edition after the date. Omit any introductory article in the newspaper's name (not *The Boston Times*). If no author is given, list all other information. If the newspaper's name does not include the city of publication, insert it, using brackets: *Sippican Sentinel* [Marion, MA].

What to include in an MLA citation for a miscellaneous source   ***MLA Works Cited Entries for Other Kinds of Materials.*** Miscellaneous sources range from unsigned encyclopedia entries to conference presentations to government publications. Give this information (as available): author, title, city, publisher, date, page numbers, and medium of publication (print, CD, Web site, etc.).

13. Encyclopedia, Dictionary, Other Alphabetical Reference—MLA

"Communication." *The Business Reference Book 2010.* Print.

Parenthetical reference: ("Communication")

Begin a signed entry with the author's name. For any work arranged alphabetically, omit page numbers in the citation and the parenthetical reference. For a well-known reference book, include only an edition (if stated) and a date. For other reference books, give the full publication information.

14. Report—MLA

Electrical Power Research Institute (EPRI). *Epidemiologic*

Studies of Electric Utility Employees. (Report No.

RP2964.5). Palo Alto, CA: EPRI, Nov. 1994. Print.

Parenthetical reference: (Electrical Power Research Institute [EPRI] 27)

If no author is given, begin with the organization that sponsored the report.

For any report or other document with group authorship, as above, include the group's abbreviated name (along with its full name) in your first parenthetical reference, and then use only that abbreviation in any subsequent reference.

15. Conference Presentation—MLA

Smith, Abelard A. "Radon Concentrations in Molded Concrete."

First British Symposium in Environmental Engineering.

London, 11-13 Oct. 2009. Ed. Anne Hodkins. London:

Harrison, 2010. 106-21. Print.

Parenthetical reference: (Smith 109)

This citation is for a presentation that has been included in the published proceedings of a conference. For an unpublished presentation, include the presenter's name, the title of the presentation, the conference title, and date, but do not italicize the conference information.

16. Interview, Personally Conducted—MLA

Nasser, Gamel. Chief Engineer for Northern Electric. Personal

interview. 2 Apr. 2010.

Parenthetical reference: (Nasser)

17. Interview, Published—MLA

Lescault, James. "The Future of Graphics." *Executive Views of*
   Automation. Ed. Karen Prell. Miami: Haber, 2010. 216-31.
   Print.

Parenthetical reference: (Lescault 218)

The interviewee's name is placed in the entry's author slot.

18. Letter or Memo, Unpublished—MLA

Rogers, Leonard. Letter to the author. 15 May 2010. Print.

Parenthetical reference: (Rogers)

19. Questionnaire—MLA

Taylor, Lynne. Questionnaire sent to 612 Massachusetts business
   executives. 14 Feb. 2010. Print.

Parenthetical reference: (Taylor)

20. Brochure or Pamphlet—MLA

Investment Strategies for the 21st Century. San Francisco:
   Blount Economics Assn., 2010. Print.

Parenthetical reference: (Investment)

If the work is signed, begin with its author.

21. Lecture, Speech, Address, or Reading—MLA

Dumont, R. A. "Managing Natural Gas." UMASS Dartmouth, 15 Jan.
   2010. Lecture.

Parenthetical reference: (Dumont)

If the lecture title is not known, write Address, Lecture, or Reading—without
quotation marks. Include the sponsor and the location if available.

22. Government Document—MLA

Virginia Highway Dept. *Standards for Bridge Maintenance.*
   Richmond: Virginia Highway Dept., 2010. Print.

Parenthetical reference: (Virginia Highway Dept. 49)

If the author is unknown (as here), list the information in this order: name
of the government organization, name of the issuing agency, document title,
place, publisher, date, and medium.

For any congressional document, identify the house of Congress (Senate or House of Representatives) before the title, and the number and session of Congress after the title:

```
United States Cong. House, Armed Services Committee. Funding for
     the Military Academies. 108th Cong., 2nd sess. Washington:
     GPO, 2010. Print.
```

Parenthetical reference: (U.S. Cong. 41)

GPO is the abbreviation for the U.S. Government Printing Office.

For an entry from the *Congressional Record,* give only date and pages:

```
Cong. Rec. 10 Mar. 2004: 2178-92. Print.
```

Parenthetical reference: (Cong. Rec. 2184)

23. Document with Corporate or Foundation Authorship—MLA

```
Hermitage Foundation. Global Warming Scenarios for the Year
     2030. Washington: Natl. Res. Council, 2005. Print.
```

Parenthetical reference: (Hermitage Foun. 123)

24. Map or Other Visual—MLA

```
"Deaths Caused by Breast Cancer, by County." Map. Scientific
     American Oct. 1995: 32D. Print.
```

Parenthetical reference: ("Deaths Caused")

If the creator of the visual is listed, give that name first. Identify the type of visual (Map, Graph, Table, Diagram) immediately following its title.

25. Unpublished Dissertation, Report, or Miscellaneous Items—MLA

```
Author (if known). "Title." Sponsoring organization or publisher,
     date. Medium of publication.
```

For any work that has group authorship (corporation, committee, task force), cite the name of the group or agency in place of the author's name.

What to include in an MLA citation for an electronic source

MLA Works Cited Entries for Electronic Sources. Electronic sources include Internet sites, reference databases, CD-ROMs, computer software, email, and blogs. Any citation for an electronic source should allow readers to identify the original source (printed or electronic) and trace a clear path for retrieving the material. Provide all available information in the following order:

1. Name of author, editor, or producer of the work or site. If no author is given, begin with item 2. For works with multiple or anonymous authors, follow the guidelines for print sources.

2. Title of the work. For online postings such as email discussion lists, give the title of the posting. Italicize the title unless it is part of a larger work; in that case, enclose the title in quotation marks and italicize the larger work's title.
3. Title of the Web site (in italics) if this differs from item 2.
4. Version or edition of the site, if relevant.
5. Publisher or sponsor of the site (often listed at the bottom of the Web page). If this information is not given, use *n.p.* (for *no publisher*).
6. Publication date (day, month, and year, if available). If no date is given, use *n.d.*
7. Medium of publication that you accessed. For all online sources, this would be *Web.*
8. Date you accessed the source (day, month, and year).

> Kent, Maureen. "The Glass Ceiling." *Businessmonthlyonline.com.*
>
> n.d. Web. 4 Oct. 2010.

If the work you have accessed electronically exists in a print or other version, you can include the publication information for that medium if you decide readers would find it useful. Begin with (1) the citation format for the other medium, followed by (2) the title of the database or Web site (in italics) from which you retrieved the content, (3) the medium of publication (Web), and (4) your access date (day, month, and year).

> Cayer, Kevin. "The Silent Depression." *Cashflow Magazine.*
>
> *Moneyline,* 1 June 2009. Web. 5 April. 2010.

Only include URLs in works-cited entries if your reader will have difficulty locating the source without the URL. This would be the citations's final item, enclosed in angle brackets (< >) and followed by a period. (When in doubt, include the URL.) When a URL continues from one line to the next, break it only after a slash or a period; do not insert a hyphen.

> "Filing Your Taxes Online." *IRS.gov.* Internal Revenue Service.
>
> June 2009. Web. Oct. 2010 <www.irs/gov/factsheets/
>
> online-filing.htm>.

Start the URL with www. and not http:// (unless the URL actually starts with http, as in http://ezinearticles.com).

26. Online Abstract—MLA

> Lane, Amanda D., et al. "The Promise of Microcircuits." *Journal*
>
> *of Nanotechnology* 12.2 (2009): n.pag. Abstract. Web. 11 May
>
> 2010.

> ***Parenthetical reference:*** (Lane et al.)

The *n. pag.* designates no page numbers.

27. Print Article Posted Online—MLA

```
Jeffers, Anna D. "NAFTA's Effects on the U.S. Trade Deficit."

     Sultana Business Quarterly 3.4 (2004): 65-74. Web.

     5 Apr. 2010.
```

Parenthetical reference: (Jeffers 66)

28. Online Scholarly Journal

For scholarly journal articles available only online (no print equivalent), use the citation format for an article from a print journal. Use *Web* as the publication medium, followed by date of access. If page numbers are not available, use *n. pag.*

```
Andres, Richard. "Public Accounting and the Legal Process."

     Public Policy 3.3 (2010): n. pag. Web. 28 May 2010.
```

Parenthetical reference: (Andres)

29. Online Newspaper Article

```
Rhode, Abbey. "Episodes of Oil Spills in the U.S. Mark a New Era

     in Accountability." Star Tribune 30 March 2009. n. pag.

     Web. 5 May 2010.
```

Parenthetical reference: (Rhode)

30. Reference Database—MLA

```
Sahl, J. D. "Power Lines, Viruses, and Childhood Leukemia."

     Cancer Causes Control 6.1 (Jan. 1995): 83-85. MEDLINE.

     Web. 7 Nov. 2010.
```

Parenthetical reference: (Sahl 83)

For entries with a print equivalent, begin with print publication information, then database title (italicized, as in *MEDLINE*, above), *Web* designation to indicate the medium, service provider, and date of access. Access date is important because frequent updatings of databases can produce different versions of the material.

For entries with no print equivalent, give the title and date of the work in quotation marks, followed by the electronic source information:

```
Argent, Roger R. "An Analysis of International Exchange Rates

     for 2009." Accu-Data. Dow Jones News Retrieval. Web. 10

     Jan. 2010.
```

Parenthetical reference: (Argent)

If the author is not known, begin with the work's title. If the Web document has page numbers, include them in your entry and in your parenthetical reference.

31. Computer Software—MLA

Virtual Collaboration. Software. New York: Pearson, 2010.

Parenthetical reference: (Virtual)

Begin with the author's name, if known.

32. CD-ROM—MLA

Canalte, Henry A. "Violent Crime Statistics: Good News and Bad
News." *Law Enforcement* Feb. 1995: 8. *ABI/INFORM.* CD-ROM.
ProQuest. Sept. 2010.

Parenthetical reference: (Canalte 8)

If the material is also available in print, begin with the information about the printed source, followed by the electronic source information: name of database (italicized), *CD-ROM* designation, vendor name, and electronic publication date. If the material has no print equivalent, list its author (if known) and its title (in quotation marks), followed by the electronic source information.

For CD-ROM reference works and other material that is not routinely updated, give the work title followed by the place, electronic publisher, date, and *CD-ROM* designation:

Time Almanac. Washington: Compact, 2008. CD-ROM.

Parenthetical reference: (Time Almanac 74)

Begin with the author's name, if known.

33. Email Discussion Group—MLA

Kosten, A. "Major Update of the WWWVL Migration and Ethnic
Relations." 7 Apr. 1998. *ERCOMER News.* E-mail.

Parenthetical reference: (Kosten)

Begin with the author's name (if known), followed by the title of the message (in quotation marks), date of message, title of discussion group (italicized), and medium. Do not include the date of your access.

34. Personal Email—MLA

Wallin, John Luther. "Frog Reveries." Message to the author.
12 Oct. 2009. E-mail.

Parenthetical reference: (Wallin)

Cite personal email as you would printed correspondence. If the document has a subject line or title, enclose it in quotation marks. For publicly posted email (say, a newsgroup or discussion list), include the address and the date of access.

Wikis, blogs, and podcasts, if needed as source material, should also be cited. Begin with the name of the communicator and topic title (in quotation marks), followed by the posting date, name of forum blog, wiki, or podcast (in italics), medium, and access date.

35. Wiki

"Printing Press." *Wikipedia.* Wikimedia Foundation, 2010. Web.

    1 June 2010.

Parenthetical reference: ("Printing")

36. Blog

Hecht, Jeff. "How Galveston Weathered the Storm." *New Scientist*

    Environment Blog. 15 Sept. 2008. Web. 22 Oct. 2010

    <www.newscientist/blog/environment>.

Parenthetical reference: (Hecht)

37. Podcast

"Countdown to Mars Touchdown." *NASA Solar System Audio Podcasts.*

    NASA, 16 May 2008. Web. 19 May 2010.

Parenthetical reference: ("Countdown")

38. General Reference to a Web Site—MLA

In referring to an entire site instead of a specific item, include the following information, as available:

Name of author, editor, or compiler; title of the site (in

    italics); site sponsor; date of publication or latest

    update; medium (Web); and your date of access.

MLA Sample Works Cited Pages

On a separate page at the document's end, arrange entries alphabetically by author's surname. When the author is unknown, list the title alphabetically according to its first word (excluding introductory articles). For a title that begins with a digit ("5," "6," etc.), alphabetize the entry as if the digit were spelled out.

On pages 447–449, you will find a list of works cited in the research report by Shirley Haley.

APA DOCUMENTATION STYLE

Another common citation style is one published in the *Publication Manual of the American Psychological Association,* 6th ed., Washington: American Psychological Association, 2009. Called "APA" for short, this method emphasizes the date. APA style (or some similar author-date style) is preferred in the sciences and social sciences, where information quickly becomes outdated. A parenthetical reference in the text briefly identifies the source, date, and page number(s):

Reference cited in the text

> In one study, mice continuously exposed to an electromagnetic
> field tended to die earlier than mice in the control group (de
> Jager & de Bruyn, 1994, p. 224).

The full citation then appears in the alphabetical listing of "References," at the report's end:

Full citation at document's end

> de Jager, L., & de Bruyn, L. (1994). Long-term effects of a 50
> Hz electric field on the life-expectancy of mice. *Review of*
> *Environmental Health, 10*(3-4), 221-224.

APA Parenthetical References

How APA and MLA parenthetical references differ

APA's parenthetical references differ from MLA's (pages 388–389) as follows: The APA citation includes the publication date. A comma separates each item in the reference; and "p." or "pp." precedes the page number. When a subsequent reference to a work follows closely after the initial reference, the date need not be included. Here are specific guidelines:

- If your discussion names the author, do not repeat the name in your parenthetical reference; simply give the date and page numbers:

Author named in the text

> Researchers de Jager and de Bruyn explain that experimental mice
> exposed to an electromagnetic field tended to die earlier than
> mice in the control group (1994, p. 224).

When two authors of a work are named in the text, their names are connected by "and," but in a parenthetical reference, their names are connected by an ampersand, "&."

- If you cite two or more works in a single reference, list the authors in alphabetical order and separate the citations with semicolons:

Two or more works in a single reference

(Gomez, 2005; Jones, 2007; Leduc, 2002)

- If you cite a work with three to five authors, try to name them in your text, to avoid an excessively long parenthetical reference.

A work with three to five authors

> Franks, Oblesky, Ryan, Jablar, and Perkins (2008) studied the role of electromagnetic fields in tumor formation.

In any subsequent references to this work, name only the first author, followed by "et al." (Latin abbreviation for "and others").

- If you cite two or more works by the same author published in the same year, assign a different letter to each work:

Two or more works by the same author in the same year

> (Lamont, 2009a, p. 135)
>
> (Lamont, 2009b, pp. 67–68)

Other examples of parenthetical references appear with their corresponding entries in the following discussion of the reference list entries.

INDEX TO SAMPLE ENTRIES FOR APA REFERENCES

APA Reference List Entries

How to space and indent entries

The APA reference list includes each source you have cited in your document. Type the first line of each entry flush with the left margin. Indent the second and subsequent lines five character spaces (one-half inch). Skip one character space after any period, comma, or colon. Double-space within and between each entry.

Following are examples of complete citations as they would appear in the References section of your document. Shown immediately below each entry is its corresponding parenthetical reference as it would appear in the text. Note the capitalization, abbreviation, spacing, and punctuation in the sample entries.

What to include in an
APA citation for a book

APA Entries for Books.   Book citations should contain all applicable information in the following order: author, date, title, editor or translator, edition, volume number, and facts about publication (city, state, and publisher).

1. Book, Single Author—APA

Kerzin-Fontana, J. B. (2010). *Technology management: A handbook*

(3rd ed.). Delmar, NY: American Management Association.

Parenthetical reference: (Kerzin-Fontana, 2010, pp. 3-4)

Use only initials for an author's first and middle name. Capitalize only the first word of a book's title and subtitle and any proper names. Identify a later edition in parentheses between the title and the period.

2. Book, Two to Seven Authors—APA

Aronson, L., Katz, R., & Moustafa, C. (2009). *Toxic waste dis-*

posal methods. New Haven, CT. Yale University Press.

Parenthetical reference: (Aronson, Katz, & Moustafa, 2009)

Use an ampersand (&) before the name of the final author listed in an entry. As an alternative to parenthetical reference, name the authors in your text and include date (and page numbers, if appropriate) in parentheses.

Give the publisher's full name (as in "Yale University Press") but omit the words "Publisher," "Company," and "Inc."

3. Book, Eight or More Authors—APA

Fogle, S. T., Gates, R., Hanes, P., Johns, B., Nin, K., Sarkis,

P.... Yale, B. (2009). *Hyperspace technology.* Boston, MA:

Little, Brown.

Parenthetical reference: (Fogle et al., 2009, p. 34)

List the first six authors' names, insert an ellipsis, then add the last author's name. The Latin abbreviation "et al." stands for "et alia," meaning "and others."

4. Book, Anonymous Author—APA

Structured programming. (2010). Boston, MA: Meredith Press.

Parenthetical reference: (Structured Programming, 2010, p. 67)

In your list of references, place an anonymous work alphabetically by the first key word (not *The, A,* or *An*) in its title. In your parenthetical reference, capitalize all key words in a book, article, or journal title.

5. Multiple Books, Same Author—APA

Chang, J. W. (2010a). *Biophysics.* Boston, MA: Little, Brown.

Chang, J. W. (2010b). *MindQuest.* Chicago, IL: John Pressler.

Parenthetical references: (Chang, 2010a) (Chang, 2010b)

Two or more works by the same author not published in the same year are distinguished by their respective dates alone, without the added letter.

6. Book, One to Five Editors—APA

Morris, A. J., & Pardin-Walker, L. B. (Eds.). (2010). *Handbook of new information technology.* New York, NY: HarperCollins.

Parenthetical reference: (Morris & Pardin-Walker, 2010, p. 79)

For more than five editors, name only the first, followed by "et al."

7. Book, Indirect Source—APA

Stubbs, J. (2010). *White-collar productivity.* Miami, FL: Harris.

Parenthetical reference: (cited in Stubbs, 2010, p. 47)

When your source (as in Stubbs, above) has cited another source, list only your source in the References section, but name the original source in the text: "Kline's study (cited in Stubbs, 2010, p. 47) supports this conclusion."

8. Anthology Selection or Book Chapter—APA

Bowman, J. (1994). Electronic conferencing. In A. Williams (Ed.), *Communication and technology: Today and tomorrow* (pp. 123-142). Denton, TX: Association for Business Communication.

Parenthetical reference: (Bowman, 1994, p. 126)

The page numbers in the complete reference are for the selection cited from the anthology.

What to include in
an APA citation for a
periodical

APA Entries for Periodicals. Give this information (as available), in order:
author, publication date, article title (no quotation marks), periodical title,
volume or number (or both), and page numbers for the entire article—not
just page(s) cited.

9. Article, Magazine—APA

DesMarteau, K. (1994, October). Study links sewing machine use

to Alzheimer's disease. *Bobbin, 36*, 36-38.

Parenthetical reference: (DesMarteau, 1994, p. 36)

If no author is given, provide all other information. Capitalize the first word
in an article's title and subtitle, and any proper nouns. Capitalize all key
words in a periodical title. Italicize the periodical title, volume number, and
commas (as shown above).

10. Article, Journal with New Pagination for Each Issue—APA

Thackman-White, J. R. (2010). Computer-assisted research.

American Library Journal, 51(1), 3-9.

Parenthetical reference: (Thackman-White, 2010, pp. 4-5)

Because each issue for a given year has page numbers that begin at "1," readers need the issue number (in this instance, "1"). The "51" denotes the volume number, which is italicized.

11. Article, Journal with Continuous Pagination—APA

Barnstead, M. H. (2008). The writing crisis. *Journal of Writing*

Theory, 12, 415-433.

Parenthetical reference: (Barnstead, 2008, pp. 415-416)

The "12" denotes the volume number. When page numbers continue from
issue to issue for the full year, readers won't need the issue number. (You can
include the issue number if you think it will help readers retrieve the article
more easily.)

12. Article, Newspaper—APA

Baranski, V. H. (2010, January 15). Errors in technology assess-

ment. *The Boston Times*, p. B3.

Parenthetical reference: (Baranski, 2010, p. B3)

In addition to year of publication, include month and day. If the newspaper's
name begins with "The," include it. Include "p." or "pp." before page numbers.
For an article on nonconsecutive pages, list each page, separated by a comma.

What to include in
an APA citation for a
miscellaneous source

APA Entries for Other Sources.   Miscellaneous sources range from unsigned encyclopedia entries to conference presentations to government documents. Give this information (as available): author, publication date, work title (and report or series number), page numbers (if applicable), city, and publisher.

13. Encyclopedia, Dictionary, Alphabetical Reference—APA

```
Communication. (2010). In The business reference book. Boston,
     MA: Business Resources Press.
```

Parenthetical reference: ("Communication," 2010)

For an entry that is signed, begin with the author's name and publication date.

14. Report—APA

```
Electrical Power Research Institute. (1994). Epidemiologic stud-
     ies of electric utility employees (Report No. RP2964.5).
     Palo Alto, CA: Author.
```

Parenthetical reference: (Electrical Power Research Institute [EPRI], 1994, p. 12)

If authors are named, list them first, followed by publication date. When citing a group author, as above, include the group's abbreviated name in your first parenthetical reference, and use only that abbreviation in subsequent references. When the organization and publisher are the same, list "Author" in the publisher's slot.

15. Conference Presentation—APA

```
Smith, A. A. (2009, March). Radon concentrations in molded
     concrete. In A. Hodkins (Ed.), First British Symposium
     on Environmental Engineering (pp. 106-121). London, UK:
     Harrison Press, 2010.
```

Parenthetical reference: (Smith, 2009, p. 109)

In parentheses is the date of the presentation. The symposium's name is proper and so is capitalized. Following the publisher's name is the date of publication.

For an unpublished presentation, include the presenter's name, year and month, presentation title (italicized), and all available information about the conference: "Symposium held at…." Do not italicize this last information.

16. Interview, Personally Conducted—APA

Parenthetical reference: (G. Nasser, personal interview, April 2, 2010)

This material is considered a nonrecoverable source, and so is cited in the text only, as a parenthetical reference. If you name the respondent in text, do not repeat the name in the citation.

17. Interview, Published—APA

Jable, C. K. (2009). The future of graphics [Interview with
James Lescault]. In K. Prell (Ed.), *Executive views of
automation* (pp. 216-231). Miami, FL: Haber Press, 2010.

Parenthetical reference: (Jable, 2009, pp. 218-223)

Begin with the interviewer's name, followed by interview date and title (if available), the designation "Interview" (in brackets), and publication information, including the date.

18. Personal Correspondence—APA

Parenthetical reference: (L. Rogers, personal correspondence,
May 15, 2010)

This material is considered nonrecoverable data, and so is cited in the text only, as a parenthetical reference. If you name the correspondent in your discussion, do not repeat the name in the citation.

19. Brochure or Pamphlet—APA

This material follows the citation format for a book entry (pages 403–404). After the title of the work, include the designation "Brochure" in brackets.

20. Lecture—APA

Dumont, R. A. (2010, January 15). *Managing natural gas.* Lecture
presented at the University of Massachusetts at Dartmouth.

Parenthetical reference: (Dumont, 2010)

If you name the lecturer in your discussion, do not repeat the name in the citation.

21. Government Document—APA

Virginia Highway Department. (2010). *Standards for bridge maintenance.* Richmond, VA: Author.

Parenthetical reference: (Virginia Highway Department, 2010, p. 49)

If the author is unknown, present the information in this order: name of the issuing agency, publication date, document title, place, and publisher. When the issuing agency is both author and publisher, list "Author" in the publisher's slot.

For any congressional document, identify the house of Congress (Senate or House of Representatives) before the date.

U.S. House Armed Services Committee. (2010). *Funding for the
military academies.* Washington, DC: U.S. Government
Printing Office.

Parenthetical reference: (U.S. House, 2010, p. 41)

22. Miscellaneous Items (Unpublished Manuscripts, Dissertations, and so on)—APA

```
Author (if known). (Date of publication.) Title of work.
        Sponsoring organization or publisher.
```

For any work that has group authorship (corporation, committee, and so on), cite the name of the group or agency in place of the author's name.

What to include in an APA citation for an electronic source

APA Entries for Electronic Sources. In 2009, the APA published the *Publication Manual of the American Psychological Association*, 6th edition. This manual provides instructions for citation of print and electronic sources. For electronic sources in particular, the APA notes that "in general... include the same elements, in the same order, as you would for a reference to a fixed-media source and add as much electronic retrieval information as needed for others to locate the sources you cited" (187). Including the Web address (URL) is still recommended. However, one new feature is the use of *digital object identifiers* (DOIs). These are unique identifiers designed to last longer than URLs, which often disappear or get changed when Web pages are moved or renamed.

Identify the original source (printed or electronic) and give readers a path for retrieving the material. Provide all available information in the following order.

1. Author, editor, creator, or sponsoring organization.
2. Date the item was published or was created electronically. For magazines and newspapers, include the month and day as well as the year. If the date of an electronic publication is not available, use "n.d." in place of the date.
3. Publication information of the original printed version (as in previous entries), if such a version exists. Follow this by designating the electronic medium [CD-ROM] or the type of work [Abstract], [Brochure]—unless this designation is named in the work's title (as in "Inpatient brochure").
4. Database names. Do not list database names (unless the database is obscure or the material hard to find), but do include the URL (or DOI, discussed below).
5. URLs and DOIs. Provide the full electronic address. For Internet sources, only provide the URL if the source would be impossible to locate without it. APA recommends only using home page URLs. For CD-ROM and database sources, give the document's retrieval number (see entry 23, below). Start the URL with http://, but do not underline, italicize, use angle brackets, or add a period at the end of a URL. When a URL continues from one line to the next, break it before most punctuation (except for http://, which should not be broken).

The APA now recommends using the DOI (digital object identifier), when available, in place of a URL in references to electronic texts. DOI numbers are found on some recent scholarly journals, especially in the sciences and social sciences. Here is a sample reference for a journal article with a DOI assigned:

Schmidt, D., et al. (2009). Advances in psychotropic medica-

tion. *Boston Journal of Psychotherapy, 81*(3), 398-413. doi:

10.1037/0555-9467.79.3.483

Parenthetical reference: (Schmidt, 2009)

23. Online Abstract—APA

Stevens, R. L. (2010). Cell phones and cancer rates. *Oncology*

Journal, 57(2), 41-43. [Abstract]. Retrieved from http://

nim.mh.gov/medlineplus. (MEDLINE Item: AY 24598).

Parenthetical reference: (Stevens, 2010)

Ordinarily an APA entry ends with a period. Entries with a DOI, however, omit the period at the end of the electronic address. If you are citing the entire article retrieved from a full-text database, delete [Abstract] from the citation.

24. Print Article Posted Online—APA

Alley, R. A. (2009, January). Ergonomic influences on worker

satisfaction. *Industrial Psychology, 5(12)*, 672-678.

Retrieved from http://www.psycharchives

Parenthetical reference: (Alley, 2009)

If you were confident that the document's electronic and print versions were identical, you could omit the URL and insert "[Electronic version]" between the end of the article title and the period.

25. Book or Article Available Only Online (no DOI)—APA

Kelly, W. (2009). *Early graveyards of New England.* Retrieved

from http://www.onlinebooks.com

Parenthetical reference: (Kelly, 2009)

This source exists only in electronic format.

26. Journal Article with DOI

Tijen, D. (2009). Recent developments in understanding salinity

tolerance. *Environmental & Experimental Botany. 67*(1), 2-9.

doi:10.1016/j.envexpbot.2009.05.008

Parenthetical reference: (Tijen, 2009)

27. Online Encyclopedia, Dictionary, or Handbook—APA

Ecoterrorism. (2009). *Ecological encyclopedia.* Washington, DC:

    Redwood. Retrieved May 1, 2010, from http://www.eco

    .floridastate.edu

Parenthetical reference: ("Ecoterrorism," 2009)

Include the retrieval date for works that are routinely updated. If a work on CD-ROM has a print equivalent, cite it in its printed form.

28. Personal Email—APA

Parenthetical reference: Fred Flynn (personal communication, May 10,

    2009) provided these statistics.

Instead of being included in the list of references, personal email (considered a nonretrievable source) is cited fully in the text.

29. Blog Posting—APA

Owens, P. (2010, June 1). How to stabilize a large travel trailer

    [Web log comment]. Retrieved from http://rvblogs.com

Parenthetical reference: (Owens, 2010)

30. Newsgroup, Discussion List, or Online Forum—APA

LaBarge, V. S. (2009, October 20). A cure for computer viruses

    [Online forum comment]. Retrieved from http://www.srb/forums

Parenthetical reference: (LaBarge, 2009)

Although email should not be included in the list of references, postings from blogs, newsgroups, and online forums, considered more retrievable, should be included.

31. Wiki—APA

Skull-base tumors. (n.d.). Retrieved June 10, 2009, from the

    Oncology Wiki: http://oncology.wikia.com

Parenthetical reference: ("Skull-Base," n.d.)

Notice the "n.d." ("no date") designation for this collaborative Web page that can be written or edited by anyone with access.

What to include in an APA citation for gray literature

APA Entries for Gray Literature. Gray literature is material that is not peer reviewed but, according to the APA, can play an important role in research and publication. Examples of gray literature include annual reports, fact sheets, consumer brochures, press releases, and technical reports (each type is so named in the title, in brackets, or elsewhere in the citation). In the sample citation in entry 32, the type of item is identified in brackets; in entry 33, it is part of the titling information.

32. Press Release—APA

American Natural Foods Association. (2009, January 20). *Newest food additive poses special threat to children, according to the upcoming issue* of Eating for Health [Press release]. Retrieved from American Natural Foods Association Website: http://www.anfha.org

Parenthetical reference: (American Natural Foods Association, 2009)

33. Technical or Research Report—APA

Gunderson, H., et al. (2007). *Declining birthrates in rural areas: Results from the 2005 National Census Bureau Survey* (Report No. 7864 NCB 2005-171). Retrieved from the National Center for Population Statistics: http://ncps.gov

Parenthetical reference: (Gunderson, 2007)

Notice that the report number, if available, is given after the title.

APA Sample List of References

APA's References section (pages 430–431) is an alphabetical listing (by author) equivalent to MLA's Works Cited section. Like Works Cited, the reference list includes only those works actually cited. (A bibliography usually would include background works or works consulted as well.) Unlike MLA style, APA style calls for only "recoverable" sources to appear in the reference list. Therefore, personal interviews, email messages, and other unpublished materials are cited in the text only.

RESPECTING COPYRIGHT

Definition of copyright

A *copyright* is the exclusive legal right to reproduce, publish, and sell a literary, dramatic, musical, or artistic work. Written permission must be obtained to use all copyrighted material. Protection begins as soon as a work is created, whether or not it is published. The purpose of copyright laws is to balance the reward for intellectual labors with the public's right to use information freely.

How copyright infringement differs from plagiarism

Although the two issues are often confused, plagiarism and copyright infringement are not the same. You can plagiarize someone's work without actually infringing on the copyright. Plagiarism (representing the words, ideas, or perspectives of someone else as your own) is primarily an ethical issue, whereas copyright infringement is a legal and economic issue.

The limits of copyright protection

Copyright protection covers the exact wording of the original but not the ideas or information it conveys. For example, Einstein's theory of relativity has no copyright protection, but the exact wording does (Abelman 33; Elias 3). Paraphrasing Einstein's ideas but failing to cite him as the source of those ideas would constitute plagiarism.

The Doctrine of Fair Use

Fair use is limited use of copyrighted material without permission as allowed by law. The source should, of course, be acknowledged. Fair use does not ordinarily apply to case studies, charts and graphs, author's notes, or private letters. In determining whether the use of copyrighted material is fair, the courts view nonprofit educational use more favorably than for-profit use. Use of published work is viewed more favorably than use of unpublished essays, correspondence, or the like. The smaller the part of the original, the more favorably its use will be viewed. Never considered fair, however, is the use of a part that "forms the core, distinguishable, creative effort of the work being cited" ("Copyright Protection" 30). Any use that reduces the potential market value of the original is viewed unfavorably.

Fair use of material in the public domain

Public domain refers to material not protected by copyright or material on which copyright has expired. Works published in the United States ninety-five years before the current year are in the public domain. Most government publications and commonplace information, such as height and weight charts or a metric conversion table, are in the public domain. These works might contain copyrighted material (used with permission and properly acknowledged). If you are not sure whether something is in the public domain, request permission ("Copyright Protection" 31).

Using Material in Electronic Form

Fair use of material in electronic form

The question of how fair-use restrictions apply to material used in multimedia presentations or to text or images that have been altered or reshaped to suit the user's specific needs is a tricky one. Information obtained via email or discussion groups presents additional problems (Howard 40): Sources often do not wish to be quoted or named or to have early drafts made public. How do we protect source confidentiality? How do we avoid infringing on works in progress that have not yet been published? How do we quote and cite this material without violating ownership and privacy rights?

Present status of electronic copyright law

The answer is that most works are considered copyrighted as soon as they are produced in *any* tangible form, even if they carry no copyright notice. Fair use of electronic information is generally limited to brief excerpts that serve as a basis for response—for example, in a discussion group. Except for certain government documents, no Internet posting is in the public domain unless expressly designated by its author (Templeton).

Until specific laws are enacted, the following uses of copyrighted material in electronic form can be considered copyright violations (Communication Concepts 13; Elias 85, 86; Templeton):

- Downloading a work from the Internet and forwarding copies to other readers.
- Editing, altering, or incorporating an original work as part of your own document or multimedia presentation.
- Placing someone else's printed work online without the author's written permission.
- Reproducing and distributing original software or material from a privately owned database.
- Copying and forwarding an email message without the sender's authorization. The exact wording of an email message is copyrighted, but except for "proprietary information" in the business world, its content may legally be revealed.

When in doubt, assume that work is copyrighted, and obtain written permission from the owner.

DIGITAL TIP

Take Notes and Keep Track of Sources on Your Computer

Note-taking software programs such as Evernote and Springnote are available for purchase online. These programs offer various options for organizing your research notes and exporting and sharing them. However, you can simply use your computer's word processing program to take notes and keep track of source information. Here are suggestions:

- *Create a folder for your research project.* Give the folder an easily recognizable title and keep everything related to your project in this folder.

- *Create a separate document file for each source consulted.* Give each file an easily recognizable name.

- *At the top of each document, include the complete source information.* Check that each citation conforms to the latest conventions of MLA or APA style (pages 388, 401). If your word processor does not provide an automatic citation option, make sure you record all the information you will need later (author, title, publisher, URL and/or DOI, publication date, city of publication, editor, issue and/or volume number, page numbers, etc.). When in doubt, record more information than you may actually need to include in your citations.

- *Summarize each source consulted and describe its significance.* Under the source information, provide yourself a reminder describing what the source was about and how you plan to use it in your paper. Be specific enough to refresh your memory when you return to the source later.

(continues)

- ■ *Copy and paste or keyboard only the information you really need.* Unless they are crucial to your research, omit graphic, sound, and video files when you download

- ■ *Do not alter original text to be quoted or paraphrased.* To avoid possible plagiarism, make sure to download all text exactly as originally written or, if you are working with a print source, keyboard the material completely and accurately.

- ■ *Obtain permission to use copyrighted material in a paper that will be published or for any commercial purpose.* (Generally, use of copyrighted material in a course paper can be considered fair use and will not require permission. However, each source must always be cited.)

APPLICATIONS

23.1   Read the following excerpt, and then consider the examples that follow. Explain why each is an example of plagiarism.

> To begin with, language is a system of communication. I make this rather obvious point because to some people nowadays it isn't obvious: they see language as above all a means of "self-expression." Of course, language is one way that we express our personal feelings and thoughts—but so, if it comes to that, are dancing, cooking and making music. Language does much more: it enables us to convey to others what we think, feel and want. Language-as-communication is the prime means of organizing the cooperative activities that enable us to accomplish as groups things we could not possibly do as individuals. Some other species also engage in cooperative activities, but these are either quite simple (as among baboons and wolves) or exceedingly stereotyped (as among bees, ants and termites). Not surprisingly, the communicative systems used by these animals are also simple or stereotypes. Language, our uniquely flexible and intricate system of communication, makes possible our equally flexible and intricate ways of coping with the world around us: in a very real sense, it is what makes us human. (Claiborne 8)

PLAGIARISM EXAMPLES

(a) One commentator makes a distinction between language used as a means of self-expression and language-as-communication. It is the latter that distinguishes human interaction from that of other species and allows humans to work cooperatively on complex tasks (8).

(b) Claiborne notes that language "is the prime means of organizing the cooperative activities." Without language, we would, consequently, not have civilization.

(c) Other animals also engage in cooperative activities. However, these actions are not very complex. Rather they are either the very simple activities of, for example, baboons and wolves or the stereotyped activities of animals such as bees, ants, and termites (Claiborne 8).

23.2 **COMPUTER PROJECT** Electronic documentation presents special problems. First, authors or sponsoring organizations for material posted directly to the Internet can be hard to find. Material on the Internet may have appeared somewhere else first, and this original source is sometimes not indicated clearly. Internet addresses won't take you back to the same site if you fail to copy them exactly—even though they may be several lines long. Pages often aren't numbered. Finally, it's sometimes hard to verify the quality of Internet sources because on the Internet, *anyone* can claim to be an expert.

As you conduct your own electronic searches, use the problems just listed as a starting point and compile your own list of documentation issues in electronic research. For your classmates, compose a set of guidelines that will help them deal with these difficulties. Then examine the MLA and APA formats for electronic documentation. Which seems more useful? Why? Can you suggest changes that will make the formats more effective for students like you as they try to document their work?

Works Cited

Abelman, Arthur F. "Legal Issues in Scholarly Publishing." *MLA Style Manual.* 2nd ed. New York: MLA, 1998. 30–57. Print.

Claiborne, Robert. *Our Marvelous Native Tongue: The Life and Times of the English Language.* New York: New York Times, 1983. Print.

Communication Concepts. "Electronic Media Pose New Copyright Issues." *Intercom* Nov. 1995: 13+. Print.

"Copyright Protection and Fair Use of Printed Information." *Addison Wesley Longman Author's Guide.* New York: Longman, 1998. 29–30. Print.

Elias, Stephen. *Patent, Copyright, and Trademark.* Berkeley: Nolo, 1997. Print.

Gibaldi, Joseph, and Walter S. Achtert. *MLA Handbook for Writers of Research Papers.* 3rd ed. New York: Modern Language Association, 1988. Print.

Howard, Tharon. "Property Issue in E-Mail Research." *Bulletin of the Association for Business Communication* 56.2 (1993): 40–41. Print.

Templeton, Brad. "10 Big Myths about Copyright Explained." 29 Nov. 1994. Web. 6 May 1995 <http://www.law/copyright/FAQ/myths/part1>.

CHAPTER 24

Composing the Research Report, with a Sample Report in APA Style

LEARNING OBJECTIVES FOR THIS CHAPTER

■ Develop a working thesis and outline for a research report
■ Draft and revise a research report in APA style

DEVELOPING A WORKING THESIS AND OUTLINE

Don't expect to arrive at your thesis until you have evaluated and interpreted your findings (as discussed on pages 340–341). Your thesis should emerge from the most accurate and reliable information you have been able to find.

On page 338 you phrased your topic as a question:

Research topic | *Violent crime on college campuses: How common is it?*

416

Nearing the completion of your research, you should have at least a tentative answer to that question:

Tentative thesis

> Violent crime on college campuses is more common than many people like to believe.

As your research continues, you might revise this tentative thesis any number of times.

Now you need a road map—a working outline. Perhaps your topic itself or your reading suggests a rough, working outline:

A working outline

I. The extent of the problem
   A. Recent examples of highly publicized campus crimes
   B. National crime statistics
   C. The 1992 Campus Awareness and Security Act
II. Direct causes of campus crime
   A. Alcohol and drug use by students
   B. Offenders from off-campus
III. Indirect causes of campus crime
   A. Naive assumptions by parents
   B. Carefree student attitudes
   C. Deceptive publicity by some colleges
   D. Special treatment for athletes and fraternities
   E. Denial and cover-up by administrators
IV. Actions required
   A. Greater candor and publicity
   B. Change in student habits
   C. Prevention programs

Of course, by the time you have composed your final outline, the shape of your report may have changed radically (see pages 423–429).

DRAFTING YOUR REPORT

When you have collected and reviewed your material, organized your note-cards, and settled on a workable thesis, you will be ready to write the first draft of your report.

Begin by revising your working outline. At this stage, try to develop a detailed formal outline, using at each level either topic phrases or full sentences.

A formal outline needs logical notation and a consistent format. *Notation* is the system of numbers and letters marking the logical divisions; the *format* is the arrangement of your material on the page (indentation, spacing, and so on). Proper notation and format show the subordination of some parts of your topic to others. The general pattern of outline notation looks like this:

The logical divisions
of a formal outline

    I.
      A.
        1.
        2.*
      B.
        1.
        2.
          a.
          b.
            (i)†
            (ii)
      C.
    II. etc.

(For a discussion of a sample formal outline, see pages 34–36.) When your outline is complete, check your tentative thesis to make sure it promises *exactly* what your report will deliver.

Now you can begin to write. Students often find this the most intimidating part of research: pulling together a large body of information. Don't throw everything on the page simply to get done; concentrate on only one section at a time.

Begin by classifying your notecards or electronic notes in groups according to the section of your outline to which each note is keyed. Next, arrange the notes for your introduction in order. You are ready to write your first section. As you move from subsection to subsection, provide commentary and transitions, and document each source.

---

*Note that each level of division yields at least two items. If you cannot divide a major item into at least two subordinate items, retain only your major heading.

†Carry further subdivisions as far as needed, but keep notation for each level individualized and consistent.

REVISING YOUR REPORT

When you have completed and documented a first draft, use the revision checklist for essays in Chapter 4, along with the following research report checklist, to revise the report.

Pages 421–431 show the completed report, documented according to the APA style guidelines described in Chapter 23.

DIGITAL TIP

Plan, Draft, and Revise a Research Report on Your Computer

Refer back to the Digital Tip boxes in Sections I and II of this book for planning, drafting, and revising on your computer. The same tips apply to writing a research report:

- *Planning on Your Computer* (see page 36): Using online thesis creators, mind-mapping software, and computerized outliners can help you discover and organize your ideas.

- *Drafting on Your Computer* (see page 58): Save your work often, keeping separate files for different drafts. Concentrate on getting the content down on the page rather than getting bogged down with details.

- *Revising on Your Computer* (see pages 74, 89, 108, 127, and 145): Recall that you can revise efficiently on your computer by using your word processor's editing application; using the "cut," "copy," "paste," and "move" options; and saving multiple revisions as separate files.

✔ A CHECKLIST for a Research Report

(Numbers in parentheses refer to the first page of discussion.)

Content

☐ Does the report grow from a clear thesis? (416)

☐ Does the title offer an accurate forecast? (49)

☐ Is the report based on reliable sources and evidence? (362, 365)

☐ Does the evidence support the conclusion? (341)

☐ Is the information complete? (341)

☐ Does the report avoid reliance on a single source? (337)

☐ Is the evidence free of weak spots? (373)

☐ Are all data clearly and fully interpreted? (366)

(continues)

☐ Can anything be cut? (33)

☐ Is anything missing? (365)

Organization

☐ Does the introduction state the purpose and thesis clearly? (423)

☐ Does the report follow the outline? (417)

☐ Is each paragraph focused on one main thought? (94)

☐ Is the line of reasoning clear and easy to follow? (33)

Documentation

☐ Is the documentation consistent, complete, and correct? (386)

☐ Is all quoted material clearly marked throughout the text? (382)

☐ Have all sources not considered common knowledge been documented? (381)

☐ Are direct quotations used sparingly and appropriately? (383)

☐ Are all quotations accurate and integrated grammatically? (383)

☐ Is the report free of excessively long quotations? (383)

☐ Are all paraphrases accurate and clear? (384)

☐ Are electronic sources cited clearly and appropriately? (396, 408)

A SAMPLE REPORT IN APA STYLE

The following report was written in response to the scenario on page 337. As you read the report, evaluate its content, organization, and documentation by referring to the checklist starting on page 419.

Running head: CAMPUS CRIME   1

Campus Crime: A Hidden Issue

Julia Schoonover

University of Massachusetts, Dartmouth
Professor J. M. Lannon

Intermediate Composition
Section 1

May 5, 2011

A research report in APA style

CAMPUS CRIME

2 — Place the abstract on a separate page, following the title page.

Provide a one-paragraph abstract (roughly 100 words) that previews the main points and shows how they are related.

ABSTRACT

Despite increasing publicity, crime on college campuses is not merely a recent phenomenon. Violent crime on college campuses, usually student-on-student and often triggered by alcohol and drugs, is far more common than people like to believe. Until recently, campus crime has remained largely a hidden issue because of naive assumptions by parents, carefree attitudes of students, deceptive publicity by some colleges, and frequent denial and cover-up by college administrators. New government legislation, improved security measures, and prevention and support programs offer partial solutions. Most needed, however, is more responsible behavior from students and greater candor and publicity from college officials.

Center the heading; double-space the abstract; use no paragraph indent.

A research report in APA style (*continues*)

Include the shortened title as a running head on each page.

Repeat the title exactly as it appears on the title page and center it.

Campus Crime: A Hidden Issue

Begin the first paragraph two lines below the title, and double space throughout.

Use the introduction to invite readers in and present your thesis.

Until the recent mass murders at Virginia Tech and Northern Illinois University, parents, students, and school administrators have largely viewed college campuses through rose-colored glasses. We tended to think that college is a fairyland in which good prevails and, on rare occasions, evil briefly invades and then quickly retreats. As early as 1993, journalist Anne Matthews described the denial problem: "When aware of campus crime at all [we] frequently attribute it to faceless, hit-and-retreat invaders from beyond the ivy curtain" (p. 38). Like characters in a make-believe world, we enjoyed feeling content and secure. As we have witnessed, however, the reality tells a different story. Violent crime on college campuses, usually student-on-student and often triggered by alcohol and drugs, is far more common than we like to believe.

Introduce brief quotes by naming the source.

For credibility, include brief quotations from authorities.

Show readers that your topic has meaning to them *personally* (our writer uses "we").

How Secure Is the Typical College Campus?

Indent the first line of each paragraph ½ inch.

Combine quoted material grammatically with your own words.

Benign images of campus life often conceal a pattern of violence that covers decades and for which no end is in sight. For example, journalist Alex Kingsbury (2007) reminds us that in 1966, 15 people were killed and 31 wounded at the University of Texas-Austin by a student ex-marine firing from a 300-foot tower on campus. In 1986, a female student at Lehigh University was "raped, tortured, and murdered in her dorm room by a fellow student" (p. 48).

Use section headings to orient readers and show them what to expect.

CBS reporter David Morgan (2007) has compiled a list of fatal shootings at thirteen U.S. campuses from May 1970 thru April 2007. And, according to more recent statistics, violent crime on campuses—including robbery, assault, and forcible rape—continues to pose grave dangers to students as well as to faulty and staff. The Federal Bureau of Investigation (FBI) provides detailed accounts and current campus attack statistics on its Web site (2010).

A research report in APA style (*continues*)

On the national front, the statistics on campus crime seem to offer cause for slight optimism. For example, the National Institute of Justice (2008) has reported a minor decrease in forcible sex offenses. However, such a decrease, between 2004 and 2006, amounted to less than 1%. The Federal Bureau of Investigation meanwhile reports that violent crime nationwide fell by roughly 5.3% between 2008 and 2009 (2010). Although these small deceases are encouraging, countless additional crimes occur routinely on college campuses and, on some campuses, offer a mixed picture. On our own campus, for example, robberies decreased by 75% between 2007 and 2009, while forcible sex offenses and aggravated assaults doubled in number during that same period (UMASS Dartmouth, 2010).

Why Has Campus Crime Received Scant Attention?

When you use questions as headings, phrase the questions as readers might ask them.

Phrase all section headings consistently.

To find the right college for their child, parents look for many qualities in a school: a strong academic program, an accomplished faculty, an attractive campus, clean and roomy dormitories, and so on. Traditionally, however, parents have rarely considered campus crime because they have assumed that college campuses are safe. Safety experts attribute such naiveté to parents' belief in the notion of *in loco parentis*—the assumption that a college or university stands in for a student's parents. One safety official at Rutgers claims that too many parents expect the university to provide the same type of care their child received at home; "that is just not possible," he explains (McClarin, 1994, p. A1). Also, the peaceful, picturesque setting of a typical campus seems reassuring, according to New York City safety consultant Harry Nolan (2008): "Students see guards patrolling at night or a video camera monitoring the dorm entrance and think, Nothing bad can happen to me.... People don't know that safety controls are often very lax."

Feeling secure in their setting, students often do not realize that 80% of campus crime is student-on-student ("Is Your College Student Safe?" 2008). According to federal statistics, more than 2,600 sexual assaults were reported in 2004, a tiny fraction of the actual number that occurred (Kingsbury, 2007, p. 49). Also college students are the most frequent victims of stalking (Truman and Mustaine, 2009). As many as one in eight female students are stalking victims, yet 83% do not file a report with campus police because many of them say they believe it would be ignored (Motia, 2007, p. 106).

In addition, like their parents, students have traditionally assumed they will be safeguarded from any danger by administrators or security personnel. They often consider themselves immune and have the attitude "'I get to do whatever I want but you have to protect me'" (Mathews, 1993, p. 42). But students make themselves vulnerable by drinking and partying and then plopping down, wherever they may be, and sleeping until they sober up.

Furthermore, experts point out that colleges are not required to provide security services, including "locks, alarms, and adequate lighting," for students who live off campus, no matter how nearby. These students therefore become particularly easy targets for crime (Motia, 2007, p. 105).

What Role Does Alcohol Play?

College crime statistics consistently show that carefree attitudes about alcohol contribute heavily to campus crime. In 1993, alcohol was declared by one journalist as "the drug of use at American colleges, and a fuel for campus crime" (Matthews, 1993, p. 41). In 2006, the National Survey on Drug Use and Health defined "binge drinking" as "five or more drinks on the same occasion on at least one day in the past 30 days," and "heavy alcohol use" as "five or more drinks on the same occasion on each of five or more days in the past 30 days."

Cite each source in parentheses, inside the period, but outside any quotation marks.

A research report in APA style (*continues*)

This survey of underage college students found that from 2002 to 2005, an average of "57.8 percent…used alcohol in the past month, 40.1 percent engaged in binge alcohol use and 16.4 percent engaged in heavy alcohol use" (U.S. Office of Applied Studies, 2006, p. 1). These findings are summarized in Figure 1.

> Consider page numbers optional in citing paraphrased material but required in citing direct quotations unless from a single-page or an unpaginated source.

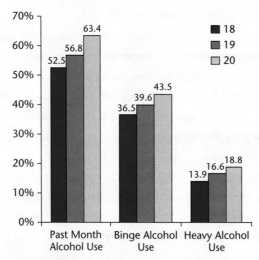

> Provide a caption that serves as the figure title and explains the figure clearly.

FIGURE 1 **Past Month, Binge, and Heavy Alcohol Use Among Full-Time College Students Aged 18 to 20, by Age, 2002–2005.**

*From "Underage Alcohol Use among College Students," *National Survey on Drug Use and Health, 31,* 2006, p. 3. U.S. Office of Applied Studies.

> Include a full source note for your data or for a figure used from another source.

> If the figure is from a copyrighted source, provide complete copyright information.

One of many troubling implications of these findings is revealed in a study sponsored by the National Institute on Alcohol Abuse and Alcoholism, which estimated that abuse of alcohol in colleges accounts for more than 70,000 sexual assaults annually (Wechsler, 2003).

What Role Does Cover-Up Play?

Administrators know the exact dangers that exist on any college campus, but too often they choose to ignore the unpleasant facts to avoid scaring off prospective students. Bright, glossy brochures promote every aspect of a particular school but rarely mention campus safety, let alone crime statistics.

Transcripts of congressional hearings (U.S. House of Representatives, 1990) revealed that when campus crime does hit home, administrators often deny that any of their students are involved.

Since 1990, federal law (the Crime Awareness and Security Act) has required that all colleges receiving federal student aid must "report campus crimes to the federal Office of Postsecondary Education in a timely fashion and notify students of threats" ("Is Your College Student Safe?" 2008). However, one recent study by the Department of Justice "found that only 37 percent of schools report sexual-assault crimes in accordance with the [requirement]" (Motia, 2007, p. 104). FBI statistics on underreporting of crimes on campus confirm these findings and indicate, in the words of one journalist, that "colleges may be portraying themselves as safer than they really are" (Seward, 2006).

> Use brackets to signal any significant alteration of the original quotation.

What Role Does Student Apathy Play?

Any violent crime on a college campus causes temporary wariness among parents, students, and faculty. For a few weeks following a rape, assault, or other crime, everyone behaves more cautiously. Parents warn students to be careful. Administrators post fliers with police numbers in large, bold print. Students walk in groups and avoid usual shortcuts through poorly lit areas.

A research report in APA style (*continues*)

CAMPUS CRIME   8

Extra police are on patrol; emergency phones are repaired; dorm security is increased. But as the immediate shock wears off, students again take their safety for granted. They begin walking alone again at night; they resume their usual shortcuts.

At our school, only four weeks after a student was nearly raped while awaiting a bus outside the library and another student was assaulted by a knife-wielding attacker, most students seemed to have resumed their carefree ways. On any late evening, males and females alike can be seen walking or jogging alone.

Is Enough Being Done?

In addition to the passage of the Campus Awareness and Security Act in 1990, the Campus Sexual Assault's Victim's Bill of Rights, passed two years later, requires all colleges to establish set policies for assisting victims. Also passed in 1992 was the Buckley Amendment Clarification Act, designating campus police records as no longer confidential. In 2002, the Campus Sex Crimes Prevention Act was enacted to track registered sex offenders who turn up on campus as students, campus workers, or volunteers. Also, in 2010, Congress passed the Campus Violence and Security Act to further enhance prevention efforts (Security on Campus, 2010).

Until recently, one problem with tracking campus crime has been the lack of an official repository for campus crime statistics, similar to the FBI's Uniform Crime Reporting Program for cities. Since October 2000, all schools have been required to report their crime statistics online to the Department of Education (Moran, 2000). To compare schools nationwide, users can visit http://www.ed.gov and click on the "Research and Stats" link. In 2011, the U.S. Department of Education published an official handbook to guide schools in reporting annual incidents affecting safety and security.

Additional resources are increasingly available online. For example, Security on Campus, Inc., a nonprofit organization for preventing campus violence, has helped victims and families take legal action against various schools for negligence and "failure to protect" (Security on Campus, 2010).

The Internet also makes it easier for parents and students to find out about crime at particular colleges. Harvard University, for example, devotes a portion of its Web site to its police department (http://www.hupd.harvard.edu). Campus crime statistics, as well as safety tips and guidelines on crime reporting, are available, as is information on self-defense courses offered by the university.

In the wake of the Virginia Tech and Northern Illinois University tragedies, schools are aggressively taking various defensive measures—for example, drop-in counseling offices in dorms, automatic screening for depression and other mental health issues at campus health centers, and improved communication among faculty, counseling and health centers, and security officials (Shute, 2007, pp. 62–63). Other measures include campuswide text systems and anonymous hot lines for reporting suspicious behavior (Wingert, 2007). At Montclair State University, students carry cell phones that have GPS locators and are programmed to sound an alarm at the police station (Murr, 2007).

Recent or planned improvements on our campus include additional police officers; an instant messaging system for emergencies; an expanded shuttle-bus system; increased lighting; more emergency call boxes; monthly safety sessions for faculty, staff, and students, and a police Tip Line (UMASS Dartmouth, 2011). Clearly, the emphasis on enhanced safety measures should reduce campus crime. But the best overall defense requires individual awareness and institutional honesty.

College students have every right to feel safe on campus, but they must recognize that campus crime is real. Although the specter of campus crime should not taint the freedoms and joys of college life, parents must become more realistic, students must take more responsibility for their actions, and colleges must be more candid—perhaps even publishing weekly crime statistics in the campus newspaper.

On campus or in the real world, crime is a fact of life. The sooner parents, students, and administrators accept this fact, the safer college campuses might become.

A research report in APA style (*continues*)

Continue the running heads and page numbers.

Center "References" at the top of a new page.

References

Include only recoverable data (material that readers could retrieve); cite interviews, lectures, email, and other correspondence parenthetically in the text only.

Double-space entries, and list them alphabetically by author's last name.

Federal Bureau of Investigation. (2010). Violent crime. *Crime in the United States 2009.* Retrieved from http://www2.fbi.gov/ucr/cius2009 /index.html   [*online newspaper*]

Kingsbury, A. (2007, April 30). Toward a safer campus *U.S. News & World Report,* 48–50. Retrieved from http://www.usnews.com

Use initials only for authors' first and middle names.

Matthews, A. (1993, March 4). The campus crime wave. *The New York Times Magazine,* 30–42.   [*magazine article*]

Capitalize all key words in magazine, journal, or newspaper titles.

Capitalize only the first word in article and book titles and subtitles and any proper nouns.

McClarin, K. (1994, September 7). Fear prompts self-defense as crime comes to college. *The New York Times,* pp. A1, A4.   [*newspaper article*]

Moran, K. J. (2000, September 2). Higher crime statistics at U-Mass due in part to reporting change. *Hampshire Gazette,* p. B1.

For a magazine or newspaper article on nonconsecutive pages, list each page number, separated by a comma.

List only the home page URL.

Morgan, D.S. (2007, April 16). Other campus shootings [Press release]. *CBS News.* Retrieved from http://www.cbsnews.com   [*press release*]

Do not omit any digits in ranges of numbers.

Motia, S. (2007, September). 10 things campus security won't tell you. *Smart Money,* 104–106.

Write out names of all months.

Murr, A. (2007, August 27). Is your campus safe? *Newsweek,* 74.

Nolan, H. (2008, February 6). Is your college student safe at school? *Reader's Digest.* Retrieved from http://www.rd.com

Italicize periodical and book titles.

Do not enclose article titles in quotation marks.

Security on Campus, Inc. (2010). *History, accomplishments, and programs.* Retrieved April 7, 2011, from http://www.securityoncampus.org   [*online article*]

Include retrieval date for content that can be updated.

Use the first main word in the title to alphabetize works whose author is not named.

Seward, Z. M. (2006, October 23). FBI stats show many colleges understate campus crime. *The Wall Street Journal.* Retrieved from http://online.wsj.com/public/article

Provide the electronic address for all Websites.

Shute, N. (2007, September 24). A wake-up call on campus. *U.S. News & World Report,* 62–65. Retrieved from http://www.usnews.com

A research report in APA style (*continues*)

CAMPUS CRIME   11

Truman, J. L., and Mustaine, E.E. (2009). Strategies for college student stalking victims. *American Journal of Criminal Justice, 34*(1–2), 69–83. doi: 10.1007/s 12103-008-9051-1

UMASS Dartmouth. Department of Public Safety. (2010). *Campus crime reports.* Retrieved from http://www.umass.edu

U.S. Department of Education. (2011). *The handbook for campus safety and security reporting.* Retrieved from http://www.ed.gov

U.S. House of Representatives. (1990). *Hearing on H.R. 3344: The Crime Awareness and Security Act.* Washington, DC: U.S. Government Printing Office.

U.S. Office of Applied Studies, Substance Abuse and Mental Health Services Administration. (2006). Underage alcohol use among full-time college students. *National Survey on Drug Use and Health, 31,* 1–3. Retrieved from http://www.oas.samhsa.gov/   *[government report online, no author named]*

Wechsler, H. (2003, November). Is student binge drinking a serious problem? *AFT on Campus,* 4.

Wingert, P. (2008, January 7). How to prevent a tragedy. *Newsweek,* 22.

Indent the second and subsequent lines of an entry ½ inch.

Use the DOI instead of the URL, if available, for online versions of print sources.

If no author is named, list the organization sponsoring the site in the author slot.

Omit punctuation after an electronic address that ends the entry.

Do not include *p.* or *pp.* before journal or magazine page numbers (but do so for a newspaper).

For additional information and practice with the learning objectives in this chapter, go to www.mycomplab.com, Resources>Research>Writing the Research Paper.

A research report in APA style (*continues*)

CHAPTER 25

Case Study: A Sample Research Project in MLA Style

This chapter follows one student writer's problem solving, from the day her report was assigned until she submitted her final draft. You can adapt the approach presented here to your own research project.

DISCOVERING A WORTHWHILE TOPIC

As soon as Shirley Haley learned that a research report was due in 6 weeks, she began to search for a worthwhile topic. Although many of Haley's college friends had adjusted to the hectic pace of the first-year student, others were not doing so well: Some had developed insomnia; others had gained or lost a good deal of weight; one friend was sleeping more than 12 hours a day. Other disorders ranged from compulsive eating and indigestion to chronic headaches and skin problems—all seemingly since the beginning of the semester. Haley wondered why, beyond the obvious pressures of college life, so many of her friends had become so unhealthy.

A psychology major, Haley had recently read about *stress* in an introductory textbook. She wondered about a connection between stress and the problems her friends were experiencing.

FOCUSING THE INQUIRY

To find the right answers, Haley knew that she would have to ask the right questions. Here is the tree chart she developed during her initial planning:

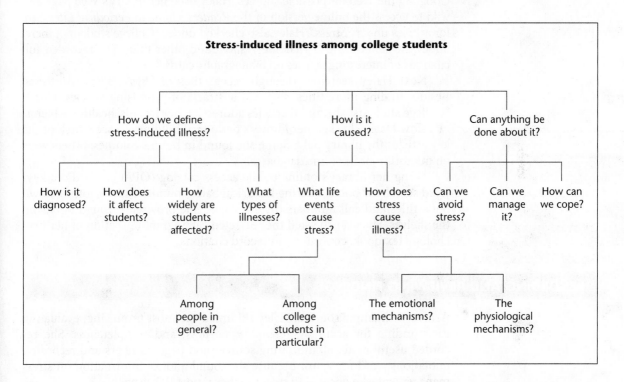

Once she knew what information she was looking for, Haley focused on the viewpoints that would give her a balanced picture:

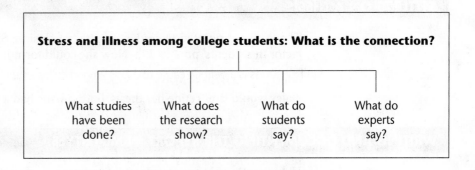

Now that she knew what questions to ask, Haley was ready to begin her search for answers.

SEARCHING THE LITERATURE

Because Haley had already read a description of stress in her psychology text-book, she needed no general reference works such as encyclopedias. After Googling the Web for possible sources, Haley used her library's Web page and wiki to access the online version of the *Readers' Guide to Periodical Literature* for articles under "Stress." Haley also checked under "College students"; there, under the subheading "Psychology," she found other titles. She recorded full citations of interesting articles on bibliography cards.

Next Haley searched through recent files of *Psychological Abstracts.* Besides finding more titles, she read abstracts of promising articles. Under "College students" she found articles addressing her friends' health problems.

Now Haley checked her library's periodical holdings to see which of the key articles the library held. Some she found in bound volumes; others were on microfilm or in online databases.

Using her library's online public access catalog (OPAC), she did a key-word search for books offering historical background on stress, jotting down book titles and call numbers. In the stacks, she browsed through books on the shelves. She also checked the "Selected Bibliography" section of her psychology textbook, continuing to record citations.

RECORDING AND REVIEWING FINDINGS

Armed with ample sources, Haley skimmed the most promising, evaluating each finding for accuracy, reliability, fairness, and completeness. She recorded useful material, indicating sources and page numbers and recording quotations word for word. Because she found a lot of information on stress management, she decided to structure her report this way:

Problem ⟶ causes and effects ⟶ solutions

SETTLING ON A THESIS

The evidence pointed toward a definite conclusion: Stress was indeed a real factor in students' poor health. Now she could formulate a tentative thesis:

| Stress is a definite cause of illness among college students.

Haley would later refine her thesis, but now she had a good focal point.

WRITING AND DOCUMENTING THE REPORT IN MLA STYLE

Haley continued to read, record information, outline, and organize her notes. Finally, she decided she knew enough to write a first draft. Using the revision checklists on pages 375 and 419–420, she reworked her first and second drafts into the final draft that appears on the following pages.

title page
cludes these
ems: report
le, author's
ame, course
department,
cipient's
ame, and
te.

The title
page is not
numbered.

enter and
ace these
ems for visual
peal.

Students Under Stress: College Can Make You Sick

by
Shirley Haley

English 101, Section 1432
Professor Lannon

May 8, 2011

A research report in MLA style

Haley i

The running head gives the author's last name, followed by one space and the page number (small Roman numerals for the outline, Arabic for the rest of the paper).

OUTLINE

Preface the sentence outline with your thesis.

<u>Thesis</u>: Disruptive changes and pressures in their personal, social, and academic lives make college students highly vulnerable to the physical effects of stress.

Here, three major sections ("*The Problem*," "*Causes and Extent of the Problem*," and "*Possible Solutions*") follow an effect-to-cause sequence (see page 239).

Each level of division in the outline contains *at least two* items.

I. <u>The Problem</u>: Stress is increasingly recognized as a cause of physical illness.
    A. The mechanisms have been studied for years, but stress is still making us sick.
    B. Stress has a technical and a personal definition, and both are accurate.
    C. More and more of us suffer the physical effects of stress.
    D. College students are among the groups most affected.
II. <u>Causes and Extent of the Problem</u>: Stress-induced illness is caused by emotional responses that have physical consequences.
    A. Stress originates when the body works too hard to maintain equilibrium.
        1. If the alarm reaction persists, the body is forever ready for action.
        2. Psychosomatic illness is not imaginary.
    B. A classic study shows a connection between the stress of common life events and illness.
    C. Even a series of ordinary events in the lives of college students can cause dangerous levels of stress.
    D. Various studies of college students confirm the stress-illness link.
    E. Cases of stress among students are worsening in number and intensity.
III. <u>Possible Solutions</u>: Now that the problem is recognized, solutions are being found.
    A. The effect stress has on us depends on how well we cope.
        1. We need both coping strategies and help from others.
        2. Without coping mechanisms, we are almost certain to be overwhelmed.
    B. Students need to develop more realistic expectations of college life.
        1. College orientation should be more realistic.
        2. Stress management courses should be offered by more colleges.
    C. Stress management training should be available to every student.

A research report in MLA style (*continues*)

When you use a title page, do not repeat your title on page 1. Instead use section headings.

Haley   1

Assign an Arabic number to each page after the author's last name as running head.

The Problem: Stress-Induced Illness

Stress can cause physical illness. The mechanisms have been studied for years, but stress is still making us sick.

Provide adequate background information to set the scene.

Researchers Dohrenwend and Dohrenwend point out that the search for a link between stress and illness began some 80 years ago. Walter Cannon identified the "fight or flight" response in 1929. Showing that emotional arousal causes physical reactions such as increased respiration and pulse rate and elevated blood pressure, Cannon laid the groundwork for stress research. In the 1930s, Dr. Adolf Mayer, who began charting patients' life events to aid his medical diagnoses, recorded "the changes of habit, of school entrances, graduations or changes, or failures; the various jobs...and other important events" (3). And Hans Selye in 1936 described the body's reaction to stress as "the syndrome of just being sick" ("Stress Concept" 72).

Introduce a brief quotation by naming the author and blending the quotation grammatically with your own words.

Cite each source in parentheses, before the sentence period but after any quotation marks.

Stress has a technical and a personal definition. Technically, stress is a psychological and physiological response to life events that disrupt the physical being. This response evolved as a primitive and necessary defense against physical danger (Hall). But in the modern world, stress takes on a broader, more personal definition: Stress occurs, for example, when a person falls in or out of love, receives good or bad news, drives a car, receives a traffic ticket, takes final exams, or graduates. All life experiences, major or minor, entail stress and too often provoke an overreaction. One Mayo Clinic expert observes that many of today's stressors usually last longer than the threat of physical danger; the resulting fight-or-flight reaction can have serious physical consequences: "Your body's stress reaction was meant to protect you. But when it's constantly on alert, your health can pay the price" (qtd. in Mayo Clinic). Although some degree of anxiety is a good motivator, excessive stress endangers our health.

Define your topic before discussing it, and clarify your definition with concrete examples.

More and more of us seem to suffer the physical effects of stress: ulcers and other digestive problems, fatigue and exhaustion, high blood pressure, headache, and so on. Prolonged stress makes us susceptible to infectious diseases and autoimmune diseases such as lupus by either suppressing or overstimulating our immune system (Mayo Clinic). Lab studies indicate that stress

Relate the material to the readers, who want to know what something means to them personally.

A research report in MLA style (*continues*)

Haley   2

can lower our resistance to cancer. University of Chicago researchers Cavagelli and McClintock found that some lab rats in new and unpredictable environments are shy and cautious while others are bold and curious. Compared with their adventurous counterparts, the shy rodents produce higher levels of stress hormones, which ultimately lower their resistance to tumors and shorten their life span by 20% (Bower 373).

Stress has its warning signs, cues telling us to seek help before our bodies break down. Among the most common signs are an overpowering urge to cry or run away, persistent anxiety for no reason, insomnia, and a feeling of being "keyed up." (See Appendix A for other signs.) Overeating and alcohol or drug use are often the result of stress beyond endurance, an attempt to escape (Selye, *Stress of Life* 175).

Refer to appendixes at report's end for detail readers might find useful but interruptive in the report itself.

Among the groups most exposed to life changes, and thus most affected by stress, are college students, whose battles with stress can begin early. Even before graduating from high school, students worry about admission to the right college. Or they feel pressure to measure up to parents' achievements and expectations or keep up with successful older siblings. "Second-rate doesn't rate at all in a majority of the households from which these [students] come—and they know it" (Brooks 613). Transition to college creates more stress as students leave a friendly and familiar environment for one that seems impersonal and demanding, academically and socially. Moreover, today's students struggle with increasing debt, reductions in financial aid, and anxiety about finding decent jobs after graduation (Whittle). University of Rhode Island counselor Jim Campbell observes that "people often assume that college is a fun, carefree time, but that is usually not the case.... In a lot of ways college is a high-risk environment" (qtd. in Ablasser). Disruptive changes and pressures in their personal, social, and academic lives make students vulnerable to the physical effects of stress.

Offer a clear and definite thesis.

A research report in MLA style (*continues*)

Haley   3

Causes and Extent of Stress-Induced Illness

> Introduce each major section.

Stress originates when the body works too hard at maintaining the equilibrium necessary for good health. Any disruption or demand, good or bad, triggers an "alarm reaction," causing adrenaline to prepare the body for action: Blood pressure rises to increase blood flow to muscles; digestion temporarily shuts down; blood sugar rises to increase energy; perspiration increases; and other physical changes occur, all to prepare the body for "fight or flight" (Selye, "Stress Concept" 76).

> Interpret your research findings.

If the alarm reaction persists, the body is forever ready for action. That is when stress becomes destructive. We can run from a speeding car as we cross the street, and when the danger passes, so does the stress. But we can't run away from some inner threat such as the pressure for good grades. And as the stress endures, our bodies become less able to maintain the equilibrium needed for health.

A connection between the stress of common life events and illness was first demonstrated in a 1967 study. First, researchers assigned point values to 43 specific life events (divorce, illness, marriage, job loss). After collecting health histories, the researchers asked their subjects to total the points for recent events in their lives. (The scale ranged from 100 points for the death of a spouse to 11 for a traffic violation—see Appendix B for a full listing.) Comparing the health histories to point totals, the researchers discovered that for 93% of the subjects, any group of life events totaling 150 or more points in one year was connected to a major illness requiring a physician's care. And the harmful effects of a high point total lasted as long as two years (Holmes and Masuda 50-56).

> Refer to an appendix for complex data.

Studies of college students confirm the stress-illness link. Even a collection of ordinary events in students' lives can place them in a danger category, as shown in Table 1.

> Number and title each visual, introduce it, cite your source, and interpret the data.

> Continue to interpret findings in relation to college students specifically, leading into a detailed discussion of studies on college students.

A research report in MLA style (*continues*)

Haley   4

Table 1   A Life-Events Scale for College Students

Event	Points	Event	Points
Beginning or ending of school	26	Change in church activities	19
Change in living conditions	25	Change in social activities	18
Revision of personal habits	24	Loan of less than $10,000	17
Change in work hours or conditions	20	Change in sleeping habits	16
Change in residence	20	Change in eating habits	15

Source: Adapted from Thomas H. Holmes and R. H. Rahe, "The Social Readjustment Scale," *Journal of Psychosomatic Research* 11 (1967): 213-18; table 3.

Place tables longer than one text page in an appendix.

Always give full source credit directly below the borrowed material.

The life events in Table 1 total 200 points, disregarding any other points students collect from out-of-school experiences. But one study showed that among students who also have to work to pay for college costs, nearly two-thirds considered the job an additional source of stress (Ross, Niebling, and Heckert 315).

More than half of the medical students in one study experienced "major health changes" within two years after entering school. A college life-events scale was given to 54 incoming first-year medical students; those with the highest scores reported most illness before the end of the second year (Holmes and Masuda 64). The stress of starting school can strongly affect one's health.

Cite a selective cross section of sources.

In a related study, Holmes and Masuda found a connection between life changes and the number of injuries sustained by 100 college football players. High scores on the life-change survey equaled more injuries on the field. Of the ten players who had multiple injuries, seven were from the group with highest scores in the life-events survey (66). One study of women collegiate soccer players found that the harder they trained, the more susceptible to illness they became (Putlur et al. 240).

Pressures of college life often produce stress-induced insomnia. For instance, one survey at a Virginia university found that 35% of students sleep

Haley 5

no more than six hours nightly—largely because of sleep disruption caused by stress (Ganeshananthan). Students who procrastinate in their college work are particularly prone to insomnia, as a Canadian study of 374 undergraduates has found (Glenn A1).

Experts at Iowa State University point out that many students tend to be overwhelmed by the stress of "balancing conflicting demands" from self, family, and school "that pull them in different directions: 'I must do it all well'; 'I must experience it all now'; 'I cannot say no'; 'I feel so guilty.'" An excerpt from their counseling advice to stressed-out students: "Proceed through your days in college with a positive attitude that you can do it all...just not at the same time" (Dean of Students Office).

Regardless of their cause, cases of stress among college students are worsening in number and intensity. For example, psychologist Sherry Benton, lead researcher in a long-term study (1981–2001) of Kansas State University students describes the problem: "We have seen staggering numbers of anxiety, depression, and...suicidal intent.... Years ago we dealt mainly with developmental issues in campus mental health services; now the problems have become more serious" (qtd. in Ablasser). One nationwide student poll by the Associated Press and the college television network mtvU found that 40% of respondents feel stress "often" and 20% "most of the time" (Fram and Tompson).

A 2010 survey of more than 200,000 incoming college students confirms these findings: "The emotional health of college freshman...has declined to the lowest level since an annual survey of incoming students started collecting data 25 years ago," reports columnist Tamar Lewin. Pat Carey, New York University psychologist and dean for student affairs, sums up the causes this way: "There are many pressures to compete and succeed these days.... Students are also bringing a lot of emotional needs to college with them" (qtd. in "College Students").

This crisis has so widened that it has overwhelmed campus counselors who, in this era of budget cuts, are understaffed and often undertrained to deal with ever-increasing and more complex student problems ("More

When you use ellipses to show you have omitted material from a direct quotation, be sure the resulting passage in grammatical

A research report in MLA style *(continues)*

Haley   6

Students"). Finally beginning to recognize the extent of the problem, the U.S. Congress is taking supportive action: Recent congressional bills include the Campus Counseling Act, a federal program to provide grants for enhancing campus counseling services (Dittmann). But legislation alone cannot solve the problem. More proactive steps are needed.

> Whenever possible, offer specific recommendations.

Possible Solutions

Because stress is unlikely to disappear, our only solution is to learn to cope. "It is our ability to cope with the demands made by the events in our lives, not the quality or intensity of the events, that counts. What matters is not so much what happens to us, but the way we take it" (Selye, "Stress Concept" 83).

For students, coping depends on realistic expectations of college life. A 1984 counseling study at Kansas State University found that students tend to be unrealistic about their chances of succeeding in college. They suffer from what Harvard professor Arthur Levine calls the "Titanic Ethic": "They see doom in the world around them but still feel they [personally] will somehow survive" (qtd. in Newton et al. 541). Students are so certain of survival, they make few plans for coping with anticipated problems; instead they rely on the hope that problems will take care of themselves (540-42).

> Include the indirect source (here, Levine) in your Works Cited list.

To help incoming students avoid shattered expectations, counselor Fred Newton and his colleagues suggest that college orientation should be more realistic: It should include stress management counseling and a no-nonsense look at all sides of college life (541).

> Paraphrase and summarize throughout your report. (See pages 384–385 for guidelines.)

Realistic approaches to college life must include exercise, adequate sleep, relaxation (say, listening to music), a healthy diet, and management of time and finances, according to one popular student blog ("Top 5"). Dr. Gregory Hall of Bentley College emphasizes the importance of "maintaining a balance between your intellectual, social, and personal development."

To cope with stress and learn to relax and care for themselves, students need to realize that no one solution fits all. Accordingly, the health services

A research report in MLA style (*continues*)

Haley   7

Web site at the University of Georgia capitalizes on linked resources to address individual student problems; an excerpt from its stress home page notes that "managing stress is individual; you need to find the strategies that work for you. What helps one person…may not be helpful for someone else. As you look through this site, think about what appeals to you and what you think you can use" (University Health Center). This is a good example of the power of the Internet for customizing a site to the needs of a given user.

Indeed, resources for stressed-out students are proliferating. Useful advice is available online from a great many colleges, including the University of Florida's "Stress and College Students" page at <http://www.counsel.ufl. edu>. Online discussions, including blogs and podcasts, on stress-related issues are found at <http://www.deja.com> or via Google. And various organizations, such as the American Institute of Stress at <http://www.stress.org>, offer advice, newsletters, and links to additional resources.

In conclusion, although stress in college is unavoidable, it can be managed. Stress management training should be offered to all students, to make them aware of the realities of college life and of their responsibility for their own well-being. All students should make it a point to explore the resources offered by their schools. As the research clearly shows, students who learn to manage stress will be less likely to find that college makes them sick.

Key your conclusion specifically to your thesis, summarizing the discussion and reemphasizing major points.

A research report in MLA style (*continues*)

Use an appendix for material that is important but difficult to integrate into the report text. Include, for example, measurements, maps, long quotations, photographs, literary passages, and so on.

Appendix A: Warning Signals of Stress

Stress has definite warning signals, emotional and physical. These are the most common.

Emotional Signs of Stress

- being emotionally very "up" or very "down"
- impulsive behavior and emotional instability
- uncontrollable urge to cry or run away
- inability to concentrate
- feelings of unreality
- loss of "joy of life"
- feeling "keyed up"
- being easily startled
- nightmares; insomnia
- a general sense of anxiety or dread

Be sure readers won't have to turn to appendixes to understand the report; distill the essentials from your appendixes and include them in the main text.

Physical Signs of Stress

- pounding heart (may indicate high blood pressure)
- constantly dry throat and mouth
- weakness; dizziness
- feelings of tiredness
- trembling; nervous tics
- high-pitched, nervous laughter
- grinding of teeth
- constant aimless motion
- excessive perspiring
- diarrhea; indigestion; queasy stomach
- headaches
- pain in the neck or lower back (because of muscle tension)
- excessive or lost appetite
- proneness to accidents

Source: Adapted from Hans Selye, *The Stress of Life,* rev. ed. (New York: McGraw, 1976), p. 175.

A research report in MLA style (*continues*)

Haley   9

Label each
appendix
clearly, and
use a separate
one to provide
for each major
item.

Appendix B: Stress Values of Common Life Events

Holmes and Rahe ranked life events in descending order according to their stress value. This table shows the rating scale.

Social Readjustment Rating Scale

Rank	Life Event	Mean Value
1	Death of spouse	100
2	Divorce	73
3	Marital separation from mate	65
4	Detention in jail or other institution	63
5	Death of a close family member	63
6	Major personal injury or illness	53
7	Marriage	50
8	Being fired at work	47
9	Marital reconciliation with mate	45
10	Retirement from work	45
11	Major change in the health or behavior of a family member	44
12	Pregnancy	40
13	Sexual difficulties	39
14	Getting a new family member (e.g., through birth, adoption, oldster moving in, etc.)	39
15	Major business readjustment (e.g., merger, reorganization, bankruptcy, etc.)	39
16	Major change in financial state (e.g., a lot worse off or a lot better off than usual)	38
17	Death of a close friend	37
18	Changing to a different line of work	36
19	Major change in the number of arguments with spouse (e.g., either a lot more or a lot less than usual regarding child rearing, personal habits, etc.)	35
20	Taking out a mortgage or loan for a major purchase (e.g., for a home, business, etc.)	31
21	Foreclosure on a mortgage or loan	30
22	Major change in responsibilities at work (e.g., promotion, demotion, lateral transfer)	29

A research report in MLA style (*continues*)

Place appen-
dixes at the
end of the text
but before the
Works Cited
pages.

Appendix B: (Continued)

Social Readjustment Rating Scale

Rank	Life Event	Mean Value
23	Son or daughter leaving home (e.g., marriage, attending college, etc.)	29
24	Trouble with in-laws	29
25	Outstanding personal achievement	28
26	Wife beginning or ceasing work outside the home	26
27	Beginning or ceasing formal schooling	26
28	Major change in living conditions (e.g., building a new home, remodeling, deterioration of home or neighborhood)	25
29	Revision of personal habits (dress, manners, associations, etc.)	24
30	Trouble with the boss	23
31	Major change in working hours or conditions	20
32	Change in residence	20
33	Changing to a new school	20
34	Major change in usual type and/or amount of recreation	19
35	Major change in church activities (e.g., a lot more or a lot less than usual)	19
36	Major change in social activities (e.g., clubs, dancing, movies, visiting, etc.)	18
37	Taking out a mortgage or loan for a lesser purchase (e.g., for a car, TV, freezer, etc.)	17
38	Major change in sleeping habits (a lot more or a lot less sleep, or change in part of day when asleep)	16
39	Major change in number of family get-togethers (e.g., a lot more or a lot less than usual)	15
40	Major change in eating habits (a lot more or a lot less food intake, or very different meal hours or surroundings)	15
41	Vacation	13
42	Christmas	12
43	Minor violations of the law (e.g., traffic tickets, jaywalking, disturbing the peace, etc.)	11

Source: Thomas H. Holmes and R. H. Rahe, "The Social Readjustment Scale," *Journal of Psychosomatic Research* 11 (1967): 216.

A research report in MLA style (*continues*)

Use one-inch margins all around.

Continue running heads and page numbers.

Works Cited

Double space and indent second and subsequent lines ½ inch.

Ablasser, Catharina. "Creating Healthy Campuses." *APA Monitor* 35.10 (2004): Web.

11 Apr. 2011.

[*article from a professional Web site*]

List entries alphabetically.

Bower, Bruce. "Worried to Death: Lifelong Inhibitions Hasten Rodents' Deaths."

Science News 13 Dec. 2003: 373. Print.   [*article in a magazine*]

Enclose article titles in quotation marks.

Brooks, Andre A. "Educating the Children of Fast-Track Parents." *Phi Delta Kappan*

Apr. 1990: 612-15. Print.

Italicize book and periodical titles.

Do not cite volume numbers for magazines or use punctuation to separate title and date.

"College Students Screaming for Stress Relief." *MSNBC.com.* 12 Dec. 2007.

Web. 30 Mar. 2011.

[*online newspaper*]

Give the work's title (in quotation marks), site's title (italicized), posting date and your access date—in that order.

Dean of Students Office. Iowa State U. "Multiple Priorities: Balancing Self, Family,

and School." 2005. Web. 4 Apr. 2011.

Dittmann, M. "Provisions from APA-Spearheaded Campus Counseling Act Become

Law." *APA Monitor* 36.1 (2005):20. Web. 6 Apr. 2011.

Dohrenwend, Barbara Snell, and Bruce Dohrenwend, eds. *Stressful Life Events: Their*

Omit the introductory article *The* in the newspaper's name.

Nature and Effects. New York: Wiley, 1974. Print.   [*edited anthology*]

Fram, Alan, and Trevor Tompson. "Poll: Stress Hurts College Students' Motivation."

Detroit News 19 Mar. 2008. Web. 30 Mar. 2011.

Capitalize all key words in a title.

Use three- letter abbreviations to denote months spelled with five or more letters.

Ganeshananthan, Sugi. "Nightmare on Whittier Blvd. Leaves Whitmanites

Sleepless." *Black and White* Nov. 1996. Web. 14 Apr. 2011.

Glenn, David. "Procrastination in College Students Is a Marker for

Unhealthy Behaviors, Study Indicates." *Chronicle of Higher Education*

26 Aug. 2002: A1. Print.

A research report in MLA style (*continues*)

Haley   12

Hall, Gregory. "College Students and Stress." Ulifeline 2006. Web. 30 Mar. 2011.

Holmes Thomas H., and Minoru Masuda. "Life Change and Illness Susceptibility."
    Dohrenwend and Dohrenwend. 45-72. Print.

Levine, Arthur. *When Dreams and Heroes Died: A Portrait of Today's College Student.*
    Jossey, 1980. Print.

Lewin, Tamar. "Record Level of Stress Found in College Freshmen." *New York Times*
    26 Jan. 2011. Web. 30 Mar. 2011.

Mayo Clinic. "Constant's stress Puts Your Health at Risk." 11 Sept. 2010. Web.
    30 Mar. 2011.

"More Students Bring Troubles to College." *AFT on Campus* Apr. 2003: 2.

Newton, Fred B., et al. "The Assessment of College Student Needs: First Step in a
    Prevention Response." *Personnel and Guidance Journal* 62 (1984): 537-43.

Putlur, Praveen, et al. "Alteration of Immune Function in Women Collegiate
    Soccer Players and College Students" *Journal of Sports Science and Medicine* 3
    (2004): 234-43. Abstract. Web. 31 Mar. 2008.

    [online abstract]

Ross, S. E., B. C. Niebling, and T. M. Heckert. "Source of Stress among College
    Students." *College Student Journal* 33 (1999): 312-17. Print.

Selye, Hans. "The Stress Concept: Past, Present, and Future." *Stress Reseach Issues*
    for the '80s. Ed. Cary L. Cooper. New York: Wiley, 1983. 63-91. Print.

    [anthology]

---. *The Stress of Life.* Rev. ed. New York: McGraw, 1976. Print.

"Top 5 College Student Stressors." 15 June 2007. College and Finance Discussion
    List. Web. 3 Apr. 2011.

Since this essay appears in an anthology cited earlier in this list, the only information needed is the editors' names and the page numbers.

Begin a citation for a Web source with the author's name (if known).

For a work with four or more authors or editors, cite only the first person's name, followed by *et al.*

Include only the final two digits of the second number if the first digits are identical.

Use three hyphens followed by a period to denote a second work by the same author.

List multiple works by the same author alphabetically according to title.

Shorten publishers' name ("McGraw" for "McGraw Hill," "Harper" for "Harper-Collins").

A research report in MLA style (*continues*)

University Health Center. U of Georgia. "Managing Stress: A Guide for College

  Students." 1 Feb. 2011. Web. 2 Apr. 2011.

Whittle, Adrian. "Common Causes of Stress among College Students." *Ezine*

  Articles 20 Mar. 2007. Web. 5 Apr. 2011.

                     [*article in an online magazine*]

A research report in MLA style (*continues*)

Special Issues in Writing

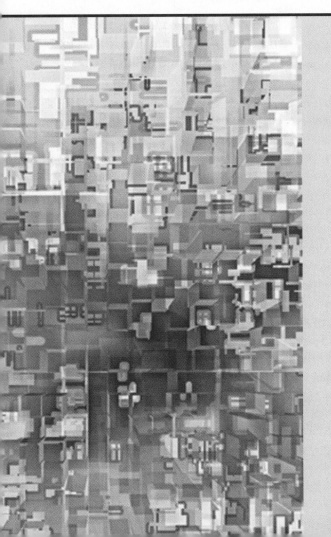

Writing at Work

LEARNING OBJECTIVES FOR THIS CHAPTER

- Understand how writing is a lifelong, daily process in one's career
- Identify the characteristics of workplace writing
- Write effective hard copy and electronic résumés
- Write persuasive solicited or unsolicited application letters

- Create a professional dossier, portfolio, or Webfolio
- Communicate using everyday workplace correspondence (memos, emails, IMs, blogs, and wikis)
- Write customer relations and sales letters

D espite the importance of meetings, phone calls, videoconferences, and face-to-face conversations, *writing* remains the core of workplace communication, whether in the form of letters, reports, emails, IMs, memos, or other documents. In workplace writing, you share information with readers who will use it for a practical purpose. Readers might use your information to perform a task, answer a question, solve a problem, make a decision, or take some other form of action. Your value to any organization will depend on how well you communicate what you know in a way that leads to action.

WRITING IN YOUR CAREER

Writing is a daily part of most careers

In any field, almost anyone in a responsible position writes daily. Managers write progress reports, personnel evaluations, requisitions, and instructions, among other documents. Computer specialists write documentation explaining to customers how to use software and hardware. Contractors write proposals, bids, and specifications for banks and customers. Engineers, technicians, and architects plan every detail of a project before contracts are awarded and construction begins. In this era of rapidly changing technology, good communication is more crucial than ever in any career.

Your writing skills are a measure of your value as an employee

When you enter the work world, employers first judge your writing by your application letter and résumé. If you join a large organization, your retention and promotion may be decided by executives you have never met. Your letters, memos, reports, and other written correspondence will be regarded as a measure of the overall quality of your work. As you advance, your ability to communicate may become even more important than your technical background. The higher your goals, the more skill in writing you will need.

CHARACTERISTICS OF WORKPLACE WRITING

The four characteristics of workplace writing

Whether you are writing a memo, a letter, an email, a report, or any other type of document, all workplace writing has these characteristics: It is reader-focused, efficient, ethical, and professional.

Reader-Focused Writing

All workplace writing is focused on the needs of the reader

In speaking with customers, clients, colleagues, or supervisors face to face, you unconsciously modify what you say as you read the listener's signals: a smile, a frown, a raised eyebrow, a nod. In a phone conversation, the voice on the other end of the line provides cues that signal approval, dismay, anger, or confusion. In writing a letter, however, you can easily forget that a flesh-and-blood person will be reacting to what you are saying—or seem to be saying. Readers are more likely to side with you when they feel as if *they matter.*

The "you" perspective

Placing the reader's needs first is known as *adopting a "you" perspective.* A letter displaying a "you" perspective subordinates the writer's interests to those of the reader. The "you" perspective conveys respect for the reader's feelings and attitudes.

To achieve a "you" perspective, put yourself in the place of the person who will read your correspondence, and ask yourself how this recipient will react to what you have written. Even a single word, carelessly chosen, can offend. For example, in corresponding with a customer who complained about a billing error, you might feel tempted to write this:

A needlessly offensive tone

> Our record keeping is very efficient, so this is obviously your error.

Such a message not only signals that you have not bothered to investigate the complaint but the tone is also condescending. Here is a more considerate version:

A tone that conveys the "you" perspective

> Thank you for your letter. We will investigate this matter immediately and will be in touch with the results within three business days.

Instead of talking down to the reader, this second version conveys a tone of respect for the reader's viewpoint and responds to the customer's request for action.

Efficient Writing

How workplace and school writing deffer

Professors read to *test* our knowledge. They read our writing from beginning to end. However, in the U.S. workplace colleagues, customers, and supervisors read to *use* our knowledge. There readers want only what they need to get the job done. Instead of reading from beginning to end, workplace readers ofter use various parts of the document for reference. These readers expect efficient writing that gets to the point and saves them time and energy.

Efficiency = an equal ratio of output to input

In any system, "efficiency" is the ratio of useful output to input. For the product that comes out, how much energy goes in?

> Energy (input) $\longrightarrow$ system $\longrightarrow$ product (output)

When a system is efficient, the output equals (or nearly equals) the input.

Similarly, a document's efficiency can be measured by how hard the user works to understand the message.

| User spends energy (input) ⟶ document ⟶ user gets the message (output)

No one should have to spend 10 minutes deciphering a message worth only 5 minutes, as in this example:

An inefficient message

> At this point in time, we are presently awaiting an on-site inspection by vendor representatives relative to electrical utilization adaptations necessary for the new computer installation. Meanwhile, all staff are asked to respect the off-limits designation of said location, as requested, due to liability insurance provisions requiring the online status of the computer.

Notice how hard you had to work to extract information that could be expressed this efficiently:

A more efficient version

> Hardware consultants will soon inspect our new computer room to recommend appropriate wiring. Because our insurance covers only an *operational* computer, this room must remain off limits until the computer is fully installed.

Documents may be inefficient in many ways. Even when the information is accurate, errors like the following create needless labor:

Causes of inefficient documents

- more (or less) information than people need
- irrelevant or uninterpreted information
- overreliance on feelings rather than facts
- confusing organization or layout
- jargon or technical expressions people cannot understand
- more words than people need

Efficient documents establish purpose and audience

Inefficient documents are produced by writers who lack a clear sense of their audience and purpose. Before writing, ask yourself *who* will use the document, *why* they will use it, *how* they will use it, and *what* you want to achieve.

Ethical Writing

Workplace writing should be ethical

Workplace writing needs to be ethical. Writers who ignore ethical considerations lose credibility at best and face legal action at worst. Ethical workplace documents are original, accurate, and honest.

Ethical writing is original

The first rule of ethical workplace writing is *originality*. No document should ever be plagiarized. Using someone else's work and claiming it as your own is plagiarism. When you do base your writing on the work of others, thoroughly document your sources, and be careful about violating copyright. For more on plagiarism, documentation, and copyright, see Chapter 23.

Ethical writing is accurate

The second ethical rule for workplace documents is *accuracy.* Readers use your documents to make decisions and take action. Names, dates, places, costs, and measurements have to be spelled out and exact. A business letter can be considered a contract; therefore, if you write to a customer or client to offer a service or product at a specified cost, you are making a legal commitment. Tell the recipients exactly what they will and will not get for their money. Workplace writing should convey only *one* meaning for all parties involved.

Ethical writing is honest

Finally, workplace documents must display honesty. Beyond outright lies, distortion or manipulation of the facts mislead readers into making bad decisions.

Professional Writing

Workplace writing is professional

Whenever you prepare a workplace document, you represent your employer. Always maintain professional standards: Follow the accepted formats for emails, memos, letters, and reports outlined in this chapter. Use high-quality stationery (usually 20-pound 8½-by-11-inch white bond) and envelopes. Also write in a tone that is neither too informal ("What's up, dude?"—and so on) nor packed with *letterese,* the stuffy, puffed-up style some writers mistakenly think sounds important. Here are examples of letterese:

Examples of letterese

Letterese	**Plain English**
as per your request	as you requested
contingent upon receipt of	as soon as we receive
please be advised that	for your information (*or omit*)
in accordance with your request	as you requested
due to the fact that	because
aforementioned	previously mentioned
pursuant to	concerning

RÉSUMÉS AND OTHER JOB–SEARCH MATERIALS

In today's job market, many applicants compete for few openings. Whether you are applying for your first professional job or changing careers, you need to market your skills effectively. At each stage of the job search, you must stand out among the competition.

Résumés

Essentially an applicant's personal advertisement for employment, a résumé gives an employer an instant overview. In fact, employers initially spend only 15 to 45 seconds looking at a résumé; during this scan, they are looking for a persuasive answer to the essential question: "What can you do for us?"

What employers
expect in a résumé

Employers are impressed by a résumé that looks good, reads easily, appears honest, and provides only the relevant information an employer needs in order to determine whether the applicant should be interviewed. Résumés that are mechanically flawed, cluttered, sketchy, hard to follow, or seemingly dishonest simply get discarded.

What to include—
and not include—
in a résumé

Parts of a Résumé. Résumés contain these standard parts: contact information, career objectives, education, work experience, personal data and interests, and references. A résumé is not the place for such items as your desired salary and benefits or your requirements for time off. Also omit your photograph as well as information that employers are not allowed to legally request (such as race, age, or marital status).

As you read through this section, refer to Figure 26.1 (page 458), which includes all the required parts of a résumé.

CONTACT INFORMATION   Tell prospective employers how to reach you. If you are between addresses, provide both addresses and check each contact point regularly. Be sure that your email address and phone number are accurate. If you use an answering machine or voice mail, record an outgoing message that sounds friendly and professional. If you have your own Web site (professional, not personal), include the URL. Remember that employers may access your Facebook or MySpace pages, so be sure to keep those pages professional in tone and content.

CAREER OBJECTIVES   Spell out the kind of job you want. Avoid vague statements such as "A position in which I can apply my education and experience." Be specific: "An intensive-care nursing position in a teaching hospital, with the eventual goal of supervising and instructing." Tailor your career objective statement as you apply for different jobs, in order to match yourself with each position. State your immediate and long-range goals, including any plans to continue your education. If the company has branches, include *Willing to relocate.*

One hiring officer for a major computer firm offers this advice: "A statement should show that you know the type of work the company does and the type of position it needs to fill" (Beamon, qtd. in Crosby, 3).

Below career objectives, you might insert a summary of qualifications. This section is vital in a computer-scannable résumé (Figure 26.3), but even in a conventional résumé, a "Qualifications" section can highlight your strengths. Make the summary specific and concrete: replace "proven leadership" with "team and project management," "special-event planning," or "instructor-led training"; replace "persuasive communicator" with "fundraising," "publicity campaigns," "environmental/public-interest advocacy," or "door-to-door canvassing." In short, allow the reader to **visualize** your activities.

EDUCATION   Begin with your most recent schooling and work backward. Include the name of the school, degree completed, year completed, and your

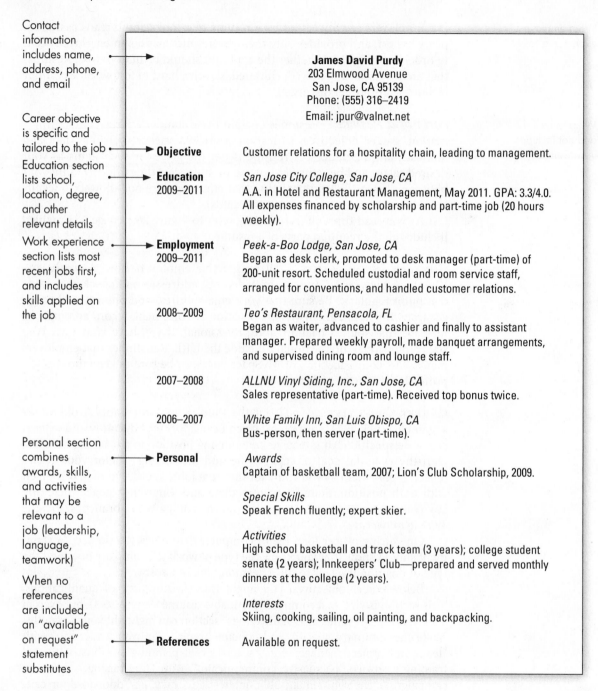

Contact information includes name, address, phone, and email

Career objective is specific and tailored to the job

Education section lists school, location, degree, and other relevant details

Work experience section lists most recent jobs first, and includes skills applied on the job

Personal section combines awards, skills, and activities that may be relevant to a job (leadership, language, teamwork)

When no references are included, an "available on request" statement substitutes

James David Purdy
203 Elmwood Avenue
San Jose, CA 95139
Phone: (555) 316–2419
Email: jpur@valnet.net

Objective   Customer relations for a hospitality chain, leading to management.

Education   *San Jose City College, San Jose, CA*
2009–2011   A.A. in Hotel and Restaurant Management, May 2011. GPA: 3.3/4.0. All expenses financed by scholarship and part-time job (20 hours weekly).

Employment   *Peek-a-Boo Lodge, San Jose, CA*
2009–2011   Began as desk clerk, promoted to desk manager (part-time) of 200-unit resort. Scheduled custodial and room service staff, arranged for conventions, and handled customer relations.

2008–2009   *Teo's Restaurant, Pensacola, FL*
Began as waiter, advanced to cashier and finally to assistant manager. Prepared weekly payroll, made banquet arrangements, and supervised dining room and lounge staff.

2007–2008   *ALLNU Vinyl Siding, Inc., San Jose, CA*
Sales representative (part-time). Received top bonus twice.

2006–2007   *White Family Inn, San Luis Obispo, CA*
Bus-person, then server (part-time).

Personal   *Awards*
Captain of basketball team, 2007; Lion's Club Scholarship, 2009.

Special Skills
Speak French fluently; expert skier.

Activities
High school basketball and track team (3 years); college student senate (2 years); Innkeepers' Club—prepared and served monthly dinners at the college (2 years).

Interests
Skiing, cooking, sailing, oil painting, and backpacking.

References   Available on request.

FIGURE 26.1 A reverse chronological résumé
Use this format to show a clear pattern of job experience.

major and minor. Omit high school, unless the high school's prestige or your achievements there warrant its inclusion. List courses that have directly prepared you for the job you seek. If your class rank or grade point average is favorable, list it. Include specialized training during military service. If you finance your education by working, say so, indicating the percentage of your contribution.

WORK EXPERIENCE   If your experience relates to the job, list it before your education. List your most recent job and then earlier jobs. Include employers' names and dates of employment. Indicate whether a job was full-time, part-time (hours weekly), or seasonal. Describe your exact duties for each job, indicating promotions. If it is to your advantage, state why you left each job. Include military experience and relevant volunteer work. If you lack paid experience, emphasize your education, including internships and special projects.

PERSONAL DATA AND INTERESTS   List any awards, skills, activities, and interests that are *relevant* to the given position, such as memberships in professional organizations, demonstrations of leadership, languages, special skills, and hobbies that may be of interest to the employer.

REFERENCES   List three to five people who have agreed to provide strongly positive assessments of your qualifications and who can speak on your behalf. Never list as references people who haven't first given you express permission. Your references should not be family members or non-work-related friends; instead, list former employers, professors, and community figures who know you well. If saving space is important, simply state at the end of your résumé, "References available on request," to help keep the résumé to one page. But if the résumé already takes up more than one page, you probably should include your references. If you don't list references, prepare a separate reference sheet that you can provide on request. Include each person's job title, company address, and contact information.

PORTFOLIOS   To illustrate your skills and experience in areas such as marketing, engineering, or other fields that generate actual documents or visual designs, assemble a portfolio showing samples of your work. If you do have a portfolio, indicate this on your résumé, followed by "Available on request," as in Figure 26.3. (See the Guidelines for Preparing Dossiers, Portfolios, and Webfolios on pages 470–471.)

Résumés from a Template.   Programs such as *Microsoft Word* provide electronic templates that can be filled in with an individual's own personal data. Such programs organize the information keyed into the template, and the organization can be easily changed as needed.

While templates can help you organize your résumé, you still need to be aware of which organizational pattern is most appropriate.

Organizing Your Résumé.   Organize your résumé to convey the strongest impression of your qualifications, skills, and experience. A résumé like the one in Figure 26.1 is known as a *reverse chronological résumé*, listing the most recent school and job first. If you have limited experience or education, gaps in your work history (e.g., due to illness, raising children), or if you have frequently switched career paths, create a *functional résumé* (Figure 26.2) to highlight skills relevant to a particular job.

GUIDELINES for Hard-Copy Résumés

- **Begin your résumé well before your job search.**

- **Tailor your résumé for each job.** Read the advertised job requirements, and adjust your career objective accordingly—but realistically. Tailor your work experience, personal data, and personal interests to emphasize certain areas for certain jobs—but do not distort the facts.

- **Try to limit the résumé to a single page but keep it uncluttered and tasteful.** If the résumé looks cramped, you might need to go to a second page—in which case you could have room to list your references (with their permission).

- **Stick to experience relevant to the job.** Don't list everything you've ever done.

- **Use action verbs and key words.** Action verbs (*supervised, developed, built, taught, installed, managed, trained, solved, planned, directed*) stress your ability to produce results. If your résumé is likely to be scanned electronically or if you post it online, list keywords as nouns (*leadership skills, software development, data processing, editing*) below your contact information and your statement of objective (see Figure 26.3).

- **Use bold, italic, underlining, colors, fonts, bullets, and punctuation thoughtfully, for emphasis.** Do not use highlighting or punctuation to be artsy. Keep punctuation consistent and as simple as possible.

- **Never invent or distort credentials.** Make yourself look as good as the *facts* allow. Companies routinely investigate claims made in résumés, and people who lie will certainly not be hired.

- **Use quality paper and envelopes.** Use white paper of high quality.

- **Proofread, proofread, proofread.** Don't rely on a computer spell checker. Famous résumé mistakes include winning a "bogus award" instead of a "bonus award" and "ruining" rather than "running" a business.

Today's résumés are often submitted electronically

Electronic Résumés.   Expect to submit your résumé electronically as well as (or instead of) in hard copy. Even if you are only asked to submit a hard copy résumé, prospective employers may want to scan the hard copy into their computer systems, which requires special formatting. Many employers ask that résumés be submitted as email attachments, and you may want

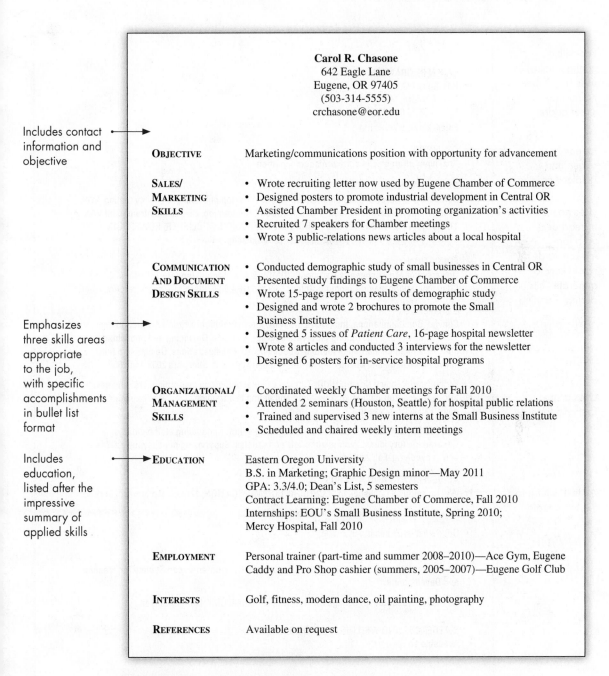

Includes contact information and objective

Emphasizes three skills areas appropriate to the job, with specific accomplishments in bullet list format

Includes education, listed after the impressive summary of applied skills

Carol R. Chasone
642 Eagle Lane
Eugene, OR 97405
(503-314-5555)
crchasone@eor.edu

OBJECTIVE   Marketing/communications position with opportunity for advancement

SALES/ MARKETING SKILLS
- Wrote recruiting letter now used by Eugene Chamber of Commerce
- Designed posters to promote industrial development in Central OR
- Assisted Chamber President in promoting organization's activities
- Recruited 7 speakers for Chamber meetings
- Wrote 3 public-relations news articles about a local hospital

COMMUNICATION AND DOCUMENT DESIGN SKILLS
- Conducted demographic study of small businesses in Central OR
- Presented study findings to Eugene Chamber of Commerce
- Wrote 15-page report on results of demographic study
- Designed and wrote 2 brochures to promote the Small Business Institute
- Designed 5 issues of *Patient Care*, 16-page hospital newsletter
- Wrote 8 articles and conducted 3 interviews for the newsletter
- Designed 6 posters for in-service hospital programs

ORGANIZATIONAL/ MANAGEMENT SKILLS
- Coordinated weekly Chamber meetings for Fall 2010
- Attended 2 seminars (Houston, Seattle) for hospital public relations
- Trained and supervised 3 new interns at the Small Business Institute
- Scheduled and chaired weekly intern meetings

EDUCATION   Eastern Oregon University
B.S. in Marketing; Graphic Design minor—May 2011
GPA: 3.3/4.0; Dean's List, 5 semesters
Contract Learning: Eugene Chamber of Commerce, Fall 2010
Internships: EOU's Small Business Institute, Spring 2010;
Mercy Hospital, Fall 2010

EMPLOYMENT   Personal trainer (part-time and summer 2008–2010)—Ace Gym, Eugene
Caddy and Pro Shop cashier (summers, 2005–2007)—Eugene Golf Club

INTERESTS   Golf, fitness, modern dance, oil painting, photography

REFERENCES   Available on request

FIGURE 26.2   A functional résumé
Use this format to focus on skills and potential instead of employment chronology.
(Note that certain items in the above skills categories overlap.)

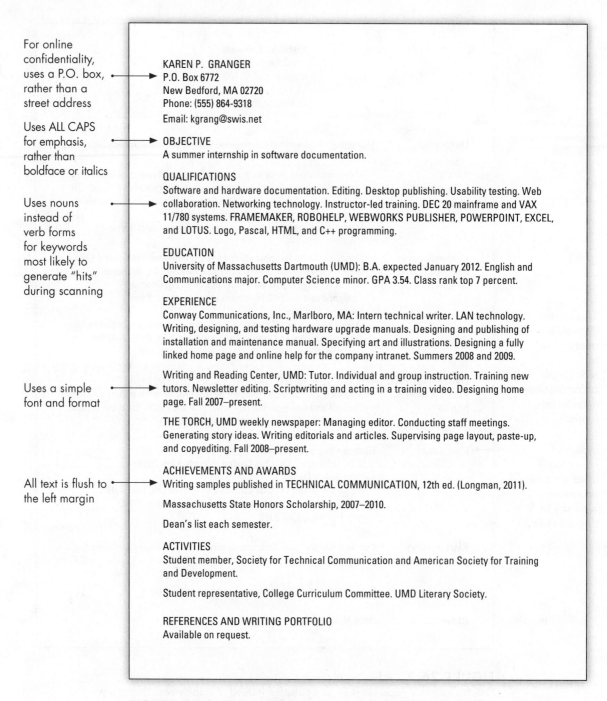

For online
confidentiality,
uses a P.O. box,
rather than a
street address

Uses ALL CAPS
for emphasis,
rather than
boldface or italics

Uses nouns
instead of
verb forms
for keywords
most likely to
generate "hits"
during scanning

Uses a simple
font and format

All text is flush to
the left margin

KAREN P. GRANGER
P.O. Box 6772
New Bedford, MA 02720
Phone: (555) 864-9318
Email: kgrang@swis.net

OBJECTIVE
A summer internship in software documentation.

QUALIFICATIONS
Software and hardware documentation. Editing. Desktop publishing. Usability testing. Web collaboration. Networking technology. Instructor-led training. DEC 20 mainframe and VAX 11/780 systems. FRAMEMAKER, ROBOHELP, WEBWORKS PUBLISHER, POWERPOINT, EXCEL, and LOTUS. Logo, Pascal, HTML, and C++ programming.

EDUCATION
University of Massachusetts Dartmouth (UMD): B.A. expected January 2012. English and Communications major. Computer Science minor. GPA 3.54. Class rank top 7 percent.

EXPERIENCE
Conway Communications, Inc., Marlboro, MA: Intern technical writer. LAN technology. Writing, designing, and testing hardware upgrade manuals. Designing and publishing of installation and maintenance manual. Specifying art and illustrations. Designing a fully linked home page and online help for the company intranet. Summers 2008 and 2009.

Writing and Reading Center, UMD: Tutor. Individual and group instruction. Training new tutors. Newsletter editing. Scriptwriting and acting in a training video. Designing home page. Fall 2007–present.

THE TORCH, UMD weekly newspaper: Managing editor. Conducting staff meetings. Generating story ideas. Writing editorials and articles. Supervising page layout, paste-up, and copyediting. Fall 2008–present.

ACHIEVEMENTS AND AWARDS
Writing samples published in TECHNICAL COMMUNICATION, 12th ed. (Longman, 2011).

Massachusetts State Honors Scholarship, 2007–2010.

Dean's list each semester.

ACTIVITIES
Student member, Society for Technical Communication and American Society for Training and Development.

Student representative, College Curriculum Committee. UMD Literary Society.

REFERENCES AND WRITING PORTFOLIO
Available on request.

FIGURE 26.3   **A résumé that can be scanned, emailed, or posted online**
Notice the standard print and the absence of fancy highlighting.

to post your résumé online, either on your own Web site or on a job search database (such as *Monster.com* or *Yahoo! HotJobs*). As you read through this section, refer to the sample résumé in Figure 26.3.

Emailed résumés

EMAILED AND SCANNABLE RÉSUMÉS   Typically, résumés are submitted to employment sites (see below) or sent as email attachments. When submitting as an email attachment, format the résumé using a word processing program that is compatible on both Macs and PCs. Or if your word processing software allows, save the résumé as a PDF document, to ensure that the formatting and page breaks will look identical on any computer.

Scannable résumés

Some organizations still request résumés be submitted on paper. In these cases, companies will often scan the paper résumé so it can be saved electronically. Electronic storage of hard copy résumés enables employers to screen applicants, to compile a database of applicants (for later openings), and to evaluate all applicants fairly. An optical scanner feeds in the printed page, stores it as a file, and searches the file for keywords associated with the job opening. Résumés containing the most keywords ("hits") make the final cut.

To design a résumé that can be scanned or sent as an email attachment use the following Guidelines.

GUIDELINES for Emailed and Scannable Résumés

■ **Use keywords.** Use words that are likely to get "hits" in keyword searches of a scannable résumé. You may want to create a "qualifications" section at the top of your résumé. Include keywords for general skills (conflict management, report and proposal writing), specialized skills (graphic design, XTML), credentials (B.S. in electrical engineering, Phi Beta Kappa), and job titles (manager, technician, intern). Use nouns for keywords whenever possible.

■ **Consider making your scannable résumé slightly longer than your standard, hard copy version.** The longer the résumé being scanned, the more hits possible.

■ **Use a simple font.** Stick with those fonts that are the easiest to scan, such as Courier, Times, and Helvetica (Ariel).

■ **Use simple formatting.** Avoid boldface, shading, italics, underlining, tabs, and centering. Place all text flush to the left margin. For emphasis, use ALL CAPS instead of boldface, italics, shading, or underlining.

■ **Save your résumé in "text only" or "rich text" format.** This will ensure that all fancy fonts and formats are removed and will allow for smooth scanning and emailing.

■ **Proofread your résumé.** Make sure the résumé is free of errors and that it emphasizes your most important skills and qualifications.

■ **Do not staple or fold pages of a scannable résumé.**

ONLINE RÉSUMÉS   You may also want to place your résumé online, either on your own Web site (which might include a *Webfolio*, see page 471) or on an employment Web site. For an employment Web site, follow the site's posting guidelines. For your own site or social networking page (such as LinkedIn or Facebook), use the following Guidelines.

GUIDELINES for Online Résumés

- **Add hyperlinks, if desired, for a searchable résumé.** If you post your résumé on your own Web site, consider adding hyperlinks so that readers can link to specific documents elsewhere on your page, such as scanned samples from your portfolio (see Figure 26.4).

- **Be sure your searchable résumé can download quickly.** Complex graphics and multimedia download slowly. Also verify that all links are functioning.

- **Include the searchable résumé's Web address on your hard copy or scannable résumé.**

- **Prepare alternative delivery options.** In case an employer refuses to track down your résumé on a Web page, be prepared to email an attached copy.

- **Avoid personal information.** Do not expose yourself or your references to identity theft by posting photographs, home addresses (use a P.O. box or simply your city and email address), or birth dates. Also avoid frivolous personal information. Post only on sites that offer privacy options, such as Zoominfo, LinkedIn, or Ziggs.com; at these sites you can check, update, and correct your profile anytime.

Application Letters

An *application letter*, also known as a *cover letter*, complements your résumé. The letter's main purpose is to explain how your credentials fit the particular job and to convey a sufficiently informed, professional, and likable persona for the prospective employer to decide that you should be interviewed. Another purpose of the letter is to highlight specific qualifications or skills; for example, you might have listed "C++ programming" on your résumé, but for one particular job application you may wish to call attention to this item in your cover letter:

> My résumé notes that I am experienced with C++ programming. I also tutor C++ programming students in our school's learning center.

Solicited and unsolicited application letters

Sometimes you will apply for positions advertised in print or by word of mouth (*solicited applications*). At other times you will write prospecting letters to organizations that have not advertised an opening but that might need someone like you (*unsolicited applications*). In either case, tailor your letter to the situation.

Email link for
quick contact

Link to
department site

Links to WRC
site and
documents
produced

Links to
company site
and documents
produced

Links to
newspaper
and documents
produced

Link to sample
documents

Links to
professional
societies

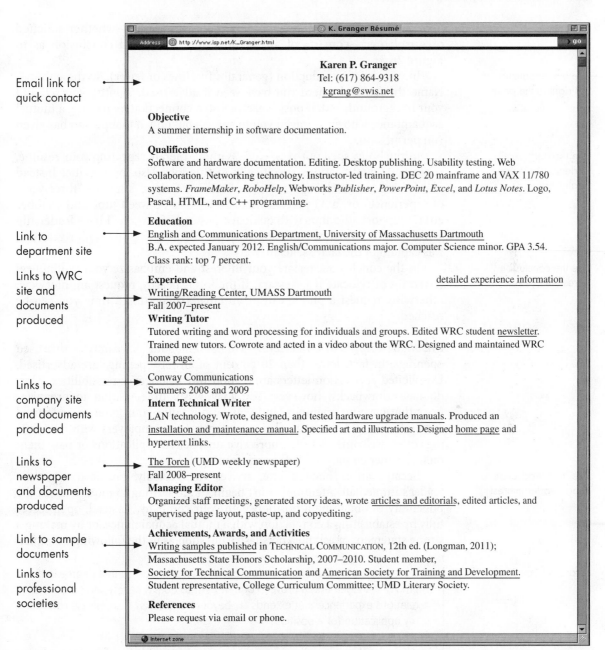

Karen P. Granger
Tel: (617) 864-9318
kgrang@swis.net

Objective
A summer internship in software documentation.

Qualifications
Software and hardware documentation. Editing. Desktop publishing. Usability testing. Web collaboration. Networking technology. Instructor-led training. DEC 20 mainframe and VAX 11/780 systems. *FrameMaker, RoboHelp*, Webworks *Publisher, PowerPoint, Excel*, and *Lotus Notes*. Logo, Pascal, HTML, and C++ programming.

Education
English and Communications Department, University of Massachusetts Dartmouth
B.A. expected January 2012. English/Communications major. Computer Science minor. GPA 3.54. Class rank: top 7 percent.

Experience   detailed experience information
Writing/Reading Center, UMASS Dartmouth
Fall 2007–present
Writing Tutor
Tutored writing and word processing for individuals and groups. Edited WRC student newsletter. Trained new tutors. Cowrote and acted in a video about the WRC. Designed and maintained WRC home page.

Conway Communications
Summers 2008 and 2009
Intern Technical Writer
LAN technology. Wrote, designed, and tested hardware upgrade manuals. Produced an installation and maintenance manual. Specified art and illustrations. Designed home page and hypertext links.

The Torch (UMD weekly newspaper)
Fall 2008–present
Managing Editor
Organized staff meetings, generated story ideas, wrote articles and editorials, edited articles, and supervised page layout, paste-up, and copyediting.

Achievements, Awards, and Activities
Writing samples published in TECHNICAL COMMUNICATION, 12th ed. (Longman, 2011); Massachusetts State Honors Scholarship, 2007–2010. Student member, Society for Technical Communication and American Society for Training and Development. Student representative, College Curriculum Committee; UMD Literary Society.

References
Please request via email or phone.

FIGURE 26.4   An Online Résumé
Links connect to various types of information, including several links to Karen's writing portfolio. For security reasons, personal contact information is limited to the applicant's phone number and email address.

Solicited Application Letters.   An application letter—whether solicited or unsolicited—consists of an introduction, body, and conclusion as in Figure 26.5.

Use the introduction to get right to the point

In your brief introduction (generally, five lines or fewer), do these things: Name the job and where you have seen it advertised; identify yourself and your background; and, if possible, establish a connection by naming a mutual acquaintance who encouraged you to apply—but only if that person has given you permission.

Use the body section to demonstrate your qualifications

In the body, spell out your case. Without merely repeating your résumé, relate your qualifications specifically to this job. Also, be specific. Instead of referring to "much experience" or "increased sales," stipulate "three years of experience" or "a 35 percent increase in sales between June and October 2011." Support all claims with evidence. Instead of saying, "I have leadership skills," say, "I served as student senate president during my senior year and was captain of the lacrosse team."

Use the conclusion to restate interest

In the conclusion, restate your interest and emphasize your willingness to retrain or relocate if necessary. If the job is nearby, request an interview; otherwise, request a phone call or an email, suggesting a time you can be reached.

Unsolicited Application Letters.   Do not limit your job search to advertised openings. In fact, fewer than 20 percent of all job openings are advertised. Unsolicited application letters are a good way to uncover possibilities. They do have drawbacks, however: You may waste time writing to organizations that have no openings, and you cannot tailor your letter to advertised requirements. But there are also advantages: Even employers with no openings often welcome and file impressive unsolicited applications or pass them on to another employer who has an opening.

Use the introduction to spark reader interest

Because an unsolicited letter arrives unexpectedly, you need to get the reader's immediate attention. Don't begin, "I am writing to inquire about the possibility of obtaining a position with your company." Instead, open forcefully by establishing a connection with a mutual acquaintance, or by making a strong statement or asking a persuasive question as in the following example:

A forceful opening

> Does your hotel chain have a place for a junior manager with a degree in hospitality management, a proven commitment to quality service, and customer relations experience that extends far beyond textbooks? If so, please consider my application for a position.

Address your letter to the person most likely in charge of hiring. Always write to a specific person—not to a generic recipient such as "Director of Human Resources." To find out the name of the person who should receive your application, consult the company's Web site and then call the company to verify the person's name and title. Also, consider using a "Subject" line to attract a busy reader's attention and to announce the purpose of your letter, as in Figure 26.6.

203 Elmwood Avenue
San Jose, CA 10462
April 22, 2011

Sara Costanza
Personnel Director
Liberty International, Inc.
Lansdowne, PA 24153

Dear Ms. Costanza:

Writer identifies self and purpose

Please consider my application for a junior management position at your Lake Geneva resort, as advertised in the April 19 *Philadephia Enquirer*. I will graduate from San Jose City College on May 30 with an Associate of Arts degree in hotel and restaurant management. Dr. H. V. Garlid, my nutrition professor, described his experience as a consultant for Liberty International and encouraged me to apply.

Establishes a connection

Relates specific qualifications from his résumé to the job opening

As you can see from my enclosed résumé, for two years I worked as a part-time desk clerk, and I was promoted to manager at a 200-unit resort. This experience, combined with earlier customer relations work in a variety of situations, has given me a clear and practical understanding of customers' needs and expectations.

Applies relevant personal interests to the job

As an amateur chef, I know of the effort, attention, and patience required to prepare fine food. Moreover, my skiing and sailing background might be assets to your resort's recreation program.

Expresses confidence and enthusiasm throughout the letter

I have worked hard to hone my hospitality management skills. My experience, education, and personality have prepared me to work well with others and to respond creatively to challenges, crises, and added responsibilities.

Makes follow-up easy for the reader

If my background meets your needs, please phone me any weekday after 4:00 p.m. at (555) 316-2419 or email at jpur@valnet.net.

Sincerely,

James D. Purdy

James D. Purdy

FIGURE 26.5 **A solicited application letter**

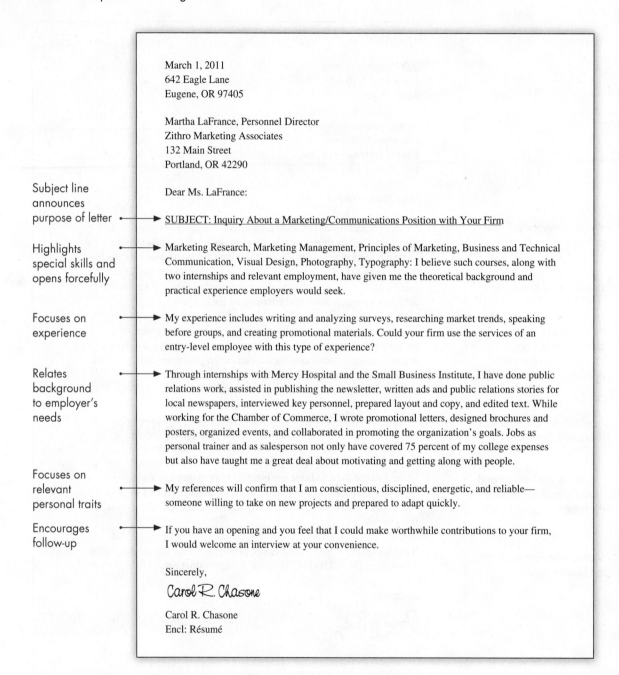

March 1, 2011
642 Eagle Lane
Eugene, OR 97405

Martha LaFrance, Personnel Director
Zithro Marketing Associates
132 Main Street
Portland, OR 42290

Dear Ms. LaFrance:

SUBJECT: Inquiry About a Marketing/Communications Position with Your Firm

Marketing Research, Marketing Management, Principles of Marketing, Business and Technical Communication, Visual Design, Photography, Typography: I believe such courses, along with two internships and relevant employment, have given me the theoretical background and practical experience employers would seek.

My experience includes writing and analyzing surveys, researching market trends, speaking before groups, and creating promotional materials. Could your firm use the services of an entry-level employee with this type of experience?

Through internships with Mercy Hospital and the Small Business Institute, I have done public relations work, assisted in publishing the newsletter, written ads and public relations stories for local newspapers, interviewed key personnel, prepared layout and copy, and edited text. While working for the Chamber of Commerce, I wrote promotional letters, designed brochures and posters, organized events, and collaborated in promoting the organization's goals. Jobs as personal trainer and as salesperson not only have covered 75 percent of my college expenses but also have taught me a great deal about motivating and getting along with people.

My references will confirm that I am conscientious, disciplined, energetic, and reliable—someone willing to take on new projects and prepared to adapt quickly.

If you have an opening and you feel that I could make worthwhile contributions to your firm, I would welcome an interview at your convenience.

Sincerely,

Carol R. Chasone

Carol R. Chasone
Encl: Résumé

Labels (left margin):
- Subject line announces purpose of letter
- Highlights special skills and opens forcefully
- Focuses on experience
- Relates background to employer's needs
- Focuses on relevant personal traits
- Encourages follow-up

FIGURE 26.6   An unsolicited application letter

GUIDELINES for Application Letters

- **Customize each letter for the specific job opening.** If you'd like, create a prototype application letter, but be sure to adapt it for each prospective job. Don't look for shortcuts.

- **Use caution when adapting sample letters.** Plenty of free, online sample letters provide ideas for approaching your own situation. But never borrow them whole. Most employers are able to spot a "canned" letter immediately.

- **Create a dynamic tone with active voice and action verbs.** Instead of "Management responsibilities were steadily given to me," say "I steadily assumed management responsibilities." Be confident without seeming arrogant. (For more on tone, see pages 139–143.)

- **Never be vague.** Help readers visualize: Instead of saying, "I am familiar with the 1022 interactive database system and RUNOFF, the text-processing system," say "As a lab grader, I kept grading records on the 1022 database management system and composed lab procedures on the RUNOFF text-processing system."

- **Never exaggerate.** Liars get busted.

- **Convey some enthusiasm.** An enthusiastic attitude can sometimes be as important as your background (as in Figure 26.6).

- **Avoid flattery.** Don't say "I am greatly impressed by your remarkable company."

- **Be concise.** Review pages 118–124. Limit your letters to one page, unless your discussion truly warrants the additional space.

- **Avoid being overly informal or overly stiff.** Avoid informal terms that sound unprofessional ("Your company sounds like a cool place to work") as well as stuffy language ("Hitherto, I request the honor of your acquaintance").

- **Never settle for a first draft—or even a second or third.** The application letter is your one chance to introduce yourself to a prospective employer. Make it perfect by trimming excess wording, double-checking the tone, and ensuring that you have connected your qualifications directly to the job. After you are satisfied with the content, proofread repeatedly to spot any factual errors or typos.

- **Never send a photocopied letter.**

DOSSIERS, PORTFOLIOS, AND WEBFOLIOS

An employer impressed by your résumé and application letter will have further questions about your credentials and your past work. These questions will be answered, respectively, by your dossier and your portfolio (or Webfolio).

Dossiers

What a dossier contains

Your dossier contains your credentials: college transcript, recommendation letters, and other items (such as a scholarship award or commendation letter) that offer evidence of your achievements. Prospective employers who decide to follow up on your application will request your dossier. By collecting recommendations in one folder, you spare your references from writing the same letter repeatedly.

Your college placement office will keep the dossier (or placement folder) on file and send copies to employers. Always keep your own copy as well, including any nonconfidential recommendation letters. Then, if an employer requests your dossier, you can photocopy and mail it, advising your recipient that the official placement copy is on the way, as dossiers are not always mailed immediately from a busy placement office.

Portfolios and Webfolios

What a portfolio contains

Your portfolio (or Webfolio, Figure 26.7) contains an introduction or mission statement explaining what you've included in your portfolio and why. Among the included items are your résumé, uploaded or scanned examples of your work, and anything else pertinent to your job search (such as copies of documents from your dossier). An organized, professional-looking portfolio or Webfolio shows that you can apply your skills and helps you stand out as a candidate. It also gives you concrete material to discuss during job interviews.

As you create your portfolio or Webfolio, seek advice and feedback from professors in your major and from other people in the field. If you have a portfolio, indicate this on your résumé, followed by "Available on request." If you have a Webfolio, provide the URL on your résumé, but also bring printed copies of its contents to your interview. Keep copies of these items on hand to leave with the interviewer if requested.

GUIDELINES for Dossiers, Portfolios, and Webfolios

- **Always provide an introduction or mission statement.** Place this page at the beginning, to introduce and explain the contents.

- **Collect relevant materials.** Gather documents or graphics you've prepared in school or on the job, presentations you've given, and projects or experiments you've worked on. Possible items: campus newspaper articles, reports on course projects, papers that earned an "A," examples of persuasive argument, documents from an internship, or visuals you've designed for an oral presentation.

- **Include copies of dossier materials.** Although they won't be official unless they go directly from your campus placement office to your prospective employer, post copies of your college transcript and recommendations on your Webfolio.

- **Assemble your items.** Place your résumé first (after your introduction/mission statement), and use divider pages or electronic files to group related items. Follow the same structure for a Webfolio. Aim for a professional look.

■ **Omit irrelevant items.** Personal photographs and other items more appropriate for a MySpace or Facebook page do not belong in a portfolio or Webfolio.

■ **Omit your street address or phone number from your Webfolio.** To maintain privacy and security, post only your email address. If you post your references, include only their names and the text of their letters, not their contact information.

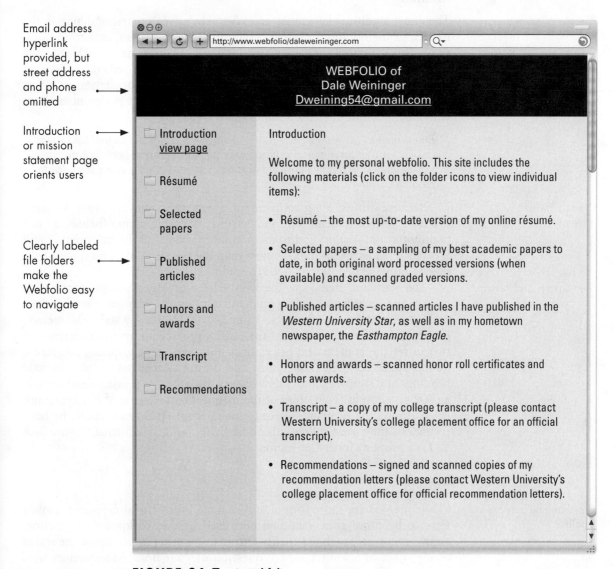

Email address hyperlink provided, but street address and phone omitted

Introduction or mission statement page orients users

Clearly labeled file folders make the Webfolio easy to navigate

WEBFOLIO of
Dale Weininger
Dweining54@gmail.com

Introduction
view page

Résumé

Selected
papers

Published
articles

Honors and
awards

Transcript

Recommendations

Introduction

Welcome to my personal webfolio. This site includes the following materials (click on the folder icons to view individual items):

• Résumé – the most up-to-date version of my online résumé.

• Selected papers – a sampling of my best academic papers to date, in both original word processed versions (when available) and scanned graded versions.

• Published articles – scanned articles I have published in the *Western University Star*, as well as in my hometown newspaper, the *Easthampton Eagle*.

• Honors and awards – scanned honor roll certificates and other awards.

• Transcript – a copy of my college transcript (please contact Western University's college placement office for an official transcript).

• Recommendations – signed and scanned copies of my recommendation letters (please contact Western University's college placement office for official recommendation letters).

FIGURE 26.7   A Webfolio
Be sure that your Webfolio is up to date. Check routinely to ensure that all links are functioning.

EVERYDAY WORKPLACE CORRESPONDENCE: MEMOS, EMAILS, INSTANT MESSAGES, TEXT MESSAGES, BLOGS, AND WIKIS

Whereas in the past, the bulk of everyday workplace correspondence occurred over the telephone or face to face, today's workplace communication happens mostly in written form, in a variety of media and formats discussed below.

Memos

Purpose of memos

The most traditional form of everyday workplace correspondence is the memo, or memorandum. Memos typically give directives, make inquiries, provide instruction, and relay various kinds of information. Despite the explosive growth of email, paper memos continue to be used widely because they provide formality, emphasis, ease of posting in a workstation or office, and a paper trail. Different organizations have different preferences about when memos should be used rather than email.

> **Note**
>
> *Email memos leave their own trail. Although generally less formal and more quickly written than paper memos, email memos are saved both as hard copy and online—and can be inadvertently forwarded to someone never intended to receive or read them.*

What to include in a memo

Because it must often compete for a busy recipient's attention, a memo needs to be easy to scan, file, and retrieve. A usable memo focuses on *one* main topic and is short and to the point. It provides all the information and analysis a reader needs, but *no more* than the reader needs, and it is distributed to only the people who need to read it.

Memo parts and format

The standard memo has the word *Memo* or *Memorandum* centered at the top and includes a heading guide identifying the recipients, sender, date, and subject (make sure the subject line is brief but clearly states the memo's purpose). In the text portion of the memo, provide an opening sentence or two to set the context and get right to the point; single-space paragraphs, double-space between paragraphs, and do not indent paragraphs; include headings and simple graphics if necessary to clarify the message; and include a copy notation at the bottom of the memo if copies are sent to anyone not listed among the recipients. Because memos are often read rapidly by busy recipients, they must follow this consistent, predictable format. Figure 26.8 shows a properly formatted memo.

Emails

The changing purpose of emails

While memos are more formal and designed for official messages, emails tend to be more conversational and used in the workplace for routine, simple messages, such as quickly letting a coworker know about the status of a project or asking a simple question of your boss. Even writers who are extremely careful with traditional paper correspondence sometimes ignore spelling and grammar as they dash off various emails. However, as

MEMORANDUM

To: All Marketing Assistants, Cincinnati Office Web
           Marketing Group
From: Marilyn Zito, Purchasing <m.zito@adco.com> *MZ*
Date: October 25, 2011
Subject: Your choices for new multifunction printer

As you requested at our October 12 meeting, I have gathered all the manufacturer information needed to order a new multifunction printer to replace the inefficient one in your area. As you know, since the MAs typically make the most use of the printers, I would appreciate your input as to which printers from the attached options seem most suitable for your purposes.

Please note that I was required to select from options under $8,500 in order to stay within your department's 2011 purchasing budget, a substantial portion of which was used to purchase your new high-speed optical scanners in March. However, I think you will find that the multifunction printers selected are state-of-the-art and should more than meet your needs in terms of capacity, speed, quality, precision, and durability—all of which you indicated were important attributes.

Please take a careful look at the models attached, consider your impressions of each model, pick your top three preferences, and email me your lists individually by November 5. I will tabulate your votes, contact you with the results, and order accordingly.

Thank you very much for taking the time to help me make an informed decision that meets your genuine needs.

Copies: J. Herrera, Director of Marketing
           M. Ziolkowski, Vice President, Purchasing

FIGURE 26.8   A properly formatted memo

the uses for email broaden and as the software evolves, workplace email messages are starting to look more polished. Writers are paying greater attention to style and correctness, and they are making their emails look more professional.

The standard email format resembles that of the paper memo, with "To," "From," "Date," and "Subject" fields. Unlike in a memo, the copy notation appears as a "Cc" (courtesy copy) or "Bcc" (blind courtesy copy) in the heading

GUIDELINES for Memos

- **Do not overuse or misuse memos.** Use email or the telephone when you need to ask a quick question or resolve a simple issue. For a sensitive topic, prefer a face-to-face conversation whenever possible.

- **Use memos for in-house purposes only.** When sending a message to a client, use email if the message is informal and a letter if the message is more formal.

- **Be brief but sufficiently informative.** Recipients expect memos that are short and to the point but not at the expense of clarity.

- **Be sure the tone of your memo is polite and respectful.** Don't make enemies by "sounding off."

- **Avoid sounding too formal or too informal for the topic or audience.** A memo to the person in the next cubicle to ask for help on a project, for example, would be more informal than a memo to a company executive.

- **Check spelling, grammar, and style.** Run the spelling and grammar checkers, but also proofread or ask a colleague to proofread the memo.

- **Be sure to initial your memo.** Initials beside your typed name certify that you are the author.

- **Determine whether to use paper or email to send your memo.** Paper memos take longer to reach the reader but may convey a more serious purpose, whereas digital distribution (such as email) is quicker but may be overlooked by the recipient.

- **Distribute to the right people.** Do not "spam" people with your memo. Whether you are sending the memo on paper or as an email attachment, be sure it reaches only those who need the information. At the same time, don't leave out anyone who needs to read your message.

guide, not at the end of the message, and enclosures can be sent as email attachments. In addition to these standard features, workplace emails use the introduction-body-conclusion format and headings, bullets, and other graphic highlights to breaks up passages of text at the bottom. A signature block (includes sender's contact information) and a complementary closing. See Figure 26.9 for an example.

Note *Any email message you receive is copyrighted by the person who wrote it. Under current law, forwarding this message to anyone for any purpose, without permision, is a violation of the owner's copyright. The same is true for reproducing an email message as part of any type of publication, unless your use of this material falls within the boundaries of fair use (see pages 412–413).*

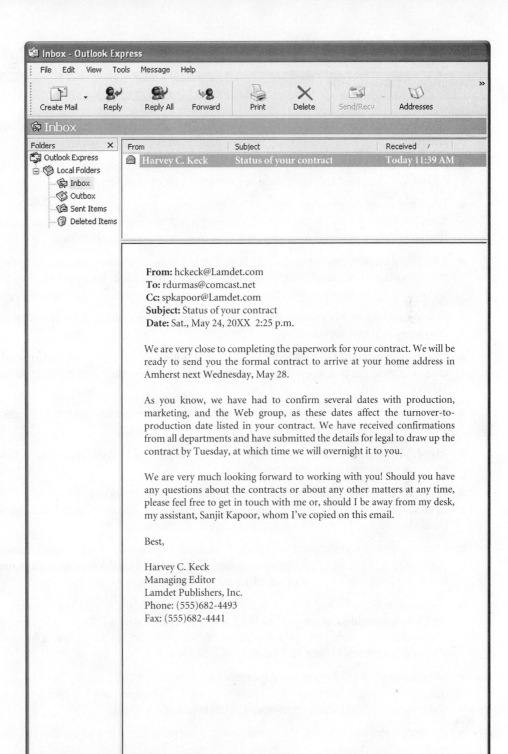

Header contains From, To, Subject, Date, plus Courtesy Copy (Cc)

Introductory paragraph gets right to the point

Body text explains background details

Conclusion invites further action

Complimentary closing Signature block appears at the very end

Inbox - Outlook Express

File   Edit   View   Tools   Message   Help

Create Mail   Reply   Reply All   Forward   Print   Delete   Send/Recv   Addresses

Inbox

Folders
Outlook Express
Local Folders
Inbox
Outbox
Sent Items
Deleted Items

From	Subject	Received
Harvey C. Keck	Status of your contract	Today 11:39 AM

From: hckeck@Lamdet.com
To: rdurmas@comcast.net
Cc: spkapoor@Lamdet.com
Subject: Status of your contract
Date: Sat., May 24, 20XX 2:25 p.m.

We are very close to completing the paperwork for your contract. We will be ready to send you the formal contract to arrive at your home address in Amherst next Wednesday, May 28.

As you know, we have had to confirm several dates with production, marketing, and the Web group, as these dates affect the turnover-to-production date listed in your contract. We have received confirmations from all departments and have submitted the details for legal to draw up the contract by Tuesday, at which time we will overnight it to you.

We are very much looking forward to working with you! Should you have any questions about the contracts or about any other matters at any time, please feel free to get in touch with me or, should I be away from my desk, my assistant, Sanjit Kapoor, whom I've copied on this email.

Best,

Harvey C. Keck
Managing Editor
Lamdet Publishers, Inc.
Phone: (555)682-4493
Fax: (555)682-4441

FIGURE 26.9   A workplace email
This email includes all the required components and is organized in an introduction/body/conclusion structure.
Source: Outlook Express frame used with permission from Microsoft.

GUIDELINES for Emails

- *Don't use email for confidential information.* Avoid complaining, evaluating, or criticizing, and handle anything that should be kept private in some other way.

- *Don't use email when a more personal medium is preferable.* Sometimes an issue is best resolved by a face-to-face discussion, a phone call, or even voice mail.

- *Don't use email for the most formal correspondence.* Don't use email to apply for or to resign from a job, send a thank-you letter following a job interview, request a raise, respond to a formal letter, or respond to something that may have legal implications.

- *Check and answer your emails daily.* If you're really busy, at least acknowledge receipt of your emails and respond later. If you will be out of the office, set your email to auto-reply, so senders know that you are away.

- *Before you forward a message, obtain permission from the sender.* Also, do not edit the sender's message when forwarding.

- *Don't use your employer's network for anything not work-related.* If you must send personal emails during the day, keep them to a minimum and use a separate email system, such as Yahoo, Hotmail, or Gmail.

- *Assume that your email is permanent and readable by anyone at any time.* "Forensic software" can find and revive deleted files.

- *Avoid "flaming," wisecracks, and rude remarks.* Any email judged harassing or discriminatory can have legal consequences.

- *Write a clear subject line.* Instead of "Test Data" or "Data Request," be specific: "Request for Beta Test Data for Project 16." This line helps recipients decide whether to read the message immediately, and it helps for filing and future reference.

- *Use appropriate formatting.* Don't indent paragraphs; instead, double-space between them. Avoid ALL CAPS, which make your message appear to SCREAM. Use bullets, headings, numbered lists, italics, and other formatting features for readability.

- *Use appropriately formal or informal salutations and closings.* If you know your recipient well, use informal salutations ("Hello") and informal closings ("Regards," "Best"). However, when addressing someone you don't know or someone in authority, use a formal salutation ("Dear Dr. Gomez") and a formal closing ("Sincerely").

- *Use emoticons and abbreviations sparingly.* Use emoticons and smiley faces :-) only in very informal messages to people you know very well. The same goes for common email abbreviations (FYI, ASAP) and "text-speak" abbreviations (OMG).

- *Be concise and to the point.* Recipients are important and do not want to scroll through long screens of information.

- *Don't send huge or specially formatted attachments without first checking with the recipient.* Large files can crash the recipient's computer or overfill his or her inbox. In addition, email recipients may be unable to open specially formatted attachments.

- *Proofread thoroughly before hitting "send."* Every message reflects your image, so double-check any email with your name on it. Also be careful that the email goes only to your intended recipients.

Instant Messages and Text Messages

Workplace uses of IMs and texts

While instant messages and text messages have long been popular for personal communications, they have recently become common in the workplace.

Instant messages (abbreviated as "IMs") allow for text-based conversation in real time. The user types a message in a pop-up box, and the recipient can respond instantly. IM groupware enables multiple users to collaborate from various locations.

Text messages (often called "texts" for short) allow quick communication using a cell phone or smart phone (such as Blackberry, Droid, or iPhone).

When not to use IMs and texts

Although they are useful for brief, rapid exchanges, IMs and texts are not appropriate for the kind of written communication that requires careful planning, composing, and editing. Also, IMs and texts are generally used only for conversations within a company or organization. Until guidelines for external use develop, avoid IMs and texts with customers or clients.

Blogs and Wikis

Functions of blogs

Interactive online forums, or *blogs* (short for *Web logs*), began as social networking sites and have for the last several elections played key roles in the national political debate, including the development of "citizen journalism." At their worst, blogs are opinion-based chat rooms for raving about the issues; at their best, they are knowledge-based resources for assembling useful information, helping get things done, and bringing people together.

Blogs as business tools

Corporate blogs play an increasingly large role in mainstream workplace communication. Major companies including Intel, Boeing, Xerox, and Texas Instruments have their own blogs that are used both to help employees network with each other (internal blogs) and to help companies network with their customers and clients (external blogs).

How a blog can enhance a company's internal conversation

Internal Blogs. Internal blogs enhance workflow and morale. In large organizations, blogs can provide an alternative to email for routine in-house communication. Anyone in the network can either post a message or comment on other messages. In the blogging environment, meetings can be conducted without the time and location constraints of face-to-face meetings; employee training can be delivered, and updates about company developments can be circulated. Blogs are especially useful for collaborating. For example, someone in personnel can ask employees if they are interested in yoga workshops to relieve stress. Colleagues can then weigh in with their suggestions.

How a blog can enhance a company's public conversation

External Blogs.   External blogs facilitate customer feedback on products and services, enhance marketing and public relations, and help personalize a large corporation. Blogs give businesses a chance to show a personal, informal side, to respond amiably and quickly to customer concerns, and to allow customers to provide ideas and feedback. Tone, of course, is critical in a corporate blog; it needs to sound friendly, welcoming, and sincere. The blog should invite readers in.

How wikis differ from standard blogs

Wikis.   Wikis are a type of blog in which users can not only comment on earlier postings but edit them as well. Despite the potential for abuse created by such alterations, a well-managed wiki network can be a valuable tool for collaboration among trustworthy users. To ensure that serial edits do not end up distorting the original posting, copies of the original along with each subsequent edit can be filed for later reference.

LETTERS: CUSTOMER RELATIONS LETTERS AND SALES LETTERS

Purpose of letters

Writers often have good reason to correspond in a more formal and personal medium than a memo or email message. A well-crafted letter is appropriate in situations like these:

- To personalize your correspondence, conveying the sense that this message is prepared exclusively for your recipient
- To convey a dignified, professional impression
- To present a reasoned, carefully constructed case
- To respond to clients, customers, and anyone outside of your organization
- To provide an official notice or record (as in a letter announcing legal action or confirming a verbal agreement)

Here we cover letter parts and formats, and two types of letters you are likely to write on the job: customer relations letters and sales letters.

Standard and occasional parts of a letter

Parts of a Letter

Most workplace letters have the same basic components. This conventional and predictable arrangement enables readers to locate what they need immediately, as shown in Figures 26.10 and 26.11: sender's address, date, inside address, salutation, body text, complimentary closing, signature, and the sender's typed name. In addition, many letters also include a heading, the typist's initials, an enclosure notation, and a copy notation.

Sender's address

Date

Inside address

Salutation

Starts on a positive, friendly note

Eases into the bad news but makes the company's stance clear

Buffers the bad news by offering an alternative solution

Concludes on a positive, friendly note

Complimentary closing

Signature

Sender's typed name

LEVERETT LAND & TIMBER COMPANY, INC.
18 River Rock Road
Leverett, MA 01054

creative land use
quality building materials
architectural construction

January 17, 2011

Mr. Thomas E. Shaler
19 Clearwater Drive
Amherst, MA 01022

Dear Mr. Shaler:

Thank you for bringing the matter of the ruptured water pipe to my attention. I was pleased to hear from you again these months after our firm completed the construction of your living room extension, though I was, of course, sorry to hear about the extensive water damage not only to the new construction but to the living room as a whole.

Naturally, I understand your desire to receive compensation for your home's damage, especially taking into account how recently the extension was completed. In reviewing the blueprints for the extension, however, I find that the pipes were state-of-the art and were fully insulated. In fact, it is the practice of Leverett Land & Timber not only to use the best materials available but also to exceed piping insulation requirements by as much as 50 percent. For this reason, we cannot fulfill your request to replace the piping at no cost and repair the water-damaged areas.

Undoubtedly, your insurance will cover the damage. I suspect that the rupture was caused by insufficient heating of the living room area during this unusually cold winter, but homeowner's insurance will cover damages resulting from cold-ruptured pipes 95 percent of the time.

Our policy is to make repairs at a 20 percent discount in situations like this. Though the pipe rupture was not our fault, we feel personally close to every project we do and to every client we serve. Please get in touch if you would like to discuss this matter further. I would also be happy to speak with your insurance company if you wish.

Sincerely,

P.A. Jackson

Gerald A. Jackson

FIGURE 26.10   A bad news customer relations letter

Jimmy's Greek Kitchen
24-52 28th Street
Astoria, NY 11102
Phone: (555) 274-5672
Fax: (555) 274-5671
Email: Jimmysgreek@comcast.net
Web site: http://www.jimmysgreekkitchen.com

July 16, 2011

Adriana Nikolaidis
26-22 30th Street #5
Astoria, NY 11102

Dear Ms. Nikolaidis:

Are you in the mood to sample the best Greek food in the neighborhood absolutely free of charge? We at the newly opened Jimmy's Greek Kitchen would like to say "Thank you for having us in your neighborhood" by inviting you to sample a variety of our authentic Greek specialties.

If you've heard of or visited the famous Jimmy's in Chicago, you know that our fare has been pleasing Chicago diners for over 40 years. At long last, we have opened a companion restaurant in Astoria, and we are proud to offer you the same high-quality appetizers, entrees, and desserts, prepared to perfection. In fact, I trained our Astoria chef myself.

Ranging from charbroiled meats and grilled seafoods to vegetarian specialties and Greek favorites like tzatziki, pastitsio, and moussaka, Jimmy's is truly the best in town. Please have a look at the enclosed menu to see the full range of tasty foods we offer.

Please take advantage of this special offer while it lasts. Until August 31, just bring this letter to Jimmy's and lunch or dinner is on the house. You may choose any appetizer, entree, side order, beverage, and dessert on the menu—all free. We hope that you will not only enjoy the dining experience but will tell others and come back to see us often.

Thank you,

Jimmy Lekkas

Jimmy Lekkas

Marginal annotations:

Opens with an attention-grabbing question

Describes the long history and appeal of the restaurant

Further maintains appeal by describing the menu

Ends by asking the reader to take action

FIGURE 26.11 A sales letter

Sender's Address.   The sender's address appears at the top of the letter, in the form of either a company letterhead or a typed mailing address. When you use your personal address, omit your name because that will appear below your signature at letter's end. On the first line, include the full street address, and on the next line, the city, state (abbreviated), country (if applicable), and postal code (ZIP code or other postal code).

Date.   Place the date immediately below the sender's address. Spell out the month completely.

Inside Address.   Double-space between the date and inside address, (the address of the recipient). Include a courtesy title ("Mr.," "Ms.," "Dr.") and the recipient's full name on the first line, the person's job title (if applicable) on the second line, company name (if applicable) on the next line, street address on the next line, and the city, state, country (if applicable), and postal code on the last line.

Salutation.   Double-space between the inside address and salutation. The salutation includes a greeting (usually "Dear"), followed by a courtesy title and the recipient's last name. If you don't know the recipient's gender, use the full name ("Dear Sandy Martin:") or the position title ("Dear Manager:"). Use a colon at the end of the salutation, not a comma.

Body Text.   Double-space between the salutation and the body text. The introductory paragraph should get right to the point. The middle paragraphs should present the details. The concluding paragraph should summarize and encourage action.

Complimentary Closing.   Double-space between the body text and the complimentary closing. Use a standard, businesslike closing such as "Sincerely," "Respectfully," or "Best regards."

Signature.   Type your name four lines beneath the complimentary closing. Sign in the space between the complimentary closing and typed name.

Other Elements.   Most company letters feature a preprinted company logo at the very top of the page, providing the name and address of the company (or employee), along with contact information. If the letter was not typed by its author, provide a notation by placing the author's capitalized initials first, followed by a slash and the typist's initials in lowercase letters. If anything was sent in the same envelope, provide an enclosure notation, using the abbreviation "Encl." and provide a brief description. If anyone is copied on the letter, provide a copy notation, using the abbreviation "cc," followed by a colon and the name of each recipient. If multiple notations are required, the typist notation appears first, followed by the enclosure notation and then the copy notation.

Letter Format

Using block format for a letter

Several formats are acceptable for business letters, and your company may have its own. The most popular format is the *block* format, as illustrated in Figures 26.10 and 26.11. In the block format, margins on the left, right, top, and bottom are all 1½ inches. Every part of the letter begins at the left margin. Each paragraph in the body text is separated by a blank line, and paragraphs are not indented.

Types of Letters

The variety of business letters

There are many types of business letters—routine correspondence letters, complaint letters, inquiry letters, claim letters, request letters, collection letters, and so on. This chapter will focus on the two most common types of letters you will be expected to write as an employee: customer relations letters and sales letters.

Types of customer relations letters

Customer Relations Letters. Customer relations letters can cover a variety of topics, from answering an inquiry to responding to a complaint to either granting or rejecting a request or demand.

Writing positive and negative customer relations letters

Replying to a customer positively (agreeing to refund money, providing information requested) is easy: Put the good news in the first sentence. The tricky part of customer relations letters, however, is ensuring that you retain the customer's goodwill even if you have to say no or deliver bad news. When you must send a negative message, do not open with the bad news. Begin with something positive (such as thanking the customer for his or her business), ease into the bad news (but make your point clear), and conclude positively (thanking the customer again or offering to answer further questions). Figure 26.10 shows a customer relations letter that delivers negative news but is phrased diplomatically.

Purpose of sales letters
Writing a persuasive sales letter

Sales Letters. Sales letters are written to persuade a current or potential customer to buy your company's product or try its services. Because people are bombarded by sales messages—in magazines, on billboards, on handouts, on television, on the Internet—your letter must be genuinely persuasive and must get to the point quickly. Engage your reader immediately with an attention-grabbing statement or an intriguing question. Describe the product or service you offer and explain its appeal. Conclude by requesting immediate action. Chances are, if the reader does not take action within minutes of reading a sales letter, he or she never will. Figure 26.11 shows a persuasive sales letter.

GUIDELINES for Letters

- *Determine if a letter is the best approach.* Save letters for recipients outside the company. When writing to a coworker or supervisor, use an email or a memo.

- *Make sure your letters are reader-focused, efficient, ethical, and professional.* Draft the letter and revise it to make sure it displays all these characteristics.

- *Follow a standard letter format.* Unless your organization has its own guidelines, use block format and the parts discussed earlier.

- *Maintain a professional but friendly tone.* Even bad news letters need to keep the reader's needs at the forefront, while at the same time keeping your message clear.

- *Check spelling, courtesy titles, addresses, and facts.* A letter that misspells the recipient's name, uses an incorrect courtesy title, or includes factual errors will be ignored. And if you send the letter to the wrong address, it won't even be read.

- *Proofread for style, grammar, and spelling.* Letters that are overly informal or stuffed with letterese will alienate the recipient, as will letters full of grammatical or spelling errors and typos.

- *Don't forget to sign the letter.* Once you've proofread and are ready to mail the letter, remember that your signature must make it official.

A FINAL WORD ABOUT WRITING AT WORK

This chapter has introduced the characteristics of workplace writing and some common types of documents you will need to write for and on the job. You can also expect to write more complex documents: short reports, proposals, grant requests, long reports, presentations, instructions, and much more. But this introduction can help you get a good head start as a workplace writer.

APPLICATIONS

26.1 If you have not already prepared a standard hard copy résumé, prepare one following the guidelines in this chapter. If you already have a résumé, revise it to follow this chapter's guidelines and to update your work experience, educational background, and other details.

26.2 Write a letter applying for a part-time or summer job in response to a specific ad, and tailor your résumé for the job. Choose an organization related to your career goals. Identify the exact hours and calendar period during which you are free to work. Submit a copy of the ad along with your letter and résumé.

26.3 Make your résumé scannable and ready for sending via email or posting online. Use an easily scannable font; remove headers, boldface, underlining, bullets, tabs, and other formatting, and proofread after you've converted the document to "text only" or "rich text" format.

26.4 A friend has asked you for help with the following application letter. Read it carefully, evaluate its effectiveness, and rewrite it as needed.

Dear Ms. Brown,

Please consider my application for the position of assistant in the Engineering Department. I am a second-year student majoring in electrical engineering technology. I am presently an apprentice with your company and would like to continue my employment in the Engineering Department.

I have six years' experience in electronics, including two years of engineering studies. I am confident my background will enable me to assist the engineers, and I would appreciate the chance to improve my skills through their knowledge and experience.

I would appreciate the opportunity to discuss the possibilities and benefits of a position in the Engineering Department at Concord Electric. Please phone me any weekday after 3:00 p.m. at (555) 568-9867. I hope to hear from you soon.
Sincerely,

26.5 Write an unsolicited application letter to the human resources director of a company that interests you and for which you qualify for an entry-level position. Go to the company's Web site to research the various positions for which you may qualify, select one, and name that position in your letter. Also find out the name of the human resources director, and address your letter to that recipient.

26.6 Write a memo from the sales director of a company to both in-house sales department employees and the sales representatives announcing and outlining a new dress code policy and diplomatically explaining why the policy is more strict for the sales reps. Maintain an informal but professional tone, format the memo properly, and keep it brief but complete.

26.7 **COLLABORATIVE PROJECT** Individually or in a small group, decide whether each of the following documents would be appropriate for transmission via a company email network: 1) a personal note to a colleague; 2) a summary to your boss explaining where you are on a project; 3) criticism of an employee or employer; 4) a note of praise or thanks; 5) an evaluation or performance review of an employee; and 6) a reminder about a meeting. Be prepared to explain your decisions.

26.8 **WEB-BASED PROJECT** Do some online research to learn how corporations are using blogs for workplace communication and what functions these blogs are serving. Write a brief analysis of a chosen blog, its content areas, and its value to customers and that corporation. You might begin with the following sites (but find others on your own):

<http://www.blogsouthwest.com/>
<http://fastlane.gmblogs.com/about.html>
<http://csr.blogs.mcdonalds.com/>
<http://blog.zopa.com/>
<http://blogs.sun.com/jonathan/>

26.9 Assume that you are an executive at a company that provides gas heat to all residents of a small city in the Northeast. A complaint letter has been forwarded to you from a heating customer who claims she was overcharged for the month of December. Write two customer relations letters to the customer, one offering a refund for the difference between what she was charged and the amount she should have been charged and another denying a refund because the charges in fact were correct. Be courteous and professional in both letters, paying special attention to diplomacy in the bad news letter. Carefully explain your reasoning for offering or denying the refund.

26.10 Assume that you own a company that produces neon signs, and you want to drum up business during a slow season. Write a sales letter that you will distribute to various businesses in the area, persuading them to take advantage of the many sign options you can offer them. Be sure to get reader attention immediately, maintain interest throughout and close with a realistic call to action.

Work Cited

Crosby, Olivia. *Resumes, Applications, and Cover Letters.* Washington DC: U.S. Department of Labor, 1999. Print.

For additional information and practice with the learning objectives in this chapter, go to www.mycomplab.com, Resources>Writing>Writing Samples.

Taking Short-Answer, Paragraph, and Essay Exams

LEARNING OBJECTIVES FOR THIS CHAPTER

■ Understand how to manage your time, read questions accurately, and settle on an exam strategy

■ Know how to respond to various types of exam questions

What exams measure

When grading a short-answer (a sentence or two), paragraph-length, or essay-length exam, your instructor will be reading to evaluate your knowledge and understanding of the material. These qualities will be indicated by how accurately you focus on the required material, how effectively you organize your thinking, and how clearly and concisely you craft your response. In short, taking these types of written exams involves a version of the writing process.

BEFORE YOU WRITE

Strategize and organize before you write

You will actually craft a better response if you don't begin writing immediately. Before you write, consider how best to manage your time; then read the questions carefully and organize your thoughts strategically.

Managing Your Time

Ways to save time

One big difference between an in-class and an out-of-class assignment, whether you are writing short answers, paragraphs, or essays, is, of course, the time factor. You don't have the luxury of extensive planning, drafting, and revising, but you still need to do those activities—in a shorter time frame, in addition to proofreading. When you sit down to take the test, consider the varying lengths of the questions (if there are multiple questions), keep the overall time period at the forefront of your mind, and work accordingly. Avoid getting bogged down by one question. Save the bulk of your time for the essay response, if there is one. But don't ignore the quality of your shorter responses.

Reading the Questions and Settling on a Strategy

Look for key words to plan your strategy

As you read—and reread—the test questions, consider the essay strategies discussed in earlier chapters: *description, narration, illustration, division and classification, process analysis, cause-and-effect analysis, comparison and contrast, definition,* and *argument.* The required primary strategy is usually signaled by one or more *key words* in the question. Like the responses you write for composition classes, exam questions generally rely on one primary strategy. Note how the key words (underlined) in the following sample test questions signal which strategy to employ:

Key words can directly or indirectly indicate which strategy to take

- Description paints a word picture: *<u>Describe</u> the earliest symptoms of autism.*

- Narration depicts a series of related events, usually in chronological order: *<u>Trace</u> the major events leading up to the War of 1812.*

- Illustration employs examples—concrete and specific instances: *How did public attitudes about gender <u>evolve in</u> twentieth-century North America?*

- Division and classification sort things into parts and group these parts into categories based on similarities: *What are the <u>major components</u> of a passive solar heating system, and how to they <u>interrelate</u>?*

- Process analysis explains the steps in a procedure or the stages in something that happens: *What are the <u>major steps</u> in cardiopulmonary resuscitation (CPR)? How did the 2008 subprime-mortgage crisis <u>develop</u>?*

- Cause-and-effect analysis traces the reasons for an event or incident or its results: *What are the possible <u>reasons</u> for the dramatic increase in cases of autism? What are the possible neurological <u>consequences</u> of adolescent marijuana use?*

- Comparison and contrast examines how two or more things are similar or different: *What are the <u>benefits</u> and risks of stocks <u>versus</u> bonds in a diversified investment portfolio?*

- Definition specifies the precise meaning of a term in its particular context: *What is mad cow disease, and how did it <u>originate</u>?*

■ Argument takes a stance on a controversial topic by supporting or refuting a given position: *Evaluate* this claim: *Reinstituting the draft is the only fair solution to the problem of an overextended military.*

Questions that call for multiple strategies

Of course, some questions will contain key words that suggest more than one development strategy. Consider, this question: *Is X a better alternative than Y? Explain and illustrate.* That question seems to call for comparison and contrast as well as supporting illustrative examples.

WRITING YOUR RESPONSES

Once you have planned how you will use your time, have carefully read the questions, and have devised a strategy by pinpointing key words, you are ready to start writing. The following sections provide tips, with examples, for writing accurate and concise short answers, well-developed paragraph-length responses, and fully developed essays.

Short Answers

Tips for writing short answers

For short answers, of course, try to be as concrete and specific as possible. When there are multiple short-answer questions, start with the easiest. Skip a hard one and move on to the next. Even short answers can involve more than one strategy.

Consider this sample question on an Introduction to Business Law test: *Define "mediation" and briefly explain how it differs from "arbitration."* *Define* and *differs* are the key words in that question to indicate that the response should rely on the two strategies of definition and comparison and contrast.

A short answer using comparison and contrast

> Mediation, like arbitration, is a negotiating process in which a legal dispute between two parties is resolved by a third party; however, mediation differs from arbitration in that the disputing parties are not required to abide by the mediator's decision.

Paragraph-Length Responses

Tips for writing paragraph-length responses

For paragraph-length responses, you are asked to write only one fully developed paragraph with a topic sentence, thesis, body, and conclusion. Be sure to follow the question's guidelines regarding length, too.

Consider this sample question from an Introduction to Sociology test: *Briefly identify the major causes of juvenile crime, and explain how these causes are related.* *Major causes* and *related* are the key words here, indicating that you should take a causal analysis strategy in your response. Also note that the question uses the word *briefly,* so keep it short:

Topic sentence/thesis (1)

Supporting details/causal
analysis (2–4)

Conclusion (5)

[1]Parental indifference, negative peer pressure, and lenient court systems all contribute to juvenile crime in a kind of circular relationship. [2]Juvenile crime seems most often triggered by parental indifference—in all socioeconomic brackets—which leaves young people with no clear-cut rules for behavior. [3]As parental influence diminishes, the peer group steps in with its own rules, often reinforcing antisocial behavior. [4]Completing the pattern is a family court system in which there are no jurors, only a judge, who often hands down lenient decisions, thus allowing relatively "lesser" crimes to go unpunished. [5]In this dysfunctional cycle, most young offenders are allowed to quickly return to the streets and commit crime all over again.

—*Betty Marenda*

Essay-Length Responses

Tips for writing essay-length responses

For essay-length answers, employ the structure used for essays in your composition course, with small differences: a brief list of points to cover rather than a full outline, a briefer introduction and conclusion, and—because of time constraints—less polished writing.

Consider this next sample question for an Introduction to Environmental Science test: *Define "organic pest control," and explain in order of effectiveness how various organic alternatives can substitute for synthetic chemical control.* The key words here are *define, explain,* and *in order of effectiveness,* so the strategies to use here are definition, classification, and illustration. The question asks that you first define organic pest control and then classify and illustrate the alternatives, so the best strategy is to introduce your essay with a one-sentence definition, followed by your thesis. Then sort by category (classify) each alternative to synthetic pest control and illustrate each with examples.

Once you have determined your overall strategy, make a list of the points you want to make or the types of information you want to cover. In this case, you want to organize by the organic alternatives to synthetic pest control specified in the question.

A rough list of areas to be covered

- mechanical or physical control
- biological control
- natural chemical control
- cultural control
- spontaneous control

Then figure out how to organize this list in a clear and logical order that follows the "in order of effectiveness" guidelines of the question. You decide to organize on the basis of methods that require *increasing levels of human involvement* (from least to most):

The working outline

- definition of OPC/thesis
- spontaneous control
- cultural control

- biological control
- mechanical or physical control
- natural chemical control
- conclusion

Note

Obviously, you could fill a book with writing about these topics. But you have only, say, 50 minutes for this essay; therefore, you need to find a good balance between how much ground you can cover and the amount of detail you can provide.

Here is your finished essay:

Definition (1)

Thesis (2)

Support paragraphs in categorized (classified) order

Brief illustrative examples (4–5)

Each support paragraph begins with a topic sentence (3, 6, 8, 12, 14)

Brief conclusion (17)

[1]Organic pest control is a method for decreasing weeds, insects, and plant disease by using natural substances and farming practices that are not disruptive to the environment. [2]Unlike the synthetic—and often harmful—chemical pesticides and herbicides, organic control employs a number of safer alternatives that require varying degrees of management.

[3]The simplest deterrent is "spontaneous control," which includes anything normally occurring in the environment to hold back the pest population. [4]For example, climatic factors such as light moisture, temperature, and topography are important in pest control. [5]Another form of spontaneous control includes natural pest enemies such as predators and parasites that are indigenous instead of having been introduced by humans.

[6]Next is "cultural control," achieved by normal farming practices designed to reduce pest populations to the point where they no longer pose a threat or to prevent certain types of pests entirely. [7]Examples include the use of pest-resistant plant species, certain tillage practices, field sanitation, crop rotation, and intercropping.

[8]"Biological control" occurs when natural pest enemies (living organisms) are introduced by humans. [9]Certain birds, spiders, and beneficial insects can be used to control weeds and other insects. [10]A single ladybird beetle, for instance, consumes up to fifty harmful insects per day. [11]Bacteria and other organisms also can be used to limit pest populations.

[12]In certain cases, "mechanical or physical control" can be effective. [13]Examples include using logs or fences as pest barriers; setting trapping devices for insects and rodents; weeding; or manipulating air supply, temperature, and moisture in silos and produce bins.

[14]Finally, "natural chemical control" involves the use of certain plant substances that have insecticidal or herbicidal properties. [15]Examples of these naturally occurring chemicals are pyrethrum (derived from chrysanthemums) and rotenone (derived from various legumes). [16]These natural chemicals are less harmful than the synthetic chemical pesticides (such as DDT and malathion) because they have low toxicity to humans and wildlife and they also degrade rapidly.

[17]Each of these organic control methods is increasingly included in pest management programs to promote biodiversity and to limit the possibility of environmental disruption.

—Eva Yohn

Notice that terms such as *tillage, field sanitation, crop rotation,* and *legumes* are not defined in the essay because this was not part of the question—and in this situation it can be assumed that both reader (instructor) and writer (student) know what these terms mean. The writer has not only demonstrated a strong understanding of the topic but also carefully followed the directions in the question.

GUIDELINES for Taking Short-Answer, Paragraph, and Essay Exams

- *Know the material.* Essay exams leave little or no room for "faking it." Take good notes in all your courses, and study the material thoroughly before you take the test. If your instructor lets you know what topics will be covered on the exam, focus on those areas.

- *Read and reread the questions.* Make sure you fully understand what type of response is expected. If something is unclear, ask the instructor to clarify.

- *Manage your time.* Usually you will have 50 to 75 minutes for the entire exam, whether it consists of a series of shorter questions, a variety of questions, or just one essay-length question. If there are multiple questions, avoid getting bogged down on one question.

- *Identify which writing strategy or strategies to take.* In most cases, key words in the question (**evaluate, describe, compare, trace, illustrate,** and so on) will provide clues as to which strategy to take. Keep in mind that certain development strategies can overlap (for example, process analysis as a primary strategy may require some combination of description, narration, illustration, and cause-and-effect analysis).

- *Make a list of major points, and develop a rough outline.* For both paragraph- and essay-length responses, first jot down the major points as they occur to you, and then develop a very brief outline to keep you on track as you write.

- *Develop a clear and definite thesis.* Both paragraph- and essay-length responses require a thesis, "the one sentence you would keep if you could keep only one" (United States Air Force Academy). Try restating the exam question as your thesis. See pages 22–27 for additional thesis guidelines.

- *Compose your response.* Follow your outline, and modify it as needed. Begin each support paragraph with a topic sentence. Be as specific as the question requires—does the question call for a broad overview or nitty-gritty detail? Find the right balance between extent of coverage and specificity of detail.

- *Proofread and revise your response.* Even if you finish early, take all of the allotted time to proofread and to make minor revisions. Turn in the most polished exam you possibly can.

APPLICATIONS

27.1   **COLLABORATIVE PROJECT** Divide into groups on the basis of shared academic interests or majors. In your group, develop one or more questions that call for a fully developed essay. Based on the key words in your question, identify the strategy or strategies that would be required to compose the response. Write a clear and definite thesis statement for your response. Appoint one of your group's members to present the group's material to the class.

27.2   Identify the key words in the following test questions, along with the strategies these words suggest:

1. Explain how a laser works.
2. Trace the origins and development of the Ku Klux Klan.
3. Justify or refute this proposition: All students should spend one year in mandatory service to their country or community before attending college.
4. What broad political differences do mainstream Republications and Democrats typically embody?
5. Analyze the major unintended consequences of the most recent war in Iraq.
6. What political and strategic reasons motivated Abraham Lincoln to issue the Emancipation Proclamation?
7. What is the Castle Doctrine, and why is it so controversial?
8. Justify the unlimited role of women in modern combat.
9. In your view, what constitutes "patriotic" behavior? Explain and illustrate.
10. Evaluate the effectiveness of meditation as a treatment for hypertension.
11. Summarize and evaluate the arguments for and against euthanasia.
12. Why is diabetes on the increase in the United States?
13. How do cancer cells originate?

Work Cited

United States Air Force Academy. *Executive Writing Course.* Washington: GPO, 1981. Print.

A Brief Handbook

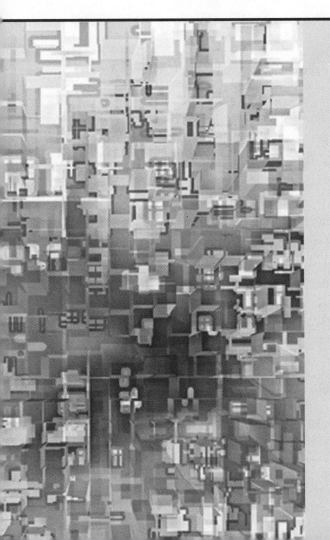

The last page of this book displays editing and revision symbols and their page references. When your instructor marks a symbol on your paper, turn to the appropriate section for explanations and examples.

COMMON SENTENCE ERRORS

The following common sentence errors are easy to repair.

Sentence Fragment

A grammatically complete sentence consists of at least one subject and verb. Your sentence might contain several complete ideas, but it must contain at least one!

> [INCOMPLETE IDEA]   [COMPLETE IDEA]   [COMPLETE IDEA]
>
> Although Mary was injured, she grabbed the line, and she saved the boat.

Omitting some essential element (the subject, the verb, or another complete idea) leaves only a piece of a sentence—a *fragment*.

> Grabbed the line. [*a fragment because it lacks a subject*]
>
> Although Mary was injured. [*a fragment because—although it contains a subject and a verb—it needs to be joined with a complete idea to make sense*]
>
> Sam an electronics technician.

This last statement leaves the reader asking, "What about Sam the electronics technician?" The verb is missing. Adding a verb (with other elements, if desired) changes this fragment to a complete sentence.

Simple verb	Sam **is** an electronics technician.
Verb plus adverb	Sam, an electronics technician, **works hard.**
Dependent clause, verb, and subjective complement	**Although he is well paid,** Sam, an electronics technician, **is not happy.**

Do not, however, mistake the following statement—which seems to contain a verb—for a complete sentence:

> Sam being an electronics technician.

The -*ing* forms do not function as verbs unless accompanied by such other verbs as *is, was,* and *will be.*

> **Sam**, being an electronics technician, **was responsible for checking the circuitry.**

Likewise, the "*to* + verb" form (*infinitive*) is not a verb.

Fragment	To become an electronics technician.
Complete	To become an electronics technician, **Sam had to complete a two-year apprenticeship.**

Sometimes we inadvertently create fragments by adding subordinating conjunctions (*because, since, it, although, while, unless, until, when, where,* and others) to an already complete sentence.

> **Although** Sam is an electronics technician.

Such words subordinate the words that follow them; that is, they make the statement dependent on an additional idea, which must itself have a subject and verb and be a complete sentence. (See also "Subordination" on pages 497–498.) We can complete the subordinate statement by adding an independent clause.

> Although Sam is an electronics technician, **he hopes to become an electrical engineer.**

Note   *Because the incomplete idea (dependent clause) depends on the complete idea (independent clause) for its meaning, you need only a pause (symbolized by a comma), not a break (symbolized by a semicolon).*

Here are fragments from students' writing. Each is repaired in two ways. Can you think of other ways of making these statements complete?

Fragment	She spent her first week on the job as a researcher. **Selecting and compiling technical information from digests and journals.**
Revised	She spent her first week on the job as a researcher, selecting and compiling technical information from digests and journals.
	In her first week on the job as a researcher, she selected and compiled technical information from digests and journals.
Fragment	**Because the operator was careless.** The new computer was damaged.

Revised	Because the operator was careless, the new computer was damaged.
	The operator was careless; as a result, the new computer was damaged.
Fragment	**When each spool is in place.** Advance your film.
Revised	When each spool is in place, advance your film.
	Be sure each spool is in place before advancing your film.

Acceptable Fragments

Not all fragments are unacceptable in all circumstances. A fragmented sentence is acceptable in commands or exclamations because the subject ("you") is understood.

Acceptable fragments	Slow down.
	Give me a hand.
	Look out!

Also, questions and answers are sometimes expressed as incomplete sentences.

Acceptable fragments	How? By investing wisely.
	When? At three o'clock.
	Who? Bill.

In general, however, avoid fragments unless you have good reason to use one for special tone or emphasis.

APPLICATION

VI.1 Correct these sentence fragments by rewriting each one in two ways.

1. Fred is a terrible math student. But an excellent writer.
2. As they entered the haunted house. The floors began to groan.
3. Hoping for an A in biology. Sally studied every night.
4. Although many students flunk out of this college. Its graduates find excellent jobs.
5. Three teenagers out of every ten have some sort of addiction. Whether it is to alcohol or drugs.

Faulty Coordination

Give equal emphasis to ideas of equal importance by joining them with coordinating conjunctions: *and, but, or, nor, for, so,* and *yet.*

Correct	This course is difficult, **but** it is worthwhile.
	My horse is old **and** gray.
	We must decide to support **or** reject the dean's plan.

But do not confound your meaning by coordinating excessively.

Excessive coordination	The climax in jogging comes after a few miles **and** I can no longer feel stride after stride **and** it seems as if I am floating **and** jogging becomes almost a reflex **and** my arms and legs continue to move **and** my mind no longer has to control their actions.
Revised	The climax in jogging comes after a few miles, when I can no longer feel stride after stride. By then I am jogging almost by reflex, nearly floating, my arms and legs still moving, my mind no longer having to control their actions.

Notice how the meaning becomes clear when the less important ideas (*nearly floating, arms and legs still moving, my mind no longer having*) are shown as dependent on, rather than equal to, the most important idea (*jogging almost by reflex*).

Avoid coordinating two or more ideas that cannot be sensibly connected:

Faulty	I was late for work **and** wrecked my car.
Revised	Late for work, I backed out of the driveway too quickly, hit a truck, and wrecked my car.

Faulty Subordination

Proper subordination shows that a less important idea is dependent on a more important idea. A dependent (or subordinate) clause in a complex sentence is signaled by a subordinating conjunction: *because, so that, if, unless, after, until, since, while, as,* and *although.* Consider these complete ideas:

Joe studies hard. He has severe math anxiety.

Because these ideas are expressed as simple sentences, they appear coordinate (equal in importance). But if you wanted to indicate your opinion of Joe's chances of succeeding, you would need a third sentence: *His handicap will probably prevent him from succeeding* or *His willpower will help him succeed* or the like. To communicate the intended meaning concisely, combine the two ideas: Subordinate the one that deserves less emphasis, and place the idea you want emphasized in the independent (main) clause.

> Despite his severe math anxiety [*subordinate idea*], Joe studies hard [*independent idea*].

The version just given suggests that Joe will succeed. The following subordination suggests the opposite:

> Despite his diligent study [*subordinate idea*], Joe is unlikely to overcome his learning disability [*independent idea*].

Do not coordinate when you should subordinate:

> **Faulty**   Television viewers can relate to a person they idolize, and they feel obliged to buy the product endorsed by their hero.

Of the two ideas in this sentence, one is the cause and the other the effect. Emphasize this relationship through subordination.

> **Revised**   Because television viewers can relate to a person they idolize, they feel obliged to buy the product endorsed by their hero.

When combining several ideas within a sentence, decide which is most important, and subordinate the other ideas to it:

> **Faulty**   This employee is often late for work, and he writes illogical reports, and he is a poor manager, and he should be fired.
>
> **Revised**   Because this employee is often late for work, writes illogical reports, and has poor management skills, **he should be fired.** (*The last clause is independent.*)

Do not overstuff sentences by excessive subordination:

> **Overstuffed**   This job, which I took when I graduated from college, while I waited for a better one to come along, which is boring, where I've gained no useful experience, makes me eager to quit.
>
> **Revised**   Upon college graduation, I took this job while waiting for a better one to come along. Because I find it boring and have gained no useful experience, I am eager to quit.

APPLICATION

VI.2   Use coordination or subordination to clarify relationships in these sentences. (Review pages 497–498.)

1. Martha loves John. She also loves Bruno.
2. You will succeed. Work hard.
3. I worked hard in calculus and flunked the course.
4. Now I have no privacy. My cousin moved into my room.
5. The instructor entered the classroom. Some students were asleep.

cs

Comma Splice

In a comma splice, two complete ideas (independent clauses) that should be *separated* by a period or a semicolon are incorrectly *joined* by a comma:

| Sarah did a great job, she was promoted.

You can choose among several possibilities for repair:

1. Substitute a period followed by a capital letter:

| Sarah did a great job. She was promoted.

2. Substitute a semicolon to signal a relationship between the two items:

| Sarah did a great job; she was promoted.

3. Use a semicolon with a connecting (conjunctive) adverb (a transitional word):

| Sarah did a great job; **consequently,** she was promoted.

4. Use a subordinating word to make the less important clause incomplete, thereby dependent on the other:

| **Because** Sarah did a great job, she was promoted.

5. Add a connecting word after the comma:

| Sarah did a great job, **and** she was promoted.

The following revisions show that your choice of construction will depend on the exact meaning or tone you wish to convey:

| **Comma splice** | This is a fairly new product, therefore, some people don't trust it. |
| **Revised** | This is a fairly new product. Some people don't trust it. |

This is a fairly new product; therefore, some people don't trust it.

Because this is a fairly new product, some people don't trust it.

Comma splice	Ms. Gomez was a strict supervisor, she was well liked by her employees.
Revised	Ms. Gomez was a strict supervisor. She was well liked by her employees.

Ms. Gomez was a strict supervisor; **however,** she was well liked by her employees.

Although Ms. Gomez was a strict supervisor, she was well liked by her employees.

Ms. Gomez was a strict supervisor, **but** she was well liked by her employees.

APPLICATION

VI.3   Correct these comma splices by rewriting each one in two ways.

1. Efforts are being made to halt water pollution, however, there is no simple solution to the problem.
2. Bill slept through his final, he had forgotten to set his alarm.
3. Ellen must be a genius, she never studies yet always gets A's.
4. We arrived at the picnic late, there were no hamburgers left.
5. My part-time job is excellent, it pays well, provides good experience, and offers a real challenge.

ro   Run-on Sentence

The run-on sentence crams too many grammatically complete ideas together.

Run-on	The hourglass is more accurate than the waterclock for the water in a waterclock must always be at the same temperature in order to flow with the same speed since water evaporates it must be replenished at regular intervals thus not being as effective in measuring time as the hourglass.
Revised	The hourglass is more accurate than the waterclock because water in a waterclock must always be at the same temperature to flow at the same speed. Also, water evaporates and must be replenished at regular intervals. These temperature and volume problems make the waterclock less effective than the hourglass in measuring time.

APPLICATION

VI.4   Revise these run-on sentences.

1. The gale blew all day by evening the sloop was taking on water.
2. Jennifer felt hopeless about passing English however the writing center helped her complete the course.
3. The professor glared at John he had been dozing in the back row.
4. Our drama club produces three plays a year I love the opening nights.
5. Pets should not be allowed on our campus they are messy and sometimes dangerous.

Faulty Agreement—Subject and Verb

The subject should agree in number with the verb. Faulty agreement seldom occurs in short sentences, where subject and verb are not far apart: "Jack eat too much" instead of "Jack eats too much." But when the subject is separated from its verb by other words, we sometimes lose track of the subject-verb relationship.

> **Faulty**   The lion's **share** of diesels **are** sold in Europe.

Although *diesels* is the noun closest to the verb, the subject is *share*, a singular noun that needs a singular verb.

> **Revised**   The lion's **share** of diesels **is** sold in Europe.

Agreement errors are easy to correct once subject and verb are identified.

> **Faulty**   There **is** an estimated 29,000 **women** living in our city.
> **Revised**   There **are** an estimated 29,000 **women** living in our city.
>
> **Faulty**   **A system** of lines **extend** horizontally to form a grid.
> **Revised**   **A system** of lines **extends** horizontally to form a grid.

A second problem with subject-verb agreement occurs with indefinite subject pronouns such as *each, everyone, anybody,* and *somebody.* They usually take a singular verb.

> **Faulty**   **Each** of the crew members **were** injured during the storm.
> **Revised**   **Each** of the crew members **was** injured during the storm.
>
> **Faulty**   **Everyone** in the group **have** practiced long hours.
> **Revised**   **Everyone** in the group **has** practiced long hours.

Collective nouns such as *herd, family, union, group, army, team, committee,* and *board* can call for a singular or a plural verb, depending on your intended meaning. To denote the group as a whole, use a singular verb.

> **Correct**   The **committee meets** weekly to discuss new business.
>
> The editorial **board** of this magazine **has** high standards.

To denote individual members of the group, use a plural verb.

> **Correct**   The **committee disagree** on whether to hire Jim.
>
> The editorial **board are** all published authors.

When two subjects are joined by *either…or* or *neither…nor,* the verb is singular if both subjects are singular and plural if both subjects are plural. If the subjects are mixed (one plural and one singular), the verb agrees with the one closer to the verb.

> **Correct**   Neither **John** nor **Bill works** regularly.
>
> Either **apples** or **oranges are** good vitamin sources.
>
> Either Felix or his **friends are** crazy.
>
> Neither the boys nor their **father likes** the home team.

For two subjects (singular, plural, or mixed) joined by *both… and,* the verb is plural.

> **Correct**   **Both** Joe and Bill **are** resigning.

A single *and* between subjects calls for a plural subject.

Faulty Agreement—Pronoun and Referent

A pronoun must refer to a specific noun (its *referent* or *antecedent*), with which it must agree in gender and number.

> **Correct**   **Jane** lost **her** book.
>
> The **students** complained that **they** had been treated unfairly.

When an indefinite pronoun such as *each, everyone, anybody, someone,* or *none* is the referent, the pronoun is singular.

> **Correct**   **Anyone** can get **one's** degree from that college.
>
> **Anyone** can get **his** [or **her**] degree from that college.
>
> **Each** candidate described **her** plans in detail.

Faulty Modification

Modifiers explain, define, or add detail to other words or ideas. Prepositional phrases, for example, usually define or limit adjacent words:

the foundation **with the cracked wall**

the journey **to the moon**

So do phrases with *-ing* verb forms:

the student **painting the portrait**

Opening the door, we entered quietly.

Phrases with "*to* + verb" limit:

To succeed, one must work hard.

Some clauses also limit:

the person **who came to dinner**

the job **that I recently accepted**

If a modifier is too far from the words it modifies, the message can be ambiguous.

| Misplaced modifier | At our campsite, **devouring the bacon,** I saw a huge bear. |

Who was devouring the bacon? Moving the modifier next to *bear* clarifies the sentence:

| Revised | At our campsite, I saw a huge bear **devouring the bacon.** |

The order of adjectives and adverbs also affects meaning:

I often remind myself to balance my checkbook.

I remind myself to balance my checkbook **often.**

Position modifiers to reflect your meaning:

| Misplaced modifier | Jeanette read a report on using nonchemical pesticides **in our conference room.** [*Are the pesticides to be used in the conference room?*] |
| Revised | In our conference room, Jeanette read a report on using nonchemical pesticides. |

Dangling modifier	**Dialing the phone,** the cat ran out the door.

The cat obviously did not dial the phone, but because the modifier *Dialing the telephone* has no word to modify, the noun beginning the main clause (*cat*) seems to name the one who dialed the phone. Without any word to join itself to, the modifier dangles. Inserting a subject repairs this absurd message.

Revised	**As Mary dialed the telephone,** the cat ran out the door.

A dangling modifier can also obscure your meaning.

Dangling modifier	**After completing the student financial aid application form,** the Financial Aid Office will forward it to the appropriate state agency.

Who completes the form, the student or the Financial Aid Office? Here are some other dangling modifiers that obscure the message:

Dangling modifier	**By planting different varieties of crops,** the pests were unable to adapt.
Revised	By planting different varieties of crops, **farmers** prevented the pests from adapting.

Dangling modifier	**As an expert in this field,** I'm sure your advice will help.
Revised	**Because of your expertise in this field,** I'm sure your advice will help.

APPLICATION

VI.5   Revise these sentences to make subjects and verbs agree in number, to make pronouns and referents agree in gender and number, and to clarify relations between modifiers and the words they modify.

1. Ten years ago, the mineral rights to this land was sold to a mining company.
2. Each of the students in our dorm have a serious complaint about living conditions.
3. Neither the students nor the instructor like this classroom.
4. Neither Fred nor Mary expect to pass this course.
5. Anyone wanting to enhance their career should take a computer course.
6. Wearing high boots, the snake could not hurt me.
7. Having two hours left to travel, the weather kept getting worse.
8. Only use this phone during a red alert.

ca   ## Faulty Pronoun Case

A pronoun's case (nominative, objective, or possessive) is determined by its role in the sentence: as subject, object, or indicator of possession.

If the pronoun serves as the subject of a sentence (*I, we, you, she, he, it, they, who*), its case is *nominative*.

> **She** completed her graduate program in record time.
>
> **Who** broke the chair?

When a pronoun follows a version of the verb *be* (a linking verb), it explains (complements) the subject, and so its case is nominative.

> The killer was **she.**
>
> The professor who perfected our new distillation process is **he.**

If the pronoun serves as the object of a verb or a preposition (*me, us, you, her, him, it, them, whom*), its case is *objective*.

Object of the verb	The employees gave **her** a parting gift.
Object of the preposition	To **whom** do you wish to complain?

If a pronoun indicates possession (*my, mine, our, ours, your, yours, his, her, hers, its, their, whose*), its case is *possessive*.

> The brown briefcase is **mine.**
>
> **Her** offer was accepted.
>
> **Whose** opinion do you value most?

Here are some frequent errors in pronoun case:

Faulty	**Whom** is responsible to **who?** [*The subject should be nominative and the object should be objective.*]
Revised	**Who** is responsible to **whom?**
Faulty	The debate was between Marsha and **I.** [*As object of the preposition, the pronoun should be objective.*]
Revised	The debate was between Marsha and **me.**
Faulty	**Us** students are accountable for our decisions. [*The pronoun accompanies the subject, "students," and thus should be nominative.*]
Revised	**We** students are accountable for our decisions.

Faulty	A group of **we** students will fly to California. [*The pronoun accompanies the object of the preposition, "students," and thus should be objective.*]
Revised	A group of **us** students will fly to California.

Deleting the accompanying noun from the two latter examples reveals the correct pronoun case ("We...are accountable"; "A group of us...will fly").

APPLICATION

VI.6   Select the appropriate pronoun from each pair in parentheses.

1. By (who, whom) was the job offer made?
2. The argument was among Bill, Terry, and (I, me).
3. A committee of (we, us) concerned citizens is working to make our neighborhood safer.
4. (Us, We) students are being hurt by federal cuts in loan programs.
5. The liar is (he, him).

shift

Sentence Shifts

Shifts in point of view damage coherence. If you begin a sentence or paragraph with one subject or person, do not shift to another.

Shift in person	When **one** finishes such a great book, **you** will have a sense of achievement.
Revised	When **you** finish such a great book, **you** will have a sense of achievement.
Shift in number	**One** should sift the flour before **they** make the pie.
Revised	**One** should sift the flour before **one** makes the pie. (*Or better: Sift the flour before making the pie.*)

Do not begin a sentence in active voice and then shift to passive voice.

Shift in voice	**He** delivered the plans for the apartment complex, and the building site **was also inspected by him.**
Revised	He **delivered** the plans for the apartment complex and also **inspected** the building site.

Do not shift tenses without good reason.

Shift in tense She **delivered** the blueprints, **inspected** the foundation, **wrote** her report, and **takes** the afternoon off.

Revised She **delivered** the blueprints, **inspected** the foundation, **wrote** her report, and **took** the afternoon off.

Do not shift from one verb mood to another (as from imperative to indicative mood in a set of instructions).

Shift in mood **Unscrew** the valve; then steel wool **should be used** to clean the fittings.

Revised **Unscrew** the valve; then **use** steel wool to clean the fittings.

APPLICATION

VI.7 Revise these sentences to eliminate shifts in person, mood, voice, tense, or number.

1. People should keep themselves politically informed; otherwise, you will not be living up to your democratic responsibilities.
2. Barbara made the dean's list and the Junior Achievement award was also won by her.
3. As soon as he walked into his dorm room, George sees the mess left by his roommate.
4. When one is being stalked by a bear, you should not snack on sardines.
5. First loosen the lug nuts; then you should jack up the car.

EFFECTIVE PUNCTUATION

pct

Punctuation marks are like road signs and traffic signals. They govern reading speed and provide clues for navigation through a network of ideas; they mark intersections, detours, and road repairs; they draw attention to points of interest along the route; and they mark geographic boundaries.

Let's review the four marks used most often, in order of their relative strength.

1. *Period.* A period signals a complete stop at the end of an independent idea (independent clause). The first word in the idea following a period begins with a capital letter.

Jack is a fat cat. His slim friends catch all the mice.

2. *Semicolon.* A semicolon signals a brief stop after an independent idea but does not end the sentence; instead, it announces that the forthcoming independent idea is *closely related* to the preceding idea.

> Jack is a fat cat; he eats too much.

3. *Colon.* A colon usually follows an independent idea and, like the semicolon, signals a brief stop but does not end the sentence. The colon and semicolon, however, are never interchangeable. A colon symbolizes "explanation to follow." Information after the colon (which need not be an independent idea) explains or clarifies the idea expressed before the colon.

> Jack is a fat cat: He weighs 40 pounds. [*The information after the colon answers "How fat?"*]

or

> Jack is a fat cat: 40 pounds' worth! [*The second clause is not independent.*]

4. *Comma.* The weakest of these four marks, a comma signals only a pause within or between ideas in the sentence. A comma often indicates that the word, phrase, or clause set off from the independent idea cannot stand alone but must rely on the independent idea for its meaning.

> Jack, **a fat cat,** is a jolly fellow.
> **Although he diets often,** Jack is a fat cat.

A comma is used between two independent clauses only if accompanied by a coordinating conjunction (*and, but, for, nor, or, so, yet*).

> **Comma splice**   Jack is a party animal, he is loved everywhere.
> **Correct**   Jack is a party animal, **and** he is loved everywhere.

End Punctuation

The three marks of end punctuation—period, question mark, and exclamation point—work like a red traffic light by signaling a complete stop.

Period.   A period ends a sentence and is the final mark in some abbreviations.

> Ms.   Assn.   Inc.

Periods serve as decimal points in numbers.

> $15.95
> 21.4%

?/

Question Mark.   A question mark follows a direct question.

| Where is the essay that was due today?

Do not use a question mark to end an indirect question.

Faulty	Professor Grey asked whether all students had completed the essay?
Revised	Professor Grey asked whether all students had completed the essay.
	or
	Professor Grey asked, "Did all students complete the essay?"

!/

Exclamation Point.   Use an exclamation point only when the expression of strong feeling is appropriate.

| **Appropriate** | Oh, no! |
| | Pay up! |

;/

Semicolon

Like a blinking red traffic light at an intersection, a semicolon signals a brief but definite stop.

Semicolons Separating Independent Clauses.   Semicolons separate independent clauses (logically complete ideas) whose contents are closely related and are not connected by a coordinating conjunction.

| The project was finally completed; we had done a good week's work.

The semicolon can replace the comma-plus-conjunction combination that joins two independent ideas.

> The project was finally completed, and we were elated.
> The project was finally completed; we were elated.

The second version emphasizes the sense of elation.

Semicolons Used with Conjunctive Adverbs and Other Transitional Expressions.   Semicolons must precede conjunctive adverbs or phrases such as *besides, otherwise, still, however, furthermore, moreover, consequently, therefore, on the other hand, in contrast,* and *in fact.*

> The job is filled; **however,** we will keep your résumé on file.
> Your background is impressive; **in fact,** it is the best among our applicants.

Semicolons Separating Items in a Series.   When items in a series contain internal commas, semicolons provide clear separation between items.

> I am applying for summer jobs in Santa Fe, New Mexico; Albany, New York; Montgomery, Alabama; and Moscow, Idaho.
>
> Members of the survey crew were Juan Jimenez, a geologist; Hector Lightfoot, a surveyor; and Mary Shelley, a graduate student.

Colon

Like a flare in the road, a colon signals you to stop and then proceed, paying attention to the situation ahead. Usually, a colon follows an introductory statement that requires a follow-up explanation.

> We need this equipment immediately: a voltmeter, a portable generator, and three pairs of insulated gloves.
>
> She is an ideal colleague: honest, reliable, and competent.

Except for salutations in formal correspondence ("Dear Ms. Jones:"), colons follow independent (logically and grammatically complete) statements.

> **Faulty**   My plans include: finishing college, traveling for two years, and settling down in Sante Fe.

No punctuation should follow *include.*
Colons can introduce quotations.

> The supervisor's message was clear enough: "You're fired."

A colon can replace a semicolon between two related, complete statements when the second one explains or amplifies the first.

> Pam's reason for accepting the lowest-paying job offer was simple: She had always wanted to live in the Northwest.

APPLICATION

VI.8   Insert semicolons or colons as needed in these expressions.

1. June had finally arrived it was time to graduate.
2. I have two friends who are like brothers Sam and Daniel.
3. Joe did not get the job however, he was high on the list of finalists.
4. The wine was superb an 1898 Margaux.
5. Our student senators are Joan Blake, a geology major Helen Simms, a nursing major and Henry Drew, an English major.

Comma

The comma is the most frequently used—and abused—punctuation mark. It works like a blinking yellow traffic light, for which you slow down briefly without stopping. Never use a comma to signal a *break* between independent ideas.

Comma as a Pause Between Complete Ideas. In a compound sentence in which a coordinating conjunction (*and, but, for, nor, or, so, yet*) connects equal (independent) statements, a comma usually precedes the conjunction.

This is an excellent course, **but** the work is difficult.

Comma as a Pause Between an Incomplete and a Complete Idea. A comma is usually placed between a complete and an incomplete statement in a complex sentence when the incomplete statement comes first.

Because he is a fat cat, Jack diets often.

When he eats too much, Jack gains weight.

When the order is reversed (complete idea followed by incomplete), the comma is usually omitted.

Jack diets often **because he is a fat cat.**

Jack gains weight **when he eats too much.**

Reading a sentence aloud should tell you whether or not to pause (and use a comma).

Commas Separating Items (Words, Phrases, or Clauses) in a Series. Use commas after items in a series, including the next to last item.

Helen, Joe, Marsha, and **John** are joining us on the term project.

He works hard **at home, on the job,** and even **during his vacation.**

The new employee complained **that the hours were long, that the pay was low, that the work was boring, and that the supervisor was paranoid.**

Use no commas if *or* or *and* appears between all items in a series.

She is willing to study in San Francisco **or** Seattle **or** even Anchorage.

Comma Setting Off Introductory Phrases. An infinitive, prepositional, or verbal phrase introducing a sentence is usually set off by a comma, as are interjections.

Infinitive phrase   **To be or not to be,** that is the question.

Prepositional phrase	**In Rome,** do as the Romans do.
Participial phrase	**Being fat,** Jack was slow at catching mice.
	Moving quickly, the army surrounded the enemy.
Interjection	**Oh,** is that the verdict?

Commas Setting Off Nonrestrictive Elements. A *restrictive* phrase or clause modifies or defines the subject in such a way that deleting the modifier would change the meaning of the sentence.

I   All students **who have work experience** will receive preference.

Without *who have work experience*, which restricts the subject by limiting the category *students*, the meaning would be entirely different.

I   All students will receive preference.

Because the phrase *who have work experience* is essential to the sentence's meaning, it is *not* set off by commas.

A *nonrestrictive* phrase or clause could be deleted without changing the sentence's meaning and *is* set off by commas.

I   Our new manager**, who has only six weeks' experience,** is highly competent.

Modifier deleted	Our new manager is highly competent.

I   This house, **riddled with carpenter ants,** is falling apart.

Modifier deleted	This house is falling apart.

Commas Setting Off Parenthetical Elements. Items that interrupt the flow of a sentence (such as *of course, as a result, as I recall,* and *however*) are called parenthetical and are enclosed by commas. They may denote emphasis, afterthought, clarification, or transition.

Emphasis	This deluxe model**, of course,** is more expensive.
Afterthought	Your essay**, by the way,** was excellent.
Clarification	The loss of my job was**, in a way,** a blessing.
Transition	Our warranty**, however,** does not cover tire damage.

Direct address is parenthetical.

I   Listen**, my children,** and you shall hear . . .

A parenthetical expression at the beginning or the end of a sentence is set off by a comma.

> **Naturally,** we will expect a full guarantee.
>
> **My friends,** I think we have a problem.
>
> You've done a good job, **Jim.**
>
> **Yes,** you may use my name in your advertisement.

Commas Setting Off Quoted Material.   Quoted items within a sentence are set off by commas.

> The customer said, **"I'll take it,"** as soon as he laid eyes on our new model.

Commas Setting Off Appositives.   An *appositive,* a word or words explaining a noun and placed immediately after it, is set off by commas when the appositive is nonrestrictive. (See page 512.)

> Martha Jones, **our new president,** is overhauling all personnel policies.
>
> Alpha waves, **the most prominent of the brain waves,** are typically recorded in a waking subject whose eyes are closed.
>
> Please make all checks payable to Sam Sawbuck, **school treasurer.**

Commas Used in Common Practice.   Commas set off the day of the month from the year, in a date.

> May 10, 1989

Commas set off numbers at three-digit intervals.

> 11,215
>
> 6,463,657

They also set off street, city, and state in an address.

> Mail the bill to J. B. Smith, 18 Sea Street, Albany, IA 01642.

When the address is written vertically, however, the omitted commas are those that would otherwise occur at the end of each address line.

> J. B. Smith
>
> 18 Sea Street
>
> Albany, IA 01642

Commas set off an address or date in a sentence.

> Room 3C, Margate Complex, is my summer address.
>
> June 15, 2009, is my graduation date.

They set off degrees and titles from proper nouns.

> Roger P. Cayer, **MD**
>
> Sandra Mello, **PhD**

Commas Used Erroneously.   Avoid needless or inappropriate commas. Read a sentence aloud to identify inappropriate pauses.

Faulty	The instructor told me, that I was late. [*separates the indirect from the direct object*]
	The most universal symptom of the suicide impulse, is depression. [*separates the subject from its verb*]
	This has been a long, difficult, semester. [*second comma separates the final adjective from its noun*]
	John, Bill, and Sally, are joining us on the trip home. [*third comma separates the final subject from its verb*]
	An employee, who expects rapid promotion, must quickly prove his or her worth. [*separates a modifier that should be restrictive*]
	I spoke by phone with John, and Marsha. [*separates two nouns linked by a coordinating conjunction*]
	The room was, 18 feet long. [*separates the linking verb from the subjective complement*]
	We painted the room, red. [*separates the object from its complement*]

APPLICATION

VI.9   Insert commas where needed in these sentences.

1. In modern society highways seem as necessary as food water or air.
2. Everyone though frustrated by pollution can play a part in improving the environment.
3. Professor Jones who has written three books is considered an authority in her field.
4. Amanda Ford of course is the best candidate for governor.
5. Terrified by the noise Sally ran never looking back.
6. One book however will not solve all your writing problems.

VI.10   Eliminate needless or inappropriate commas from these sentences.

1. Students, who smoke marijuana, tend to do poorly in school.
2. As I started the car, I saw him, dash into the woods.
3. This has been a semester of happy, exciting, experiences.
4. Sarah mistakenly made dates on the same evening with Joe, and Bill, even though she had promised herself to be more careful.
5. In fact, a writer's reaction to criticism, is often defensiveness.

Apostrophe

Apostrophes are used to indicate possessives, contractions, and the plurals of numerals, letters, and symbols.

Apostrophe Indicating the Possessive.   At the end of a singular word or a plural word that does not end in *s*, add an apostrophe plus *s* to indicate the possessive. Single-syllable nouns that end in *s* take the apostrophe before an added *s*.

> The **people's** candidate won.
> The chainsaw was **Emma's.**
> The **women's** locker room burned.
> I borrowed **Chris's** book.

For words that already end in *s* *and* have more than one syllable, add an *s* after the apostrophe.

> **Aristophanes's** death

Do not use an apostrophe to indicate the possessive form of either singular or plural pronouns.

> The books were hers.
> Ours is the best school in the county.
> The fault was theirs.

At the end of a plural word that ends in *s*, add an apostrophe only.

> the **cows'** water supply
> the **Jacksons'** wine cellar

At the end of a compound noun, add an apostrophe plus *s*.

| my **father-in-law's** false teeth

At the end of the last word in nouns of joint possession, add an apostrophe plus *s* if both own one item.

| **Joe and Sam's** lakefront cottage

Add an apostrophe plus *s* to both nouns if each owns specific items.

| **Joe's** and **Sam's** passports

Apostrophe Indicating a Contraction.   An apostrophe shows that you have omitted one or more letters in a phrase that is usually a combination of a pronoun and a verb.

I'm	they're
he's	you'd
you're	who's

Don't confuse *they're* with *their* or *there*.

Faulty	there books
	their now leaving
	living their
Correct	their books
	they're now leaving
	living there

Remember the distinction this way:

| Their friend knows they're there.

It's means "it is." *Its* is the possessive.

| It's watching its reflection in the pond.

Who's means "who is," whereas *whose* indicates the possessive.

| Who's interrupting whose work?

Other contractions are formed from the verb and the negative.

isn't	can't
don't	haven't
won't	wasn't

Apostrophe Indicating the Plural of Numerals, Letters, and Symbols.

The **6's** on this new printer look like smudged **G's, 9's** are illegible, and the **%'s** are unclear.

Quotation Marks

Quotation marks set off the exact words borrowed from another speaker or writer. The period or comma at the end is placed within the quotation marks.

Periods and commas belong within quotation marks

"Hurry up," Jack whispered.

Jack told Felicia, "I'm depressed."

A colon or semicolon is always placed outside quotation marks.

Colons and semicolons belong outside quotation marks

Our student handbook clearly defines "core require- ments"; however, it does not list all the courses that fulfill the requirement.

When a question mark or exclamation point is part of a quotation, it belongs within the quotation marks, replacing the comma or period.

Some punctuation belongs within quotation marks

"Help!" he screamed.

Marsha asked John, "Can't we agree about anything?"

But if the question mark or exclamation point pertains to the attitude of the person quoting instead of the person being quoted, it is placed outside the quotation mark.

Some punctuation belongs outside quotation marks

Why did Boris wink and whisper, "It's a big secret"?

Use quotation marks around titles of articles, paintings, book chapters, and poems.

> **Certain titles belong within quotation marks**   The enclosed article, "The Job Market for College Graduates," should provide helpful insights.

But titles of books, journals, magazines, and newspapers should be italicized. Finally, use quotation marks (with restraint) to indicate your ironic use of a word.

> **Quotation marks to indicate irony**   She is some "friend"!

APPLICATION

VI.11   Insert apostrophes and quotation marks as needed in these sentences.

1. Our countrys future, as well as the worlds, depends on everyone working for a cleaner environment.
2. Once you understand the problem, Professor Jones explained, you find its worse than you could possibly have expected.
3. Can we help? asked the captain.
4. Its a shame that my dog had its leg injured in the accident.
5. All the players bats were gnawed by the cranky beaver.

Ellipses

Three spaced dots in a row (...) indicate that you have omitted material from a quotation. If the omitted words come at the end of the original sentence, a fourth dot, immediately following the last quoted word, indicates the period. (Also see page 383.)

> "Three spaced dots ... indicate ... omitted material.... A fourth dot indicates the period."

Italics

Use italics or underlining for titles of books, periodicals, films, newspapers, and plays; for names of ships; and for foreign words or technical terms, especially terms being defined. Use italics sparingly for special emphasis.

The *Oxford English Dictionary* is a handy reference tool.

The *Lusitania* sank rapidly.

She reads the *Boston Globe* often.

My only advice is *caveat emptor.*

Bacillus anthracis is a highly virulent organism.

Do not inhale these fumes under any circumstances!

Our contract defines a *work-study student* as one who works a minimum of 20 hours weekly.

( )/ Parentheses

Use commas to set off parenthetical elements, dashes to give emphasis to the material that is set off, and parentheses to enclose material that defines or explains the statement that precedes it.

An anaerobic **(airless)** environment must be maintained for the cultivation of this organism.

The cost of running our college has increased by 15 percent in the past year **(see Appendix A for a full cost breakdown).**

This new calculator **(made by Ilco Corporation)** is perfect for science students.

Material between parentheses, like all other parenthetical material discussed earlier, can be deleted without harming the logical and grammatical structure of the sentence.

[ ]/ Brackets

Brackets in a quotation set off material that was not in the original quotation but is needed for clarification, such as an antecedent (or referent) for a pronoun. (Also see page 383.)

"She **[Amy]** was the outstanding candidate for the scholarship."

Brackets can enclose information taken from some other location within the context of the quotation.

"It was in early spring **[April 2, to be exact]** that the tornado hit."

Use *sic* ("thus" or "so") between brackets when quoting an error in a quotation.

The assistant's comment was clear: "He don't **[*sic*]** want any."

Dashes

Dashes can be effective—if not overused. Parentheses deemphasize the enclosed material; dashes emphasize it.

> Have a good vacation—but watch out for sand fleas.
>
> Mary—a true friend—spent hours helping me rehearse.

APPLICATION

VI.12   Insert parentheses or dashes as appropriate in these sentences.

1. Writing is a deliberate process of deliberate decisions about a writer's purpose, audience, and message.
2. Have fun but be careful.
3. She worked hard summers at three jobs actually to earn money for agricultural school.
4. To achieve peace and contentment that is the meaning of success.
5. Fido a loyal pet saved my life during the fire.

EFFECTIVE MECHANICS

The mechanical aspects of writing include abbreviation, hyphenation, capitalization, the use of numbers, and spelling.

Abbreviation

Avoid abbreviations in formal writing or in situations that might confuse your reader. When in doubt, write the word out.

Abbreviate some words and titles when they precede or immediately follow a proper name, but not military, religious, or political titles.

Correct   Mr. Jones

Dr. Jekyll

Raymond Dumont, Jr.

Reverend Ormsby

President Kennedy

Abbreviate time designations only when they are used with actual times.

Correct   400 B.C.

5:15 a.m.

Faulty   Plato lived sometime in the B.C. period.

She arrived in the a.m.

Most dictionaries provide an alphabetical list of other abbreviations. For abbreviations in the documentation of research sources, see pages 388–411.

Hyphenation

Hyphens divide words at line breaks and join two or more words used as a single adjective if they precede the noun (but not if they follow it):

I spent the entire evening at the computer.

a full-time job

an all-too-human error

She works full time.

The error was all too human.

Other commonly hyphenated words fall into the following categories.

- Most words that begin with the prefix *self-* (check your dictionary):

self-reliance

self-discipline

- Combinations that might be ambiguous:

re-creation [*a new creation*]

recreation [*leisure activity*]

- Words that begin with *ex,* meaning "past" or "former":

ex-faculty member

excommunicate

- All fractions, ratios that are used as adjectives and that precede the noun (but not those that follow it), and compound numbers from *twenty-one* through *ninety-nine*:

a **two-thirds** majority

In a **four-to-one** vote, the student senate defeated the proposal.

The proposal was voted down **four to one.**

Thirty-eight windows were broken.

Capitalization

Capitalize the first words of all sentences; the titles of people, books, and chapters; languages; days of the week; months; holidays; names of organizations or groups; races and nationalities; historical events; important documents; and names of structures or vehicles. In titles of books, films, and the like, capitalize the first word and all those following except articles, coordinating conjunctions, and prepositions.

Items that are capitalized		
	Joe Schmoe	Russian
	A Tale of Two Cities	Labor Day
	Protestant	Dupont Chemical Company
	Wednesday	Senator Barbara Boxer
	the *Queen Mary*	France
	the Statue of Liberty	the War of 1812

Do not capitalize the seasons (*spring, winter*) or general groups (*the younger generation, the leisure class*).

Capitalize adjectives derived from proper nouns.

Chaucerian English

Capitalize titles preceding a proper noun but not those following.

State Senator Marsha Smith

Marsha Smith, state senator

Capitalize words such as *street, road, corporation,* and *college* only when they accompany a proper noun.

Bob Jones University

High Street

Pearson Publishers

Capitalize *north, south, east,* and *west* when they denote specific locations, not when they are simply directions.

the South

the Northwest

Turn east at the next set of lights.

Use of Numbers

Numbers expressed in one or two words can be written out or written as numerals. Use numerals to express larger numbers, decimals, fractions, precise technical figures, or any other exact measurements.

543	2,800,357
$3\frac{1}{4}$	15 pounds of pressure
50 kilowatts	4,000 rpm

Use numerals for dates, census figures, addresses, page numbers, exact units of measurement, percentages, times with a.m. or p.m. designations, and monetary and mileage figures.

page 14	1:15 p.m.
18.4 pounds	9 feet
12 gallons	$15

Do not begin a sentence with a numeral. If your number needs more than two words, revise your word order.

Six hundred students applied for the 102 available jobs.

The 102 available jobs brought 600 applicants.

Do not use numerals to express approximate figures, time not designated as a.m. or p.m., or streets named by numbers less than 100.

about seven hundred fifty

four fifteen

108 East Forty-Second Street

Spelling

Always use the spell-check function in your word processing software. However, don't rely on it exclusively. Double-check spellings in your dictionary. When you reread your writing assignments, note the spellings of words that give you trouble. Compile a list of troublesome words for future reference.

VI.13   In these sentences, make any needed mechanical corrections in abbreviations, hyphenation, numbers, and capitalization.

1. Dr. Jones, our english prof., drives a red maserati.
2. Eighty five students in the survey rated self-discipline as essential for success in college.
3. Since nineteen ninety seven, my goal has been to live in the northwest.
4. Senator tarbell has collected forty five handmade rugs from the middle east.
5. During my third year at Margate university, I wrote twenty three page papers on the Russian revolution.
6. 100 bottles are on that shelf.

Format Guidelines for Submitting Your Manuscript

Format is the look of a page, the visual arrangement of words and spacing. A well-formatted manuscript invites readers in, guides them through the material, and helps them understand it.

FORMAT GUIDELINES for Submitting Your Manuscript

- *Use the right paper.* Type or print in black ink, on 8½-by-11-inch, low-gloss, white paper. Use rag bond paper (2 pounds or heavier) with a high fiber content (25 percent minimum).

- *Use high-quality print.* Try to print your hard copy on a letter-quality printer or a laser printer.

- *Use standard type sizes and typefaces.* Standard type sizes for manuscripts run from 10 to 12 points, depending on the typeface. Use other sizes only for headings, titles, or special emphasis.
  Except for special emphasis, use conservative typefaces (or fonts); the more ornate ones are harder to read and inappropriate for most manuscripts.

- *Number pages consistently.* Number your first and subsequent pages with arabic numerals (1, 2, 3), ½ inch from the top of the page and aligned with the right margin or centered in the top or bottom margin. For numbering pages in a research report, see pages 421 and 435–437.

- *Provide ample margins.* Narrow margins make a page look crowded and difficult and allow no room for peer or instructor comments. Provide margins of at least 1½ inches top and bottom and 1¼ inches right and left. If the manuscript is to be bound in some kind of cover, widen your left margin to 2 inches.

(continues)

- *Keep line spacing and indentation consistent.* Double-space within and between paragraphs. Indent the first line of each paragraph five spaces from the left margin. (Indent five spaces on a word processor by striking the Tab key.)

- *Design your first page.* If your instructor requires a title page, see pages 421 and 435. For the first page of a manuscript without a separate title page, follow the format your instructor recommends.

- *Cite and document each source.* Consult Chapter 23. For designing Works Cited or References pages in a documented essay, see pages 430 and 447.

- *Proofread your final manuscript.* Spell checkers and grammar checkers can reveal certain errors but are no substitute for your own careful evaluation. See pages 73–74 for proofreading advice.

How to Insert Corrections on Final Copy

If you need to make a few last-minute handwritten corrections on your final copy, use a caret (^) to denote the insertion:

make

If you need to^a few handwritten...

Any page requiring more than three or four such corrections should be reprinted.

- *Bind your manuscript for readers' convenience.* Do not use a cover unless your instructor requests one. Use a staple or large paper clip in the upper left-hand corner.

- *Make a backup copy.* Print out or photocopy a backup paper, which you should keep just in case the original you submit gets lost or misplaced.

✔ A CHECKLIST for Formatting

Before submitting any manuscript, evaluate its format using the following checklist.

- ☐ Does the paper meet quality standards?
- ☐ Is the print neat, crisp, and easy to read?
- ☐ Are type sizes and typefaces appropriate and easy to read?
- ☐ Are pages numbered consistently?
- ☐ Are all margins adequate?
- ☐ Are line spacing and indentation consistent?
- ☐ Are the first and subsequent pages appropriately designed?
- ☐ Is each source correctly cited and documented?
- ☐ Has the manuscript been proofread carefully?
- ☐ Is the manuscript bound for readers' convenience?
- ☐ Has a backup copy been made?

December 31, 1971. Reprinted by permission of the author.

Updike, David. "Clothes Woes" originally appeared as "I Don't Like What You're Wearing" by David Updike, *Newsweek,* May 24, 1999. Copyright © 1999 by David Updike, used with permission of The Wylie Agency LLC.

Watts, Alan. *In My Own Way.* New York: Pantheon Books, a division of Random House, Inc.

Wright, Frank Lloyd. Excerpt adapted from Frank Lloyd Wright, "Away with the Realtor" in *Esquire,* October 1958. Copyright © 1958 by Esquire Publishing Inc. Reprinted courtesy of Esquire and the Hearst Corporation.

INDEX

A Guide to the Digital Tip and Beyond the Writing Classroom Boxes

DIGITAL TIPS

The Digital Tips boxes are a new feature. The boxes (in Sections I, II, and IV of the book) offer practical tips on using your computer as a writing and research tool.

BEYOND THE WRITING CLASSROOM BOXES

The Beyond the Writing Classroom boxes in Section III (Essays for Various Goals) have been updated to enhance the text's practical, "real world" approach to writing. Balancing with the book's special emphasis on sample essays with topics of interest to students (social networking, online education, popular culture, multiculturalism, the workplace, campus life) and its chapter on the writing at work (resumes, application letters, portfolios, emails, memos, and letters), the BTWC boxes show how the various t essays students are asked to write aren't merely academic exercises but also apply to other courses, the workplace, and the community.

Editing, Revision, and Proofreading Symbols

Symbol	Problem	Page*	Symbol	Problem	Page*	Symbol	Problem	Page*
ab	incorrect abbreviation	520	num	error in the use of numbers	523	shift	inconsistent tense, voice, mood, or point of view	506
agr p	error in pronoun agreement	502	over	overstatement or exaggeration	132	short	short sentence(s) needed for emphasis	126
agr sv	error in subject-verb agreement	501	par	parallel phrasing needed	115	sp	misspelled word	523
apl	missing or misused possessive apostrophe	515	pct	error in punctuation	507	spec	more specific word or phrase needed	497
av	active voice needed	116	[ ]/	brackets	519	sub	subordination needed or faulty	521
bias	biased language needs rephrasing	144	:/	colon	510	Th	ineffective "There" or "It" to begin a sentence	119
ca	pronoun in the wrong case	505	,/	comma	511	tone	inappropriate tone for topic or reader	138
cap	capital letter needed	522	--/	dash	520	trans	transition needed, to connect related ideas	105
cl	word that merely adds clutter	123	.../	ellipses	518	trite	overused term or phrase	132
			!/	exclamation point	509	var	variety needed in structure/ length of sentences	126
comb	choppy sentences need to be combined	124	-/	hyphen	521			
			( )/	parentheses	519			
coord	coordination needed or faulty	497	./	period	508	w	too many words, too little meaning	119
cram	overstuffed sentence	114	?/	question mark	509	wo	word order needs rearranging	115
cs	comma splice, links two sentences only by a comma	499	"/"	quotation marks	517	wv	weak verb, denotes no specific action	120
			;/	semicolon	509			
euph	euphemism that misleads	132	pref	needless preface, delays the point	123	ww	wrong word	133
frag	a fragment used as a sentence	494	prep	needless preposition, creates wordiness	121	¶coh	paragraph lacks coherence	98
ital	italics needed for emphasis	518	pv	passive voice needed	117	¶ts	topic sentence inadequate or missing	95
mod	a modifying word or phrase misplaced	114	qual	needless qualifier, conveys uncertainty	123	¶un	paragraph lacks unity	97
			red	redundant phrase, says the same thing twice	119	∧	insert whatever is missing	526
neg	negative construction needs rephrasing	122	ref	unclear referent (word a pronoun refers to)	113	#	insert one letter space or line space	
nom	nominalization (nouns made from verbs)	121	rep	a word or phrase repeated needlessly	119	ℐ	delete this word or phrase	
np	a needless phrase, creates wordiness	120	ro	run-on, no break or link between sentences	500	⌒	close up the space	
			sexist	potentially offensive word choice	143	~	reverse these elements	

*Numbers refer to the first page of major discussion in the text.